The Inter

CENTRAL EUROPEAN DEMOCRACY AND ITS BACKGROUND

Founded by KARL MANNHEIM

The International Library of Sociology

POLITICAL SOCIOLOGY
In 18 Volumes

I	The American Science of Politics	*Crick*
II	The Analysis of Political Behaviour	*Lasswell*
III	The Analysis of Political Systems	*Verney*
IV	Central European Democracy and its Background	*Schlesinger*
V	The Decline of Liberalism as an Ideology	*Hallowell*
	(The above title is not available through Routledge in North America)	
VI	Democracy and Dictatorship	*Barbu*
VII	Dictatorship and Political Police	*Bramstedt*
VIII	Federalism in Central and Eastern Europe	*Schlesinger*
IX	History of Socialism	*Laidler*
	(The above title is not available through Routledge in North America)	
X	How People Vote	*Benney et al*
XI	The Logic of Liberty	*Polanyi*
	(The above title is not available through Routledge in North America)	
XII	Pacifism	*Martin*
XIII	Patterns of Peacemaking	*Thomson et al*
XIV	Plan for Reconstruction	*Hutt*
XV	Politics of Influence	*Wootton*
XVI	Politics of Mass Society	*Kornhauser*
	(The above title is not available through Routledge in North America)	
XVII	Power and Society	*Lasswell and Kaplan*
	(The above title is not available through Routledge in North America)	
XVIII	Process of Independence	*Mansur*

CENTRAL EUROPEAN DEMOCRACY AND ITS BACKGROUND

Economic and Political Group Organization

by

RUDOLF SCHLESINGER

Routledge
Taylor & Francis Group
LONDON AND NEW YORK

First published in 1953
by Routledge

Reprinted in 1998, 1999, 2000
by Routledge
2 Park Square, Milton Park, Abingdon, Oxon, OX14 4RN
711 Third Avenue, New York, NY 10017

Transferred to Digital Printing 2007

Routledge is an imprint of the Taylor & Francis Group, an informa business

First issued in paperback 2013

© 1953 Rudolf Schlesinger

All rights reserved. No part of this book may be reprinted or reproduced or utilized in any form or by any electronic, mechanical, or other means, now known or hereafter invented, including photocopying and recording, or in any information storage or retrieval system, without permission in writing from the publishers.

The publishers have made every effort to contact authors/copyright holders of the works reprinted in *The International Library of Sociology*. This has not been possible in every case, however, and we would welcome correspondence from those individuals/companies we have been unable to trace.

British Library Cataloguing in Publication Data
A CIP catalogue record for this book
is available from the British Library

Central European Democracy and its Background
ISBN13: 978-0-415-17539-5 (hardback)
ISBN13: 978-0-415-86322-3 (paperback)
Political Sociology: 18 Volumes
ISBN 0-415-17820-7
The International Library of Sociology: 274 Volumes
ISBN 0-415-17838-X

Publisher's Note
The publisher has gone to great lengths to ensure the quality of this reprint but points out that some imperfections in the original may be apparent

CONTENTS

CONTENTS

PART TWO
THE PERIOD OF CRISIS (1905–1923)

PART THREE
CENTRAL EUROPEAN DEMOCRACY AND ITS FALL (1924–1938)

PREFACE

THIS book is concerned with a particular type of social organization and a particular stage in the development of certain countries. Some, among my readers, may reproach me for describing phenomena which they regard as characteristic only of a few individual countries in terms of a general trend of modern society. My only answer must be to endeavour to carry out my task in such a way as to make it clear that the problems discussed are not of merely historical interest, and may yet have their relevance even for Britain. All nations at a certain stage of their development have to face certain general problems, though these problems take on very different shapes in different national settings.

The regional framework of the investigation has its own importance. It was chosen not only because of my conviction that contributions to political science are most useful if the authors have had some experience of the political life of the countries they write about, but also because the matters investigated mark an important stage in the development of the modern labour movement. As I have explained elsewhere, I consider the application of Marxism by the Central European Social Democrat parties as a distortion of its original meaning. We cannot, however, neglect the fact that it was in this application or distortion, that Marxism displayed the more popular aspects of its impact during the period of the Second International; even Russian Bolshevism grew up as a direct reaction against this kind of Marxism.

The institutional forms of the experience here discussed should not be thought of as mere reflexions of a local failure to apply Western democratic concepts, not to speak of the naïve belief that that failure resulted from mere misunderstandings. Local conditions, which made it inevitable, were reflected in the institutions; but those institutions were shaped by a basic trend found in all countries—at least all those within the Western political tradition—whose economic system is based upon private ownership of the means of production. Experience shows that in all these countries, though with differing rates of speed, mass parties based upon the organization of sectional groups are replacing parties which grew out of the social conflicts in which the system was formed or out of oligarchic cliques which survived from still earlier periods. The result is that the place of most citizens in political life is defined *a priori* by their economic status, and what real democracy exists must be democracy within the socio-political group. In analyzing the experience of Central Europe we are analysing an extreme and locally coloured instance of a trend generally observable.

This book has grown out of diverse lines of study, pursued at different periods of my life, and the reader must judge for himself whether I have succeeded in bringing them together. Thirty years ago, at the suggestion of my teacher, Prof. Grünberg, I wrote my thesis on the relationship between political Socialism and Trade Unionism in Germany and Austria; from that time on I have never ceased to be interested in the history of the Central European labour movement, in whose activities I took part right up to, and after, the Hitlerite conquest. I have never believed in the primitive explanation of the Social Democratic policies, after the vote for the War Credits in 1914, as a betrayal of Marxist principles by a mere degenerate clique of bureaucrats; I was interested in the kind of 'Marxism' which could be produced by such a movement as pre-1914 Social Democracy, and in the reasons for which such a party continued to oppose the Revisionism of Bernstein, who correctly foretold its course. In my thesis of 1922 I submitted that 'orthodox' Social Democracy merely expressed the need for an all-embracing organization of labour as against the trends which would restrict trade unionism to a narrow aristocracy of workers; in my book on *The Agrarian Problem in Social Democracy*, written in 1926 and published in Russian, I attempted to find the additional roots of Revisionism in the impact made by the lower middle classes on the only serious opposition party that existed in Imperial Germany. During the subsequent years I followed up the development of a specific ideology of Economic Democracy in German Social Democracy, at a time when such an ideology clearly implied the reception of monopoly capitalist developments into the outlook of the Labour movement. I cannot say that I was in any way surprised by the behaviour of German Social Democracy in the catastrophe, nor can I claim that I, or the school of thought whose views I shared, have made more than critical contributions to the analysis of the situation.

A very different line of thought was started amid the conditions of the emigration. After 1932 we learned to orientate the revolutionary labour movement towards the defence of existing democratic institutions, and perhaps after 1934 towards a post-Hitlerite régime based upon such institutions. I think the turning-point came as a result of the failure of the German working class to react to the crisis of June 1934, which destroyed any illusions as to the merely short-term transitional character of the Hitlerite régime which might have survived our experiences in reorganizing the German underground movement in 1933. Since then it has become fashionable to explain all developments in political ideology by considerations of international politics. But although the international conditions necessarily produced the framework, it would be a mistake to describe the concepts of the *Front Populaire* period as mere manœuvres conditioned by an international emergency; the very triumph of Hitlerism which necessitated the *rapprochement* between the Powers threatened by its aggression also demonstrated that a prolonged period of organic growth of democratic institutions was needed during which the German people could transform its social structure. The attempts made by the Central European labour movement to find a solution of its own for the problems of our time have been brought to an end by the development of an international situation wherein each of the two halves of Europe has a clear-cut solution backed by the leadership of one of the two World Powers and shaped according to its pattern. Only the wishful thinker can refuse to face the facts. But it would have been most unnatural for German left-wing exiles to turn their thoughts towards such a prospect until it became a reality.

In the atmosphere I have described, there was an obvious need to argue with British friends who were unable to take seriously any democracy but their own, and to segregate, in my own mind, the truly democratic elements in the post-1919 institutions from the tradition which led to the catastrophe of 1933. From this line of thought arose a number of studies on Austrian and Central European democracy. One of them, *Federalism in Central and Eastern Europe*, was published in this series in 1945; others are more or less integrated in the present book, though here the main interest has shifted from the institutional to the historical field. Although I have tried to write without any preconceived sociological assumptions—except, perhaps, the very important one that a theoretical analysis covering different societies is possible—I owe my readers an explanation of the theoretical interests pursued in this study.

During a war which was not foreseen by the ruling classes of the Western democracies, was fought in undesired alliance with, and was inspired by, ideas abhorrent to those still holding social power, and resulted in the triumph of one 'totalitarian' power over another, there grew up that cynical attitude towards political ideologies which has been characteristic of the aftermath of all great revolutions in the past; it is promoted by the external dilemmas in which many intellectuals find themselves in a time of 'cold war'. From the characteristically 'pink' concept that 'power-politics' are evil—as if politics could have any other subject than power—the conclusion was drawn that sociology deals mainly with the application of that abstraction, power, and that all that is taking place in our days is the establishment of new forms of the eternal rule of men over men. It would be dishonest of me not to say that I fight this concept, not only because it is bad sociology and (so far as the emotional aspect of the issue is concerned) because it implies worship of all established power, but also because I think that this small contribution is the best I can make towards preventing the death of scores of millions of men and the destruction of those cultural values of our civilization which can survive the present social structure of western Europe and the politico-economic hegemony of the white peoples if they are divorced from what is bound to die. The prospect of 'pure power' is to be broken.

But my feelings about formalist sociology do not prevent me from seeing that there is an element of truth in the case it has to make. When I found Burnham praising Michels, I looked into the old Michels again; and I realized not only that there was a consistent path from the syndicalist criticism of the bureaucracy of the labour movement to fascism, i.e. to the building up of a hierarchical bureaucracy to manage the State machinery of monopoly capitalism (I never regarded Mussolini as a *mere* renegade), but also that to explain unwelcome facts as results of the treacherous behaviour of mere 'bureaucracies', 'workers' aristocracies', etc., leads into a maze of wishful thinking and propagandist assertion about the behaviour of other peoples. There is no sense in analysing the behaviour of masses except in connexion with the conditions and the institutional framework—official and unofficial—in which they can form and express their opinions, or in analysing institutions except in connexion with the real interests of the people they represent and without whose support they are bound to break down at the first serious crisis.

The treatment varies as between the three parts of this book. The first is in the main an introduction to the two following; and even in Part Two some aspects of general politics and ideology are but briefly touched on, to be discussed more thoroughly in Part Three. Similarly, the space allotted to the treatment, say, of German and Austrian developments respectively expresses my estimate, not of the immediate importance for world history of the events described, but of their suitability as illustrations of the general trends I wish to discuss, with a certain bias in favour of evidence not yet otherwise available to the British student. It has not been my intention to provide a history of Central Europe, or even of its labour movement, during the period concerned; I wished to follow a certain trend of social development, illustrating what I have to say from the original sources for the simple reason that this is the only way of exposing my interpretations and conclusions to scholarly criticism. Such a procedure implies some judgement as to the value of the existing secondary sources; if, by taking illustrations from the original source-material, I have given some help to the future historian of the period, so much the better. But it is not from this standpoint that I would wish my attempt to be judged; what matters is whether the evidence given is sufficient, not to prove my interpretations, for to claim that it does so would be preposterous, but at least to make their discussion fruitful and to invite more thorough attempts at verifying them.

Dealing only with a particular trend in Central European development and its expressions in institutions, the book naturally devotes less attention to other factors that, in a history of the period, would have to be covered much more thoroughly. To avoid misunderstandings on the part of readers who take it up in the absence of such a history, I would make it clear that: (1) I do not suggest that the trend here investigated became at any time the predominant element in Central European politics, but I deal with the surviving elements of the past and with the origins of fascism only as opponents of the democratic movements; (2) in this study the Communist movement appears only in its elementary stages as one of the possible alternatives, and later as a limiting factor in the activities of the trend which proved predominant within the labour movement; a full appreciation of Central European Communism is possible only in connexion with the developments both of Soviet Communism and of the Central European framework.

Much of the source material used arose in the course of disputes: some in the struggle between the labour movement and its opponents, some in factional conflicts within that movement or other groups discussed. Obviously we must avoid the pitfall of taking the tenets of the ideological framework of a movement for granted, or of accepting at their face value the statements of historians whose sympathies lie with a particular group. Even statements which originated at different moments from a single source must be appreciated in the light of the conditions under which they were made: the interpretation of the German Trades Unions predominant at the various Congresses of the Social Democratic party depended greatly on the relationship existing at that moment between the Unions and the Party.

Difficulties of this type are found in the study of any controversial problem; in our field, however, they tend to be perpetuated by the stabilization of competing trends within the labour movement which is so characteristic of our day. In the present international situation the factional myth of one country (which, so far as that country is concerned, can still be checked by the facts and by the contentions of the opposite faction) may easily become the almost unquestioned tradition of all the publications dealing with the subject in another country. West European readers who find that some facts in this book are presented in a light very different from that which they have been used to take for granted are invited, not necessarily to accept my exposition, but first of all to devote some thought to the question how they came to be informed about an evidently controversial problem in such a way that they might not even notice that it was controversial.

Every student of the history of political parties will agree that the documentation available for facts or organization (as distinct from phraseology) is incomparably better for working-class than for bourgeois parties. The former depend upon the contributions and unpaid activities of their members, who would not come forward unless proper reports were made as to their use and unless the rank and file were given some critical voice in the organization of those activities. Disputes in the sectional camp, which I referred to above as a potential source of distortion, are responsible for the incomparably better documentation of events in the left-wing than in the right-wing organizations, where disputes, though no less frequent, can more easily be concealed from the public. On such an issue as bureaucratism working-class organizations may differ from others mainly in that even a comparatively moderate growth of the phenomenon will provoke articulate criticism. It may be true that party life is developing to-day from the fresh air of controversy predominant even in the twenties towards a more authoritarian pattern —a tendency quite independent of the existence of authoritarian elements in the professed ideology of the parties concerned. For the countries and the period treated in this book, however, I would confidently state that there is enough evidence, sufficiently varied in character, to allow for historical statements that involve no greater measure of dependence upon the historian's bias or error than do those about more remote periods which are less 'controversial' because fewer people feel the topicality of the issues they involve.

My sincere thanks are due to all my friends whose suggestions and criticisms have helped me in the various stages of the preparation of this work, and to Mr. James T. Craig and Mr. A. S. B. Glover who undertook the correction of the style.

Invereoch
Kilmun
Argyllshire

February 28th, 1953

PART ONE

THE PERIOD OF FORMATION
1862–1905

CHAPTER ONE

THE HISTORICAL FRAMEWORK

THE subject of this study is the growth of sectional organization in connection with the development of political democracy in Germany, Austria, and Czechoslovakia. The choice of geographical framework is not dictated solely by the fact that these three republics developed similar régimes during the period 1918–33; the area is that of the activities of the parties which led the Second International before 1914. Any treatment of pre-1914 Austrian Social Democracy which made no reference to Czechoslovakia would be highly artificial; but the inclusion of that country, though it preserves the essentially industrial character of the framework, destroys its purely German nature and introduces so important an aspect of modern developments as the problem of nationalities. Examples of extreme and continuous repression of the labour movement occurred on occasion even within the region we are considering, e.g. in Prussia east of the Elbe; but the whole picture would be altered were we to include Hungary, not to speak of the more backward parts of the former Hapsburg monarchy, where such repression was the rule.

The *terminus ad quem* is the Fascist conquest of democracy, brought about in Germany by the establishment of the Hitler régime, in Austria by the dissolution of Parliament in 1933, and in Czechoslovakia by the Munich betrayal of 1938. The starting-point of the investigation is the sixties of the nineteenth century, when the outcome of the Prussian Army conflict decided that Germany's unification was to take place under Junker leadership, with the bourgeoisie in a merely subservient position and the young labour movement taking the lead in representing the democratic ideals of 1848, and when Prussia's triumph of 1866 forced on the Hapsburg monarchy an internal reorganization which set the social as well as the national forces of opposition in motion.

Some fifteen years earlier these countries, like all continental Europe west of the Russian frontier, had taken part in the revolution of 1848. Professor Namier has called this the 'revolution of the intellectuals', and there is some truth in the description. Eighteen-forty-eight marked the fruition of ideas current since the days of the French Revolution. Resistance to those ideas had become so weak that in most cases armed students, by the side of suburban workers, without calling for a peasant insurrection, were able to play an important part in breaking the resistance of the *ancien régime*, although these very limitations of the movement restricted the thoroughness of the transformation which followed. Eighteen-forty-eight was also the birthday of the ideas realized during the century that followed: modern nationalism and the *Communist Manifesto*. But the Frankfurt Assembly and the Slav Congress at Prague became mere memories, to be eventually followed up by more realistic trends in German and Czech nationalism, and the uninfluential League of Communists survived only in the traditions of movements that started about the time with which our study is concerned. Since 1848 was primarily a year of seed-sowing, it will be mentioned only on one occasion[1] as the starting-point of an organization which continued throughout the period with which we are to deal.

But 1848 was not only a year in which lofty ideals were born. The easy initial triumph of the movement indicated the complete decay of the system of feudal-romantic reaction artificially imposed as a result of the pattern of international politics prevailing at the time of Napoleon's defeat. Its rapid collapse showed to what an extent bourgeois nationalism had been taken over by the traditional ruling classes. The bourgeoisie had become so afraid of the labour movement, unripe and far away as it was in the Paris of 1848,[2] that it was prepared to shelter under the protection of still semi-feudal and absolutist régimes which were prepared to look after its economic interests without admitting it to a share of power. Thus the defeated revolution from below became the starting-point for a 'revolution from above' carried out by the traditional ruling classes.

In 1848 the last feudal institutions of the Central European countryside were abolished, and, save for the post-1919 Czechoslovak land reform, the gradual rise of industry marked the only change in social structure during our whole period. Agriculture declined in importance, but even in 1918 it was still the chief occupation of 25 per cent of the German and 40 per cent of the Czechoslovak and Austrian peoples. In Germany, the decision to abolish feudal dues[3] had been taken during the Napoleonic period, and as far as French power extended, the peasants retained most of their land. But in Prussia the reform was very

[1] See p. 28 below.

[2] Cf. the references given in my *Federalism in Central and Eastern Europe*, p. 49 note 2.

[3] Serfdom had already been abolished in the era of Enlightened Absolutism, before the French Revolution, except in some minor German States, where its abolition was enforced by the French armies.

long drawn out; freedom had to be purchased by the transfer of land to the Junkers, and the poorer peasants, who had to transfer all their land, became landless labourers. In Austria, including the Czech parts of what was to become Czechoslovakia, the reform was delayed until 1848, but under pressure of the revolution it was carried out in such a way as to preserve peasant ownership, the main burden of the compensation payable to the lords being borne by the State. In the Alpine provinces of Austria, later to be the western parts of the Austrian republic, substantial numbers of peasants had successfully resisted enserfment since medieval times. Hungary, to which Slovakia belonged, remained until 1945 the big owners' paradise.

The result was that peasant ownership[1] became widespread in western and southern parts of the region, while the landlord remained predominant in the last. In 1895, taking Germany as a whole, nearly a quarter of the cultivated land was occupied by 25,000 agricultural holdings each over 100 hectares (250 acres) in area; in the eastern provinces of Prussia more than half. In Pomerania the share occupied by large holdings was two-thirds, in Poznania and Mecklenburg three-fifths. This picture fails to distinguish the Junker who managed his own estate from the core of the landowning aristocracy; the following table, for the year 1905, shows the biggest estates, those of more than 5,000 hectares (12,500 acres) each:

Province	*No. of landlords*	*Area owned (thousand hectares)*	
		total	*agricultural*
East Prussia	11	68	34
West Prussia (now Pomorze)	13	106	48
Poznania	33	301	147
Pomerania	24	183	103
Silesia	46	672	192

The share of the Silesian latifundia-owners amounted to a quarter of the available land, and a considerable portion of this land was in the hands of the three biggest of them: the Prince of Pless (52 estates, amounting to 130,000 acres); the Duke of Ujest (52 estates, 100,000 acres); the King of neighbouring Saxony (50 estates, 78,000 acres). In some provinces of Prussia the entails of the nobility embraced 22 per cent of all the available land.

In Austria, for reasons already given, latifundia were less developed. But even there they included 20 per cent of the available land and 5 per cent of the agricultural population. Latifundia-ownership of the forests was most important, for the peasants depended upon them for wood and firing, and the interests of the game-owners could cause serious harm to

[1] As a rule, on average land, the owner of 25 acres is regarded as a self-supporting peasant, the owner of 50 to 80 acres as a rich one. In mountain regions the corresponding figures are of course higher, and in regions of vineyard, etc., much lower.

peasant economy. Between 1903 and 1912 the aristocratic forest-owners, together with their associates from the commercial class, appropriated 7 per cent of all the peasant land in Upper Styria and 4·5 per cent in Middle Styria.[1] In all the Alpine provinces of Austria other than Tyrol the number of cattle decreased during that period owing to the replacement of peasants by deer.

In what was to become Czechoslovakia the distribution was not much more favourable to the peasants than in Prussia. Owners of more than 500 acres controlled two-fifths of the available land in Slovakia, nearly a third in Moravia, and 27·6 per cent even in Bohemia. The core of the Czech latifundia-owners was formed by the descendants of the servants of the Hapsburgs who had received the land confiscated from the Bohemian nobles after the triumph of the Counter-Reformation in 1621,[2] while in Slovakia the list was headed by German and Hungarian aristocrats.[3]

The position of the landowning aristocracy was of great importance, but in a period of rapid industrialization it could not establish economic control. It did, however, form the backbone of the existing political régime, the essentials of which remained unaltered until 1918. In Austria, State power was exercised by a kind of 'second nobility', the professional military and civil servants of the house of Hapsburg; behind these stood an inner circle of the higher nobility, the big estate owners, who were the intimate friends of the Court. They controlled the Church, the civil service, and the diplomatic service; and they managed every government, although only occasionally did one of them, and then usually not one of the most powerful, himself assume the office of Prime Minister. In Prussia, and to a lesser extent even in the South German States, the Junkers or their younger sons controlled all the key positions in the army and civil service. No less important was the fact that, because of the army's key position in German social life, the class which controlled the Prussian core of the German army thereby controlled the German intelligentsia. No member of the middle class or intellectual had any social standing without being a commissioned officer in the Reserve, and commissions were granted only when an officers' corps consented to co-opt the candidate. As a matter of course no commissions, and therefore no posts commanding social prestige in civil life, were granted to Socialists, Jews, or those who were not members of a church. Although most of the civilian posts were held by persons of non-

[1] In one district of neighbouring Lower Austria, the peasant's losses amounted to 23 per cent of their lands. See O. Bauer, op. cit. (1925).

[2] The Schwarzenbergs, whose 'kingdom' made a major contribution to the Bohemian emigration to the U.S.A., owned 187 estates totalling 493,000 acres, Prince Liechtenstein 360,000 acres, four other aristocratic families and two bishoprics over 75,000 acres each.

[3] Prince Schönborn 325,000 acres, Duke Philipp of Coburg-Gotha (the later Nazi leader) 195,000 acres, Count Andrassy 105,000 acres.

Junker origin, the institution conditioned them to share the Junker outlook.

Such realities of social life were transformed into political practice by an elaborate system of sham constitutionalism. A tripartite constitutional structure existed in Prussia from 1849 onwards, and in Austria after the conclusion, in the late sixties, of the manifold constitutional experiments that followed the defeat of 1859. It consisted of the Crown —which meant the actual person who wore it; an Upper House with a majority of hereditary nobles but including some higher civil servants and the like; and a House of Deputies elected on a complicated suffrage which ensured a safe majority for the most wealthy groups.[1] In Prussia the suffrage was indirect. Equal manhood suffrage was not introduced there until the end of the monarchy, and in Austria it did not come until 1906. As in Austria, national antagonisms might threaten the working of the parliamentary façade, an 'emergency' article provided for government and legislation without Parliament. In Germany, the gradual establishment of national unity under Prussian leadership made the constitutional practices of the Empire a mere cover for its control by the forces in power in Prussia. The Imperial Parliament was elected by manhood suffrage, but the Imperial government was not responsible to it, and the Federal Chancellor also held the office of Prussian Prime Minister, thus depending on the Prussian combination of one house of large estate owners and one controlled by the most wealthy taxpayers. There was no Imperial veto,[2] and Parliament was held in check only by the Federal Council. But the Emperor commanded the army and, as King of Prussia, through his influence on the other princes was sure of a safe majority in the Federal Council, which was composed of representatives of the individual State governments. The rights of the separate German States, not very extensive and increasingly encroached upon by the effects of economic centralization, were still effective enough to nullify whatever real power might be left to a progressive majority in the Imperial Parliament.

Before the rise of the modern labour movement, there was no force in opposition to the traditional régime other than liberalism, to which should be added in Austria the growing middle classes of the Slav nations. As early as the summer of 1848 the German bourgeoisie decided in favour of the Prussian way of unifying Germany; all further argument was restricted to the question of what should be the relative shares of the Junkers and the middle class in the government of the

[1] Hungary, with which we are concerned only because it then included Slovakia, was ruled completely by the gentry; but they enjoyed some degree of parliamentarism, as the government was responsible to the gentry-parliament. The details of the mechanism do not interest us, as the Slav minorities were completely without rights.

[2] But influential lawyers believed that it could be exercised in an indirect way, if necessary; the necessity never arose. See my *Federalism*, p. 76, note 3.

Prusso-German State. In 1859 German liberalism was organized in the *Nationalverein* (National Association) in order to advocate the Greater Prussian solution of the German question; and from 1862 to 1866 the Progressive party aimed at real power in Prussia. Bismarck defeated the Progressive Parliament, but, against the predominant mood of the Junkers and the hesitations of his king, he led Prussia on the path of diplomatic manœuvres and wars which resulted in the establishment of the Prusso-German empire. The institutions of that empire were so shaped as to satisfy the economic needs of the bourgeoisie without admitting it to a share in political power: this was enough to ensure the political collaboration of the bulk of the Liberals, known after 1866 as the National Liberals. Only a small group, which co-operated with the People's Party in Saxony and Southern Germany (which continued to oppose the Prussian solution of the German problem), remained in opposition. The leaders of the National Liberals aimed at 'preserving Liberalism' by 'waiving certain liberal doctrines',[1] by attracting enough Conservatives to make the party acceptable to the Court and the Army,[2] and even by preventing the 'premature' admission of Southern Germany to the North German Federation because this might strengthen left-wing liberalism, which in Prussia was condemned to play the part of a hopeless minority.[3] The ascendancy of National Liberalism among the German middle classes and in the German Parliaments was firmly established by the events of 1870–1. It ended only in 1878, when Bismarck again turned to the Conservatives. In 1879 nearly all the Liberals, except the South German People's Party, supported Bismarck's demand for oppressive measures against Social Democracy. But they strongly opposed the measures for social insurance introduced during Bismarck's last period of office and intended, in his policy towards the working class, to counterbalance the oppressive aspect. Their ranks were eventually split over the issue of Bismarck's reconciliation with the Junkers' demands for high corn duties and with the Catholic Church. Half of them remained in the National Liberal Party, which still followed Bismarck after the liberal episode in his policy had ended, but nearly half rallied to a Liberal Progressive Party. In 1893, on the issue of armaments and colonial policies, this party also split, the pro-militarist minority forming the Liberal Association, which in 1903 united with the National Social Party organized by Naumann, a former right-winger. In 1910 the Liberals reunited, except for the National Liberals, who meanwhile, to quote Rathenau,[4] had become 'another Conservative Party, the heavy-industry and big-business wing of Conservatism'.

[1] Duncker to Treitschke, in *Deutscher Liberalismus*, p. 385.
[2] Roggenbach to Oetker, ibid., p. 408.
[3] Wehrpfennig to Treitschke, ibid, pp. 415 ff.
[4] In a draft of a platform for a 'Party of German Freedom'; Nachlass, vol. I, p. 70.

The history of Austrian liberalism is even shorter. As in Prussia, 1848 brought the decisive cleavage, but with the difference that the obvious contradiction between the multi-national character of the Hapsburg monarchy and its leading role in the unification of Germany made the democratic and republican Left much stronger. In the insurrections of June 1848 in Prague and October 1848 in Vienna the Left was defeated, and the stage was left to the Liberals. In the National Assembly at Kremsier the Czech and German Liberals, inspired by the increasing threat of reaction, achieved a compromise on the constitutional issues; but the very prospect of a working Parliament caused the Court to hasten the abolition of the constitutional façade. The outcome was a military-bureaucratic dictatorship.[1] Part of the Viennese bourgeoisie directly collaborated with absolutist centralism; representatives of the 'progressive' wing of the bureaucracy such as Schmerling remained in the background until the French victory of 1859 forced on the dynasty a return to sham-constitutionalism. Schmerling's tenure of office from 1861 to 1865 proved to be more centralist than Liberal, and failed in consequence of the resistance of all the non-German peoples. But after the defeat of 1866, Francis Joseph appeased the Magyar gentry by the Dual Constitution, which offered them half the empire as ruling space. To prepare for a renewed fight for German hegemony, a Liberal government, this time including some real representatives of the bourgeoisie, came into office in the Austrian half of the empire. It did carry out some reforms, especially in the field of education, including the repeal of the Concordat of 1856. But the political influence of Austrian liberalism was broken by the economic depression of 1873, which deprived it of the support of the Austro-German lower middle classes which now turned anti-Semite. Its tenure of office came to an end in 1878, when the Austro-German middle-class politicians declined to support the annexation of Bosnia, for fear of increasing the Slav majority in the Dual Monarchy and thus undermining the joint Austro-German and Magyar hegemony. The role of the Hapsburg monarchy within the system of German imperialism consisted precisely in serving as an organ of indirect rule over the Slavs. This function fitted in well with Francis Joseph's interest in ruling as many peoples as he could; he thus got his opportunity to isolate the Austrian Liberals from their erstwhile protector, Bismarck, who, meanwhile, had dropped his own Liberals. A Conservative-Slav government, under Taaffe,[2] was installed with Prussian permission.

[1] See my *Federalism*, pp. 171 ff.

[2] A similar attempt had been made under Hohenwart in 1871, when the first German victories had proved the hopelessness of the Austro-German programme as embodied in Austrian liberalism. It had to be dropped when the new German empire, together with its Magyar allies, proved strong enough to establish political control of the Hapsburg monarchy.

After the removal of the Liberals from office, and the installation of the Taaffe government, part of the Austro-German lower middle classes turned towards political Catholicism;[1] others found expression for their aspirations in the Linz programme of 1882, which, while retaining the liberal anticlericalism, called for the creation of an artificial German majority within Austria by excluding Galicia from the Austrian half of the Dual Monarchy. From this point, Austro-German nationalism soon developed in a chauvinist direction, foreshadowing many features of Hitlerism. Anticlericalism, from opposition to the Church's support of feudal backwardness, became simple anti-Catholicism, partly in view of the Protestant character of the new German Empire and partly in search for an expression of 'racial' mystique in a revival of the cult of Wotan. Liberalism was now criticized, not for having compromised with the Court and the nobles, but for being Jewish, 'un-German', and so on. The Czechs were no longer expected to submit to constitutional changes which would create a German parliamentary majority, but were to be treated as 'under-men', to be excluded from all posts in the administration, from the professions, and even from skilled jobs in industry. In 1895 the Badeni government introduced regulations which, by allowing the use of Czech as well as German for official purposes in the purely Czech parts of Bohemia, improved the opportunities for Czechs to enter the civil service,[2] but because of Austro-German resistance the attempt ended in the nearest approach to revolution which Austria experienced between 1848 and 1918. Badeni's successor had to withdraw the regulations.

There was an obvious difference between the situation of the already prosperous middle class of an oppressor people, backed by a nearby Great Power, and that of the young middle class of an oppressed people, reduced until lately to the status of peasants and unskilled workers. But there are also remarkable similarities between the development of Czech and of Austro-German nationalism. In both camps the defeat of the democratic attempts of 1848 to overthrow the *ancien régime* was followed by more moderate middle-class attempts to win its favour in order to get as much satisfaction as possible for the national claims, and in both camps the tendency to fit their own national claims into a broader framework of reconstruction on liberal principles was replaced by nationalism pure and simple, though that of the Czechs was in open opposition to the powers that be. After the second half of the sixties the 'Old Czech' leading group round Palacky was opposed by the Young Czechs because of its tendency to appease the Court and the established Church, which since 1621 had been regarded as the symbol of national oppression.[3] Following the 1848 traditions, Palacky declined to sym-

[1] See below, p. 46.
[2] See my *Federalism*, pp. 201–5.
[3] For the split between Young and Old Czechs see Denis, op. cit., vol. III, pp. 560 ff.

pathize with Tsarist Russia: 'If ever', he wrote, 'we ceased to be Czechs, it would be quite indifferent to us whether we became Germans, Italians, Magyars, or Russians.'[1] The Young Czechs, not so devoted to liberal principles, were rather vague on this point; but the 'rule of the knout' in Tsarist Russia which Havliček, writing in 1846, had resented, deprived Pan-Slavism of much of its potential appeal among a people of peasants and workers. So the Young Czechs had to seek their nationalist utopia in the past, and the romantic nonsense they produced or revived could stand competition with any of that cherished by their German opponents. However, it must not be forgotten that their opposition to the Old Czechs, who on this as on other issues were cautious diplomats, began in declarations of sympathy for the anti-Tsarist Polish insurrection of 1863, and that in the turbulent demonstrations of 1893 the singing of the *Marseillaise* played as great a part as the display of Pan-Slav emblems.[2] With the enfranchisement of the popular masses nationalism pure and simple, in the Czech as well as in the Austro-German camp, receded in favour of sectional mass-parties influenced by nationalism. On the other hand, as we shall see, nationalism proved strong enough to split the existing all-Austrian sectional organizations.

[1] Cf. Palacky, op. cit. (1872), pp. 28 ff., and Masaryk, op. cit. (1898), p. 57.
[2] Denis, op. cit., vol. III, p. 610.

CHAPTER TWO

THE ORIGINS OF SECTIONAL ORGANIZATION, POLITICAL AND ECONOMIC

(*a*) *Schultze-Delitzsch, Lassalle, and the Origins of the German Political Labour Movement*

AFTER the defeats of the German middle and lower middle classes in their political struggles of 1848–9 and 1862–5, co-operatives of craftsmen's and small traders became popular. The 'social question', which even in those days attracted the attention of bourgeois opinion, however, was how to avoid a struggle between the new proletariat and the middle classes. Schultze-Delitzsch, who added his home and centre of activities to his name in order to distinguish himself from the many other Schultzes in German Parliaments, whatever his ambitions, could be no more than the inspirer of the lower-middle-class co-operative movement. A man who, when asked by workers for his advice on how to organize, was capable of replying: 'Gentlemen, have you saved?' was not likely to earn much working-class support. But bourgeois opinion, which would have been very glad to find the workers in the state of mind he attributed to them, hailed him as 'king in the social realm'.[1] Lassalle, indeed, began his propaganda in opposition to Schultze, an approach for which he was strongly taken to task by Marx, who did not think opposition to a Liberal the most suitable starting-point for the labour movement in a country such as Prussia, nor believe that Schultze's concepts could divert the workers from the path of class-struggle.

Although Schultze was one of the leaders of the Left Centre in the Prussian National Assembly of 1848, he never took part in the revolutionary movement, and soon returned to his experiments in co-operative organization. Freedom of competition was, to him, the essence of economic freedom; interference was evil. From what he could grasp of the Proudhonist current of those days Schultze accepted the 'principle of solidarity', not valid on a national level and in connexion with the State, but as between the members of a small co-operative who knew

[1] Cf. Brentano's introduction to Riehn, op. cit., and Zeidler, op. cit., p. 133.

each other and would act as mutual guarantors so that they could stand up better to the test of competition on the market. A not unfriendly critic of his work[1] remarked that, in spite of the balance Schultze claimed to keep between socialism and individualism, he was much more of an individualist than a socialist, but that this very limitation enabled him to help the small entrepreneur whose economic existence was threatened in his day. On the other hand, even when we come to speak of co-operatives of working-class consumers and of peasant producers, we shall meet his name and tradition only as a starting-point in opposition to which the actual mass-organization grew up.[2] Schultze-Delitsch concerns us here as the opponent against whom the German labour movement's first ideology was formulated.

The Prussian constitutional crisis of the early sixties was accompanied by a new birth of working-class organizations,[3] which since the defeat of the 1848 revolution had been virtually non-existent. The first of these were educational, with a strong interest in issues of co-operation and insurance; the possibilities of circumventing the legal prohibition of trade unions were hardly used.[4] Political interest centred on two issues: manhood suffrage, which in view of the record of its use in France for Bonapartist purposes was a highly controversial issue, and was rejected not only by the bourgeois Liberals but by progressive workers such as Bebel; and the collection of membership fees of the National Association (the Liberal-Progressive party caucus) by monthly instalments so that workers might be able to join. In 1862, when a national organization of the Workers' Associations was proposed by a committee elected by the Leipzig associations, the Progressives, who had just entered on the constitutional conflict with the Prussian Government, were faced with the question whether they would support manhood suffrage and concede the monthly collection of party fees. They turned down the demands, and the committee then approached Ferdinand Lassalle, a Socialist publicist who, unlike the founders and all the other active members of the League of Communists, had escaped imprisonment or exile after the defeat of 1849. In the war of pamphlets which accompanied the Austro-French-Italian crisis of 1859 he had taken part as an open supporter of the Greater Prussian solution of the German problem.[5] His next appearance on the political stage was de-

[1] Zeidler, op. cit., pp. 37–8.

[2] See below, pp. 40–1 and 44–5.

[3] Bebel's statement on the 'mushroom-like growth' of workers' associations (op. cit., vol. I, p. 55) betrays the optimistic standards of a young movement; as late as 1863 the Liberal wing of the labour movement, to which at that time he belonged, rallied 54 associations at its national congress. At Bebel's own election to the congress in the largest centre, Leipzig, 127 votes had been cast (ibid., p. 81).

[4] Professional educational associations originated as late as 1864, and evidently only in connexion with the Lassalleans. Cf. ibid., p. 91.

[5] Cf. his polemic with Engels, reported in my *Marx*, pp. 309–10.

voted to attempts to drive the Liberals further than they wished to go in their conflict with the Prussian government. On 12th April 1862, in a speech later published as the Workers' Programme, Lassalle had explained that what Hegel had called the moral idea of the State would be realized once the State, through the operation of manhood suffrage, was based upon the idea (evidently in the Hegelian sense) of the *Arbeiterstand*:[1] the workers, he said, represented the Church of our times. So it was not unnatural for the leaders of the Leipzig committee to seek Lassalle's advice when, like him, they found themselves rejected by the Progressive party.

In drafting his answer Lassalle had to make a basic political decision. The young workers' movement might rally as a political pressure group round the programme of the Left of 1848, i.e. the German democratic republic, to be established by the overthrow of all existing governments, with freedom of combination and other guarantees for the free development of the labour movement; the expected betrayal of the liberal cause by the Progressive-Liberals would be followed by the formation of an independent political party of the workers. The Marxists' distrust of Lassalle grew into the conviction that he was a traitor, because he chose the other alternative, that of dissociating the workers from the liberal cause so that they might maintain a bargaining position between the Liberals and the Prussian government. Lassalle's biographer, Oncken, agrees with Engels's description of him as a 'Tory Chartist'; Bismarck stated later that he did not doubt Lassalle's monarchist convictions, though he might prefer a Lassalle dynasty to a Hohenzollern one. Lassalle's main interest was clearly in manhood suffrage, which Bismarck eventually introduced in order to steal 'the most powerful ingredient known at the time to liberty-mongers'; but Lassalle would hardly have agreed with Bismarck that that ingredient was best when used in combination with the Junkers' electoral whisky and with ample scope for 'the play of God-willed dependences' by the open ballot.[2] Lassalle's bargaining position in relation to Bismarck, however, consisted precisely in the chance that, if an agreement entered into by him was supported by the workers, Bismarck could dissolve the oppositional Parliament without risk of serious disorder; in compensation Lassalle hoped to obtain manhood suffrage, thereby enabling the workers' party to become a powerful partner in a coalition with either of the major parties. In his answer to the Leipzig workers' committee, dated 1st March 1863, Lassalle developed the plan of his political campaign. He had to show that the workers needed a political party which could obtain, and operate with, manhood suffrage; any diversion from this

[1] Literally 'workers' estate'. The term had not in those days acquired its modern Fascist implications, but it is clear that Lassalle, a former member of the League of Communists, quite deliberately avoided the term 'working class'.

[2] Bismarck's *Memoirs*, Engl. ed., vol. II, pp. 62–4.

objective was an evil. Hence his concentration upon a polemic with Schultze-Delitzsch, who had said that the workers needed 'self-help' in the economic field, and should leave politics to the Liberals.

Schultze-Delitzsch had taught the German lower middle classes that they should not look for the help of the Prussian State to preserve the patriarchal order of things in which there was an appropriate place for the guild-master, but should help themselves by co-operative effort. There was no inherent reason why a Socialist should refute this statement: Socialist criticism was invited by Schultze's interpretation of the position of the working class as identical with that of the lower middle class. But in order to refute Schultze, Lassalle produced the formula 'State help versus self-help', the State help being that of a State brought under pressure by manhood suffrage, the Self-help that of Schultze-Delitzsch. Marx and Engels, whose main message in those years was that 'the emancipation of the working class can only come from the workers themselves', quite apart from their hostility to the Prussian State with which Lassalle was bargaining,[1] were bound to reject a propaganda which denounced 'self-help' in order to criticize the co-operative utopia. The argument Lassalle used to prove the futility of 'self-help' implied also that of trade unionism—at a time when, though non-existent in Germany, it was already important in England and was developing in France. Lassalle's argument was based on those economists who had stated that wages were bound to remain at the minimum physiological subsistence level, 'the iron law of wages'; it followed that within capitalist society no improvement in working-class conditions was possible. In discussing alternatives to capitalism, Lassalle replaced Schultze's co-operative utopia by another, namely, Producers' Associations with State help, which Louis Blanc had demanded as early as 1848. In the Paris of that time, this demand had raised the issue of public support for the unemployed; in the Germany of 1863 it made no sense except as a suggestion for the establishment of 'Socialist' cells within the existing society without interference with the rights of existing entrepreneurs, and it was so interpreted by Bismarck as well as by Bishop Ketteler,[2] who saw no harm in offering support to such experiments. But Lassalle was inviting the workers to form a political party of their own in order to extort from the Prussian State large-scale support for that very panacea!

If the intensity of the German workers' urge for a political party of their own needs proof, it is provided by the fact that an ideology such as we have described, in spite of its complete divorce from reality, could serve as the banner under which that party rallied. Those of Lassalle's

[1] They did not know how far Lassalle had gone in his negotiations with Bismarck (cf. Gustav Mayer, *Bismarck and Lassalle*, Berlin, 1928), but grasped enough to realize the position. Cf. Engels's Letter to Kautsky, 23rd February 1891.

[2] See below, p. 32.

tenets which were in clear contradiction to the needs of the working-class struggle were passed over or reinterpreted; a few years after Lassalle's death, Fritzsche, one of the leaders of the Leipzig committee which had sought his advice in 1862 and one of the Lassallean M.P.s, organized the first German trade union, that of the cigar-makers. When its strength was tested in a big strike, producers' associations (without State help), were formed as a means of employing the strikers, and later the blacklisted.[1] In the minds of the German workers, the conception of the society to come as a complex of producers' associations served as propaganda for the rejection of capitalist exploitation; the polemic against 'self-help' meant only the rejection of utopian dreams that workers might turn into capitalists by saving; and the 'iron law of wages' was but another way of saying that maximum achievement in the industrial field could not dispense with the need for political action. This interpretation of Lassalleism was eventually accepted by the German labour movement, and Bebel, the man who contributed most to the overthrow of the Lassallean sect and its specifically Prussian-oriented policies, wrote forty years later that he, like nearly all those who became Socialists during that period, had come to Marx through Lassalle.[2] Lassalle's attraction to the Prussian method of achieving German unity, as well as his personal qualities, gave his organization a dictatorial constitution. This was obviously necessary for delivering the goods promised in negotiations with such strange partners as Bismarck. On the other side, South German and Saxon Liberals, organized in the People's Party, continued to resist Prussian hegemony even after their Government had submitted to it in 1866. Since the foundation in 1862 of Lassalle's *Allgemeiner Deutscher Arbeiterverein*, the left-wing Liberals had opposed it by the Union of German Workers' Associations, but at its Nuremberg congress, in 1868, that Union, until then dominated by the People's Party, declared its solidarity with the International and accepted Socialism as its theoretical platform while continuing to oppose the centralist and pro-Prussian Lassalle organization. It was soon joined by an opposition which had grown up within the latter.

As a result of the factional struggles which followed Lassalle's death, a new leadership challenged his clique: Schweitzer, while accepting the Prussian method of unifying Germany, attempted to transform the Lassalle organization into an up-to-date Socialist party, while retaining its centralist organization. Evidently this was regarded as necessary for

[1] An interesting monograph on this movement, with some bias in favour of the Liberal opponents of the Socialist leaders of the cigar-makers' union, was published by F. Klüss, in *Volkswirtschaftliche Abhandlungen der Badischen Hochschulen*, 1905.

[2] Op. cit., vol. I, p. 118. At the Nuremberg Congress (see below, in text) of the anti-Lassalle wing of the German labour movement, Schweidel (*Proceedings*, p. 38) stated that he, 'like this whole Congress', took the Iron Law of Wages for granted. According to Mehring (op. cit., vol. IV, p. 57), Grillenberger said, of an even later period, that 'in organization we were Eisenacheans [see below, p. 20], in theory Lassalleans'.

the control of a caucus used to authoritarian management.[1] Schweitzer, however, realized that leadership could not derive its authority from the founder's will, but had to be tested by ensuring the party's political leadership of the masses. In 1868 several strikes were in progress, one of them, as we have just seen, led by Schweitzer's fellow-partisan Fritzsche. The movement was modest enough, but it surpassed anything experienced in Germany up to then and demonstrated that that country was to face the problem of industrial conflict familiar in Western Europe.[2] In order not to be left behind by its competitor, the Union of German Workers' Associations, and perhaps also to find some cover in the event of the police dissolving the Lassalle party,[3] which actually happened even before the trade unions were formed, Schweitzer considered that the party should take the lead in organizing trade unions. This was not easy, in view of the Lassallean tenets of State help and the Iron Law of Wages.

In speaking to his sect,[4] Schweitzer had to show that the workers would eventually be convinced of the truth of these tenets and of the need for political action by their very failure to improve their conditions

[1] Lassalle actually transferred the presidency of his organization (which implied its almost autocratic control) by his will, and in the same way ordered the expulsion of potential opponents of the clique to which he entrusted the continuation of his work. Such rulings, though observed at first by his devoted followers, were the source of internal conflicts under which his clique eventually broke asunder.

[2] The propensity of some academic historians of the labour movement (Kulemann, op. cit., p. 184, as opposed to Brentano and Mayer, op. cit., pp. 242–4) to repeat uncritically the organization myths of such bodies as are regarded as moderate and 'reasonable' is illustrated by the widespread assertion that at any rate the immediate incentive to the formation of German trade unionism was given by the Liberal leader, Max Hirsch, in his contributions to the *Berliner Volkszeitung* on British trade unionism. Better knowledge than that of Dr. Hirsch was available to people such as Liebknecht, who had spent years as an exile in England, and Schweitzer, who was corresponding with Marx on *Kapital*, and needed no external incentive to realize the potentialities of the strikes in which members of his own party took part. As was most natural for a follower of Schultze-Delitzsch, Hirsch went to England to study co-operation, and only there noticed the existence of trade unions. His reports were published immediately before the Hamburg Congress of the Lassalle party, and were evidently written later than the articles in the *Sozialdemokrat* by which Schweitzer prepared opinion regarding that Congress (see below).

[3] The anti-Lassalleans in the labour camp reproached Schweitzer for advocating centralism in the future trade unions for this very reason, as against his assertion that it would be required by the very needs of industrial conflict (see below, pp. 18 and 20). Engels (letter to Marx of 30th September 1868) and Marx (writing on this suggestion to Schweitzer on 13th October), regarded the practical needs of trade unionism, especially the need for democratic control, as a main argument against extreme centralization. The argument would hardly have been emphasized had they not disapproved of those political uses which Schweitzer was regarded as likely to make of centralized power concentrated in his hands.

[4] In a series of articles in the *Sozialdemokrat*, 1868, Nos. 77 ff., reprinted by Bringmann, op. cit., Annex, pp. 316 ff., summarized ibid., pp. 114–15, and by Mehring, op. cit. (1898), pp. 316 ff.

by industrial action. Socialists, believing that only the conquest of political power could solve the social problem, should not organize strikes; but as the strikes were the workers' spontaneous reaction to the growth of capitalism, Socialists should help the workers in their struggle so that they might draw the appropriate lessons from the inevitable failures. By acquiring the habit of defending their interests themselves the masses would be prepared for democracy, which was the essential condition of the introduction of Socialism by State help, unless the latter were interpreted in a reactionary sense.[1] They would also recognize the benefits of centralist organization, a specific Lassallean tenet, as demonstrated by the experience of British trade unions; in comparison with the latter, however, German trade unionism would enjoy the benefit of permeation with the spirit of Socialism from the very start. But when speaking to the trade unionists themselves, Schweitzer and Fritzsche naturally emphasized the more positive sides of their attitude to industrial action. In the motion submitted to the Hamburg Congress and accepted by it, it was stated that strikes could not change the existing economic structure, and so were incapable of *fundamentally* improving the conditions of the working class, but they were a suitable means of developing class consciousness and breaking down police tutelage. If organized in the proper, i.e. centralist manner, trade unions could remove specially oppressive social evils, such as long hours, child labour, etc. The enumeration of the possible achievements was obviously dictated not only by respect for the sanctity of the Iron Law of Wages but also by the desire to concentrate the workers' attention on issues which demanded solution by legislation, i.e. political action.

While the specific form in which Schweitzer put forward his argument was naturally conditioned by the specific tenets of the group to which it was made, and by the desire to concentrate all attention on political action, its basic contents were quite current in the world of labour of that time. The description of strikes as due to a delusion of the working class which could be overcome only by experience had been propagated by the Geneva section of the International in 1865 and 1866,[2] and the alternative of Producers' Associations was also available to those who rejected State help for their foundation.[3] So the Geneva Internationalists shared with their Lassallean contemporaries the grudging admission of the inevitability of strikes, and, like the Lassallean Schweitzer, eventually found consolation in the hope that the experience that the workers

[1] This rider, added by Schweitzer, shows that he was quite conscious of the dangers involved in orthodox Lassalleism; this puts his subsequent agreement therewith (below, p. 20) in a not very favourable light.

[2] Bringmann, op. cit., p. 124, and Annex, p. 314 ff.

[3] Cf. the memorandum submitted by the Geneva section to the London conference of the International (*Vorbote*, 1866, No. 4), and the proceedings of the Geneva Congress, 1866 (*Vorbote*, 1866, No. 10, p. 145).

acquired in strikes would be applied in more advanced activities.[1] Nor were all of Schweitzer's trade unionist fellow-partisans more enthusiastic about trade unionism than he was himself.[2] The low degree of development of industrial action and the disillusionment caused by its initial failure, which was in sharp contrast to the urgency of national unification, must be kept in mind in order to understand how much the formation of the first German trade unions was governed by moves on the political chessboard of factional disputes.

Schweitzer had to wage a hard fight within his caucus for the mere convention of the trade union congress. His motion was passed by his Party congress by 3,417 votes to 2,589, but orthodox Lassalleism was strong enough to prevent the calling of the trade union congress on behalf of the party, and the two presidents, Schweitzer and Fritzsche, had to threaten resignation in order to get the party's permission by a small majority to convene the congress in their private capacity as M.P.s. The congress itself was a success, though the number of workers claimed to be represented, 142,000, was certainly exaggerated;[3] the competing Internationalist Trade Unions, formed by the Nuremberg majority of the Association of German Workers' Associations, were much weaker. A third group was formed by the official leaders of the Liberal party,[4] one of whom, Max Hirsch, had returned from a trip to Britain just in

[1] Ibid., 1867, No. 12 (Memorandum to Lausanne Congress); 1868, No. 5, p. 67; 1869, No. 3 (p. 63) and No. 8 (p. 118).

[2] In the tailors' appeal to establish their trade union (*Sozialdemokrat*, 1868, No. 9), the need for combination and friendly society benefits is emphasized, with the rider that they believed themselves 'to have found a way which, while not directly helping us to achieve our aims, may lead us into the right road'. There were some protests (Nos. 13 and 15), including one from the Hamburg tailors, who declined to participate 'because our pockets are empty and we do not wish to be turned aside from the main thing, the political party, as were the cigar makers'. On the other side, a communication by the Elberfeld workers (in No. 18) hails the Berlin Cigar Makers' Co-operative 'because they have thrown off the yoke of capital and have challenged the Iron Law of Wages'. This seems clearly to indicate that this producers' co-operative was not regarded as a mere emergency measure of workers on strike, and that the Lassalle programme was not interpreted to mean an immediate nation-wide re-organization of production.

[3] The calculation was based on the statements of the 206 delegates as to the number of workers who had taken part in their election; although (outside Berlin) rather large numbers of workers must be supposed to have subscribed to the travelling expenses of every delegate, in view of the level of wages at that time, it is most unlikely that 700 workers took part in the election of the average delegate. After the split (see below, p. 20), which involved only a small minority but may have repulsed other sympathizers, the representatives of 21,000 trade union members voted at the Third Congress on so decisive an issue as amalgamation (see below, pp. 20–1).

[4] Cf. Bringmann, op. cit., p. 131 ff., Mayer, op. cit., p. 245, and Bringmann, op. cit., p. 335, for the opinion of an independent left-wing liberal, Jacobi, who suggested participation by the Liberal workers in the trade-union movement initiated by that party which undoubtedly enjoyed the confidence of the majority of prospective trade unionists.

time to be impressed by the attempt of some Trade Union leaders, as against the campaign which followed the Sheffield outrages, 'not only to dissociate themselves from the turbulence of the old-fashioned trade unionists, but also . . . to persuade the public that the Junta and their friends, not the strike-jobbers or the outrage-mongers, were the authorized and typical representatives of the Trade Union movement'.[1] With such statements in their minds, Hirsch and his friends produced the afterwards familiar juxtaposition of British trade unionism, alleged to be based upon the principle of social peace, with the Socialist concepts of class struggle. Schultze-Delitzsch, the apostle of 'self-help' by saving, and the convinced opponent of strikes, was a main speaker at the foundation meetings of the Liberal unions, later known from the name of the two conveners as Hirsch-Duncker unions. Duncker later admitted that his only purpose was to prevent the workers from joining the Lassallean unions.[2] Notwithstanding their intentions, the Hirsch-Duncker unions, on the recognition issue, were involved in the largest strike of the early period, that of the Waldenburg miners in 1869, which ended in defeat, the disillusioned miners joining the Social Democratic camp. Although they were the only early unions not dissolved under the Anti-Socialist law, in later periods the Hirsch-Duncker unions were important only as organizations of part of the black-coated workers.

But a major crisis arose in the Socialist camp within nine months from the foundation Congress of the Lassallean trade unions as a result of one of those unprincipled manœuvres in which the Lassalle party seemed so prolific. Confronted by an increasing internal opposition to his dictatorship, Schweitzer changed sides and attempted a reconciliation with the orthodox Lassalleans; part of their price was an undertaking to end his support of trade unionism. The opposition, headed by York and Fritzsche, united with the Association of German Workers' Associations to form, at the Eisenach Congress of 1869 (whence the name Eisenacheans for the anti-Lassallean faction of Social Democracy) the German Social Democratic Party. Most of the Lassallean Trade Unions lost their Presidents, who had formed the hard core of the anti-Schweitzer opposition, but retained a large majority of their members.[3] When the secession was an accomplished fact, Schweitzer found it convenient to re-emphasize the Iron Law of Wages and to deduce from it the necessary subordination of the unions to the Party; he soon suggested the amalgamation of the trade unions into 'one big union'.[4] A motion

[1] S. and B. Webb, op. cit., pp. 264–5.

[2] Mehring, op. cit. (1878) (written from the anti-Socialist standpoint), p. 103.

[3] Mehring, op. cit., 1898, vol. III, p. 381. Mayer's (op. cit., p. 341) explanation of this by the reluctance of members to part with the contributions already paid (less than one year after the foundation of the unions) is a transference of later attitudes into that early period. See below, p. 66.

[4] Cf. his articles in *Sozialdemokrat*, 14th September 1869 (reprinted by Bringmann, op. cit., p. 156), and 29th December 1869.

to this effect was indeed carried in January 1870 by the Lassallean Trade Union Congress by 12,500 votes to 9,000; the objections were only for reasons of propagandist convenience. York, reporting to the Stuttgart Congress of the Eisenach party in June 1870, opposed amalgamation with the sole argument that, since the time of the guilds, the workers had been accustomed to professional organization; he introduced a motion in favour of the concentration of the trade unions' interest on the establishment of Producers' Co-operatives, which was accepted.[1] When protests were made against the return to 'self-help' apparently implied in this resolution,[2] the editors of the Eisenachean paper replied that nobody thought of establishing the new society without 'State help', i.e. before the conquest of political power: the trade unions, however, as the organizational centres of the society to come, should devote some attention to acquiring organizational experience which whould eventually help in its construction.

Mehring is certainly right in explaining this increased interest in the society to come by a number of unsuccessful strikes,[3] and this factor was bound to influence both the competing factions of the labour movement. Apart from this, however, there was in the Lassallean camp also a conscious anti-trade unionist tendency which aimed at complete absorption of the unions by the Party, and, indeed, carried motions to that effect at the Party congresses of 1870 and 1872. But they failed to influence Lassallean trade unionists other than those whose unions broke down in any case because of lack of means. The Party's main strength rested upon the workers of the Berlin building trades; in view of the importance of the seasonal element and of skilled labour, rapid action might be more important than funds, and Schweitzer's argument in favour of centralization as furthering rapid action may have been accepted at its face value. At the Party congress of 1874 an official motion was defeated which denounced trade unions as 'self-help without prospects other than that of splitting the working-class forces', and demanded their dissolution within a year on pain of expulsion from the Party; instead, the Congress—the last held by the separate Lassallean party—adopted the motion proposed by the unions, which emphasized not only the need for centralizing friendly society benefits but also the possibilities of industrial struggle, including that for wage increases.[4] Thus, ten years after Lassalle's death, orthodox Lassalleism was defeated within his own

[1] Mehring, op. cit., vol. III, p. 386, Stuttgart (1870), Müller on Dresden Congress of Social Democratic Party (*Protocol*, p. 122). York's report was characteristically called 'On Co-operatives'; the only type of co-operatives not rejected at that time as 'Self-help' were Producers' Associations formed by workers on strike.

[2] Kreacker in *Volksstaat*, 1870, No. 52, also Hillmann.

[3] Op. cit., p. 387; see also Bebel, op. cit., vol. I, pp. 191–2.

[4] Report of the Cologne Party Congress, p. 190. Mehring (op. cit., p. 58) has apparently overlooked these events, which happened at a time when he stood outside the party.

organization. The defeat, however, concerned his one-sided emphasis on political action, not the direction of that action.

Partly because of their origins in the opposition to Schweitzer, and partly, perhaps, for the simple reason that they were the weaker of the two competing factions, the Eisenacheans defended the principle of political neutrality of trade unions, and had it accepted by their Trade Union Congress at Erfurt in 1872. In this atmosphere, though only in the minds of a few more advanced thinkers, more definite ideas of the part eventually to be played by trade unions could grow up; it is interesting to note that they developed very much on the lines characteristic of the later Guild Socialism in Britain. Hillmann's 'Practical Suggestions on Working-Class Emancipation',[1] published in the *Volkstaat*, May 1873, and described by Mehring twenty-five years later as 'still instructive and helpful reading', represent an attempt to reinterpret the Iron Law of Wages as dealing with the customary standard of living, an idea similar to Marx's 'historical and moral element' in the definition of wages; it followed that successes in the industrial struggle can become definitive if upheld over a sufficient period. Just as the medieval guild unconsciously emancipated bourgeois society, trade unions are the means of the economic, social, political, and intellectual emancipation of the working-class; their organizational achievements inspire working-class demands for political equality. Just as the feudal State had to recognize the guilds, so will the bourgeois State eventually be forced not only to recognize trade unions but to model political and municipal organization after their pattern. Thus a people's democracy will be achieved.

(*b*) *United Social Democracy under the Anti-Socialist Law*

In 1875, after it was realized that the Prussian method of unifying Germany had to be accepted by the Eisenacheans as an accomplished fact, and Bismarck in 1873 had dissolved the Lassalle organization, the two factions united in the Gotha Congress.[2] Political reunion was not

[1] Reprinted by Bringmann, op. cit., pp. 382 ff. There was some opposition to the publication, which refutes a description of it as characteristic of the intellectual level of those days. On the other hand the quoted approval by Mehring, one of the leaders of the left wing of Social Democracy, shows how far Hillmann anticipated the insight available at a much later stage of development.

[2] Marx's disappointment about the extent to which the Eisenacheans' declarations of solidarity with the International represented actual understanding of his theories found expression in his *Critique of the Gotha Programme*. When Engels published it twenty-seven years later, the Party leaders protested, allegedly because of mere tactical consideration for the cult of Lassalle which was still current in the Party. Such 'tactical' considerations on the part of people such as Bebel, who during their struggle with the Lassalleans had not refrained from giving the least charitable explanation of any move of their opponents, merely proved the absence of fundamental opposition to Lassalleism as a political theory. A few years after the Gotha Congress, Engels's critique of Dühring (whose theories were supported by some of the

sufficient to revive the weak plant of German trade unionism in view of the current economic depression; in 1877 there were not more than 50,000 trade unionists, or 1·5 per cent of the workers employed in the trades where unions existed. But the political labour movement, as the only serious and consistent opposition party, made rapid progress; in the national elections of 1877 it polled half a million votes, 9 per cent of the total cast. Bismarck meanwhile had decided on a definitely right-wing course, and looked on oppression of the extreme left as a suitable device for splitting liberalism. To accomplish this he used two attempts on the Emperor's life made in 1878 by madmen without political connexions as his pretext for outlawing the Socialist Party, the trade unions, and all publications in sympathy with Socialism or even republicanism. The repression, though not to be compared with modern fascist efforts,[1] was enough to bring about a temporary crystallization of the diverse trends which coexisted within Social Democracy. On the one side, the official Party institutions solemnly dissolved themselves, and some intellectuals deplored the errors of class struggle by which the Party had forfeited the sympathy of respectable bourgeois opinion. On the other, the demand of the active party workers for an underground organization and the fact that German left-wing oppositionists had started periodicals abroad with encouragement from Marx and Engels, eventually forced the leaders to start an official Party organ, the *Sozialdemokrat*, to be published abroad.[2] Although its editors were chosen for their moderate outlook, and were eventually to become outstanding representatives of the Party's right wing,[3] the situation caused them to move far to the left

Social Democratic leaders) provoked sharp reactions, including a motion at the Party Congress of 1877 which deplored the publication of *Anti-Dühring* in the Party organ. The situation characterized by these reactions to the *Critique of the Gotha Programme* and *Anti-Dühring* was the background against which Kautsky's works of the eighties and early nineties might appear as a triumph of Marxism.

[1] The party retained its parliamentary representation, which worked as a main channel of its activities; and the banishment of Social Democrats from their place of domicile—which in those days played the part assigned in modern techniques of repression to the concentration camp—was an efficient agency for the spread of Socialism outside the industrial centres.

[2] Bebel (op. cit., vol. III, p. 27) argues against the assumption, widespread in his day, that the leaders had lost their direction and the Party had been saved by the masses (Mehring's chapter on the first period of the Anti-Socialist Law is headed: 'A Year of Disorientation'). But Bebel's argument itself elucidates the concepts of leadership held by himself and his fellows of what was later described as the Party Centre: he agrees that among the leading officials there was a good deal of inactivity and cowardice, but excuses this by the material difficulties caused by the loss of their jobs; he adds that there was also quite a lot of depression among the rank and file.

[3] Bernstein was one of the three members of the Zürich group who after the publication of the Anti-Socialist Law had written the famous article opposing the concept of class struggle which, they alleged, was responsible for the Party's loss of bourgeois sympathy; Vollmar enjoyed so much sympathy among the right-wing Social Democratic leaders that they dropped in his favour the demand for control of

of the Party's official attitude. At the Party Congress of August 1880, held in Switzerland, the word 'legal' was unanimously deleted from the clause of the programme stating that the Party would pursue its aims by all *legal* means. Bebel explained the amendment as being directed only against the Anti-Socialist Law; once the Party regained its legal status it would obey the laws. But there can be no doubt that many supporters were convinced that Socialism could be achieved only by overthrowing the existing régime. These conditions explain the triumph of Marxism, though in a vulgarized version, as the predominant Party ideology. During the period of the Anti-Socialist Law it was prepared for by the Party publications abroad and such restricted publication of books and periodicals as after a time became possible; it was accepted in the Erfurt Programme of 1891, immediately after the Party's triumphant emergence from underground.[1]

The two general elections which took place during the terror campaign that preceded and followed the passing of the Anti-Socialist Law had cost the Party about a third of its former voting strength; but the losses were made good as early as 1884. In 1890 Social Democracy, still in a semi-legal state, polled 1·4 million votes, or 20 per cent of the total, i.e. more than any other party, though majority representation, together with the anti-socialist blocs arranged for the second ballot, prevented it from getting more than thirty-five seats. Bismarck's conflict with his new royal master, Wilhelm II, on the question whether to meet the Socialist tide by bullets or by social reforms contributed greatly to his dismissal, after which the Anti-Socialist Law was not renewed. During

the editorship of the *Sozialdemokrat* which they had made when Hirsch, a friend of Marx and Engels, was the likely candidate for the post (cf. Bebel, vol. III, p. 63). Most of the relevant correspondence is available in English in Marx-Engels, *Selected Correspondence*, vol. 9 of the Marxist-Leninist Library. Bebel's letters were inspired by an obvious tendency to smooth over the differences between Marx and Engels and the German Party by minimizing the importance of the latter's right wing (cf. his op. cit., vol. III). Mehring, in 1893, gives a fairly comprehensive picture of events. Bernstein's and Vollmar's development under the impact of their responsibility for the Party organ issued abroad is shown by the fact that Bernstein's editorial policy not only met with the approval of Marx and Engels as well as of the large majority of Party members, but also provoked the disavowal of the organ by the parliamentary Party (Bebel, op. cit., vol. III, p. 185). Vollmar wrote the famous article in the *Sozialdemokrat*, in which prolongation of the Anti-Socialist Law was welcomed as a means of keeping the workers conscious of the eventual need for a decisive struggle; this article was welcomed by Engels, but disowned by Bebel—who wrote an answer on behalf of the Party leaders—allegedly for tactical reasons (op. cit., p. 190 ff.). On Vollmar's and Bernstein's later attitude see below, pp. 83 and 90.

[1] In order to judge of the extent to which Marxism was received in official Party theory we may mention that, while in 1875 Marx had criticized the Gotha Programme for promising the workers social emancipation once a democratic republic (the 'free people's state') was achieved, Engels in 1891 had to criticize the Erfurt Programme for not raising the demand for a democratic republic even in such a veiled form as was compatible with Prussian legality.

the currency of this Law the position of the parliamentary Party, as the only Party organ which could work in the open and which scored visible successes, encouraged a tendency in its ranks to restrict the prospects of Social Democracy to what could be achieved within the framework of Prusso-German legality; added to this was the fact that the Party organ published abroad tended to reflect more radical trends in the membership than did the official Party leaders, and that the parliamentary Party used every suitable opportunity to disown it. As early as 1882 even the temporizing Bebel foresaw that a split might become necessary; some of the Party leaders and especially of the M.P.s, he thought, preserved the appearances of membership either because they were not conscious of the contradictions between the Party view and their own attitude, or were afraid to speak their minds knowing that the masses would not follow them.[1] In 1885 a more definite hint of things to come was given when the parliamentary Party, with appropriate phrases about the 'civilizing functions of German commerce', supported State subsidies for some German shipping lines of little commercial importance, but essential for colonial expansion in Africa and the South Seas.

Though with less elaborate theoretical foundations than in later years, during the early period of the Anti-Socialist Law three trends became visible in the Party: a left wing, some of whose extreme representatives, when expelled from the Party, went over to anarchism as apparently the most radical and anti-bureaucratic attitude available,[2] but the bulk of which was made up of a clear majority of the active Party members and provided the basis for the reception of Marxism as the Party ideology; a right wing, which even in those days followed the lines that eventually led to the decision of 4th August 1914 and which, in the absence of trade unions, was supported by a major part of the parliamentary Party; and in the centre, a term not then in use,[3] Bebel and a few other leaders who temporized in either direction but supported the right wing on the essential point that they prevented its expulsion.

(c) *The Growth of Trade Unionism*

The references made above to the origins of German trade unionism illustrate the growth of the ideology of the political labour movement

[1] See letter to Auer of 7th January 1882, reproduced, op. cit., vol. III, pp. 186 ff.

[2] Of those leaders who developed along these lines during the first years of the Anti-Socialist Law, most (according even to Bebel's statement, op. cit., vol. III, p. 48) as late as the spring of 1879, edited his paper in such a way as to win Marx's and Engels's approval; his anarchism developed when the German Party leaders started abroad a paper of their own, in competition with which outsiders such as Most wanted to keep to the extreme left. Hasselmann had been a Lassallean who opposed to the last the union with Eisenacheans; in modern Marxist terms, his 'deviation' had been rather right wing. After the repeal of the Anti-Socialist Law the 'Wild men', and, in the Trade Union field, the Localists (see below, p. 61) embraced anarchism only when they were driven out of the official framework of the Labour movement.

[3] See below, p. 93.

rather than of that of trade unionism itself. Trade unionism after 1890, with very few exceptions, marked a new start, not only formally because of the Anti-Socialist Law, but also as regards the actual formation of at any rate the more important unions. In Austria the right of combination was granted under the pressure of a powerful mass demonstration on 18th December 1868. Austrian trade unionism, little disturbed at first by factional disputes,[1] developed at least as well as its German counterpart:[2] at its first high-water mark, before the depression of 1873, there were in Austria 33,000 trade unionists and about the same number of members of associations for mutual assistance in case of illness and disablement,[3] most of which served as legal camouflage for trade unionism which was exposed to repression by the administration. The documentation on the first steps in Austrian trade unionism available in Deutsch's history shows a remarkable absence of political dogmatism, or rather a strong readiness to use the available political terminology for trade unionist purposes, however this might fit its original content. We find the Iron Law of Wages being quoted in negotiations with employers to demonstrate that the increase demanded was just necessary to keep the workers in a state of good health,[4] and the 'Producers' Associations with State Help' as a mere definition of the final Socialist aim and quite compatible with very realistic demands for immediate reform.[5] In the early eighties, the political labour movement in Austria was split into two factions. The Radicals, who were supported by most of the trade unionists, roughly corresponded with that wing of German Social Democracy which enforced resistance to the Anti-Socialist law, and like it were described by their opponents as 'anarchists', with not much greater justification. The Moderates, like the right wing of the German party, hoped for improvement from rulers whose benevolence might be increased as a result of some pressure exerted by constitutional means. Strange as it might seem to such an author as Deutsch, who saw through the spectacles of later disputes,[6] Radicals might elaborate quite concrete programmes of trade unionist action,[7] while Moderates might oppose the introduction of friendly society benefits, even in favour of the unemployed, with very dogmatic arguments,[8] especially if the union's chest were empty. Empty it was, and remained for a long time,

[1] The internal struggle between Lassallean and the internationalist Eisenachian factions very soon resulted in the triumph of the latter.

[2] Doctrinaire Lassalleans who opposed trade unionism in Germany might describe it, with some exaggeration, as 'imported from Austria' (Bringmann, op. cit., vol. I, p. 190).

[3] Deutsch, op. cit., vol. I, pp. 73–4.

[4] Ibid., pp. 68–9.

[5] Ibid., pp. 77–8.

[6] See below, pp. 55 and 61.

[7] See Deutsch, op. cit., p. 114.

[8] Cf. ibid., p. 116.

for only the class-conscious minority dared to join the organizations. In the Alpine districts, apart from Vienna and Lower Austria, trade union membership on the very eve of the 1918 revolution did not exceed that of the political Party, which itself was only a small fraction of those who supported it by their votes at elections.

Under these conditions, only two types of industrial movement could be effective: those of small groups, mainly of skilled workers, relying on disagreements among their employers coming into the open during a strike, which might be prolonged by whatever support other sections of the labour movement that regarded the strikers as its protagonists could afford,[1] and those of workers in important centres whose working conditions were so appalling that even when the strike was suppressed by bloodshed, pressure of public opinion and the respect of the rulers for the consequences might compel improvements.[2] In the first stage, only movements of the former type could be consolidated as organized unions. The turning-point was reached when trade unionism entered the basic industries dominated by the most powerful monopolies, whose labour force was recruited from among the most backward strata of the population. The origins of the German Miners' Union afford a classical illustration of this process.

In the Ruhr, during the spring of 1889, small nuclei of Socialist and, it would seem, Catholic miners began to agitate for a wage increase of 15 to 25 per cent, and for the eight-hour day calculated from pithead to pithead. No immediate action was planned, and a delegates' meeting was called for June 2nd, but the agitation was sufficient to bring the accumulated tension to a spontaneous outbreak. On May 8th 40,000 miners came out, and six days later 110,000 were involved, with 30,000 more on the Saar and in Silesia. Catholic influence induced the Ruhr miners to send a delegation to the Emperor, who promised sympathetic investigation of their demands on condition that Social Democratic influences should be expelled. An agreement was concluded on May 19th, but 'a recurrence of the strike, which was threatened in consequence of its ambiguous terms, was prevented by the arrest of the strike committee', to quote a by no means subversively-minded historian.[3] Neither the partial success nor the betrayal by the Government was likely to reduce the influence of the Socialist groups. A trade union of the Ruhr miners was formed; in the following year it was transformed into a general German Miners' Union, with 58,000 members. The mine-owners' failure to keep the agreement led to another strike in February 1891; it also started spontaneously, just as a committee of Socialist and Catholic delegates was preparing to present its demands. It never attained the

[1] Cf. ibid., p. 179.

[2] Cf. Deutsch's (op. cit., p. 152) report on the strike of 30,000 miners and furnace men at Vitkovice, 1890.

[3] Kulemann, op. cit., p. 296.

extent of the previous strike, and was defeated, but it was alleged that the Miners' Union rose to a temporary strength of 100,000, or two-thirds of all the miners. A setback reduced this inflated figure to 11,000 in 1895,[1] and its gradual recovery in numbers did not fundamentally affect the union's character as an organization of an *élite*; continuous emigration from the Polish parts of Prussia and the strong influence of the clergy prevented its consolidation in what were not times of acute struggle. But that the majority of the miners continued to support it was shown in 1894 by the mass meetings called to nominate delegates to the International Miners' Conference, against which the Catholics reacted by the formation of the Christian Trade Union.[2]

The counterpart to this dynamic development was represented by the German Printers' Union, an almost isolated representative of its type, but the model for those who advocated an imitation of the British pattern. Even before the revolution of 1848 the printers had been organized in local brotherhoods, supervised by the guild, which entered into agreements ('Postulats') with the guild on the basic conditions of employment. The revolution was unlikely to create strong antagonisms between an exclusive group of skilled workers and employers with an obvious interest in the success of a movement of which one of the chief demands was freedom of the press; but it did encourage the workers to demand that the former patriarchal arrangement should be replaced by a 'national Postulat'. In the course of a number of strikes for this demand the formation of a trade union on a national scale was attempted under the leadership of Stefan Born, a member of the League of Communists who had returned from exile; the failure of these movements soon resulted in the re-establishment of joint organizations of employers and employees, with a central committee composed of representatives in equal numbers from both sides. During the period of reaction after 1848 the *Gutenbergbund* was established, mainly to administer friendly society services, but despite this it became the object of repression. Local professional educational associations[3] were started as early as in any other trade; a modern trade union, on a national scale, came into being in 1866—shortly after that of the cigar-makers[4]—in anticipation of the repeal of the Anti-Combination Law. The specific characteristics which were to distinguish the Printers' Union from the rest of Central European trade unionism were present from the very start,[5] and association

[1] Müller (op. cit., p. 46) explains the setback partly by the bankruptcy of a Consumers' co-operative in which the union funds had been invested. Kulemann even speaks of a mere 8,000 members in 1895.

[2] See below, p. 36.

[3] See above, p. 13.

[4] See above, p. 16.

[5] Bebel (op. cit., vol. I, p. 102) reports that in 1865 the Leipzig printers, whose active members were out of jobs after an unsuccessful strike, refused to accept material aid from non-printers because to do so would oblige them eventually to

with either of the competing factions of Social Democracy was avoided; Bebel,[1] however, takes it for granted that no considerable number of members was in sympathy with non-Socialist parties. As early as 1877 the union achieved its long-proclaimed aim, collective bargaining; two years later, however, under the pressure of the Anti-Socialist Law, it had to dissolve and form itself into a friendly society in order to preserve its funds.

When the Law had expired, the Printers' Union was re-established, and demanded revision of the collective agreement, as its terms provided, by 1st January 1892, so as to secure the nine-hour day. The strike that followed was defeated, as a liberal historian of German trade unionism[2] points out, because 'the moral support given to the printers by Social Democracy deprived them of the support of public opinion'. The police confiscated the strike funds, and the Union was prohibited from levying special funds. The Union's appeal on this point was upheld, but by then the strike had been lost. The Union leaders themselves contributed to the defeat of the strike by preventing its extension to those undertakings which, having the most urgent orders in hand, had declared their willingness 'in principle' to negotiate; the other employers were able to wait until, after three months, the strike had to be called off.[3] The masters refused to negotiate a new agreement with the existing Union leaders; they demanded the right to nominate four of the nine 'employees' representatives'. In March 1896 a compromise was reached, providing for direct election of all the representatives under the direct supervision of the Industrial Court. The elections resulted in a complete triumph for the union, causing the employers to drop their aspiration to form a 'yellow trade union'. The new agreement provided for a central body, on terms of parity; the agreements were to be concluded for a term of three (soon prolonged to five) years.

The establishment of such machinery for settling industrial disputes was hailed by the whole right wing of the German labour movement and all its well-wishers in the middle classes as a great achievement. But the union leaders had to defend it continuously against keen criticism from Social Democracy and even from within the union itself.[4] So far as concerned the workers' immediate interests the results were moderate; the 10 per cent wage increases of 1906 and 1911 were both absorbed by

support strikers in other trades, and thus increase the demands on their pockets, heavy enough already. This narrow-mindedness does not seem to have had a political background; the mediation of the General Council of the International was used to make contact with the London printers, though not with other British workers, whose support would have been refused.

[1] Ibid., p. 182.

[2] Kulemann, op. cit., p. 269.

[3] A. Braun, op. cit. (1900), p. 622.

[4] See below, p. 66.

the rising cost of living, and in the matter of hours all that was achieved was a half-hour reduction on Saturdays in each of these renewed agreements.[1] The eight-hour day did not come until the 1918 revolution. More important from the critics' point of view was the fact that the strike of 1892 was the last as well as the first to be organized by the Printers' Union on a more than local scale.

(*d*) *Political Catholicism and its Labour Movement*

The differences between the bodies discussed in the last section, whatever their political inspiration, had their direct origin in the needs of the sectional struggle. We have now to deal with organizations inspired by a body whose professed aims and purposes lay outside the sectional conflict and which were produced only in reaction against that conflict.

Political Catholicism, in Germany at any rate, had a twofold origin. On the one hand, it may be described as the Catholic wing of extreme conservatism; its origins in Bavaria date from the opposition to eighteenth-century Enlightened Absolutism on such matters as compulsory elementary education and the emancipation of the Jews. Even after 1866 Bishop Ketteler, its theoretical parent, took a definite stand against constitutionalism as well as against any transfer of historically based allegiances from one prince to another. Political Catholicism was Greater German only inasmuch as it advocated Hapsburg hegemony throughout Germany. But, being a minority in Prussia, it was also an opposition movement which, because of its specific forms of expression, could find a voice even when all other opposition forces had been driven underground. In the Rhine provinces it arose, as a definite movement, in 1838 in protest against the arrest of the Archbishop of Cologne, Droste-Hülsdorff, who had refused to obey the Government's orders regarding mixed marriages. Radical liberals, like Marx, who were in favour of complete disestablishment, for that very reason defended the Church's right to decide what marriages it should bless in accordance with its own principles, without having to obey the concepts of the Erastian State as regards the necessary conditions of social life in a country of mixed religions. This attitude was preserved when Social Democracy, in the name of civic freedom, demanded the repeal of Bismarck's laws expeling the Jesuits.

The Church never reciprocated this attitude; it always combined the demand for its own freedom with the claim to mould legislation on such matters as education and marriage according to its principles, with binding force even for non-Catholics.[2] Its support was willingly given to reactionary dictatorships if they concluded Concordats enacting such principles. This was done in Austria in 1856 as well as in 1934, and in both instances the Church played a large part in bringing about the

[1] *Deutscher Buchdruckerverband*, p. 38.

[2] See below, p. 276.

dictatorship. The fact that the Church claims supernatural authority for this type of bargaining[1] and that it regards a monopoly of influence over the young generation as an essential part of its freedom obviously invites counter-propaganda on the part even of those progressives who do not consider the decision of metaphysical issues to be in our age a topical task. This causes additional friction with an organization which was capable, for example, of breaking off diplomatic relations with the Czechoslovak Government because the latter honoured the national hero Hus, burned by the Council of Constance 500 years before. In many cases 'threats to religious freedom', against which the Catholic population has to be defended, seem to be invited in view of the fact that political Catholicism thrives on such grievances, which are almost the only uncontroversial issues within its camp.

Apart from the contradiction between its highly authoritarian philosophy and the fact that it may be exposed to repression by definitely right-wing governments, political Catholicism is beset with a much more general problem: how to secure unity of action by a denomination made up of social groups with openly antagonistic interests. In Austria, where the Church's solidarity with the established régime was beyond question, a Catholic party could in modern times operate only on a social platform. In 1870, when Francis Joseph made a short-lived attempt to settle domestic issues with the German Liberal bourgeoisie by establishing a Conservative government supported by the non-German part of the nobility and attempting some social reforms,[2] a Catholic writer, Baron Vogelsang, suggested that small-scale enterprises should be protected by subjecting large-scale industries, and those alone, to diverse measures of regulation in favour of even the adult male worker: as a long-term aim he looked to the establishment of democratically organized peasants' co-operatives, such as eventually helped to bring the main basis of political Catholicism into being,[3] and the transformation of industrial employment into corporative shareholdership—a suggestion which is now excluded from the purview of Catholic reformers by the Encyclical *Quadragesimo Anno*.[4]

In Bismarck's Germany, however, political Catholicism, after 1871 called the Centre Party, found itself for a moment the main party of the opposition. Bismarck, whose fatherland, like the Catholic Church,

[1] I am quite conscious that the dogma of papal infallibility is formulated with sufficient care to preserve some freedom of manœuvre under changing circumstances for the head of the hierarchy; but what actually counts is how the average Catholic interprets it, and his interpretation is in no way discouraged by the hierarchy. What is actually offered by the ecclesiastical partner in political agreements of the kind described is political advice tendered from pulpit and confessional to people who regard obedience to such advice as essential for the salvation of their souls.

[2] See note 2 above, p. 9.

[3] See below, pp. 45–6.

[4] Jostock, op. cit., pp. 112–14.

always needed some supposed threat in order to mobilize its supporters, did not hesitate to win Liberal sympathy for Prussian dictatorship by denouncing as 'public enemy number one' a party with reliable monarchist principles whose federalist demands did not go beyond the wish to restore the electoral dynasties of Hanover and Hesse under Hohenzollern suzerainty and to oppress the Catholic Poles less brutally than he did himself. So he launched the 'Kulturkampf' against the 'enemies of German unity'. All over West Germany, the persecuted priest became the local symbol of resistance, as he did once again in Hitlerite days. As soon as Bismarck turned from Liberal to Conservative support on the issue of Protection, he was backed by the Centre party because of its strong agrarian element.[1] It voted for the Anti-Socialist Law, and in the late eighties and nineties a Conservative-Catholic coalition formed the parliamentary basis for German right-wing government. As late as 1889 the Centre leaders, Windhorst and Count Hertling, opposed Bismarck's compulsory social insurance bill with the argument that State subventions would make the workers look for help to the State rather than to the Church.

But there was another aspect of the problem. Unlike Austria, a compact Catholic country where the Church supported the government, and political Catholicism could not affect the working class, the party of the religious minority in Germany could retain working-class support provided it made the right appeal. Its intellectual leaders were conscious of this. In a letter to Lassalle, Bishop Ketteler expressed his agreement with the proposal for producers' co-operatives, while objecting to Lassalle's basic demand for State help in view of the limits to State interference set by 'the divine economy of the temporal life of man'.[2] In 1877 Count Galen, on behalf of the Centre Party, introduced a social reform bill which did not accept the principle of State regulation in the interest of the adult male worker, but touched only on the questions of Sunday rest, restriction of female and abolition of child labour. But in the interest of the small craftsman 'restriction of industrial freedom' and the regulation of the relations of apprentices and journeymen to their masters were suggested, agriculture being protected by restricting the labourer's right to change his domicile. This was not quite what the workers desired, but even this restricted social reform policy ended, so far as the 'respectable' section of political Catholicism was concerned, with the formation of the Taaffe government in Austria and the Conservative-Catholic bloc in Germany. The hierarchy and the Catholic nobles now took their place in the ruling stratum of a society economi-

[1] During the whole period of the Empire, landowners (amongst them some owners of latifundia) never formed less than a quarter, and at times a half, of the parliamentary Centre party; the workers were represented only indirectly through a few priests active in their organizations.

[2] Erdmann, op. cit., p. 29.

cally dominated by monopoly capitalism and freed from the delusions of the Liberal period; so the Church need no longer oppose Liberalism. But now the more plebeian elements of political Catholicism became articulate. In section (*f*) below we shall discuss the lower-middle-class aspect, which became most conspicuous in Austria.

The preliminary stage of the Catholic workers' movement in Germany was marked by organizations mainly concerned with welfare work; the prevention of political dangers threatening the Catholic worker, though not forgotten, was only in the background.[1] The outstanding body at this period was the Catholic Journeymen's Association, founded on the eve of the 1848 revolution by Kolping, a former journeyman who had managed to study for and reach the priesthood in order to attack the wretched material and moral conditions under which his former fellows suffered in their leisure time. In its formative years, the Association began from the assumption that journeymen were merely masters in embryo; as late as 1902 its friendly attitude to the Christian Trade Unions was qualified by the observation that these bodies had no interest in the eventual economic independence of their members, and therefore exercised a levelling influence, while the Journeymen's Association sought 'to prepare young craftsmen, even if for the time being they have to work in factories, for their future status as masters'.[2] Such a concept, together with the body's character as a welfare organization looking after young men who were supposed frequently to change their residence, might explain the fact that all powers of decision were concentrated in a hierarchy of priest-presidents, nominated by the bishops on the suggestion of committees composed of priests and Catholic notables. In administering the local centres of activity, the hostels, the priest-president was supported by a consultative body elected by the journeymen and by a Council of Protectors, many of them employers, some ex-journeymen. The Council shouldered the financial responsibilities, and special precautions were taken to keep the control of property in the hands of the hierarchy, lest Socialist influence might lead to its use in ways contrary to the donors' intentions.[3] The Association's non-interference in economic conflicts was honestly due to the presence of masters in its midst[4] and not to any supposed contradiction between Christian morality and participation in economic disputes. Its purely denominational character was derived from its specifically educational activities.

The Catholic Church's answer to the modern labour movement was the formation of the Catholic Workers' Associations, to which the

[1] Erdmann, op. cit., pp. 178 ff. and 198.

[2] Ibid., p. 197.

[3] Ibid., p. 187.

[4] Ibid., p. 199. The quotations refer to official pronouncements of the Journeymen's Association, especially H. F. Schweitzer's *Handbuch für Presides* (Manual for Presidents of Local Groups), Cologne, 1905.

Encyclical *Rerum Novarum* gave the sanction of the supreme ecclesiastical authority. In the late seventies attempts were made to create a Catholic workers' organization in the Ruhr, but ecclesiastical support was given only with reluctance, while the employers threatened with dismissal all workers who joined it. The attempt was dropped even before the Anti-Socialist Law destroyed the legal basis of worker's associations.[1] When Bismarck's police measures failed, organization of the Catholic workers for economic purposes within a Catholic framework became more popular in anti-Socialist circles. But the work had a logic of its own, and Catholic organizers who began with the main intention of fighting Socialism, with the employers' sympathies,[2] began to regard economic reforms as an objective worth achieving for their own sake.[3] In 1885, within the Social Insurance Organization in the Ruhr, a campaign was started to repeal the changes introduced to the disadvantage of the miners when the Anti-Socialist Law was enacted; in April 1886, on the initiative of the Centre Party, an Association for Legal Aid to Miners was formed, said to have 20,000 members. These attempts, cautious as they were, were answered by the dismissal of the participants and by support by the employers for Protestant Professional Associations with an anti-Catholic bias, and they came to an end when the (free) Miners' Union was formed.[4]

The Amberg Congress of German Catholics, in 1887, recommended the general formation of Catholic Workers' Associations, reconciliation of the rights and duties of masters and employees being described as their main economic purpose, alongside religious instruction and devotion. Control by the hierarchy was established through the institution of priest-presidents, nominated by the local bishop; only in conjunction with the national assemblies of the presidents was a meeting of workers' delegates allowed to share in the management of the body. In a group of adult workers with a stable membership, mainly concerned with social policies, such an organization could be defended only on the basis of an authoritarian approach to basic social issues. Apart from its religious activities, among which the cultus of St. Joseph, 'Patron of Workers', was emphasized in papal pronouncements, the Association operated as a supporting organ of the Centre party.

None of these activities was likely to impress anyone who was not a convinced member of the Catholic Church and the Catholic party, nor were they likely, even for Catholics drawn into industrial life, to counteract the attractions of Socialism and Socialist-sponsored Free Trade Unionism.[5] Organized as they were on a territorial basis, the Catholic

[1] Müller, op. cit., pp. 32–3.
[2] Erdmann, op. cit., pp. 269–70.
[3] Müller, op. cit., p. 17.
[4] See above, pp. 27–8.
[5] Since these unions, in all the countries dealt with in these pages, formed by far

Workers' Associations were only occasionally affected by industrial conflicts. In order to oppose the Free Trade Unions more effectively, professional groups were formed in the Catholic associations, but these were strictly subordinated to the territorial organization and to its priest-president,[1] who was instructed to discourage immoderate economic demands and to explain to the members the misery caused by strikes.[2]

There was, however, one field in which even a purely territorial organization with an ideology so opposed to industrial strife as contemporary Catholicism was could render its members service. As the labour front of the Centre Party, the Associations discussed social policies and provided the main lever for that party's eventual acceptance of a more positive attitude than that which lay behind Count Galen's proposals.[3] Their salaried Workers' Secretaries helped members to realize their rights under the existing legislation. In the legal field, the Catholic Workers' Secretary might differ from his Socialist counterpart by holding to some delusions about the ability of bourgeois justice to grant the worker his rights, but such delusions need not make him a less efficient advocate. The fact that he belonged to a conservative rather than a subversive party might help to secure his client a more attentive hearing. But new problems could arise when a Catholic employer used political or ecclesiastical channels to prevent the effective formulation of a claim directed against himself.

From the point of view of our investigation, the Legal Aid activities of the Catholic Workers' Secretary are important as an instance where basic functions of sectional organization were performed by an institution which did not originate from that section's own efforts, although this would hardly have happened had it not been for the competition of real sectional organizations. By promoting the application of the law most favourable to the worker, even if he does so in order to prevent the Church losing adherents to the Socialist party, the Catholic Secretary takes part in the class struggle; yet he may still believe that he is merely ensuring the just application of a law standing above classes. This distinguishes him from the Christian Trade Unionist shop steward who recognizes that he is defending the interests of his fellows against the clearly opposed interests of his employer. Naturally the Church disliked

the most important section of trade unionism, and their national representations the closest counterpart to the British Trades Union Congress, we shall not in future use the qualification 'free' except when they are mentioned in direct opposition to their competitors. References to 'Trade Unions' (capitalized) will mean this dominant group, as distinct from references to trade unions (without capitals) in general, which will include the minority unions. The 'yellow' trade unions, whose *bona fides* was denied by all other groups (see below, pp. 59–60) will always be so called.

[1] Müller, op. cit., p. 18.

[2] Erdmann, op. cit., p. 373.

[3] See above, p. 32.

the Catholic workers entering into such a position, especially as employers were so well represented among its supporters. In fact, Christian Trade Unions, as distinct from Catholic Workers' Associations, took their rise, to put it mildly, without the Church's support, and had eventually to force recognition from it.

The abortive attempt to form a Catholic Workers' Association on the Ruhr[1] was followed by efforts made 'by the non-working leaders of the Christian workers rather than by the workers themselves'[2] to form an inter-denominational Christian trade union. They also failed, in view of the employers' threat to dismiss every worker who took part in any form of industrial organization. When the Miners' Union was formed[3] the Catholics offered to participate on condition that all Socialists were excluded from leadership, but this, of course, was refused, and the Catholics kept aloof. After the setback which followed the Miners' Union's first triumphs the Christian Miners' Union could be started, characteristically enough with a protest, in a loyal telegram to the Emperor, against the election of delegates to the International Miners' Conference by meetings convened by the Free Miners' Union.[4] At the foundation congress, the possibility of conflicts with the employers which might involve a need for occasional collaboration with the Free Miners' Union was envisaged by the Catholic priests, though not by the Protestant pastors who took part.[5] But peaceful agreement between employers and employees was described as the organization's purpose.[6] Discussions of political and denominational matters was barred, and there were guarantees for equal representation of the two denominations on the Executive Council, but 'by joining the Union every member declares himself an opponent of Socialism'.[7] The Union started with about half the membership of its Free competitor; the proportion seems not to have changed, and after four years of activity it claimed no more than 28,000 members. The authorities preserved a comparatively friendly attitude, but 'from the very start the employers behaved towards

[1] See above, p. 34.

[2] Müller, op. cit., p. 33.

[3] See above, p. 27.

[4] The interpretation of the spirit of British Trade Unionism at that time current in Germany (see also p. 20 above) is illustrated by the fact that the leaders of the Catholic Miners explained the task of their organization, started after this manner by the need 'to organize ourselves according to the example of the British miners'—whose delegates at the International Congress had, indeed, just defeated a resolution in favour of the nationalization of the mines (Müller, op. cit., p. 42).

[5] Kulemann, op. cit., p. 303; Erdmann, op. cit., pp. 402–4. This attitude of the ministers, which was hardly surprising in view of the position of both denominations within Prussia, should not be confused with that of the miners belonging to either denomination; occasionally Protestant miners played a leading part in opposition (from the Left) against the (Catholic) Chairman of the Union (ibid., p. 411).

[6] Article 2 of the Rules.

[7] Articles 3 and 8.

the new union in much the same way as if it had been Socialist-inspired'.[1] The Union leaders forbade action in solidarity with dismissed members;[2] some strikes, however, had inevitably to be supported. The immediate cause of the first of these was a reduction in the number of Church feasts recognized as miners' holidays; but the substance was the issue of recognition by the employers of the (Christian) Trade Union.[3] More favourable conditions than in the heavy industries were found in the long-standing industries of the Catholic Rhineland, particularly textiles, and here the movement might be regarded rather as a Centre-inspired parallel[4] to that called forth in most of the industrial centres by Social Democracy.

Whatever the founders' intentions, the workers joined even Christian trade unions with the intention of defending their own interests. The advice of the national congress at Frankfurt (1900) was needed to instruct local Union leaders that the justice of a strike was not in all cases a measure of its chance of success;[5] at that congress the Free Trade Unions were criticized rather for their propensity to call more strikes than the Christian Unions could support than for their alleged 'Godlessness'. As concerned the winning of recruits for Christian Trade Unionism, organization of the hitherto passive sector of the Catholic workers was much more promising than competition with the Free Trade Unions;[5] even in the Mainz programme (1899) it was laid down that it was not a trade union's job to fight a political party, not even Social Democracy.[7]

The coexistence of trade unions divided from one another by theological issues was from the sectional viewpoint an evil, and this fact was openly stated at the Frankfurt congress; once it was recognized, in either camp, that questions of world outlook were not among the legitimate issues of trade unionism, and Catholic members of the Free Trade Unions were no longer exposed to rationalist propaganda, a united front of the workers would oppose the united front of capitalism.[8] Only a small minority[9] rejected the aim of trade union unity and even refused to co-operate with the Free Trade Unions in particular conflicts unless equal status in all decisions was accorded them—a large demand

[1] Kulemann, op. cit., p. 302.
[2] See also p. 34. There were counterparts to such an attitude in Free Trade Unionism (see below, p. 56).
[3] Kulemann, op. cit., p. 308.
[4] As there was no official discrimination against the Centre Party, such allegiance would be proclaimed with an outspokenness inconceivable in the Free Trade Unions. Cf. ibid., p. 397.
[5] Müller, op. cit., p. 111.
[6] Ibid., p. 229.
[7] Ibid., p. 109.
[8] Brest and Giesberts on the Frankfurt Congress, Elm, op. cit., p. 358; Müller, op. cit., pp. 114 ff.; Erdmann, op. cit., pp. 455–6.
[9] Erdmann, op. cit., p. 454; Müller, op. cit., p. 117.

from the smaller partner. In order to prevent a split, the congress avoided a decision on the issue, but the opposition found expression in the publications of the East and North-east German Catholic Workers' Associations, which were controlled by a Baron von Savigny, a member of the Catholic nobility close to the Court and the hierarchy.[1] But even within the ranks of Christian Trade Unionism a trend was not made more attractive merely by being sponsored by a millionaire and a nobleman.

Christian Trade Unionism, however, was not merely one aspect of the labour movement; it owned its very existence to facts which from the sectional point of view were irrational. The type of worker who needed a trade union to defend his sectional interests but hesitated to join the Free (Socialist-dominated) Trade Unions because they were denounced from pulpit and confessional, would not join the weaker and less efficient Christian Trade Unions unless he was assured that spiritual security would compensate for organizational shortcomings. A Union, however, which was acceptable to employers who regarded its Christianity, about whose spiritual and sectarian aspects business men were not likely to bother overmuch, as a mere synonym for submission to their will, would be no serious trade union at all, but a mere testimony to the truth of the Marxist assertion that Catholic social reform was only a device of the employers to betray the workers. There could be no Christian Trade Unionism unless it had the backing of the ecclesiastical authorities even when employers (and among them Catholics who might operate with Conservative-Catholic arguments behind them) demanded its suppression. But the hierarchy was dominated by the Catholic part of the nobility, and—at least since Bismarck's swerve to the right—was one of the established powers within the German empire. So it struck against the Christian Trade Unions in a way from which they never recovered.

The bishops could not condemn strikes and coalitions as such without exposing themselves to the reproach that they were taking sides with the employers in the economic struggle; but they could oppose the only framework within which working-class organization could be efficient in a country where the majority of the workers were rallied under the banner of a Marxist philosophy and the minority opposing it was split on denominational lines. The Catholic workers could share in efficient sectional action on the assumption that, metaphysics apart, they had something in common with their non-Catholic fellows; but this basic assumption the bishops rejected. Following Savigny's suggestions,[2] the Fulda Pastoral of 9th August 1900 warned the Catholic workers against the error of assuming that observance of the rules of Natural Law in economic life was enough, and that the concrete teachings of

[1] Müller, op. cit., p. 120.
[2] Ibid.

Catholic Christianity might be neglected. In order to make it clear that the Pastoral was meant as an answer to the Frankfurt congress of the Christian Trade Unions, the Archbishop of Freiburg explicitly stated that it was necessary to protect the workers who belonged to those Unions against the unchristian influences that used Christianity as a cover for helping Social Democracy.[1] The Christian Trade Unions protested that their separate existence was due to their very desire to protect the Christian workers against unchristian influences, and that a united trade union movement would not be formed without obtaining guarantees against possible collision with Christian principles.[2] But this was no answer to the Archbishop, who, when speaking of 'unchristian influences', had had in mind not the Marxist philosophy, whose supporters would not 'use Christianity as a cover', but the very principle of sectional struggle. He could not do this explicitly without thereby subscribing to all the Marxist statements about the social function of his Church. In the purely theological field, however, his position against the Christian Trade Unions was stronger, because since the Encyclical *Rerum Novarum* Catholics did not doubt that the Church had a theologically-based answer to the social problem; Christian Trade Unions formed in conjunction with heretics were clearly unsuitable instruments for applying that teaching. On the other hand, even on the assumption that a Christian counter-offensive could overcome the Marxist tendency of the German workers, the Protestant majority precluded the Catholic Church organizations from embracing the bulk of the workers, and to pursue this utopia was simply to say in other words that Catholic workers should keep aloof from any efficient form of trade unionism. *Rerum Novarum* had left the issue open, by stating that the actual form and content of Workers' Associations might vary according to conditions. Its emphasis on the need for agreements with employers and its defence of the right of coalition within certain limits suggested that its authors had in mind real trade unions, with a specific philosophy, but its demands as to the promotion of devotional activities could hardly be satisfied by organizations of an undenominational character. There was a contradiction between these two aspects in a country of mixed religions, and an Encyclical addressed to the Church as a whole was not bound to give an unequivocal answer. There was thus ample scope for the political sympathies of the hierarchy to operate.

The Bishops of Breslau and Trier, to whose dioceses belonged respec-

[1] Müller, op. cit., p. 121 ff.; Erdmann, op. cit., pp. 461–3.

[2] At the Krefeld Congress (1901), forty delegates representing 99,460 Union members supported this protest, against eleven delegates (for 7,730 members) who voted against the Executive Committee and thus supported Savigny's attempt to form purely Catholic 'Unions' (see below, in text). The different proportion as between electors and delegates—and it should be remembered that the expenses of the opposition delegates, who came from the east, were much heavier—illustrates the difference in the means available.

tively the heavy industries of Silesia and the Saar, forbade within their jurisdictions the extension of the activities of the München-Gladbach Centre of the Catholic Workers' Associations, which supported the development of interdenominational Christian Trade Unions. As a substitute, Baron von Savigny and Cardinal Kopp of Breslau established a Centre of 'Trade Departments' of the Catholic Workers' Associations in Berlin—a city where Catholic workers were an insignificant minority, and any attempt they made to keep to themselves was bound to render their organization completely harmless from the employers' point of view.[1] Expansion of the activities of this centre all over Germany was attempted. On the Saar 'King Stumm' was consistent enough in his opposition to labour organizations of any kind to suppress even the Trade Departments;[2] elsewhere they met with distrust even from the Catholic workers. The official historian of the Centre Party states that the workers resented having the stability of their religious faith questioned by the bishops; this was regarded as a reactionary pretext applied in order to prevent them from fighting for better conditions.[3]

(e) The German Consumers' Co-operatives

Schultze-Delitzsch's interpretation of the small craftsman's position as that of a mere entrepreneur allowed Consumers' Co-operatives only a subordinate place in his scheme, and led him into a successful fight against their attempts at independent centralization.[4] On the other hand, the workers were unlikely to join bodies recommended by the Liberal leader, Eugen Richter, as a useful device 'to check the honesty of our domestic servants and the proper use of their time'.[5] While the Anti-Socialist Law was still in force, Kautsky, in an attack on Consumers' Co-operatives, said that they could be of help to only a minority of the working class, and that only to a imited extent.[6] Clearly, in those years only a minority of the workers could get along without credit from shopkeepers towards the end of the week, and even more in cases of illness or unemployment. Statements such as Kautsky's were not expected to limit the use of co-operatives, but were intended to prevent the growth

[1] For these very reasons they were advertised to employers by their literary representatives such as Prof. Hintze, quoted by Kulemann, op. cit., p. 375.

[2] Cf. Max Payer, op. cit.

[3] Bachem, op. cit., vol. VII, p. 193. Cf. also Jostock, op. cit., pp. 149–50.

[4] Cf. Zeidler, op. cit., pp. 224–5.

[5] Riehn, op. cit., pp. 16–17.

[6] The very small part played by Consumers' Co-operatives among Social Democratic workers is illustrated by the fact that a motion 'on Co-operatives' accepted as late as 1891 by the Hamburg organization, and subsequently by the national Party congress (cf. Zeidler, op. cit., pp. 456–7, and Proceedings of the 1892 Party Congress, pp. 223 ff.) devoted its attention mainly to Producers' Co-operatives, in terms of the old argument against Schultze-Delitzsch's 'Self-Help'. They are said to be useful only in exceptional cases, as a way of finding some means of subsistence for workers dismissed after strikes. See above, p. 21.

of ideologies which might turn aside the active workers from the Party's struggle. In this they were completely successful: although, eventually, Germany did not lag behind other countries in developing working-class co-operatives, no ideology of 'co-operative Socialism' was able to develop except among the keener Co-operative officials.

The membership of German Consumers' Co-operatives rose from 88,000 in 1873 to 120,000 in 1885, 244,000 in 1892 and 469,000 at the end of the century: the increase due to new social strata entering the Co-operatives evidently began in 1885.[1] The average sales per member remained remarkably stable over the whole period at about Mk. 250 per annum, and while this represented only a moderate portion of the budget of an average lower-middle-class family even in the seventies, it suggests that by the nineties a predominantly working-class membership bought almost everything it could at the Co-op. The influx of working-class elements and the formation of new co-operatives based upon them centred in Saxony, a region with an almost entirely working-class population which, before and long after our period, remained remarkably immune to the reformist tendencies within the Party. To provide for strikes, unemployment, illness, etc., the new and mainly working-class co-operatives after the nineties developed special funds, fed by special contributions from every member.

In 1902, the Liberal majority of the management of the Central Association of Consumers' Co-operatives, faced with a Social Democratic majority among the delegates just elected to the National Delegate Conference, expelled the left-wing majority of the Co-operatives from the Association,[2] arguing that they 'aim at undermining the position of the lower middle classes'. The left-wingers formed the Central Association of German Consumers' Co-operatives, which, in 1912, embraced 1·63 million of the 1·91 million organized consumers in Germany. Attacks against the threat to throne, altar, and the living standards of the lower middle classes[3] had accompanied the rise of the co-operative movement ever since the days when it emerged from the narrow confines in which Schultze-Delitzsch's fear of such developments had kept it, but with Social Democracy in a key position and the typical Co-op employee appointed by a Social Democratic manager, such attacks became more serious; the defence of the Co-ops against legislative interference became a live issue, strengthening the links with the political party.

[1] This refutes any explanation (see Riehn, op. cit., p. 10) of the long period of stagnation of Consumers' Co-operation by the Anti-Socialist Law. Obviously an underground party has not less but more interest than a legal one in using even forms of organization whose immediate value is regarded as questionable. The German workers became interested in co-operatives just when the law had closed other forms of organization to them. Cf. Braun's comment in Bringmann, op. cit., vol. I, p. 210.

[2] Herkner, op. cit., vol. I, p. 466.

[3] Cf. Riehn, op. cit., pp. 94–5 and 127 ff.

The rise and impressive initial success of Consumers' Co-operatives was due to the small retailer's inability to reflect consumers' demands or even to defend his own interests in his relations with his wholesaler; even purchasing co-operatives of the small retailers did not come into being until the pressure of the Consumers' Co-operatives was evident.[1] The more justified the retailers' complaints, the more obvious was their need to relieve the pressure at the consumers' expense by selling those goods which carried the highest margins. Consumers' Co-operatives react upon this process both by large-scale purchasing and by undertaking production themselves. The former is efficient only in competition with the isolated small-scale retailer, not with a privately-owned Department Store or a Purchasing Co-operative of small retailers; it results in the elimination of an obsolete form of retailing, and the process cannot be repeated. *If* Co-operative production can be carried out in real independence of monopolies controlling the private production of commodities sold, including banks which are creditors of competing enterprises, it may result in cheaper prices and/or better quality in the goods supplied, provided the Co-operative is prepared to let its members enjoy the profits in their capacity as consumers. But the tendency to attract members with maximum dividends is as old as the Co-operative movement itself, and it is bound to result in price-increases in excess of the cost of distribution.[2] In the incidence of these price-increases the Co-operative's interest in developing those branches of its business on which its power to attract mainly depends may easily overrule social considerations.[3] The statement that the indirect effect of co-operative organization on the general relations between working-class consumers and their suppliers is much more important than the dividend may be quite true, and reads prettily in propagandist pronouncements by the Co-operative movement; but the average housewife will join the Co-operative only if she expects to receive therefrom some benefit she cannot get otherwise, and not in recognition of the fact that Co-operative competition has forced her private capitalist supplier to reduce prices.

A glance at any of the statistics available shows that in conditions of fairly wide membership[4] the various departments of some co-operatives

[1] Ibid., pp. 49 ff.

[2] Cf. the tables given ibid., p. 32.

[3] Cf. Schär, op. cit., pp. 337 and 367.

[4] Assuming family of average size, the membership of the Basel co-operative reported on by Schär comprised 95 per cent of the total population; co-operative elections, which were strongly contested, showed results similar to those of political elections under manhood suffrage—a narrow Labour majority. This suggests that all classes were represented fairly equally among the members, the absence of some fanatics of the lower middle class interest compensating for that of the poorest strata of the working class.

are frequented to a quite different degree.[1] There may be opportunities for increasing sales by improving service, though these are not nearly so extensive as enthusiastic supporters of Co-operatives hope;[2] in a fairly efficient Co-operative, however, no fundamental improvement can be expected unless completely new fields are opened up. Now it is just in the field of new 'luxury' and semi-luxury commodities that Co-operative expansion meets its limits, because it lacks the mechanism necessary to 'create new demands' or the informal social pressure that a powerful monopoly can exert. Once the obvious gaps are closed, the very fact that increased working-class consumption finds expression in a proportionately smaller share of the recognized staple goods in mass consumption may result in Consumers' Co-operatives taking a diminishing part in satisfying consumers' demands. By its very nature, the benefit arising to consumers as a whole from the Co-operatives' entering into competition in a given field is non-recurring; and once Co-operation ceases to be on the offensive, it is a mere question of efficiency whether the static appeal of the dividend can be taken over by some shrewd business man, as was quite usual in the Germany of the Weimar Republic. In no case is there any chance of improvement in working-class standards comparable with those achieved by trade unions.[3] This fact, and not any ideological prejudice, was the limiting factor in the development of Consumers' Co-operation compared with other aspects of the labour movement.

(f) Extension of Sectional Organization to Other Social Groups

The very existence of a strong opposition party, the only serious one in Germany, which was based on the labour organizations, was bound to serve as a focus for other opposition elements. As early as 1905 a critical student, Dr. Blank,[4] stated that a quarter of the Socialist votes polled in 1903 were non-working class; this implied that the lower middle classes were represented by the Socialist party at least as much

[1] In Schär's example (p. 370) 15 per cent of the members bought their bread, and 90 per cent their milk at the Co-op, the percentages for other commodities ranging between these figures.

[2] Schär (ibid.) compares the 550 francs per year spent by the average member of the Basel Co-operative with the 1,500 francs which might have been spent, assuming an average income of 3,000 francs per family. In fact, the Co-operative paid its own employees an average salary of 2,100 francs; from what is known of the average structure of the pre-1914 working-class budget hardly more than a third (in the middle classes, to which Schär's estimate of average income appears to refer, even less) of the annual income could be spent on goods sold at the Co-op.

[3] From the data given by Riehn (op. cit., p. 69) as well as by Schär, an increase of 4 per cent in the family's real income may be taken as the possible result of the activities of a Consumers' Co-operative continued over many years. Clearly a trade union, to be regarded as efficient, would be expected to show very different results after some decades of activity.

[4] *Archiv für Sozialwissenschaft*, vol. XX/3, pp. 507 ff.

as by the Liberals;[1] they formed a no less important element in the Socialist vote than did the workers in the large factories, the only real supporters of orthodox Marxism. Even had all the industrial workers voted for Social Democracy, they could not have made up more than two-thirds of the total Socialist vote polled in 1903 in Halle, Königsberg, Leipzig, Bremen, and Chemnitz; or more than three-fifths in Berlin, Frankfurt-on-Main, Dresden, Hamburg, and Munich; only a narrow majority in Altona, Stettin, and Nuremberg, and a mere minority in Berlin-Charlottenburg. Bebel[2] refused to accept Blank's suggestion that the avoidance of an appeal to class struggle in the Party's electoral manifesto in 1903 was due to an electoral structure of this kind, but he could correct Blank's estimates of numbers only in details, reducing his estimate of a non-working-class Socialist vote from three-quarters to half a million. Bebel himself noted that at the elections to the Berlin Merchants' Court in May 1905 the Socialists had polled 21 per cent of the total vote and emerged as the second strongest party.

However strong the political influence of Social Democracy among the lower middle classes, it had no success as an organizer of their economic struggles. Even in the days of the Weimar Republic an attempt, undertaken jointly with Liberals, to create a left-wing Smallholders' Association, proved a conspicuous failure so far as the peasants were concerned, in spite of its being joined by large numbers of workers and craftsmen with small allotments. It is obvious that, as soon as any lower middle class group is organized, those elements within it which are comparatively prosperous are bound to play a leading part, and thus to acquire additional means of spreading their political views. But while Social Democracy failed in the role of organizer of non-working-class groups, its very existence forced sectional organization upon even the most conservative forces. They could easily work upon the fact that modern capitalist developments had made co-operative organization essential for lower-middle-class producers, and especially for the peasants.

Schultze-Delitzsch's prescriptions for the formation of Producers' Co-operatives did not meet the needs of the peasants, who were unwilling to risk their homesteads under the system of unrestricted liability, but on the other hand were quite ready to do without large dividends if this enabled them to avoid Schultze's formula, clearly unfit for agricultural conditions, that no co-operative should grant credits for longer terms than those of its own debts. Raiffeisen, a former civil servant with a distinctly conservative outlook, tried to solve these problems by an organization *for* the peasants rather than *of* them; in order to check the solidity of prospective debtors, his co-operatives were formed

[1] Both Liberal factions (see above, p. 8), but not, of course, the National Liberals, being included.

[2] *Neue Zeit*, vol. XXIII/2, pp. 332 ff.

for small districts and were led by priests, teachers and so on, with the peasant member in a somewhat subordinate position.[1] Profits were accumulated to back the co-operatives' debts; as this could hardly be managed within a local framework, the local co-operatives were backed by, and were dependent upon, central banks. This made for more bureaucratization even before the officials of the local Raiffeisen societies began to receive salaries,[2] and it was not difficult for Schultze to denounce this shortcoming; but it remained questionable whether the freedom of the individual group was threatened more by Raiffeisen's system of paternal supervision or by the progress of 'free' internal differentiation within Schultze's co-operatives. In his struggle against his competitors Schultze went so far as to denounce their non-compliance with all the finesses of the law and the alleged unsoundness of their basis of credit.[3] He did not succeed in destroying them, but his attacks helped to force on them an even higher degree of centralization; in 1877 a central organization in Neuwied was established. The very success of the Raiffeisen co-operatives, however, provoked the rise of competition in their own field.

From 1866 the Agricultural Associations of the Rhine Province accepted the Raiffeisen system, and historians of political Catholicism[4] have noticed the connexion between this reception of a device intended to deliver the peasant from Jewish usury and the formation of the Associations under the leadership of Catholic nobles and latifundia-owners. Whatever the new organization owed to Raiffeisen's principles, it looked on them as a means for strengthening its own hold on the peasantry. Attacks on the solvency of the Raiffeisen banks were regarded as a quite legitimate means of competition; the difference between the reactions of prospective co-operators to such methods and those of workers to strike-breaking by competing trade unions provides a useful illustration of the basic difference between what was meant by solidarity in the two classes.

Political Catholicism, which in Germany had opened the era of political co-operation, in Austria produced the classical example of its application for purposes of real mass organization. In the late nineties a generation of young village priests opened an attack on the traditional political control of the peasantry by the noble owners of large estates, the very people who controlled their own superiors, the bishops;[5] thus did the Christian Social Party, whose urban origins we shall soon be noticing, receive its mass basis. Certainly this was a democratic achievement, enhanced by the fact that the village priest's role was that of

[1] Zeidler, op. cit., p. 125.
[2] Ibid., p. 286.
[3] Ibid., pp. 263–77.
[4] Bachem, op. cit., vol. III, pp. 422–3.
[5] O. Bauer, op. cit., 1925, p. 145.

initiator, and control was soon handed over to the peasants themselves. But with the advance and centralization of co-operation a leading stratum developed, mostly made up of lawyers, priests, and Catholic politicians, providing wide opportunities for patronage and even corruption; the prestige of a party which worked with co-operative support was obviously threatened by the bankruptcy of the co-operatives. The importance of this factor as a lever to the control of political parties by high finance will be illustrated later.[1]

Long before this stage, political co-operatives came to be regarded as a necessary tool for any party with influence among the peasantry. In Austria, national antagonisms had split the co-operative movement from its very start; the future Czechoslovakia began with parallel Czech and German co-operative centres in each province, as well as a Polish one in Silesia, and a separate Catholic one in Bohemia.[2] In Prussia, in 1893, the Junkers replied to a lowering of the corn duties by Bismarck's successor Caprivi by forming the League of Agriculturalists and making use of whatever influence and pressure the Junker could bring to bear upon his peasant neighbour, and of the opportunities for material bribes inherent in the Raiffeisen system of agricultural co-operation. The stock-farming peasants of the West, organized in the Catholic-led Peasants' Associations, did not want high tariffs on the foodstuffs they used; hence there was friction in matters of detail. But over major issues there was collaboration, and the very move which established the agrarian character of the Conservative party also strengthened the predominance of the right wing within the Centre party.

The urban lower middle classes were the last to find their modern form of political expression; but it was to be the most vocal of all, and in phraseology, if not in politico-economic content, was the forerunner of the régimes which eventually were to succeed reformist democracy. Austria, which was to give Central European fascism its Führer, was also the first country to produce its ideological antecedents. In 1883 the lower middle classes were granted a restricted suffrage by Taaffe, who in many respects followed on the lines of the Hohenwart government, among whose ideologues was Baron Vogelsang.[3] Karl Lueger, a demagogue of outstanding capacity, succeeded in creating a mass party for political Catholicism on an anti-Semite basis, the Christian Social Party. Its success among the lower middle class was instantaneous; the Liberal Associations of some sections of Vienna joined it *en bloc*. But it completely failed in its attempts to draw workers away from Social Democracy, though it went much further in such appeals than did the German Centre; the Christian Social Workers' Programme, issued in 1894, called for manhood suffrage, the ten-hour day, nationalization of the

[1] See below, pp. 312–3.
[2] Digby, op. cit., p. 286.
[3] See above, p. 31.

banks and the mines, and the prohibition of anonymous holdings in joint-stock companies. The police soon noticed Lueger's failure to win working-class support, while his successful propaganda among the lower middle classes might mobilize the latter against the vested interests.[1] For years Imperial assent to Lueger's election as Mayor of Vienna was refused. But once accepted, he proved a capable administrator, and no implacable enemy of big business, whether baptized or not.

The rural aspect of the Christian Social offensive has already been mentioned.[2] The bishops and the Court appealed to Rome to repress what they interpreted as a revolt of the village priests against the vested interests, but Cardinal Rampolla declined to oppose a movement which was clearly within the limits set by *Rerum Novarum* and was actually to provide the Church (and all the other vested interests) with their main bulwark after Emperor, nobles, and the primitive identification of social order with the right of the deer to eat the peasants' corn and of the game-preserving lord to dispossess his peasants had disappeared.[3] In spite of the very unequal suffrage the Christian Socials conquered the Diet of Lower Austria in 1902, and that of Tyrol soon after; in 1907, after the introduction of manhood suffrage, the Old Conservatives of Upper Austria, Salzburg, and Styria had to join them. In the general elections of that year, the Christian Socials all over Austria polled 1·04 million votes, just as many as the Centralist majority of Austrian Social Democracy.[4] While among the Sudeten Germans it remained one out of many competing factions, the Christian Social Party was now, and continued to be, the only party representing the Alpine peasantry as well as the Viennese lower middle class. Laws intended to protect the peasant against the game-preserving lord were regularly enacted by the Christian Social majorities in the Diets, and with equal regularity refused imperial assent. But any original radicalism soon disappeared, under the twofold influence of Lueger's big-business connexions and of the Heir Apparent, Francis Ferdinand, who sought to suppress the democratic elements in 'his' party in order to make it a safe foundation for the replacement of parliamentarism by bureaucratic dictatorship, and for foreign policies dictated by the German alliance.

In Bohemia, the hotbed of nationalist struggles in the Hapsburg

[1] Cf. the documents published by Bruegel, op. cit., vol. IV, pp. 264 ff. and 310.

[2] P. 45.

[3] Rampolla's refusal to disown the Christian Socials contributed to Francis Joseph's veto against his election as Pope in 1903. Cf. Bruegel, op. cit., vol. IV, and Bachem, op. cit., vol. VI, p. 196. The evidence as to the dispute between the Viennese government and the Vatican has recently been collected in F. Engel-Janosi's paper 'The Resignation of Count Kalnoky' in the *Journal of Central European Affairs* (University of Colorado, U.S.A.), vol. XI, no. 3, pp. 265 ff.

[4] Less than Social Democracy if the Czech Separatists, who played a much more important part among the Socialists than among the Catholics, are added on either side.

dominions, the interplay of national and sectional conflicts brought about a complete transformation of the traditional party system. The introduction of manhood suffrage for a few of the seats in the Austrian Parliament resulted in the first splits in the Young Czech party,[1] which up to then had enjoyed a near-monopoly in the representation of the non-Socialist parts of the Czech nation. On the one side the Czech Agrarian Party, based upon the Peasants' Co-operatives, opposed the urban interests which dominated the Young Czech party; on the other, that party itself started the Czech National Socialist Party as a shrewd device to detach the workers from Social Democracy. Unsuccessful in its immediate aim, the new party soon became a competitor of the Young Czechs themselves,[2] all the more dangerous because there was little Czech bourgeoisie to appeal to beyond the black-coated workers and the intelligentsia. The introduction of manhood suffrage in 1906 did not weaken Czech nationalism in general, which grew strong enough to split the Socialist as well as the Catholic party, but it sounded the knell of traditional bourgeois nationalism; the Young Czechs, National Democrats after the 1918 Revolution, were reduced to a comparatively small party of Big Business, supporting pro-Tsarist pan-Slavism as opposed to democratic conceptions of Czech independence.

Among the Sudeten Germans, resistance to the Czech emancipation movement resulted in the formation of a radical pan-German wing of German nationalists which aimed at the complete repression of the so-called 'undermen' and anticipated Hitlerism in such features as racialism and the cult of Wodan, unlike the ordinary German bourgeois parties which were satisfied with constitutional means of discriminating against the Czechs and which again were split on sectional lines by the formation of an Agrarian Party. National prejudice was strong even among the Socialist workers of German nationality,[3] and contributed to the subsequent split in the labour movement on national lines; but in highly industrialized Bohemia it was virtually impossible to win working-class support for a middle-class party, such as all groups of official German nationalism then were. Nor was it possible to divert the lower middle-class disappointment by mere anti-Semite phraseology of Lueger's Viennese type, because of the strong non-Jewish bourgeoisie which existed here, unlike other parts of the Hapsburg monarchy. It was in such an environment that the German Workers' Party in Austria appealed to workers who, while pursuing their social interests, were prepared to forsake 'international Jewish Social Democracy'. The programmed opposed 'narrow-minded class parties' and claimed to represent 'the interests of all honest productive labour', evidently including well-intentioned employers; it demanded the nationalization or com-

[1] See above, p. 11.

[2] Cf. Chmelar, op. cit., pp. 10–11.

[3] Cf. O. Bauer, op. cit. (1907), pp. 574 ff.

munal ownership of 'all those capitalist enterprises whose private ownership impairs the common weal', especially the mines and railways —most of the latter nationalized long since—and some more definite reforms in social insurance and protection of labour.[1]

Again, the intended 'National Labour Party' proved a conspicuous failure so far as Labour was concerned.[2] It success came among those strata of the black-coated workers who would never have supported Social Democracy but disliked the official middle-class parties. On the eve of World War I Jung, the real founder of Nazism, gave the party the name under which its imitation became world-famous, and a programme definitely intended to appeal to the lower middle classes, with suggestions for inflationary currency reform, protests against speculation in land, etc. In its local framework, even this attempt failed; the German National Socialist Party entered the era of the Czechoslovak republic as a sectional representation of the Sudeten-German black-coated workers, railway officials, etc., together with agrarians, small traders and similar groups into which—apart from Social Democrats and Christian Socials—the Sudeten German camp was split.

(g) *The Politico-Ideological Background of the Formation of Economic Groups*

The experiences described in this chapter refute some widespread views about the relation between political and economic factors in the origins of modern mass-organization. Clearly, it cannot be asserted that economic needs, as represented for example by trade unions, are the necessary background of political organization: we have seen that not only had the German workers[3] a political party long before there were any trade unions of importance, but that even the spread of peasants' co-operatives was due to organizers inspired by political or sectarian religious motives. At the same time we cannot subscribe to the frequently-held view that in Central Europe, unlike Britain where things took the opposite course, the political labour party created the trade unions. We have seen that not only did it meet with the greatest difficulty in intellectually digesting the phenomena of industrial conflict, but that even when it had made its choice, trade unions created by party decision remained uninfluential until growing industrial conflict had impressed the need for organization on a large part of the working class.

It would seem that, although economic mass organization must be

[1] Cf. J. Krebs, *Kampf in Böhmen*, Berlin, 1936, p. 38.

[2] In Reichenberg, an industrial centre which was also a centre of Sudeten German nationalism, the National Socialists polled a mere 14,000 votes against 30,000 for the Social Democratic leader, Viktor Adler. In the general election of 1911 they won, in all Bohemia, three seats, but only by arrangement with other German Nationalist groups.

[3] In Austria the development of the political party and of trade unionism proceeded side by side; cf. the data given by Deutsch, vol. I, pp. 44 ff.

based upon sufficiently developed enonomic needs, it cannot come into being without some ideological incentive produced in the course of political conflict. The opposite view seems to be due to the fact that in Anglo-American trade-unionist tradition (which also influenced Marxism) the 'prehistoric' ideological stage—Chartism in Britain, the Knights of Labour and so on in the U.S.A.—was written off as an infantile disorder, happily overcome. There is an obvious need for political neutrality in trade unions, and hence a tendency to say little of political influences, such as that of German Social Democracy, in their formation; but only bad logic could draw the conclusion that trade unions, or any other form of sectional organization, could come into being without some political ideology for a background.

The reasons for such a relationship are not difficult to understand. Every strike, and every instance of a co-operative surviving a crisis in which its existence and its members' deposits are threatened, presupposes a kind of behaviour which from the standpoint of the 'good husbandman', that is, from the pattern which has been impressed upon the worker's mind by all the ideological devices of the society in which he lives, is irrational. The leaders shoulder much bigger risks than their followers; but even the latter have to face a situation very different from that of later days, when the organization has become an accepted element in society. The inspiration needed to face those risks must come from the acceptance of an ideology which appeals to values higher than the member's immediate economic interests; but it must also appeal to a circle much wider than the prospective members of a young organization. No body at its start can have the support of more than a small fraction of those it aspires to lead and eventually to organize; but its capacity for becoming a mass-organization depends upon its basic appeal being approved by people outside its nucleus, and on their sympathy depends the possibility of even the smallest initial success. On the other hand, the strength of economic interests in modern society is far too great to permit any political or even religious ideology to remain aloof from economic organization; a nationalist or sectarian party would lose all its mass-support if it offered its followers the alternative of dropping either their political affiliations or their sectional interests.

Some readers may consider the evidence mentioned in sections (*d*) and (*f*) of this chapter as a proof of the 'abnormal' character of Central European conditions, with religious and national issues crossing the 'normal' lines of modern capitalist development. But these details are important for us only in that they show how the political or sectarian 'disturbances' of 'normal' group antagonisms carry mass-organization, once it has arisen in the 'classical' way, into strata which otherwise it would hardly reach. Conflicts between the ideologies inspiring German trade unionism and the political labour movement respectively are about as old as the movements themselves; but it seems clear that without such struggles neither of them could have arisen. Even the struggle in the 'non-political' co-operative camp between Schultze-Delitzsch and Raiffeisen cannot be understood except in connexion with the general relations between liberal and conservative attitudes in nineteenth-century Germany. The problems of the emancipation of the lower middle classes can be appreciated only if we realize that those features of the Raiffeisen system which made it the more suitable of the two for peasant mass-organization were deeply bound up with the conservative attitude not only of Raiffeisen himself, but even more of the parties that made greatest use of his system.

Nor would it be correct to say that, although *some* ideological incentive, and the interest of some political group, may be needed to bring about the organization of economic groups, the concrete character of that incentive is unimportant. At a certain stage of development economic organization is applied as a means to strengthen the position of almost every political group that can put forward a claim to power in the days of mass suffrage; but not every group's appeal has been successful, and few groups have rallied all the strata to which they sought to appeal. And the literal meaning even of successful appeals does not of necessity coincide with the sense in which they are received. A young and uneducated working class may accept any ideology that can be shown to be a symbol of its emancipation; but it is remarkable with how true an instinct even a very young and raw labour movement chooses from the ideologies offered to it those elements which it can find useful.[1] The 'iron law of wages', after having served its purpose of proving to the worker that he needed a political party, was dispensed with when it opposed the needs of rising trade unionism. But there would have been no trade unionism in Prussia without an independent working-class party, and no German working-class party could arise without being dominated for some time by what was then the dominant issue in German political life, national unification. In a country whose bourgeoisie accepted the leadership of the Prussian military autocracy in order to solve that problem, such an attitude was bound to be reflected in the camp of the politically nascent working class; the contests of the various factions over that issue were a main incentive for the prospective organizers of the working classes. Certainly, Catholic organizers of labour were inconsistent in building up interdenominational Christian Trade Unions which were inefficient from the trade unionist point of view and unsuitable from that of the Catholic Church; but the working-class inhabitants of the Catholic ghetto could not enter trade unionism unless under the guidance of leaders drawn from their familiar surroundings, and, the framework of the Catholic Church being what it was, the initiators of Catholic working-class organization could

[1] See above, p. 26.

hardly behave otherwise than they did without being expelled from that framework.

The course of the politico-ideological influences which we have followed has its own logic: it is the bourgeois-democratic transformation of social relations in countries whose middle class failed to assume political power, and thus left its political and economic interests in the care of the *ancien régime*. It is bourgeois because it not abolish private ownership of the means of production; it is democratic because it led to to a regime in which the political and economic organi zations of the workers and peasants, i.e. the large majority of the population, played an important part. The workers, repressed by military-autocratic régimes in the interest of the bourgeoisie, could not create their own sectional organizations without raising the demand for political freedom. This was in sharp opposition to the bourgeoisie, and was therefore connected with a demand for the abolition of capitalism. Nor could the vested interests hold their own without mobilizing the lower middle classes, and part of the workers, within the framework of ideologies that could split the labour camp, and those ideologies were made popular by anti-capitalist phraseology. The outcome was that all the major social groups became organized, and *laisser-faire* capitalism inevitably became a ghost; though this ghost is occasionally revived by representatives of the vested interests, especially when they are appealing to the appropriate protectors abroad. The struggle between the social groups as to how society should be reorganized could not be replaced by ideological statements about the society to come made in the course of the competition between prospective organizers of the masses, but the internal development of the organizations was bound to herald the prospects of reorganization.

CHAPTER THREE

STABILIZATION OF ACTIVITIES AND FORM OF THE SECTIONAL ORGANIZATION

(*a*) *Development of the Non-combatant Activities of Trade Unions*

TRADE unionism in its original form[1] appealed to the workers' need to be prepared for industrial conflict; the worker is supposed to join the union because he understands the need for long-term preparation,[2] or at any rate because he sees the industrial conflict developing and dislikes the alternative of starvation or strike-breaking.[3] Even had the trade unionists been far-sighted enough to undertake the support of unorganized workers who joined in a strike,[4] those who had contributed to union funds would have first claim to whatever frugal support was available; the intelligent worker was expected to avoid a situation in which he would have to ask for benefit from funds to which he had made no contribution. With the exception of the German printers, who, in consequence of their background, were closer to the pattern

[1] In some documents issued before the rise of trade unionism (cf. the resolution of the Nuremberg Congress of the anti-Lassalle Workers' Associations, 1868, reproduced by Bebel, op. cit., vol. I, p. 177), insurance against sickness, old age, etc., was described as a main purpose of the trade unions because of lack of faith in the chances of industrial struggle, as well as to prevent State authority being strengthened by taking on itself such popular tasks. But such tasks were for a long time materially impracticable for the trade unions, with the possible exception of the printers. Such statements refute the description of the friendly society benefits as a mere later 'degeneration'; but they are irrelevant in describing the actual appeal of the first unions.

[2] Cf. the classical definition by S. and B. Webb, op. cit., p. 1.

[3] The difference between these attitudes in itself implies some inequality in the members' conformity with the union's basic standards, long before the introduction of friendly society benefits.

[4] This was suggested even in the strike regulations issued 1st August 1894 by the Austrian Trade Union Centre, a document directed against a light-minded approach to strikes (cf. Deutsch, op. cit., pp. 207 and 201). Such support was suggested, of course, as a means of recruiting the unorganized workers for the union; some differentiation in the amount of strike pay given to members and non-members respectively would conduce to such a result.

of a friendly society, the typical trade unionist of the early period undoubtedly joined for the reasons given;[1] in a few instances, where Austrian workers were offered the opportunity of acquiring trade union status in strikes without having to shoulder the other expenses, the opportunity was taken up by a majority of the workers concerned.[2]

Yet from the trade union organizers' standpoint the original appeal, however well it might correspond to the principles of class struggle, suffered from the disadvantage that it failed to stabilize the membership. The need for economic struggle is felt with varying strength from one period to another. When masses of new workers with a non-industrial background enter industrial life, large fluctuations in union membership are inevitable.[3] Even representatives of a union of highly skilled workers with a long tradition of political activity regarded a membership which varied according to the expectation of industrial dispute as the most natural thing in the world; occasionally the union lost members even after a successful strike.[4] In the light of British experience, the introduction of friendly society benefits seemed an obvious device to stabilize membership, and unemployment seemed the most suitable risk for trade unions to cover. Unlike some other risks, there was no public Social Insurance against it, and the introduction of public insurance might seem suspect so long as the State was clearly hostile to the labour movement;[5] in any case it would have to be supplemented by trade union activities in order to safeguard the interests of those unemployed persons who were most deserving from the trade union point of view. There was an obvious connexion between unemployment and industrial conflict, and there was a long tradition of unemployment benefit even in the unions of the building trades, which had a radical history.[6]

For a long time a fundamental distinction was made in nearly all the trade union publications between 'combatant' benefits against the risks

[1] For the different position in Britain, see S. and B. Webb, op. cit., *passim*, especially pp. 445 and 457–8, also p. 383.

[2] Deutsch, op. cit., p. 182, states that up to 1898 the 'second class' of the Lower Austrian engineering workers (i.e. those who preferred to manage without unemployment benefit) was in the ascendant; it lost its importance only a decade later.

[3] See above, pp. 27–8.

[4] Rohrbach, op. cit., on the Metal Workers' Union, which at that time comprised mainly the engineering workers.

[5] In the different political setting of the Christian Trade Unions, which discussed the introduction of unemployment benefit at their Krefeld Congress in 1901, a not very numerous *right-wing* minority, composed of opponents of the policy of 'neutralizing' the Christian Trade Unions (see above, p. 37), opposed the suggested benefit because it could safely be left to the State (on the attitude of the right-wing trend in Free Trade Unionism to this matter see below, p. 57). The majority favoured the introduction of the benefit because it would strengthen union discipline as against the employers. Cf. Müller, op. cit., p. 123.

[6] See above, p. 21.

of unemployment and change of residence, not to speak of strikes and victimization, and the ordinary friendly society benefits.[1] To the critical historian, such distinctions may seem to be rationalizations of the need to make some compromise with the financial limitations of the young unions if their appeal was not to be restricted to the small minority which in those days could afford high contributions, and with the opposition in their own ranks. In fact, the kind of fellow-worker whose union membership was dependent merely upon a claim to unemployment benefit was not likely to play the part of a strike-breaker in times of industrial conflict, even if he were not a member. The real contribution of unemployment benefit to the sectional struggle lay in the stabilization of membership figures, and any friendly society benefit served that purpose. Indeed, once the resistance to introducing such services as unemployment benefit was broken, trade union propaganda came to be largely based upon the help that was granted to the loyal member in every conceivable difficulty.

The opposition in the Free Trade Unions to the introduction of unemployment benefit was based on the twofold argument that the rise in contributions which it would occasion would prevent the Union from becoming all-embracing, and there was the threat that the once combatant body might develop into a mere friendly society, or at any rate attract an inert membership undesirable from the standpoint of trade unionism's original tasks. These two arguments, despite first appearances, did not necessarily contradict each other; a rise in contributions combined with the offer of benefits might deter the worker whose difficult conditions made him a desirable recruit[2] from the point of view of the class struggle, while attracting the 'good husbandman' with but a moderate propensity to vote in favour of strike action. In the end the Union would obviously have to include both, but its future character might be determined by whichever type was predominant during the formative period.

[1] The distinction was made even in the early nineties by the Socialist minority of the Austrian printers and by the Socialist majorities of the other unions (Deutsch, op. cit., pp. 155 and 165 ff.). The resolution of the Party Congress of 1891 described benefits other than those for unemployment and strike-pay as alien to trade unionism and belonging properly to the sphere of the State; but there was some opposition in trade union circles even to the introduction of unemployment benefit (ibid., pp. 174–5). For the completely different attitude in Britain, where even representatives of the 'New Unionism' began their friendly society activities with funeral benefits, see the Webbs, op. cit., p. 420 note.

[2] The upholders of the opposite viewpoint had a different conception of the *élite*. As late as 1924 the German Printers' Union (op. cit., p. 29) quoted with pride the compliment paid to its institutions by the moderate Liberal, Tiedemann: 'A Union whose friendly society benefits make such demands upon its members can be sure of embracing the *élite* of the trade, to be supported by whatever moral strength is available. . . . Efforts like those which bear fruit in services of this kind cannot be made by blind masses inspired by agitators.'

Even in the nineties we find in trade union publications[1] descriptions of the various kinds of trade unionist, with an evident bias against the active union member whose mobility and propagandist activities, followed by frequent dismissals and perhaps by costly solidarity strikes, might cause his union trouble and expense. Such an attitude to the kind of member without whose effort and sacrifice the union could not grow was not typical of German trade unionism at that time; but once unemployment benefit was introduced, mere necessity required that its abuse should be prevented by the enumeration of those causes of unemployment, ranging from drunkenness and lateness at work to 'manifestly bad workmanship',[2] which would bar a claim to benefit; members whose behaviour resulted in their frequent unemployment might be rendered harmless to union funds by being transferred to a group which paid lower fees but had no claim to benefit.[3] Such a policy would bring strong pressure on the slightly under-average worker, with a propensity to disputes with his foreman and to being one of the first to be dismissed in times of depression, to mend his ways and preserve his means of livelihood by compensating for his below-par productivity by a below-par tendency to quarrel with his master. From the standpoint of the 'good husbandman' whose loyalty to his union and readiness to ask a good wage for good work were merely different aspects of his professional pride, such behaviour was natural; the under-average worker might be tolerated if he kept in his proper place and did not support radical proposals. But from the standpoint of the class struggle, a trade union policy which drove the under-average worker to behave in this way, if not to join the yellow trade union, could not but seem treacherous.

So long as conditions in the heavy and mass-production industries prevented the introduction of friendly society services in the most important unions, the existence of such services in a few favoured trades increased the already enormous differentiation within the labour movement. In the mid-nineties the annual membership fees collected[4] ranged from Mk. 1·96 in the Miners' to 53·10 in the Printers' Union, 42·71 in the Hatters' and 19·24 in the Coppersmiths'. Most of the unions collected Mk. 5 to 10 per member. In 1896 the average unemployment benefit per member was in the Printers' Union Mk. 6·10, in the Hatters' 5·49, and in the Moulders' only Mk. 0·55.[5] This last figure, typical for

[1] The organ of the German Metal Workers' Union as quoted by Hänisch, op. cit.

[2] R. and G. Michels, op. cit., p. 457.

[3] Herkner, op. cit., vol. I, p. 238.

[4] The weekly contribution was Mk. 0·20 in the Miners' and Mk. 1·10 in the Printers' Union. In the former case the difference between the theoretical annual contribution (Mk. 10·40) and the sum actually collected may be explained, apart from temporary unemployment, by the Union's reluctance to recognize in its statistics the fluctuations in its membership (see above, pp. 27–8).

[5] On the average a member of the Printers' Union received Mk. 17·41 and a member of the Hatters' Union Mk. 14·43 annually in illness or invalidity benefit.

most of the unions which paid such benefits, could hardly be regarded, even in years of moderate unemployment, as a serious contribution towards lessening the pressure of unemployment on the members concerned. Substantial benefits—and then not only for the unemployed but even more for the 'non-combatant' friendly society services—were paid only in those unions where there were 'closed shop' conditions in a large proportion of the enterprises covered. From the data given[1] it appears that two types of Union coexisted; most of them embraced some 5 to 10 per cent of the workers in the trade concerned (in the union strongholds perhaps 20 to 30 per cent were organized), and paid little attention to friendly society services of any kind, while a few aristocratic unions of the mid-nineteenth-century British type held a very large part of the movement's total funds, but for clearly non-combatant purposes.[2]

In the first years of the twentieth century the position of the workers had improved sufficiently to enable them to bear somewhat higher contributions, but the ideological resistance to purely friendly society services remained strong enough to prevent experiments in them outside the Printers' Union. In 1900 the Metal Workers introduced unemployment benefit, and in 1904 the Miners. By 1908 it had been established in three-quarters of the German Free Trade Unions.[3] In the typical cases the amount paid weekly was 6 to 10 Mk., which was enough to alleviate the worst hardships, provided it was paid over a prolonged period. But it lasted only for 30 to 60 days, save for the Printers, who paid it for 280 days. These benefits, such as they were, could not have been paid had unemployment reached the level it attained in even the more prosperous phases of the post-war period; and, especially in the mass-unions, even in pre-1914 conditions the benefits paid could not have been provided by the contributions exacted had not the continuous increase in membership covered the benefits due to members of long standing. Any setback would have confronted the unions with the alternative of reducing the promised benefits or increasing contributions, and that in times of depression. Either course might easily turn the setback into a catastrophe. These limitations to friendly society services were fully recognized; but while the Austrian Miners' Union, looking on social insurance as a public concern, demanded the reform of the State system so as to ensure democratic self-government and freedom of combination,[4] the Stuttgart Congress of the German Free Unions in 1902 demanded State support for the unemployment services of the trade unions—later called the

[1] Sources: Legien, op. cit., and Hänisch, op. cit.

[2] In 1896, out of a total expenditure of 3·6 million marks by all the Free trade unions, 1·1 million was spent by the Printers. This union excluded the unskilled workers, who had a union of their own, resembling the mass-unions in character.

[3] The Hirsch-Duncker Unions (see above, p. 20), in which there was no opposition on grounds of principle and little strike expenditure to act as a limiting factor, had introduced unemployment benefit as early as 1895.

[4] Deutsch, op. cit., p. 177.

Ghent system.[1] No one could seriously expect anything of this kind from the Hohenzollern monarchy; but serious problems were implied in such an appeal even to a reformed State, which could certainly not support a trade union service without appropriate guarantees for the unions' behaviour.

There is, however, only a moderate amount of truth in the assertion that the unions' propensity to strike action was restricted by their concern to preserve the funds needed to carry on their friendly society services. A comparison for the year 1912 between the expenditure per member in the main trade union groups for combatant purposes and for unemployment benefit[2] suggests that the amount spent for either purpose was a function of the financial strength of the union concerned rather than of its ideological principles. The very existence of large funds might make those who administered them reluctant to enter into serious conflict with the authorities, whether those funds were destined for the support of strikers or for paying unemployment or sickness benefit. To say that the growth of the non-combatant activities of the unions caused them to betray their Socialist principles is only a reflection of the delusion that their combatant activities were necessarily directed against the existing order of society.[3]

More important than the influence of the unions' non-combatant activities on their behaviour in the industrial field were the potentialities they involved of eventually replacing trade unionism by some other kind of organization managed by the workers' sectional antagonists. We have already noticed[4] the opportunities possessed by the Catholic Workers' Secretaries to fulfil one of the functions of the trade union, i.e. to supply legal aid in conflicts arising out of their members' employment; but what is significant is that they acted on behalf of the workers in opposition to the employers, even though they did so on the basis of an ideology very different from that which inspired trade unionism. But the non-combatant services could be supplied as well, or better, out of the employers' funds in order to 'buy off' the workers' right to strike.[5]

[1] See below, p. 299.

[2] According to Herkner, op. cit., p. 242, the amounts were (in marks):

	Trade Unions:		
	Free	*Christian*	*Hirsch-Duncker*
Strike and victimization benefit	5·46	1·90	3·19
Unemployment and travelling benefit	3·53	0·86	2·61

[3] See below, p. 92.

[4] See above, p. 35.

[5] Weber, op. cit., p. 373. A few pages later the same writer suggests that the *bona fide* unions should retort to the 'yellows' by introducing more non-combatant services, such as old age pensions. But, obviously, the support of an old trade union member, who presumably during his active life would have already received large sums in strike and unemployment benefit, would cost the unions more in relation to

This was one of the basic ideas of 'yellow' pseudo-unionism.

As every trade unionist knows from experience, so-called 'small grievances'—which may be more important in a worker's life than a few pence more or less per week—are a most important element in fomenting movements even for larger issues. Experience of the Italian *Dopolavoro* and the German *Strength through Joy* has made it a commonplace that improvements gained in those fields may even help to destroy bona fide trade unionism. Liberal critics might be right in saying that only the large-scale enterprise could afford the expenditure needed for such improvements as might influence the workers' morale; but this was only another way of saying that one of the most fruitful of trade union activities could prosper mainly in small and medium-sized enterprises where, because of the larger part played in them by skilled labour, trade unionism had taken its rise. Memories of the old truck system might still handicap the appeal of 'works co-operatives' backed by the support of the employers, but to satisfy the workers' housing needs was clearly beyond the power of the organized labour movement. Liberal critics of the 'yellow' organizations[1] would concede that economic liberalism had conspicuously failed in that field, while housing schemes initiated by the employers were notably successful.

Academic sociologists have noticed that the analogies between the position of a yellow 'trade unionist' and a civil servant employed during good behaviour were bound to appeal to large sections of the German people; but as in a capitalist society full employment was impossible, in the event of a triumph of yellow trade unionism its supporters would lose that scarcity value for which employers were still prepared to pay.[2] Before such forecasts could be tested, yellow trade unionism was defeated by the elementary class-consciousness of the German workers; indeed, it admitted its defeat from the very beginning by the mimicry it deemed necessary to hide the fact of its support by the employers. Although the close connexion between the 'yellow' unions and the Employers' Associations was obvious,[3] the former claimed to be merely a variety of trade unionism differing from other varieties only in its organizational principles, just as those other varieties differed among themselves. Indeed, the 'yellow' movement was split in its search for efficient mimicry, as is illustrated by the Berlin organizations' emphasis on the need for at any rate the appearance of self-government: this

his contributions than superannuation benefit for a yellow trade unionist with a long record of unbroken service, some of it presumably as a useful strike-breaker, would cost his employer.

[1] Heiss, op. cit., p. 378.

[2] Weber, op. cit., p. 374 ff.; Herkner, op. cit., p. 216.

[3] In the instance quoted by Herkner, op. cit., pp. 218–19, a mere 4 per cent of the funds were raised by the members, 6 per cent by 'extraordinary members' (mostly Churches and other bodies with right-wing sympathies), the rest by the employers.

made them exclude the salaried employees, who managed the labour organizations established by a number of the biggest undertakings such as Krupps, the Chemical Trust, and the Munich-Augsburg-Nuremberg engineering works. In fact, the workers joined yellow Unions only where they could be forced to do so. The Siemens Works in Berlin, where a quarter of the employees were formally members, became famous as the home of the 'blood-oranges'—yellow outside, red inside; perhaps a deeper root of the evil was correctly indicated in the Berlin workers' witticism that their fellows at Siemens' had a deplorable tendency to 'enter the works in the pram and leave it in the hearse'. The vote polled by the 'yellows' at their original home, the Augsburg engineering works, in the secret ballot for the election of workers' representatives in the Industrial Court, dropped from 2,300 in 1907 to 1,400 in 1912, while that of the Free Unions increased from 4,000 to 6,500.

The employers recognized the failure of the 'yellow' Unions when, in the Working Community Agreement of November 1918,[1] they had to undertake to withdraw support from them. With the conspicuous exception of agriculture, where the League of Agriculturists had its own 'workers' ' section, the employers' support was transferred to the right wing of Christian Trade Unionism and similar trends. When eventually the Nazis realized the actual content of yellow pseudo-unionism, they carefully avoided paying any tribute to their unlucky precursors. As we have seen and shall see later, the German workers proved to be accessible to appeals which were not based upon their own class-ideology; but not to organizations evidently started by their sectional opponents.

The yellow attempt, however, had shown that, once sectional organization dropped its purely combatant outlook, it also lost its monopoly of offering the workers an answer to their grievances. What it had offered as bribes in the field of welfare services and housing accommodation would eventually be sought in the services of the welfare State; but there was no inherent reason why such services should depend on the political complexion of the Government. The tendencies to 'industrial feudalism' implied in the offer of services by their employers individually had been rejected by the workers; but there was no inherent reason why they should be rejected when brought into being by the employers' State.

(b) *Centralization and Institutionalization of Free Trade Unionism*

The tendency to centralization which in all countries springs from the practical needs of trade unionism[2] took on certain specific aspects in Germany because the Associations Law prohibited the amalgamation

[1] See below, p. 152.
[2] For Britain see S. and B. Webb, op. cit., chapters iii and iv.

on a nation-wide scale of organizations whose activities might be called political, at least in a sense suspect to the Government.[1] Under the Anti-Socialist Law the local 'non-political' labour organizations had proudly served as the rallying-point for all sides of the labour movement; with the end of that law nation-wide amalgamation of trade unions became possible provided identification with Social Democratic politics was avoided. There was no serious disagreement about the practical usefulness of centralizing trade unionism, but the Party naturally felt some sympathy with those who had carried its banner through the most difficult years. Quite apart from the experience of Austria, where similar arrangements were the norm,[2] the compromise between the German Metal Workers' Associations and the Berlin engineering workers' Localist group showed that it was possible to combine the necessary centralization with some degree of autonomy, at least in the larger local organizations, and to set aside a large proportion of the funds collected[3] for financing local strikes and benefits. Thus the German Party leaders may have been justified in ascribing the less reasonable behaviour of most of the trade union centres to political, anti-Party, prejudice.[4]

Yet even in Austria, where political antagonism between Party and Trade Unions might be considered as non-existent, the need for central control of industrial conflicts was recognized by the issue of 'strike regulations'. The first, issued by the T.U.C. on 1st August 1894, was very moderate: a claim by strikers for support from the central body was recognized only if the strike had been previously approved by that body and lasted for more than eight days, or if the need for a strike in defence of existing working conditions was admitted; but even non-authorized strikes *might* be supported by the national body if it thought fit. Support for strikes of local importance was left to the local organizations.[5] But in the resolution accepted by the Trade Union Congress of 1900 strikes begun against the advice of the trade union centre concerned were denied any kind of support, even moral, and material

[1] For the greater freedom enjoyed by the Christian Trade Unions see preceding chapter, p. 37 note 4.

[2] Cf. Deutsch, op. cit., p. 173.

[3] According to Rohrbach, op. cit., in the Berlin compromise mentioned in the text local groups with more than 3,000 members (of which at that time there were none outside Berlin) were allowed to retain 25 per cent of their members' contributions for local administration and another 50 per cent for local strikes and benefits. This may be compared with the relations between central and local organizations considered normal 20 years later; 80 per cent of the contributions collected were then paid into the central funds, strikes had to be conducted by the local organizations under central direction, and the regional organizers were appointed by the central Committee (Herkner, op. cit., p. 231).

[4] Auer on the Berlin Party Congress (1892), *Proceedings*, p. 243, and Report of the Central Committee to the Cologne (1893) Party Congress.

[5] Deutsch, op. cit., pp. 207–10.

support by the whole labour movement was restricted to large-scale strikes conducted by unions which had properly prepared their funds but had exhausted them; support for unorganized workers was made dependent on the decision of the T.U.C.[1] In the same year the T.U.C. refused to support a strike generally considered legitimate and likely to succeed, because its funds were already earmarked for the support of another strike conducted by the same union. This attitude was upheld when the strike had actually started, and was supported by the union concerned as well as by the provncial T.U.C.[2]

Before 1918, strike-breaking was not regarded as a legitimate means of enforcing trade union discipline. Nor did any Central European T.U.C. of the nineties control sufficient funds to make a strike's success dependent on its support. Its power to 'regulate' strikes, therefore, depended on its ability to convince working-class opinion of the merits of unconditional discipline.[3] But the strikers also could appeal to that forum: an obvious lever for such an appeal was afforded by local solidarity between the various trades. In the middle nineties the German dispute with the Localists was followed by a quarrel as to the competence of the local Trades Councils. Defenders of established trade union authority[4] emphasized that, in protecting their funds against expensive strikes, the unions were also protecting the rights of members in smaller centres who had little hope of being able to resort to the 'abuse' of collections among the general working-class public. Interference with the union centre's established right to authorize or prohibit strikes reached its height when the local Trades Councils supported strikes even in other towns, thus replacing mutual obligations by favours, or, as Trades Councils would see it, promoting working-class solidarity. The Trades Councils would claim that they could allow for local conditions better than anyone else,[5] and the defenders of the bureaucracy would reply that, while the Trades Councils were composed of workers still at the bench and likely to be impressed by temporary working-class enthusiasms, the national leaders of a trade union were free from such sentimental bias; they were immunized against the danger of being impressed by enthusiastic strikers by the consideration that people who had done little in advance to strengthen the organization needed for the strike were unlikely to make serious sacrifices when the time for action came. Successful strikes presupposed funds accumulated in advance, and such accumulation was impossible in the local Trades Councils.[6] True, it was impossible even in the national unions at that time; but if enthusiasm was excluded and support made conditional upon members having

[1] Ibid., pp. 164 ff.
[2] Ibid., p. 243.
[3] Ibid.
[4] Legien, op. cit.
[5] Stumm, op. cit.
[6] Pörsch, op. cit.

joined the union before the actual strike issue was in sight,[1] there would be fewer strikes and more opportunity to accumulate funds for a still unforeseen future.

The democratic structure of the local Trades Councils led to a chain of political and organizational conflicts with the central trade union bureaucracy. The Trades Councils might condemn the policies of the Printers' Unions,[2] they could discuss political issues while the national unions were barred from so doing by existing legislation, and their relations to the local Party organization might be closer than the advocates of 'neutralization of the trade unions'[3] would like. Clearly, they provided competing centres; therefore Legien suggested that their members should be nominated by the local Committees of their unions, which were, of course, subject to national headquarters, instead of being elected at public meetings of their trades, a procedure which favoured the election of persons well known in the local labour movement. The assumption that, in the conditions of those days, the local committee of a trade union represented a broader outlook than that of a leadir g factory representative from the bench[4] was rather fantastic; but the conflict was not merely a struggle for organizational forms and political power.

A national wages policy with its implications was then hardly within the reach of the unions; trials of strength in individual factories were the commoner method of procedure. Although the immediate issue varied, the common background was the demand that the employers should recognize, if not the national trade union, which before 1918 was exceptional, at least the local group and the 'men of confidence' in the factory. In an average-sized town, the prestige and strength of the labour movement in every factory would increase if a success were scored by the workers in a factory of local importance, and the Trades Council would react accordingly. But in a Union such as the Metal Workers', the stabilization of its position in a factory which from the national viewpoint was of third-rate importance would not be regarded as justifying the considerable depletion of the Union funds by a lengthy strike. In any case the Union had little to give apart from Marks and Pfennigs, and in the event of a broad wave of strikes, not many of them.[5] The solidarity of fellow-workers in the town, however, might supply not only money, bread, and fuel, but also moral backing, which would increase the value of such material supplies. A woman textile worker who would be very glad to earn a quarter of the wages over which the carpenters

[1] According to Rohrbach, op. cit., the Metal Workers' Union supported during strikes only members of at least six, or in exceptional cases three, months' standing.

[2] See below, p. 66.

[3] See below, p. 67.

[4] Pörsch, op. cit.

[5] As late as 1907 the Free trade unions had total funds averaging 20 marks per member, part of which, especially in the richest Unions was earmarked for friendly society benefits.

had struck might still feel that their struggle would hasten the coming of the day when women workers, even if not earning carpenters' wages, would yet be dealt with as human beings acting as a group, instead of being played off by the foreman against each other. She would therefore make an effort to save a few Pfennigs for the subscription list, and also bring what pressure she could as a customer on the baker round the corner to spare a few loaves for the strikers' children. Obviously this kind of solidarity was manifested between the local trades rather than in the national industrial sphere.

Had the national trade union been able to develop a national wages policy, it could have allowed workers who were calling for a strike which was not thought important enough to justify the use of national funds to go ahead with what local support was available, and with the merely moral support of the union centre. But the national Unions had no considerable funds, and would never amass any if working-class capacity for sacrifice was absorbed by such strikes as happened to command the necessary enthusiasm and local sympathy whether they happened to accord with Trade Union policies or not. Therefore national Unions criticized the practice of deciding on strikes in enthusiastic factory meetings instead of in the quieter atmosphere of the worker's home, where he would face all the difficulties involved before marking his ballot-paper in favour of a strike.[1] In later days, when, because of the stronger position of the national Unions in funds and discipline, workers were no longer inclined to strike with only local support, little more was heard of these disputes; the Cologne Trade Union Congress (1905) abolished the right of the Trades Councils to collect money for strikers and demanded that the individual Unions should regulate their strike policy in accordance with their own financial resources. With the important exception of Rosa Luxemburg's theory of spontaneity[2]—whose importance, however, lay mainly in its influence upon later Communist thought—all further disputes concerned the tactics to be applied within the centralized organizations.

The very fact that recognition by the employers had been the basic issue in the preceding struggles strengthened the internal discipline of the organization of labour; the movement's democratic ideology lent further authority to the rules and regulations. Even if a minority for a moment considered secession as the last resort of those who believed that they had been overruled by a cooked majority, the memories of past splits, in Austria as well as in Germany, were bitter enough to banish the thought. There were more recent memories of groups which had resisted centralization, and the very consciousness of the fact that the Localists' original platform[3] had been loyal to the Party lent additional strength

[1] On the Practice of the Decision to Strike, *Neue Zeit*, vol. XVI/1, pp. 372 ff.

[2] See below, pp. 105–1.

[3] See above, p. 61.

to the observation that those of them who had failed to enter the centralist framework were driven into the anarchist deviation. But once unity at any price was accepted as a basic tenet, the Unions' rules and strike regulations became a fetish, like the law of an ordinary bourgeois State. To organize strikes successfully, it was not enough to assess the situation correctly, to inspire the sympathies needed to get support, and, in case of success, to be clever at the negotiating table; it was more necessary to be astute in dealing with the senior officials of the Union in order to get sanction for the strike. One who opposed the 'high-ups' could do well if he knew all the intricacies and subtleties of the rules, for the same reasons as in most countries it is a help to an opposition leader to be a good lawyer. For the same reasons, his opposition might end by his being admitted into the inner circle. No special turpitude on his part or on that of those who 'corrupted' him with a prize which appealed to his ambitions, though hardly to his material interests,[1] need be involved; he tried to gain influence in the organization which stood for all the values accepted in his world, and they looked around in the lower organizations for active members who deserved promotion because of their knowledge of Trade Union affairs. His argument, even if distasteful, was sound, for he knew how to interpret the rules and how to manage a ballot; such knowledge distinguished the experienced trade unionist, whether within or outside the leading clique, from the enthusiastic but inexperienced and unreliable new-comer. The ranks of potential opposition leaders within the Trade Unions might be further drained by the competition of the Party whose activities were bound to attract precisely those who reproached trade unionism with neglecting the interests of the most depressed sectors of the working class.

Because of the specific conditions of Central Europe, collective bargaining on a national scale did not come into vogue during this period. Yet it was envisaged very soon, and the individual facts we are now to discuss were generally disputed precisely because of the widespread and justified assumption that they indicated the direction in which the minds of trade union leaders were working. Collective bargaining in itself was regarded, in the political Party as well as the Trade Unions, as an achievement if it testified to the workers' strength;[2] the point at issue was whether this achievement, in the sense of mere recognition of the Unions as bargaining partners by the employers, justified far-reaching concessions. Only because this issue was clothed by the workers concerned in all kinds of radical phraseology could the impression be created that collective bargaining itself was a contested issue. In the general framework of Christian Trade Unionism it was quite natural for

[1] See below, p. 72.

[2] Cf. Deutsch, op. cit., p. 258. For the same attitude in Germany, cf. Fischer's report on the Jena Party Congress (1905), *Report*, pp. 235 ff.

the desire for collective agreements to be emphasized;[1] in that of Free Trade Unionism, however, the issue came into the open in the aftermath of a dispute within the only Union which had succeeded in concluding a collective agreement.

Middle-class disapproval of the collaboration of the Printers' Union with Social Democracy had played its part in defeating the strike of 1892;[2] the Union leaders' move towards collective bargaining was accompanied by the dismissal of the editor of the Union's weekly, who reproached them for taking up an attitude hostile to the Party. That reproach was, to say the least, not refuted by the leaders' statements in defence of their action at the following Congress. The opposition, inspired by the desire to preserve the connexion with the political party of the labour movement but wishing to define clearly its attitude in the industrial field, over-emphasized this criticism by passing from a rejection of the conditions of the agreement of 1896, to positive suggestions[3] which, though the fact was not stated, really implied a rejection of the principle of collective bargaining. When the opposition leaders published a journal of their own they were expelled from the Union by a referendum; but in view of the Union's record as a friendly society rather than a fighting organization the majority of 13,251 against 5,164 was not very impressive. When the opposition tried to form an organization of its own, it failed to rally more than a few hundred members, most of them employed in the Party's printing enterprises. During the conflict the Leipzig Trades Council, dominated by the Party's left wing, admitted the delegates elected at the meetings of the opposition while rejecting those chosen at the much better attended meetings of the official Union, because the latter 'was based upon the principle of collective agreement community,[4] which contradicts the principles of the modern labour movement'. Such support, while it prevented the dissenters from being called 'blacklegs' from the standpoint of accepted class ideology, could not prevent their having to submit eventually to the official Union. The issue of principle was not likely to be cleared up so long as it was obvious that collective agreements on a more than local scale were attainable only by unions which pursued a course not favoured by the bulk of the working class, either by undercutting the latter's demands, as the Christian Trade Unions did, or by enjoying a privileged position and adopting attitudes consistent with being an *élite*, as did the Printers.

The connexion of the Free Trade Unions with Social Democracy

[1] Müller, op. cit., pp. 229–30.

[2] See above, p. 29.

[3] Cf. Kulemann, op. cit., pp. 280 ff.

[4] The translation of *Tarifgemeinschaft* as 'collective agreement', i.e. the natural outcome of collective bargaining, would obscure the essential point that the institution under criticism included the possibility that, in theory, at any rate (see above, p. 29), one party together with a minority of the other could enforce against a majority of the latter a supposed super-class will of the industry.

raised obvious difficulties in their acceptance by the employers of Imperial Germany as partners in collective bargaining; the weakening of that connexion seemed a necessary task to those Union leaders who envied the Printers' achievement. Right-wing Social Democrats, though they might resent suggestions from the Printers' Union that they should nominate separate Trade Union candidates for Parliament, disapproved not only of any Socialist propaganda in the Unions, however discreet, and of collaboration between the local Trades Councils and the Party;[1] they even argued that, as the strength of the labour movement as a whole was more important than that of one of its components, Britain with its powerful but non-partisan Trade Unions might represent a more powerful development for labour than Germany with its model Social Democracy.[2] (A few years later, the same author complained of the tendency of German trade unionists to imitate the British pattern by gradually dropping the ideology of the labour movement.[3]) Kautsky emphasized that in a country with a strong Social Democratic Party the concept of non-political trade unionism was a delusion: the German unions had only the choice between collaborating with the political party of the working class, or opposing it, and relying on the bourgeois parties as the only ones which had a chance to take part in the government. There was evidence of a tendency on the part of Trade Union leaders to pursue the second path; the Cologne Trade Union Congress[4] adopted a resolution moved by Bringmann in which the trade unions were described as the *only* means available for the improvement of working-class conditions. A little later, Bringmann,[5] speaking at a private meeting of the Trade Union leaders, described Marxism as the disease from which the German labour movement suffered; the unions should replace it by an ideology of their own. Such a policy, while somewhat weakening Social Democracy as a whole, would have strengthened its left wing. In view of later developments it is interesting to imagine the consequences which it would have had in August 1914 and in the critical days of the Revolution.

Yet the Union leaders did not turn aside from Social Democracy. In a country where even the tamest attempts at industrial organization provoked repression by the employers,[6] and the State machinery was closely connected with the most reactionary social forces, no independent labour movement was possible without the protection of a strong political labour party. Nor could the internal cohesion of the labour movement be seriously threatened by the Free Trade Union leaders'

[1] Elm, op. cit., p. 358.
[2] Ibid., p. 362.
[3] See below, p. 104.
[4] See also above, p. 64, and below, p. 104.
[5] Quoted by Winnig, op. cit., p. 108.
[6] See above, p. 40.

flirtations with their colleagues of the Christian Trade Unions so long as the Church threatened the latter with excommunication even for collaboration with Protestants.[1] The 'Academic Socialist' school of liberal economists as well as the theoretical instigators of Bringmann's search for non-Marxist trade unionism[2] might deplore the German rulers' lack of understanding of moderate unionism, which prevented its separation from the Socialist party; but such complaints could not alter German realities.

Nor could the Unions preserve their internal cohesion without the Party's support in view of the difficulties with their own members which the growth of centralist organization involved. They repeatedly complained of the Party's tendency to see in the Localist movement more than a rebellion against their legitimate authority; but they would not have won the struggle so easily without the support, however moderating in nature, of the Party which, as distinct from themselves, enjoyed the prestige of having defeated the Anti-Socialist Law. When their opposition to the spontaneous strike movement, combined with their inability to organize strikes on a centralist basis, induced them to propagate escapist utopias such as the enforcement of improved working conditions by the pressure of working-class consumers, they got quite a lot of punishment at the Party congresses.[3] Their confessions of weakness encouraged the Party's self-assertion and even provoked doubts about the prospects of trade unionism in general.[4] Yet if they had failed to co-operate with the Party which was supported by the vast bulk of the German working class, the breaking-off of a strike distasteful to most of the strikers would not have been hailed as a great triumph of working-class discipline.[5] A mere ten years after the Printers' dispute Winnig[6] demanded that the Party organizations and press should support the Trade Union leaders whenever their views differed from those of the majority of the Union members; as modern conditions called for diplomacy at the negotiation table, this was the only means of rallying the masses behind their competent leaders and of avoiding conflicts between Party and Unions. At that time such views were unlikely to be accepted by the Party. But the very opportunity to make such a case

[1] See above, pp. 38–9.

[2] Winnig, op. cit., pp. 96 and 69 ff.

[3] e.g. Proceedings of the 1892 Berlin Party Congress, pp. 230 ff.

[4] See below, p. 88.

[5] Cf: e.g. Michels', (op. cit., pp. 168–9) description of the calling off of a miners' strike as an illustration of the helplessness of the masses against the bureaucracy with Luise Zeitz's praise of the discipline shown by the Saxon anthracite miners on such an occasion (Jena Proceedings, 1905, p. 326).

[6] In *Neue Zeit*, vol. XXV/2 (1907), replying to an argument (ibid., vol. XXV/1) between Backhaus, the representative of the Printers' Union, and Kautsky concerning an agreement in which the union had sacrificed the interests of the machine composers for the benefit of the skilled craftsmen.

within an organization that enjoyed the loyalty of virtually the whole working class might be a sufficient reason for Union leaders to say what they had to say in terms of the Party's ideology, that is, to appeal to the class-discipline familiar to the German workers.

(c) *Democracy and Bureaucracy in the Organization of Labour*

Apart from the authoritarian tendencies found in the government of some Catholic organizations,[1] democracy, in the sense that in theory at any rate all organizational activities were based on majority decisions of the members, was an undisputed tenet in all the bodies under discussion, as distinct from the later fascist bodies based on the leadership principle. Without it neither the activities needed for the body's life, most of them unpaid,[2] nor the necessary discipline would have been secured. Nor could a bureaucracy not evidently authorized by those whom it claimed to represent expect to possess any authority in negotiations and public appeals.

The permanent shortage of members suitable for filling the greatly increased[3] number of offices resulted in ample opportunity for every member who had belonged to the body for some time and attended its meetings with more or less regularity to be elected to minor office; if he did not accept such a task he was likely to be blamed for failing to shoulder his part in management. Active members look upon themselves as private soldiers in the army of their class; they assume that an earnest member, duly educated, will do his part in a similar way, and feel that members so recruited as to be unlikely to become true 'activists' are to be thought of as mere makeweight.[4] The active member, who looks on the preparation of his fellows for such efforts as his first duty, is the main representative of the concept of mass organization as a *union of effort*, as distinct from the lower-middle-class concept of it as a combination of monetary contributions from which a dividend is expected. This concept of intra-Union, or intra-Party, democracy as equal opportunity for all active members to have their voice in the community's decision strikes the keynote in the ideology of the labour movement. The dictatorship of the working class, which will ultimately lead to a classless democratic society, is a State run by the activists of the labour movement.[5] The expectation that the activist minority will eventually become

[1] See above, pp. 33–4.

[2] Even in large organizations such as the Berlin branch of the Metal Workers' Union collection of fees by the 'man of confidence' was not replaced by the use of paid house-to-house collectors until after 1918.

[3] The introduction of friendly society benefits greatly increased the amount of work to be done, while not correspondingly increasing the number of members prepared to take a share in it.

[4] See above, p. 55.

[5] The Austrian Social Democratic Party, not conspicuous for radicalism, preferred to speak of its members, Ministers in Coalition governments, as 'men of confidence', using the term familiar to every factory worker.

identical with the community of those on whose behalf it has to act[1] may be utopian; but it warns the minority not to move too far ahead of those it has to lead. No narrow-minded approach, say, to the support of unorganized workers in the event of a strike and to their participation in the necessary decisions is usually associated with the 'activist' conception of democracy within an organization.

But once trade unionism was established as an element in the existing economic framework, administering benefits according to the rules of accountancy and being gradually admitted as a party in collective bargaining, the membership became a subject of administration rather than of mobilization. The 'men of confidence' in the factories ceased to be regarded by the Union leaders as the natural representatives of the membership and of those unorganized workers who followed the Union's lead, as they were in trade unionist theory;[2] the relations between the central leaders, the local activists, and the mass of the membership took on the character of a three-cornered fight, in which the first element used the third as a dead weight to turn the scale in its favour.[3] In the period of the Weimar Republic, when the prevention of strikes was looked upon as a main function of trade unionism, even members who failed to take part in a strike ballot because they were ill were considered as having voted 'No' in order to make it more difficult to achieve the very large majority required for an affirmative vote.[4] Long before this the local groups were described as bodies established by the Central Committee, and their elected leaders had to be confirmed by that body.[5] Before the split in the political labour movement and the identification of the Trade Union bureaucracy with one of the competing labour parties, however, such confirmation could hardly be refused in the face of a firm decision of the electors.[6]

The increasing centralization and the growing amount of administrative work made necessary an increased number of paid officials. Because of the influence of the syndicalist myth, which regards the 'corrupt' bureaucrat, as opposed to the 'democratic' ranker, as the root of all the evils which have befallen the labour movement, the importance of this factor has been much overrated. For this very reason I have preferred to demonstrate the rise of bureaucratic functions before turning to the issue of 'bureaucrats'. In 1898, with just under half a million members, the German Free Trade Unions had 104 salaried officials; six years later, with more than a million members, the number was

[1] Cf. Lenin's expectation that eventually every washerwoman would learn how to govern the State.
[2] Nestriepke, op. cit., vol. I, p. 322.
[3] See above, pp. 62 and 64.
[4] See below, p. 333.
[5] Nestriepke, op. cit., p. 316.
[6] For conditions under the Weimar Republic see below, p. 239.

677;[1] not all of these were employed in executive work. During the following decade the number of union employees rose to 2,867;[2] 482 in the central offices, 429 in regional administration, 1,956 in the local offices; while the membership had just trebled. As a material interest within the German labour movement directly influencing its supporters, the publicans, as practically the only suppliers of accommodation for meetings, were hardly less important than the bureaucracy, with which they shared a lower-middle-class standard of life, as well as the fact that most of them had deserved it by sacrificing their original livelihood as skilled workers at the bench in the interest of the movement. Even Social Democratic publicans, however, had a strong tendency to accommodate themselves to the political views of their patrons, oppositionally-minded workers amongst them. On the other hand, it was the function of 'bureaucrats' to issue orders provoking opposition; no wonder that they became the scapegoats for the whole middle-class and lower-middle-class influence upon the labour movement.[3]

The material conditions of the labour bureaucracy have been described in very different terms. Michels[4] interpreted it as a channel through which workers rose into the middle class, betraying the interests of their former comrades; but their own idea is seen in their complaints that they were definitely worse off than the average skilled worker and badly exploited by their fellows.[5] The fear that something like the first interpretation might be realized, much more than parsimony with the 'workers' pennies', contributed to such facts as might support the second interpretation. In those days, before the assimilation of the standard of life and social habits of the skilled worker to those of the lower middle classes, there was something to be said in favour of a policy which prevented the workers' representatives from being socially separated from those they represented,[6] and from growing accustomed

[1] Herkner, op. cit., p. 232. The figure corresponds to that given by S. and B. Webb (op. cit., p. 466) for British unionism in 1892, when its numerical strength was about equal to German in 1898.

[2] Nestriepke, op. cit., vol. I, p. 323. This 1914 number of paid officials was already considerably larger than that reached in Britain in 1920 (cf. S. and B. Webb, op. cit., pp. 517–18); the percentage of union officials mainly employed in political activities was much smaller in Germany, with its strong Social Democracy, than in Britain. On the other hand, the average German trade union official, at least before 1914, spent a very considerable part of his time in Party activities; at least in the tense atmosphere created by the Cologne Trade Union Congress (see above, p. 67), the Party would denounce union leaders who complained of such activities (cf. Fischer on the Jena Party Congress (1905), Proceedings, p. 236).

[3] The extent to which the opposition trends within the labour movement influence the terminology of opponents outside it is well illustrated by the acceptance of the term 'bureaucracy' (which makes sense in the Trotskyist, but not in a conservative ideology) as a description of the ruling stratum in the U.S.S.R.

[4] Op. cit., pp. 291 ff.

[5] As reported by Milhaud, op. cit., pp. 351 ff., even for an early period.

[6] For the same issue in Britain see S. and B. Webb, op. cit., pp. 469–71.

to standards which they would lose if not re-elected, or if their organization carried out a policy which might lead to its suppression by the authorities.[1] On the other hand, the widespread prejudice against bureaucrats hindered their recruitment from among the most active members of the working class, and attracted the most bureaucratically-minded type of worker to at any rate the lesser positions in Union service: the really capable and ambitious working-class politician would prefer to remain at the bench as long as this was compatible with the offices he held in Party and Trade Union. Even in the Christian Unions, exposed as they were to the pressure of their Free competitors, it might be held that a miners' leader could not be taken away from the pit without losing his authority among his comrades.[2]

After the financial difficulties of the start were overcome, the salaries of officials in the labour movement other than the managerial staff in the co-operatives[3] were calculated on the principle that they ought not to exceed the maximum earnings of a skilled worker.[4] One of the more serious aspects of the trade union officials' complaints was that they became articulate at the very time when the principle was being applied with some degree of broadmindedness. The salaries paid to the Berlin secretaries of the Woodworkers' Union rose from 28 Marks per week in the middle nineties to 35–40 Marks in 1906; most of the officials of the Metal Workers' Union earned in 1909 from 165 to 200 Marks per month (maximum 250, minimum 125). In 1914 the typical Trade Union salary was 180 to 240 Marks per month, the leaders getting perhaps 300 Marks.[5] The whole morale of the labour movement was threatened when people who had risen to their position because they had done unpaid work in their comrades' interests in addition to their day at the bench, and who daily exhorted the activists to similar efforts, now complained of the inordinate hours they had to work as paid officials, of the insecurity of tenure implied in the elective principle, or of the

[1] In view of the whole intellectual climate of the Continental labour movement, where martyrdom on its behalf was held in the highest esteem, this argument could have force only when the preceding one had become effective, that is when the bureaucrat, or his family, had moved into social surroundings where these values no longer held. As long as a general optimism prevailed as to the labour movement's prospects, the argument might move the minor officials more strongly than the union leaders, who could be fairly sure of stepping from prison into Parliament.

[2] Herkner, op. cit., p. 233.

[3] There was no reason for paying them on a scale different from what the unions thought proper for other commercial employees doing similar jobs; if, because of insufficient reward, a co-operative employee should transfer to private employment, his behaviour would not appear as a betrayal of the basic standards of the labour movement, unless in the mind of a fanatical co-operator.

[4] Tribute was paid to this principle as late as 1920 by so conservative a Union as the Printers', which in 1868 had been the first to pay its President an annual salary of 1,200 marks, quite a large amount in those days.

[5] Herkner, op. cit. pp. 233–5; Nestriepke, vol. I, p. 327.

possibility that they might on occasion have to advocate the claims of a group of highly skilled workers better paid than they were themselves.[1] The whole ideology of the German labour movement prevented comparisons with the rewards which a worker with organizing capacity might reap by betraying his class allegiance and entering on a managerial career, as discussed by the Webbs for Britain;[2] but comparisons with the salaries paid by Party and Co-operatives, and complaints that the best qualified Trade Unionists were attracted into the Party's service, were quite frequent. Comparison with co-operatives betrayed a confusion of organizational with managerial activities;[3] as to the Party, its service attracted gifted Trade Unionists not so much because the principle that officials should earn no more than the best-paid workers needs a wider interpretation in an organization comprising workers of all trades, but because of the higher prizes, such as seats in Parliament, which the Party had to offer to the ambitions of the working-class activist, and perhaps also because work in its ranks would accord better with the strictest concepts of the generally accepted class ideology.

The Trade Unions had many more jobs to offer than the Party in those days;[4] so they were likely to be the first to offer employment to the worker blacklisted because of his Union activities. If he had journalistic ambitions beyond editing the Union's periodical, which hardly anyone but the activists read, he eventually had to change to a Party daily, to which he would have already contributed on behalf of his Union; parliamentary ambitions might be satisfied as a reward for organizational and propagandist activities to an extent hardly compatible with a full-time job in a Union office. The process was quite legitimate from the standpoint of the accepted ideology according to which Trade Unions and Party were both branches of a single labour movement; indeed, it was the mere expression, in the higher ranks, of the description of the Unions as 'recruiting schools for Social Democracy', of which in those days they would not complain.[5] The very possibility of argument on such issues proved that there was emerging not only a professional body of working-class organizers—a necessary implication of the growth of the movement—but also a distinct body of officials with a corporate consciousness of their own, in potential opposition to that of the movement they had to serve.

The danger of bureaucratic degeneration was much canvassed in all the factional conflicts within the labour movement; safeguards against a divorce between centre and members were among the accepted in-

[1] See f.n., [5] on p. 71.

[2] S. and B. Webb, op. cit., pp. 588–9.

[3] See f.n., [3] on p. 72.

[4] Under the Weimar Republic, conditions changed because the Party had many municipal and similar jobs at its disposal; but at that time no one was likely to be black-listed for Social Democratic activities.

[5] See below, p. 88.

gredients of a Trade Union constitution. Usually the Central Committee had a small majority of workers still at the bench, elected by the members of the town where the headquarters were, and wider councils had to be consulted before important decisions were taken. The importance of the first device might be less when the salaried members of the Committee formed an inner board, meeting much more frequently and preparing the issues for discussion by the wider body; in cases of conflict the authority of those elected by the trades of a single town might prove inferior to that of those elected by the national congress.[1] A consultative council might be dominated by the Union's own regional organizers nominated and paid by the Central Committee;[2] even the periodical congresses might well deserve the description of 'parliaments of paid officials'.[3] An analysis of the statistics of the Printers' Union shows that, at any rate since its reconstruction when the Anti-Socialist law ended, and deducting a moderate number of delegates elected on a single occasion only, the more stable representatives were re-elected throughout their trade unionist lives. Obviously they were unlikely to support opposition to the implications of a policy with whose traditions they were closely connected. On the other hand, members would be reluctant to replace such a traditional delegate if he worked as well as a salaried employee of the Union, and failure to re-elect him would imply a vote of no confidence.[4]

In these circumstances, a defeat of the established Union leaders at a national congress was inconceivable unless widespread opposition by the rank and file was supported and organized by some force with an ideological appeal superior to the habits of subordination established by Unionist tradition.[5] Before 1914 the test was never applied, because the Union leaders avoided actions which would meet with the disapproval of all the political trends coexistent within the Party,[6] and because the

[1] The issue became current after the War, when, on the whole, the Berlin workers proved more radical than the German average as expressed at a national congress.

[2] Nestriepke, op. cit., p. 316. In the Regional Organizers' conferences of the Printers, which functioned largely as a substitute for national congresses, only Regions with over 3,000 members (in 1924 just a quarter of the Regions) were granted a second representative, over and above the Regional Organizer.

[3] Nestriepke, op. cit., p. 311.

[4] In the Printers' Union there was a long-standing demand (since 1896) to deprive Regional Organizers of the right of election as delegates and to give them a consultative vote instead. The issue was settled in 1924 by transferring one of the decisive votes of each Region to the Organizer, who no longer had to go through the process of election.

[5] Herkner's observation (op. cit., vol. II, p. 355) that the rigidly centralized Unions with their highly developed friendly society services and their large bureaucracy held a disciplinary power over their members far superior to that of the Party appears to be a generalization from that peculiar Union, the Printers'. Its origins were not, as were those of the others, manifestly due to Party initiative, and it had a tradition of potential solidarity with the masters.

[6] Only in 1905 did they approach this point; see below, p. 104.

influential trends in the Party avoided interfering with what was regarded as the sphere of trade union autonomy.[1] After the split in the political labour movement the hold of the right-wing leaders, who were supported by all the reformist tradition, proved no stronger than might be expected from the skilled workers' attitude: in some Unions the hold of the Independent Socialists was no weaker than in the working-class electorate as a whole. Conditions changed once more when the political trends compatible with reformist trade unionism rallied against the Communists and proclaimed Social Democracy 'the political support of Trade Unionism'.[2]

(*d*) *Peasants' Co-operatives: Bureaucracy and Control by the Banks*

The position of the members of a Peasants' Co-operative, when once agricultural producers' co-operation has become comprehensive, differs from that of those of a Consumers' Co-operative in that the former depend on the organization for their whole livelihood. But the co-operative, unlike a trade union whose aim it is to reduce the exploitation of labour to a minimum, *has* to take something away from its members. Whatever there might be to be said against the private dealer whom the peasant co-operative replaced, what he took from the peasants' pockets—sometimes even from out of the mouths of their children—was the necessary means for the industrialization of the eastern parts of Central Europe. The co-operative system allows this function to be fulfilled in two ways. In consequence of his social position as a quasi-entrepreneur, the peasant is generally prepared to accept the leadership of the most prosperous of his fellows who, in their capacity of small-scale capitalists, may use their control of the co-operative to accumulate funds; the inability of peasant co-operatives to develop large-scale activities in other ways compels them to bind themselves to the banks, which dominated the economic life of all Central European countries. The former channel will promote only the agricultural enterprise of the kulak and such auxiliary industries as minister to its prosperity; the second permits of of the exploitation of agriculture as a whole.

The well-off peasant's leadership within the co-operative, which took the place of the paternal authority which stood by its cradle,[3] is not necessarily bound up with statutory rulings which increase his voting power, although very wide differences in economic strength are hardly compatible with an equal vote in the affairs of the co-operative.[4] It can

[1] See below, pp. 111–3.

[2] See below, pp. 239 and 241.

[3] See above, pp. 44–5.

[4] Digby (op. cit., pp. 293 and 309–10) describes two types of peasant co-operative. The local Credit Association, with its hundred or two hundred members—most of them peasants with ten to fifty acres—was open to all who owned a house or land in the village and did not compete in business with the co-operative; each member had equally limited liability for the co-operative's debts, and each had one vote, so that

be exercised through the other members' moral and material dependence upon him, and it is strengthened by such moderate bureaucracy as can develop within the local co-operative (usually a man with a pension or other small means who receives an honorarium for his services varying with the time he is expected to give to the work). This little bureaucrat, subservient to the whims of the local notables to whom he owes his appointment, will find himself, together with those notables who attend the annual conferences with him, completely helpless when representing the needs of the local co-operative before the Central Co-operative Bank with its huge bureaucratic machinery tackling complicated issues which few of them are capable of understanding, and none of them of replying to by alternative suggestions. If, as in Czechoslovakia after 1918, the Central Co-operative is identified with a political party which commands key positions and has rewards for faithful servants at its disposal, there will be little opportunity and no great urge to oppose its management of affairs. Its resolutions on agricultural policy are actual law, enacted by Parliament as a matter of form,[1] and it is responsible for whatever help the peasant gets from the State; it may be relied upon to use its influence in such ways as to make those branches of agricultural production of which it has a safe monopoly the most profitable for the peasant producer. The well-to-do peasants, who are in actual control of local co-operatives, are likely to be satisfied at least so far as to feel that the best bargain has been struck compatible with protecting other interests equally legitimate in their conservative outlook, and to suggest to dissenters that they shall keep silent rather than risk the economic and social boycott reserved for those who 'threaten co-operative unity'.

The gradual diversion of the funds raised by co-operative banks from the purposes originally pursued is illustrated by evidence from Czechoslovakia.[2] Before 1914, 90 per cent of the resources of the local banks in Bohemia-Moravia were lent to their own members; ten years later it was only 15 per cent, while 76 per cent of the assets were deposited with the Central Co-operative Banks. To some extent these deposits were transferred from the agriculture of the predominantly depositing districts to that of the areas which made the largest demands for loans, and the fact

the total vote expressed the village's collective judgment as to the soundness of a prospective debtor. In Warehouse Co-operatives the stakes of the individual peasant are different, and two different types of solution were sought for the problem. In the one, each member had only one vote, though he had to take up shares in proportion to the size of his holding and received a dividend up to a maximum of 5 per cent; in the other every share carried a vote—with a limit to the number of votes any one member could exercise—and the interest paid on shares was occasionally increased. It was certainly no mere chance that in the village described as typical for the former kind the acreage of the individual farms varied from 15 to 50, as compared with 8 to 240 in the second.

[1] Polin-Claron, op. cit., p. 87.

[2] Digby, op. cit., pp. 295 ff.

that the Central Co-operative Banks appropriated most of the difference between the interest paid on deposits and that received for loans[1] might still be explained by the need for insurance against emergencies. But it was certainly not in the interest of agriculture that the ratio between deposits and loans to agriculturists and co-operatives, which from 1900 to 1913 had been fairly stable at 10 to 8, should change in 1927 to 17 to 7. Digby's explanation—or that of his Czech Agrarian sources—of the low demand for agricultural credits by the slow development of co-operative industries[2] simply begs the question. The Agrarian Party, which owed its existence to the co-operatives but remained their master after it had become the main middle-class party, together with the great private banks,[3] controlled the policies of the Central Co-operatives and prevented agricultural co-operation from entering such obviously suitable fields as hop-marketing and sugar-refining,[4] and this in a country which certainly had greater need of improvements in agriculture and in the industries working up its products than of additional banks and insurance companies. In the industrial field, something comparable to this process could happen only under Hitlerism, when the trade unions continued to collect fees in order to cover strike and employment benefits, which had become obsolete, without taking on new functions that called for any comparable outlay: they thus became collectors of additional taxes for rearmament. But while Hitler, in order to achieve this, had to confiscate the trade unions,[5] in agricultural co-operation a similar change of function could be brought about without interference with its democratic government through a mere appeal to the interest of its members in safe investments.

(*e*) *The Marxist Explanation of the Rise of the Workers' Bureaucracy*

Marxists explain the phenomena discussed in the last section as a particular instance of the processes by which small-scale capitalist enterprise comes under the control of monopoly capitalism, whatever the phraseology used. But the developments mentioned earlier in this chapter have always provided a much more difficult problem: the very organization of labour, from the activities of which working-class emancipation was expected to follow, developed along lines which were bound to be interpreted as a betrayal of its principles, at least by those who upheld the class-ideology of the movement.

The official representatives of the labour movement before 1914 denied the very existence of a problem of bureaucracy save for the obvious fact that the growth of the labour movement called for an in-

[1] Ibid., pp. 292 and 296.
[2] Ibid., pp. 298–9.
[3] Cf. Polin-Claron, op. cit., pp. 89–90.
[4] Digby, op. cit., p. 331.
[5] See below, p. 335.

creasing number of paid officials. Bebel, writing his memoirs as late as 1910, spoke of the position of employed Party official as an ideal one for the Social Democrat, who could thus work for his cause without fear of dismissal; if he put all his effort into his job, he might be sure of his comrades' appreciation.[1] There is no hint of the possibility that the diligent paid official might work in a direction other than that which a majority of the organized workers looked upon as the right one, or that, while working in accordance with his own convictions and those of a majority of the workers, he might yet come into conflict with his senior colleagues.

The formalist school of sociologists, as represented by Pareto and Michels, rejects this democratic utopia: it sees organizations as means for the exercise of oligarchic power by one group of individuals over another. Michels[2] elaborated this point by comparing the opportunities of social advancement open to gifted workers in the labour movement with those offered by the Catholic Church to peasants' sons, who can become bishops, though not governors or generals. The fallacy in this argument is easy to see; the authority of bishops is not derived from the fact that occasionally a peasant's son may become a bishop, but from the basic teaching of the Roman Church. The way in which bishops are selected may help to assure those who believe in bishops that the sacred office will be exercised with due regard to the needs of the common man, but in no way explains the origins and character of the Catholic Church. But the worker who joins a trade union is not expected to ascribe to union officials some superior authority; the way in which they are recruited is mere matter of fact which does not increase their authority in any way. The sociologist's interest in such issues starts just beyond the establishment of commonplaces such as that in every organization there are leaders and led, that similarity of origin between leaders and led is conducive to those leaders' authority, and that leadership is occasionally misused to promote the private interests of individuals in positions of power. He starts with the question whether a given situation contains elements conducive to the use of established power for such

[1] Op. cit., vol. II, pp. 90–1. This was written in connexion with the experiences of the period before the Anti-Socialist Law. At that time the maximum salary paid by the Party was 200 marks per month, and salaries of even 70 marks per month were paid to officials holding responsible positions. The Party official might expect to spend a fair share of his life in prison; so the issue of 'lower-middle-class degeneration' hardly arose. But Bebel's statement was quite a general one, made at a time when a widespread opposition to 'bureaucrats' was already evident. He does not seem to have grasped the possibility that during the forty years of his leadership and of the Party's growth the type of man who was out to work for his convictions might have been replaced by another who was out for a satisfactory job, with some spare time in which to enjoy life, and that, when the average active Social Democrat had become fairly safe from dismissal in an ordinary job, the Party post would have to offer other attractions.

[2] Op, cit., p. 291 ff.

purposes that tensions on a mass scale—the only ones that interest him—are likely to arise. In this he differs from the disappointed idealist who, once the behaviour of the working class has failed to come up to his expectations, looks for a scapegoat and finds it in the assumption that millions of people who have organized themselves and made all kinds of sacrifices to emancipate their class can be misled by a few hundred[1] clever fellows who have managed to climb above working-class conditions.

The only existing theory that attempts a sociological interpretation of the activities of the workers' bureaucracy is the Marxist-Leninist, which seeks to explain them by an economic phenomenon, namely, the rise of an aristocracy of workers which supplies sufficient backing for the bureaucracy's policies. This theory is not free from the utopian approach; it starts, like that of Michels and other disappointed syndicalists, from the standpoint that the ideal mass organization ought to be democratic but in practice is not. In the 'pure concept of power' it is simply stated that democracy is a utopia and that hence power should be applied according to standards other than that governed ought to have a share in making the rules by which they are governed.[2] But in the Marxist-Leninist concept definite conditions are laid down the removal of which would allow of democratic development in a realist sense, realism having undergone some evolution between the earlier and the later writings of both Marx and Lenin.[3]

Because of the enormous influence exercised by post-Chartist British trade unionism on the formation of more conservative opinion within the German trade union camp, the concept of a workers' aristocracy, made up of people with high earnings who could afford expensive friendly society benefits and show a corresponding contempt for their

[1] See above, p. 71.

[2] The theoretical connexions between fascism and syndicalism should not be thought of as restricted to the origins of the concept of the 'corporative state', which is something of a showpiece in the ideological armoury of fascism. The reaction against the nineteenth-century democratic Utopia produced a cult of power exercised by *élites* amongst those who kept some of their original ideals as well as amongst those who regarded the social content of the power exercised by the *élite* as irrelevant, and looked on the myth created to justify it as a mere propaganda device, which needed only to be effective.

[3] This evolution should not be interpreted as a disillusioned abandonment of original Utopianism; the most Utopian writings of Marx and Lenin respectively are the pamphlet on the Paris Commune (1871) and *The State and Revolution* (1917). Both served to emphasize the Utopian criticism of bourgeois democracy as a counterpoise to its identification with the ultimate political ideals of Marxism. In their practical approach to the problems of democracy within the labour movement both Marx and Lenin moved from practical neglect of those problems conditioned by underground work and factional strife in an underground movement (and in the case of Marx, perhaps also by the ideological impact of Jacobin traditions) to the sober but positive approach illustrated in Marx's struggles against Schweitzer and Lenin's last fight against Trotsky in the Trade Union discussion of 1920.

less fortunate fellows, was current in Germany. It was accepted by those who regarded such a development as desirable[1] as well as by those to whose Marxist views it was anathema. In his postscript to the German edition of the Webbs' *History of Trade Unionism* Bernstein, the German Revisionist leader, said that 'Trade unionism will always rely mainly on those strata of the working class that are usually described as the "workers' aristocracy" '. From this statement Kautsky[2] drew the logical conclusion that a trade union movement which was concerned merely with raising the standards of the privileged sectors of the working class above those of other groups for whom it felt no concern, was bound to split the labour movement. To the Marxist Kautsky it was obvious that the progress of industrialization was bound to destroy that exclusive position of which the right-wing British trade unionists and the German Printers were so proud, notwithstanding all the attempts to preserve an obsolete monopoly by apprenticeship rules and by forbidding printers who had not been apprenticed to work on machines.[3] The problem of bureaucracy, say in the British Transport Workers' Union, which was formed as part of the reaction of the 'New Unionism' against the obsolete aristocratic pattern, and in most of the Continental unions, is outside the cope of Kautsky's theory. But were it not for the implied unpopularity of 'workers' aristocracy' within the labour movement, the Leninist attempt at explanation could hardly have been made, and would certainly have failed to make the strong appeal it did.

The Marxist theory of the workers' aristocracy is composed of two elements, neither of them very controversial; thus Lenin could quote not only from classical Marxist writings but also from contemporary liberal authors. In a number of utterances[4] (the first being a letter of 7th October 1858), Engels stated that Britain's vast colonial possessions and her monopolist status in world markets enabled even the working class of that country to enjoy a privileged position; and in the Preface of 1892 to his *Condition of the Working Classes in England*,[5] he wrote that the benefits to the English workers arising from the country's industrial monopoly were shared among them very unequally, the privileged minority pocketing most, but even the masses having a temporary

[1] See note 6, p. 68 above.

[2] Op. cit., 1900.

[3] Cf. Fischer on the Jena Party Congress, Proceedings, p. 240. See also note 2, p. 67 above.

[4] Quoted in Lenin's *Imperialism* (*Selected Works*, vol. 5), p. 98.

[5] The connexion is important; for Engels the concept of Britain's monopolist extra profits explained the failure of British industrial and political conditions to develop in the way expected by himself and others in 1844, and refuted the expectations of those who hoped to see the German and other workers attain a prosperity similar to that experienced in the nineties by at least the upper strata of the British working class. This attitude is excluded by Lenin's conception of imperialism as a phenomenon common to all fully-developed, that is, monopoly-capitalist, countries.

share from time to time. Lenin corrected this statement by the assertion that only the upper strata of the British working class were 'corrupted'. He was perhaps influenced by wishful thinking as to the chances of a Communist mass-party in Britain; but he could base his statement on a bourgeois authority,[1] and it will hardly seem controversial to Continental socialists who have had the opportunity of seeing a British slum.

But the real issue starts when the obvious fact of social stratification is put side by side with its supposed explanation, the theory of imperialism. What, in concrete sociological terms, is the definition of the workers' aristocracy? Occasionally[2] Lenin identified it, as a matter of course, with the skilled workers. This was done in connexion with the relations between ruling and oppressed nations in a multi-national state or a colonial empire, and in this context such an identification is quite correct: national inequality manifests itself within the working class precisely as inequality of access to skilled and well-paid jobs. But this does not prove that the workers' aristocracy in Germany or Britain can profitably be identified with the skilled workers—unless the chain of causation could be reversed to assert that worker-aristocrats are those who succeed in establishing a monopoly for their trade by elaborate rulings on apprenticeship and so on; to which a Marxist would have to add a workers' aristocracy of this type is bound to disappear in the natural course of capitalist development. To assert that the most developed capitalist countries with the highest propensity to monopoly in a given industry should have the highest proportion of skilled workers is, for a Marxist, a contradiction in terms, because he regards the replacement of the medium entrepreneur by monopolist giants and the destruction of craft-privileges within the working class as two aspects of a single social process. The kind of workers' aristocracy likely to be produced by imperialism in a group of advanced industrial nations, whose upper classes drew vast tribute from Asia and Africa, has been correctly described by Hobson[3] as 'great tame masses of retainers, no longer engaged in the staple industries of agriculture and manufacture, but kept in the performance of personal or minor industrial services under the control of a new financial aristocracy'. To say that the butcher

[1] Schulze-Gävernitz, quoted pp. 96–7.

[2] *A Caricature of Marxism and 'Imperialist Economism'*, *Selected Works*, vol. 5, p. 291. The argument is directed against the thesis that the position of the workers in oppressing and oppressed nations was the same, and its first half (as to 'crumbs of the supra-profits which the bourgeoisie of the oppressing nations obtain by the extra exploitation of the workers of the oppressed nations') could be applied to imperialism in general. But the following statement, on the different percentage of workers in oppressing and oppressed nations who become skilled workers 'and thus rise to the position of a labour aristocracy' makes sense only in the connexion mentioned in the text. Possibly Lenin was not conscious that in the course of an argument intended to deal with imperialism in general he had slipped into his familiar Russian (and also Austro-Hungarian, Southern-United-States, colonial, etc.) conditions.

[3] *Imperialism*, 3rd edition, 1938, p. 364.

interested in his lordship's custom and in good domestic jobs for his relatives, or even the skilled engineering worker employed by some radio manufacturer, should provide the main stronghold of the conservative tendencies in British trade unionism is obvious nonsense.

If we exclude direct participation of the working classes in income derived from imperialist expansion, there remains only one possible connexion between imperialist 'supra-profits' and stratification of the working classes, namely, that which existed in nineteenth-century England; by having made satisfactory profits the capitalists are enabled to meet trade unionist demands—among which might be demands for the artificial preservation of the position of some groups of workers; and thus the position of the workers who are best organized, or most capable of appealing to accommodating sympathies in the employers' counsels, will improve in relation to that of other groups. In this case, the 'supra-profits' are distributed as a premium on trade unionist organization and seem to the workers concerned to be achievements of their struggle; and the more supra-profits are available in a given country at a given time, the less need there is for the bourgeoisie to restrict its tactics of appeasement to mere small minorities of the workers who have demanded better conditions. The ideal type of workers' aristocracy, with its scope smallest and its differentiation from the bulk of the working classes greatest, is seen not in the leading imperialist countries, but in their colonies, where small minorities of white foremen and skilled workers treat the black or yellow workers as 'undermen'. In this case, too, no tension arises within the trade unionist organization, which has to serve only the whites. The whole argument about workers' aristocracy, however evident its merits in such a case, is a mere refutation of the white men's union's insolent claim to be regarded as representation of 'the workers'.

Although in every country the workers who are first drawn into the trade union movement form a kind of aristocracy in relation to other workers, and in many countries the first trade union bureaucracies to come on the scene are engaged in preserving this aristocratic position of their patrons, the concept of the 'workers' aristocracy' provides no explanation for the rise of bureaucracy and the potential tension between it and the rank and file. If the 'workers' aristocracy' be thought of merely as the privileged section of well-paid workers able to pay high membership fees and to enjoy the benefits of a tactic which enhances the scarcity-value of their individual labour-force, this fails to explain the rise and importance of bureaucracy after that privileged position has become obsolete. The introduction of imperialist 'supra-profits' into the picture could explain only some delay in that obsolescence, perhaps some degree of ability and willingness on the part of important bourgeois groups to allow some monopolies of skilled labour to linger on as a recognition of their sound attitude towards the existing order and in the hope of creating a moderating influence within the labour movement as a whole. If the workers' aristocracy be defined as those who directly profit from imperialist expansion and the supra-profits derived from it, it is obvious that this stratum is far too small, and, with a few exceptions, too far removed from the labour movement's main centres of strength to explain any important developments. If it is thought of as the group of those who are capable of gaining material improvements in consequence of their employers' prosperity, it is clear that an increase in the sum of profits distributable will tend to turn that group from a mere minority aristocracy into a majority of the whole working class.[1] Supposing that it embraced the whole of the working class, there is no reason why in the labour movement, and also in the body politic, of such an imperialist State democracy in the full sense of any formal definition could not flourish—Imperialist democracy in Arthur Rosenberg's terminology. It would be destroyed only by the revolt of the underdog nations—and by the Imperialist States' own preparations to meet this threat.

Failure to realize these simple truths was due to the unpreparedness of the socialist *élite*, during and after World War I, to face the fact that in the leading Western countries it had to 'swim against the current', not only of a propaganda wave, but also of the interests, at any rate the short-term interests, of a majority of those whom it tried to win, and that consequently the obstacles found in its way were not necessarily always of an anti-democratic character. The very existence of numerous undemocratic traits in the life of existing mass-organizations invited them to be used as an explanation for the failure of those organizations to come up to the standards expected by the revolutionaries, the more so as those expectations had been encouraged by declarations made by the representatives of those organizations during the pre-war period.[2] To Marxists, betrayal by individual leaders would not seem a sufficient explanation, and would not fit in with Communist tactics, which demanded not merely the removal of some individual leaders but a thorough purging of the labour movement from the forces responsible for the betrayal of 1914. The corrupted workers' aristocracy, backing a bureaucracy which betrayed the principles of the labour movement, was just broad enough for an object of general attack and yet not powerful

[1] In original Comintern tactics, the connexion was honestly represented by the statement that, independently of the ability of national revolutions in backward colonial countries to establish actual progressive régimes—a chance which, at that time, was regarded with less optimism than after the success of the Soviet collectivization of agriculture—they had to be supported by the revolutionaries of the advanced countries because they reduced the extra-profits of the national bourgeoisie and the implied opportunities to corrupt part of their own working class. In view of their long-term interest in establishing socialism the workers of the imperialist countries were invited to act against their own short-term interests.

[2] See below, p. 113.

enough for Communists of an imperialist country to despair of rallying the bulk of the working class within their country. But its comparatively limited size might be merely a product of wishful thinking.

(f) Social Democracy and the Diverse Trends in the Labour Movement

As we have seen in Chapter Two, all aspects of labour organization in Central Europe took their origin in the impulse given by the formation of the Socialist Party. This Party also provided the stage on which the different trends arising in the world of labour found their expression and were assimilated.

Because of the different political framework, the internal development of Social Democracy in Germany and in Austria proceeded on very different lines. In the latter country the two factions, Radicals and Moderates,[1] were brought together in 1888 on the initiative of a young physician, Dr. Adler, who a few years earlier had helped to draw up the Linz programme of Austro-German nationalism.[2] On New Year's Day, 1889, they reunited on the Hainfeld Congress. The programme, on Marxist lines with due emphasis on the demand for adult suffrage, rejected the anarchist concept of individual application of violence; 'apart from this' (i.e. on the decisive issue of mass action) 'the party's tactics will depend on the behaviour of the ruling classes and their organs.'

Now this behaviour was marked by the denial of the most elementary political rights as well as by the chronic crisis of the multi-national empire: the latter caused the conservative bureaucracy, and even the Court, to be constantly on the lookout for possible counterpoises to the national oppositions, and especially to whatever potential power of opposition might be left in the bourgeois-national parties. In 1885 Taaffe's government extended a restricted suffrage to the lower middle classes and thus gave Lueger his opportunity;[3] without its benevolent toleration[4] the Hainfeld Congress would have been impossible. But manhood suffrage, on a very restricted basis, was not granted in Austria until 1897; if Austrian Social Democracy wanted to be a factor in political life it had to resort to non-parliamentary action, i.e. to do the very thing from which German Social Democracy refrained in order to escape threats to its legal and parliamentary existence. On the other hand, for the reasons just mentioned, Austrian Social Democracy might be sure that careful application of non-parliamentary action would involve little risk of a collision with the State machine as such. The German trade unions, backed by the party leaders who feared a renewal of the Anti-Socialist Law, failed to celebrate May Day on its introduc-

[1] See above, p. 26.
[2] See above, p. 10.
[3] See above, p. 46.
[4] See the documentation in Bruegel, op. cit.

tion in 1890, and thus created a precedent whose observance led to continuous disputes with the party and their own more advanced groups; the Austrian workers, by mass strikes on that same day, established a precedent which was not afterwards seriously contested. A German right-wing Social Democrat, himself not inclined, even after Hitler's triumph, to learn from his and his party's record,[1] compared the German slogan 'Comrades, do not let yourselves be provoked, the reactionaries want some shooting', with the Austrian workers' song 'Right will be conquered on the streets, so have we learnt from Belgium'. From 1893 onwards the Austrian workers, speaking 'Belgian' or 'Russian' according to the current fashion in the world of labour, in either case by political mass-strikes and demonstrations, advanced step by step until, under the impact of the Russian Revolution of 1905 and the complete standstill to which parliamentarism had been brought by the competing bourgeois national parties, equal manhood suffrage was won.[2] Disillusionment followed when not only the new democratic parliament but the Socialist party itself was split on national lines.

German Social Democracy emerged from the underground united, but with a formidable crisis near at hand. Under the Anti-Socialist Law there had already been a series of internal conflicts, the most important of which concerned the Party's attitude to imperial expansion.[3] In June 1891, immediately after the Party regained its legality, Vollmar, who during the first part of the repression period had moved to the left, spoke offering conciliation with the régime provided it enacted additional social reform legislation and recognized the trade unions; he even acknowledged the Triple Alliance as a 'guarantee of peace'. He was mildly rebuked at the Erfurt Party Congress, which, however, expelled the 'Wild Men' for having come under anarchist influences. Engels commented on the political demands of the Party programme adopted at this Congress that the demand for a democratic republic had been omitted; he was afraid this might be due to a tendency, after the experiences of the Anti-Socialist Law, to accept the legality of Bismarck's Empire as a framework within which the working class could achieve its aims.[4] Seven years later Heine, in a speech as parliamentary candidate, offered the ruling classes parliamentary votes for more guns in exchange for more popular rights; when challenged because of this speech at the Stuttgart Party Congress he replied that to win democratic rights there were only two alternatives: the actual use of the guns in insurrection, which the Party rejected, or using the ruling classes' need for additional armaments as an occasion for parliamentary bargains. Not even Rosa

[1] Stampfer, op. cit., p. 14.
[2] See below, pp. 123–4.
[3] See above, p. 25.
[4] Letter to Kautsky of 26th June 1891 (*Neue Zeit*, vol. XX/1, pp. 5 ff.).

Luxemburg[1] answered this alleged alternative by the most elementary statements of Marxism.

Being the only real opposition party, and therefore rallying all such forces as opposed the existing régime,[2] the Party made its way towards asserting even its most elementary tenets. The desire to win the votes of the peasants, including those who were well-to-do, resulted in the acceptance at the 1894 party congress of an agrarian platform drawn up with great consideration for the peasants' protectionist interests, and making suggestions for credit reform and so on. A commission was set up to work out a detailed agrarian programme. In its deliberations, and in the literary productions which accompanied and followed these discussions, a right wing, led by Vollmar and David, came to the conclusion that the Marxist tenet of the superiority of large-scale enterprises was not valid for agriculture; in this field the Party should replace its programme of socialization by one of promoting medium and small enterprises. The majority of the commission would not go so far as this, but even the eventual report, though backed by the Party leaders, was rejected at the Breslau Congress of 1895 by 156 votes to 63. The left-wing majority, represented at the Congress by Kautsky and Clara Zetkin, deemed that the proletarization of the small-holders was unavoidable under a capitalist system and that any attempt to promise them protection against the unavoidable would land the Party in mere reformism, or even in competition with anti-Semites and similar lower-middle-class demagogues. The party organizations of Silesia and Posen (not very important in those days) had been the first to reject the Commission's report, but only a few speakers at the Congress[3] noticed its failure to cater for the needs of the agricultural labourers of Prussia beyond the Elbe: on the whole, the Party majority's attitude simply reflected the reluctance of a sectional organization of industrial workers to tackle the problems of the countryside. The Congress was followed by a literary discussion in which David for the right wing and Kautsky for the orthodox Marxists contributed major books on the validity or otherwise of the Marxist tenet of concentration of enterprises in agriculture.

There was no further vote on the subject at a Party Congress, but the Marxists, who in 1895 had had a clear majority and retained their position up to the eve of the First World War,[4] rallied on a platform which

[1] *Coll. Works*, vol. III, pp. 159–60. Rosa Luxemburg simply states that there was a third weapon, apart from the two Heine mentioned, namely 'proletarian class consciousness' as a means of moral pressure.

[2] See above, pp. 43–4.

[3] O. Braun (*Proceedings*, p. 159) and Schippel (ibid., p. 173).

[4] The 1913 Party Congress decided to establish a new Commission to draw up an agrarian programme, and rejected a motion by the East Prussian Organization which would have excluded the Revisionists from that Commission: the latter, as installed by the Central Committee, would have gone very far to meet the right wing's standpoint had the War not intervened.

was clearly negative towards the peasants' interests, including land reform, which would destroy progressive large-scale enterprise and also harm the labourers' interests; the Party's concern with the countryside was restricted to trade unionism, which proved a pious hope, as the labourers remained practically unorganized till the 1918 revolution. The Party's right wing, on the other side, argued from the standpoint of the peasant interest, including that of the well-to-do peasants of South and West Germany, which demanded a cautious approach to the improvement of the conditions of agricultural labourers. This fitted in well with the policy of the majority of the Social Democrats in the South German States, where there was a little more liberalism than in Prussia; the parliamentary parties, in the Diets of those States, duly voted for the Budget and took part in such Court ceremonial as befitted members of the parliamentary majority; the procedure was repeated till 1914 with the same regularity with which it was disapproved by the Party's congresses.

The Party and trade unionism in Austria were defined by Victor Adler[1] as two aspects of a single unity, the organizations of two different activities of one class; this may support the assumption that the less harmonious character of the relations between the 'two aspects' in Germany was due to ideological distortions rather than to objective conditions. But the ideological disputes recorded in the first section of Chapter Two belonged to the past: and a bridge from Lassalleism, were there one, would lead to the pro-trade-unionist right wing of the Party, not to its Marxist critics. In fact, there was a marked differentiation in basic attitudes within the Trade Unions as well as within the Party, disputes between the two organizations being caused by the fact that the specific weight of either trend within each of them was different; the contrast with Austria was mainly due to its less advanced conditions which made the varying trends within the labour movement less articulate.

German Socialist theorists, not unimpressed by the attempts made by the 'Academic Socialists' and other respectable Liberals to find 'reasonable' elements in trade unionism while joining in the official condemnation of 'subversive' Social Democracy,[2] expressed a fear that some evidently anti-socialist trends within the Trade Union camp, such as the Printers' policy, might foreshadow the eventual reception of the supposed British pattern of non-political trade unionism.[3] Sharp controversies arose whenever trade union leaders demanded more than the Party would willingly grant,[4] and especially when they tried to back

[1] In his Introduction to Deutsch, op. cit., p. vii.

[2] Cf. Kautsky, op. cit., p. 431.

[3] For the description of that pattern as a real threat, cf. apart from Kautsky, also Liebknecht (Proceedings of the Jena Congress, 1905, p. 251), and even the Revisionist von Elm, see below, p. 104.

[4] See above, pp. 61 and 67–8. For the attitude of the Party's left-wing cf. Rosa Luxemburg, op. cit., pp. 209 ff. (reprinted from *Neue Zeit*, 1901), where, for reasons

their demands by excessive self-assertion.[1] There was counter-assertion on behalf of the Party; at its Cologne Congress in 1893 Liebknecht and Bebel stated that trade unionism as developed in Britain was bound to fail in Germany: once monopoly dominated the whole of industry, political struggle would be the German workers' only defence. Legien[2] answered that trade unionism would survive as long as the capitalist mode of production. Bebel's and Liebknecht's attitude was not shared by the whole Party majority: Molkenbuhr[3] even suggested wide unions without political affiliations. But there certainly was some wishful thinking at least as regards the eventual removal of conflicts on competence between Party and Trade Unions by the dynamics of capitalism. It was not just weakened by the Unions' search for substitutes for industrial action.[4]

From the Party's point of view, the educational merits of trade unionism lay mainly in the experience it gave the workers in the organization of their daily struggles; even Legien, speaking on behalf of the unions in a highly controversial mood,[5] described them as preparatory schools for the political movement and recognized the merely palliative character of their successes; but he did complain of the Party members' tendency to emphasize this point.[6] There was some justification for such complaints: Kautsky, clearly influenced by the current interpretation of British 'Old Unionism' as typical, went to the length of questioning the prospects of strikes by unskilled workers;[7] evidently his scepticism as to the prospects of old-fashioned trade unionism applied to those of unionism in general.

A new stage in the disputes about the relations between Party and Unions opened in the later nineties, when the unity of German trade unionism, especially among the miners, was threatened by the current identification of Free Trade Unions with Marxism, this being interpreted in a popular way and including the description of religion as

of principle, Party support against the dissenting group of Trade Unionists was refused although, in Rosa Luxemburg's own opinion, the trade union leaders were undoubtedly right.

[1] At the Cologne Party Congress—three years after the end of the Anti-Socialist Law—Legien provoked keen argument by his statement that the average trade unionist, by risking his material existence in conflict with his employer, made more serious sacrifices than the Party member. A year before (Proceedings, Berlin Party Congress, p. 139) he had explained the opposition met with by the Trade Unions within the Party caucus (see note 3, p. 68) by an invasion of the latter by small entrepreneurs with an anti-trade-unionist outlook.

[2] Proceedings, p. 295.

[3] Ibid., p. 206.

[4] See above, p. 68.

[5] Proceedings, p. 295

[6] See Cologne Proceedings (1893), p. 183.

[7] Quoted by Herkner, op. cit., pp. 213–14.

opium for the people. In his concluding speech in the discussion on Revisionism at the Hanover Party Congress of 1899, Bebel declared that it was a supreme interest of the Trade Unions to keep as much aloof from the political Party as possible and to avoid Party politics lest they should be incapable of winning over the Catholic workers. In his speech at the meeting of the Berlin party activists which followed the Congress, Bebel explained his attitude; trade unions should pursue 'working-class politics, but not party politics'; to convinced Social Democrats it was obvious that under German conditions the defence of the political interests of the workers as such would lead the trade unions into a united front with the only party which defended those interests. A few years later,[1] when the 'neutralization' issue had ceased to be topical because of the open lining up of the leaders of the Christian Trade Unions with the policies of a bourgeois bloc,[2] Bebel explained his attitude of 1899 as implying that the Trade Unions should rally the workers independently of their political creed, and that the Party comrades working in the Unions should explain to the members that as workers they were citizens and interested in all the issues of State and legislation; 'If trade unionists', he continued, 'are educated in such a spirit I am prepared to publish a trade union weekly without mentioning the word Social Democracy for a whole year, but with the result that the readers will become Social Democrats.'

Such an attitude was a necessary implication of a Socialist's confidence in the historical role of his party; but it was not general amongst the Trade Unionists who, under the Christian impact, advocated 'neutralization'. The Miners' leader, Hué,[3] while explaining his attitude in the Party periodical as intended to prevent reactionary influences from being exercised on the pretext of religion, on other occasions[4] said that a trade unionist, as such, should not be interested in the political outcome of trade union neutrality; any other attitude would merely prove that he was not interested in trade unionism for its own sake.

Thus there were two explanations of trade union neutrality; one tactical, relying on the objective implications of industrial conflict, and another which refused to recognize any greater historical connexion in the unions' activities. In theory, a third attitude would have been possible within the Party; while recognizing the unions' political neutrality, it might have ordered its members to raise the trade unionists' consciousness to the level of all the political implications of their economic struggles. But this attitude was forbidden because the Party's left wing, the only potential author of such an approach, never during the whole period under discussion overcame its suspicion of trade

[1] On the Jena Party Congress, 1905, Proceedings, p. 313.
[2] See below, p. 120.
[3] *Neue Zeit*, vol. XX/2.
[4] Quoted in Mannheim Party Congress (1906), Proceedings, p. 272.

unionism as a source of aristocratic deviations. The Party as a whole, while believing in certain automatic implications of industrial conflict, failed to ascribe to its members any separate task distinct from that of the average trade unionist, apart from enlightening him on the need for political as well as industrial struggle. Clearly it had to accept trade unionism as it was, discussing no issues other than its interpretation.

The discussions on 'neutralization' of the Unions proceeded without bitterness: it was implied in the Party creed that no decision on the issue could prevent the Unions from actually becoming Socialist. A different position arose when the representatives of the day-to-day, avowedly reformist, activities of the sectional organizations attempted to explain their needs in terms of the sectional world-outlook; this implied the demand for its 'revision'. Bernstein, the leader of revisionism, actually said very little which was not bound to be a commonplace amongst practical Trade Unionists and co-operators: such people would not like to interpret their everyday work against the gloomy background of an impending catastrophe of capitalism, to the eventual happy outcome of which they would have contributed some practical schooling of their members in the arts of discipline and self-government, with the practical experience that their everyday activities necessarily failed to solve fundamental social problems and were another proof of the need for revolutionary activities (which involved the risk of confiscation of the Trade Union funds). In Marxist theory there were quite a few statements on the likely developments of working-class conditions apparently pessimistic in the eyes of sober observers, not to speak of the wishful thinking of Trade Unionists and co-operators working in a prosperous imperialist country. Hence the need for 'revising' Marxism. There was wishful thinking amongst academic economists about the ability of capitalism to overcome periodical depressions by means of an improved credit system and of monopolist organizations; Revisionists such as Bernstein did not fail to transfer such ideologies into the fold of the labour movement. On the other side Rosa Luxemburg felt that the periodical depressions observed in contemporary capitalism provided insufficient foundation for the Marxist expectation of a situation where the working class would have to face the alternatives of starvation or the overthrow of capitalism; she suggested that the Marxist theory of crises was a theoretical abstraction from trends which developed only when capitalism had exhausted the possibilities of conquering new foreign markets.[1]

[1] This theory, as explained in the first edition of *Sozialreform oder Revolution* (in Luxemburg's *Collected Works*, vol. III, p. 48) although in its author's mind it certainly led to her further theoretical statements, should be clearly distinguished from her later theory according to which capitalist accumulation, *independently of the industrial cycle*, would come to a standstill (involving the catastrophe of capitalism) once all the possibilities of capitalist expansion at the expense of pre-capitalist formations were exhausted.

Bernstein[1] considered that, for a long period, the only task of Social Democracy was to organize the workers and to promote democratic reform in the existing State. In this sense he regarded the 'ultimate aim' of Socialism as irrelevant, and the actual movement of gradualist progress as the only thing that mattered. It was true, though not polite, when he went on to describe the actual activities of Social Democracy as in conformity with his concept, as distinct from the revolutionary prospects proclaimed in the Party creed, and called upon the Party to dare to show itself in its true character.

Bernstein in some respects overstated his case. He attacked Hegelian dialectics, which was popular among German Social Democrats in the sense of a (very mild) theory of historical evolution, and made propaganda for Neo-Kantianism as the philosophical foundation of the labour movement. Such argument was both inaccessible and unacceptable to the average trade unionist, who, however, was able to appreciate the simple consistency of the Party creed even in its current vulgarized form; it had no sense apart from transferring current bourgeois fashions of thought into the labour movement and depriving the latter of a main source of its moral strength, namely the conviction that the future belonged to it. Recurrences of the Lassallean concept of the transforming power of the existing State, together with a proclamation of the democratization it was supposed to be undergoing, might flatter the South German Social Democrats who compromised with their local pseudo-parliamentary monarchies, but were bound to provoke the feelings of Prussians, who formed the great majority of German Social Democrats,[2] and were conscious that a thorough transformation of existing political machinery was the preliminary condition for even moderate democratic reform. To state that the Marxist theory of value was a one-sided abstraction no better than the academic abstraction of marginal utility might have been legitimate in an academic discussion on the history of economic thought; but it could not fail to provoke the Trade Unionists who knew very well that the second abstraction did not provide a sensible approach to the everyday problems of piece-work and hours. To reject Social Democracy's traditional opposition to colonial expansion and to regard colonial policies as having merits in civilizing backward areas[3] might be a correct reflexion of the eventual trends of German reformist socialism[4] and might even appeal to the narrow-minded trade union leader's nationalist outlook; it contradicted the fact that Social Democracy, even were Bernstein correct in considering

[1] *Zur Geschichte und Theorie des Sozialismus*, p. 234.

[2] Conditions in the other North German States were similar, suffrage in Saxony and two of the Hanseatic towns being restricted as soon as a Social Democratic majority was on the cards.

[3] Op. cit., p. 235.

[4] See below, pp. 114.

it a party of progressive liberal reform, had to appeal to pacifist feelings in Prussia; Bernstein himself, in 1915, when his theoretical concepts had conquered the Party, opposed its policies from the standpoint of pacifist opposition to the War.

Bernstein's fundamental thesis that he spoke for actual Social Democracy as opposed to its ideological self-deception was correct. But, being restricted to the outlook of that privileged minority of well-paid workers and the liberal intelligentsia which, lacking an opposition party of its own, tried to adapt Social Democracy to its needs, he failed to grasp the sociological reasons for that self-deception: the sectional world-outlook that he criticized was implied in the conditions of the German working class. How could a Berlin woman homeworker, dependent on the confectioner's whim and on the grocer's credit, or a miner, or an iron-worker in the 'kingdom of Stumm', who was prevented from joining even the tamest variety of Christian Trade Unionism, be helped by Bernstein's assertion that co-operatives and trade unions implied gradual growth into a democratic society, and that the growing monopolist organization of capitalism—Stumm's 'kingdom' being part of it—would gradually remove the misery implied in its periodical depressions? Social Democracy was the party of more than a small and comparatively easy minority of well-organized workers just because it represented the expectation that the misery of capitalism and the Prussian autocracy would be replaced by a new and better society, granting equal rights to all the workers. Had it not been identified with that expectation it would not have rallied the millions of voters on whom Bernstein's own expectations of a gradual democratization of Imperial Prussia depended. So it was bound to reject the attack on its ideological foundations.

This reaction, however, was surprisingly slow. Bernstein's basic statements[1] passed unnoticed even in the *Neue Zeit*, edited by Kautsky, until Rosa Luxemburg and Parvus, representatives of the Party's extreme left, beat an alarm. At the Party Congress of 1899 the discussion started,[2] but did not lead to a rejection of the Revisionist principles as contradicting the Party creed; even Rosa Luxemburg dropped the demand for the expulsion of Bernstein and his group, made in the first edition of *Sozialreform oder Revolution*, from the later editions of the book. In 1903, after the electoral triumph of Social Democracy, Bernstein, supported by a large part of the parliamentary party, suggested that the latter should make the visit to Court—involving a cheer for the emperor Wilhelm II—which was not prescribed by the law and which

[1] We have intentionally based the above explanation of Bernstein's view on his *Zur Geschichte und Theorie des Sozialismus*, i.e. on the collection of his articles from which the discussion started, as distinct from his *Evolutionary Socialism*, written during its course.

[2] On the Heine incident, see above, p. 85.

the party had avoided, in order to deprive the bourgeois parties of the pretext on which they refused to elect a Social Democrat Vice-President of the Reichstag, a post to which the party's strength in Parliament now entitled it. At the same time a dispute arose about the Revisionists' collaboration in the Liberal press; the Revisionists answered by rather disloyal attacks on the political past of leading left-wingers such as Mehring. In such an atmosphere, Bebel, at the Party Congress of 1903, sharply attacked the Revisionists and even threatened them with expulsion from the party; but they were eventually allowed to escape by voting for the resolution condemning their views—on the pretext that they were misrepresented—and continued to propagate them.

Bernstein's Revisionism, however, had not been defeated by revolutionary Marxism; apart from a few outsiders such as Rosa Luxemburg, Marxism meant to German Social Democracy hardly more than an economic theory justifying the workers' protest against exploitation and conducive to efficient trade union tactics; a concept of history useful as a counterpoise against the schoolmaster's patriotic legends, and a general philosophy which might counter the priest's defence of the established order, assuring the workers of the ultimate triumph of their cause. Revisionism was defeated because the Party could not fulfil its most elementary political tasks without the support of the Berlin home-worker and the Ruhr miner, who demanded their legitimate place in the world of labour and did not wish to wait till the printers were able and willing to enforce their emancipation. It was defeated because the world of labour—including the more intelligent and far-sighted printer—could not be integrated without a common outlook which distinguished the class to which the future belonged from the rotten world of to-day. But, as we saw in the previous section, it could not be taken for granted that those who needed that outlook in order to claim their place in the existing world would be prepared to make the supreme efforts needed to bring a new one into being: they might prefer to be called to the inheritance of an estate which had become vacant because of the inherent laws of its own decay. In his article 'Socialism in Germany', written in 1891, Engels, while rejecting premature insurrection, developed the analogy of the triumph of Christianity within the Roman empire; the new social organization, inspired by a new outlook, which had grown up within a decaying world, would in due course assume responsibility for its estate. Engels was realistic enough to mention the part played in the eventual triumph of Christianity by the attitude of the Army.

The group which described itself as the 'Marxist Centre' of German Social Democracy[1] and was supported by the large majority, proclaimed that by the mere strengthening and defence of their organization the

[1] The term was coined by Kautsky, during the discussions to be followed in the next chapter, but accepted, during and after World War I, by the left-wingers in order to denounce the Centre's unprincipled vacillations.

working classes would be prepared for taking over a responsibilty which would be theirs because of the expected automatic breakdown of capitalism, possibly on an occasion brought about by a desperate attack by the reactionary régime on working-class organization. The Revisionists rejected the concept of a revolutionary crisis involving a fundamental change of régime: the very process, they said, in which the existing political and economic régime was adapted to the growing influence of the working class involved its gradually turning socialist. To Bernstein the ultimate aim was nothing, the movement towards it everything. We have seen that the majority of the labour movement was bound to reject such a concept as a threat to the coherence and moral strength of the movement; but its own ideological assertions as to the outcome of its activities were soon exposed to the test of history.

PART TWO

THE PERIOD OF CRISIS
1905–1923

CHAPTER FOUR

SECTIONAL ORGANIZATION IN THE AGE OF MONOPOLY CAPITALISM

(a) *The Economic and Political Setting*

THIS is not the place to discuss the question whether there was a definite break between the pre-monopoly and the monopoly-capitalist stages in the development of Central European capitalism.[1] There certainly was such a break in the development of the labour movement, and some at least of its leaders were conscious of this.[2] The statistics of German industrial development, however, show a fairly continuous line of growth.

[1] In principle, the correctness of describing monopoly capitalism as a new stage in the development of capitalist society does not depend on whether the change can be observed equally in English and in German life, or coincided with a transition of industrial leadership from one nation to another which even at its start was nearer to the new pattern. The change was bound to be emphasized in German literature because more tribute had been paid to the British pattern by nineteenth-century German economists than German economic reality justified.

[2] Cf. Bebel's statement (above, p. 88) that with the general triumph of large-scale enterprise trade unionism would come to an end, and the very serious attention devoted, from the point of view of similar expectations, by Trade Unionists and 'academic Socialists' to even such meagre growth of 'yellow trade unionism' as we have met with (above, pp. 59–60). The Revisionists held more optimistic views as to the survival of workers' economic organizations in the monopoly capitalist age, the special merits of which they were to discover much later (see below, p. 98), and paid more attention to the new attitudes supposed to be called for from the workers in an age of imperialist politics (they would deny that monopoly capitalism was imperialist). It would be quite a mistake to conclude from the much later elaboration of a definite theory of imperialism by the non-German Leninists that the recognition of a break between pre-monopoly and monopoly capitalism was a factional issue; Hilferding, the founder of the modern theory of monopoly capitalism, which found no expression within the Party majority, never belonged to its extreme left, while Rosa Luxemburg, the left-wing leader, throughout her life worked with a concept of capitalist breakdown to which the monopoly character of modern capitalism was not essential (cf. my *Marx*, etc., pp. 193 ff.).

	1882	1895	1907
Percentage of total population employed in, or dependent upon:			
Agriculture	42·0	35·6	28·5
Industry	35·1	38·9	42·5
Commerce and Transport	9·9	11·5	13·3
Undertakings employing more than 50 workers: percentage of the total	0·3	0·6	0·9
Percentage of industrial workers employed by these	22	30	37

The giant enterprises characteristic of the age of monopoly capitalism had their origin at the very beginnings of modern German and Austrian capitalism. The Diskonto-Gesellschaft was established in 1856, the Deutsche Bank in 1870, and the Dresdner Bank in 1872. As early as 1882, with the support of the Diskonto-Gesellschaft, the Gelsenkirchen Bergwerksgesellschaft was established; in 1888 it embraced all the mines controlled by its patron bank and was responsible for the formation of the Rhine-Westphalian Coal Syndicate, which by 1893 controlled 86·7 per cent of the coal output of the two provinces, increasing to 95·4 per cent in 1910. In that year, according to Werner's data, of the Ruhr's total coal output of 89·3 million tons and its 354,200 miners, 19·3 million tons and 72,600 workers were from mines controlled by the Deutsche Bank, 17·6 million tons and 69,000 employees from those controlled by the Diskonto-Gesellschaft; 12·5 million tons and 44,200 employees were controlled by the Berliner Handelsgesellschaft; and 7·2 million tons and 28,000 miners by the Dresdner Bank and the Schaffhausen Bankverein. A further output of 16·9 million tons produced by 63,500 employees was controlled by the three biggest of the remaining entrepreneurs, Thyssen and Krupp among them, thus leaving less than 16 million tons and 77,000 employees for all the minor undertakings. Krupp, Thyssen, Stinnes, and Kirdorff in the Ruhr, and Stumm in the Saar, also led in the organization of the German steel industry. From the beginning they were joined by that traditional element in German society, the big Silesian latifundia-owners; the Pless and Ujest[1] interests controlled many of the mines and much of the other industrial interests connected with them. The production of electrical instruments and machinery from the first days of its growth was associated with two giants, the Allgemeine Elektrizitätsgesellschaft and Siemens-Halske-Schuckert. Similar conditions prevailed in the chemical industry, though its complete fusion was reserved for the post-war years. From the very beginning of the development of shipping in modern Germany, by far the largest part in it was played by the Hamburg-Amerika Line. At the end of 1912 the nine biggest banks, all with headquarters in Berlin, controlled 49 per cent of all deposits, and the six largest of them were

[1] See above, p. 5.

represented on the Supervisory Councils of 751 joint-stock companies; on the other hand, 51 of the leading industrialists were members of their own Supervisory Councils. Undoubtedly the banks controlled, if not the larger, at any rate the most important share of German industrial capital. In Austria the control of industry by High Finance was even more advanced.[1]

In order to restrict competition, cartels grew up by the hundred even in the nineties; whenever industrial depression hardened competition they broke up, to be re-formed when returning prosperity invited precautions against excessive expansion. From the beginning of the twentieth century, however, most cartels became fairly stable, if only because the big banks now controlled most of the competitors, and would not allow a cartel or syndicate to break up, unless the banks had a quarrel among themselves.

In 1893 German steel production exceeded British, and in 1910 was double the British production, which itself had grown almost twofold. Germany's attempt to conquer the world market for her increased production had to be supported by the control of her domestic market by monopolist bodies, for which the preliminary conditions had been created by the tariff policy inaugurated in 1879. The basic features of German imperialism were not the clumsy and ill-assorted choice of colonial symbols for her expansion, nor her rulers' special ability to find the most provocative methods of expression whenever she made an attempt at external expansion; these traits merely reflected the difficulties felt by a late-comer in the struggle for the distribution of the colonial world and the way in which Greater Prussia had been formed. What mattered was that the new tradition of national unification and the fresh experience of industrialization were immediately fused in an attempt at world conquest.

Bernhardi, in his book *Germany and the Next War* (1914), posed the alternative: world power or decay. There was, indeed, no other, if not from the point of view of the German nation, at any rate from that of an obsolete social structure which had been preserved by the Prussian method of establishing German unity and which based its foreign policy on an even more backward régime in Austria-Hungary. The great opportunity of the Junker-Heavy-Industrialist combination which ruled Germany lay precisely in its capacity to establish a firm link between the nation's apparent need to expand and its own need to repress all potential opponents of such expansion. German Social Democracy was not an underground movement like the Russian; it feared the link instead of cutting it. Against the lure of prosperity in the Greater German Empire it had little to offer except an outworn nineteenth-century utopia of Free Trade and International Conciliation, which would not necessarily exclude a recognition of the civilizing mission of the colonial politics of

[1] See below, pp. 180, 322 and 360–1.

advanced bourgeois-democratic countries.[1] Social Democratic speakers opposed German colonial policy because of its barbaric and aggressive methods, which were not rewarded by material results other than the acquiring of military bases which would further complicate the international situation, because of the inroads it implied into the taxpayer's pocket, and because it set up an antagonism to Britain, thought to be in the interest of Russian Tsarism which was still considered as the inspiration and support of the German ruling class. The first two arguments were commonplace among many Liberals. The fiction of a Germany still subservient to Russian Tsarism and driven as its tool into an anti-British policy was a direct continuation of the traditions of 1848 and the radical-democratic concept of modern foreign policies as a struggle between the feudal East and the advanced West, which was shared by the founders of Marxism.[2] Such an argument turned into direct support of the German war effort as soon as German imperialist expansion collided with the imperial policies of Tsarist Russia.

If these were the attitudes of Germany's most definitely opposition party, all the others proved an easy prey to the lure of imperial expansion. As early as 1898 the Catholic Centre voted for the naval building programme. When in 1906 Erzberger, a representative of the Centre's left wing, attacked the corrupt policies of the Colonial Office[3] he earned not only the hatred of Helfferich, then Colonial Minister and later leader of the National Conservative Party,[4] but also official disavowal by the leader of the parliamentary party, Dr. Spahn: Civil Service discipline would be undermined if M.P.s were to interfere with the Executive's business by criticizing civil servants. Chancellor Bülow, however, used the opportunity for a dissolution against the 'anti-Empire' parties, Socialists and Catholics. In an atmosphere closely approaching that of the nationalist plebiscites under the Weimar Republic, Social Democracy suffered its closest approach before 1914 to an electoral defeat: it added only a quarter of a million votes to the three million it had polled in the 1903 elections, and lost most of its parliamentary seats to the compact front formed by all the bourgeois parties at the second ballot.

[1] Cf. Liebknecht's speech in the Reichstag, 21st June 1899 (vol. III, 2707–9), commented on by Yerusalimsky, op. cit., pp. 596–7. But see Bebel on the Stuttgart Congress of 1898, reported ibid., pp. 501–2, with his direct declaration of solidity with the 'backward' peoples, victims of imperialist aggression.

[2] Cf. my *Marx*, etc., p. 312.

[3] In Erzberger's biography, published in 1925 by Prof. Bauer on behalf of the Windhorst League (the comparatively left-wing Catholic Youth organization: right-wing Catholics would never have thought of honouring the memory of the 'traitor'), the hero was defended against the 'calumny' of having been an opponent of Wilhelm II's naval and colonial policies. Bauer, however, found it inopportune to use the convincing evidence produced by Erzberger during the War, e.g. his article in *Die Tat*, no. 30, 1915, where it was said that the destruction of the whole city of London would be justified if a single German soldier's life could be spared thereby.

[4] See below, p. 217.

In 1899 the concession for the building of the Baghdad Railway was secured from Turkey by the German government for a finance group led by the Deutsche Bank, whose manager, Siemens, was the founder of a leading electrical machinery combine. After an abortive attempt at competition, with British backing,[1] Austria-Hungary turned into the closest supporter and immediate agent of German south-eastward expansion; German permeation of the Turkish State machinery and army began immediately the agreement was concluded. Some years were to pass before the line-up for early twentieth-century imperialist conflicts became obvious. The 1906 crisis concerned that unfavourably situated object Morocco; but from 1908 onwards political crises in the Balkans, with Austria-Hungary and Russia as the apparent protagonists of the two blocs of Great Powers, followed each other in rapid succession up to the general conflagration in 1914.

Increasing awareness of the danger of war coincided with increasing social tensions. After 1906, protectionism and the progress of monopoly resulted, in Germany as well as in Britain, in a continuous rise in the cost of living. From 1910 real wages began to fall—and this in a period of industrial prosperity. There were many demonstrations, strikes, and disorders: 1910 in Berlin-Moabit, 1911 in Vienna (where the demonstrations resulted in shooting and the building of barricades), in France and Britain. In 1912 the strikes which followed the massacres in the Lena gold-fields heralded the second wave of the Russian revolution; it had already led to mass strikes and barricades in St. Petersburg when it was interrupted by the outbreak of World War I. In Germany the increasing dissatisfaction of the masses with their standard of life collided with the increasing caution of the Trade Union bureaucracy, whose attitude was governed by solicitude for their funds and fear of large-scale political conflicts; the result was a number of big unofficial strikes. In the summer of 1913, 40,000 workers from the Hamburg shipbuilding yards were out for nine weeks; to get rid of this movement, the leaders of the German Metal Workers' Union even called an extraordinary Congress and prohibited their subsidiary organizations from issuing strike pay. In view of the record of the Printers' Union it is no surprise to learn that it was to the fore in developing these new methods of trade union 'leadership'; in 1911 it broke a strike of the Berlin printers, which defied the collective agreement, by expelling the strikers from the Union and introducing Union members from other areas who were prepared to fill their places. Yet such methods were not characteristic of all German trade unionism; in a pamphlet published by the Carpenters' Union, the Printers' Union was even described as 'an executive organ of the will of the organized employers'.

Such conflicts were still isolated. Political tension within Germany

[1] Cf. Yerusalimsky, op. cit., pp. 620–1

developed at a rather moderate pace. In 1910 the Liberal factions[1] were reunited under Naumann's leadership on a platform less protectionist and more favourable to social reform and educational progress than that of their National Liberal competitors. But it was not averse to militarism and imperialist expansion, of which in fact Naumann, during the war, became a principal advocate. As the Revisionist trend within Social Democracy developed, Naumann could suggest a political combination 'from Bassermann (the leader of the National Liberals) to Bebel'; in the days of the Weimar Republic such a combination was to be known as the 'Great Coalition'. It was not very stable: in 1906, as we have seen, nearly all the Liberals were to be found in Bülow's Conservative-Liberal bloc. Nor did it provide an alternative to imperialism; in 1912 all the Liberals voted for the new armament programme, while the Social Democrats, who did not, at least voted for the new taxes destined to raise the necessary funds so far as those taxes fell upon the wealthier classes.

On the eve of the 1912 elections Kautsky developed the theory of the 'new middle class', meaning thereby, like Bernstein ten years earlier, the black-coated workers whose ranks had been swollen by modern industrial development and who were supposed to have produced the 'new Liberalism', as illustrated by the fushion of the Liberal groups. The Social Democratic Party, after its triumph in the first ballot, concluded an agreement with the Liberal groups on the tactics for the second ballot. This agreement was ominous for the further development of the labour movement: the Liberals were promised not only Socialist support in all those constituencies where they faced right-wingers, but also the sacrifice of sixteen constituencies where Socialists faced Liberals. The agreement did not overcome the deeply-rooted class instinct on either side; the Social Democratic workers in the sacrificed constituencies went to the polls, though in most cases without success,[2] and most Liberal voters supported the Conservatives, whatever their leaders might have agreed to. Nor did the 'left' majority which resulted from the

[1] See above, p. 8.

[2] In one constituency the Social Democratic organization, evidently controlled by the Left wing (see below, p. 115), failed to refrain from election propaganda, and won the seat. This affords a sufficient illustration of the falsity of the leaders' argument. Under the pre-1918 German and Austrian electoral system a second ballot decided between the two candidates with the largest vote in the first ballot. The disputes between the left wing and the majority of the Socialist Party thus centred on the questions: (*a*) whether, in the event of a Liberal-Conservative combination, all the second ballots in which that bloc was represented by a Liberal would be lost for Social Democracy—the alternative was that in a straightforward struggle on clear class lines additional voters might be mobilized for Social Democracy—and (*b*) whether a 'left' bloc with a party which had to be compensated for not combining with the Conservatives was worth any sacrifice, were it merely that of a good opportunity for clear-cut class propaganda, supposing the Party leaders were right on issue (*a*).

elections to what was to become Germany's wartime parliament prove specially stable: within four weeks the Social-Democrat Vice-President, Scheidemann, was dropped by the Liberals because he carried out the decisions of his Party Congress and refused to pay the traditional tribute of loyalty to Wilhelm II.[1]

(*b*) *The Pre-War Alignment in the German Labour Movement: Social Democracy and Trade Unions*

The full importance of these developments was hardly realized within the labour movement until after World War I. The Russian revolution of 1905, however, was generally regarded as an event of outstanding importance, though not as a forerunner of the establishment of the first Socialist régime and of the definitive cleavage within the labour movement, which no one at that time foresaw.[2] Tsarism had been looked upon as the traditional stronghold of European reaction since the days of the Holy Alliance; its obvious weakening encouraged offensive action against the Central European monarchies. Political activity in Germany seemed the more urgent because of the danger that the German Government might intervene in support of Tsarism. The issue never became a live one, because of the defeat of the Moscow insurrection in December 1905, though the full importance of this was realized much later in the Socialist than in the Conservative camp.

On the other hand, the fact that backward Russia, with its record of 'underground' fighters, undisciplined though heroic, was now drawing the revolutionary implications of Marxism would not encourage the respectable German Trade Unionist, or Revisionist Social Democrat, to 'speak Russian',[3] particularly since the further development of German monarchy into an ordinary Western conservative régime seemed possible after the defeats its Tsarist backer had suffered. So the first reaction to the great event was a trial of strength between the various trends within the German labour movement. Within the Social Democratic Party the political mass strike, whose effectiveness as a weapon of class struggle had become evident in Russia,[4] grew popular as a means of winning new political rights, especially equal suffrage in the key State

[1] It is characteristic of the conditions of that time in Germany that the claim of the strongest parliamentary party to the post of first President was not even considered. As the son of the then leader of the Centre Party, Spahn (see above, p. 100), bore witness before the post-War *Untersuchungsausschuss* (vol. VII, p. 233), his father took the initiative in the complete removal of the Social Democrats from the Praesidium by insisting that Scheidemann must take part in the Court ceremony, which was in no way prescribed by law.

[2] See my *Marx*, etc., p. 294.

[3] See above, p. 85.

[4] The 1905 military, and especially naval, mutinies in Russia which made so great an impression on public opinion did not give rise to any discussion on the tactical issues of the class struggle in Central Europe.

of Prussia, and of defending those that already existed, such as equal manhood suffrage in elections for the Imperial parliament. But respectable trade unionists grew horrified at the possible implications of the Party ideology, now illustrated by a real revolution. The Cologne Trade Union congress of May 1905 discussed the May Day strikes, which in many factories were regarded as a trial of strength, but were deplored by the Unions as causing unnecessary expenditure because of the lock-outs that followed them. Bringmann, speaking for the T.U.C., rejected the celebration of May Day in any form; not a single Trade Union member had been recruited because of it. Since social legislation had come to a standstill, the German workers had lost their interest in politics: trade unionism was now the only available means of improving their conditions. In this spirit all the main issues of the day were discussed at the congress; accounts were definitely settled with those who advocated low membership fees and a strike tactic based on support from outside the Union concerned;[1] the political general strike was described as an anarcho-syndicalist utopia.

To understand the outcome of the dispute, we must bear it in mind that Trade Unions and Party were organizations of practically the same group of people; the Trade Unions, outnumbering the Party threefold in membership, included most of its electoral supporters so far as they were employed in trades not prevented by German conditions from organizing,[2] and except in a few aristocratic Unions, such as the Printers, nearly every active Unionist was a Party member. The Union leaders' reaction to the increasing self-confidence of the labour movement was deplored not only by the official Party leaders but also by the more moderate of the Revisionists. At the Party congress in Jena Fischer, speaking for the Central Committee, described both the Cologne resolutions on the May demonstrations as deplorable symptoms of a disease still latent in the body of the German labour movement and of a loss of Socialist faith on the part of some Trade Unionists.[3] Von Elm, rather more outspoken, had written in the *Sozialistische Monatshefte*, the Revisionist organ, that the Cologne congress showed the danger that German trade unionism would follow the British pattern, the idealist approach being gradually replaced by a mere accountant's attitude to problems of general importance. Fischer's formulation of the funda-

[1] See above, p. 64, and Nestriepke, op. cit., vol. I, pp. 426–7.

[2] In 1907, when most of the lower middle class were rallied against it under nationalist slogans, the Party, with 530,000 members, polled three and a quarter million votes, while the Unions had 1,873,000 members (many of them aged between 18 and 24, and therefore voteless). Women, who had no vote, formed no large part in either figure, but about a sixth of the Party's vote must still have come from the lower middle classes. Agricultural workers, Civil Servants, railwaymen, and most workers in the heavy industries could not join trade unions, although many voted Socialist.

[3] Proceedings, p. 234.

mental relations between Party and Unions[1] should have been acceptable to any not too narrow-minded Trade Unionist. Both organizations were equally important and had equal rights within the labour movement; but in relation to its ultimate aim of socialism, Trade Unions and co-operatives, however great their importance in improving working-class conditions, should be regarded as palliatives. Trade Unionists should keep it in mind that all their achievements might be brought to nought by a single law increasing the import duties on food; therefore it was in their best interest to support the political Party which was the only force that could avert such dangers.

Festive speeches about ultimate aims apart, such an attitude implied that Unions and Party were equally important representatives of the workers' interests in different fields of action, distinct from but dependent on each other. In the following year Rosa Luxemburg, the intellectual leader of the Party's left wing, wrote in *Massenstreik, Partei und Gewerkschaften* that this was the only approach correct on the reformist level; the Party's claims to supremacy were based on its task, not only of fighting the parliamentary battle for day to day reforms, but also of preparing for the overthrow of capitalism by revolution. She rejected the Bolshevist idea of a party which would support the sectional interests of labour while continuously representing before it the tasks implied in a future revolutionary situation; so he rclaim for a leading role for the Party depended on the assumption that a socialist revolution was impending. When, at the Jena Party congress, she asserted that the Russian revolution heralded the time, foreseen by Marx and Engels, when evolution would become revolution, she was speaking for every convinced Socialist in Germany; and she was not alone when, against the Revisionist lawyer Heine, who had warned off the unorganized masses from entering the contest in the course of a political general strike, she stated that in a revolutionary situation control was necessary not over the masses but over lawyer M.P.s, to prevent them from betraying the revolution.[2] But, as we are soon to see, she was almost alone, perhaps because of her Russo-Polish background, in having any conception of a revolution more definite than memories of 1848. And her conception was purely negative.

Rosa Luxemburg's theoretical approach was governed by the combination of a Menshevist attitude to Russian organizational problems with a strictly anti-bureaucratic attitude to those of Germany: her reply to the institutionalization of the German labour movement was simply a denunciation of institutionalization as evil. Making spontaneous mass-action the object of all that devotion to great causes of which she was capable, she failed to see that even 'spontaneity' is not

[1] Ibid., p. 274.

[2] Jena, Proceedings, p. 320. At the following congress (Mannheim, Proceedi ngs, p. 298) Bebel dealt with Heine in terms that hardly differed

pure democracy, but is only action under *ad hoc* leadership; she was at least convinced that such leadership would meet the needs of a revolutionary situation better than anything that the Party, including the trend she herself led, could provide. In *Massenstreik, Partei und Gewerkschaften* she wrote that the direction of the political general strike, which to her was a synonym of the revolutionary process, so far as concerned giving the word for its start, shaping its organs, and covering its expenses, should be left to 'the revolutionary period itself', i.e., to spontaneous mass action. Apparently she confused the refutation of obvious nonsense, such as the trade union leaders' assertion that before a great political mass action was started the funds available for it should be estimated, with an answer to the very serious question whether a nation which needs a revolution can expect the proper decisions to be taken by an *ad hoc* meeting of workers in a factory, or of some comrades working in related factories, the correctness of their decision being checked by the reactions of other *ad hoc* meetings in other factories, military units, etc., after the first shots have been fired. Perhaps she was not even conscious that the people's 'spontaneity' in all actual revolutions, the Russian included, was quite distinct from its mythology;[1] probably she was horrified by the prospect that a group of people who regarded themselves as competent to 'organize a revolution' on a national scale might also look upon themselves as competent to establish a revolutionary dictatorship.[2] She certainly had reason to doubt whether any organized

[1] The analysis of 'spontaneity' in modern revolutions—the older ones are insufficiently documented—would be a most promising task for a historian prepared to tackle a problem with general sociological implications. As regards the *grands journées* of the French revolution, the very first of them included, it is comparatively easy to follow, in any good history, the process of organization by definite persons with definite connexions, though in those days they would not be described as a political party; for the Russian revolutions of 1905 and March 1917 a close scrutiny of the sources, and of the actual importance of the events reported in them, would be needed. In an atmosphere of factional struggle, each faction claimed for its organizational activities whatever part its individual members might have played in *ad hoc* groupings fitting even Rosa Luxemburg's pattern (she would not have denied that it is well for the participants in such groupings to be prepared by the educational activities of their party); but it is for historical argument to determine what part either of the Russian factions, as an organized body (even if only locally) played, say, in giving to the demonstration organized by Gapon on 22nd January 1905, the character that led to its further implications. Sorel, as a historian of the French Revolution, was certainly not unaffected by his tendency, as a sociologist and politician, to insist on the importance of *élites*; but even less attention should be paid to the purely ideological ascription of any historical event to anonymous action of 'the people'. Trotsky's *History of the Russian Revolition* (English edition, 1932, vol. I, pp. 119 and 129), the tendency of which is quite definite opposition to party claims, nevertheless takes *ad hoc* organized leadership in the February revolution of 1917 for granted.

[2] A definite line is traceable from her article 'Organizational Problems of Russian Social Democracy', reprinted from the Menshevist *Iskra* in *Neue Zeit*, vol. XXII/2 (1904), to her posthumous critique of the Bolshevist revolution (including such state-

body in the world of labour as she knew it[1] was indeed superior to the live initiative of some local *ad hoc* body which acted when it found that the feelings of its fellows demanded action. Such a body would describe as 'spontaneity' its belief that similar conditions would probably have created similar feelings everywhere else, so that all that was necessary was to make a start. In contrast, any centralized body shouldering national responsibilities might be handicapped either by the shortcomings of the information available when the movement was an underground one, as in Russia, or by its own bureaucratic conceptions of proper financial provisions, legal safeguards, etc., as in Germany.

Rosa Luxemburg restricted the task of the Party to the development of general tactical concepts[2] so that 'in every phase of the struggle the sum-total of all the activized proletarian strength is fully realized, so that the slogans proposed never lag behind the level of the actual relation of strength between the fighting class-forces, but always go beyond it.' The actual realization of those slogans was left to the initiative of the 'spontaneously' created mass organs. Evidently she was convinced that this task could be performed by some small group of revolutionary propagandists who would, if necessary, defy the Party's discipline. She never seriously tackled the problem of how the obvious interconnections between the diverse parts of a revolutionary country, the different conditions in different industries, and so on, can be reconciled with a type of national leadership which aims only at offering slogans suitable to the most advanced parts of the battlefield, leaving the fighting units to make their choice. She herself was eventually to die in conditions created by a local insurrection of her fellow-partisans, started against her own advice, while the operation of 'spontaneity' had just failed to set in motion latent forces in the rest of the country which a few months later might have secured a triumph.

In 1905–6 many German Social Democrats were convinced that the

ments as she cannot be proved to have corrected in the last months of her life, as was done with some others in Clara Zetkin's counter-critique).

[1] Including both the Russian factions, whose performance in the events of 1905 were not outstanding, though to any sincere revolutionary they must have seemed infinitely superior to Rosa Luxemburg's German surroundings.

[2] This statement in the 1906 pamphlet marks a certain development from that in the article of 1904 just quoted, wherein the existence of tactical principles, apart from the most general concepts of the class struggle, which the working class could be taught by a central committee, was denied. In *Massenstreik, Partei und Gewerkschaften* Party decisions on such questions as whether general strikes, or armed insurrection, should be considered as appropriate at the moment and encouraged according to the country's circumstances are regarded as quite legitimate; only their actual application is left to 'spontaneous' initiative. The change is evidently due to the 1905 revolution.

Russian Revolution, with its possible international implications,[1] might result in mass strikes[2] for the conquest of democratic rights, as had just been seen in Austria;[3] but there were completely different ideas as to what such a mass strike actually implied. Rosa Luxemburg[4] regarded it as 'the specific form of mass movement characteristic of revolutionary periods': street demonstrations and armed conflicts with the existing State machine were mere incidents in its general progress. Evidently revolution to her was mere disorganization of the existing State machinery, with the prospect that the mass organs which had arisen 'spontaneously'—an example of which had just been provided in the shape of the St. Petersburg Soviet, which was dominated by left-wing Mensheviks—would eventually step into the gap left by the breakdown of government resistance. The concept of revolution by planned military action, after preparation by strikes, demonstrations, etc., disorganizing the government and increasing the prestige of the revolutionaries, presupposes the Bolshevist concept of Party, which she rejected. Without considering such details,[4] the Revisionists would heartily agree with Rosa Luxemburg's identification of mass strike with revolution, in order to conclude from Germany's manifest unpreparedness for the latter the utopian character of the former.

The official Party leaders[5] rejected the inherent necessity of such a

[1] The issue of a possible German intervention in favour of Tsarism played a large part in the discussions at the Mannheim congress (1906), and the controversy was made more bitter by Rosa Luxemburg's natural dissatisfaction with Bebel's reluctance to commit the Party to mass strikes on any definite *political* occasion (in the event of attacks on trade union rights even the right-wing trade unionist, Bommelburg, regarded mass strikes as unavoidable). In the summer of 1906, Bebel was probably convinced of the impending defeat of the Russian revolution by the Tsar's own resources; his refusal to endanger the Party's legal opportunities by a statement about hypothetical cases which would, however, be used by the Government as a proof of impending Socialist treason, need not be interpreted as a refusal to risk much in a decisive situation. Rosa Luxemburg, still, like all the other Russian revolutionaries, an optimist in the summer of 1906, would have liked the Party to be committed to a revolutionary course whether a Russian or some other crisis provided the opportunity.

[2] All the German documents speak of 'mass strike', to avoid confusion with the anarchist utopia of a hundred percent general strike.

[3] See below, pp. 123–4

[4] *Massenstreik*, etc., op. cit., pp. 437–8. Clara Zetkin, Rosa Luxemburg's closest follower, had stated that the general strike could become effective only when backed by the ghost of revolution, to which the Revisionist Heine agreed (Proceedings of Jena Congress, p. 315).

[5] Their point of view was explained by L. Zietz (Proceedings of the Jena Congress, p. 327), but is implied also in Bebel's statement, made at the same congress in arguing against the right-wing opponents of a mass strike, that, for large issues, the German workers were prepared even to starve for a fortnight if trade union funds for their support were not available, and in his warnings against demonstrations involving the risk of massacres (Mannheim Proceedings, p. 239). In a letter to Roland-Holst (reprinted in Paul Fröhlich's introduction to Rosa Luxemburg's, op. cit., p. 67), Rosa Luxemburg explained the 'exoteric' character of her references to Bebel's

connexion; they regarded the political mass strike as a disciplined and well-organized action carried out for limited objectives. Trade Unionists might accept such a concept at least verbally,[1] and prove by the enumeration of the trades prepared for such action[2] that the force available was insufficient to bring actual pressure to bear upon the government: it followed that the strike would have to be supplemented by street demonstrations which were likely to result in bloody collisions with police and army. From Rosa Luxemburg's point of view, the obvious answer[3] was that massacres of peaceable demonstrators might bring into action important trades absent from Legien's list, such as miners and railwaymen, as well as putting the conscript army out of action. But if these implications had been made explicit, it would have been clear to most Party members as well as Trade Unionists that the logical implications of the Party creed contradicted their actual attitude. In his concluding speech at the Jena congress,[4] Bebel however, quoted—or misquoted[5]—as an authority by Rosa Luxemburg, with an unsubstantiated reference to Engels, questioned the concluding sentence of the Communist Manifesto which she had quoted: the German workers, said he, had more to lose than their chains. If this was true, it was unreasonable to make supreme sacrifices, possibly in support of the revolution in another country, in order to conquer a world which might become theirs in due course by the gradual process of history.

The only counter-argument which Rosa Luxemburg could explicitly put forward was a reference to the large masses of German workers who were excluded from the benefits of well-developed organization but whose class-conscousness might awake in a revolutionary wave: the agricultural labourers, the railwaymen, the subjects of 'King Stumm' and other monopolists, the home-workers, etc. Since they were unorganized, these masses did not count in the eyes of practical organizers;

authority at the Jena Party Congress: she was conscious of the difference existing between the two points of view, but had, for tactical reasons, quoted the supreme Party authority for what were actually the policies of a small minority group.

[1] Legien in Mannheim Proceedings, p. 244. A year before (Jena Proceedings, p. 322) he had joined with Heine and the other Revisionists in accepting the identification of mass strike and revolution.

[2] Engineering, woodworking, building, and in part textile workers; the printers, the only well-organized group a strike of which would have made an immediate impression on public opinion, being conspicuously absent. If post-1918 Communists had disposed of such a force, which in Berlin made up the majority of the working class, for demonstrative action, they would not for a moment have hesitated to use it when only limited aims were envisaged, as was the case with the Party majority in 1905–6.

[3] It is clearly implied in *Massenstreik*, etc. To explain it fully would have been impossible, not only because of the feelings of the average Party member, but also because of the risk of its being described as a threat to the legality of the Party.

[4] Proceedings, p. 339.

[5] See f.n. [4], p. 108.

but on the basis of the experiences of the Russian revolution, Rosa Luxemburg argued that their organizations would arise in the course of the struggle itself. From the point of view of hardened trade unionists, this was no argument; *ad hoc* organizations which came to birth in the course of an actual conflict did not count.[1] But here Rosa Luxemburg would join issue and compare the elemental energy of the unorganized workers rising to self-consciousness in the heat of the struggle with the cautious and short-sighted approach of the well-disciplined trade unionist 'husbandman'. Two worlds confronted each other, as the trade unionists'[2] outbreaks of hatred would certify; and Rosa Luxemburg's assessment of the potential of the as yet unorganized masses was important mainly as a forerunner of later Communist attitudes.[3] Her case was implied, however, by that very Party creed that had defeated the Revisionists.

Against this background, the conflicts provoked by the Cologne Trade Union Congress proved to have only ideological foundations. By 287 votes to 14 the Jena Party congress of September 1905, inspired by the progress of the Russian revolution and shocked by the trade unionists' pretensions to leadership on a political question, answered the Cologne arguments about the alleged identity of the political mass strike with the anarchist general-strike-utopia by asserting that a political mass strike would be the answer to interference with manhood suffrage for the imperial parliament.[4] There was no risk of the issue's becoming a live one immediately; the only achievement of the left wing was that the Party had explicitly recognized what in Austria was a commonplace, namely that the political general strike was one weapon in the proletarian class-struggle, legitimate if it suited its purpose.[5] But the Jena resolution denoted a more radical approach even by the Party leaders. In October, the editors of *Vorwärts*, the Party's

[1] See above, pp. 62–3.

[2] Not only those who became open renegades like Winnig, op. cit., p. 108. Complaints of her failure to get killed during the Russian revolution were fairly common among the right-wing Social Democrats.

[3] See below, pp. 373–4.

[4] Similar to the restrictions already imposed in some of the States. See above, p. 91.

[5] In making comparisons with the predominant British attitude towards 'direct action' (cf. S. and B. Webb, op. cit., pp. 665 ff.), the absence of political democracy in Central Europe before 1918, and the existence of imperial vetoes based on the actual disposition of the State machinery, should be kept in mind. Bernstein, the Revisionist leader, stated that 'the right of resistance is a truism like the right to breathe', though it would not necessarily be emphasized every day. Under the conditions prevailing, the German workers could easily be deprived of essential rights under legal forms, e.g. by disfranchisement by a bourgeois majority convinced that it was sure to lose the next general election (a procedure which, by the way, is current in present France and Italy). If they reacted to such a course, to restriction of the right of combination, etc., by 'direct action', their action would differ from the case envisaged by the Webbs only in so far as German legality differed from British.

central organ, were replaced by left-wingers, and there were plans to celebrate 21st January 1906, the anniversary of the Russian revolution, by street demonstrations in favour of general suffrage in Prussia, though these demonstrations were in the end called off in order to avoid collisions with the Police, perhaps under the influence of the defeat of the Moscow insurrection in December 1905. Unfounded rumours concerning an impending attempt to force the issue by a political general strike caused some apprehension in the Trade Union camp, which was appeased by a secret conference between the Central Committees of the Party and the T.U.C. The Party leaders explained that they did not regard a political general strike as suitable at the moment, but if conditions should change, they would contact the T.U.C. and, after an unofficial agreement with it, conduct the strike on the Party's responsibility, thus avoiding any direct danger to the Trade Unions' funds and legal status.[1]

The Party had conceded all that the Trade Union leaders could reasonably demand: the basic right of co-decision without the risks of formal responsibility. But the Report of the Conference was published in a Localist paper, in a distorted version which invited an interpretation of Bebel's questioning the topicality of a general strike in February 1906 as a basic retreat from his acceptance of this weapon, in principle, at the Jena Party congress. The suggestion has been made that the indiscretion had its origin with the Trade Union leaders, who were eager to prove the Party's insincerity, and also to hint at the probable consequences of an attempt to carry out the decisions of the Party congress. If this was the intention, the indiscretion would only have made explicit what was implied in Bebel's attitude, as distinct from the claims made upon it by the left wing.[1] The Jena resolution had not committed the Party to a general strike on any definite occasion, apart from the rather academic case of the abolition of manhood suffrage; and it had concluded with the demand for 'thorough propagandist and organizational efforts' as a preliminary condition for political general strikes. Bebel, who regarded such strikes as a disciplined organizational activity, could hardly have regarded that condition as sufficiently fulfilled a few months after the Jena congress. The Party tried to get the Union leaders' assent to joint publication of the proceedings of the secret conference. When, suspiciously enough, that assent was refused, the Party proceeded on its own responsibility, earning the Union leaders' sharp reproaches and the suggestion that it should have protected their authority by simply proclaiming the harmless character of the actual proceedings and demanding that the Party members take its word for this.[2]

Such criticism implied a demand that the Party should be subordin-

[1] Paul Fröhlich's Introduction to Luxemburg, op. cit., pp. 70–1.
[2] Legien in Mannheim, Proceedings, p. 243.

ated to the T.U.C., and was rejected by Bebel;[1] but together with the leading Trade Unionists he moved a resolution at the Mannheim congress, explaining that there was no contradiction between the resolutions of the Cologne Trade Union and the Jena Party congresses, and that Party and Trade Unions were equally important organizations of the working class. This implied that a political general strike,[2] which at Jana had been declared necessary in certain circumstances, could not be proclaimed without the permission of those who, at Cologne, had described it as anarchist nonsense. An amendment moved by Kautsky, and accepted by Bebel as well as by the Trade Unionists, stated that unity of action between Party and Trade Unions presupposed that the latter were dominated by the spirit of socialism; every party member must work in this sense within the Unions.[2] If, however, there was no contradiction between the Party's policies and those of the Union leaders it was clearly unnecessary to exert the Party's influence in the Unions in favour of a change in their policies. The left wing, led by Kautsky and Luxemburg, was incapable of pressing its own point without provoking misunderstandings,[3] and was probably even incapable of conceiving organized activities by the Party members in the Unions in opposition to the Union leaders. No vote was forced, except on the alleged absence of contradictions between the Cologne and Jena resolutions. This left-wing amendment was defeated by 323 votes to 62, although a glance at the resolutions submitted to the Party congress by the local organizations shows that the demand for control of the unreliable Union leaders by closer collaboration between the Party members had been predominant on the eve of the congress.

But these resolutions also indicated a unanimous demand for greater activity by the Party members in Trade Union life; and Rosa Luxemburg, inspired as she was by deep distrust of any kind of stable organization, was the last to satisfy that demand. So the socialist activists who looked for a trade unionism different from that represented by the Cologne resolutions were given no guidance; Rosa Luxemburg's reluctance to apply Party discipline in order to enforce conformity with accepted principles of trade union organization represented merely an outsider's position. There was a strong demand that trade unionism should conform to socialist principles; there was also something like

[1] Ibid., p. 294.

[2] See f.n. [2] p. above 108.

[3] Kautsky's original amendment had continued with the demand that Party members in their Union as in all their other activities should be governed by the decisions of the Party congresses (which was either a matter of course, or an acceptance of the Bolshevist conception of Party with which Kautsky and Luxemburg clearly disagreed); it concluded with the declaration that the Party was the highest and broadest representative of the proletarian class struggle. It was argued that a resolution of this type, while actually uncontroversial, would cause unnecessary difficulties for the Unions on the neutrality issue; so it was withdrawn.

unanimity on the issue that no action was feasible that was not endorsed by both the main organizations of the labour movement. Revisionism, as a specific ideology, had been defeated, and trade union leaders were expected to conform with the Party's ideology; but they were allowed to interpret it as they liked, and they had an established right to veto any action which they considered detrimental to the interests of their organization.[1] The class-conscious worker was expected to be a Party member as well as a Trade Unionist, and before long a co-operator as well; but in both these bodies his inspiration was only a machinery whose democratic façade hardly veiled the domination of the bureaucracies. And these had agreed that any action which might bring either of them into undesirable conflict with the existing State was to be avoided. Bebel had argued clearly enough against some motions which demanded the declaration of a political general strike in the event of German armed intervention against the Russian revolution; if a Central Committee was foolish enough to call a general strike in such a situation, a state of emergency would be proclaimed, and jurisdiction would pass from the ordinary courts to courts-martial.[2]

One year after Mannheim the most important implications of what had happened became explicit, or would have done so had not lip-service to radical phraseology and the left wing's tactics of quoting from established authority resulted in an unholy alliance against recognition of the facts. At the Stuttgart congress of the Second International, Bebel, on behalf of the German Party, explained that it would not reject armaments if there was a guarantee that they were intended merely for defence; this could easily be checked, as, under modern conditions, there was no great difficulty in distinguishing aggressor from victim. In no event would the Party allow its fight against militarism to develop in ways 'dangerous to the Party's life and perhaps even to its very existence'; an evident hint at the existing State's probable reactions to propaganda in the army. After these explanations, the German delegation voted for the resolution, which was drawn up by a sub-committee of the congress under the leadership of Lenin and Rosa Luxemburg—who, of course, would not fail to establish the betrayal of that resolution by the Party majority's behaviour in 1914—and which demanded, in the clearest possible terms, the use of the approaching war as an opportunity for a working-class revolution. In the same year, Karl Liebknecht published a pamphlet on *Militarism and Anti-Militarism*, calling for socialist propaganda in the army; this was immediately disowned by the Party's Central Committee. The Socialist Youth Movement, organized under Liebknecht's leadership, was deprived of its autonomy and transformed into a bureaucratic welfare

[1] For this interpretation of the Mannheim decision on the political general strike, see also Umbreit, op. cit., p. 170.

[2] See f.n. [1] p. 108.

organization, managed, on behalf of the Central Committee, by Friedrich Ebert. Noske, Ebert's future colleague, earned only mild criticism by declaring, in that very year 1907 in the parliamentary discussions on the defence Budget, that Social Democracy was not opposed to army discipline, intended to make Germany's defence as strong as possible, and in the event of war would prove no less patriotic than any other section of German society. Fear, if not of the Government's hypothetical sanctions against anti-militarist propaganda, at least of the reactions of the German electorate to an anti-imperialist attitude on the part of Social Democracy,[1] might provide one explanation of such developments, immediately after the Russian revolution and the Morocco crisis; the predominance in the Party organization of people who had much more to lose than their chains[2] another; but neither force could have delivered the whole body of the German labour movement into the hands of German imperialism had not organizational unity been turned into a fetish by the left perhaps even more than by the right wing of the Party.[3]

In spring 1910, in view of impressive street demonstrations for equal manhood suffrage in Prussia, Rosa Luxemburg renewed her suggestion that the Party should contemplate political general strikes as a means of forcing this burning issue. In the summer, after the Moabit disorders,[4] Kautsky replied with sociological analyses of the behaviour of 'unorganized masses', and described the political general strike as a weapon permissible only at the decisive stage of the revolution;[5] for the present, the Party should devote all its attention to the coming 1912 elections. It was only consistent for Molkenbuhr in 1911, on behalf of the Central Committee, to reject the organization of protest meetings against German policy in Morocco: such action would allow the government to describe Social Democracy as 'anti-national' and thus to turn the lower-middle-class vote against it, as in 1906. The Magdeburg Party congress, 1910, turned down Rosa Luxemburg's suggestions on the general strike issue; the Left, afraid of the possible implications of a sharp cleavage, avoided a division. This did not prevent Kautsky from recognizing in

[1] See above, p. 100.

[2] In 1907 the Party's Berlin organization, probably more working-class in its outlook than most others, and in the whole subsequent period a main stronghold of the left, numbered amongst its members 10 per cent of definitely lower-middle-class status, half of them publicans (see above, p. 71), 75 per cent skilled workers and their wives, and a mere 15 per cent unskilled workers.

[3] See below, p. 116.

[4] See above, p. 101.

[5] In his article 'Was nun?', published in *Neue Zeit*, Kautsky, who two years before (ibid., vol. XXVII/1) had published Engels's letter of protest against the falsification of his Preface to the *Class Struggle in France* (cf. my *Marx*, etc., pp. 252 and 254), used that so-called 'political testament of Engels's as a weapon against Rosa Luxemburg, clothing the above argument in military language.

his book *Der politische Massen sterik*[1] that, since 1910, what he called the Marxist Centre had been formed; the old-standing cleavage against the Revisionists was supplemented, and soon overshadowed, by another against the Left; in view of growing social tensions the dangers threatening the Party from 'revolutionary impatience' tended to increase, while those originating from 'impatience to enter the government' decreased (the book was published six months before August 1914). In 1912 the Chemnitz Party congress, in a bitter argument against Rosa Luxemburg and the Left, approved the Second Ballot agreement with the Liberals; at the same time, the new parliamentary Party was granted (by a majority of eight votes) powers to decide in favour of special taxes to cover the cost of armaments.[2] Heine's old slogan 'Guns for the people's rights'[3] was now accepted in the more modest form of 'Guns, provided the rich pay their fair share'.

In the discussions in the Party Press, and at the Chemnitz congress, Kautsky and Haase argued, against Rosa Luxemburg and Radek, that modern capitalism was not in itself imperialist but produced tendencies that counteracted war; Haase, speaking at the congress, spoke of international trusts as one of them. Alliance with 'peaceful' groups within the bourgeoisie was to be desired; and we have already seen that, *faute de mieux*, the German Liberals and an armaments programme that weighed heavily on the rich might serve the purpose. If, as had been said, it was quite easy to distinguish aggressor from victim, it was even easier to listen to one's own Government when it asserted that it was not the aggressor; on the eve of World War I David, speaking in the Reichstag on behalf of Social Democracy, certified the peaceful intentions of the imperial government. On 28th July 1914 *Vorwärts*, the Party's principal organ, still described Austrian government policy as the main threat to peace; but at the Prussian cabinet meeting of July 30th the German Chancellor, after negotiations with the Social Democrat M.P., Südekum, was able to promise that Social Democracy would not interfere with the war effort. On July 31st the Prussian Ministry of Defence withdrew the secret orders for the arrest of the Social Democratic leaders in the event of war 'because, according to reliable information, the Social Democratic party intends to behave in the way fitting for every German'. On August 2nd, a conference of the trade unions decided to call off all outstanding wage disputes; on the 3rd the parliamentary party, by 78 votes to 14 (the remains of the 'Centre' and

[1] His main article against Rosa Luxemburg had been headed 'Between Baden and Luxemburg', the Baden Social Democrats having again voted for the budget, as, of course, they continued to do, notwithstanding the mild censure they received at the Magdeburg congress; see above, p. 87. The geographical parallel was provocative; it had no meaning as applied to the quite irrelevant Duchy of Luxemburg, but very much in relation to Rosa Luxemburg's native Poland.

[2] See above, p. 102.

[3] See above, p. 85.

the few left-wingers) decided to vote for the war credits. The Revisionists, not yet sure of their majority, had prepared for a split in the event of an adverse vote by the parliamentary party; no similar violation of Party discipline was to be feared from the fourteen. The 'Marxist Centre's' last struggle was waged, successfully, for the right of Haase, the Party Chairman, to pronounce in Parliament the parliamentary party's decision against which he had himself voted. Karl Liebknecht, who for the moment himself kept discipline in parliament,[1] described the comedy which set the stage for a greater tragedy:

'Even on that occasion the Revisionist wing was not to be allowed to represent the Party; the "radical" wing was afraid that the public might realize its defeat and annihilation. Its last ambition was to preserve the delusion for its survival after its death.'[2]

More than three years later, when the Centrists had seceded, driven to do so, as we shall see, by external pressure rather than of their own volition, the right-wing Social Democrats, at their Würzburg congress in October 1917, could honestly explain what had happened. Reporting for the parliamentary party, David, a Revisionist of old standing, said:

'Our decision of 4th August 1914 determined the whole further course of the German labour movement. This was the cross-roads at which two possible lines for its development parted. By deciding as we did, we chose a road from which there can be no return.' (*Proceedings*, p. 316.)

That decision was defined even more clearly in David's reply to the debate, in which many speakers had emphasized the importance of 4th August 1914 as a conclusion of the discussions with the left wing of Social Democracy:

'On that day those who set their expectations on an imminent catastrophe (of capitalism) could vote against the war credits; whoever looked towards such a catastrophe was bound to see its great hour approaching. . . . This would have been the consistent attitude of that trend [i.e. of the radical phraseology of pre-war Social Democracy—R.S.] but it is precisely this that was rejected by the parliamentary party. By voting for the credits the Party declared that the present State deserves to be defended.' (Ibid., p. 390.)

While the Party leaders drew the appropriate conclusions as to the merits of constitutional monarchy, coalition government with bourgeois parties, a gradual transformation of the national economy through 'organized capitalism', etc., one of the lesser-known delegates stated the truth that 'the German working class, instinctively perhaps rather than consciously, is closer to Lassalle's attitude to the State than to scholastic Marxism'.[3]

[1] But, conjointly with Rosa Luxemburg, Clara Zetkin, and Franz Mehring, published a declaration to the foreign Press.

[2] *Reden und Aufsätze*, p. 131.

[3] Hug-Rüstringen, Proceedings, p. 267.

The immediate consequences of the decision that had been taken were explained immediately after the event by the conservative Professor Delbrück:

'Let us imagine, for a moment, that instead of these mass organizations (Social Democratic Party and Trade Unions) millions of workers had faced the State as individuals; in such a case many of them would have been likely to offer passive if not active resistance to mobilization. Before 1870 the application of armed force was necessary in not a few places in any case of mobilization; even in 1813 such things happened here and there. Nothing of the kind has happened this time (1914). . . .'

Social Democracy had turned into a civilian organization of the rear for the very war to whose denunciation it had paid lip-service. But it had to survive as a separate party, and we may quote another conservative statement (from the *Preussische Jahrbücher*, April 1915, pp. 50–1) to give the reasons:

'True, it will not be possible to train Social Democracy as a parliamentary good boy. It must preserve its character as a workers' party proclaiming socialist ideals, for on the very day when it forsook these ideals a new party would arise to take up the dropped platform of Social Democracy in a more radical formulation.'

As events have shown, in the conditions of post-1918 Germany the mere continued existence of a party of social reform in the workers' interest was not sufficient to prevent the formation of a more radical workers' party; yet the mere prevention of the latter party from enlisting a majority of the working class was important enough for the German bourgeoisie to encourage concessions which gave Social Democracy another spell of life till the Great Depression changed the bourgeoisie's basic approach.[1]

The decision German Social Democracy took on 4th August 1914 was one of the most portentous in world history: in Marx's own country, his idea of a Socialist world revolution beginning with the industrial countries of Western Europe was defeated. This decision was confirmed by the behaviour of the majority of the German Social Democratic workers in the crisis following World War I, at a time when allowance could no longer be made for the suggestive power of nationalist propaganda and when the example of the Russian revolution was available; and then it inspired Lenin's observation that 'ultimate victory is assured because the Russians, Chinese and Indians, taken together, form a majority of mankind'.[2]

Yet the event had been prepared for by a long chain of decisions each of which was deeply rooted in the day-to-day life of the mass organization; only in a few cases, such as the Second Ballot Agreement of 1912, had these decisions been open to criticism within the current frame-

[1] See below, note [1] on p. 363.

[2] *Better Fewer, but Better*, in *Selected Works*, vol. IX, p. 400.

work. Twelve years before, in *What Is to be Done?*, Lenin had stated that there are two kinds of class-consciousness, and that the higher and revolutionary, as distinct from the lower and trade unionist kind,[1] was not produced by the immediate experience of the workers' class-struggle: it had to be brought to them from outside, by an organization of professional revolutionaries closely connected, but not identical, with the working class.[2] He did not recognize that the Marxism current within the Western Labour movement might belong to the lower type of class-consciousness; certainly even the extreme left of that movement rejected his conclusions. Lenin tried to explain the difficulty by his concept of a workers' aristocracy corrupted by a share in imperialist surplus profits, discussed in the last chapter; this theory was clearly incapable of explaining the failure of the whole German, and indeed Western, labour movement to come up to the Bolsheviks' expectations.

A long time was to pass before the real importance of the decision of pre-1914 Social Democracy was realized. Some people believed, during the first period of the war, that they were actually fighting Tsarism, the traditional backbone of European reaction; others, at least in 1918, recognized that the war policy of German Social Democracy had been mistaken even from the German national point of view; only a few dared to say that they had been right on 4th August 1914 because even to err with the leaders of one's nation was better than splitting its unity. The left-wingers came to believe that, in pre-1914 days, they had committed a big tactical mistake which, however, could be corrected: the division between the Bolsheviks and the Mensheviks, which in Russia had enabled the former to triumph, should have been transferred to Germany. They overlooked the fact, however, that their own pre-1914 record was opposed to that of the Bolshevists not only in tactics but even in principles; the unity whose preservation was *ex post facto* deplored had been, in Russian terms, the unity between the different trends of Menshevism. (In Russia too there had been Menshevist internationalists.)

(c) *Other Labour Organizations in Germany*

Whatever contribution earlier discussions on co-operation had made to clarifying fundamental attitudes,[3] no group in the Party would dispute the possibility of partial improvements in working-class conditions when the Party Congress of 1910 found time to discuss the work of Consumers' Co-operatives. Nor was Germany a fertile soil for the growth of utopias of 'co-operative socialism'. The view that co-operatives would be an element of the society to come was not explicitly

[1] Lenin included in the term such parliamentary reform politics as are implied in the needs of the sectional struggle. Ibid., vol. II, pp. 65 and 81–2.

[2] See my *Marx*, etc., pp. 230–1.

[3] See above, pp. 15 and 40–1.

rejected, as in 1899; this might be interpreted as toleration, if not as endorsement, of a basic Revisionist tenet. Positive approval, however, was given to co-operatives only for reasons already familiar; they offered their active members opportunities to gain administrative experience, and provided emergency funds which might be useful in times of labour conflict.[1] Their undertakings, in agreement with the trade unions, might provide model working conditions, and their influence could be exercised to enforce such conditions on the private enterprises supplying them with goods; this was the very suggestion which the Party Congress of 1892 had rejected as utopian.[2] Actual production by the co-operatives of the goods they sold was recommended, and the egotistic attitude of members who preferred high dividends to investments rebuked.

The only one of these points that could be verified by the day-to-day activities of the labour movement was the co-operatives' influence upon labour conditions. The contradiction between the trade unionists' demand for model conditions of labour and the co-operators' demand for high dividends had been noticed years before. The Fourth Congress of Consumers' Co-operatives had rejected 'utopian' demands for working conditions more favourable than in competing private enterprises; the reporter on these decisions in the Party's leading periodical[3] had said that 'in many cases the worker is not the most pleasant of employers'. This statement might refute the concept of co-operation as a nucleus of reform socialism as well as an auxiliary of trade unionism.

More interesting from our point of view were the developments in the Christian labour movement parallel with Free Trade Unionism, where the effect of imperialist developments could be felt without the consolidating influence of Marxist ideology. In the political field, the left tendency within the Centre party, that counterpart to the development of Christian Trade Unionism, became conspicuous: on the eve of the 1906 elections Bachem proclaimed that the party must 'leave the turret',[4] i.e., its sectarian limitations. Erzberger dared cautiously to attack the brutal and corrupt Imperial colonial administration.[5] Bülow, by inflicting a serious electoral defeat on the Party, gave it a definitive lesson on the inadvisibility of criticizing whatever could be represented to chauvinist Germans as the national cause and of disputing the leader-

[1] See above, p. 41.

[2] Proceedings of the 1910 Party Congress, pp. 456, 458, 463.

[1] Fleissner, in *Neue Zeit*, vol. XXV/2, esp. p. 539.

[4] In German political jargon the 'Centre turret' denoted the impossibility of making serious inroads into the strongholds of the denominational minority, which was supported by the confessional, and usually indicated a respectful acknowledgement by the opponents of the Centre. Bachem, of course, used the term in the opposite sense; he wanted his party to be transformed into a Christian Democratic one, to use modern terms, which could manage without the help of the confessional.

[5] See above, p. 100.

ship established in the Prusso-German empire; presumably the Centre's ecclesiastical backers were not too angry at such a taming of ambitious politicians. The Christian Trade Unionists had already submitted.

Within the limits of ecclesiastical discipline, the Fulda Pastoral[1] could be questioned only as to its 'interpretation'; the defenders of Christian Trade Unionism had to explain that the danger against which it warned was purely a hypothetical one, i.e. the Union neutral towards Socialism as well as Christianity would never arise.[2] Thus the bishops were granted their decisive point (only, it is true, *qua* right-wing politicians, not *qua* theologians; from the latter point of view the interdenominational unions were no better than really neutral ones would have been). At the Breslau congress of 1906, when Bülow's campaign against all opponents of colonial expansion and against anyone who might collaborate with Social Democracy was already in full swing, even such Trade Union leaders as Giesberts tried to prove that interdenominational Christianity was a synonym not only of anti-Socialism but also of German nationalism.[3] The need for unity between Protestant and Catholic workers, which was opposed by Savigny's 'Catholic Unions', was explained by the unity of the opponents of the religious *and patriotic* ideals which inspired the Christian Trade Unions (that is, of Social Democracy), with the rider that, within the framework of the fatherland as thus defined, the lower classes must defend their rights.

After a decade of dispute, Pius X's encyclical of 24th September 1912, *Singulari quadam*, decided the issue for half a dozen years. The supporters of the interdenominational Christian Trade Unions had to be satisfied with a '*tolerari posse*', that is, with the absence of a condemnation, while papal approval was restricted to the purely Catholic Workers' Associations. This was not a very great achievement from the standpoint of those who believed that their Church had a message for workers in the trade union field; they were left in charge of such of the Catholic workers as were not devout enough, or indifferent enough to their worldly needs, to follow the path suggested to them by their supreme spiritual authority, but were still reluctant to sin against its explicit commands. The Catholic worker, however, got his spiritual guidance not from a Latin encyclical but from its interpretation by the priest in the confessional, whose origins were often not very dissimilar to his own.

The living forces of German Catholicism gathered behind the München-Gladbach Centre and the Christian Trade Unions. These lost their specific Catholic appeal, namely the claim that more than the individual conscience stood behind their suggestions, just as, by the very fact of being interdenominational, they had lost that specific handicap of the Catholic Workers' Association, the president nominated by the local

[1] See above, p. 38; Erdmann, op. cit., pp. 467 ff.
[2] See above, p. 37.
[3] Erdmann, op. cit., pp. 499 ff.

Bishop. Meeting their fellow Trade Unionists on equal terms, without the conscience that they were backed by their Church's doctrine, they might be induced to search for foundations for sectional organization independent of any ecclesiastical teaching. After World War I, the 1918 revolution, and the rise of comprehensive Trade Unionist organization, the Church's attitude changed, and the Trade Departments of the Catholic Workers' Associations joined the Christian Trade Unions.

The organizational dispute occasionally rose to the proportions of an intra-ecclesiastical scandal, but it did not prevent the numerical increase of the Christian Trade Unions. In 1907 they had 300,000 members, and the Trade Departments (Berlin Centre) some 160,000.[1] In a comparison of these numbers it should be remembered that, for good reasons,[2] the Trade Departments did not everywhere have to manage without the favour of employers. The Christian Trade Unions, on the other side, contained not only Catholic supporters of the Centre Party but also mainly black-coated workers whose political sympathies were likely to lie with the Conservatives or National Liberals, and, at least in the overwhelmingly Catholic textile industries of the West, even some rationalist-minded workers with Socialist sympathies, who had no alternative trade unionist organization. At that time, the industrial vote of the Centre Party numbered about half a million; the percentage of the politically Catholic workers who belonged to one kind of Catholic industrial organization or another seems to compare not unfavourably with the 60 per cent of the Socialist vote then organized in Free Trade Unions, especially if the unquestionably pro-Trade-Unionist attitude of the Socialist party, and the greater attractive power of an organization six times as large, are taken into account. The climax, with 350,000 members of the Christian Trade Unions, was reached as early as 1911 (that is, before the clarification of the Church's attitude); it was followed by a drop to 218,000 in 1914. Between 1907 and 1914 the membership of the Free Trade Unions increased from 1·9 to three millions; so it is obvious that, to some extend, Christian Trade Unionism actually worked as a 'harbinger of Social Democracy'.[3] Part at least of the rank and file, after having taken the first steps in sectional organization in their familiar surroundings, turned to the more efficient body.

(*d*) *The Pre-War Crisis of the Austrian Labour Movement*

The development of the Austrian labour movement between the Russian revolution of 1905 and the beginning of World War I differs

[1] The total membership of Catholic Workers' Associations rose from only 80,000 as late as 1895 to 350,000 ten years later; so it was obviously stimulated by the development of Christian Trade Unionism, quite apart from the Trade Departments which were regarded as a Trade Union surrogate.

[2] See above, p. 40.

[3] See above, p. 39.

from that of its German counterpart in two important respects. Firstly, the position in the multi-national empire prevented its having to face a united front of the vested interests and even allowed for occasional parallelism between its own interests and those of part of the bureaucracy and the Court;[1] secondly, because of the much larger freedom of action it thus enjoyed, there was no cleavage, as there was in Germany, between the advocates and the opponents of action for the enforcement of democratic reforms. Instead, there were cleavages within the labour movement, following the lines of national cleavage in Austrian political life.

In general, it might be said that the Social Democrat who sided with his bourgeois co-nationals even against his fellow Social Democrats of other nationalities showed in so doing the same attitude as a German Revisionist who supported German imperialist expansion. But the issue was complicated by the fact that the Empire, and Austrian Social Democracy, was under the predominant influence of the Austro-Germans. A Czech Social Democrat who rejected Czech nationalism and preserved unity with his Austro-German comrades might thereby be supporting the centralism of the Hapsburg monarchy; indeed, during the War the Czech 'Centralist'[2] group which took up this attitude supported the war-effort of the dying Empire. A Czech Social Democrat who sided with his national middle class and, in general, with the radical lower middle classes who favoured radical measures to enforce national self-government betrayed by so doing the internationalist principles of Social Democracy and was likely to disrupt the unity of working-class action in the Empire; but, as regards the burning issues raised by the crisis of the Empire, he was more likely to favour revolutionary solutions. An Austro-German Social Democrat was bound to support centralism within the Party and to oppose separate action by its national sections; only small verbal nuances would indicate whether he did so because he was a nationalist German who wished to preserve his nation's position of leadership—had he been a chauvinist who supported direct oppression of the Slavs he would not have joined Social Democracy—making whatever use he could of internationalist terminology in order to defend his people's claim to a leading part in the community of nations, or, alternatively, because he aimed at real equality between the members of the Union that was bound to replace the Empire, and opposed the

[1] See above, p. 84.

[2] The name is derived, not from support of centralism within the Hapsburg monarchy—every Czech Social Democrat, and, in theory at least, every Austro-Hungarian Social Democrat, was a federalist on issues of constitutional reform—but from the attitude taken towards the internal structure of the Labour movement. Correspondingly, a Czech 'Separatist' Social Democrat was a supporter of separate Party and Trade Union centres for the Czech workers, but not necessarily of the secession of the Czech lands from the future federation.

Czech Separatist[1] Social Democrat's nationalism because it disrupted working-class unity.

The answer of Social Democracy to the most burning issue of the Austrian Empire was defined in the nationalities programme adopted by its Brno Congress in 1898.[2] Pursuing the line of compromise achieved by the moderate Liberals of the diverse Austrian nationalities at the end of the abortive 1848 revolution,[3] and meanwhile abandoned by the bourgeois parties in favour of straightforward nationalism, the Brno programme demanded the transformation of Austria into a 'democratic federation of nationalities', each administering autonomously the territory it predominantly inhabited, with safeguards for the national minorities therein. There was a definite tendency to restrict national self-government to cultural matters, and to preserve centralism in all the basic economic issues; but only later was the Brno programme interpreted as implying mere *personal* cultural autonomy for the members of the diverse nationalities (in a sense similar to the autonomy granted to religious sects) and denying them the government of autonomous territories of their own.

The Russian revolution of 1905 had an enormous influence on the Austrian labour movement, which was used to mass action on the suffrage issue. It also increased the cleavages within the ruling camp; the Hungarian gentry turned from the Dualist compromise of 1867 towards a demand for a mere personal union, destroying the unity of the army—the very institution in which Francis Joseph was most interested. When the question of equal manhood suffrage in Austria arose, resistance was restricted to the big estate owners, the Austro-German Nationalists and 'Liberals' (as we know,[4] another name for Big Business), and their Polish allies who had long since subordinated Slav solidarity to their contempt for Ukrainians and Czechs, plus the supporters of all these groups within the higher bureaucracy. All resistance rallied to the House of Peers, while all the active pressure needed to overcome that resistance came from Social Democracy. The Court, the Government, and the Catholics readily gave way to what they had no reason to oppose, and the outcome was a constitutional change which the labour movement could ascribe to its pressure, exercised outside Parliament. It was from precisely this type of circumstances that Austrian Marxism, as a definite trend within the international labour movement, arose.[5]

In September 1905 the Social Democratic Party began its mass campaign for equal manhood suffrage. Shortly afterwards, passive resistance

[1] f.n. [2] on previous p.

[2] Full text in Bauer's *Nationalitätenfrage*, pp. 527–8; see also my *Federalism*, etc., pp. 210–11.

[3] Ibid., pp. 172 ff.

[4] See above, pp. 9–10 and 48.

[5] See also below, p. 371.

by the Czech Nationalists began on the North Bohemian railways, behind the back of the Social Democratic Trade Unions, and at first with purely economic demands. On October 31st, during the meeting of the Social Democratic Party congress, news arrived of the Tsar's concessions to the Revolution, and on the same evening organized street demonstrations began. Within a few days the whole country was involved, and there were even barricades in Prague. On November 3rd the railwaymen's passive resistance, which had spread throughout Bohemia-Moravia, was headed by the Trade Union which, at the same time, raised the demand for equal manhood suffrage; on the next day the demand was accepted 'in principle' by the Government. Martial law was proclaimed in Prague and Kladno on November 6th, and a few days later all the railways 'worked to rule'. On November 12th the economic as well as the political demands were accepted.

So far as mass-pressure was concerned, the Government had capitulated to the threat of a Czech national revolution rather than to the demonstrations organized by Social Democracy, which was even looked upon as a moderating factor.[1] Social Democracy, however, could not control the mass movement except by guiding it along the channels of short-term strikes and well-organized demonstrations, while the Government could not secure the passage of the bill through the Upper House before a general strike was threatened by its Social Democrat allies.

The triumph was short-lived. The rise of a Catholic mass party which as well as Social Democracy, was likely to benefit from manhood suffrage,[2] had contributed to the Court's willingness to tolerate the enforcement of the reform against the body of the vested interests; when, at the 1911 elections, the Catholics were definitely reduced to the second place, imperial interest in democratic parliamentarism as an agency of imperial unity was reduced. Count Stürck, who in 1906 had led the opposition in the Upper House to suffrage reform, became Prime Minister, and early in 1914 he succeeded in provoking the Czech nationalists into parliamentary obstruction, thus getting an opportunity to adjourn Parliament *sine die* and to govern under the 'emergency article' of the Constitution.

On the other side, it was no longer a united Social Democratic Party which triumphed at the polls in 1911; its centralized organization comprised only the Austro-Germans and the 'Centralist' minority of the Czechs; the 'Separatist' majority split not only the political party but

[1] Cf. the proceedings of the Cabinet meeting of 23rd November, reported by Bruegel, op. cit., vol. IV, pp. 367 ff. Troop reinforcements were sent to Bohemia, where the movement was described as all-national; in the other Czech provinces it was restricted to the working class. It was noted that the (Vienna) Central Committee of Social Democracy could influence only the internationalist section of the Czech labour movement, while the nationalist groups were completely out of control.

[2] See above, p. 47.

even the Trade Unions in 1908 after its demand for reorganization of the T.U.C. as a federation of national units had been rejected. Negotiations for a compromise were demanded by the International, but failed in 1910–11; when the majority of the Czech Social Democratic organization sided with the autonomous Czech Trade Unions, the Centralist minority seceded in order to preserve international unity. In the 1911 elections the two Czech Social Democratic factions were in open opposition to each other; Polish and Italian Social Democrats acted as—not even moderate—members of their respective national groups, linked with their 'fellow Social Democrats' of other nationalities by very loose bonds. On Marxist principles there was little to be said in favour of unity with a group led by Pilsudski, and even on the Czech issue right, within the concepts of working-class unity, was formally on the Centralists' side; the Separatists even rejected compromise proposals for granting national autonomy for the Unions' educational activities, while preserving strict centralism in the field of economic struggles.[1] But as close inter-connection between trade unionist and political organization was taken for granted all over Central Europe, there was little point in reproaching the Czech Separatists for undermining Trade Union unity unless the Party which uttered such reproaches worked with a programme likely to satisfy reasonable Czech demands for national emancipation, including a full share in the control of industry and in the skilled jobs. But Austro-German leaders such as Bauer reduced the Slavs' claim to mere educational facilities in the mother tongue.

[1] Cf. Bauer, op. cit., p. 552.

CHAPTER FIVE

WAR AND REVOLUTION

(a) *The War Crisis of German Social Democracy*

HOWEVER surprising may have been the marriage between the Prussian Government and the majority section of German Social Democracy,[1] it was easily consummated. The Trade Unions, after calling off all wage agitations, ceased to pay most of their friendly society benefits except for unemployment and personal emergencies, to which were added benefits for the families of mobilized men. Among the benefits suspended were those for travelling, change of residence, sickness, and in three-quarters of the Unions, for being black-listed.[2] It was evidently taken for granted that the War was bound to mean a setback for the labour movement; Trade Union membership, 2½ million on the eve of hostilities, dropped to one million in 1916; and the lesser Unions, with smaller funds and exposed to the power of attraction of the big war industries, would soon have gone bankrupt had they not been protected by a special emergency rule forbidding transfer of membership to other Unions belonging to the T.U.C.[3] Few functions were left to the unions, and none that distinguished the Free Unions from their Christian and Liberal competitors; after 4th August 1914 there was no ideological obstacle on either side to collaboration. Joint meetings in February 1915 agreed on the organization of the employment exchanges and in the following August on a common front against the Yellow

[1] See above, p. 115. The Trade Unions, though in the forefront of the trend within Social Democracy that supported the war effort, expected to be dissolved on the outbreak of war and had made some preparations to protect their funds. There was welcome disappointment on both sides when, at the first meeting with the War Ministry, the T.U.C. leaders, who had expected 'difficulties' with the Government, were told: 'Well, if you cause no difficulties to us . . .!' (Umbreit, op. cit., p. 158).

[2] The obvious assumption was that, in the atmosphere of wartime unity, a black-isted man would find a job—unless his behaviour in the Party disputes on war policy, which in an active fighter might not coincide with that of the Trade Union leaders, caused additional suspicion.

[3] Umbreit, op. cit., p. 160.

Unions, for whose promotion the biggest employers found good opportunities under wartime conditions. The most important of these agreements was that of 12th December 1916, which provided for joint support for the Law for Industrial Mobilization. 'United by a common determination to defend the Fatherland to the last', and expressing their solidarity with the Government after the German peace offer had been rejected by the Allies, the Unions agreed to joint proposals for the lists of workers' representatives on the various committees provided for by the Law.[1] They had good reason to be satisfied; after having prevented for more than two years what some of their members would have deemed proper in the event of war, they were now given a positive part to play in the organization of the war economy. The Employers' Associations, which as late as 1915 had rejected the Trade Unions' offer to set up joint committees for the settlement of disputes,[2] now had to meet them within a legally prescribed framework. From this moment the fall in union membership came to an end; the increasing mobilization of new workers for industry, women especially,[3] and the revival of strike activities, however much the unions opposed them, resulted in an increase of membership to 1½ millions on the eve of the revolution.

No similar achievements, from the standpoint of the Social Democratic majority, could be expected in the political field, so long as there was any chance of a German victory. The demand for a reform of the Prussian suffrage[4] was put forward with the claim that 4th August 1914 had proved the patriotic unity of the German people: to this the Junkers, if sufficiently honest, might have replied that it had proved the readiness of those whose political rights were restricted to support Prussia as she was. Under the impact of the Russian revolutions of 1917, Emperor and Government suggested concessions; Ludendorff's High Command, and the Junker majority in the Prussian Diet, knew quite well, however, that if the war was won their rule would be safe, even without concessions, and if it was lost, minor constitutional niceties would not matter.

Actual political trouble arose for Social Democracy in defending its attitude before its own members. The first protests had been weak, and restricted to the extreme Left;[5] the bulk of the minority of August 4th (the 'Marxist Centre') even indulged in theoretical justifications of what had happened. Characteristic of this attitude was Kautsky's pamphlet *Die Internationalität und der Krieg*.

After the 'Marxist Centre' had for so long based its attitude towards

[1] Umbreit, op. cit., p. 167.

[2] Ibid., p. 169.

[3] During the war the percentage of women amongst the reduced membership of the unions increased from 9 to 25.

[4] See above, p. 114.

[5] See note 1 on p. 116.

war on the assertion that in modern warfare a distinction between aggressor and victim was easy to make,[1] Kautsky now found that in this particular war, which was fought under the very conditions anticipated in all the pre-war Socialist discussions, such a distinction failed; accordingly, every Socialist in every country was entitled to protect his own fatherland against hostile invasion. True, such a policy set the workers of the different countries in opposition to each other, and 'it is difficult to distinguish the activities of internationalist from those of chauvinist patriotism';[2] but this simply implied that the International was incapable of preventing a split among the proletarians: 'It is essentially an instrument of peace, *not an effective instrument in war*'.[3] Struggle for peace, that is, support of all the groups within one's own country which were trying to bring the war to a speedy end by compromise, class struggle in peacetime—these were Kautsky's conclusions. The labour movement was supposed to look after its immediate group-interests which, in peace-time, were described as 'class struggle' and in war-time in terms of the pacifist desire for a quick end by compromise. There was not the slightest idea of an independent policy for labour in those very situations which provided the opportunity for revolutionary change, as the International had proclaimed[4] and Kautsky himself in his *Way to Power*, published five years yearlier,[5] had at least indicated. Kautsky's present position differed from that of the right wing of his party only in the expectation that after the war, as distinct from the dreams of the Greater German Empire in whose administration nationalist Socialists would be admitted to share as junior partners by the Prussian High Command, the traditional plurality of European Great Powers would still exist; German labour should look forward to coexisting in post-war Europe with other national labour parties.

The true measure of German Social Democracy is seen in the fact that this was the very carefully considered approach of a critic of the Party majority, even more than in the outbreaks of war hysteria which German and other Social Democrats shared with other chauvinists. Opposition to the war on principle was restricted to Rosa Luxemburg's group; from December 14th onwards its only M.P., Karl Liebknecht, voted against the war credits, and in 1915 it started to issue publications —Rosa Luxemburg's *Junius* pamphlet, and the *Internationale*, whose title served to describe the group. Much later, when the merits of the case ought to have been clear from the Socialist as well as from the national point of view, the Independent Social Democrats found in

[1] See above, p. 113.
[2] Op. cit., p. 34.
[3] Op. cit., p. 38.
[4] See above, p. 113.
[5] Page 105 in the third edition of 1920.

Liebknecht's having started an anti-war propaganda as early as 1914 a good illustration of Communist 'putschism'.[1]

The Party Centre regarded its opposition to the war as dependent on military events. As late as 17th May 1915, at a meeting of the parliamentary party, Haase described Hoch's suggestion of a parliamentary interpellation on the peace issue as ridiculous, in view of the Italian declaration of war.[2] But at that time the Russian front in Poland was already being broken. On 9th June 1915 some hundreds of active Party workers, belonging to the Centre, appealed to the Central Committee and the parliamentary Party to end the policy of August 4th, in view of the fact that the war had ceased to be a defensive one. Immediately afterwards, a joint article was published, as a platform, by Kautsky, Haase, and Bernstein, the last of whom showed the honesty of his pacifism by not sharing in the triumph of his theoretical child, Revisionism. Once more, the whole of the criticism was directed against 'annexationist war aims'; and the attitude of the Social Democratic majority was shown by its official disavowal of an analogous statement by Haase, in December 1915. This, at last, was too much for the opposition's patience: when the next vote on war credits was taken, on December 29th, twenty of the forty-three M.P.s who at that time already opposed them within the Parliamentary Party crossed the floor against the Government. Their argument, again, centred on Germany's military security and her favourable position which laid on her the onus of initiating peace negotiations. Nearly a year later, at the Kienthal conference of the Socialist left-wingers, Ledebour, the representative of what was to become the Independent Socialist Party of Germany, denied that there was a general obligation on Socialists to refuse war credits to an imperialist government independently of the military situation. Evidently no use of military defeat as an opportunity to overthrow the Government was considered.

Such an approach provided no justification for definitely splitting the Party; it was natural that the Centre should reject all the suggestions for building up an organization, contesting by-elections, and so on, made by Rosa Luxemburg's group (soon to be called the Spartacus group from the name of their underground publication). The right-wing majority of the Social Democrats found toleration of the Centre within the Party incompatible with its own good relations with the High Command; gradually, the split was enforced against the will of the Centre. On 24th March 1916 it had to secede from the Parliamentary Party, which had denied it the right to address the Reichstag; in the autumn repressive measures were taken within the Party organization itself. In October 1916 his Prussian Majesty's G.O.C. Berlin closed down the Berlin *Vorwärts*—the Party's central organ, though controlled by the Berlin

[1] Cf. Prager, op. cit., pp. 42 and 76.

[2] Scheidemann, *Memoiren* (German edition), vol. I, p. 345

organization—which was in sympathy with the Centrist group, and transferred it to the right-wing Central Committee. Even now, the Centre's reaction was restricted to a suggestion to stop subscribing to the paper; but the effect of the scandal was strong enough to cause many Berlin workers to follow Spartacus's slogan, that is, to cease their contributions to the Party funds. On 7th January 1917 a conference of representatives of all the left-wing groups (113 of the Centrist *Arbeitsgemeinschaft*, 42 of *Spartacus* and the allied groups) was called 'to discuss the tactics of the opposition M.P.s and the measures necessary to defend the Party's constitution and the members' ownership of their newspapers'.[1] Meanwhile a new political issue had arisen through the enactment of the Law on Industrial Mobilization, which was supported by the Majority Socialists though it involved the abolition of the right to strike; it was unanimously opposed by all those who were represented at the conference. The fundamental issues involved in Spartacus's different approach to the war were regarded as untopical by the Centrists until the war ended, because they could not be discussed under conditions of martial law.[2] Suggestions for forming a new party, or even ceasing to pay contributions to the old one, were rejected; the motion accepted by the Centrist majority of the Conference looked to no more than an organization of the opposition faction, in order to prepare for the struggle to regain control of the Party by constitutional means when the war had ended. For the right-wingers, however, this was reason enough to expel the opposition as early as January 16th; three more months passed before the opposition drew the obvious conclusions.

March 12th–14th (New Style) saw the fall of Tsarism, by accepted Socialist tenets the stronghold of European reaction, and, in any case, the main pretext used by the Majority Social Democrats for their support of the German war effort. Their attitude to the war, of course, did not change; but *Vorwärts* now appealed to the Hohenzollern monarchy to prevent revolutionary agitation by constitutional reforms, and Wilhelm II replied with vague promises in his Easter message. The Centrists would not drop republicanism, but the *Mitteilungsblatt* of

[1] The Proceedings of this conference and of the Foundation Congress of the Independent Social Democratic Party have been published, by Emil Eichhorn, on the basis of his personal notes. Minor mistakes in detail are not excluded, but there has been no protest against the presentation. Eichhorn himself was a left-wing Independent who later joined the C.P.

[2] Merkel-Solingen, ibid., p. 105. Even the Spartacus delegates voted for the Centrists' manifesto on the peace issue, moved by Kurt Eisner, which included criticism of 'unsuitable methods' applied in the Imperial Government's 'peace move', and demanded 'a European, democratic and Socialist propaganda for peace'. Rosa Luxemburg's friends (Ernst Meyer was their main speaker at the Conference) may have voted for such a resolution for mere tactical reasons (cf. Heckert's speech at the Foundation Congress, mentioned below); even this would prove that the Left wing regarded any but a purely pacifist propaganda as hopeless in the given conditions.

their Berlin organization warned the German workers against 'schematic transfer of the revolutionary methods of one country to the quite different conditions of another'. In Germany, the effect of the Russian events had already been felt in the parliamentary discussions on the details of the reform announced in Wilhelm's Easter message. April 6th saw the opening of the National Conference of the Opposition, which was to become the Foundation Congress of the Independent Socialist Party; the Spartacus group took part 'in order to get a protecting roof over our heads'. But the 'protecting roof', for the time being, counted no more than fifty to sixty thousand members; though it must be remembered that the Majority Socialist Party had no more than 230,000 in 1917.[1] The Russian Bolsheviks, whose tactics were anathema to Rosa Luxemburg,[2] would not have hesitated to make a start on even a much smaller basis, especially under conditions where the prestige of the heroes of the anti-war struggle, Liebknecht and Luxemburg, was on the side of the extreme Left.

The speeches of the Centrist leaders at the Foundation Congress moved on the lines already laid down. Discussions on principle were to be regretted because they might split working-class unity yet further; even the description of the new body as an Independent Socialist *Party*, instead of a mere 'Opposition of the Social Democratic Party', was accepted against the advice of the Centrist leaders.[3] Ledebour emphasized the importance of *democratic* Socialism; mass-action could not be initiated by the leaders; the masses, when they arose spontaneously, would act of themselves, and the leaders should follow and defend them.[4] This statement glorified in advance all the tragic weakness of the German revolution to come, but Rosa Luxemburg herself had supplied its theoretical foundations; her pupils could distinguish their attitude from that of the Centre only by theoretical arguments about the background of the war.[5] Kautsky explained imperialism by the desire of capitalists for extra profits, but this was not implied in the very nature of capitalism; capitalists could be prevented by political pressure from such disastrous attempts. Heckert, speaking for Spartacus, answered: 'The Centre wants peace, only because war is no beanfeast. The Centre represents the bourgeous pacifism, the weariness of the masses.' Afterwards

[1] Its membership declined from 433,000 in March 1916 to 234,000 a year later, when the split was just coming; in the Greater Berlin region alone, with central Germany, parts of Saxony, and the Ruhr a main stronghold of the Opposition, 70,000 members were lost.

[2] See above, pp. 106–7.

[3] The influence of the Spartacus group was also felt in the organizational decisions of the Congress, which left to the lower organizations of the new party a wide degree of autonomy, evidently because of the experience of centralism in the old party; and even the right to form groups within the party. Centrists were left in control of the whole Central Committee; possibly this was for external reasons.

[4] Proceedings, p. 52.

[5] Ibid., p. 72.

the whole Congress voted for Kautsky's manifesto, which expressed sympathy with the Russian March resolution and with the Zimmerwald anti-war wing of the International, and called for Democracy, Peace by Negotiation, Disarmament, and International Arbitration. The Foundation Congress of the Party of the German left wing, in this most decisive hour of German history, closed with exhortations not to be discouraged if the young Party should meet with defeat at the post-war general elections.

(*b*) *The Russian and Central European Revolutions*

April 1917 brought not only the split in the organization of German Social Democracy, but also the first political general strikes. In Berlin 125,000 ammunition workers, and in Leipzig and Brunswick nearly all the workers, came out in protest against a reduction in the bread ration, against the war and martial law. In the summer occurred the first major mutiny in the Navy; when, on 9th October 1917, the Chancellor tried to use it as a means of attack on the Independent Socialist Party, that Party demanded clemency and objected to the terrorist verdicts of courts-martial, but did not fail to protest its innocence. Whatever the fundamental difference was between German and Russian conditions, it showed itself in the fact that German conditions had failed to produce that organized and resolute leadership whose existence might on more than one occasion during the next six years have made all the difference between victory and defeat.

Before following the course of events in Germany, we must return to the Dual Monarchy. Its labour movement was spared the dramatic turns and crises of its sister German party, if only for the reason that, when the war approached, bureaucratic-military dictatorship had replaced a parliament unlikely to provide unanimous support for a war against a coalition some of whose members enjoyed sympathies amongst some of the nations making up the Empire.[1] But the trends which dominated German Social Democracy were also predominant in the leadership of at least the Austro-German, Polish, and Czech-'Centralist'

[1] In the initial stage of the war, those who still regarded Tsarism as the main threat to European Socialism had some reason for supporting the Austrian war effort; an openly defeatist attitude was adopted by large numbers of the Ukrainians and the Czechs, culminating in the open desertion of the Prague regiment during the battle in the Carpathians, and, of course, by the Serbs, whose revolt against the Hapsburg empire stood at the cradle of the war. From the battle of Gorlice on 2nd May 1915, which removed any danger of a Russian invasion, to the last battle on the Isonzo in October 1917, which removed the Italian threat strongly resented by the Southern Slavs, especially the Croats, support of the war effort for reasons other than inertia collapsed among all the nationalities with the exception of the right wing of the Germans, Magyars and Poles; among the two last-mentioned the larger part of the soldiers might be influenced by the Right Wing. At the time of the Bolshevist revolution in Russia practically the whole body of the Czechs, Ukrainians, Rumanians, and Southern Slavs (the Slovenes excepted) were very near rebellion.

sections of Austrian Social Democracy. The German Party's decision of 4th August 1914 was greeted in the central organ of Austrian Social Democracy by an editorial, 'The Day of the German Nation'. On May Day 1915 the Prague Party organ published an editorial whose text, for simplicity's sake, had been supplied by the police.[1] For the political outcome it mattered little whether the social-patriotic utterances originated from honest German nationalism, as in the former case, or from fear lest refusal to accept the productions of such strange contributors might endanger the survival of the Party press, as in the second. At the two Party conferences in May 1915 and March 1916 overwhelming majorities voted against an opposition group, led by Friedrich Adler (Viktor Adler's son), corresponding to the official German Opposition (the later Independent Socialists): it demanded that the Party should protest against *annexationist* war aims and the German Majority Socialists' support of them. The Party leaders based themselves mainly on the argument that the Austrian Party ought to avoid the German split and thus preserve its unity; but this argument would have been irrelevant had not the German majority enjoyed strong support among them. As Friedrich Adler was to point out, the main differentiation among the leaders was that between Great Austrian defenders of the Hapsburg empire pure and simple like Renner, and German nationalists like Leuthner and Pernerstorfer who remembered their political origins,[2] with Viktor Adler and a majority of the leaders attempting to combine these attitudes. At the March conference in 1916 the Party majority rallied on a platform for the post-war reconstruction of the Hapsburg monarchy; autonomous national districts should combine in unions of each nationality for autonomy in *cultural* matters[3] within the Empire. The extension of even such moderate reforms to the Hungarian half of the Dual Monarchy was not mentioned, since within the framework of the existing constitution it was clearly impossible. The opposition maintained a policy of 'strict neutrality' towards the Austrian 'constitutional problems'; it neither wished to support the national revolutions against the multi-national State, nor to defend that State against them. It wanted Social Democracy to oppose the war strongly;[4] it obviously thought too little of the labour movement's chances to bother about anything except general propaganda for the continuation of the class struggle in a framework which would not be of its making.

The inherent weakness of the left-wing opposition was shown by the fact that it found its most notable expression in the action of an individual, and though intended as a demonstration on behalf of the

[1] The incident was mentioned by Friedrich Adler, at his trial, as an instance of the baseness of the censorship as well as of the weakness of official Social Democracy.

[2] See above, p. 84.

[3] See above, p. 123.

[4] Otto Bauer, *The Austrian Revolution*, English edition, p. 29.

revolutionary class struggle and so accepted by broad masses of the Austrian workers, this action was conditioned by a conflict within the Austrian ruling class. The Austrian Prime Minister, Stürck, whose dictatorship[1] rested on Hungarian support, had betrayed Austrian economic interests in the negotiations for the renewal of the Austro-Hungarian agreements and had resisted the calling of Parliament which, for fear of excessive concessions to Hungary, the Austrian political parties—above all the Social Democrats—and even the aristocratic leaders of the Upper House were demanding. Adler killed Stürck after the latter had prohibited any mention of the constitutional problems in the Press and even forbidden a meeting called by the Professors of Public Law at Vienna University (not Left-Wingers). The immediate impression was strong: the meeting of the parliamentary leaders, which Stürck had forbidden to discuss constitutional issues, demanded the recall of Parliament. Francis Joseph, who in his long life had accumulated enough experience of the chances of resisting the inevitable, in its last month drew the conclusions by nominating as Stürck's successor Körber, one of the leaders of the liberal wing of the bureaucracy. Francis Joseph's own successor, Karl, attempted to restore the dictatorship under Count Clam-Martinitz, a representative of the latifundia-owners and the Conversative wing of the bureaucracy. He was supported by the Austro-German nationalists and the Catholics, who followed their aristocratic leaders and did not wish to lag behind anyone else in showing their German nationalism; constitutional reforms intended to secure German hegemony in Austria were to be introduced by imperial decree before Parliament should be allowed to meet.

But the Russian revolution of March 1917, while offering the Empire some hopes of a negotiated peace, set the masses of its nationalities into motion. The Social Democratic leaders, invited to use their international connexions in the interest of the Empire, answered that this was impossible so long as the idea of an anti-Slav *coup d'état* and non-parliamentary government continued in being. Count Czernin, Karl's Foreign Minister, warned his master that a negotiated peace was the only alternative to revolutionary movements in Germany as well as in Austria during the coming winter.[2] Parliament was recalled and used to the full as a platform for denouncing Stürck's terrorist régime as well as for proclaiming the non-German peoples' demands for self-government. The existing constitution of the Dual Monarchy was openly denounced, at least by the Czech left-wingers; but none of the Slav declarations denied the possibility of continuing the multi-national State as a democratic federation.[3] Even the Czech Separatists'[4] declara-

[1] See above, p. 124.
[2] Cf. his book *Im Weltkrieg*, Berlin, 1919, pp. 200–1.
[3] Cf. my *Federalism*, etc., pp. 236–7.
[4] See note [2] above, p. 122.

tion at the International Socialist Peace Conference in Stockholm foresaw the right to full national self-determination, including the right to separation, as demanded by them resulting in a free federation of national States of the principal peoples of the former empire, the smaller ones being satisfied with cultural autonomy. The Austro-German Social Democratic representatives were the only ones who defended the existing State as the protector of the freedom of the small Slavonic nations, and even looked to its extention: Poles, Ukrainians and Southern Slavs, since the majority of them lived beyond the Austro-Hungarian frontiers, should be satisfied with cultural autonomy within the reformed monarchy![1]

Such was not the attitude of a majority of Austrian Social Democracy. At its congress, in October 1917, a clear majority of the delegates were in sympathy with the Left, and an address of fraternal greeting, unanimously adopted, was sent to Friedrich Adler in his prison cell. In the interest of Party unity, however, the Left refrained from asking for a declaration of solidarity with the German Independent Socialists. In his concluding speech, Seitz, the right-wing chairman of the congress, recognized the necessity and relative legitimacy of the two trends in the party, 'one of which reminds us of the needs of the present, the other of those of the future'.[2] On the decisive issue, the Left confined itself to a declaration denouncing 'social patriots' like Renner and 'National Socialists' like Pernerstorfer, and the Polish Socialists and some Czech Separatists; its positive demands differed from Renner's standpoint merely in adding that the coming federation should be established by Constituent National Assemblies of the various peoples. Accordingly, the Left accepted the official resolution, moved by Renner, which was confined to his old programme of preserving the Hapsburg monarchy by some liberal reforms.[3]

The immediate impact of the Bolshevist revolution in Russia reached

[1] Bruegel, op. cit., vol. IV, p. 245. Smeral, for the Czech Centralists, would have been satisfied with far-reaching Czech autonomy within a reformed Austria, but was honest enough to concede in private negotiations with Masaryk's representatives that the latter's standpoint was shared by a majority of the Czech nation.

[2] Ibid., p. 322.

[3] Otto Bauer (*Die österreichsche Revolution*, German ed., p. 61) says that, at that time, the Left was convinced that in the case of a revolution the Brno nationalities programme (see above, p. 123) as reflected in Renner's resolution, would prove obsolete and that the only alternative to support of the reactionary régime of the monarchy against the national revolutions was support of the national movements in favour of complete separation (including *Anschluss* for the Austro-Germans). This policy certainly corresponds to that of the Left a few months later, during the January strikes (see below in text); but from its point of view the vote of the Left for Renner's motion was, to say the least, inconsistent—unless the consistency lay in the fact that the proclamation of a separatist policy was avoided at the Party congress, when it might disrupt unity with the Party's right wing, but envisaged during the strike, when it conformed to the attitude of the bourgeois Czech leaders. See note [4], below, p. 137.

Central Europe through the peace negotiations at Brest-Litovsk. On 12th January 1918, General Hoffmann, driven into a corner by Trotsky's propagandist statements, replaced all the democratic phrases with which the German delegation had made play during the first stage of the negotiations by laying his German sword openly on the negotiating table. The move displeased everyone in Austria, including the government, which would have been glad if the monarchy could have escaped from its crisis by a negotiated peace; the Social Democratic Party called mass meetings for January 13th to protest against Hoffman's conduct. But a small group of radical workers in the Wiener Neustadt industrial region decided to begin a political strike the following day, on which the bread ration, already meagre, was to be halved. This move coincided with the start of a political strike by the workers of the Czepel works in Budapest, organized by the 'Left-Radical' group.[1] The strike spread like wildfire; when Renner called for a return to work, and the head of the Ministry of Food promised concessions on the bread issue, the Wiener Neustadt workers answered that they were more interested in peace than in bread; a programme of political demands was adopted. On January 17th the strike became general in Vienna, Lower Austria and Styria. The Central Committee of the Social Democratic Party decided to head the movement,[2] with the obvious intention of limiting it; all

[1] In order to be distinguished from the ordinary 'Left' which, as we have seen, corresponded to the German and international Centre, the Austro-Hungarian groups which supported the standpoint of the Zimmerwald Left and were in general sympathy with the Russian Bolshevists called themselves 'Left-Radical'.

Borkenau (*The Communist International*, p. 92) asserts that the strike spread from the Czepel works over Austria; this is impossible in view of its simultaneous start. Even a planned start in the two centres is unlikely: on January 13th the Vienna Committee of the Left Radicals suggested to their friends in the Wiener Neustadt region that they should delay the movement in order to get a better start in connexion with the expected breakdown of the engineers' wages negotiations; this clearly excludes the possibility of a simultaneous start in Vienna and Budapest. Cf. the pamphlet *Der Januaraufstand der österreichischen Arbeiterschaft*, published 1918 by the Zürich publishing agency of the Bolsheviks, which collaborated closely with the Left radicals (copy in British Museum). According to the same source the strike, after having been called off by the Vienna Workers' Council, was continued by the radical workers *against* the advice of the Left Radical committee; and the number of workers continuing the strike, which the publishers of the pamphlet had no interest in underestimating, is given as smaller than in the government-official *Neue Freie Presse*. All this points to isolation even of the Left-Radical leaders from a large part of the striking workers.

[2] The demands proclaimed in this conexion, in comparison with the Wiener Neustadt resolution of January 16th, excluded points such as the immediate release of Friedrich Adler, the introduction of the eight-hour day, and the confiscation and distribution of food reserves by Workers' Committees (which had no point except in connexion with revolutionary action), but included the demand for general suffrage at municipal elections, which hardly needed to be specially emphasized unless the continuation of the monarchy was presupposed. On the decisive issue of peace the demands of the Central Committee appeared the more radical, in that not only were

the essential services, including the railways, were to continue at work, and street demonstrations were to be avoided. The Government had no more than 3,000 reliable troops in the capital, where nearly 100,000 soldiers in training and on leave were prepared to join the revolution.[1] Workers' Councils on the Russian Soviet model were elected to decide on the course of the strike; the Social Democratic Central Committee had no delusions about its continued authority over the workers. The Left (to be distinguished from the Left Radicals) was in control of the Vienna Workers' Council. On January 20th, after the Government had made some concessions—which did not affect the control of the State machinery or the course of the Brest-Litovsk negotiations—it decided to call off the strike, but to work for the eventual dissolution of the Hapsburg monarchy and its replacement by independent national States,[2] agreeing on this basis with the Czech Centralists and some Polish and Slovene Socialists.[3] But decisions as to the future had no relation to the calling off of the strike; the initiative was left to the bourgeois nationalists[4] who would produce separate national States with the proper international backing.

A few days after the strike was officially called off—the workers of many important factories continued it for some days[5]—the Austrian

annexations rejected, but participation by 'the workers' men of confidence' in the peace negotiations was demanded also. This demand, in the existing political structure and in view of the German alliance obviously utopian, was pointless unless it was supposed that Count Czernin would continue as chief Austrian representative at Brest-Litovsk, some Social Democratic advisers being added.

[1] Julius Deutsch, *Aus Österreichs Revolution*, Wien, 1921, p. 5.

[2] See f.n. [3], p. 135.

[3] Otto Bauer, *Die österreichische Revolution*, pp. 66 ff.

[4] Bauer describes the reluctance of the Czech leaders to support a revolutionary movement which might be suppressed by German troops (with fatal consequences for Czech nationalism) as a main reason for his friends' decision to avoid a revolutionary upheaval. Actually, the workers of Brno, where the Centralist Trade Unions were predominant, went on strike as early as the 18th, and the calling off of the strike in Vienna was immediately followed by movements in Moravska Ostrava, Kladno, Plten, and Prague. With the possible exception of the last-mentioned, the part played by the Czech nationalist leaders, if any, was restricted to swimming with a current not of their own making. Even in Prague the atmosphere was so little nationalistic that Vrbensky promised self-determination to all the Austrian peoples, including the Sudeten Germans, and concluded with a *Slava* for the workers of Vienna and Budapest, the working-class members of the oppressing nationalities of the Dual Monarchy. Obviously Masaryk and his friends did not like revolutions, and preferred Czech independence to come as a by-product of an Allied victory without revolutionary upheavals. As we are here discussing events from the point of view put forward in Bauer's book, we need not ask what the Czech nationalists would have liked; the question is what they would have been forced to do if Bauer and his friends had pursued a different policy.

[5] This fact refutes Bauer's assertion (English ed., p. 36) that the strike had to be ended before hunger forced the strikers to capitulate. The risk of starvation, with a bread ration of three ounces a day, threatened them in their ordinary lives; the risks in question at that moment were those of civil war.

battle-fleet at Cattaro mutinied, led by a group of Socialists and Yugoslav national revolutionaries, and the intervention of German submarines was necessary to subdue it.[1] A few days later, under the influence of the events in Austria, a general strike was started in Berlin; the absence of German support was one of the reasons mentioned by Bauer for calling off the Austrian movement. There can be little doubt that a revolutionary initiative in Vienna and Budapest would have carried with it the Austro-Hungarian monarchy, including the Czech territories[2] and centres such as Cracow, where as early as the 28th street demonstrations had increased to such an extent that the Government imposed a curfew. The railway strike, had it not been prevented by the Social Democratic Central Committee, would have spread the movement over the whole of the monarchy and defeated all the Government's attempts to concentrate reliable troops.[3]

The Government's own interpretation of the situation is made sufficiently clear by the fact that it dropped the suggestions for a military dictatorship elaborated at Karl's headquarters,[4] and by its negotiations with the Vienna Workers' Council. A full-scale invasion of Austria by the German Army was possible—but at the cost of delaying, if not calling off, Ludendorff's planned offensive on the Western Front; little is to be gained by speculating whether such an invasion would have sufficed to turn the German January strikes into an actual revolution. No speculation is necessary to see that a different decision taken on January 20th in Vienna, whatever its immediate outcome, would have changed the course of history.

About a week after the end of the January strikes in Vienna similar events occurred all over North Germany, especially in Berlin. The initiative lay not with a political party,[5] but with a body of unofficial shop stewards in the principal Berlin factories, the *Revolutionäre Obleute*, who were connected with the Independent Socialists only by being Party members, as were most 'class-conscious' Berlin workers. Leadership was assured by the official Party leaders, after a keen dispute, on the workers' side, as to whether the Majority Socialist leaders should be allowed to participate—a dispute decided in the affirmative by the

[1] Strong (op. cit., p. 69) gives many examples of mutinies of whole regiments, of all nationalities, from February 1918, i.e. the period immediately following.

[2] See f.n. [4], previous p.

[3] See f.n. [1], previous p.

[4] It is interesting to pursue the later careers of the candidates. Prince Schönburg-Hartenstein, the proposed dictator, had to wait another sixteen years before, as Dollfuss's Minister of War, he got his occasion to shoot Austrian workers. Generals Kraus and Bardolff—candidates for the Ministries of Food and the Interior respectively—later became active Nazis, and leading officials after the *Anschluss*.

[5] No influence by the Spartacus group (which did not become influential in Berlin until the *Revolutionäre Obleute* combined with it—see below, note [2] on p. 159) has ever been claimed, even to the extent that influence was exercised in Austria by the Austro-Hungarian 'Left Radicals'.

influence of the Independent leaders—and on the side of the Majority Socialists on the question whether it was necessary to join. It was necessary; and many years later Scheidemann, in the witness-box in support of Ebert, then President of the Weimar Republic, assured the monarchist judges who had to try Ebert's libel suit against their fellow monarchists[1] that 'if we had not taken that decision it would be most unlikely that this court would be sitting here to-day, and the war and many other things would have been eliminated as early as January 1918 by a Socialist revolution'.[2] This was not intended as a self-criticism but as a profession of Ebert's loyalty, if not to Wilhelm's government, to the things it stood for; and no hasty conclusions about the real prospects of a German revolution in January 1918 should be drawn from such an interested statement. However, it illustrated not only the character of German Social Democracy, in that it was made at all, but also the difference between German and Austrian conditions, in that it had to be made; while the Austrian government allowed the strikers the appearance of a successful demonstration, the German considered them as traitors who, fortunately, could be removed from the streets before irreparable damage was done and the reckoning with those who had treated their action as a legitimate demonstration could be postponed to the proper time.

(*c*) *The Fall of the Monarchies*

The strikes of January 1918, though overshadowed by the more spectacular events of the autumn, represented the Central European labour movement's nearest approach to mass action against an apparently still stable régime. In successful as distinct from abortive revolutions, the importance of such events lies in their making evident the vulnerability of the régime and thus encouraging subsequent action of a more decisive character. Nothing of that kind came to the fore in the Central European revolutions: the destruction of what was bound to fall was left to the armies of the opposing military coalition, and the interpretation of the democracy to be built on the ruins of autocracy was left to the leader of that coalition's propaganda.

The revolutionary forces in Austria, by failing to stike during the January movements, lost, not one opportunity which would be followed by others, as in Germany, but the one occasion when they could still combine to shape a common future. The failure of international Social Democracy left the field to the competition of the national bourgeoisies

[1] See also below, f.n. [5] on p. 156.

[2] Cf. the memorial publication *Friedrich Ebert* (op. cit.), pp. 353–4. The inclusion of the statement which proved Ebert's loyalty to Imperial Germany but was bound to lend support to the sharpest of the reproaches levelled by the Communists against Ebert and Social Democracy, in an official Social Democratic publication, is in itself remarkable.

for a interpretation of the Wilsonian principles favourable to their particular nationality. Emperor Karl had grasped that a quick peace was his dynasty's only chance of survival, but also that the German bayonets were his only protection against the forces of revolution. So, together with his Foreign Minister, Count Czernin, he manœuvred between secret negotiations with the Western Allies, which involved the prospect of at least threatening Germany with the possibility of a separate peace, and unconditional subservience to his German masters. When the double game was called by Clemenceau's disclosures, Czernin, impressed by the early successes of Ludendorff's Western offensive, preferred to play the German card. His royal master joined in submission to Ludendorff, preferring a cheap and ephemeral triumph over Czernin to the already prepared alternative of withdrawing from political responsibility for the last act of the drama.[1] His friends assert that he was already convinced that an Allied victory was inevitable; if these are not merely after-the-event explanations, his behaviour can be explained only by his consciousness that the monarchy's future rested on the continued loyalty of the Austro-German middle classes and bureaucracy and that of the Hungarian gentry, neither of whom would have supported a dynasty restored by the conquerors of Prussia. Karl, however, survived on the throne for a few months longer only at the price of being mortally compromised with all the parties; with the pro-Germans because of his attempted betrayal, and with the others because of his eventual submission. Not only the German Nationalists, but even the Austro-German Catholics now protested against the 'private diplomacy of irresponsible cliques'. Little confidence was restored in these quarters, and few delusions among the Austrian Slavs had to be destroyed, by an internal policy which promised reconstruction of the monarchy in the Austro-German interest.[2]

[1] Cf. Czernin, *Im Weltkrieg*, pp. 230 ff.; Werkmann (Karl's secretary), *Deutschland als Verbündeter*; and Allizé (French military representative in 1919), *Ma mission à Vienne* (Paris, 1933), whose exposition of events we here follow as it appears to be the most plausible and did not originate from one of the parties to the Karl-Czernin dispute. Allizé's sources of information assert that the Empress Zita, who simply reproached Czernin for his failure to support unconditionally his royal master's private diplomacy, induced Karl to withdraw his assent to retire for a time on alleged medical grounds, with a pro-German archduke as deputy. Unless Zita is supposed to have preferred the appearance to the reality of power—which in a person of her background and outlook might be just possible, but can hardly be assumed in all those who must have taken part in such a decision—her behaviour can be explained only on the assumption that she interpreted the Hapsburg régime as a hierarchical organization demanding unconditional obedience from its servants and itself obediently serving the Great Power which dominated the region. Such obedience included the functioning of the Hapsburg monarchists as German agents in early 1918 as well as in 1938–45, and also professions of their pro-Allied sympathies in the years of Western hegemony.

[2] On May 19th Karl's last Austrian Prime Minister but one, Seidler, announced local autonomy for Bohemia, which was a long-standing demand of the Sudeten

A new wave of army mutinies started in May, and continued with increasing strength until the fall of the monarchy; in June a further reduction in the bread ration was followed by another mass strike in Vienna. But political initiative was no longer on the side of the Socialist workers, nor, for that matter, of the Slav national revolutionaries, unless and until they were brought into action by the logic of the military situation. The breakdown of the Bulgarian front, in September 1918, faced the Yugoslav nationalists in Austria with the alternative of taking the initiative or of letting the new Yugoslavia be dominated by a Greater Serbian régime—which was eventually to happen under the French hegemony, and to survive as long as that lasted. Carefully enough, they assumed power when any resistance by the Hapsburg monarchy was rendered impossible by mutinies of the troops which were sent to restore the south-eastern front; after a few weeks the monarchy itself transferred the navy to the Southern Slavs to prevent its falling into Italian hands. The Czechs, more remote from the scene, delayed action until not only German intervention (which in October 1918 was impossible) but also the risk that a revolutionary struggle might strengthen their left wing and alienate conservative sympathies in the Allied camp, were ruled out. When demonstration strikes and mass meetings in favour of an independent republic were announced for October 14th, the National Council asked the Czech Social Democratic leaders to prevent disturbances. They readily obliged, and thus defeated the taking over of power which their left wing had prepared for that day.[1]

The Austro-German Social Democrats had no agreed programme;[2] Otto Bauer advocated *Anschluss* with a democratic Germany, but the Party conference of October 3rd decided in favour of the right to self-determination of all the Austrian nations, including the Austro-Germans 'who according to their own needs should regulate the relations

Germans, to whom it would give regional autonomy, but not for the rest of Austria, where it would help the Slovenes, Italians, and Ukrainians.

[1] The events in some provincial towns where the countermanding order did not arrive in time, or was disobeyed, showed how easily a Czech initiative might have overthrown the Hapsburg State; in Pisek the revolutionaries took over power without any conflict, officers and soldiers of the garrison simply replacing the black-and-yellow Hapsburg cockade by the red-and-white national Czech one.

[2] Otto Bauer's later attempts to derive his *Anschluss* policies from an agreement of the Left going back to January 1918 (see above, p. 131) are refuted by his own recognition (*The Austrian Revolution*, English ed., p. 62) that before 9th November 1918 the Austrian workers were opposed to *Anschluss*, and by the way in which, at the time of the events under discussion, the slogan of a dissolution of Austria into independent national States was defended even by supporters of the Left close to Bauer. In a discussion in the *Kampf*, Nos. 6 ff. (esp. p. 528) Austerlitz answered Renner's argument that a clear delimitation between independent national states following the nationalities principle was impossible under Austrian conditions by reference to the experience of Russia, where temporary separation had resulted in voluntary, and therefore closer, federation.

of their State with those of the other Austrian nations and with Germany'. The formula, accepted against the resistance of Renner (perhaps the last serious defender of Austrian unity), left as possible alternatives complete independence, a free federation of the Austrian nations, and *Anschluss*; but the absence of explicit provision for the future of the Sudeten Germans, who supplied the larger part of Austro-German Social Democracy, perhaps supports the assumption that the prospects of federation were not taken very seriously. The declaration was acceded to on the following day by the German Nationalists, and on October 9th by the Catholics who added the rider that self-determination should result in the transformation of Austria into a federation of free national States. This was accepted by Karl, who on October 16th published his manifesto on the transformation of the Austrian monarchy.[1] In this, of course, more emphasis was laid on national autonomy, within a unity whose continued existence was taken for granted, than on self-determination, tribute to which was paid only by accepting the long-standing Social Democratic proposal[2] for the constitution of the administrative bodies of the national units. This made the formal bridge for what legal continuity was to survive; Provisional National Assemblies were formed by the M.P.s belonging to the various nationalities, though they assumed functions very different from those envisaged in the manifesto.

The Austro-Germans' National Assembly, meeting on October 21st, restricted itself to declarations of programme on behalf of the parties, the Socialists still giving their first preference to federation, the Catholics to a federation headed by a monarch, the German Nationalists to *Anschluss*; an Executive Council of twenty-three members was elected, by the events of the following days it was forced to assume responsibility for the administration. On October 23rd the Yugoslavs assumed power in Fiume, on October 28th the Czechs in Bohemia and Moravia. Karl, still blind to the realities of the situation, ordered the Army, on October 29th, to vote on the alternative of monarchy or republic; the outcome could easily have been foreseen. When on October 30th the Austro-German National Assembly again met, the nationalist speeches of the bourgeois M.P.s were overshadowed by the workers' mass demonstrations. In the evening hours the black-and-yellow cockades were removed from the soldiers' caps, to be replaced by new ones matching the wearer's political outlook: red for most of the privates, the black-red-yellow of German Nationalism for most of the reserve officers, and blank for those professional officers who did not wish to

[1] The Hapsburg rulers' complete divorce from reality, or at least their complete incapacity to see any elements of reality other than the structure of their State machine (see note above p. 140) is illustrated by the fact that the 'Lands of St. Stephen's Crown' were explicitly excluded from the proposed reconstruction, which was thus obviously out of the question for Czechoslovaks, Yugoslavs, and Rumanians, whose co-nationals would have been left under the rule of the Magyar gentry.

[2] See above, pp. 123 and 133.

betray their monarchist convictions. On the next day State power was formally taken over by a coalition government of all the parties, the key positions being gradually concentrated in the hands of Social Democrats. In some of the provinces the transfer of State power was delayed for a few days longer; so the Hapsburg monarchy in the Austro-German parts of the empire broke down after all the rest had deserted it. There was no attempt at resistance; the army—with or without red cockades—dissolved spontaneously within a few days; only with great difficulty could the nucleus of a new one be created from the organized workers. Karl's government, without a State, still continued on paper, and the new Austro-German government was clever enough to leave to it the responsibility for signing the armistice.

Not until the German monarchy had fallen was Austria declared a republic; when on November 11th Renner and Seitz moved the proclamation in the State Council, they tried to win the assent of the bourgeois parties with the explanation that otherwise, however much they preferred the coalition, under the workers' pressure the formation of a purely Socialist government, like that just established in Germany, would be unavoidable.[1] Even after the Social Democrats had threatened to proclaim the Republic, by a breach of the existing legal status, the Vienna wing of the Catholic party, backed by the Church leaders, still resisted until their fellow-partisans from the Provinces cabled the peasant's demand for Karl's abdication. One hour later the decision in favour of the 'legal revolution' was announced, to be carried out the next day to the accompaniment of well-disciplined mass demonstrations. A small group of intellectuals which had just formed the Communist Party had connexions with one of the military formations which organized themselves as 'Red Guards'; it arranged a demonstration before the Parliament building, which would have passed unnoticed had not some shooting taken place through a misunderstanding, and occupied the offices of the leading bourgeois newspaper for an hour, to call, in a special edition, for the proclamation of the *Socialist* republic.[2] The way

[1] Bruegel, op. cit., p. 393 ff.

[2] Ruth Fischer (op. cit., p. 64, note), gives her personal account of the incident, which seems inexact at least in that the occupation is said to have gone on for two or three days, and the shooting to have started from the guards in the building (but it is probable that the Red Guards started shooting because of a clumsy move by the guards in the building). There was probably less spontaneity than Ruth Fischer asserts. During the incidents before the Parliament building, a demand that the red flag should be hoisted was made by some officers of the Red Guard to the Christian Social Mayor of Vienna. He agreed 'in order to pacify public opinion' on condition that it was hoisted jointly with the red-white-red flag of the new Republic (*Neue Freie Presse*, 13th November 1918—the day after the incident). The tendency to seize editorial offices common at that time among Central European left-wingers was undoubtedly promoted by the idea that the absence of a revolutionary orientation of the masses was due to the bourgeois monopoly of their sources of information: proper information, plus some symbolic gestures, would bring their latent spon-

in which such incidents passed is the best illustration of the complete absence of any revolutionary trend in those days.

Another possibility was more serious. Because of the very way in which the new States had originated from the struggle of nationalities within the old monarchy, the whole movement might easily turn into a continuation of those struggles between State machines with some 'Socialist' colour. When, on 4th November 1918, a delegation of Sudeten Germans, led by the Socialist Seliger, tried to negotiate an agreement with the Czech Provisional Government, on the basis of voluntary federation, Rašin, the Czech nationalist leader, answered the Sudeten Germans with the words: 'We do not negotiate with traitors'; they were regarded as traitors because they appealed to the principle of national self-determination, for the defence of which against the Hapsburgs Rašin himself had a few months earlier been under sentence of death, against the claims of the new Czech State to unconditional control of all the territories which belonged historically to Bohemia or Moravia but at that time were controlled by local Sudeten German governments under the Austrian Republic. Soukup, the leader of the Czech Social Democrats, deplored the unavoidable armed conflict but regarded it as impracticable for his party to 'leave, at that moment, the united front of the Czechoslovak nation', while Seliger now came to regard 'the liberation of his nation from threatening oppression . . . as the predominant issue of the present time'.[1] The Austro-German government, if only to deprive its own nationalists of an easy line of attack, sent arms and military specialists. They were not used;[2] the Sudeten-German bourgeoisie was interested in maximum use of nationalist phraseology but not at all in the working-class leadership evident in Austria and in the local resistance movement.[3] As early as November 2nd the mayors of Aussig and Litomerice called for Czech occupation 'so as to preserve public order'. At that time, the Czech Provisional Government was still too cautious to attempt armed intervention; Beneš prepared the decision by a series of notes to the principal Allied Powers. Always prepared to represent the Czech national interest in whatever phraseology was current in the councils of the mighty, he made ample use of the 'Bolshevist danger' (evidently embodied in the Austro-German Social Democrats) against which 'public order in Central Europe had to be pre-

taneity into being. In spite of their belligerent appearance, which, to an opponent more aggressive than the Austrian Social Democrats, might serve as a welcome provocation (see below, pp. 161–2), such actions should be clearly distinguished from attempts to seize public buildings, etc., as military objectives during the course of an insurrection, as in Russia in October 1917. Nothing of that kind happened in Central Europe in 1918.

[1] E. Strauss, *Die Entstehung der tschechoslovakischen Republik*, Prague, 1935, p. 298.
[2] Deutsch, *Aus Osterreichs Revolution*, p. 69.
[3] Strong, op. cit., p. 173.

served'.[1] He had his way, and on November 28th the Czechoslovak occupation of the territories[2] began, against a mere token resistance ordered by the Austrian government and carried out by the industrial workers. On 4th March 1919, Social Democratic manifestations for national self-determination resulted in a massacre; 52 workers were killed and four wounded. The victims eventually served as martyrs for Henleinism, that is, for the destruction of Social Democracy and the Czechoslovak republic; such was the impasse into which the Austrian labour movement had been led by its failure to develop a political line of its own.

Notwithstanding the preservation of some appearances of legality, at least in Austria,[3] what happened in the countries which had made up the Hapsburg empire was certainly a revolution. From the economic point of view, the destruction of the privileged position of Vienna High Finance involved the emancipation of the Czech and other national

[1] Cf. his *War Memoirs*, English ed., pp. 482–3.

[2] The more important of them bordered on Germany (not Austria) which, at that time, was no more interested in this issue than in *Anschluss* in general.

[3] Of course, the Emperor had no constitutional power to dissolve the Empire by a manifesto, and the fact that the national sections into which its Parliament was dissolved began functioning, on lines very different from those envisaged in the manifesto of October 16th, was a very poor substitute for the assent of the Lower House (the Upper House was silently abolished). In the Austrian parts of Czechoslovakia there was a continuity as regards the parties—the Czech parties of the Austrian Parliament agreeing on proportional co-option of members of the Czech National Assembly—but not as regards the persons of the M.P.s; for the representation of the Slovaks, who in Hungary had been virtually disenfranchised, resort was had to co-option according to a plan agreed by the Czech parties. The national minorities were not represented at all, for the avowed reason that the Czech parties did not want the representatives of those minorities to complicate the already very difficult sectional issues which divided them.

Karl never formally abdicated—indeed, he made repeated attempts to regain at least the Hungarian crown; but when the resistance of the Christian Social Party to the proclamation of the Republic collapsed (see above, p. 143) he signed a declaration proclaiming his withdrawal from public affairs and his submission to the people's decision. When the Constituent Assembly elected on 16th February 1919 unanimously repeated the proclamation of the Republic, Karl was invited to submit to the popular vote, as he had promised. He declined; but the coalition government was spared the trouble of forcibly expelling him from the country by the efforts of a British Military Mission which undertook, as the salvation of a crowned head from dangers supposed to threaten it, what really was an act of emigration the formal responsibility for which the salvaged emperor refused to shoulder. The diaries of Lt.-Col. Strutt, who undertook the mission, with his observations about the 'red Jews', as he called the very moderate heads of the Austrian government, his parallels to the novel *Königsmark* and his desire that British troops should enforce a restoration (reproduced in Vivian, *Life of the Emperor Karl*, pp. 185 ff.), are an amusing illustration of the kind of people through whom British influence was exercised in Central Europe after the First World War, the kind of policies expected by Central Europeans from that influence (long before Chamberlain and Lord Runciman made their additional contributions), and also of the way in which the business worked out.

bourgeoisies, and far-reaching adjustments in the rest of Austria; from the political point of view, it is obvious that parliamentary democracy was something new as compared with the sham-constitutionalism of the monarchy and that the State machine had to be replaced, however many of its elements were taken over; the behaviour of Emperor Karl during the last crisis might be explained by a desire to ease the transition of the civil servants and commissioned officers into the service of the new States without making them conscious of any break in their allegiance. The problem was much more complicated in Germany, in spite of the unquestionable existence of all the paraphernalia of a revolution.

Since the last pre-war elections, the German Reichstag had had a left-centre majority. It did not become effective during the first years of the war, when annexationist war aims were supported by all the parties with the exception of the left-wing Socialists; and it made its first appearance under the impact of the Russian revolution of March 1917. Even Emperor Wilhelm II found it advisable, in his Easter message, to announce his readiness to support a democratic reform of the Prussian suffrage, that old apple of discord;[1] but the Conservatives, backed by the High Command, resisted. In July, when the Russian slogan in favour of a peace 'without annexations or indemnities' and the Stockholm Socialist peace conference were in the public eye, the Reichstag majority, including even the National Liberals, managed to pass a resolution in favour of a negotiated peace. But now the High Command intervened, and enforced the resignation of the Chancellor, Bethmann-Hollweg, because of his collaboration with the parliamentary majority; the latter was satisfied when his successor, Ludendorff's nominee Michaelis, accepted the resolution with the rider 'in such a sense as I interpret it'.

The issue was thus settled: the parliamentary majority, including the Majority Socialists, supported the Brest-Litovsk peace and continued endless discussions with the Conservative majority of the Prussian Parliament, which was not prepared to drop its electoral privileges and could not be superseded either under the theory of Prussian constitutionalism or within the realities of Ludendorff's dictatorship. But in the last days of September 1918, Ludendorff, jumping from exaggerated hopes to exaggerated pessimism—or perhaps simply looking for some scapegoat who would sign the armistice after he had lost the war—declared that there was no hope of preserving a cohesive front for more than a few days and demanded that a parliamentary, or semi-parliamentary, government be installed to negotiate the peace. The parliamentarians, obeying this last order of Ludendorff as they had those that had preceded it, assumed 'power' under the leadership of Prince Max of Baden, a member of one of those South German dynasties which had preserved some reputation for what in the conditions of the Prusso-

[1] See above, pp. 7, 114 and 127.

German empire was described as liberalism.[1] Wilson, asked for negotiations for an armistice, drove Max and his government from one concession to another, until some constitutional amendments removed at any rate the formal obstacles to parliamentary government;[2] even a replacement of Wilhelm II by his grandson was considered.

The kind of constitutional change that took place in Germany in 1918–19 is illustrated by the fact that most authors who wrote on these events from the standpoint of the Weimar Republic[3] described the changes in October 1918, by which political responsibility was transferred from the Junker-controlled Army to the left-centre parties which formed the majority in the last Imperial Parliament as well as in the Republican ones that followed it, as the 'real' revolution; the subsequent events of November 1918 were described either as a misunderstanding caused by lack of information on the part of the masses as to what was happening on the political scene[4] or, at most, as a supplementary act necessary in order to enforce the submission of the High Command under the new parliamentary government. The sailors' revolt was caused by what a leading Conservative, Delbrück, has described[5] as a 'political mutiny' of the Naval Command against the new government's peace policy; the Admirals wanted to prevent the capitulation of the Navy by a desperate battle, which could not influence the military course of events,[6] but might be helpful in establishing the myth necessary for eventually restoring the Army's political authority. The sailors, long[7] the most revolutionary part of the German armed forces, mutinied on

[1] See above, p. 87. Participation in the coalition government was agreed to in the Social Democratic parliamentary party by an overwhelming majority; the minority's main argument was the fear, eventually justified, that the Party would be compromised by assuming responsibility for an unfavourable peace treaty (Scheidemann, *Memoirs*, German ed., vol. II, p. 189).

[2] The most important was the repeal of the prohibition of any person being a member of the Reichstag and the Federal Council at the same time, which prevented members of a parliamentary government in the Reich from representing that government in the Federal Council. The introduction of a convention according to which no government could function without having the confidence of a parliamentary majority was attempted, but as we shall see (below, pp. 265–6 and 327–8) the interpretation of the meaning of parliamentary government remained a sore spot during the whole existence of the Weimar Republic.

[3] In this respect I can see little difference between the quoted works of Rosenberg, Jäckh, and Stampfer.

[4] Rosenberg, op. cit., p. 255.

[5] *Untersuchungsausschuss*, vol. IV, pp. 162–3.

[6] It is conceivable that heavy British losses in such a battle might have resulted in an earlier transfer of naval supremacy from Britain to the U.S.A., but it is not clear whether such consequences were intended by the German admirals.

[7] The 1918 mutiny of the Austrian battle fleet (see above, pp. 137–8), though supported by the coastal forts and by the few workers at the base, was defeated because of its remoteness from the main industrial centres, which were themselves in a revolutionary mood.

L

October 31st, and order could be restored only by returning the battle squadron to its Kiel base.

But there the sailors got into contact with the workers of an industrial centre; after a demonstration for the liberation of the arrested mutineers, on November 3rd, which resulted in an armed conflict, they elected a Soviet and proclaimed their demands: abdication of the dynasty (not only of Wilhelm II personally), equal adult suffrage, and political amnesty for the imprisoned revolutionaries. By the morning of November 4th the Sailors' Council had 40,000 well-armed men at its disposal. Noske, the well-known Right Wing Social Democrat, sent to Kiel to represent Max of Baden's government, regarded the movement as a mere 'mutiny'[1] but was clever enough to collaborate with it in order to prevent its growing into a real revolution. On November 7th he was visited by Haase, the Independent Socialist leader, with whom he agreed that collaboration between the two Social Democratic parties was the only way of preventing 'immeasurable harm'.[2] He preserved control in Kiel,[3] but not over the spread of the movement. On November 5th armed sailors carried the movement to Lübeck and Brunsbüttel, on the 6th to Hamburg—where the officers attempted to resist—and to Cuxhaven, and on the 7th to Emden and Wilhelmshaven. On the following day the north-west German cities down to Brunswick, Osnabrück, Düsseldorf, Cologne, Magdeburg, Halle, Leipzig, Dresden, and Frankfurt were affected; in the first four the arrival of a few hundred armed sailors set off the local tension, in the others mere knowledge of what had happened at Kiel was sufficient. On the 7th Munich had its own revolution under pacifist slogans, carried out by the local Independent Socialist leaders and with an unmistakable tendency to preserve Bavaria's individuality within the new Germany.[4] Very differently from the French and Russian examples, Berlin, the capital, lagged behind the rest of the country; it was considered important enough for political manœuvring when it was left almost alone to represent imperial Germany. On November 7th the Social Democratic ministers presented an ultimatum, with the intention, as Scheidemann himself has explained,[5] of keeping the Berlin workers quiet for another day or two. Max of Baden relates in his Memoirs that Ebert accompanied the presentation of the ultimatum with the statement that Wilhelm's abdication was necessary in order to avoid revolution, 'but I (Ebert) hate revolution like deady sin'. The state of mind that still prevailed in official Germany

[1] Op. cit., p. 9.

[2] Ibid., p. 27.

[3] Scheidemann (*Der Zusammenbruch*, pp. 103 ff.) reports the attempts made by himself and Noske on the evening of November 6th to induce the sailors to lay down their arms; their demands, including that for an amnesty, could be fulfilled only in the proper constitutional way, with imperial assent.

[4] See my *Federalism*, etc., pp. 84–5.

[5] *Memoirs*, German ed., vol. II, pp. 292–3.

is indicated by the demands which had to be put forward in such a peremptory way: freedom of assembly, non-interference of the police with political demonstrations, an increasing share in the imperial government for the Social Democratic Party, transformation of the Prussian government so as to make its composition coincide with the majority existing (under manhood suffrage) in the Empire. Wilhelm's abdication was not mentioned, evidently so that it might appear to be a free decision, but to that issue everything had boiled down. At a meeting of the parliamentary parties on the morning of November 8th Wilhelm was dropped by all the bourgeois parties except the Conservatives—the Centre agreed only after a sharp internal discussion with its right-wing minority, led by Gröber; the next twenty-four hours passed in unsuccessful attempts to get the emperor's assent.

Whatever revolutionary initiative there was in Berlin was concentrated in the Committee of Revolutionary Shop Stewards which had been formed in the January strikes. It was composed mainly of left-wing Independent Socialists, but in opposition to that Party's leadership; as late as October 30th the Berlin Committee of the Independent Socialist Party rejected suggestions for street demonstrations with the characteristic argument that the situation was growing ripe for decisive action but that the time had not yet come: so nothing should be done at the moment.[1] On November 2nd the Shop Stewards' Committee, by 22 votes to 19, rejected for alleged technical reasons the suggestion for a rising on November 4th which, as events proved, would have coincided with the Kiel insurrection. The argument that it would be a question of 'all or nothing' was again brought forward; two members only supported Liebknecht's suggestion that, if insurrection was to be delayed, street demonstrations should begin at once. During the days following, while the revolution was spreading throughout the country, Liebknecht's daily suggestions for making a start in Berlin were with equal regularity rejected: at first because of incomplete technical preparations, later because everything had been arranged for a date as far off as November 11th. At last on November 8th the police decided the issue by arresting the proposed military leader; lest his arrest should be followed by that of the Shop Stewards' Committee, action had to be taken, and so the revolutionary demonstrations started in the morning hours of the 9th. There was no further resistance to overcome, and within a few hours the garrison had changed its allegiance. Up to the last moment Max of Baden had vainly pressed the Emperor to abdicate in favour of his grandson, with himself as regent and the Social Democratic leader, Ebert, as Chancellor. He now proclaimed this measure on his own responsibility, but it was too late. Karl Liebknecht was just proclaiming a Socialist republic when Scheidemann saw the only chance of preventing it from becoming Socialist and led by the Left Wingers in himself

[1] For a discussion of an analogous argument see below, f.n. [1] on p. 225.

proclaiming a Democratic republic on behalf of the Majority Socialists, and the transfer of government from Max of Baden to Ebert. Up to this time, and even at a later hour, Ebert had tried to preserve his combination with Max of Baden and a monarchy at least in the form, so he was angry at Scheidemann's action, but could not change the course of events.[1]

Scheidemann was proud that, by his timely action, he had broken 'the Bolshevist wave that threatened to engulf Germany'. As we shall soon see, there was no Bolshevist wave in any reasonable definition of the term; even Liebknecht moving with a procession of enthusiastic demonstrators on the Reichstag building could not have changed the course of events. What had been avoided was the risk that the Majority Socialists, up to this minute the party of the war effort and, as Ebert's efforts showed, even of the preservation of constitutional monarchy, might be excluded from the new Government originating from a definitely anti-war and anti-Hohenzollern movement. At this moment, however, authority over the masses rested with the Independent Socialists, whose anti-war record and republican sympathies could be taken for granted; if they declined this time to collaborate with the Majority Socialists they might lead a powerful opposition against a transitory government of that party and their Liberal friends. The Independents were conscious of their bargaining position, and the Majority Socialists knew that they must at least make verbal concessions; but, unlike the Independents, they knew what they stood for. In the negotiations that preceded the formation of the Provisional Revolutionary Government, on 9th November 1918,[2] the Independents demanded that Germany should be declared a Socialist Republic; the Majority Socialists answered that they, as a party, pursued the same aim, but that the decision ought to be left to the Constituent Assembly. The Independents demanded that that Assembly should be convened 'only after the achievements of the Revolution were consolidated' in order to give them constitutional sanction; the Majority Socialists agreed formally to this point, but manœuvred in such a way that the Assembly was convened at the earliest possible moment.[3] The Independents demanded 'exclusion of all bour-

[1] Scheidemann, op. cit., English ed., vol. II, pp. 578 ff. Ebert continued his efforts to keep Max of Baden in office as a *Reichsverweser* (i.e. Regent—a function not provided for by the German constitution, but monarchical in its implications), until 5 or 6 p.m., i.e. seven hours after the proclamation of the Republic, in obvious competition with the negotiations between his party and the Independent Socialists reported below.

[2] Scheidemann, op. cit., pp. 587 ff.

[3] Within the provisional Revolutionary Government, both parties agreed to 19th February 1919 as the date for the elections. But the Majority Socialists, sure of a majority at the First Congress of the Workers' and Soldiers' Councils, allowed the Government to be 'overruled', so that the elections were called for as early as January 16th. As a result, they coincided with the culmination of the White terror in Berlin (see below, p. 163); one month later they would undoubtedly have expressed the workers' reaction which led to the events of March (see below, pp. 72 and 189).

geois members from the Government'[1]; the Majority Socialists were outspoken enough to reply that this 'would greatly jeopardize, if not make impossible, the feeding of the people'; this argument implied that the bourgeois partners needed for a coalition were not the Liberals but people who were in the confidence of the Junkers and well-to-do peasants. As a face-saving proposal the Independents suggested that the bourgeois Departmental Ministers should be regarded as mere advisers of the political Cabinet, which was to be composed exclusively of 'Socialists' (people like Ebert and Noske stood rather to the right of some of the bourgeois 'advisers'); and this proposal was accepted. The Independents themselves remained silent on the essential question of the Army, but as early as November 12th this issue was decided by a telegraphed order from the new Government to the High Command: discipline and subordination under the old officers were to be maintained, and the Soldiers' Councils were restricted to acting as advisory bodies on welfare and discipline, so as to improve relations between officers and men. Instead of the realities of power the Independents insisted on the formalities of revolution; so the new Government submitted to the formality of election by an extempore mass meeting described as the 'Berlin Workers' and Soldiers' Council' (actually there were no elected representatives, apart from the Shop Stewards), and described itself as the 'Council of People's Commissars'.

These paraphernalias have greatly helped to create, even with serious historians, the impression that there was a temporary revolutionary régime in Germany; all that happened in fact was a coalition of the comparatively moderate wing of the Junker-middle-class combination which had ruled imperial Germany[2] with Social Democracy which, during the war, had definitely developed from its former status as the legal opposition into that of a labour organization supporting the Government. The reforms proclaimed, with legal force, by the new Government as the achievements of the revolution did not step outside the framework of bourgeois democracy (nor even the concessions already in fact granted under the pressure of the mass movements); restoration of civil freedom, a political amnesty, adult suffrage and pro-

[1] In Bavaria, Eisner, leader of the Independents, in his speech of November 8th (cf. Bernstein, op. cit., 1921, pp. 54 ff.) took the same line as was taken next day in Berlin by the Majority Socialists in favour of 'bourgeois specialists'.

[2] I avoid speaking of the 'bourgeois' wing, because the divisions in imperial Germany were not quite on those lines; Ludendorff's dictatorship was controlled by Heavy Industry much more than by the Junkers, and some of the bureaucrats and lawyers comparatively near to the latter had collaborated with the Left-Centre Reichstag majority during the war (see above, p. 146) and also showed themselves inclined to collaborate after 9th November 1918. In discussing the shifts in the distribution of real social power, however, I also avoid speaking of the left-centre Reichstag majority as the bourgeois partner in the coalition, as is done by most historians; the decisive change occurred when the Heavy Industrialists themselves understood that they had to drop the open shop.

portional resprsentation at all elections to public bodies, abolition of all restrictions on freedom of combination (especially those concerning the agricultural workers), the eight-hour day, and unemployment benefit. The law on obligatory industrial war service[1] was repealed with the exception of the rulings on conciliation procedure within the factories. On November 14th the *Arbeitsgemeinschaft* (Working agreement) between the Employers' Associations and the trade unions was established; the former accepted the eight-hour day and the full right of combination, dropped any support for 'yellow' trade unions and recognized the bona fide trade unions—including, of course, the Christian and Hirsch-Duncker Unions—as the only sharers in negotiations and collective agreements; the trade unions undertook to submit all industrial disputes for discussion in the *Arbeitsgemeinschaft* before resorting to a strike. The hierarchy of *Arbeitsgemeinschaften* (joint bodies of employers and trade unionists, on a basis of parity) to be formed within each industry was to be crowned by a *Zentralarbeitsgemeinschaft* formed by the central bodies of employers' associations and trade unions in order to discuss disputes involving more than one industry and general issues that arose in the drawing up of collective agreements; it came to an end in the period of reaction in the winter of 1923–4, when the employers refused to submit to it for discussion issues such as the abolition of the eight-hour day. This agreement, immediately sanctioned by the new Government, established both the full legal status of trade unionism and the readiness of trade union leaders to restrict the use of that status to the pursuance of economic aims which were reasonable within the given capitalist framework.

No less respect was shown for the existing administrative machinery; as early as November 14th the Federal Council, i.e. the representation of the State Governments, was restored, though, of course, with a changed personnel.[2] By a decree of November 16th the new Prussian Government, with the concurrence of the two left-wing Independent Socialists Ströbel and Rosenfeld, prohibited local Workers' and Soldiers' Councils from interfering with the course of justice and with the independence of the judges—eventually to prove one of the sorest points of the Weimar Republic.

It depends very much on what definition of revolution we apply whether a moderate shift in the distribution of social power within the Junker-bourgeois coalition which controlled Germany under the Hohenzollern, Weimar and Hitler—a *very* moderate shift, as the Hindenburg-Papen combination was to show—can be brought under that heading;

[1] See above, pp. 127 and 130.

[2] The decision was taken under the pressure of State Governments acting under very different motives (see my *Federalism*, etc., pp. 85 ff.). There can be no doubt that amongst these motives alliance of the new local rulers with the local bureaucracy was predominant.

the moderate bourgeois-democratic reforms which were left over from imperial Germany and carried out by Weimar hardly justify being described as a bourgeois revolution.[1] What real efforts at social change were made aimed at a Socialist transformation of society; there can be no doubt that these movements were not only defeated but failed even to conquer ephemeral political power except on a local scale. The history of the German revolution, however, is not that of the enactment of overdue bourgeois reforms, but of the defeat of the movements aiming at a revolutionary transformation of German society.

(*d*) *The First Defeats of the German Revolution*

The outcome of the coalition formed by the Majority and Independent Socialists will be better understood if we keep it in mind that the only clear difference between the two parties concerned the annexationist war aims of imperial Germany;[2] after the defeat this difference lost its importance. In the background there was a difference in attitude to the part played by the Army in traditional German society; the independents, most of the rank-and-file Majority Socialists, and some of the leaders of the latter were honest pacifists and would have preferred to dispense with the existing army as quickly as possible, while at least the Ebert-Noske group—the only section of the Majority Socialists which knew clearly what it wanted—could not conceive, any more than could the Imperial General Staff, a resurrection of Germany without the preservation of the framework of the old Army. On the very evening of November 9th, Ebert made an agreement on the telephone with Gröner, the key man in the General Staff and the head of the group which understood that the days of military dictatorship based on mere Junkerdom and Heavy Industry were over. This talk established the collaboration of the Army with the new Government for what some would call the preservation of public order, and others counter-revolution.

The Independent Socialist leaders did not like what was to come; but they had no alternative prospect. Even in private they would not say, as Ebert did, that they hated revolution like sin;[3] on the contrary, their proclamation of November 12th stated that the monarchy had been replaced by the Socialist Republic, that the new government had received its powers from the Soviets,[4] and that Socialist principles would

[1] As done by Stalin in the *History of the C.P.S.U.* (English ed., 1945, p. 231), presumably in order to preserve continuity with all the authoritative Bolshevist statements which recognized the existence of a German revolution (in the hope that eventually socialism would triumph) and yet to avoid entanglement of the idea of a Socialist revolution in the German bankruptcy.

[2] See above, p. 129.

[3] See above, p. 148.

[4] The German term *Arbeiter-und Soldatenräte* (Workers' and Soldiers' Councils exactly equivalent to the Russian Soviets) was of course applied; but the appeal was plainly based on the popularity of the corresponding Russian institution. On the formation and background of these German 'Soviets' see above, p. 151.

immediately be put into practice. But during their six weeks of participation in the coalition Government they made no attempt to realize such promises—unless their share in the establishment of the Commission for Socialization which eventually put the Coal and Potash cartels on more rational foundations[1] is to be regarded as a Socialist measure. More important than the details of the economic order to come was the actual issue of real power. We have seen that on November 12th the new Government lent its authority to the preservation of army discipline; on the following day the Executive Council, i.e. the wider body composed of Majority Socialist and Independent representatives which supervised the Government, refused to form a Red Guard from the Berlin workers because to do so would show distrust in the Berlin garrison's faithfulness to the revolution; in fact, a few weeks later, the soldiers of the Berlin garrison were attacked by the troops of the Social Democratic Government and would have been glad of as much support from armed workers as they could get.

The full confusion of the Independent policies was revealed over the question of a speedy convocation of the Constituent Assembly,[2] which was demanded by the Majority Socialists, supported by the compact body of bourgeois public opinion and by the army; the Independents would say neither on what alternative authority the Government should be based, nor what measures should be taken during the revolutionary interregnum. Naturally the majority of the First Congress of Workers' and Soldiers' Councils found that if Germany was to be an ordinary democracy in the Western sense her constitutional authority should be supplied as soon as possible. Power found in the streets after the emperor Wilhelm had run away could be made legitimate only by clear conceptions about its proper use for the regeneration of the nation; but such concepts were just what the German left-wing lacked and even despised as involving a 'dictatorship over the proletariat'. Without a leader from the Left, the majority of the German workers remained during the decisive period where they were kept by the inertia of their organizational tradition, i.e. with the Majority Socialists; the bulk of the lower middle classes, allowing for some 'swing of the pendulum' to the left, as was natural after a great war, also remained where they were, that is, behind the diverse bourgeois parties duly adapted to the changed conditions.[3] These basic facts would not have changed had Ebert and Scheidemann continued for a few more months as 'People's Commissars' instead of as Ministers, nor even had they allowed Messrs. Haase and Ledebour to continue to have a share in the job.

After the event, the Independent Socialists explained their behavour during the decisive period by the international framework imposed by

[1] See below, p. 307.
[2] See f.n. [3], p. 150.
[3] See below, pp. 165–6.

the Allied victory, and the possibility that a revolutionary Germany might have been starved: it may be added that the dependence was not only imposed but also sought. On November 14th Ebert sent Wilson his famous appeal for food 'on condition that public order in Germany is preserved'. Wilson would have been a very poor politician had he not emphasized, in his answer, that the demand could not be considered unless public order in Germany was preserved—which was just what Ebert wanted him to say. The alternative to the Western orientation was an evil to both factions of Social Democrats: to the Independents, who deplored the Bolsheviks' violation of all accepted democratic values, perhaps even more than for some Majority Socialists, who, once the internal régime in Germany was firmly established, would be prepared together with their Army friends to play the game of *Realpolitik*. At the time of which we are speaking, the unofficial war against Soviet Russia was being continued by the Baltic troops, while the Independent Socialist leaders shouldered the official responsibility for sabotaging the restoration of German-Soviet relations. At the meeting of the Government on November 19th Haase, who was responsible for Foreign Affairs, suggested dilatory treatment of the Soviet request for a restoration of diplomatic relations, which had been broken off by Scheidemann shortly before November 9th with the help of a police provocation of which he was extremely proud.[1] Kautsky supported Haase with the argument that the Soviet Government could not survive for more than a few weeks longer. Among the demands forwarded to the Soviet Government was one for the reinstatement of the monarchist Consuls-General in Moscow and Petrograd, who had been replaced by the German Soviets formed in Russia as well as in all German institutions; and amongst the measures applied to demonstrate the undesirability of an Eastern orientation was the return of fifty wagon-loads of grain which had been sent by the Soviet Government as an earnest of help. Haase explained his refusal of these by saying that Russia was starving and that Germany would be fed by the Allies. In the circumstances, no test of the question what bargaining power revolutionary Germany, in view of her position between West and East, could preserve, could ever be made. Nor was it intended that it should be; international dependence on the Allies was sought precisely because of its internal implications. True, those internal implications eventually became expensive for the Western Allies and destructive for Social Democracy; but this was not then foreseen.

There still remained two ways of securing 'public order' against any extension of the revolutionary upheaval; it could be based on forces

[1] Cf. his *Memoirs*, vol. II, pp. 532–4. In his *Zusammenbruch* (Berlin, 1921, p. 224), which is highly polemical, Scheidemann speaks of the events described below in the text as 'the Russian policy of the People's Commissars which was managed by the Independents'.

supposedly devoted to the new Government, or it could be sought by a revival of the reactionary traditions of the Prussian army. Both ways were attempted, with different results. Ebert and Wels (the new right-wing Social Democratic commander of Berlin) called sailors from Cuxhaven and Kiel, who, because of Noske's activities during the crisis,[1] were supposed to be reliable, to protect as the People's Sailors' Division the security of the capital, under the command of Count Wolf Metternich, a personal friend of Wilhelm II. The Army High Command prepared special divisions, well armed and with as high a proportion of commissioned officers as possible, all unreliable elements being removed without public scandal;[2] the wearing of revolutionary emblems and the formation of Soldiers' Councils for other than welfare purposes was prohibited. The two kinds of military preparation did not necessarily contradict each other; during the first days of December Guard formations, composed mainly of non-commissioned officers and bearing the black-white-red flag of the Empire, were introduced into Berlin; on December 6th, with the participation of Wels and probably some encouragement from Ebert himself,[3] Monarchist Volunteer Corps arrested the Executive Council and attempted to replace the collective Government by Ebert as President. The attempt failed because of the left-wingers' vigilance. The People's Sailors' Division now removed their commander, who had taken part in the *coup*, and elected a Soldiers' Council; but right-wing Socialists and High Command agreed on improving the preparations for the next attempt.

On December 6th, at the Headquarters of General Sixt von Arnim's group, a meeting of the General Staff and Commanding Officers decided on the formation of special Volunteer Corps, specially adapted for street fighting and subject to the old military discipline;[4] on December 8th Gröner and Hindenburg promised Ebert to introduce ten divisions into Berlin to purge the capital of revolutionary elements.[5] The preparations,

[1] See above, p. 148. Because of the part played in the revolution by the sailors, a corps composed of sailors and reliable from the Government standpoint was supposed to enjoy special authority.

[2] The relevant secret order of the Commanding Officer of the 11th Army, of November 16th, was read by the left-wing Independent Brass at the meeting of the First Congress of Workers' and Soldiers' Councils on 17th December 1918. Each army corps was supposed to form one special division of this kind and to exempt it from demobilization.

[3] Cf. Scheidemann, Memoirs, German ed., vol. II, p. 334.

[4] General Märcker, who commanded the first Volunteer Corps formed a few days after this decision, in his book *Vom Kaiserheer zur Reichswehr*, has described the details, including the honest professions of his monarchist loyalty made to his soldiers (op. cit., p. 57) and the inclusion in the soldiers' oath of 'the military laws as they were on 1st February 1918' (ibid., pp. 53–4).

[5] Cf. Gröner's report of his conversation with Ebert on the secret telephone, given in the Munich *Dolchstoss-Prozess* of 1925 (in order to refute the defamation of Ebert by the monarchists and Nazis who now found it convenient to call him a traitor, see

the increasing self-confidence of the professional officers, and the occasional monarchist demonstrations were noticed by the soldiers, most of whom were in sympathy with the Majority Socialists but regarded the destruction of the Prussian barrack-room order and the end of the war as the main achievements of the revolution. These feelings were expressed by the same First All-German Congress of Workers' and Soldiers' Councils which gave such short shrift to the Independents' attempt to delay the calling of the Constituent Assembly and a majority of which refused to seat Karl Liebknecht and Rosa Luxemburg, who, because they had no party organization,[1] had failed to secure mandates. Almost unanimously the Congress accepted the 'Seven Hamburg Points' which were moved by the almost exclusively Majority Socialist Hamburg delegation and by most of the soldiers' representatives; the Provisional Government itself, instead of the Prussian general whom it had appointed as 'advisory' Minister of War, had to control the Army; the officers had to be elected or at least confirmed by the soldiers, had to take an oath not to support attempts at counter-revolution, and had no authority off duty; discipline had to be maintained by the Soldiers' Councils. Eventually, the standing army was to be abolished and replaced by a People's Militia, as envisaged in the Social Democratic programme.

also above, p. 139) and quoted by Rosenberg, op. cit., p. 324. Hindenburg's letter to Ebert is given in the latter's op. cit., pp. 369–370. Cf. the sources given by Ruth Fischer, op. cit., p. 65, note 15.

[1] The elections were indirect and were comparatively easy to manage; but it should be kept in mind that the authority of Karl Liebknecht especially was so enormous tha ton November 9th Ebert and Haase had had to offer him membership of the Council of People's Commissars (he refused because his demand for thorough revolutionary measures was rejected); any left-wing Independent who in any of the 350 constituencies had moved the election of one of the two heroes of anti-war resistance could have created a most awkward position even for right-wing Social Democrat election organizers. At the Congress, apart from 288 Majority Socialists, 25 supporters of a separate Soldiers' Group, and 25 'Democrats'—i.e. Liberals, evidently elected by black-coated workers—there were 90 supporters of the Independent Socialists (among them ten members of the Spartacus League) and eleven 'Independent Communists'. Ruth Fischer's tendency in her treatment of this period is to underline the revolutionary possibilities supposed to be inherent in the January crisis; she emphasizes (op. cit., p. 70) the social structure of the Congress: 195 salaried Party or Trade Union officials, 71 intellectuals, 13 army officers, 179 workers. In any case, the motion of the left-wing Independent, Bäumig, to base the new constitution on the Soviet system received 98 votes (against 344); so there was a not unimportant left wing in existence, whose strength did not differ fundamentally from that of the Independents in the elections to the Constituent Assembly a month later (see below, p. 164) or, to take another comparison, from that of the Bolsheviks at the first Soviet Congress in June 1917. The obvious problem in any discussion of Communist policy is not to complain about the predominance of bureaucrats in conferences dominated by right-wing Social Democrats, but to explain how people who by their behaviour had become heroes of an anti-war struggle could be expected to head a revolution if they were unable or unwilling to get themselves elected to a congress of 490 delegates.

The Congress was clearly inconsistent in accepting such motions while trusting for their execution to a Government which had agreed with the Supreme Command that it would not interfere with established Army authority nor tolerate the interference of Soldiers' Councils with officers' duties. In a special order to the Army, Hindenburg protested against the Congress decision while explaining his confidence that the Government would stand by its promises to the Generals and thus enable them to continue their services; he took it for granted that the Government had regarded the provisional Constitution, according to which the Congress was the highest authority in revolutionary Germany, as a harmless scrap of paper; and he proved to be right. On December 20th, immediately after the Congress had closed, the Government agreed with Hindenburg's representative, Gröner, that the Congress decision should not be carried out.

On December 23rd, Ebert and Wels used a minor and easily composed incident to settle accounts with the People's Sailors' Division which had so thoroughly disappointed their hopes.[1] It was suddenly attacked by General Lequis's troops and artillery, but as the Government troops quickly disintegrated under the influence of the Berlin working-class population surrounding them, the attack was easily repulsed. Wels, as the one immediately responsible, had to resign, and Lequis was replaced by von Lüttwitz, the head of one of the most notorious of the Volunteer Corps who was to become famous by his share in the Kapp Putsch.[2] Most members of the People's Sailors' Division belonged to no political party; the sailors had been involved in the conflict through a mere dispute about their pay, and were satisfied with the compromise which, before the attack, the Government had refused. This outcome, however, was a moral defeat for the Government. Ebert despaired of a quick victory and expected the temporary occupation of Berlin by the left-wingers; he would, if necessary, reconstitute the Government in Potsdam where fresh troops were concentrated.

No revolutionary attack followed—none was ever intended—but a mere Government crisis; the Independent People's Commissars put before the Central Executive Committee, composed since the First Congress of Workers' and Soldiers' Councils purely of Majority Socialists,[3]

[1] See above, p. 156 For the details of the conflict, see Ruth Fischer, op. cit., p. 72.

[2] See below, p. 192.

[3] Three months later, when Haase at the National Conference in March 1919 was under pressure, he described (Proceedings, p. 84) the situation of December 24th in terms of an opportunity for the Independent Commissars to remove their compromised Social Democratic colleagues, and to govern according to their principles; this opportunity had been wasted because at the preceding Soviet Congress the Independents, under pressure from their left wing (to hit at which was Haase's obvious purpose) had declined to take part in the Central Executive Committee except under conditions of parity, as existed in the Government. In these conditions, argued Haase, it was impossible to form a purely Independent Government, because it could be

a number of questions concerning the Government's behaviour during the critical days, its failure to carry out the Congress's resolution on the Army, and the issue of economic 'socialization'; the obvious intention was to achieve a good place as the opposition in the impending elections to the Constituent Assembly. The right-wing Socialist committee evaded the delicate question, but, on its part, asked the Independent members of the Government whether they would be prepared to protect property and public order 'with all the means available', which included the old Army formations and the Volunteer Corps. Now the Independents resigned, on the most friendly terms—the Independent members of the Prussian Government, immediately before their resignation became effective, went so far as to sign a decree directed against strikes and 'exceessive wage claims' (January 2nd). In spite of their later allegation to the contrary[1] they appear never to have considered replacing the right-wing Social Democratic Government; their behaviour during the January fighting soon demonstrated that even in the most critical situations they did not dream of removing it.

Just when the Independents had become an opposition party the National Conference of the Spartacus League assembled, to found, on New Year's Day 1919, the Communist Party of Germany. Full solidarity with the Soviet Government was expressed, and Socialist Germany envisaged as a Soviet republic, but in the programme of the new party Rosa Luxemburg again proclaimed the principle of spontaneity; the Party would make no premature attempt at removing the Government, nor take part in any combinations with the Independents, or their left wing,[2] but would continue its propaganda until the masses, from their

dismissed at any moment by the Social Democratic Central Executive Committee. Dittmann (ibid., p. 75) asserted that a considerable minority of the Majority Socialist members of the Executive Committee (i.e., the soldiers' representatives) would have been prepared to support the Independent Socialist Commissars in a conflict. He blundered by saying that, for this reason, the Independents, if in possession of half the seats on the Executive Committee, could have ousted the Majority Socialist Commissars: in fact the Independent faction of the Workers' and Soldiers' Congress had refused to take part in the Executive Committee—though, curiously enough, not in the Government—precisely because its demand for half the seats had been rejected. Dittmann even asserted that had it not been for that mistake on the part of the Independent faction of the Congress the whole course of the revolution would have been different: Karl Liebknecht and Rosa Luxemburg still alive, and Socialism in being. No more has been heard since, even in Social Democratic writings, of this strange hypothesis.

[1] See preceding footnote

[2] At the foundation Congress the question arose whether the new Party should be formed conjointly with the Revolutionary Shop Stewards (the *ad hoc* organization of the left-wing Independent workers of the chief factories which had played a large part in the revolution, see above, p. 149 who now appeared ready to break with the Independent Socialist leaders, but formulated some conditions for collaboration with Spartacus; participation in parliamentary elections, joint control of programme and publications, dropping of the name 'Spartacus', 'precise instructions as regards

own experience, were convinced of the correctness of its principles, aims, and fighting methods. This meant that, for the time being, the Communist Party regarded itself as a mere propaganda group; but some efficient methods of propaganda were denied to it when, against Rosa Luxemburg's and Liebknecht's advice, participation in parliamentary elections and in existing trade union machinery, as distinct from the revolutionary Factory Councils to be created, were rejected by considerable majorities.

A few days after its foundation the new party, and with it the left wing of the German labour movement, lost its two outstanding leaders; and the conditions in which this was able to happen came about precisely because of its reluctance to assume more than advisory functions towards spontaneous mass movements. Ebert, who had learned the lessons of his defeats on December 6th and 24th, moved the Volunteer Corps of Generals Märcker and Lüttwitz to the military camps sur-

the tactics of street demonstrations'. The first of these demands coincided with the actual wishes of the Spartacus leaders, who, however, as we have seen, had been overruled by their own caucus; the second was clearly intolerable to Rosa Luxemburg and her closest associate, Leo Jogiches; if there was to be a special Communist Party at all (this was not a matter of principle for them, as they rejected the Leninist concept of the organizational functions of such a party) it had to propagate *its own* principles with the greatest possible clarity; the masses were supposed to learn by their own experience provided advanced teaching was available. The last point, in those days, was clearly intended to be a demand for definite guidance in order to avoid being provoked into civil war or, if such a war were started, to win it; this was clearly desirable from the standpoint of Leninist (or earlier Marxist) concepts of insurrection as an 'art' as well as from that of ordinary common sense. No special nearness of Karl Liebknecht to Leninist principles need be supposed in order to explain his sympathy with this point. On the other side, in spite of statements of old standing by Rosa Luxemburg about the inadmissibility of tactical advice tendered by a Central Committee (see above, p. 107), we need suppose no failure on her part to apply ordinary common sense in order to explain her reluctance to accept this principle when suggested by the revolutionary Shop Stewards and by her friend Liebknecht; all of them indeed, during the next few days, moved into a definitely adventurous position, which in view of their background it was not difficult to foresee.

Ruth Fischer's appreciation of these disputes is dominated by her bias against the Spartacists and in favour of the tradition of the Berlin Shop Stewards, with a tendency to show that the January rising was a promising attempt which with better leadership might have succeeded (see op. cit., pp. 83 ff.); this continuation of old disputes within the C.P. by an author who has abandoned the Bolshevist position—the only one from which criticism of the Spartacists gave sense—appears strange. P. Manova, in *Voprosi Istorii*, I/1949, gives the most systematic presentation of the events; she suffers from the opposite mistake, i.e. she represents the Spartacists as a party in the Bolshevist sense, subject to criticism where they failed to act consistently as behoves such a party and praised where they took decisions consistent from such a party's point of view, i.e. advising against insurrection in an evidently unfavourable situation. Manova does not even consider whether such advice was actually conditioned by sober appraisal of the situation or by reluctance to give positive counsel until the masses had acted. The evidence for the existence of an intentional provocation by the Government is given by Manova as well as by Ruth Fischer, but contradicts the latter's appraisal of the situation in January 1918.

rounding Berlin, without exposing them this time to the risk of contagion by the revolutionary population. In his deposition at the Dolchstoss trial Gröner stated that, on Noske's order, the military preparations were concluded by December 29th; on January 4th, the day when the political provocation was started, Ebert and Noske visited the Volunteer Corps assembled at the Zossen camp near Berlin.[1] The military preparations were completed, and an easy pretext for attack could be produced by forcing issues of prestige upon the left wing and handling them in such a way that peaceful settlement was made impossible without the unconditional surrender of the other side.

On December 25th, immediately after the breakdown of Ebert's attack on the People's Sailors' Division, a group of armed workers had occupied the offices of *Vorwärts*, whose transfer by the right-wing Social Democrats to the Imperial High Command[2] was an old grievance of the Independent majority of the Berlin workers. Something similar had already happened on November 9th, and there was no reason why the incident should not once more be settled by negotiation; indeed, negotiations were begun by the head of the Berlin police, Eichhorn, a left-wing Independent, who was supported by his Party caucus as well as by the Shop Stewards' Committee. From the standpoint of the right-wing Social Democrats, the very fact that a left-winger like Eichhorn occupied such a position was one of the most intolerable by-products of the revolution, all the more since Eichhorn had taken an active part in repressing the *coup* of December 6th. On January 4th, when the military preparations were completed, Eichhorn was removed from his office by the Government, on the pretext that he had failed to use force against the occupiers of the *Vorwärts* building. Eichhorn, who still clung to the revolutionary legality of the pseudo-Soviet system, declined to leave his post without an order from the Central Executive Committee which had appointed him; had the Government pursued aims other than the provocation of an armed conflict, it could easily have satisfied his condition, as the right-wing Social Democrats were in control of the Central Executive Committee. But the Government's aim was to provoke the Berlin workers into a premature insurrection;[3] an attack against a position of such prestige as that of head of the Berlin police was certainly the best means of ensuring it.

On January 4th, when Eichhorn's dismissal and his refusal to submit became known, the situation was discussed in the Central Committee of

[1] Märcker (as quoted f.n. [4] on p. 156) reports that Noske was highly satisfied and encouraged Ebert, who appears to have been depressed by his preceding setbacks.

[2] See above, pp. 129–30.

[3] This was claimed by the right-wing Social Democrat Ernst, nominated Eichhorn's successor after the Government's triumph, in an interview given on 16th January 1919 to foreign journalists (*Avanti*, 23rd February 1919, quoted by Manova, op. cit., p. 68; see also the interview with Philips Price quoted in his *Germany in Transition*).

the C.P. as well as at a joint meeting of the Berlin Committee of the Independents, the Revolutionary Shop Stewards, and two representatives of the C.P., Liebknecht and Pieck, who also took part in the meeting of their Central Committee.[1] The meeting of the C.P. decided in favour of a protest demonstration, but uttered a strict warning against a struggle for political power, for which conditions outside Berlin were not ripe; the meeting of the Independent Socialists and Shop Stewards, however, on the initiative of the two C.P. representatives, declared that decisive action was necessary in order to prevent the Government from preparing its military measures. On the following day, after a most impressive demonstration in which some regiments of soldiers took part, another meeting of the same composition was held to consider the situation; during the demonstration some arms had been distributed and some other newspaper offices had been occupied by armed workers,[2] and there were declarations of solidarity from some more barracks. So it was decided to elect a Revolutionary Committee of fifty-three members with three Presidents—Liebknecht among them—and to call an armed demonstration for the following day. From the point of view of attendance and spirit it was a complete success; Noske[3] is probably right in saying that, if there had been real leaders, they could have been in control of Berlin by midday; as was natural in his position, he fails to discuss the question how far such a local success would have fitted into the framework of his preparations for a grand show-down. But nothing was done, except to circulate a leaflet proclaiming the overthrow of the Government,[4] and to make some attempts at propaganda in the barracks, from which it was evident that Army support for the movement was much smaller than had been supposed on the preceding day. In the absence of quick and inspiring moves this support dwindled further during the following decisive days, and the workers' resolutions from the factories turned on the restoration of working-class unity.

[1] The most systematic presentation of the subsequent events is given by Manova, op. cit., pp. 66 ff.

[2] Manova, op. cit., pp. 70 ff., gives ample evidence in favour of these incidents having been caused by police agents; certainly the dispersal of the few available workers' fighting groups on quite irrelevant errands helped the Government. On the other hand, from the whole prehistory of the *Vorwärts* incident (only the continuation of which on January 5th is touched on in Manova's record) it is clear that there was some spontaneous interest on the workers' part in such objects. This was natural in view of the whole presentation of class-struggle in terms of enlightenment and the absence of any definite concepts of armed insurrection. What police agents there were could not become effective without those inclinations on the part of the public.

[3] Op. cit., p. 69.

[4] Pieck (quoted by Manova, op. cit., p. 74) later explained the origin of this leaflet, to which he and Liebknecht added the signature of the C.P., by the demand of wavering troops for a guarantee that their oath of allegiance to the former Government had now become obsolete. This explanation is characteristic enough; an irreversible step was taken in order to explore the conditions in which it might have some prospects of success.

From the beginning the Central Committee of the Independent Socialist Party had declared itself neutral in the armed conflict between its Berlin organization and the Government, and had offered its good offices for mediation; these were accepted by a large majority of the 'revolutionary committee'. In the circumstances the only possible result was to win another day for the Government. At the meeting of the Communist Central Committee on January 8th, Jogiches and Rosa Luxemburg sharply attacked the participation of Liebknecht and Pieck in the Revolutionary Committee and demanded their withdrawal; as late as January 10th the Central Committee disowned them to the extent that they were not allowed to take part except as observers. Nothing came of these steps; on January 8th the Government troops had entered Berlin and occupied all the strategic positions without resistance save from isolated workers' detachments in the newspaper offices and some railway stations; these were duly massacred. Under these conditions, the Central Committee of the C.P. joined in an appeal to the workers to offer armed resistance; on the following day, the Shop Stewards' Committee proclaimed a new Government consisting of Liebknecht and two left-wing Independents. This was no more than a gesture intended to underline that the struggle, which was going on without prospects or centralized leadership, should be directed to the overthrow of the Government.

By January 12th all was over, and on the 15th Karl Liebknecht and Rosa Luxemburg were arrested by a special squad of the Volunteer Corps and shot 'while attempting to escape', a formula to become famous in the years to follow. Much later, under the Nazi régime, responsibility was proudly claimed by the immediate instigator of the murder, Eduard Stadler, the organizer of one of those 'anti-Bolshevist' groups which sprang up in those days like mushrooms, financed by Heavy Industry and connected with the Government. The central figure among the actual organizers of the murder was Captain Pabst, prominent at General Lüttwitz's headquarters; the main reason Stadler gave to the executives was the consideration that, unhappily, the Government side had no outstanding leaders, so the Left must be deprived of its leaders.[1] Lüttwitz's Staff at first found that the incident involved no irregularities, so no special investigation was necessary. When the Government insisted on at least the appearance of an investigation, the Staff looked after such pure eyewash as remained. The Government was quite satisfied with such a position; the 'criminal prosecution' of the actual perpetrators of the murder continued for ten years—they were later promoted to the status of national heroes—and became one of the major judicial scandals of the Weimar Republic. Appeals to kill the leaders of the C.P. had been published, with the full toleration of the

[1] *Eduard Stadler als Antibolschewist* 1918–19, Düsseldorf, 1935, pp. 51–2, quoted by K. Kamenetskaya in *Voprosy Istorii* I/1949, p. 106.

Government and partly in its Press;[1] only an accident prevented the success of an attempt made by a close supporter of the Government to carry out the measure[2] shortly before the right-wing officers got their opportunity. By putting the Government in the position of abetting the murder of the outstanding leaders of the anti-war struggle and making the split between the two wings of the labour movement irremediable, the incident did great harm to Social Democracy, unless the links with German militarism be regarded as Social Democracy's main assets; in which event the murder was useful in that it destroyed whatever doubts might survive from pre-war propaganda as to its counter-revolutionary reliability.

(*c*) *Constitution and Peace*

In the shadow of these events, on January 19th, the Constituent Assembly was elected. As Berlin was not considered safe, it met at Weimar, under the protection of General Märcker's troops; even in the Thüringian neighbourhood of Weimar Märcker had to attack one working-class centre after the other. Lower middle-class opinion could not but interpret what had happened as the defeat of the anti-war revolution; in these circumstances it was remarkable that the two Social Democratic parties—the Communists abstained[3]—polled together 45 per cent of the total vote, as against a 35 per cent Social Democratic poll in the elections of 1912. Of the two working-class parties that contested the 1919 elections, the Majority Socialists polled 11·1 million votes, the Independent Socialists 2·2 million; in those industrial centres where during the war crisis the majority of the old Social Democratic organizations had joined the Independents (Berlin, Central Germany, Leipzig, Thüringia, Lower Rhineland) the Independents won more working-class votes than the Majority Socialists, though even in those regions the latter got a higher total vote because of lower-middle-class support.

[1] A poem by one Zickler, published in *Vorwärts* on the eve of the murder, became notorious: 'Many hundred workers in a row, proletarians! Karl, Rosa, Radek and all their gang, not one of them is among the killed.' According to Scheidemann, op. cit., vol. II, p. 611, similar feelings, though not the determination to carry out the murders, were widespread among the Social Democratic leaders; the Stadlers, however, could be relied upon to fill the gap.

[2] A. Fischer, Wels's deputy, sent out an expedition to arrest Liebknecht and Luxemburg; as they went to the wrong address they found, instead of the persons they sought, Ernst Meyer, member of the Communist Central Committee, and Ernst Ledebour, the leading Left-wing Independent. As was established at the trial of the latter, and is also confirmed by Fischer, the Government's sanction for their immediate execution would have been available if Liebknecht and Luxemburg had been found (Proceedings, Berlin, 1919, pp. 478 ff., and 537 ff., quoted by Kamenetskaya, op. cit., p. 105). That some orderly procedure was applied in these matters is illustrated by the fact that the Opposition leaders who were actually arrested suffered no harm, as they might have done in Hitler's day.

[3] See above, p. 160.

The bourgeois parties had rallied immediately after the November revolution, first with the demand that the Imperial Parliament should be recalled, as the constitutional organ last in existence. When the progress of the revolution made this impossible, the slogan was changed to the demand for the convocation as early as possible of a Constituent National Assembly, which would differ from the old Parliament only in detail.[1] As Social Democracy organized the necessary shooting, there was little to argue about; only the German People's Party, which, as we shall see, was the special party of Heavy Industry formed against its own intentions, entered the elections with the slogan that it would 'free the nation from Red chains'; for the moment it did not achieve very promising results. The Republic was accepted as a fact with varying degrees of enthusiasm, and by the Centre comparatively late; but even in the Conservative camp Count Reventlow, who eventually was to become a prominent figure in the 'Socialist' wing of National Socialism, changed the motto of the pan-German *Deutsche Tageszeitung* from 'For Emperor and Empire' to 'For the German Nation'. After Wilhelm's behaviour in the November crisis the monarchy was done for, and nationalists had to uphold their cause within the new political framework. This attitude, adopted in essence by all the bourgeois parties, should not be mistaken for a political realignment; when reorganizing themselves early in December 1918 as the German National People's Party and electing a leader, the Conservatives avoided choosing Delbrück, who, in the eyes of the German Patriotic Party (the extremist warmongers) was tainted by his collaboration with Bethmann-Hollweg, Ludendorff's opponent[2] and instead chose the colourless Hergt, who, as a Prussian Minister, had resisted general suffrage to the last.

Only in the Liberal camp did the fall of Bismarck's empire involve a party reshuffle. In the *Berliner Tageblatt* of November 16th a number of left-wing Liberal intellectuals, such as Theodor Wolff, Helmuth Gerlach, Albert Einstein, and Hjalmar Schacht, published a manifesto in favour of the formation of a Democratic Party; while defending private ownership of the means of production except in industries already dominated by private monopolies, its authors accepted most of the reforms suggested in the Social Democratic programme, land reform and so on. As this platform was gradually accepted by all the leaders of official Liberalism (as distinct from the National Liberals) it was correspondingly watered down; the condemnation of the preceding war policies especially, in which the Liberals had shared, was mitigated.[3]

[1] The suggestion was made in the evening edition of the *Berliner Tageblatt*, 8th November 1918, on the eve of the Berlin revolution.

[2] See above, p. 146.

[3] Cf. S. I. Lenchner's paper on 'The Attitude of the Bourgeois Parties towards the 1918 Revolution' in *Trudy po Novei i Noveishei Istorii*, Institute of History, Academy of Sciences of the U.S.S.R., Moscow, 948 (in Russian).

The National Liberals, deprived of their former privileged position, would have liked to join, but their right wing was led by Stresemann and heavy industrialists like Stinnes and Röchling, who had been collaborators of Ludendorff, and this was too heavy a burden for honest Liberals. On December 4th agreement was reached between the representatives of the moderate National Liberals, Friedberg and Leidig, and the Liberal representatives Fischbeck (before the revolution Prussian Minister of Commerce) and Schacht. The new Democratic Party was to be formed on the basis of national unity, acceptance of the Republic, and preservation of private ownership of the means of production (apart from exceptional cases where nationalization might be needed); persons who had played a leading part in propaganda for annexationist war aims and in attacks against the U.S.A., or who had voted against equal suffrage in Prussia, were to be excluded. Stresemann and his friends, against their will, had to build up a party of their own; and so they formed the German People's Party, the next of the various political instruments through which Big Business was to control Germany. Under the immediate impact of their war record, they fared badly at the polls on January 19th, receiving 1·6 million votes, against 5·7 for the Democrats. The latter absorbed the bulk of those Conservative or National Liberal voters who moved to the left under the new conditions while still preserving their traditional prejudices against Social Democracy.

The comparatively best results in the bourgeois camp were achieved by those parties which had proved stable in their conservative policies, which enjoyed solid support from sectional organizations (the League of Agriculturalists, the Christian Peasants' Unions, and the Christian Trade Unions respectively), and which could be compensated by the women's vote for the unavoidable losses due to the changed political atmosphere.[1] The Centre, including its Bavarian wing, which was soon

[1] In the May elections of 1920 in a few places the votes of men and women were counted separately; in Catholic Cologne, 60 per cent of those who voted for the Centre and 55 per cent of those voting for National Conservatives and German People's Party were women, but only 40 per cent of the right-wing Social Democrat, and 33 per cent of the Independent Socialist voters. In Protestant Spandau, near Berlin, the porportions were similar, but less marked: right-wing Social Democrat being no more, and left-wingers (Independents and Communists together) only moderately discriminated against (47 per cent of their supporters were women). In view of the war losses of men, an equal propensity of either sex to vote for a given political party would have been expressed in a small female majority among its supporters. Separate counts of this kind were strongly opposed by women's organizations, which were afraid that the obvious results might threaten sympathy for women's suffrage on the part of the Left, while the right wing might still abolish it for ideological reasons. Such fears were quite baseless; even Hitler, while promising women a return from politics and factory to their homes, still found it useful to let them have votes in his plebiscites. The Left regarded the women's vote as a means of political education; the Communists especially, who were least favoured by the women's vote, would regard such education as much more important than a few seats in Parliament.

to cause a split towards the right, polled 6 million votes, and the German National People's Party (i.e. the Conservatives) 2·9 million. The new Government was formed by a coalition between Social Democrats, Centre, and Democrats, called the 'Weimar Coalition' from the meeting-place of the Constituent Assembly. These parties held an enormous majority; the Independent Socialists formed the left opposition, the German People's Party and the German Nationals that of the right. There was little fundamental antagonism within parliament, despite the continuing civil war between the Volunteer Corps and the workers; even the Parliamentary leader of the Conservatives, Dr. Traub, in an article of 20th February 1919 greeted the rapid formation of a stable republican Government as 'the first important test successfully passed by the parliamentary parties'.

In the hour of the birth of the Weimar Republic as well as during its later career, its real problem was not smooth technical working but whether it could appeal to those driving forces which were alive in the nation. In a widely-noticed speech at the Congress of the Majority Socialists, held on 10th–15th June 1919 at Weimar, Wissell, perhaps disappointed by the Government's failure to pay more than lip-service to his 'socialization' projects, said:

> 'The Government works on a compromise platform which prevents us from doing serious work on the decisive issues. We have established formal political democracy; but by so doing we have merely fulfilled the programme of the last imperial Government, that of Prince Max of Baden (*applause*). The people takes very little interest in the shaping of the Constitution. . . . We are continuing to govern under the old forms of political life and have poured but little new wine into them. . . .The achievements of the revolution are regarded by the people as essentially negative. . . . The military government has been replaced by a new one the principles of which differ little from those of the old bourgeois ones. . . . History's judgment of us will be stern and bitter.'

David, one of Ebert's closest personal supporters, in fact merely underlined Wissel's point when he objected that the Government, for its part, had good cause 'to be dissatisfied with the people' which hindered its work by revolutionary ideologies and strikes; Eggerstädt, a right-wing trade unionist, replied that Wissel had only expressed the feelings of the masses. Stampfer commented in *Vorwärts* of June 17th that Wissel's speech and the discussion that followed had laid bare the deep crisis of Socialism which was only superficially concealed by the tactical homogeneity enforced by the circumstances.

Only occasionally did these processes affect the work of the Constituent Assembly. After the resignation of the Independent People's Commissars, the remaining (right-wing Social Democrat) Commissars had invited a Democratic professor, Hugo Preuss, to prepare a draft for the Constitution; he attempted to combine parliamentary democracy, which was generally accepted as the new framework, with elements of a Presidential Republic on the American pattern. Within the Constituent Assembly there were serious disputes on two points only. Following the traditions of German democratic liberalism since 1848, Preuss suggested redistributing the national territory into sixteen States of roughly equal size and importance, which implied the abolition of Prussia; the representatives of these States, directly elected by the people, would form a Second Chamber, and Preuss found it possible to grant such a Chamber the right of veto (in the constitution as eventually accepted the Second Chamber, which was nominated by the State Governments, had merely a suspensive veto). Thus increased powers had to be granted to the national Government which, in view of the economic development since Bismarck's days, would have been supplemented by guarantees against Prussian supremacy in the central Government. But the Constituent Assembly had not only a unitarian majority, embracing both Liberal and both Socialist parties, but also a very strong pro-Prussian camp, formed by the Conservatives, both Liberal parties (apart from a few Democratic ideologues, such as Preuss), and the right wing of Social Democracy, except for its Bavarian and allied members. Heine, the Prussian Social Democratic Minister,[1] opposed any 'dismemberment of Prussia' with arguments which any right-wing monarchist might have used with greater ideological consistency. The only large anti-unitarian party, the Centre, was much less opposed to continuing traditional Prussia than to altering the structure and borders of the existing non-Prussian States, whose bureaucratic inertia was the essence of its 'federalism'. In the outcome, the conditions for an alteration of existing State boundaries were so shaped that they were inapplicable except where State Governments themselves were convinced of the absurdity of their limits as imposed by history; thus eventually the small Thüringian States (even so, excepting the Prussian territories scattered among them) were fused into a larger unit; the most southerly of them, Coburg, was absorbed by Bavaria.[2] For the rest, the structure of Bismarck's empire was preserved, but the powers of the federation were enlarged, principally by the financial reform eventually introduced by a Centre Minister, Erzberger. Old Prussia's authority was exercised not so much through the Prussian vote in the Second Chamber as by the powers of the President, who, independently of his party ticket, was closely connected with the Prussian Army.

On the second point of dispute the Centre played a more active part because the issue involved its special grievance, religious education. The Weimar Constitution was to have a preamble consisting of a long catalogue of Fundamental Rights. This was partly for ideological reasons—in the Central European countries a mere enumeration of formal con-

[1] See above, pp. 85 and 105.

[2] For the details see my *Federalism*, etc., pp. 98 ff.

stitutional guarantees without consideration for the special needs and desires of each important social group would have had little appeal—and partly because agreement on these principles implied agreement on at least the main lines of future legislation, without which the coalition could not be kept together. The Centre had a basic interest in religious education; and those in the Social Democratic caucus who wished to meet it, for opportunist reasons, could compromise with a sectarian[1] trend within their own ranks which was strongly interested in modern schools with general moral teaching and no religious interference. During the period when the Centre, because of the dispute over the Versailles Treaty, was the only coalition partner of the Socialists, the 'first Weimar educational compromise' was agreed upon: equal rights were given to schools of three types: (a) denominational schools supervised by the State as well as by the sectarian bodies as regards all their teaching; (b) the so-called 'simultaneous' school for children of various denominations, where religious instruction was given by State-controlled teachers belonging to the denomination concerned, from which children could be excused at their parents' request;[2] (c) the 'secular' school with no religious instruction and purely State-controlled. After the Democrats re-entered the Government, the Centre had to agree to the 'second Weimar educational compromise', which was also supported by the National Conservatives and by most members of the People's Party, i.e., all the important Protestant representatives; the 'simultaneous school' (type b)

[1] It evidently represented a distortion of the Socialist programme; the latter's 'secular school' was seen as the standard of national education, non-denominational but not positively rationalist, leaving religious education to the free decision of the parents. The 'secular school' of Weimar Germany was a mere educational experiment for a restricted number of children from a definitely rationalist environment, a kind of Socialist ghetto; in Prussia, on 1st May 1927, out of 4·2 million children and 110,000 teachers in all the elementary schools, only 77,000 children with 2,025 teachers were in secular schools, all of them, of course, in large towns. For this reason the Communists would suggest that worker parents should send their children to 'simultaneous schools' but have them excused from religious instruction—as, without ideological reasons, did most Socialist parents in the larger industrial centres. The point up to which German legislation could be interpreted on the lines of Socialist principles was illustrated by experience in Saxony: an enactment of 22nd July 1919 which put religious instruction on a purely voluntary basis—the local authorities being advised to give the demominational bodies technical facilities, such as rooms, for their activities—was ruled by the Federal Supreme Court to be incompatible with the Weimar Constitution; but a second law was allowed to shift on to the parents the initiative in demanding religious instruction, which was given by State-appointed volunteer teachers, and not supervised by denominational bodies. After the events of 1923, such an interpretation of the law in the sense of left-wing principles came to an end.

[2] A policy similar to the British educational compromise of 1944 would have been inconceivable in a country where religion and political conservatism were so closely associated, so that there was a very strong rationalist trend within the working class, and where Roman Catholicism was by far the best-organized denominational group, so that there was no question of an 'agreed syllabus'.

was described as the normal type, 'schools of a certain world outlook' (types a and c) which by the first compromise would have enjoyed equal rights were to be established only if a certain number of parents demanded them (as was the rule in Catholic Bavaria before Hitler was firmly established). A Federal Law on Education was promised by the Constitution and regarded by the Catholics as the only safeguard against possible Erastian developments in the simultaneous school; as the specific Catholic demands could not be satisfied except within the framework of a right-wing coalition, the promise to enact the law, though never fulfilled, was eventually used to keep them within such a coalition.[1]

More important than these points of dispute was the ease with which the decisive articles of the Weimar Constitution were enacted. Ebert's personal ambitions[2] were supported by his collaboration with the Army. Delbrück, the National Conservative leader, speaking in the Assembly on July 7th, described the President's increased powers as an achievement of his own collaboration in the framing of the Constitution; during the debates only an Independent Socialist M.P., Cohn, noticed the danger that article 48 might eventually serve as a means for some General to supersede legislation by Parliament. Preuss, however, whose interest in limiting the rule of the parliamentary parties[3] had contributed to establishing the Presidency in its actual form, defined Presidential initiative as the designation of 'the man who, in the light of the whole political situation, appears to be the competent leader of public opinion as embodied in Parliament'.[4] In authoritative treatises on German constitutional law[5] it was stated that 'since the Constitution is intended to set up a parliamentary, and not a Presidential, Republic', the President's powers, including the suspensive veto, must be exercised as a *pouvoir moderateur*, supporting the majority Government but not seeking to frustrate it, or aiming at obtaining by pertinacity a controlling power for himself. When, in the autumn of 1923, Ebert transferred to a General his alleged power to suspend or dissolve constitutional State Governments, and in the following winter transferred his dictatorial powers

[1] See below, note [2] on p. 266.

[2] Social Democracy was not united on the issue. Scheidemann, who was Prime Minister at the time, looked to a Presidency with essentially representative functions; he therefore offered to Ebert, as Party Leader, his retirement from the Chancellorship to some other Ministry in order to let Ebert occupy the most important office; he was greatly surprised when Ebert decided in favour of keeping the Presidency. (Cf. *Memoirs*, vol. II, p. 616.)

[3] He argued (*Staat, Recht und Freiheit*, p. 387) on the basis of Montesquieu's concept of the separation of powers, perhaps without noticing that the established administrative and military machinery with which such compromises were made in his days was that of the Prussian monarchy.

[4] *Nachlass*, p. 445.

[5] R. Thoma, in *Handbuch des deutschen Staatsrechts*, vol. I, p. 508.

over all Germany to a General, Preuss[1] complained of such 'transformation of a civilian republic into a scarcely veiled dictatorship of the sabre'; but from the very beginning[2] Ebert appears to have been more correct in interpreting the potentialities of his office.

If Preuss, in 1919, did not wish things to happen as they did, he did everything to thwart his own intentions. The direct election of the President was not only bound to give him an authority at least equal to that of Parliament, but also to bring to the surface the two-party system latent in Germany: [3] the alternative was to have a *Front populaire* President,[4] not unlikely to be faced with an Army mutiny, or a President of the Hindenburg type, whose advent could be foreseen without special political genius.[5] Neither alternative was palatable to the framers of the Weimar Constitution, but it was extremely naïve to expect one and the same party system to produce a left-wing President and a coalition including the Big Business interest. The kind of Presidential candidate likely to be produced by the German coalition system was a person standing on the extreme right of the left-centre coalition, like Marx in 1925, otherwise the right wing of the coalition could not hope to be kept within the combination;[6] the fate of such a candidate, if confronted with an attractive right-wing alternative, was not difficult to foresee. If there was any wish to have a *pouvoir moderateur* in Germany, it would be satisfied by the need for coalitions within Parliament, not against it; and if there was any chance of saving democracy within the framework of the Weimar Constitution, the Constitution's rulings on the Presidency would have had to be used to rally the left wing against the Army-Big-Business combination; but this was precisely what its authors did not want.

Only one point in the Constitution went beyond the typical liberal outlook, and showed traces of the mass movements without which the Republic would not have come into being. Since the Auxiliary Service Act of 1916.[7] Workers' Committees had been established in all factories with over fifty workers, and since the Working Community Agreement of 15th November 1918,[8] in all shops with more than twenty workers. The workers' desire to have a representation of their interests in the factories, independent of their employers as well as of the Trade Union

[1] *Um die Reichsverfassung vom Weimar*, p. 42.

[2] See f.n. [2], previous p.

[3] See below, pp. 232–3 and 283.

[4] He need not be a Social Democrat; a left-wing and pacifist Catholic like Wirth who, in 1922, declared that 'for me, the Right wing is the enemy', would have been greatly preferable to another Ebert from the point of view of the Left.

[5] Stresemann made the suggestion as early as 1920 in connexion with the ideological preparation for the Kapp Putsch.

[6] See below, p. 233.

[7] See above, p. 127.

[8] See above p. 152.

leaders' collaboration policies, contributed much more to their demand for a Councils system than did the confused concepts of 'socialization', or the 'Soviets', more fictitious than real.[1] When the second wave of the German revolution started with mass strikes in the last days of February 1919, the demand for workers' control, or at least for legal recognition of workers' councils, was in the forefront. Scheidemann, who understood that it was directed against the trade union bureaucracy, on February 25th declared, on behalf of the Government, that 'none of its members contemplates, or has ever contemplated, the incorporation of the Councils system in any form in the Constitution or in the administrative machinery'. But this orthodox capitalist policy was answered by a general strike in the Berlin engineering industries, and the Catholic leader Erzberger mediated.[2] As General Märcker was just out to destroy the People's Sailors' Division in Berlin, which had remained neutral in the January fighting, some concession had to be made to the Berlin Social Democratic workers to prevent them from joining the struggle. On March 4th, Scheidemann gave to his fellow-partisans on strike in Berlin a written undertaking that 'the Workers' Councils shall be recognized as a representation of the workers' interests, and anchored in the Constitution'. For this purpose territorial Workers' Councils (Chambers) and a Federal Workers' Council were to be established. Accordingly, Article 165 was inserted in the draft Constitution: after recognizing the equal rights of employers and employed in fixing conditions of labour, their organizations and agreements (i.e. the Working Community Agreement of November 1918) the article goes on:

> 'In order to represent their social and economic interests, workers and salaried employees shall be represented in Factory Workers' Councils, District Workers' Councils for regions forming economic units, and a National Workers' Council.

District Economic Councils and a National Economic Council were to be formed by the corresponding Workers' Councils 'together with representatives of the employers, and other sections concerned' in order 'to fulfil all economic tasks and to collaborate in the execution of the laws concerning socialization'. The National Economic Council had to be consulted by the Government on draft bills 'of essential importance for social and economic policies' before they were introduced in Parliament; it could also initiate such bills independently of the Government.

Of all the promises of Article 165 only the Factory Workers' Councils[3] and a Provisional Federal Economic Council were actually set up; the latter was a consultative body made up of representatives of the

[1] See above, pp. 151 and 154.
[2] Cf. Guillebaud, op. cit., p. 9.
[3] See below, pp. 289 ff.

various economic interests, in the labour field the trade unions; interference in State or Federal politics by directly elected representatives of the workers was thus avoided. Familiar as chambers of trade and commerce, of agriculturalists, etc., had been long since, Workers' Chambers were regarded as undesirable from the employers' as well as from the trade union bureaucrats'[1] point of view: when their formation was considered by the left-wing State Governments in Gotha and Brunswick in 1919 and Saxony in 1923 it was regarded as a piece of 'legal Bolshevism' and contributed to the eventual removal of the State Governments by Federal execution.[2]

The major decision which the Constituent Assembly had to face was the acceptance of the Versailles Treaty. There was no alternative,[3] but a clever manœuvring for position was necessary in order to restrict the eventual use of the fact by the right-wing opposition and, more important, to preserve the support of the Army, without which the Government could not survive for a day, but which might easily take the Government's nationalist phraseology too seriously. Inspired by both motives, and perhaps also by the hope of bringing some pressure to bear upon the Allies who regarded the coalition Government in Germany as as the only safeguard against 'Bolshevism', some Social Democrats went rather far in verbal opposition; throughout the Republic's existence, Scheidemann's declaration that 'the hand which signs this treaty should dry up' proved a boomerang, as only he,[4] and not his party, could avoid

[1] The resistance of these latter shows their own estimate of their backing within the working class; in Austria directly elected Workers' Chambers operated as an additional representation of the trade unions (though with an insignificant Communist minority representation) and as a State-financed centre for research and similar activities.

[2] In Gotha and Brunswick Central Workers' Councils were formed as a kind of Second Chambers; they had the right to introduce bills (as envisaged in Art. 165 of the national Constitution) and to appeal by plebiscite to the electorate against enactments of the First Chamber (as the working-class parties, in view of their electoral strength, could do in any case). But the principle that Workers' Councils should not interfere with legislation was at stake; Märcker's troops entered Gotha on February 17th and Brunswick on April 9th. Cf. Cohn, M.P., in the Weimar National Assembly, 3rd July 1919, Proceedings, vol. 327, p. 1261. The Saxon law, establishing a purely consultative Workers' Chamber similar to the existing Commercial and Agricultural Chambers, was enacted immediately before the Reichswehr entered Saxony and never came into operation.

[3] There is no need to discuss the alternative available in the event—merely hypothetical, as we have seen—of a working-class triumph in January or March 1919; presumably the very fact of such a result of the German civil war would have resulted in armed collision with the Allies; some kind of 'Brest-Litovsk'—say, temporary acceptance of the secession of the occupied zones, to which Bavaria might have been added on her own initiative, would have been quite a favourable outcome from the Socialist point of view.

[4] In reading Scheidemann's *Memoirs*, English ed., vol. II, pp. 229 ff., one can hardly avoid the impression that he felt outmanœuvred by Ebert who had put him into the foreground of nationalist phraseology in order to get rid of him on occasion

signature. Noske had to make a formal resignation in order to preserve the Army's confidence; he appealed to the officers to withdraw the resignations tendered by them in protest against the treaty, so that the struggle against Bolshevism might continue. In this critical situation the Independent Socialist Party was the first of all the German parties to declare itself in favour of acceptance; to the foreign Socialists who expected the German Socialists to refuse to sign so that the revolutionary movements in their own countries might be strengthened, Haase answered that for the moment such hopes were utopian, and Germany needed immediate peace. Just as the right-wing Socialists' 'internationalism' had evaporated when the German bourgeoisie needed war, so did that of the Independents when it needed a scapegoat to shoulder the responsibility for its peace; in neither case was any attempt made to think beyond the feelings current at the moment amongst the masses. Quite consistently, *Vorwärts* on 19th May 1919 explained to the Independents the contradictions inherent in their attitude; it was nonsense to talk about World Revolution while rejecting the only measure which might—perhaps—put World Revolution into motion. The editor, Stampfer, who himself was a quite honest opponent of signature, added that, after signature, every German government, 'including a purely Socialist one', would be bound to function as the sweater on behalf of Allied capitalism; the Independent *Freiheit*, on June 2nd, answered that only acceptance could keep Germany and her hope for an eventual revision of the treaty in being. Thus the roles were changed; the right-wing Social Democrat argued from the standpoint of Socialism to show the consequences of acceptance (which his party, eventually, was quite willing to draw), while the 'left-winger' proved to be the more far-sighted bourgeois politician. For the time being, the demagogic game continued; on May 21st the Social Democrats arranged street demonstrations in Berlin against the Independents' propaganda for acceptance. The Democrats found it convenient to escape, for a time, from Government responsibility; a new coalition Government between the Social Democrats and Centre parties had to be formed. It bowed to the unavoidable; even the National Conservatives helped by promising before the division that, while voting against the Treaty, they would never question the patriotic motives of those who had decided the other way. We need hardly add that the promise was not long kept.

(*f*) *The Formation of Republican Austria*

Germany moved from the appearance of a Soviet dictatorship with bourgeois 'specialist' Ministers to an ordinary coalition Government of

of the reconstruction of the Government. Certainly the issue had two aspects; at that time there were numerous possibilities on the cards, and in some of them it would have been nice to have been the martyr both of nationalism and of resistance to the man responsible for killing 10,000 revolutionary workers.

Social Democracy and the more moderate of the bourgeois parties: Czechoslovakia and Austria arrived at the same governmental structure from the all-national coalitions with which they had started during the dissolution of the Hapsburg monarchy. The main difference arose from the fact that the old State machinery and Army had melted away with the Hapsburg monarchy. In Czechoslovakia some break with the past, which did not rule out the integration of the bulk of the old officers and bureaucrats into the new State machine, was imposed by the fact that the new State was derived from a national movement which from its predecessor's point of view was treasonable and allied with its external enemies; in Austria it followed from the fact that the old army simply disappeared; a new one could not be created except by appealing to the Socialist sympathies of the unemployed, the only persons who were prepared to join. This was clearly the only alternative to having an army of mere mercenaries; when eventually the peace treaty established the professional character of the Austrian army and Austria's internal development made the soldiers' professional future dependent on the favours of right-wing politicians, all the safeguards set up to preserve the army's republican character proved to be of only temporary value.[1]

For the time being, however, Austria had an army which took the oath to Socialist principles as well as to the constitution of the Republic, which marched under red banners, and took political advice from the Workers' and Soldiers' Councils; this made the Austrian Republic appear more radical than it was—though for better reasons than the German Republic, which had originated in the Soviet comedy but was soon controlled by the Prussian army. A political position incomparably stronger than in Germany was also granted to the Austrian working class in the field of administration; in view of the sabotage and corruption of the bureaucracy, even the necessary minimum of food supplies for the towns could not be secured without wide control of local administration by the Workers' Councils.[2] These thus became an important factor in local government long before they were centralized in order to get a discussion platform with the Communists.[3] The right wing, for its part, armed the well-to-do peasants so that they might defend their food stores and the 'freedom of trade' against requisitionings by Council-controlled food offices and the various checks set up with or without the

[1] See below, pp. 186 and 316–7.

[2] Cf. O. Bauer, *The Austrian Revolution*, p. 86.

[3] See below, pp. 182*ff*. This origin from really existent and functioning local organs, at least as much as the need to have real elections in order to be possessed of authority in relation to the Communists, also made the central organs of the Austrian 'Soviet' system much more important than were the corresponding ones in Germany, whose political role was over as soon as they had decided to transfer power to parliamentary democracy. The Austrian Councils were intended to function within such a democracy, and did so, at least as bodies which gave the Social Democratic leaders information about the feelings of their rank and file. See below, p. 202.

authority of the central Government. Because of the complete breakdown of the monarchy there was no real focal point around which those counter-revolutionary forces could rally, apart from the slogan 'Away from Red Vienna' (i.e. from the region of food shortage which was not prepared to pay the proper black market prices but exercised political pressure under horrible 'Bolshevist' slogans); this found expression in the Alpine lands in secession moves in favour of any neighbour with the desirable political outlook—Switzerland, Italy, reactionary Bavaria, and even Hungary.[1] In the international situation as it then was, a disintegration of Austria was bound to bring about open conflict between the French and Italian blocs, so that the easiest way of compromise was to keep existing Austria together; apart from this, the interest of Vienna Big Business in keeping at least the rest of Austria united was far too strong to allow the influence of the right wing of the Christian Social Party to be used for the encouragement of separatism; the days when the armed peasants could be made use of for a right-wing *coup* all over Austria were not yet. On the other hand, the connexions between the provincial Social Democrats and the left wing of the local Christian Socials were strong enough to nourish a common aversion to being drawn into experiences of the Bavarian or Hungarian type.[2]

The political slogan of *Anschluss* with Germany, which grew up in the nationalist atmosphere of disintegrating Austria, especially among the intelligentsia,[3] was accepted in the Provisional Constitution of November 12th and also in the definitive Constitution as enacted by the Constituent Assembly on 14th March 1919. But no attempt was made to realize it in November-December 1918, when the Allies would have had to accept the accomplished fact as an application of the principle of national self-determination. They might have punished Germany by settling some frontier problem even less favourably in the Versailles Treaty; the fear that this might happen was the overt argument brought forward against a *de facto Anschluss* from the German side, and by some Austrians with a strong interest in Germany's power. But the use of this argument was simply another way of saying that some Upper Silesian or East Prussian districts were more important to Germany than reunion with a people which was looked upon as one of the constituent parts of the German nation. There might be much opportunism in such an argument (it would be easier to get, by treaty revision after a few years, an *Anschluss* on a voluntary basis, for which a theoretical majority was always available in Austria, than to retrieve territory lost to Poland); but there was also a quite real aversion among the actual rulers of Germany to having a Catholic majority in the country, and, within the labour movement, a strengthening of Independent Socialism, with which

[1] See below, pp. 179 and 204.
[2] See below, p. 203.
[3] See above, p. 141.

the overwhelming majority of Austrian Social Democrats were in sympathy. In November, when 'Soviet' Germany seemed far to the left of Austria, the fear that an end of coalition parliamentarism might involve the country in the German upheaval may have been one of the main reasons which caused the Austrian Catholics to drop the Hapsburg monarchy.[1] Later, when the Austrian workers' temporary delusions about the character of the German Republic[2] had disappeared, the frontier might be regarded as a solid barrier against the entry of Noske and his Reichswehr into the country. The dispute about whether the Austrians were a distinct nation, carried on mainly among the *émigrés* during World War II, belongs to the realm of nationalist scholasticism; nations are formed, and disintegrate, precisely in that social groups for certain reasons (however opportunist in appearance) begin to draw, or cease to draw, certain political conclusions which follow from the existence of a national community. It is quite irrelevant to this process whether there is an intention to create, or to dissolve, some existing nation—such intentions are mainly found among propagandists who do not need to express the feelings of the masses—and the masses need not have any concept of nationality; certainly the Dutch and Swiss had none when they parted their ways from those of the Germans. Nor does it matter whether there has been 'external violence'; the simplest way to get some development not accounted for by nationalist ideology accepted is to 'dictate' some treaty, and see whether it is revised at the next opportunity, and even if it is revised, whether 'restored national unity' will withstand the next situation in which fidelity to the supposed nationality proves inopportune.

The political structure of Czechoslovak and Austrian government was defined through the swings in public opinion which had happened during and immediately after the war, and became evident at the next elections. In Czechoslovakia there were no national elections until 1920; as the Czech parties disliked arguing about the Constitution with the national minorities, the committee of the Czech parties, with co-opted Slovak representatives, which had been formed in October-November 1918 as a National Assembly[3] went on legislating and eventually enacted the Constitution, beginning with the preamble: 'We, the Czechoslovak people. . . .' But the municipal elections of May 1919 showed a definite trend towards the left; so the all-national coalition, in which according to the intensity of their nationalist phraseology the Young Czechs and similar parties had played parts quite disproportionate to their likelihood of support from the electorate, was replaced by the 'red-green' one —i.e. Social Democrats and Agrarians, who between them had the support of all the important mass-organizations save the Roman Catholic

[1] See above, p. 143.
[2] See note [2] above, p. 141.
[3] See above, note [3] on p. 145.

Church, which was compromised by its prolonged support of the Hapsburgs. It might be at least open to question whether a coalition of trade unions and peasants' co-operatives was capable of developing a foreign policy or making a common stand on major issues; this problem was evaded because of the existence of a group of national figures with great prestige[1] and experience whose leadership was hardly disputed during the whole existence of the Republic; perhaps precisely because they were unable to develop a political party of their own which might have competed with those already in existence.

The political party system of Austria which continued throughout the lifetime of the democratic Republic was already established in the first elections under general suffrage with proportional representation, on 16th February 1919. The two chief parties, Social Democrats and Christian Socials, were nearly equal in strength; in these first elections which were influenced by the revolutionary wave, the Social Democrats polled 1·21 million votes, the Christian Socials 1·07 million. Each of them had special strongholds; the Social Democrats Vienna, the industrial regions of Lower Austria and Upper Styria, and the more industrialized provincial towns such as Graz and Linz, and also Carinthia; elsewhere the party formed a significant minority, except in the western parts of Upper Austria, Eastern Styria, and Eastern Tyrol, the only regions where it polled less than 20 per cent. The Christian Socials were the strongest party in nearly all the non-industrial regions, and polled more than 20 per cent of the total vote even in the industrial regions other than the working-class quarters of Vienna. Even in 1919 the German Nationalists, whose later fate, for thirteen years, was to be continuous decay, proved to be a small party, with 550,000 votes; their influence was restricted to the lower middle classes and the richer peasants in Styria and especially in Carinthia where, with a third of the total vote, they held the second place after the Social Democrats, thus reducing the Catholics to an insignificant position; during the period 1919–30 the German Nationalists were reduced to a fifth of the total vote even in this most nationalistic of all the Austrian provinces. The two-party system thus established should not be thought of as a clear-cut front of town versus countryside; while the Christian Socials remained the party of most of the urban lower middle classes, the Social Democrats made extensive inroads amongst the agricultural workers, though these were overestimated by the bourgeois Press which was horrified at the loss of the conservative monopoly of the countryside.[2]

There was no doubt from the start that a coalition of the two major

[1] The prestige of the Masaryk-Benes group was partly based upon the elimination of competing political authority by the bankruptcy of the pro-Austrian orientation of Catholics and right-wing Social Democrats as well as of the pro-Tsarist part of the Young Czechs.

[2] Cf. *Neue Freie Presse*, 18th February 1919.

parties was the only alternative to civil war; in the circumstances, the German Nationalists preferred to occupy the position of chief defenders of free enterprise, left vacant by the reluctance of even the Christian Socials to appear as the protectors of Big Business, and to advocate against the left-centre coalition whatever conservative interest happened to be in the foreground.[1] So the young State was spared, for many years, an opposition which appealed to nationalist sentiment, however strong this sentiment might be within either of the major parties. With due respect for the workers' susceptibilities the coalition was described, by the Social Democratic leaders, as a 'workers' and peasants' Government'; and certainly, at least during the first period, there was some tendency on the part of the Christian Social Provincial representatives to put the interests of the Viennese bourgeoisie in the background. But as early as 30th May 1919, when during a deadlock in the discussions on the Law on the Factory Councils the Social Democrats sought direct negotiations with the 'peasants' representatives', Kunschak, the leader of the Viennese Christian Socials, reminded them that, whatever phraseology they might prefer, they had made a coalition with the Christian Social *party* as a whole, not merely with one group within it. This was true, at least so far as essentials were concerned; and, quite apart from the influence of the Viennese bourgeoisie on the Christian Social caucus, bourgeois 'specialists', as in Germany, looked after the interests of Big Business.

Nothing more than lip-service was ever paid to 'socialization'. On 7th April 1919 the workers of the Alpine Montan Company, the country's main heavy industrial combine, which held first place on the 'socialization' list, deposed the management and asked for immediate legislative action, but the 'specialist' Finance Minister, Schumpeter, arranged for sufficient delay for the shares to be acquired by the Italian Fiat combine; they thus became 'Allied property', and the Armistice Commission, headed by the Italian General Segré, intervened in the appropriate way. Even so moderate a measure as the law obliging Joint Stock Companies to allow the State to participate in any issue of additional stock, so as to give it some representation on the Boards of the major companies, was answered by extreme threats on Segré's part to enforce the resale of the State's part in a new issue of shares in the Alpine Montan Company to the Fiat group as majority holder. It was not external pressure, however, that was mainly responsible for the failure

[1] Its compatibility or otherwise with national feelings was less important. In his Memoirs Count Erdoedy, one of the leaders in the war fought by the White Hungarians in 1920–21 against the Austrian Republic, reported how, in spring 1919, when 'Chief of Police of the German National Parliamentary Party' (in Austria) he had to organize a West Hungarian movement against the Hungarian Soviet Republic; being a Hungarian landlord he did this, of course, with no pro-Austrian bias. While serving the Austro-German Nationalist party, he thus became a protagonist of the struggle against the union of the region with Austria.

to nationalize Austria's chief industries; as early as 1919 Otto Bauer in his pamphlet *Der Weg zum Sozialismus* opposed a measure so obviously conducive to State control of industry as nationalization of the big banks, which in Austria controlled all the major industries, because of the large share of their capital held abroad, and because their assets in the other Succession States of the Hapsburg monarchy could be much better used in the Austrian interest if they remained in private hands. In summer 1919 the Provinces demanded, and received from the Federal Government, control of the public rights over minerals, water power, and forests; these rights were never used by the Christian Social majorities in the Provincial governments except to sell concessions for their use to private entrepreneurs. Of the whole nationalization programme, as accepted after the February elections, even by the Christian Socials, nothing remained save a new form of management for a few State enterprises set up during the war, which otherwise would have had to close down.

Thus the achievements of the Austrian revolution remained confined to some reforms in labour legislation, most of them enacted while pressure was being brought upon the Austrian bourgeoisie by the existence of a Soviet régime in neighbouring Hungary.[1] The most important of these measures—ephemeral by its very nature—was the obligation, established by the law of May 14th, compelling all enterprises employing more than fifteen workers to increase their staff by 20 per cent, and not to dismiss workers without the consent of the District Industrial Committees (which were composed of representatives of the State, the employers, and the trade unions), and the Law on Factory Councils.[2] The eight-hour day, which in Germany was proclaimed as the first real achievement of the Revolution—although in fact soon abolished[3]—was only provisionally enacted in Austria in December 1918, but was preserved until the end of the Republic. Even the law of 20th July 1919 on Workers' Holidays, an object of special pride to the Social Democrats, and of special attack by the bourgeois side, did not go even as far as the Hitlerite German, not to speak of the Soviet Russian, laws; only for the holidays of juvenile workers was fairly satisfactory provision made. In general it may be said that Austrian social legislation, while very cautious wherever the production costs of industry were seriously concerned, aimed at removing the actual barriers that had prevented any part of the working class from sharing in the cultural activities of the labour movement (except for the agricultural workers, whose employers were the main support of the coalition on the Christian Social side). Enactments such as the abolition of night baking, limitation of working

[1] This was the well-considered tactic of the Social Democrat leaders. Cf. O. Bauer, *The Austrian Revolution*, pp. 31–2.

[2] See above, p. 179, and below, p. 289.

[3] See below, p. 228.

hours, guaranteed free time for domestic workers, protection of home workers, etc., while completely harmless to the profits of industrial enterprise, provoked the most vociferous protests on the part of the bourgeois Press, which thus demonstrated the impossibility of achieving even the most moderate reforms without continuous working-class pressure.

There was no revolutionary crisis in Austria comparable to the German events of December–March 1919.[1] The existence in spring 1919 of the Bavarian and Hungarian Soviet Republics (the former of which was divided from the Austrian centres by large conservative regions on either side of the border and never became a serious political factor) mattered not so much for any revolutionary implications it might have within Austria as because of the strengthening of the reactionary trends within Austria while those Republics existed, and particularly after their fall. There were, however, lively discussions among the Austrian workers as to whether the Russian and Hungarian examples should be followed; this argument might have developed into a split of the Social Democratic Party had not its leaders accepted the principle that the decision whether to preserve parliamentary democracy or not lay with the Workers' and Soldiers' Councils, a majority of which, if in favour of assuming power, might claim the loyalty of the army[2] and the subordination of the minority of the labour movement.[3] In order 'to fetter

[1] For Czechoslovakia, see below, p. 200.

[2] See above, p. 175.

[3] In critical situations such as that of 13th June 1919 (see below in the text) the Workers' Council did not fail to proclaim its fundamental assent to the principles of Soviet dictatorship, adding, however, that conditions at the time were unfavourable to its establishment. Such statements have frequently been taken by bourgeois critics as proof that no differences other than tactical divided Friedrich Adler and Otto Bauer from the Communists. Undoubtedly, *to their left* there was a group of Austrian Social Democrats which took such an attitude, and therefore differed from the more reasonable majority of the Austrian Communists (see f.n. [2] below p. 183) merely in their belief that they could pursue their policies within the Social Democratic Party; in view of the earlier and later (see below, pp. 202 and 343) record of the Upper Austrian labour movement it is quite possible that the Upper Austrian Workers' councils, when suggesting in March 1919 a centralization of the Councils movement, were inspired by such an attitude. Even together with the Communists this group would have formed a mere minority, though a large one, within the Soviet Congress; but it would have been bound to vote against any resolution which did not recognize, in principle, the right of the working-class organization to establish its dictatorship. Moreover, without such a recognition the main case for expecting the Communists to bow to an adverse Soviet decision would have gone. So the most leftward group which was necessary for the formation of an overwhelming majority against the Communists (at the meeting of the Vienna Workers' Council of June 13th 231 against 27 votes, with 6 abstentions) determined the terms of the resolutions; these resolutions were supported even by the right-wing group round Renner which (as their behaviour in February 1934 was to show, see p. 343) rejected not only proletarian dictatorship but even the use of violence to defend democracy. It is possible that the Bauer-Adler Centrist group regarded the Soviets not only as a safety-valve to prevent

the Communists', as Julius Deutsch has put it, or 'to create an organ of joint action for all the trends of the Socialist labour movement', to use the words of the organizing statute drawn up at the time, the Workers' Councils which had grown up locally were centralized in a national system immediately after the establishment of the Hungarian Soviet Republic; 'For over a year the Workers' Council performed most efficiently the function of a safety-valve in constant explosive use, or a ventilator turning continuously in rushing wind. It was a common ground, where all the shades of Marxist opinion met, where the violent and the impatient would let off steam and satisfy themselves with the appearance of doing something, where minorities (as the Communists were) could make their voices heard, and were therefore not wholly driven back into force.'[1] Obviously, having proclaimed the principle of Soviet dictatorship, the Communists could not attempt an armed *coup* in its favour when the Workers' Councils declined to assume power.

The most important episode in the life of the Austrian 'Soviet' was the vote of the Vienna Workers' Council of 13th June, 1920; it prevented a *coup* planned by a minority of the Austrian Communists after the Armistice Commission, on the suggestion of the Viennese bourgeoisie, had demanded a reduction of the army to a mere 12,000 men[2] and thus provoked the soldiers. The Revolutionary Soldiers' Committee led by the (Austrian) Communists successfully organized an armed demonstration of the soldiers on June 5th and prepared some kind of 'factory occupation' in case the dismissals should be carried out; the threat was sufficient to support Otto Bauer's refusal, on June 12th, to execute the Armistice Commission's order, which was directed against the Social

Communist action (this was certainly their *main* intention) but also as a bridge which might be used in case events outside Austria should suggest the establishment of a 'Soviet' dictatorship (i.e. of a monopoly of power by the organized labour movement) without the risk of civil and external war; but they did not consider such a prospect likely, nor did they desire it. All the groups in the Soviet from the Bauer-Adler group to the moderate majority of the Communists were linked by the desire that whatever moves might become necessary should be backed by an overwhelming majority of the working class, so that bloody splits on the German pattern might be avoided. They were not political children who expected adventurers such as Bettelheim (see f.n. [2] below p. 183) or former supporters of the Hapsburg monarchy such as Renner to support majority decisions taken against their will; but they may have hoped that an overwhelming vote of representatives of the working class elected in the factories would force such principal opponents to retreat grudgingly into some corner (as, in those days, did the right-wing minority of the Hungarian Social Democrats).

[1] Macartney, *Social Revolution in Austria*, pp. 131–2.

[2] The fact that the Treaty of Saint-Germain eventually allowed for an army of 30,000 men supports the explanation given in the text (which also coincides with Gen. Segrés whole attitude as illustrated, for example, on the nationalization issue—see above, p. 179). The Socialist army was the main grievance of the 'great Press' and of big business and aristocratic circles; a reduction far below the planned level would both have increased unemployment, and opened gaps for recruitment in the conservative countryside.

Democratic majority of the Army at least as much as its small Communist minority. But the Austrian C.P., at that moment, was controlled by an unofficial Hungarian emissary, and the minority he organized as a new Party Centre went on with their preparations for the *coup*. A large-scale collision could not have been avoided had not the vote of the Vienna Workers' and Soldiers' Council on June 13th supported the position of the opponents of the *coup* within the Communist camp, so that the Government's concession to the soldiers was accepted. In these circumstances, the critical day would have passed quietly had not the Vienna Police President, Schober, anxious to establish his reputation as a 'saviour of society',[1] on the evening June 14th arrested the Communist Party officials as a meeting was calling off the action planned.[2] The

[1] See below, p. 315. Erdoedy reports in his Memoirs (p. 140) that in January 1918 (see above, pp. 137–8) Schober was already in favour of shooting against the workers.

[2] This presentation of the events is based, apart from contemporary publications, on an argument with the participation of the main responsible, Ernst Bettelheim, in the Vienna periodical *Kommunismus* (1921), which was influenced by the disputes among the Hungarian *émigrés*. It seems fairly clear that even in May 1919, when Bettelheim was sent to Vienna allegedly at the request of one of the factions of the Austrian C.P., the Hungarian Communists were divided amongst themselves; who actually backed his far-reaching powers, which included the right, if necessary, 'to dissolve the Austrian C.P., in order to reorganize it', has never become clear. The most remarkable fact is that, at a time when the existence of the Comintern was purely theoretical, and it was also unwilling to back the Hungarian faction which sent this strange emissary (cf. Radek's very sharp article in *The Communist International*, vi. 9, 'The Lessons of an Attempted Coup') the elected Central Committee of the C.P. gave way so easily to a young man with mysterious credentials who neither before nor afterwards played any part in politics, and accepted the guidance of a *Direktorium* nominated by him, at least in theory. In fact, the Revolutionary Soldiers' Committee was the only part of the C.P. which counted in practical politics, because it was backed by one of the battalions which had originated from a political split in the Red Guard formed in November 1918, and commanded deep sympathy in case of provocations against the majority of the army such as that of General Segré; this Committee continued to pursue the political line of the Central Committee, as we have seen in the text.

On the night of June 12th–13th the *Direktorium* did not know that Bauer had informed Gen. Segré of the impossibility of carrying out the dismissals without meeting with serious resistance on Segré's part. It therefore decided to use the opportunity for a *coup* on June 15th; it sent one of its members to the Wiener Neustadt industrial region, where, on the initiative of the same group, the January strike of 1918 had started. He met with strong resistance from the local Communists, who regarded the adventure as nonsense and would not have carried out his orders even if he had not been recalled on the evening of June 14th. This order, responsibility for which Bettelheim disclaimed even in the discussion of 1921, had been decided upon by the *Direktorium* because the Revolutionary Soldiers' Committee—the only force on which it relied—had decided to submit to the Government's order to keep the troops in barracks during the critical days. On the same evening a near-Communist paper published a declaration that no action was planned for the following day; so it seemed clear that the meeting of party officials, whose arrest caused the bloody events of June 15th, was intended to prevent adventures, and presumably to settle accounts with the *Direktorium*. Ruth Fischer, who was strongly attacked in Bettelheim's demonstrators who assembled unarmed on the following morning marched to the prison to demand the release of their leaders. Friedrich Adler was in favour, but the Social Democrat Minister of the Interior, Eldersch, for reasons of prestige wished to delay the release until after the end of the demonstration. Meanwhile the police opened fire and twenty people were killed. The tense situation was saved by the moderates on both sides; the Revolutionary Soldiers' Committee prevented the Communist battalion from going into action, and the Executive Committee of the Workers' and Soldiers' Councils demanded the immediate discharge of the arrested men, who immediately joined in quieting the demonstrators. A more important contribution was made by replacing the police in the streets by the army, which enjoyed the workers' confidence. A prolonged discussion in the Vienna Soviet on the question of responsibility resulted in disapproval of the behaviour of the Communist organizers of the *coup* (the internal history of which the Communists were reluctant to disclose[1]) as well as of the arrests ordered without necessity; but as early as June 18th it was agreed in the coalition committee of the Government to keep Eldersch and Schober in office, though not to protest to the Hungarian Government, as the bourgeois parties had suggested.[2] Two days later the funeral of the victims of June 15th (all of them Communists or sympathizers) was arranged by the Vienna Soviet, both the working-class parties taking part.

This incident has been described in detail, not because of its immediate importance, but because it represents the most serious crisis that occurred during the Austrian revolution,[3] and shows a clear contrast to

article, has failed even to mention the June incident in her *Stalin and German Communism*; she mentions, with unverifiable generalizations, another earlier and much less important one, on p. 111. Friedländer, who spoke at the Soviet meeting of June 13th on behalf of the C.P., was an opponent of the *Direktorium*, and for this very reason could not know what, at the moment, was decided on behalf of his party; so he failed, at that meeting, to answer Adler's questions about the Communist plans for June 15th. But after the event, at the meeting of the 17th, he stated, truly, that the *coup* had been planned because of the movement within the army against the dismissals, and that after the withdrawal of the dismissals the plan was dropped.

[1] See preceding footnote.

[2] As is evident from the last note, the protest would have been somewhat unjustified in view of the rather passive role which was ascribed to the Hungarian government in the designs of Bettelheim's backers.

[3] In the records of the various 'saviours' of Austrian society numerous other occasions where great harm was prevented by their activities are mentioned. What we have learned about the first of them (above, p. 143) should be enough to dispel any conceptions about political dangers emanating from the Austrian C.P. The incidents of April 17th were clearly caused by the despair of starving unemployed, the most impressive feature being the women who literally threw themselves upon the carcasses of some dead police horses in order to get some meat, while the Bren guns were still firing. The Communist leaders as well as the Communist-controlled army battalion

the way in which comparable issues were settled in Germany. It certainly signified the culmination of the life of the Austrian Workers' Councils. While the discussions with the Communists soon grew stale, the 'Soviet' was still important as an internal check on the bureaucratic structure of Social Democracy; as late as May 1920 the decision of a national congress dominated by the Social Democratic left wing proved helpful as a signal to the leaders that the coalition policy must be brought to an end.[1] With the end of the coalition, and the submission of the majority of the left-wing Social Democrats (a minority joined the Communists in spring 1921), the Workers' Councils, whose administrative functions had meanwhile been restored to the bureaucracy, withered away; their self-dissolution in 1920 was hardly noticed.

More important than the alleged revolutionary implications of the Hungarian events were their counter-revolutionary ones. At his trial in 1935 Rintelen,[2] who in 1919 had been the leader of the Styrian right-wing Christian Socials, brought evidence to show that at that time he had supported the organizations of Hungarian White Guards for action against the Hungarian Soviets (and, incidentally, eventually against Austria also), and we have already heard[3] of the corresponding activities of the 'police chief of the German National Parliamentary Party'. On May 6th a formation of Hungarian officers who were preparing operations against Hungary was arrested at Bruck-on-Leitha by the Austrian army; on May 2nd a group of Hungarian officers even kidnapped the Hungarian Minister in Vienna from his Embassy, stole the funds, and interned him in a Vienna Franciscan convent; the Superior found the whole procedure quite in order, and accepted the prisoner. This first series of 'incidents' corresponded with the first crisis of the Hungarian Soviet Republic which was overcome in the days of May 1919; during the second, which resulted in the fall of the Hungarian Soviets, the Austrian workers' reactions were remarkably strong,[4] because of the probable implications of the event on internal developments. On August

sternly opposed the disorders; if the most drastic incidents were indeed caused by the mysterious Hungarian caucus, as is asserted by Ruth Fischer, op. cit., p. 111, it can only be said that they in no way differed from others which were to happen on this soil, precisely when the Austrian working class had no political leadership (see below, p. 207).

[1] See below, p. 202.

[2] See below, pp. 320 and 345.

[3] See f.n. [1], p. 179.

[4] When, on July 21st, demonstrations against Allied intervention in Russia and Hungary were convoked by the Second International, Friedrich Adler attempted to change the date to a Sunday (the 20th), but got only a narrow majority (115 to 76) in the Vienna Workers' Council, and the protest of the District Councils resulted in a reversal of the first decision of the Vienna Council by 142 votes to 104. In spite of these vacillations, the strike was practically complete. Reactions in the provinces were different; in Graz the Social Democratic Party organized, instead of a strike, a meeting against the Peace Treaty, conjointly with the German Nationalists!

13th all the armed forces paraded before Parliament and the Government to demonstrate their willingness to defend the Republic. Under the shadow of this demonstration, and perhaps also of the anti-Jewish pogrom already beginning beyond the Leitha, even the *Neue Freie Presse* found that *Anschluss* with White Hungary was as undesirable as *Anschluss* with Red Hungary would have been. Some shift in the relation of Austria's internal forces was unmistakable; the reshuffle of the coalition Government in October 1919 brought with it the dropping of all pretence at nationalization and of the participation of the Workers' Councils in local government; a representative of Big Business, Dr. Reisch, replaced the liberal Schumpeter as Minister of Finance. While the social reforms introduced during the preceding periods were definitively enacted, the army question was settled by a compromise which secured the position of the existing (Socialist) soldiers while making future recruitment outside Vienna and Lower Austria a matter for the provinces; in the Alpine provinces with their Christian Social Governments the village priest's recommendation eventually became a necessary qualification for enlistment.

The programme of the second coalition Government was announced on the same October 17th on which the Treaty of Saint-Germain was ratified; and in appearance at least the peace negotiations had made their contribution to Austrian domestic policies. Early in May the Christian Socials insisted that no supporter of the *Anschluss* should head the Austrian delegation; they suggested in succession two former Prime Ministers of the empire, with the obvious intention of forcing the Social Democrats, who could not accept such suggestions,[1] to shoulder the responsibility. So Renner, as judged by his antecedents a supporter of Danubian federation, headed the delegation, while Otto Bauer, the Foreign Minister, remained in the background. The negotiations proceeded on the now estabished pattern: a demonstratively severe first draft of the treaty, protests with much nationalist fervour, improvements, more moderate protests; but while this went on Bauer, on June 11th, attempted to regain some diplomatic initiative for Austria by a suggestion which fifteen years later, in a different setting,[2] was revived

[1] Quite apart from its implications as regards the interpretation of the domestic policies of the new Austria, any representation of the country which emphasized continuity with Hapsburg Austria would have strengthened the other Succession States' demand to make Austria alone responsible for the former monarchy's debts.

[2] This point should be clearly kept in mind in a political judgment on Bauer's policies. Italy, in 1919, had a Liberal Government, and Socialist influence was in the ascendant. Hungary was a 'Soviet Republic' whose internal development might encourage wishful thinking in Bauer as to its eventual transformation into a bourgeois-democratic republic with strong working-class positions on the Austrian pattern. On the other side, the French bloc was the protagonist of counter-revolution: its armies had invaded Hungary and, in Russia, the Czechoslovak legions had helped Kolchak into the saddle; so Bauer might feel that he was allying Austria with the more moder-

in the Rome protocols. Without raising the *Anschluss* question Bauer promised Italy continuous Austrian support and permanent occupation rights in the fortresses of South Tyrol provided Italy renounced its claim to complete annexation of the latter, which was bound to compromise any supporter of friendship with Italy in the eyes of Austrian public opinion, and supported Austrian demands for other mitigations of the draft peace treaty, the main hardships of which, apart from South Tirol, originated from the members of the French bloc, Czechoslovakia and Yugoslavia. This suggestion was clearly a continuation of the national traditions of Austro-German liberalism, just as the nationalities policy of the Hungarian Soviet Republic was a continuation of the tradition of 1848; unlike Schuschnigg, who eventually attempted the combination in order to create a counterweight against a forcible *Anschluss* and failed, because he overlooked the fact that Fascist Italy was bound to become a German satellite, Bauer regarded it as a support for an eventual voluntary *Anschluss* with a liberal Germany[1] which would thus have opened the door to the Balkans. In the conditions of 1919 the suggestion was bound to be turned down by Italy, and a veer towards the French bloc seemed to offer Austria the only chances of improving the conditions of the treaty. Quite apart from his *Anschluss* policies Bauer had made himself most unpopular with that bloc because of his policy of neutrality towards Soviet Hungary and his refusal to accept the German regions of Western Hungary except on the basis of a plebiscite arranged jointly with Hungary. On July 25th, when the days of the Hungarian Soviet Republic were already numbered, Bauer resigned. It was not only an issue of foreign politics; on August 3rd *Le Temps* demanded to know how soon Bauer's resignation would be followed by that of Deutsch, the Minister of Defence, who was no particular supporter of *Anschluss* but was responsible for the Socialist structure of the Army; the French and Austrian bourgeoisie had to wait another year for Deutsch's resignation. For a period, however, which ended only with France's self-effacement at Munich in 1938, opposition to French hegemony in the Danubian basin was to come from the right instead of from the left.

The course of the Austrian revolution has frequently been cited as a test of the assertion that the tragedy of the German labour movement

ate of the imperialist camps. From the point of view of Austro-German nationalism Bauer was certainly preferable to Schuschnigg; the former made Italy's renunciation of annexation of purely Austrian territories a condition of agreement, while the latter accepted the continuing Italianization of South Tyrol.

[1] A person of Bauer's intelligence, in June 1919, cannot have had any delusions about a Socialist Germany. Besides, he himself in his book has described World War I as 'the greatest bourgeois democratic revolution in history'. So it would be a complete mistake to look on his policies as an attempt to use the 'revisionist' anti-Versailles forces as a potential ally of a Socialist country a point made in Lenin's speeches at the time. Cf. *Sochinenya*, 3rd ed., pp. 14–6, translated by L. Kochan in *Soviet Studies*, Vol. II., pp. 115–6.

was due only to its split, which in Austria was avoided. That split, which was desired by the Austrian bourgeoisie,[1] was avoided only by careful manœuvring which would have been impossible if the chances of an Austrian revolution had seemed promising to any important group within the labour movement. For this very reason comparisons with Germany, i.e. with one of the key points where the relations of strength within the opposing class camps were given their shape, should be avoided. January 1919 was certainly a blunder from the Communist standpoint; but there could be no doubt that eventually swords would have to be crossed with Ebert and his ally Hindenburg. Austria's domestic conditions were likely to be equalized with those of the surrounding world; a split within the labour movement was avoided by strict avoidance of any attempt to influence those conditions, or to take sides in an international conflict in which they might be reshaped. True, a tradition governed by the conviction that clever manœuvring could find a way out of the most difficult situations was not necessarily the best preparation for the inevitable crisis.

[1] On the very eve of 15th June 1919, the *Neue Freie Presse* demanded that Austrian Social Democracy 'must clearly show its colours, as has been done in Germany'. At that time, however, few representatives of the bourgeoisie would have supported the suggestion made by one of them, Steeruwitz, in the fascist atmosphere of fifteen years later (op. cit., p. 194) that the left wing ought to have been provoked into an armed collision; this might have caused some loss of blood but, in the long run, would have been better for Austria because of the inevitable reaction. The *post eventum* advocates of such policies failed to notice that, in early 1919, it was by no means taken for granted that every Soviet government born out of some provocation would be followed by some Horthy; if supported by an Austrian Soviet Government backed by the majority of the Austrian working class, Soviet Hungary might have survived, and the whole history of Central Europe have taken a different course.

CHAPTER SIX

STABILIZATION OF BOURGEOIS RULE

(*a*) *The Kapp Putsch and the Cleavage in the German Labour Movement*

On either side of the great social cleavage, the battles of spring 1919 were to be followed by a political regrouping. Among the workers, many delusions about the social implications of parliamentary democracy were destroyed when the Berlin workers, in March 1919, combined the inscriptions on the Government's posters: 'Nationalization is going on' with those on its barbed wire: 'Anyone who goes on will be shot.' Development of a system of Workers' Councils became popular. Three different trends supported the slogan: the desire to escape from the dangers of a struggle for political power, which was to be replaced by a very refined system of economic democracy on the basis of producers' self-government; the workers' demand for control of production in the shop; and distrust of the reformist Trade Union bureaucracy.[1] Very different things might be understood by 'a system of Councils';[2] at the March 1919 congress of the Independent Socialist Party two opposing concepts collided. Däumig, speaking for the left wing, described the Councils as an alternative to parliamentary democracy and a struggle for power as inevitable; according to the majority resolution submitted by Haase the Councils should function within the framework of municipal and national administration, and should collaborate in factory management and in carrying out the measures of

[1] Cf. Radek's pamphlet *Die Entwicklung der Weltrevolution und die Taktik der kommunistischen Parteien*, written in the Lehrter prison in November 1919 (published by the Spartacus League), pp. 42 ff. Radek expressed himself comparatively politely as regards what we have called above the escapist tendency, and was very reserved in his opposition to the Trade Union bureaucracy (evidently in view of the strong tendency to *replace* any kind of trade unions by Factory Councils, which was supported by the left-wing Communists). See above, p. 160, and below, p. 160. He regarded the Factory Councils as only a reserve position in case the Trade Unions should be suppressed by the progress of counter-revolution.

[2] To translate the German *Räte* by Soviets (as has been done above on some occasions when obviously political councils were concerned), would here beg the question put below.

'socialization'. This 'integration of the councils in the framework of the Constitution' did not differ fundamentally from the promises of Article 165 of that Constitution, which was enacted shortly after the March Congress.[1] Herz, speaking for the Party's right-wing majority, even explained that integration of the Councils in municipal government was a far more practicable suggestion than nationalization of the big banks; Germany could not manage without the big private bankers' credits.[2] The differences in approach seemed to be fundamental, and Herz, speaking at the end of the Party Congress, described the split as inevitable; for the time being, they were 'bridged' by a compromise resolution calling for integration of the Councils system in the Weimar Constitution as a preparatory step to its eventual replacement by the Councils. The final row arose only because in the elections of the Party presidents Haase declined to collaborate with Däumig, who a few months before had attempted to form a new party conjointly with the Spartacus League.[3] Allegiance to the traditional leaders proved to be strong; Haase carried the congress by a large majority, although on issues of principle it had been almost equally divided.

Before nine months had passed, the leaders of the Independent Socialist Party had to accept much more radical phraseology; the Leipzig Congress, 30th November to 6th December 1919, unanimously agreed to a platform in favour of replacing parliamentary democracy by proletarian dictatorship, exercised by Soviets. Crispien, Haase's successor,[4] rejected union with the right-wing Social Democrats, the traitors to the working class and the murderers of thousands of workers. The actual attitude of the leaders who used such terms was indicated by Crispien's description of November 1918 as a model of proletarian dictatorship, with great praise for the workers' failure to wage civil war against the counter-revolutionaries and to punish the war criminals.[5] Both wings of the Congress heartily agreed about the value of organizational experiments with 'Soviet' systems before the conquest of power. The actual meaning of the radical phraseology was illustrated by the debates on the Party's international affiliations. The overwhelming majority of the

[1] See above, p. 172.

[2] Proceedings, p. 186. Cf. Bauer's analogous position, see above, p. 180.

[3] See above, note [2] p. 159 Undoubtedly Däumig, like Rosa Luxemburg, regarded participation in parliamentary elections as valuable only from the point of view of Socialist propaganda preparatory to the eventual upheaval. A motion of his, expressing this view, was rejected by the March Congress of the Independent Socialist Party by the narrow margin of 68 against 67 votes.

[4] Haase had meanwhile been killed by a White murderer. It is hardly necessary to say that the justice of the Weimar Republic let the latter escape.

[5] Proceedings, p. 225. his paean on 'non-violent revolution' was supplemented by the statement (ibid., p. 222) that Marx and Engels in their later years had dropped their 'occasional' hints at the need for destroying the bourgeois State machine. As we know (see f.n, [5] on p 115) this was the conventional way of disowning revolutionary interpretations of Marxism.

Independent Socialist workers demanded affiliation to the Comintern, which had been founded in March 1919 as a mere skeleton[1] but commanded the vast authority of the Russian Revolution, now victorious over the White generals, which was strengthened by comparison with the course of events in Germany. Hilferding, speaking for the right wing, reproached the Bolsheviks for their terrorism as well as for a definite tendency towards the restoration of capitalism (this argument was put forward at a time when War Communism in Russia was at its height—evidently as an appeal to emotional objections to Lenin's use of bourgeois specialists!); Hilferding drew the conclusion that only in the capitalist West would the decisive battles be fought out; therefore the Independent Socialist Party should not cut the links with the Western Socialists.[2] The Russians needed the world revolution to get out of their difficulties, but the German Socialists were not threatened by a catastrophe, even if the revolution were delayed; they must avoid dependence on the Russians who would ask them to force the issue.[3] Such an interpretation of the international and German situation reduced the declarations that the eventual German revolution would establish a Soviet system to a mere lip-service to Marxist principles, such as had been current in pre-1914 Social Democracy.

Representatives of the right wing such as Hilferding were alone among the Independent Socialists in knowing clearly what they wanted. Ledebour, the outstanding representative of the tendency to overthrow reactionary governments by proclamations,[4] bitterly complained of the fact that the opponents of the Soviet Government were deprived of civic freedom. An amendment expressing solidarity with the application of violence in the revolution was rejected by 'a large majority'—evidently no count was needed. Stöcker and Däumig, the representatives of the left wing, described their divergences from Hilferding as merely tactical; Stöcker's motion in favour of joining the Comintern, which had originally been signed by a majority of the delegates, was lost by 114 votes to 169. This congress, like its predecessor, ended in a political compromise (leaving the Second International and entering into negotiations with the Comintern on the conditions for joining it) and an indecisive squabble on the composition of the Central Committee. Crispien, who had headed the lists of both factions and was thus elected almost unanim-

[1] Of the major parties outside Russia, only the Bulgarian and the Italian Socialists took part; even the representative of the German Spartacus League abstained from the vote on the formation of a third International, with the explanation that conditions in the West were not yet ripe.

[2] Proceedings, pp. 313 ff. The majority of the French and Czechoslovak Socialists and a strong wing in the British Independent Labour Party, were in favour of joining the Comintern; the 'Western Socialists' whom Hilferding had in mind were evidently the 'Social patriots' of 1914.

[3] Ibid., p. 321.

[4] See above, p. 162.

ously, explained after the end of the congress, in an interview with Frossard, that in spite of the acceptance of the principle of proletarian dictatorship the Party was not interested in an early conquest of power; that would only be in the interest of the reactionaries, who were bound to triumph after the countryside had starved out the towns. For the time being the Party should restrict itself to parliamentary activities. No wonder that it proved helpless when the reactionaries decided to march.

Just as in Russia the Bolsheviks' July defeat at the hands of the Kerensky Government was followed by Kornilov's attempt to remove Kerensky to second place, so in Germany the Generals who on Ebert's behalf had defeated the workers' revolutionary movements determined that the army, which had saved the country, should also control the Government. They were in close collaboration with the German National Party (apart from its agrarian wing Bang, a collaborator of the industrial leader Hugenberg, also took a leading part in the preparations for the Putsch). A political figurehead was needed, and the army leaders were intelligent enough to look for a person closely connected with the right wing of the labour movement. Noske, their Minister of Defence, was an obvious choice;[1] but he declined, and the Generals had to look for a political head in their conventional environment. Kapp, a National Conservative who headed the economic organization of the Junker-dominated agrarian interests, and Ludendorff were chosen to head the dictatorship. A threat to the mercenaries' material interests provided the opportunity for the Putsch; when the expectations of the members of the Volunteer Corps to be fully integrated in the new Reichswehr were affected by the limitations of the Peace Treaty, von Lüttwitz issued a political ultimatum to Noske and Ebert; still hoping for a compromise, the two did not even inform their party about the ultimatum.[2] On the morning of 13th March 1920, Lüttwitz moved his troops into Berlin; Seeckt and Schleicher, the official heads of the General Staff, refused to fight the rebels.[3] When the Government escaped to Dresden, the local

[1] Cf. his op. cit. pp. 196–7. The passage, which refers to April 1919, indicates that Noske suspected other Social Democratic leaders (presumably Ebert, see above, p. 156) to be less immune to temptations from that quarter. On the very eve of the Putsch, March 10th, Noske was assured by Lüttwitz that the conspirators had no objection to him and Ebert; indeed, the documents found at a search, on March 11th, at the home of Dr. Schnitzler, a chief organizer of the Putsch, envisaged the arrest of Ebert and Noske, but with the option of their joining the new Government. Ruth Fischer (op. ci., p. 121) quotes a report by Volkmann (*Revolution über Deutschland*, p. 322) according to which the offer of the dictatorship to Noske was repeated by Capt. Pabst (see above, p., 163 and below, pp. 318 ff).

[2] Cf. Scheidemann's speech at the meeting of the Social Democratic Parliamentary Party, 19th March 1920.

[3] Otto Meissner (*Staatssekretär unter Ebert-Hindenburg-Hitler*, Hamburg, 1950, pp. 86–7) does not mention the army leaders' refusal to fight, for which there is plenty of contemporary evidence (his report that Seeckt attempted to discourage the rebels and refused to collaborate with them, but remained on leave in Berlin, does not

commanders prepared to arrest it, and again the Government did not dare to arrest them in spite of the offers made by reliable republicans; it proceeded to Stuttgart, where a few generals not involved in the conspiracy could be found and the National Assembly could be convened in the traditional atmosphere of South German liberalism.

When the Government arrived at Stuttgart, Kapp's fate was already decided. The Trade Unions and both Social Democratic Parties[1] had called a general strike; a suggestion by the Independent Socialists to arm the workers was rejected by the Majority Socialists, because this would drive the bourgeoisie and even the reliable part of the Reichswehr into the arms of the mutineers. But already the general strike was more than the rebels could stand. The Government, in evident doubt about the outcome, had left representatives in Berlin to negotiate with them, but it did not need to satisfy any of their demands, for after two days of power Kapp had to resign with the declaration that he did not wish to drive Germany into the arms of Bolshevism by clinging to his office. On that very day—March 16th—Watter and some other rebel generals returned to the allegiance of the Ebert Government which, indeed, was in need of their skill.

Against the advice of the Social Democratic leaders, the workers in the Ruhr and in Western Saxony had armed during the Putsch. In the Ruhr, the Kapp troops under Watter suffered a number of defeats; the region was soon in the hands of a local Red Army of some 50,000 men, comparatively well organized but without any political leadership. The

contradict it). According to Meissner, Ebert himself, against the sharp protests of Noske and his Chief of Staff, General Reinhardt, decided that there was no chance for armed resistance and that the Government, with the exception of its Vice-Chancellor Schiffer, who was left in Berlin as its representative, should escape. Meissner also has an evident tendency to belittle the army's collaboration with the rebels; only the Commanding Officers in Berlin and East Prussia joined the rebels openly enough not to avoid his citation; even the vacillations of the Saxon Commander-in-Chief, General Märcker (see above, p. 164) are watered down as far as possible. Meissner's book shows some absence of even the most elementary knowledge about the situation, and events, in the labour movement; so far as the world with which he ought to be familiar is concerned, his very delicate position, already evident from the title of his book, should be kept in mind. But because of his very versatility he is the last surviving witness for quite a number of important events within the Government circle, and should be consulted for those facts which he could understand and the correct presentation of which does not too greatly contradict his own interests.

[1] The Central Committee of the C.P., whose left wing had just been expelled (see p. 196), applied orthodox phraseology for escapist purposes when declaring the armed conflict irrelevant because both the parties to it were bourgeois; so the workers should not bother about it. This theoretical exercise proved harmless, since the local leaders in those regions where the Communists were influential paid no heed to their Central Committee's instructions; they behaved as well or as badly as their left-wing Independent colleagues, assuming local control without attempting any concerted action against the reactionary army, and laying down their arms as soon as the issues were decided at the centre.

Government which had allowed the Kapp party to prepare their mutiny was completely compromised; for the moment the appeals of the Social Democratic Party to end the general strike had no more success than the joint appeals of Schiffer (the Government representative left behind in Berlin) and Seeckt. The Trade Unions on March 20th negotiated with the Government terms for calling off the strike, envisaging democratization of the army and the civil service, dissolution of the army formations which had taken part in the Putsch, the resignation of Noske and Heine, and participation by the Unions in the formation of the new Government; as the Berlin workers were still not prepared to call off the strike, an additional agreement, concluded two days later, provided for the withdrawal of the mutinous troops from the working-class quarters of Berlin.[1] The Trade Unions suggested that the compromised Government should be replaced by a 'Workers' Government' formed by themselves together with their Christian and Hirsch-Duncker fellows, i.e. by comparatively left-wing Catholic and Liberal M.P.s. As Stampfer correctly noted, in *Vorwärts* of March 25th, the 'Workers' Government' would have been a reconstruction of the Weimar coalition under a different name; the name, however, was abhorrent to the bourgeois parties and the right-wing Social Democrats, while the left-wing Independents, whose participation would have been necessary, declined for reasons of principle and from aversion to a coalition with right-wing Social Democrats—or, to call the thing by another name, because they were enamoured of their position in opposition.[2] The coalition Government was restored, and only Noske was dropped (as was also Heine, who had taken a similar position within the Prussian Government); this remained the only part of the agreement with the Trade Unions which was fulfilled. At the same time an agreement was negotiated in Bielefeld by Severing, acting on behalf of the Government, with representatives of the three workers' parties (including the Communists) and of the Red Guards; the latter were to lay down their arms; administration, army and police were to be reorganized on conditions similar to those agreed upon in Berlin with the Unions; the Reichswehr would not enter the Ruhr, and the arms were to be collected by the municipalities. In a speech made a few days later, on April 3rd, Severing explained that the Bielefeld agreement had served its purpose of dividing the loyal sections of the working class from those with whom accounts must be settled; the political concessions made had been necessary to quieten

[1] Report of the Social Democratic Central Committee to the Party Congress, Kassel, 1920, p. 10.

[2] In order to correct its initial mistake, the Communist C.C. accompanied its promise of loyal opposition to a 'Workers' Government' based on the Trade Unions by theoretical considerations about its supposedly intermediate character between bourgeois democracy and proletarian dictatorship. These declarations, which, for the moment, remained without any practical consequences, heralded later disputes in the Communist camp. See below, p. 223–4.

the workers, and to win time during which troops could be assembled. Before the conditions of the agreement could be carried out, Watter's troops, acting now on behalf of the Government, took their revenge by invading the Ruhr and carrying out the usual massacres. There was no attempt elsewhere to resume the general strike; the workers who, during the critical days, had controlled Central Germany under Independent Socialist and local Communist leadership, remained inactive while the fate of the Ruhr was decided. A situation similar to that which had paved the Bolsheviks' road to the October revolution resulted in Germany in a strengthening of reaction.

In Bavaria, the right-wing Catholics had used Kapp's Putsch as an occasion to replace the coalition Government, formed after the local Soviet episode of spring 1919, by a dictatorship under Kahr, based on White Guards formed in the villages under the leadership of one Escherich (whence the name 'Organization Escherich', abbreviated to 'Orgesch'). During the following years Munich was the witches' cauldron where all varieties of fascist gangs and ideologies, Hitler's group amongst them, competed for leadership in the Fascist Germany to come. More important, for the time being, was the fact that the Army, the main force of German reaction, re-formed its ranks after the Kapp experiment. After the failure of the adventurers, the generals rallied round Seeckt, who preferred the exercise of real power behind the scenes and the proper use of existing political machinery to open attacks which would rally the German workers against rearmament; at the same time, notwithstanding all promises to the contrary made in the Berlin and Bielefeld agreements, the Army was purged of all elements which might prove unreliable in the event of conflict between it and the republican Government. The reduction of the army to half its former strength (the threat of which had brought the mutinous troops into action) was now used to get rid of all elements supposed to be 'not unpolitical' or disturbing to army discipline by complaints against their (Kappist) superiors; even in those days a non-commissioned officer who had protested against his Kappist commander might get eight months' imprisonment and, of course, be dismissed the service, while his superior who had merely mutinied against the Republic remained at his post.[1] All in all only 172 commissioned officers were dismissed for having taken too active a part in the Putsch, in which a very high percentage of the officers' corps had joined and with which the great majority had sympathized. The colourless Democrat Gessler, who replaced the scapegoat Noske as Minister of Defence, presided over these developments, which met with Ebert's full approval. In his *Memoirs*[2] Scheidemann reports that Ebert was shocked when, speaking in Parliament after the defeat of the Putsch, he had demanded the disarming of the mutinous

[1] Caro-Öhme, *Schleicher*, Berlin, 1932, pp. 122–3.
[2] Vol II, p. 658.

troops and a purge of the officers disloyal to the Republic—broad-mindedly promising, besides, financial assistance to all royalist officers who should be honest enough to retire from the Republic's service.

In the general elections of 6th June 1920 the political shifts caused by the defeats of the German revolution and by the Kapp Putsch became evident. Part of the lower middle class vote returned to the bourgeois camp, so that the share of the parties of labour in the total vote dropped from 45 per cent (in 1919) to 42; but within the workers' camp there was a powerful shift to the left. The Independent Socialists polled 4·9 million votes against 5·6 million for the Majority Socialists; so the vote of the former was more than doubled, that of the latter halved. The Independent Socialists won a majority of the working-class votes in the major industrial centres.[1] The Communist organization had been weakened by the expulsion of their left wing (which kept to the decisions of the foundation Congress against activities in Parliament and Trade Unions and was supported by majorities in the main industrial centres apart from Saxony),[2] and as during the Kapp Putsch the party had behaved no better than the left-wing Independents, it was by-passed by the left-wing swing, getting a mere 440,000 votes. In the bourgeois camp, the Centre was weakened by a general decline in its vote and by the right-wing split in its Bavarian organization, which henceforth contested all the elections as the Bavarian People's Party and got something like a million votes; the Democrats, with a mere 2·2 million votes, were reduced to the position of a third-rank party, from which they never recovered,[3] and the German People's Party (the party of Stinnes, Vögler, and Stresemann), with 3·7 million votes, became the unquestioned representative of the bourgeoisie, a position eventually to be shared with the German National People's Party when the latter, in 1924, came to take part in

[1] In Berlin city, for example, the Independents polled 437,000 against 186,000 Majority Socialist votes.

[2] Ruth Fischer (op. cit., pp. 118–19) reports that even Paul Levi, the prominent leader of the right wing of the Spartacus League, was convinced of the need for trade unionist activities only by Radek before the Heidelberg Congress. At the foundation Congress, Rosa Luxemburg's attitude to the problem had been not quite clear; she was definitely the leader of the young Party's right wing (see above, f.n.[2] on pp. 159–60), but her whole antecedents were bound to cause some sympathy on her part with people who wished to replace bureaucratic centralization by loose initiative 'from below'. The syndicalist element in her attitude was alien to Levi; if Ruth Fischer is right, Radek simply helped Levi to overcome some sentimental reluctance to fight friends of Rosa Luxemburg. Afterwards, he did it with a fervour of which Radek disapproved, and split the young party against a very strong minority. Radek's report is translated in *Soviet Studies*, vol. III, pp. 423–4.

[3] Further gradual decline brought the Democratic Party down to 1·5 million votes in the 1928 elections. An open challenge in the 1930 elections was no longer regarded as hopeful; therefore the former Democrats joined up with one of the comparatively moderate (or, at least, pro-French) semi-fascist organizations, the *Jungdeutscher Orden*, as the German State Party; they did not win, even in such disguise, more than 1·3 million votes.

the Government. Even after the collapse of the Kapp Putsch, with which they had been in sympathy, the German Nationals increased their 1919 vote by a third; People's Party, Centre (without the Bavarians), and German Nationals were about equal in strength. Evidently, the German middle classes reacted to Kapp's defeat with increased realism, but also with a definite move to the Right.

In the left wing of the labour movement, the lessons of past experiences with the 'Western and peaceful approach to Socialism' were drawn by the decision of the Independent Socialist caucus, September 1920. As we know,[1] the dispute at the Leipzig congress had resulted in a compromise according to which negotiations were to be sought with the Comintern on the conditions for affiliation. On the eve of the Second Congress of the Comintern Lenin[2] decided to keep the 'Marxist Centre' outside the organization by demanding from the parties no mere declaration of solidarity with ideological principles but also a structure which would adapt them for underground work and a centralist structure for the International which would ensure that Moscow had a say in any future dispute on the interpretation of the accepted principles. The outstanding leaders of the right wing of the Centre, such as Kautsky and Hilferding, were to be excluded, and in the election of the new Central Committees those who had supported affiliation from the very start were to be secured a two-thirds majority. This was intended as a challenge, and it served its purpose; an article by Louise Zietz against acceptance of the conditions was headed: 'We are not going into Slavery.' Sepp Örter discovered, in the *Freiheit* of September 2nd, that the Moscow régime was based upon armed force, and therefore was a reactionary power. For the Congress in Halle in October 1920, the right-wing majority of the Central Committee invited the Menshevik Martov as the chief speaker against Zinoviev, who represented the Comintern; Martov did not fail to make his case by a long diatribe against all the hardships and difficulties of the Russian revolution. This made Zinoviev's task still easier; even more than his powerful oratory, the obvious alternative of supporting or opposing the Russian revolution increased the majority in favour of affiliation which had already originated from the election of the delegates;[3] by 236 to 156 votes affiliation was carried.

It is difficult to assess the definite steps by which this decision on the part of the active workers of the Independent Socialist Party was carried by the masses backing it; the 750,000 members alleged to have existed before the fusion with the Spartacus League clearly belonged to the

[1] See above, p. 191.

[2] *Sel. Works*, vol, X, pp. 200 ff,

[3] Zinoviev himself (*Zwölf Tage in Deutschland*, Hamburg, 1921, pp. 7 and 11) reports that from the very start the left wing had a safe majority of 50, which during the Congress increased to 80. Ruth Fischer's assertion (op. cit., p. 145) that Zinoviev won over the majority by his speech is a dramatization. See also below, p. 247.

realm of organizational mythology (or to the factional struggle over the proportion of leading posts to be given to former Spartacus members and left-wing Independents respectively). The new C.P. had no more than 300,000 members,[1] of whom 50,000 may have come from the Spartacus League. The remaining right-wing Independent Socialist Party was eventually forced by a financial deficit to reunite with the Majority Socialists; even before the reunion it had to close down its central organ for lack of subscribers. In spite of the emotional importance of party membership for just the kind of worker organized in the Independent Socialist Party, the heir of the traditions of the Marxist Centre, a large number of Party members evidently ceased to be organized at all when their traditional background was disturbed; first, they had to face the alternative of either breaking with the Social Democrat tradition or opposing the Russian revolution, afterwards, so far as they remained in the 'buffer' party, they were invited by their leaders to rejoin the Noskists; the group which, under Ledebour, continued the traditions of the Independent Party survived as an uninfluential sect until the end of the Republic. The decision of the Independent voters was slower; in the elections to the Prussian Diet in February 1921, before the crisis in the C.P. caused by the March insurrection,[2] of the four millions in Prussian territory who voted Independent in the 1920 national elections, one million each joined the Communists, the Majority Socialists, remained faithful to the rump party, or simply stayed at home. Not until the 1923 crisis was the left wing of the German labour movement definitely absorbed by the C.P.

Those Independent Socialist voters who immediately returned to the Majority Socialist fold merely anticipated what their leaders were bound to do at a more moderate pace after all the exchanges of bitter words and after the failure of the attempt to retain the support of the left-wing workers. The rump party continued to use phrases about 'socialization', but little actual difference of opinion on this point divided the Majority Socialists from Hilferding, who, speaking against Zinoviev at Halle, had already interpreted Marx as saying that the typical form of a working-class revolution in Western countries was indicated by the enactment of the maximum working hours in Britain!

The interplay of domestic and foreign politics provided the opportunity for the return of the Independent Socialists. The defeat of the Social Democrats in the elections of June 1920 was followed by a formal offer to the Independents to join the Weimar coalition, on its platform

[1] The Report of the Central Committee to the Jena Party Congress of August 1921 gives a figure of nearly 360,000, but this includes fantastic figures (in round thousands) for some regions, such as 66,000 for Halle and 40,000 for the Hamburg region. The less fantastic figures of five other regional organizations are also given in round thousands.

[2] See below, p. 214.

(the promises made to the workers in March were already withdrawn), and, after its rejection, by the formation of a Government of the moderate bourgeois parties under the right-wing Catholic Fehrenbach; the Social Democrats voted against an Independent motion of no confidence, but remained outside the Government. As early as spring 1921 the nationalist demagogy of the bourgeois parties landed the country in a crisis on Reparations; to answer the London ultimatum of May 1921 a new coalition Government, under the left-wing Catholic Wirth, had to be formed. This was supported by the Independent Socialists who were already complaining that the Majority Socialists, by their clumsy negotiation tactics, had failed to secure them a place in the Government. On 30th September 1921 the readiness of the Independents to take part in coalition Governments was formally proclaimed, but rejected by the bourgeois coalition partners of the Majority Socialists. There were recurrences of leftism in the Independent Socialist Party; in spring 1922 even the editors of its central organ, headed by Hilferding, were removed because they had opposed a strike of the Berlin electricity workers directed against their employers, the Majority Socialist council. But when the nationalists' attacks on the Wirth Government resulted in the murder of Rathenau, the Independent Socialists joined the front of the coalition parties; they supported the Majority Socialists' opposition to the Communist demand that the opportunity be used to disarm the fascist gangs and to purge the State apparatus; jointly with the Majority Socialists they disowned, on July 8th, the anti-fascist 'excesses' which in some places had disturbed the peaceful character of the joint demonstrations of the workers' parties. The Majority and Independent Socialist parliamentary parties combined on July 15th to enforce Independent participation in the coalition Government. Catholics and Democrats, the bourgeois partners in the coalition, answered by a similar combination with the People's Party, the open representative of Big Business which, at that time, still professed monarchism and demanded abolition of the eight-hour day. Coalition with such a partner was too much for the Social Democratic parties; the Majority Socialists eventually left the Government and accepted the Independents in the more favourable atmosphere of opposition to a bourgeois government. It was a moderate opposition; when Levi[1] at the Independents' Berlin meeting on July 20th explained the need for fusion with the Majority Socialists, he argued that the pros and cons of coalition politics were a mere mathematical formula irrelevant for history, that a dissolution because of the unsatisfactory formulation of the Law for the Protection of the Republic would have resulted in a further fall in the exchange value of the Mark, and that therefore the Independents must vote for the law—which eventually did more harm to the labour movement than to the fascists who had murdered Rathenau. Independent tactics had of

[1] See below, p. 215.

necessity become identical with those of the Majority Socialists. Eleven hundred of the activists voted for the fusion, and a mere hundred for the motion of old Ledebour, to whom it was intolerable to be in one party with those responsible for Rosa Luxemburg's murder. Levi, her old comrade, felt cooler about such things.

Most of the Independent leaders disliked the business; when, at the last Party congress, Ledebour spoke against reunion, the delegates cried: 'It is the workers, not we, who demand reunion.' As events were to show, there were few workers left in the Independent rump; and Toni Sender, another of the comparatively Left Independent leaders, rightly pointed out that the more advanced of the Majority Socialist workers were a greater asset for a continuation of a Left opposition in the united Party than the people the Independents brought with them. One hundred and twenty-two of the 192 delegates signed a declaration against the kind of coalition policies hitherto practised by the right-wing Socialists, and reaffirmed their intention to work within the reunited party for the old principles; but not much more was heard of most of them. What moderate opposition eventually developed in the united Social Democratic Party operated mainly upon regions such as East Saxony which had never been affected by the split. In the last years of the Republic men such as Hilferding, Dittmann and Crispien were amongst the foremost leaders on the road to surrender.

(*b*) *Economic and Political Stabilization in Austria*

The return to stability after the revolutionary upheaval proved easiest in Czechoslovakia; the disturbance had been less marked as compared with the other republics, and there was no interference from outside apart from the political and economic dependence on the French system of alliances and on international High Finance with its notions of monetary orthodoxy, which were shared at that time by all the bourgeois parties and were not openly attacked even by the Social Democrats. In 1920 the Social Democratic leaders had to face the opposition of a majority in their party, which eventually was to form the C.P. In order to save what could be saved they precipitated the split, using the sympathies of Government and judiciary in order to appropriate, though a minority, the name and property of the Party. The Czech workers protested against this move in December 1920, by a general strike which was to be the most serious disturbance to the life of pre-1938 Czechoslovakia, apart from the short-lived Slovak Soviet Republic. The right-wing Social Democrats, like the German comrades after the Kapp crisis, hoped to improve their position by taking a 'respite from the external responsibilities of coalition government': a 'Government of leading civil servants', under Czerny, was formed. In reality it was a revival of the 'all-national coalition',[1] of course without the left-wing Socialists,

[1] See above, p. 177.

its parliamentary backing being secured by the *Pjetka* (committee of representatives of the five parties) which became an important instrument of government even after its immediate cause, the Government of officials, had disappeared. The Government of civil servants gave the parties a chance to reform their ranks behind the scenes,[1] but it also established the power of the bureaucracy as 'the fixed pole amid the change of events', even before this power was anchored in the predominant position of the Agrarian Party. After a year, the informal coalition was replaced by a formal one, under Beneš; another year later Beneš was replaced by the Agrarian leader Svehla. The Government, thus moved to the right, managed in 1923 to stabilize the currency by deflationary methods; as in all the other continental countries this meant abolishing a number of social achievements in the interest of economy. But not till after the elections of November 1925 were the Social Democrats eliminated from the Svehla Government and an all-bourgeois coalition formed; for the first time non-Czech (especially Sudeten German) parties which shared the social outlook of the Czech coalition parties were included. The Czech Social Democrats had been afraid to take the initiative for such a combination in the face of possible right-wing demagogy; it was left to the right-wingers, when in the Government, to establish the precedent which was followed till the end of the democratic Republic.

We left Austria in September 1919, when, after the fall of the Hungarian Soviet Republic, the balance in the governing coalition had shifted to the right.[2] As the Army was reliable from the Republic's point of view, the Kapp Putsch in Germany moved Austrian politics rather to the left: the news of it was immediately followed by a demonstration by the army and the workers. A demand in the form of an ultimatum by the Social Democrats that their Catholic partners in the coalition should cease to obstruct the enactment of parts of the agreed coalition programme, i.e. the Army Organization Law and insurance against unemployment, was acceded to within two hours. The Austrian right-wingers' leader, Seipel, speaking on March 16th, hailed the Kapp Putsch as an expression of popular dissatisfaction with the parliamentary régime, but warned against any attempt at imitation: 'Who can guarantee that it would indeed be followed by nothing more than a few days of Bolshevism?'[3] It might be questioned whether even a less cautious approach could have produced even so much as an effective provocation; when the leading right-Wing Catholic M.P., Mataja, arrived in Salzburg for

[1] J. Borovicka, *Ten Years of the Czechoslovak Republic*, Prague, 1928, p. 93.

[2] See above, pp. 186–7.

[3] The argument that a few days of Bolshevism would not be too high a price to pay for a prolonged White Terror on the Hungarian pattern seems to have been quite popular among Austrian right-wingers; for its retrospective application by a leading Catholic representative of Big Business see above, note [1] on p. 188.

negotiations with the local reactionaries (presumably in connexion with the events in nearby Bavaria) Deutsch was asked by the local Workers' Council whether Mataja should be arrested.

Kahr's establishment in Bavaria changed the situation in the neighbouring parts of Austria: the *Orgesch* served as a pattern for the *Heimwehren*. In some places violent demonstrations by the right wing already occurred; even in Vienna on June 7th precautions had to be taken against an attempted pogrom. Since all the concessions possible by participation in a coalition Government had been obtained, dissatisfaction grew amongst the Socialist workers for sharing in its responsibilities; this found expression on May 31st at the Second and last Congress of the Workers' Councils. Against the advice of Bauer and Adler, the Socialist ministers were invited to resign if their partners in the coalition rejected their amendments to the draft law on the property tax which were intended to prevent tax evasions by delaying payment until the amount was depreciated by the progress of inflation (the rejection of such demands by the Christian Socials could be taken for granted). Another resolution of this Congress shows where responsibility lay for the rise of the Austrian 'party armies'; as a reply to the formation of *Heimwehren* (literally 'home guards') on the *Orgesch* pattern the workers were invited to form *Heimwehren* of their own. At that time there was not even a special name for unofficial armed formations current in the world of labour; later, resort was had to *Ordner*, i.e. the stewards who shepherded demonstrations; eventually the *Schutzbund*—League for the Protection of the Republic—arose.

The existence of a majority to the left of the official leaders of the Workers' Councils convinced the Socialists that continuation of coalition policies threatened the unity of their party at a time when all other centrist parties were threatened by a split; by leaving the coalition, they succeeded in isolating the issue of the International from all domestic issues. No one, not even the Communists, believed that there was any chance in isolated Austria of following the Soviet example; Lenin's Twenty-one Conditions were thus bound to seem merely a demand for a split in the labour movement. They were rejected by an overwhelming majority; the minority, itself split into several factions, eventually joined the Communists, but in no way affected their character as an uninfluential sect.

The overt proclamation of the Government crisis was followed by prolonged manœuvres by both Socialists and Catholics, in which the boycott of White Hungary proclaimed by the International Transport Workers' Union as well as the final bargaining over the distribution of federal and State powers in the new Constitution played their part; some eyewash[1] was applied in order to avoid pre-election responsibilities. On

[1] As all the parties had announced their intention of leaving the Government and not entering any coalition, a provisional Government had to be elected by 'propor-

October 1st the new federal Constitution was enacted; on November 3rd the new federal Parliament could be elected. The Social Democrats lost 190,000 votes, and the Catholics gained 140,000, thereby becoming the largest party; they now had to form a coalition with the German Nationalists under the left-wing Catholic Mayr. Otto Bauer eventually summed up the position:

'At the time of the second coalition Government [i.e. after September 1919 —R.S.], the working class discovered how limited its power had become, even when our representatives sat in the Government. The working class now [after November 1920—R.S.] saw that it was not powerless even when it abandoned the Government to the bourgeoisie.'[1]

In fact, things were not very far from an unofficial coalition, as every Government had to keep on terms with its railwaymen and soldiers. In the Ministry of Transport the representative of the Railwaymen's Union enjoyed not much less influence than the Minister himself; Deutsch (the former Minister of Defence) and Smitka worked as 'civil commissaries' with the Minister of Defence, and the Army was commanded by General Körner (at present President of the Austrian Republic) whom Deutsch had nominated. Such collaboration by the 'opposition' presupposed some unofficial arrangement over the majority's nominations for the key ministries; until Seipel's advent to power all changes in the Government were preceded by unofficial contacts with the opposition, which would not misuse its power to veto persons unless they were obvious counter-revolutionaries and potential Putschists.

The precarious equilibrium, however, was threatened by the young Republic's counter-revolutionary environment. The Hungarian White Guards who had been organized with Austrian right-wing support[2] to fight the Hungarian Soviet Republic were concentrated in West Hungary, ostensibly in order to prevent its cession to Austria as envisaged by the Peace Treaty, but also to strengthen the pro-Hapsburg wing of Hungarian counter-revolution. On 26th March 1921 the ex-emperor, according to Erdoedy's report[3] with French and British backing, arrived in Oedenburg after illegally passing through Austria, from which the Hapsburgs had been expelled. From Horthy, who governed formally as Regent on behalf of the King, he asked for immediate transfer of power; as at the time, he possessed nothing but his persuasive powers, he had to return when Horthy refused. The Pretender was allowed to pass through Austrian territory to Switzerland, but, at the demand of the

tional representation' (every party voting only for its own candidates). Of course, this implied previous arrangement as to how the Cabinet offices should be distributed by 'the luck of the ballot', the strength of each parliamentary party being known in advance.

[1] *The Austrian Revolution*, p. 223.

[2] See above, p. 185.

[3] Op. cit., p. 201.

Socialists, under guard of a detachment of the Austrian army, in order to make the legal position clear to him. As a protest against the acceptance of this demand by the Prime Minister, Seipel, the leader of the monarchist right-wing of the Christian Social party, resigned from the Party chairmanship.

To avenge his defeat on traditionalist lines, Seipel found a suitable tool in the German Nationalists, with whom he had been on good terms since the days when they had been compelled to play the part of open reactionaries and advocates of capitalist orthodoxy.[1] Evidently with the knowledge of the right-wing Catholic leaders, the German Nationalists now began a campaign in favour of *Anschluss* which the major parties, especially the Social Democrats, did not dare, nor perhaps even wish, publicly to disown, though they knew very well that any step in that direction would land the country in hopeless complications with the Allies. During the last session of the old Parliament, a German Nationalist motion had been accepted, demanding a plebiscite on the *Anschluss* with the rider that the date should be fixed within six months—at a time when, as everyone foresaw, the German Nationalists would themselves be in the Government and would hardly be eager to bring about a crisis for it. In the spring of 1921, however, the Catholic right-wingers of Tyrol and Salzburg, under the attractive power of Kahr's Bavaria, in conjunction with the local German Nationalists started Provincial plebiscites on *Anschluss* in view of Parliament's failure to arrange for a national plebiscite. It was an evident campaign for the dismemberment of the Republic; but the Social Democrats did not dare to reply to it with a programme of their own for the necessary financial reforms in Austria (at that time monetary inflation had just reached the point where it ceased to create a premium on Austrian exports and would still have been manageable).[2] So the Social Democrats, and the Prime Minister Mayr with whom they collaborated, were helpless victims of the right-wing Catholic and German Nationalist initiative, which resulted in almost unanimous plebiscites in favour of *Anschluss* and increasingly sharp protests by the Allies. On May 31st Rintelen, evidently acting on Seipel's orders, had the Styrian Diet (this time against the Socialist votes) decide in favour of a Provincial plebiscite on *Anschluss*; on July 3rd his price for a repeal of that 'patriotic' decision[3] was Mayr's resignation.

The Christian Social Party Congress, on June 8th, formulated the slogans of the policy to be followed by Seipel the year following; 'a strong Government' and 'financial reconstruction with the help of the

[1] See above, p. 179.

[2] See below, pp. 207–8.

[3] i.e. for Catholic support of the Social Democratic motion to defer the plebiscite *sine die*; the German Nationalists were allowed to preserve their prestige by voting against.

League of Nations'. None of the 'strong men' recommended was ready to accept: Seipel still preferred to remain in the background. Rintelen therefore suggested a Cabinet led by the Vienna Chief of Police, Schober, a convinced monarchist but near to the Nationalists and even prepared to refrain from the application of Police power when it was more risky than on 15th June 1919, and later on 15th July 1927.[1] He, unlike other Austrian right-wingers, behaved loyally when a crisis arose in Austro-Hungarian relations because of the attack by Hungarian 'unofficial' troops on the Police which on Allied orders were to occupy Western Hungary,[2] and when the army, which he naturally disliked, had to be called in to protect the frontier; when the Hungarian 'Irregulars' were given open support by the Italian head of the Allied mission, Schober negotiated an agreement with Czechoslovakia. As small battles between the Austrian army and the Hungarian Whites developed all along the frontier, the strengthening of the former, and even the arming of the workers in the threatened regions, became a national interest; the Hungarian resistance, though it gave the Allies a pretext for revising the Treaty of Trianon in Hungary's favour, internally strengthened the Austrian Republic. Monarchist restoration in Austria, however, was only the second aim of the West Hungarian Whites; on October 21st the Pretender again arrived in their midst and moved to Budapest, this time accompanied by troops. On the outskirts of Budapest Karl's attempt broke down, but the shadow of the threatened restoration, with which Seipel would certainly have sympathized, was enough to bring about an Austro-Czech agreement.

For the time being, the right-wingers' dalliance with their external support had resulted only in strengthening Austria's independence and internal *status quo*. This is important in view of the common assumption that the Versailles Treaty, or German-Polish relations, were to any large extent responsible for the eventual triumph of German Fascism. Certainly, within the pattern of the German polity as created by Ebert's and Noske's triumph, external conflicts like that of Upper Silesia in 1921, and the invasion of the Ruhr in 1923, were bound to provide occasions for arming White Guards for use inside Germany. It is also true that the extreme pacifism of the German Independents, which resulted in indifference to army questions, created perhaps an even more serious handicap against a proper use of external complications for strengthening the German left than Bauer's admiration for *Anschluss* in the 1848 tradition did in the Austrian case. But the very coexistence, within the

[1] See below, p. 315.

[2] In view of the Austrian right-wing and Hungarian propaganda against the 'Red' Austrian army the Allies had prohibited it from entering the territory ceded to Austria and demanded occupation by 'reliable' police forces; these, of course, dispersed as soon as they came under serious attack. When the Hungarian bands attacked on Austrian territory, the attackers were repelled by the Army, not without losses.

framework of Central European Centrist Social Democracy, of the Austrians with their worker-controlled army and later their *Schutzbund*, with the helplessness of the German Independents, should put us on our guard against the too hasty assumption that there was no alternative to the actual course of events other than the triumph of Communism.

It was not political but economic events that disturbed the political equilibrium in Austria. Most Western writings on Austria's post-war economic crisis were coloured by the Austrians' own complaints about the Peace Treaty and by the experience of the Viennese bourgeoisie, if not of the aristocratic, intellectual and higher civil service circles in which most of the foreign correspondents moved, the evident sufferings of the rentiers, etc. In a sober approach, considering the country with all its industries as a whole and taking the need for radical and painful adaptations after such a catastrophe for granted, the position of the Austrian Republic after the dissolution of the Dual Monarchy was anything but hopeless. It had retained 74 per cent of the old Austria's production of paper, and 90 per cent of that of motor cars. Less agreeably, it retained nearly the whole of some of the luxury industries, but only a fraction of their internal market. Clearly the problems could be solved only by an export drive. An obvious need for readaptation was expressed by the fact that new Austria was left with 83 per cent of the former production of railway wagons, and two-thirds of the iron ore, but only with a third of the furnaces; not even this third was fully used during the existence of the Republic. She had a clear need for imported food, which could eventually be reduced by developing her own agriculture, and also for nine-tenths of her coal consumption.

On the other hand, the Viennese banks owned a very large part of the industrial assets of the other Succession States; the new States wanted to get rid of this dependence, but this desire could itself be used as an opportunity to pay for the necessary imports while Austria's industry was being adapted to the new circumstances.[1] A really unbearable burden for the new Austria was the large mass of *rentiers*, civil servants, and officers of the former monarchy, a result of the privileged position which the Austro-Germans had enjoyed in the old State and quite out of proportion to the possibilities and needs of the new; without perpetuating the financial catastrophe it could not be helped, except by reducing all these unearned incomes to a subsistence level.

The monetary inflation provided for the necessary surgery, though by an unplanned and necessarily painful procedure. It created ample opportunities for some of the superfluous elements (e.g. the staffs of the

[1] This possibility refutes Otto Bauer's argument against nationalization of the Austrian banks (see above, p. 180). Surely the Austrian State could have used their assets much more rationally than the uncontrollable shareholders did. Private ownership of banks with assets in States which paid tribute to capitalist orthodoxy was important only if these assets were meant to be preserved.

big banks which were far in excess of current needs) to indulge in speculations which made things worse, and it even helped to concentrate large blocks of shares in all kinds of enterprises in the hands of large-scale speculators, such as Castiglioni: both developments paved the way for subsequent crises.[1] But a monetary inflation, caused by the budget deficit, was the obvious outlet in a political setting where neither of the opposing classes could enforce its concepts of positive reform. The automatic reduction of rents brought about by the monetary inflation and the enormous State subsidies for bread and other staple foods promoted the competitive strength of Austrian industry as soon as the initial stoppages through shortage of raw materials were overcome. On the other hand, the food subsidies represented in 1921–2 just half the budget deficit. When they were reduced, on 1st December 1921 a general strike and demonstration was organized behind the back of both Social Democrats and Communists (the group of Factory Councillors of the Vienna suburb of Floridsdorf, who organized it, distrusted both parties equally). The manifestation, in which more than a hundred thousand workers took part, culminated in excesses such as the burning down of the Employers' Association building. The volcano quieted down as quickly as it had erupted, though nothing more had been achieved than a short delay in the increase of the price of bread.

The incident shows that even within this best organized of all the national labour movements existed energies which were wasted because no one bothered to concentrate them on realizing a practical programme. There was no inherent reason why the problem of inflation should not have been solved without accepting foreign supervision of the Austrian finances. At the end of the financial year 1920–1 the total debt corresponded to no more than an annual budget; the percentage of the deficit to the total amount budgeted, which in 1919–20 was as high as 63, was reduced to 51 in the second half of 1921 and to only 40 per cent in 1922, of which the last month alone was affected by Seipel's reforms. Throughout the crisis the Austrian banks, which could always refer to their interests in the other Succession States, stood completely aside, and kept even private industry on minimum credit lines. By moving their capital abroad, they preserved their assets during the whole crisis, unlike the German banks, which later had to be subsidized by the State. Two of the great banks became foreign-owned during the crisis; the others extended their foreign credits. This proved helpful as soon as 'confidence' was restored; on the other hand it made a solution of the currency crisis against the will of High Finance almost impossible. Nationalization of the banks might have been a practical proposition in 1919; in combination with an energetic finance policy and a production drive based on the workers' confidence it might have consolidated the position of a left-wing Government and restored Austrian economy to a

[1] See below, pp. 312–13.

level where agreements with the other Succession States on terms of equality could have been reached. But a policy which was marked by reluctance either to face political crises or to hurt the short-term interests of any important section of the electorate was bound to put the initiative in Seipel's hands. As soon as the monetary inflation had outlived its function as a subsidy for Austrian exports, any increase in money in circulation was immediately followed—and, because of the speculative element, sometimes even exceeded—by a fall in the foreign exchange rate and a rise in internal prices. There was no longer any group in Austria interested in the continuation of the inflation, and whoever did the inevitable was bound to earn the laurels of a saviour of his country.

Seipel's initiative and leadership was possible because of the widespread conviction that Austria could not stand on her own feet. Certainly she could make good use of foreign credits; but the one purpose for which they were *not* needed was to stabilize the currency. Foreign exchange (in the Austrian banks) was among the few things that were available in ample supply; the only economic argument for not using it to finance imports was to preserve the predominant position of the Viennese banks in relation to the Succession States. Least of all were foreign credits needed for the technique of currency stabilization; as events were to show, the currency reserves were restored as soon as 'confidence' returned, and no part of the League of Nations loan was eventually used for the purpose. The purpose for which foreign credits *were* needed was precisely to show that they were needed, i.e. that the country could not pursue an economic policy distasteful to potential creditors. The Austrian working class, after 1918, was in no mood to submit to the prescriptions of its domestic capitalists as to what was necessary for the country and what was not; but it had been trained by its very leaders, who alternatively spoke of *Anschluss* and of the need to wait for the ripening of the revolution in the leading capitalist countries, to accept outside conditions as something with which one had to conform. Discussions on foreign credits to be offered to Austria in compensation for dropping the *Anschluss* programme were as old as Austrian independence; but these prospects were at a deadlock because of the antagonisms between the Little Entente and the Italian group.

These premisses taken for granted, Seipel tackled his job in a masterly way. By his agreement with Czechoslovakia, Schober had incurred the wrath of the German nationalists; when another fall in the exchange rate in May 1922 was followed by a wave of big strikes which involved the railways and the post and telegraph services, Seipel, the 'strong man', had no difficulties in combining with them, and Schober had to resign. Everyone had had enough of the men of straw, and even the Social Democratic organ wrote: 'Seipel himself should govern.' On May 24th he assumed office. The bankers, headed by Rothschild, offered one million sterling as their contribution to the capital of a new bank (the other half to be raised abroad), on condition of complete freedom from taxation and the transfer of all available assets (including the State forests and a French credit already granted) to the old bank as cover for its notes; currency stabilization would be delayed until deflation had increased the value of the old currency. This was too much even for Seipel, but it served to let any possible conditions put by foreign bankers appear in a more favourable light.

Beneš, asked for help on August 21st, referred Seipel to the League of Nations; evidently he was afraid to take the initiative in purchasing Austria's collaboration at a price which would not have been very heavy from Czechoslovakia's point of view but might involve conflict with Italy. On August 23rd the Social Democrats offered a new coalition, on certain conditions, and demanded the immediate recall of Parliament. But Seipel was already on the way to Verona; on the following day he offered the Italian Foreign Minister a customs union. This was no mere diplomatic manœuvre; Carinthia and Styria were already pursuing a pro-Italian foreign policy of their own; but just because it had to be taken seriously, it forced Beneš to proceed. On September 6th Seipel was able to speak before a well-prepared Council of the League of Nations, offering Austria's readiness to accept foreign supervision as a condition of help but threatening that she would join some major economic unit if help was denied. Otto Bauer, speaking in Parliament on September 14th, rejected foreign control *to the extent* offered by Seipel. There was hard bargaining on the necessary restriction of expenditure, especially as far as the army and the railwaymen were involved, on new indirect taxation, and especially on the full powers for the Government demanded as a condition of the loan; when the Social Democrats, whose votes were essential for the necessary amendments to the Constitution, resisted the Geneva conditions, Seipel was authorized by the League of Nations' delegates to make the necessary concessions; apparently he had accepted harder conditions than were thought necessary, in order to leave some room for bargaining. On November 27th the compromise was enacted; the Government was allowed to issue the necessary emergency decrees, but needed the agreement of a special parliamentary committee.

On condition of accepting a League of Nations supervisor for her finances, promising to 'preserve her independence' (i.e. to abandon *Anschluss*) and carrying out the agreed programme of reforms, Austria was to receive a credit of 650 million gold crowns, 130 million of which were intended to repay the advances already granted while 520 million would cover the budget deficit supposed to be inevitable during the next two years. In fact only 611 million was raised; 40·3 as a reserve for the loan service, 122 for repayment of the advances. A mere 262 million was needed to cover the budget deficit up to 10th August 1925, 199 million was still payable when—after some delay—the League of Nations' control was ended.[1] The course of foreign exchange had improved on the very day Seipel went to Verona; the technical stabilization of the currency was a mere matter of the movement of the funds of the Austrian banks. There was nothing in the achievement which could not be accomplished with Austria's internal resources—except forcing the Austrian people to accept a deflationary policy and Government management according to the rules of orthodox finance, independently of the wishes of the electorate as represented in Parliament. Otto Bauer later described the acceptance of the Geneva control as the end of the Austrian revolution. The Austrian revolution had ended long before that, but Geneva marked the end of the delusions on *Anschluss* as well as of the description of the Austrian régime as a government of 'workers and peasants'.

Within the realm of Austrian realities, the League of Nations intervention marked only a short-lived triumph for the right wing. The necessary short-term credits and the capital of the new National Bank were raised by Austrian capitalists before the League of Nations loan became available, and the budget deficit disappeared as early as autumn 1923; even exports continued to rise in that year. But the stopping of public investment and the dismissal of large numbers of public employees[2] reduced the home market; private capital, which in orthodox theory had to fill the void opened by the retrenchment of public investment, moved on the broad and promising road of speculation. Not only the banks' own capital but even that of the industrial enterprises owned by them turned to the Stock Exchange, the French inflation offering the most promising field of monetary speculation. The setback caused by the stabilization of the franc was enough to cause a panic on the Stock Exchange and another escape of that very 'hot money' whose return had been Seipel's main achievement; the orthodox methods of deflation applied according to the directives of the League of Nations Commissioner made things worse. By 1st March 1923 Austria had 167,000 unemployed; 125,000 more than a year earlier, and nearly as many as at the peak point of the post-war crisis in 1919. After some vacillations the chronic unemployment, from which the Republic was never again to recover, rose by the end of February 1925 to 193,000, that is 17·6 per cent of the Austrian workers.

A general election was due in November 1923, a time when the workers were already feeling the burden of unemployment while the

[1] Layton-Rist, *The Economic Situation of Austria*, Report to the League of Nations, p. 49.

[2] The failure of the Austrian Government to dismiss quite as many as had been provided for by the League's programme furnished material for repeated complaints by the Commissioner; by 7th July 1923, however, 44,871 officials (instead of the 50,000 looked for by the plan) had been dismissed. Increase in the number of dismissals beyond the cases of obvious redundancy naturally increased the opportunity for political pressure.

lower middle classes and many of the salaried employees still enjoyed the 'prosperity' induced by the franc speculation. Although the propaganda of the Government parties centred on the success of the monetary reform and the alleged economic stabilization, the Social Democrats, the only party which had opposed it at least in appearance, increased their vote by nearly 300,000, regaining in Vienna and all the eastern provinces the percentage of the total vote they had achieved in the revolution year 1919, while in the western provinces, except Carinthia, the 1920 level was maintained. This last was the only province where the German Nationalists made a temporary advance; in general, they lost about a third (in Vienna even half) of their percentage of the total vote. The reduction of their partners in the Government to a group of merely local importance enabled the Catholics to preserve their lead over the Social Democrats; the two-party system was almost accomplished.

On 10th March 1924 the League of Nations Committee refused Seipel's request that a part of the loan should be made available for productive investments; the interests of the subscribers prohibited such a step as long as the possibility of a future deficit remained. Therefore it was suggested that the Austrian Government should attract private investments by restricting the taxation of banks and joint stock companies, and of mortgages by the abolition of the Rent Restrictions Act.[1] In September the Committee decided to prolong the financial control of Austria beyond the minimum term provided for in the Geneva agreement; true, Austria had balanced her budget sooner than was expected, but this fact was due to an increase in public revenue of 106 per cent instead of the 30 per cent anticipated, while expenditure had been reduced by a mere 4 instead of 70 per cent. Also only 68,330 public employees, instead of the 100,000 called for by the agreement, had been dismissed by July 1924. In the final compromise the Austrian Government was allowed a higher figure of expenditure than had been agreed on in 1922, and the League of Nations Commissioner was instructed to show his reports to the Austrian Government before they were sent to Geneva; this concession illustrates the existing situation. In return, the Government undertook to abolish the taxation of exchange operations, to reduce the taxation of joint stock companies by 25 per cent, to carry out an administrative and financial reform at the expense of the Provinces, and to let the National Bank's discount policy be governed by the need 'to maintain the stability of the Krone, not only in relation to gold, but also to goods'.[2] In short, to perpetuate deflation.

The experience the Austrians had of Seipel's main achievement was a shock to his prestige, and he failed to reduce the Provinces' share in the public revenue (most of them were governed by fellow partisans of his). He again attempted to force the issue by a threat of resignation, for

[1] *Report* of the Financial Committee of 15th September 1924.
[2] Ibid., p. 231.

which a strike of the railwaymen provided an occasion fitting the 'anti-Red' setting. The railway strike was settled by a compromise, but the Provincial Catholics refused to surrender and formed a new Government under Ramek, with the Catholic social reformer Dr. Resch (instead of Schmitz, the watchdog of Seipel and Vienna Big Business) as Minister for Social Affairs. Seipel's group had to submit, lest they should be completely excluded from the Government; his friends, the German Nationals, used the opportunity to quit the Government, but continued to support it.

In September 1925 the League of Nations control was lifted, although for reasons of international 'equilibrium' Zimmermann's resignation was delayed until 30th June 1926, so that it could coincide with that of his colleague in Budapest. Public finance and the rate of exchange remained stable until 1931. Some of Austria's industries, such as the production of paper and hydro-electric power, far exceeded the pre-war level; others, among them the iron, steel, and engineering industries, were stabilized in a state of depression from which they did not recover before the Hitler invasion.

(c) The German Crisis of 1923 and its Consequences

Unlike the earlier crises of the German revolution, the last one, which is usually associated with the French occupation of the Ruhr, arose between fairly well grouped and organized class forces; one of the characteristics of a revolutionary situation enumerated by Marx and Lenin, namely disorganization in the camp of the ruling class, was conspicuously absent so far as Germany's domestic policies were concerned. There were, however, vacillations in foreign policy, and some difficulties were met with in the simultaneous use of the various non-bourgeois forces without whose support no bourgeois government was possible.

The German ruling class operated upon two co-operating parties—to which, in the Catholic regions, we must add the right wing of the Centre—the German People's Party and the German Nationals, supported respectively by Heavy Industry and by the Junkers. It had an army which had gone through the disappointments of Kapp's adventure, and had purged itself of all elements suspect of taking the oath to the Weimar Constitution too seriously. It was supported by a Social Democratic Party which gathered under its banner the non-Communist majority of the working class; as a reserve, there were the rising forces of Fascism. Apart from the local conditions of the Munich stronghold of German Fascism there was the 'Black Reichswehr', that is, that part of German rearmament which was driven underground by the provisions of the Versailles Treaty and expressed the views of dissenting Big Business men (and, especially in Hitler's case, foreign influences also) who were dissatisfied with the official bourgeois policies. From the formation of the Volunteer Corps through the Upper Silesian war of spring 1921 to the Ruhr conflict of 1923 stretched the chain of events in which the unofficial army of German reaction was formed and supported out of public funds; the Government's official dissociation from its doings preserved its character as an opposition force which, if the worst came to the worst, might rally all those who despaired of Weimar Germany but were not prepared to accept proletarian dictatorship.

In opposition to the existing régime stood the Communist Party, since its fusion with the left-wing majority of the Independent Socialists a mass party whose membership rose at all the later crises of the German Republic to near the 350,000 mark; its total vote even in the aftermath of defeat (in the May 1924 elections) was 3·7 million. Unlike its predecessors, which had been the objects rather than the shapers of the preceding crises, the C.P. was pledged to the policy of bringing about a Socialist revolution in Germany as soon as possible; failure to act could not be excused by lack of mass spontaneity or of the Social Democratic leaders' will to co-operate. But what this obligation really meant did not become clear in the process of trial and error which preceded the crisis; nor was it likely to do so in the process of abstract argument without any opportunity of verification in action which followed it.

The leaders of the Spartacus League as well as those of the left-wing Independents who in autumn 1920 assumed joint leadership of the united C.P. agreed in assuming that the defeats of the German labour movement were due to lack of co-ordinated working-class action. In an Open Letter to the Social Democrats and Independents, published on 6th January 1921, they proposed joint action on behalf of such aims as were shared by all the groups within the labour movement independently of their different ideas about their further purposes; this meant, in the first place, defence of the social achievements of the revolution and a financial policy which would shift the burden of reparations from the shoulders of the proletariat on to those of the bourgeoisie. Such a proposal was quite natural in the context of later Communist policies; but in the minds of people who had not grasped that, in the Leninist framework, the issue of forming a joint party with another group was very different from that of temporary co-operation with it, the Open Letter seemed to contradict the Twenty-one Conditions.[1] A minority

[1] Ruth Fischer (op. cit., p. 171), who, strangely enough, in her present political position still reflects the emotional element of her attitude at the time of these events, puts all the responsibility for the proposal—which was logical from Levi's point of view as well as from Däumig's—on Radek, who made it; she states that the Independent neophytes 'were outraged by this proposal'. In fact, the differences of opinion cut across the former party lines. Ruth Fischer's report reflects local conditions in Berlin, where the Spartacus leaders had expelled almost the whole organization after the Heidelberg Congress (see above, p. 196), so that nearly all the Communist workers were former Independents, and nearly all the old Spartacists (with the exception of Ruth Fischer and her closest friends) supporters of the right wing of the C.P. But the new leaders of the Central Committee who shouldered the responsibility

group of the Central Committee (former Spartacus members such as Levi as well as Independents such as Däumig) resigned when the February 1921 Plenum of the C.C. (which overwhelmingly backed the policy of the Open Letter) endorsed by a narrow majority the Comintern's policy towards the Italian Socialist Party. The opportunity was seized by two delegates who had been sent by Zinoviev (apparently without the approval of the Russian Politburo)[1]; the new leaders of the German C.P. undertook to open the revolutionary offensive. They did not have to wait for an occasion; their assumption of control of the Party coincided with a provocation by the Prussian Government against the workers of Central Germany, who had played no predominant part in the crises of 1919 and 1920 and therefore had not yet been disarmed.

On Easter Eve the police invaded the Mansfeld region to search the workers' homes and disarm them. The date chosen made a protest strike impossible; so the Mansfeld miners offered armed resistance—in the opinion of one of the new party leaders, because of a misunderstanding of the party's slogans.[2] The Central Committee took no measures to break off the action, but on the contrary attempted to extend it. In Central Germany a partial insurrection was followed by bloody repression; in other parts of Germany the failure of the workers (including those who voted for the C.P.) to support the party's action became manifest.

The defeat was followed by an internal crisis: Paul Levi, the most prominent of the Party leaders who had resigned in February, attacked in a pamphlet the adventurous tactics of the Party majority and of the Comintern agents who inspired them; the Central Committee answered by expelling Levi from the Party. His attack was not meant to be directed against Soviet Russia; during the conflicts that had led to his resignation he had issued the slogan of an alliance between (existing,

for the March action were themselves old members of the Spartacus League (though opposed to Levi). The February 1921 Plenum of the C.C. censured the opposition of some Berlin leaders (Ruth Fischer and her friends) on the issue of alliance of a bourgeois Germany with Soviet Russia (see below in text) by a majority of 33 votes against 20; evidently this majority included the greater number of the former Independent Socialists.

[1] The details of the event remained a persistent subject of controversy within the C.P.; I see no reason for not following the presentation of Ruth Fischer (op. cit., p. 175) which is not just charitable to her friend Zinoviev. Levi, in his pamphlet *Unser Weg* (Berlin, Seehof-Verlag, 1921, pp. 29–30) stated that more than once delegates of the Comintern had, later, been found to have exceeded their powers; so he was not sure whether the Executive Committee of the Comintern (i.e. Zinoviev) was responsible. Lenin clearly was not, as is shown by his attitude at the Third Comintern Congress (see below in text); but even much later Zinoviev used Guralsky, one of the delegates, as his representative in Germany; this would have been most impolitic if he had regarded his action as more than, at worst, a technical mistake.

[2] This is how the facts are presented by Levi, the keenest critic of the party's action, op. cit., pp. 33–4.

republican) Germany and the U.S.S.R.; but the left wing in Berlin had answered with the declaration that no alliance with the U.S.S.R. was possible until the German bourgeoisie was overthrown.[1] Lenin disapproved of Levi's public attacks while his party was in a most difficult situation, but agreed with the actual content of his criticism; the Third Comintern Congress, July-August 1921, decided in favour of a United Front policy on the lines of the German C.P.'s Open Letter of 6th January 1921. At first, the leaders of the German C.P. had reacted to criticisms of the 'March action' by producing truly Blanquist theories on the merits of a 'revolutionary offensive' in order to develop latent class consciousness; but after some resistance they agreed to the motion of the Congress. If Levi had merely been interested in fighting adventurism, he could now easily have returned to the Party; but, as was already evident from the immediate reason for his resignation from the Central Committee, his opposition had not been merely an appeal *a Cominterno male informato ad Cominternum melius informandum*,[2] but a protest against Russian leadership in general. His supporters, soon joined by some erstwhile supporters of the Berlin left-wing opposition, such as Reuter-Friesland, the present Mayor of West Berlin, formed a separate faction. When expelled from the C.P., they joined the Independent Socialists, among whose ranks they supported reunion with the Majority Socialists; their experience seems to have convinced them that there was no half-way house between having either unity with the extreme and honestly counter-revolutionary right wing of the labour movement or a revolutionary party whose main inspiration was bound to come from the triumphant Russian comrades.

The dissenters continued to be officers without an army, and the incident, which is unduly emphasized in the current treatment of this period because of the great attention devoted by both Communist and non-Communist historians to the documentary output of factional dispute, was soon overcome. As early as the winter of 1921–2 the C.P. was evidently influential among the municipal workers and railwaymen who

[1] Cf. ibid., pp. 6 ff. On this issue the Berlin group was isolated; at the February 1921 Plenum of the C.C. (the very meeting at which Levi was disowned on the Italian issue, see above, p. 214) the slogan of alliance with Soviet Russia was endorsed by 50 votes to 3 (i.e. against the Berlin representatives).

[2] The fact that this appeal had been made in formal breach of Party discipline would, at that time, have been regarded as a mistake, but a pardonable one if the criticism had been directed only against tactical errors. At the time of Brest-Litovsk, Lenin himself had threatened resignation from his Party offices and public propaganda if he remained in the minority; and he continued to collaborate with comrades who, when they remained in a minority (and were afterwards, undoubtedly proved to have been wrong) resorted to means of resistance which went far beyond protest in public. The interpretation of every breach of Party discipline as a kind of criminal offence belongs to a much later stage of the development of Bolshevism; at the time of which we speak, it was regarded rather as the symptom of an illness whose causes had to be investigated.

went on strike, and in the mass demonstrations that followed on Rathenau's assassination in June 1922 it played a prominent part; all subsequent criticisms of the attitude of its leaders at that time were directed against their failure to continue the demonstrations in spite of the refusal of the Majority Socialist and Independent parties[1] because of the Communist leaders' excessive interest in unity with the other working-class parties; such criticisms evidently presuppose that, a few months after the end of its internal crisis, the party was strong enough to take an independent initiative. The most serious result of the crisis and its solution was the coexistence of two wings of German Communism which, each in its own way, went to the limit in misinterpreting the Bolshevik experience. The official leaders, who had gone at least in terminology to all extremes of adventurism, had been convinced by the Russians that they had been mistaken; hence they drew the conclusion that proper Bolshevist policies implied continuing to collaborate with the other working-class parties (i.e. just the opposite of what the Bolsheviks themselves had done in October 1917); the opposition, mainly based on the Berlin organization, believed that the essence of Communism was a refusal to co-operate with non-Communists for any purposes whatever, that is, avoidance of the very thing which had made the Bolshevists strong enough for the decisive break with their former allies. In actual practice, either approach reduced the C.P. to propagandist activities; the first, because any form of action would be rejected by allies without whose support the party would refrain from acting; the second, because only that form of action was admitted for which the C.P. was clearly too weak, and for which it could never become strong enough unless it successfully tackled the problem of breaking the offensive of German reaction.

The actions of German Big Business were defined by the interaction between the external restrictions on Germany's development and the fact that both to resist Reparations and to shift the responsibility for them on to left-centre Governments would strengthen the domestic position of Big Business and its political representatives. Politically, the parties alleged to be responsible for the defeat of the German empire and its glorious army would also have to bear the responsibility for extorting the tribute on the victors' behalf and for the sufferings of the small savers who were expropriated by the monetary inflation; economically, the very interest these parties felt in the recovery of German industry under its industrial leaders would secure for the latter ample credits to be repaid in money whose value had fallen to almost nothing, especially if the actual controller of German policies speeded up monetary inflation by provoking the appropriate crises in Germany's internal and external conditions. Monetary inflation freed Heavy Industry from its debts and allowed Heavy Industrialists to acquire shares in all kinds of

[2] See above, p. 199.

enterprises at almost no cost; Stinnes became especially famous for his 'empire', which included nearly everything from the Heavy Industries amid which he had grown up and the German People's Party which he had helped to found to a near-monopoly in all kinds of mass publicity, to Fascist gangs dependent on his subsidies, and many other enterprises little connected with his main activities except that their shares could be bought up cheap. A host of minor speculators accompanied the big 'combine builders' ' profiteering, and the indignation of those who saw their savings thus vanish might find an easy and, from the Big Bosses' point of view, profitable outlet in anti-Semitism.

The Left-Centre parties, who hated 'like sin'[1] the surgery which could have put an end to all this, became helpless victims; their leaders could be killed when it suited their opponents' demagogy and the murderers were safely protected by a sympathetic judiciary, interference with whose 'independence' would obviously have undermined the Rule of Law.[2] When Wirth's Government had to accept the London ultimatum, his fellow-partisan Erzberger, who had carried out the centralist finance reform and had besides long been unpopular with the National Conservatives and their leader Helfferich,[3] became the focus of nationalist demagogy; after plenty of appeal to the public to kill him the fourth attempt on 26th August 1921, was successful. The Foreign Minister, Rathenau, was the next object of the witch-hunt which went on quite openly in the Bavarian and almost without concealment in the rest of the German right-wing Press. Being, unlike Erzberger, a large-scale industrial organizer himself, he could not be said to be involved in the dirty interconnexions between German parliamentarism and Big Business, but he was a Jew, and in any case was the member of the Cabinet charged with the negotiations on reparations. The fact that, by concluding with the Soviet delegation at Genoa the famous Rapallo Agreement on 16th April 1922, he had taken the only step which could secure Germany some degree of independence,[4] did not make things any better;

[1] See above, p. 148.

[2] The procedure is repeated in the West German Republic, that second—and not improved—edition of the Weimar Republic. On 25th November 1946 Erzberger's assassin (see below in text), who since 1933 had not found it worth while to deny his deed, was re-tried and acquitted by the Freiburg-im-Breisgau Court (1) because Hitler had granted an amnesty in 1933 to all those who had committed murder for patriotic reasons, and (2) because Tilessen had in fact acted from patriotic motives. (Ruth Fischer, op. cit., p. 285, note). The French supervisory authority ordered a retrial; but I have never heard of the German Federal Republic purging its Judiciary and Civil Service of the kind of people likely to give such judgments, though there are many protests against the Russians' less diplomatic methods of handling the German Augean stable.

[3] See above, p. 100.

[4] In the atmosphere of identification of German liberalism with complete subservience to the West, Rathenau's biographer, Count Kessler (*Rathenau*, London, 1929, pp. 328 ff.) has taken great pains to shift the responsibility on to Wirth and the

evidently the business magnate, perhaps because of Jewish interconnexions, was not only a servant of the West but also an abettor of Bolshevism. Immediately after his return from Genoa on June 24th, he was killed by the patriotic gangs; the actual assassins (two of whom committed suicide in order to avoid arrest, while the rest got off with a few years in prison) became national heroes, and the instigators continued to control most of the economic life and much of the politics of the Republic.

This time the patience even of the German Left was tried almost to breaking-point. Enormous workers' demonstrations, at first spontaneous, later organized by all the three working-class parties, called for the repression of the Fascist gangs. Wirth declared in Parliament: 'For me, the enemy stands on the Right.' It was a personal declaration; the bourgeois parties, including his own, insisted on a formulation of the Law for the Protection of the Republic which would threaten anti-State activities from the Left just as much as those from the Right, and the judiciary would see to it that Communists were imprisoned and monarchists acquitted. A dissolution in the atmosphere of those days, presumably combined with some spontaneous action for disarming the Fascists, would in all likelihood have produced a Left majority; but the Social Democrats, including their newest acquisitions from the Left,[1] were horrified at such disturbance and accepted a formulation of the law that would command the support of the German People's Party. All their efforts were directed at strengthening their position in the coalition to correspond with their absorption of the Independent Socialist Party; most of the Independent parliamentarians, though very few of the party members, had joined them. The bourgeois parties, however, remained firm and insisted on the inclusion of the German People's Party in the Government, to restore equilibrium; in the resulting crisis Wirth's Government was replaced by a bourgeois minority combination headed by the General Manager of the Hamburg-Amerika line, Cuno, and relying very much more on his capacity to represent Big Business than on the uneasy parliamentary support which it might get from the German

supporters of a pro-Russian orientation in the Foreign Office; it may be noted that in a recent official Soviet publication (*Diplomatishesky Slovar*, vol. II, p. 487) Rathenau's general attitude is described as hostile to the U.S.S.R. Obviously a Soviet publication of 1950 which describes a Western Liberal's and business man's attitude to the U.S.S.R., where he undoubtedly wished to invest capital, as 'hostile', does not necessarily mean that he was hostile in the sense ascribed to the term at the time of the event. Meissner (as quoted in f.n, [3] on p. 192) who is in open sympathy with Ebert, states that the latter, whose opposition to the Rapallo agreement was well known, reproached Rathenau as well as Wirth for not having asked his opinion before concluding the agreement. Rathenau was soon killed, but Ebert's opposition to Wirth continued, and is said by Meissner to have contributed to Wirth's resignation in November 1922 (see below).

[1] See above, pp. 199–200.

Nationals or the Social Democrats, neither of whom were represented in it.[1]

The policy of the new Government was to score points over France by making proper use of British sympathy. Within six weeks it had its conflict; on January 11th the French began to occupy the Ruhr. This time the bourgeois appeal to the Left Centre was, not to shoulder the responsibility for capitulation—this also would follow in time—but to support national unity after the pattern of 4th August 1914. The Social Democrats behaved in the appropriate way; the Communists were the only party to vote against the policy of 'passive resistance' (the application of which very soon crossed the vague boundary between sabotage and guerrilla warfare by the patriotic gangs; the latters' collaboration with army and Government, including the Left-Centre government of Prussia, was strengthened by secret agreements).[2] Even the Central Committee of the C.P. dismissed an editor, Gerhard Eisler, who on his own responsibility but in accordance with the opinion of the opposition groups within the Party, had replaced the slogan 'Hit Poincaré on the Ruhr and Cuno on the Spree' by another: 'Hit Cuno and Poincaré on the Ruhr and on the Spree': the implication being that class struggle against the German Government should be carried on in the occupied territories, but Poincaré be resisted on the Ruhr.[3]

[1] Meissner (op. cit. pp. 113–14) describes the formation of the Cuno Government not only as a reaction of Ebert against his own party, whose resistance to the demands of the bourgeois parties had prevented the formation of the 'great coalition' with which Ebert was in sympathy, but also as a first break with the rules of parliamentarism, in that the Government was composed of business men and specialists and did not possess a parliamentary majority. It is possible that Meissner correctly emphasizes not only the first point, which is beyond controversy, but also the second, which would emphasize those elements in Ebert's policies to which Meissner could remain faithful in his later career; but it should be kept in mind that government by emergency legislation was not foreseen at the time, and that a bourgeois minority Government tolerated by the Social Democrats had already been in office in 1920–1.

[2] The facts, which became evident by the protests of the Fascist organizations in some German States against their dissolution, and in the course of the conflict of the Saxon with the Reich Government (see below, p. 223) are summarized by Merker, op. cit., p. 87–8.

[3] Eisler's formulation meant that the class struggle on the Ruhr ought to be directed against the German capitalists and officials as well as against the Occupation forces; the prospect of eventually getting rid of the foreign as well as the domestic exploiters should be based on revolutionary struggle in unoccupied Germany. This was the line which the bulk of those who disagreed with the right-wing leaders of the German Politburo were prepared to follow, and has also been accepted in retrospective interpretation of the period by the German C.P. Ruth Fischer's line, as expressed in her op. cit., pp. 254 ff. (i.e. development of a revolutionary movement on the Ruhr which was to spread thence to the rest of Germany) would certainly not have been supported by the bulk of the Party's left wing outside, perhaps, Berlin (I cannot check the accuracy of her report about the amount of support she enjoyed within her narrowest factional caucus). On one of the occasions mentioned (so far as I remember, when the unemployed workers of Mühlheim had occupied the Town Hall and dis-

Some of the Ruhr industrialists underwent a formal trial and imprisonment by French courts martial, and thus acquired the status of national heroes, in addition to the hundreds of millions of gold marks which were paid them partly as an indemnity for lost profits, and partly as credits to be repaid in notes which had no more value than the paper they were printed on. On the Left too, there was some vested interest in 'national resistance'; the workers were paid the wages which because of the general strike ordered by the Government they failed to earn. In order that the 'resistance movement' could function, the value of the mark had to be stabilized, and most of the gold reserve was sacrificed for the purpose. When it came near to exhaustion, on April 20th, the exchange rate was allowed to fall freely, and the greatest monetary inflation of all time, not excluding that in Russia during the civil war, was set in motion. Disorders took place on the Ruhr, where the workers, especially those in receipt of employment and other benefits, could no longer make ends meet; the internal discipline of the C.P. was severely tested by the desire to prevent these local movements, which occasionally went to the length of occupying public buildings and disarming the police, from growing into a general insurrection which would obviously have been at the mercy of the French occupation troops.

More important tensions matured in the unoccupied parts of Germany. The depreciation in value of the wage-packets resulted in an uninterrupted chain of strikes and go-slow movements, and in many parts of the country Control Committees were formed to fight profiteering in the markets, especially in Saxony and Thüringia where left-wing Social Democratic State Governments dependent on Communist support were in power. The nationalist wave inspired by the occupation of the Ruhr and the direct support given by the Government to the Ruhr saboteurs as well as to the 'Black Reichswehr' encouraged Fascist activities of all kinds, including local attempts at pogroms and at beating up meetings of workers' organizations, which rightly reciprocated. The C.P. replied to the growth of Fascism by a propaganda campaign intended to convince lower-middle-class supporters of that creed that they were betraying the national cause by following the lead of Big Business,[1] and by encouraging the formation of Red Hundreds, which

armed the police) she went down to the Ruhr, together with the Party's chairman, Brandler, to prevent a revolutional outbreak. This was done only under Party discipline but Ruth Fischer would have been the last to submit to Party discipline if more than the assessment of a local incident had been at stake.

[1] This was the whole content of the famous 'Schlageter' campaign, initiated by Radek. As is evident from the discussion in articles written later by Communists and some representatives of 'left-wing' Nationalism (Count E. C. Reventlow, *Völkisch-Kommunistische Einigung*, Berlin, 1924), neither of the parties to the dispute dropped any of its principles; the Communists demanded that the Nationalists should abandon their Big Business connexions, and the Nationalists that the Communists should drop Marxism and class-struggle. Nothing could come out of these arguments

grew up in the repeated battles for meeting-halls, but might also serve more serious purposes. There was no cleavage on these issues between the two factions of the Party, but the Left Wing was afraid of too much quasi-friendly argument with Nationalist as well as Social Democratic leaders, while the Right-wing majority was afraid that armed battles with the Fascist gangs would land the Party into a conflict with the police and Social Democracy. A 'fighting day against Fascism' was organized for 29th July 1923, and it was clear that local armed conflicts would result; but when the police prohibited street demonstrations a majority of the Central Committee, not clearly divided on factional lines, restricted the demonstrations to indoor meetings, since the Comintern, to which the issue had been submitted, had failed to give a lead.[1]

(which continued during and after the preparations for the anti-Fascist day mentioned below in the text without anyone's noticing any inconsistency) except some opportunity for the younger members of both parties to regard their mutual relations in terms other than those of stick and revolver: clearly whichever of the opposing sides gained the initiative in actual struggle would profit from such opportunities. So far as Ruth Fischer's own activities in the campaign are concerned, she gives (note 16 on p. 282) a correct record; it should, however, be added that no speaker at this and similar meetings went further than she did in making an emotional appeal to the Fascists to separate their ways from those of Big Business, whose policy implied the betrayal of the nation. I still think this policy was the only one by which the Communists could avoid complete isolation from the lower middle classes. Naturally it was and is not popular in the West; but those who write as historians ought not to use such unpopularity as a means of settling accounts with old factional opponents. The issue of principle, whether the German Communists should be ready to collaborate *with the bourgeoisie* in a struggle for revision of the Versailles Treaty, had been settled as early as summer 1919 by the expulsion of the Hamburg National Bolshevists, Wolfheim and Lauffenberg, even by their closest friends, the left-wing Communists, who eventually were expelled by Levi (see above, p. 196). Levi himself, on the eve of his expulsion from the Party, made a strong case for supporting a bourgeois left-wing Government prepared to strengthen relations with Soviet Russia (see above, pp. 214–15 and f.n.[1]). All the argument put forward at the time by Lenin (quoted by L. Kochan, in *Soviet Studies*, vol. II, pp. 114 ff.) and even all the later statements by Soviet writers who tried to discover some progressive traits in German Revisionism (amply quoted by Ruth Fischer) aimed at justifying an alliance between the Soviet and the bourgeois German *states* from the standpoint of Communist principles: the arguments with German rank-and-file Fascists in summer 1923 served the purpose of winning lower-middle-class support for a socialist *revolution* in Germany, which, if successful, would naturally have involved an alliance with Soviet Russia. Nothing in that propaganda excluded temporary concessions to the Western Powers similar to those which Soviet Russia had made at Brest-Litovsk.

[1] Stalin's letter to the Politburo, reproduced in J. Deutscher's *Stalin*, p. 394, and by Ruth Fischer, op. cit., p. 306, though loosely dated 'Summer 1923'; appears to belong to these inconclusive discussions within the Comintern; certainly it does *not* represent 'an accurate presentation of the Politburo line' (as asserted by Ruth Fischer) which was in the process of development. Ruth Fischer's reference to Stresemann is groundless even if Stalin's letter had originated immediately before the anti-Cuno strikes, i.e. early in August 1923. Cuno at least as much as Stresemann 'turned towards Britain'.

Having experienced these events on the spot, I think it just possible that it was by this decision—little noticed at the time outside the C.P. and hardly mentioned at all in the later literature on the 1923 crisis—that the C.P. lost whatever moderate chances existed of a revolutionary outcome of the crisis: at that time, as distinct from later months, parts of the Army were unreliable from the Government's point of view and working-class activity was at a high level. Armed conflicts with Fascists and police, which in some places would probably have resulted in a conquest of power by the workers, might easily have precipitated the events which were to develop a week later after the C.P. had lost the initiative.

Within the bourgeois camp the impasse produced by 'passive resistance' and its failure was soon realized; Stresemann[1] came to the conclusion that the only practicable alternatives were the 'great coalition' (from his own party to the Social Democrats), a restored Wirth Government supported by the moderate Left, or a Socialist Workers' Government of revolutionary character. Naturally he preferred the first alternative. The new Government which was to replace Cuno was almost formed when a general strike in Berlin, precipitated by shortage of wages money resulting from a printers' strike at the National Bank, caused Cuno to resign. The main demands of the strikers were economic, but culminated in the call for his resignation;[2] during the following weeks the movement involved most regions of unoccupied Germany, but faded out in its original centres as its immediate demand was met.

After the necessary diplomatic soundings, the new coalition Government, on 26th September, formally broke off 'passive resistance' on the Ruhr; on October 3rd, two days after an abortive mutiny of parts of the Black Reichswehr, who had taken the nationalist phraseology too seriously, it replaced the Social Democratic Minister of Finance, Hilferding, by Luther, a banker belonging to the People's Party and more suitable for encouraging the confidence of Big Business, as was necessary for a stabilization of the currency by orthodox methods. A few

[1] *Vermächtnis*, vol. I, p. 78.

[2] In the existing conditions, it was quite natural that the movement should be led by a committee elected by mass meetings of the shop stewards, the legally recognized alternative to the Trade Union bureaucracy available to the German workers; Ruth Fischer's reference (op. cit., p. 298) to the avoidance of the term Soviet is therefore misleading. The German term, at the time, would have been *politische Räte* as distinct from *Betriebsräte*, 'Shop stewards', or committees elected by them in the above case. It would have been applied only in a situation supposedly ripe for a decisive struggle for power (the term was used by Brandler, the representative of the C.P., at the Chemnitz conference mentioned below in the text), according to the decision of the Central Committee that the time had come for a decisive test of strength. If the name *Räte* was compromised, it was not by the Russian but by the German record (see above, p. 151); the Party, in any case, took it for granted that the workers would understand by *politische Räte* something different from, and closer to the Russian pattern than, the comedy of 1918.

days later the Communists joined the State Governments of Saxony and Thüringia, which hitherto had been composed only of Social Democrats—most of them belonging to the left wing of their party—but were dependent on Communist support. This step, represented as a measure of defence against the increasing Fascist threats from Bavaria, was also at the same time an answer to the right-wing course of the Reich Government. Zeigner, the Saxon Prime Minister, openly protested against the Reichswehr's collaboration with the Fascists. A trial of strength was inevitable, and the Communists had joined the Saxon and Thüringian State Governments precisely in order to bring it about on an issue on which they could expect a wide measure of support.

During this whole critical year, the C.P. had been split to its very foundations. At the national Congress in Leipzig, which was in session just as the French invaded the Ruhr, two well-organized factions faced each other; the right-wing majority, whose main strongholds were in the Central German States where the Governments depended on Communist support and pursued a policy of such moderate reform as was compatible with the actual relations of strength existing in republican Germany,[1] and the left wing, with concentrations in Berlin, Hamburg, and the Ruhr—the main industrial areas outside Central Germany, and the very regions whose Spartacist organizations had once been expelled because of their leftist opposition.[2] The struggle centred on the definition of a Workers' Government, as the party's next aim. The Party majority defined it as 'an attempt of the working class to defend its interests within the framework and by the methods of bourgeois democracy'; almost everything depended on whether the word 'attempt' was to be taken seriously (i.e. whether the working class was prepared to go further once it became evident that its interests collided with the set-up of Weimar Germany) or whether the whole thing was to be interpreted as a Communist-Socialist coalition of the kind suggested by Legien in 1920[3] or simply of the contemporary Central German pattern, to be

[1] See above and below, f.n. [1] on p. 169. The reader will remember that even in pre-war Social Democracy the apparently favourable conditions for social reforms existing in some German States encouraged the development of a local branch of the party's right wing (see above, p. 87).

[2] See above, p. 186.

[3] See above, p. 194. Ruth Fischer (op. cit., pp. 300–1) reports a meeting between the Berlin Trades Council and the political parties, at which substantially the same line was taken. Without entering into argument on the question whether she may not overestimate the chances of agreement that existed at the time, and whether her present assessment of the situation quite coincides with that she made in those days, the example may be useful as an illustration of the misleading character of all descriptions of the cleavages between the German Communist factions in terms of the 'United Front'. Two of the three C.P. delegates mentioned by Ruth Fischer (she herself and Herr Geschke) belonged to the left wing, and I do not remember that any reproaches were levelled against them even by their own followers for this attempt at reaching an agreement with the Social Democratic leaders. What was actually matter

followed by withdrawal into opposition if the Social Democratic parties refused their collaboration. The Comintern gave some support (qualified by definite discouragement of all attempts by the right-wingers to expel the left wing) to the Party majority because it took the first interpretation for granted. The left wing described the slogan 'a Workers' Government' as 'a synonym of the demand for proletarian dictatorship'. As the right wing's definition led to the catastrophe of October 1923 and proved not to differ substantially in its actual content from ordinary coalition policies, the left wing's definition was accepted by the Fifth Comintern Congress in the summer of 1924 and maintained for more than a decade, until it was superseded by *Front Populaire* policies. But before this point was reached, the test of the concepts of the German Party majority had to be made: ambiguous as they were, they did offer some hope of action, while the Left might easily confine the party to radical propaganda until the conditions for wholesale upheaval had matured without its intervening.[1]

When the anti-Cuno strike had shown how critical was the German situation, the Russian Politburo decided to support those groups in the German Party (the Left together with a large part of the Party majority) which were calling for a trial of strength. A compromise with Brandler, leader of the Party majority, seemed to have been found in the decision to let the upheaval start with a defence of the Saxon and Thüringian 'Workers'' Governments against the inevitable intervention by the Reich Government; in order to make full use of the opportunities to arm the workers which were said to exist in the Central German States, the Communists had to join the Governments of those States. In fact, the local Communists, including Brandler himself and some of his closest followers, did not use their ministerial posts for any subversive activity; one of them became famous because of his attempts to alleviate the unemployed workers' sufferings by letting them fish for carp in the public ponds. The Reich Government needed only to let the Commun-

of controversy in the Party was what kind of government was to be aimed at, which involved different answers to the question whether it could be achieved by mere negotiation.

[1] Op. cit., p. 383, Ruth Fischer asserts her (present) conviction that a proletarian dictatorship established in 1923 would have remained 'a historical episode' and that 'Germany would have found equilibrium in democratic government'. Such views, expressed at the time, would obviously have prevented her own capacities from influencing whatever chances of survival such a régime might have had; the left wing of the party would have been the first to repudiate her. A person who is capable of expressing such views even in a very different setting, instead of simply saying, if she so wishes, that she was mistaken when a Communist, may actually have interpreted the functions of the Communists in the German revolution as similar to those of the Levellers in the English, or the Paris Commune of 1792–3 in the French revolution; so far as she was typical of the German Left—which was only very partially—such an attitude clearly excluded any but a purely propagandist approach to the revolution.

ists carry on with activities of this kind in order to defeat their claim that they had a solution to the crisis. An offensive move, though contemplated in the Moscow negotiations, was clearly beyond the scope of the German C.P. True, Brandler, whose aim, like that of any left-wing Social Democrat, was the defence of the democratic Republic, had found it necessary in Moscow to clothe his policy in the current revolutionary phrases; the fact that the two Central German States were nearest to his idea of the future of the Weimar Republic had to be expressed in terms of the assertion that they were suitable bases for an all-German revolution. But no amount of military preparation by the party could produce an armed conflict unless the Reich Government began the conflict on the basis on which it was prepared.[1] Ebert and the coalition Government could be relied on not to tolerate left-wing State Governments; on 14th October 1923 Federal execution with the purpose of removing the Communist ministers was ordered on the basis of the famous emergency article of the Constitution.[2]

On the eve of General Müller's actual invasion of Saxony, a conference of Saxon workers' organizations was called, ostensibly to discuss the State Government's economic policies. The party had decided that a general strike should be called and that the workers should be invited to elect *politische Räte* (Soviets) which would act as the political basis of the revolution. Representatives of the Central Committee were sent out to all the important centres so that armed insurrection in support of the Saxon workers' resistance could begin.[3] Brandler, with moderate en-

[1] The left wing and some other members of the party, demanded a broadening of the proposed basis of action by mass propaganda for strikes, etc. all over the country. Actually all the party's activities were diverted into technical preparations for the armed upheaval. It is difficult to say whether, without such diversion, many more strikes, unemployed demonstrations, etc. would have occurred in October 1923 than actually happened. There are situations in which large parts of the working class are convinced that nothing short of a struggle for power can promote their cause, and the absence of big strikes and so on was conspicuous among the arguments brought forward in the Bolshevist councils against Lenin's suggestion to start the insurrection in October 1917. (Cf. the materials on the Bolshevik meetings of 28th or 29th October 1917, published in Bunyan-Fisher, *The Bolshevik Revolution*, 1917–18, Stanford University Press, 1934, pp. 72–5). But even in such situations the average worker is not prepared to support insurrection except under the circumstances in which he has been taught to regard it as appropriate. In autumn 1923 there was no appropriate issue apart from the defence of the Central German workers' Governments; when these were allowed to fall, all ideas of Communist resistance to the further moves of reaction were dropped, though the Communists, involved in factional struggle, were not ready to recognize this for some weeks longer.

[2] See above, p. 170.

[3] This fact, which is also reported by Ruth Fischer, refutes her assertion (op. cit., p. 336) that the mere proclamation of a general strike 'to see what reactions there would be in the Reich' was contemplated. Such a move was suggested by Radek (see op. cit., pp. 371–2), and eventually even made by the Saxon Social Democrats (see below in text); but the executive committee of the Central Committee of the C.P., on the critical day, undoubtedly, however inconsistently, urged a decisive stroke.

thusiasm, submitted the party decision to the conference; when the left-wing Social Democrat leaders declared that they would withdraw from the Conference if the Communist motion were adopted, Brandler withdrew, and new couriers were sent out to cancel the first order. The one sent to Hamburg missed his train, and the party representative who had set out with the original order, Ernst Thälmann, started the insurrection. Though sympathy was widespread, only 300 members of the fighting formations took an active part (it would have been more if the isolation of the rising had not become known so soon). The results of the fighting proved in any case that in an all-German rising the police would have been no match even for the mere fighting formations of the C.P., and that large parts of the army could have been diverted from Central Germany.[1] As things stood, their withdrawal from action had to begin after only twenty-four hours, nothing more having been achieved than the establishment of a symbol of the fighting power of the C.P., if not of its recognized leaders. General Müller invaded Saxony with some bloodshed, but without meeting any resistance except a

[1] There are short treatments of the episode by P. Merker (op. cit., pp. 91–2) and Ruth Fischer (op. cit., pp. 338–9), and in an article by D. D. Davidovich in *Voprosy Istorii*, II/1948. The last is evidently based on the extensive and reliable investigations of the military course of the events issued, under the Weimar Republic, in the underground publications of the Communist fighting organizations. Merker uses misleading terminology for the events he describes, owing to his writing in an atmosphere of *Front Populaire* policies where he is evidently afraid of the fact that the C.P. prepared the insurrection (for such purposes had it been founded), and thereby he does it great injustice (for example, he describes the Chemnitz conference, which, as a local Saxon event, was bad enough, as a 'National Workers' Conference', as which it would have been ridiculous). Ruth Fischer (whose presentation of the military events is coloured by factional feeling against Thälmann, who in fact ordered the withdrawal as soon as he was sure that Hamburg would remain isolated) is mistaken in describing Remmele as having gone with Thälmann: in fact Remmele was the courier indirectly mentioned by Merker who was ordered to bring the countermanding order to Hamburg. The circumstances in which he failed to arrive in time, as well as Thälmann's earlier departure from Chemnitz, are open to interpretation as attempts to force the course of events independently of Brandler's well-known hesitations: in view of the later view of the Hamburg rising as the one heroic episode in the sad story of 1923, neither of them would have been horrified at such an explanation.

More important than the nuances in the presentation of the episode are the differences in its evaluation. Davidovich, with a bitterness not usual in the pre-1933 C.P., where the question whether the decisive opportunities were missed in August or in October 1923 was left open, continues the Party tradition according to which a revolutionary situation was missed because of the Party leaders' betrayal. Ruth Fischer, whose report on the Chemnitz conference is correct, and even more Merker, whose presentation is charitable to the left-wing Social Democrats, and even more so to Brandler, whose refusal to fight without them is regarded as a matter of course, appear not only to criticize the transfer of the party's main attention to the Central German States, as has been general since that time, but even to question the correctness of contemplating a decisive trial of strength. Merker (p. 99) criticizes the attention devoted to Saxony precisely from this point of view, and speaks of 'raising extravagant hopes among the workers'.

general protest strike proclaimed by the Social Democrats and Communists when he occupied Dresden. With questionable legality he dismissed the Government and replaced it by the leader of the bourgeois minority in the Diet as Reich Commissioner. Eventually, this minority turned into a majority in later elections, and all the progressive legislation of the former Governments was repealed; later still, Saxony and Thüringia became strongholds of Nazism. For the time being, what was important was that the left-wing Social Democrats as well as the Communists, who had behaved as an appendage to them, had proved unwilling to join battle with Ebert's army.

The Communist defeat was followed by the boiling over of the Bavarian witches' cauldron. The Ruhr crisis was used as an opportunity for strengthening the local right-wing régime; on the day when passive resistance in the Ruhr was called off by the Reich Government, dictatorial powers were assumed by Kahr, and the commanding officer of the Bavarian Reichswehr, von Lossow, openly threw off subordination to Berlin. This gave the Reich Government occasion, on September 29th, to proclaim a state of emergency, which, as we have seen, was used as an opportunity for settling issues with the left wing. Von Seeckt's army did not like to cross swords with right-wingers; so long as the opposition remained a local Bavarian affair—whatever phrases of protest against the 'betrayal of the Ruhr' were used, and whatever appeals were made to the sympathies of the North German extreme right wing—things would be, and eventually were, settled by its integration into the new German régime reformed on the lines of the right wing's ideas. But Kahr and Lossow worked with the support of the Fascist organizations with all-German aspirations which had now rallied under Hitler and Ludendorff. In the scramble for position between the Bavarian group, which wanted to use the local armed potential as a means of pressure to shift the Federal settlement as far as possible to the Right with increased autonomy for Bavaria, and the Nazi group which desired a centralist Fascist dictatorship over all Germany, the Nazis secured the initiative: on the night of November 8th–9th they forced the Kahr-Lossow group to join in proclaiming an all-German dictatorship. Ebert transferred dictatorial powers to Seeckt, who was no more eager for an armed conflict than were his Bavarian colleagues; after a few hours Kahr and Lossow disowned Hitler's *coup*, which broke down in a hopeless attempt to mobilize the Munich lower-middle-class public against their betrayal.

Hitler's *coup* thus proved an even less suitable starting-point for a future attack against the Reich régime than, from the other side, did the Communist insurrection in Hamburg, which at least was defeated in honest battle against its natural enemy and might be interpreted as an indication of what the Communists could be capable of under a leadership which made a proper use of their energies. Hitler's moral position, however, was saved by his trial, which was properly used to unmask the length to which Kahr and Lossow, whose Government were now trying Hitler and Ludendorff, had themselves gone on the path of treason. It is hardly necessary to say that, under the justice of republican Germany, Ludendorff got off scot-free and Hitler with a few months' internment in a fortress; just long enough to write his book and to gain the prestige of a martyr, at least from the lower middle class, among whom it was to be had cheap. Kahr, who was eventually killed by Hitler on 30th June 1934, was finally compromised from the point of view of republican legality as well as from that of Fascist insurrection; the explosion resulted in turning Bavarian political Catholicism definitely into an ordinary right-wing bourgeois party.

Seeckt used his emergency powers to outlaw, while they lasted, both the Communist and Fascist parties; this caused them some little organizational inconvenience but gave them the prestige of not being responsible for what was to follow. Stresemann himself later spoke of the 'deeply tragic' situation of the Social Democrats whose whole political authority rested on the social achievements of the revolution but who now had to take the responsibility for abolishing them. It should be added that even what little relief from that responsibility they got was against their own intentions. After the Reichswehr, on the orders of a Government in which they took part, had invaded Saxony and deposed their fellow-partisan ministers, the Social Democrats could not avoid moving a vote of censure, but it was framed in such a way that the German Nationals should for reasons of principle be unable to support it; the calculation proved a mistaken one, as the Conservatives were more interested than the Social Democrats in a fall of the Government. Hergt, the National Conservative leader, was quite right in stating that, according to their own declarations, the Social Democrats were not on the retired list but in the reserve of the Cabinet,[1] which was now formed by a bloc of all the bourgeois parties. Making use of the extraordinary powers voted, and duly prolonged, with Social Democratic support, this Cabinet now abolished, by 'emergency procedure', all such achievements of the revolution, or even of the liberal legislation in existence before it, as did not fit into the framework of stabilization of the budget by orthodox deflationary methods, or could at least be connected with it by the fact that they involved public expenditure—from the eight-hour day, the rights of civil servants, and many improvements in social insurance, down to trial by jury. During the last period of the monetary inflation, the standard of living had fallen so low that the very fact of stabilization, at whatever level of wages and hours and combined with whatever amount of unemployment, was greeted by broad masses as a deliverance; when the working class had failed to impose its solution for

[1] Stampfer, the leading Social Democratic authority on this period (op. cit., pp. 353–4) agrees with this interpretation.

the crisis, Big Business, with such support from abroad as soon became evident in the Dawes Plan, had its chance.

With the ending of the political crisis of 1923, and the stabilization of the currency, the German revolution had reached its end. One after another the three mass parties in which German labour had found its political representation had failed; only moderate satisfaction for the C.P., in which all left-wing opposition to the régime was now rallied, could be derived from the fact that the Majority Socialists had 'failed' by joining hands with the bourgeoisie in suppressing the revolt of the workers, while itself had only failed through reluctance to cross swords with the bourgeoisie's supporters. For an estimate of the situation existing at that time within the labour movement it is almost irrelevant whether, with other concepts, tactics, and leadership, the C.P. could have secured power, a very different shape for the Weimar régime,[1] or at least a starting-point from which, whatever its temporary losses, all the opposition to bourgeois rule that was bound to grow up during the Great Depression could be rallied. The Communist workers felt that they had been betrayed by Brandler as they had earlier by Ebert, Scheidemann and Hilferding; an attempt by the Comintern and the more moderate members of the Party majority to effect a combination of the moderate wings of both factions simply failed; by an overwhelming majority, control of the Party passed to the Left, at that time lead by Ruth Fischer and Maslow. Great efforts were needed even to prevent the Communist workers from simply leaving the Trade Unions in favour of anarcho-syndicalist experiments, as many of the radical workers, disappointed by the loss of the eight-hour day and by the betrayal of the Trade Union leaders, did at that time. Whatever the afterthoughts, or the contemporary secret thoughts of the Left leaders,[2] they assumed power within the Party precisely because they made themselves mouthpieces of the widespread feeling that 'the specific German way to Socialism' had failed, and that a comparison between the German October of 1923 and the Russian October of 1917 proved the superiority of the Bolshevist methods. It was *they* who raised the demand for 'Bolshevization of the West European parties' and rallied the German C.P. in the struggle against Trotskyism.[3] When in 1925 they fell out with that group

[1] As we have seen above (p. 222), this was even Stresemann's opinion.

[2] The writer, who took an active part in the events here described, and also in the subsequent discussions, has learned from Ruth Fischer's book a great deal about the actual character of her Russian affiliations.

[3] Ruth Fischer's and Maslow's personal resentment against Radek, which is evident in many parts of Fischer's book, and the question to what extent he was the initiator of, or merely acquiesced in, Brandler's mistakes, are irrelevant in an assessment of their heading the struggle against Trotskyism, which was more than a person, and certainly more than the factional associations of a person (in their contributions to the literary argument which followed the publication of Trotsky's *Lessons of October*, Maslow and Fischer specially made the point that it was not individual

in the anti-Trotskyist Russian Party majority which proved to be the stronger one, they could easily be ousted by an Open Letter of the Comintern which met with little serious resistance outside the Berlin organization; this happened notwithstanding the fact that they had not even been extremist representatives of the trend which made United Front policies in general responsible for the defeat of October 1923.[1]

Complete reliance on guidance from the Russian Politburo and whatever influence such reliance may have had on the German C.P.'s later failure to form in time a united front with the Social Democrat workers against the growth of Hitlerism[2] was not a cause but a consequence of October 1923; it followed from the experiences with a leadership shaped by Rosa Luxemburg's opposition to Lenin's concepts of the Party and its tasks, and from the fact that the Trotskyist Radek, acting at that time as the representative of the Comintern, had supported the mistakes of the German leaders. What Ruth Fischer and Maslow, in the German discussion of those days, reproached the Russian leaders for was not intervention in German affairs, as was asserted later, but failure to intervene on behalf of the Russian Party majority.

That an opportunity of decisive importance was lost because of dependence on advice from a brother party which failed to come forward, and that the loss of prestige caused by failure to head the German revolution could be compensated only by borrowing from the prestige of the victorious Russian revolution, is about the worst thing that can be said of a revolutionary party, and possibly even of the capacity of the German people to regenerate itself by a Socialist revolution (since no one, certainly not the dissenting factions, has produced in Germany a revolutionary party more sincere than the K.P.D.). It cannot be amended or mitigated by complaints about the fact that the Soviet leaders eventually fulfilled the additional task put upon their shoulders as well as they could and, quite naturally, on the assumption that from the standpoint of international Communism the preservation and strengthening of their own system was essential.

During the months which followed Seeckt's laying down of the formal dictatorship and the stabilization of the currency, the German Republic assumed its definitive shape—if the word 'definitive' can be applied to a

leaders but organized parties that mattered). Ruth Fischer's struggle against Trotskyism, which, at the time the events occurred, could only be interpreted as being waged from the standpoint of Stalin, Zinoviev, or a person not quite sure which of the two she should support, appears in a peculiar light as we learn from her book (pp. 247, 311–12, and 359–60) that her actual Russian affiliations were with the groups usually described as left of Trotsky and that her disapproval of Trotsky's attitude in the Russian discussions of 1923 was mainly based upon his limiting himself to a demand for intra-party democracy instead of introducing a many-party system as demanded by the Workers' Opposition.

[1] See below, p. 232.
[2] See below, pp. 378 ff.

state of things which began to be overthrown only six years later. In the economic field, the stabilization of the currency put an end to combines such as that of Stinnes, the growth of which had been based on the acquisition of 'real values' by credits which had to be repaid in depreciated paper; circulating capital was now required to keep the undertakings going. An enormous concentration of wealth had taken place during the inflation period because of the expropriation of the masses; Lederer[1] estimates that small savers had lost 50 milliard gold marks during the inflation, and employees some 24 to 28 milliards from the reduction in their real wages; to this must be added the profits made by entrepreneurs because of the low incidence of the taxes paid by them in depreciated currency. Most of these, roughly 100 milliards, were concentrated in the hands of Big Business: in part, they replaced the depreciation of capital goods (in real terms), another part had to cover the losses involved in dumping exports. In addition, the material costs of counter-revolution, including the passive resistance in the Ruhr, must have been considerable; yet enough remained to reorganize the financial oligarchy controlling business, headed by the big banks, the two largest of which were fused into the giant D.D. Bank (Deutsche Bank und Diskontogesellschaft). Backed by American credits, the inflow of which began immediately the inflation had ended, large-scale finance started reorganizing the great industrial monopolies; these were headed by the Chemical (IG Farben) and the Steel Trusts, with a capital of 1,100 and 800 million marks respectively, and the Hamburg-Lloyd Combine which practically monopolized the merchant navy.

On the parliamentary scene, the new order was stabilized when the German Nationals dropped as much of their nationalist demagogy as was necessary in order to have a share in bourgeois coalition governments collaborating with other countries. By opposing the Dawes Plan in the Reichstag elected in May 1924, they enforced a dissolution from which they emerged, in December, with 6·7 million votes together with the Reichslandbund,[2] i.e. as the second largest party next after the Social Democrats, the main supporters of the Dawes Plan, whose vote had risen to 7·2 millions, while the Communist vote was reduced to 2·7 millions. This increased weight was cashed by a turn round to support of the Dawes Plan; the German Nationals thus became the largest partner in the bourgeois coalition Governments which, under moderate right-wingers such as Luther and Jarres, ruled Germany for nearly four years. Control of the caucus of the German People's Party soon passed into the hands of Vögler, the leader of the Steel Trust, another asset of the Stinnes estate. In order to promote collaboration with the German Nationals Vögler organized within his party a 'National Liberal Association'; still, Stresemann's prestige and competence as leader in foreign

[1] *Strukturwandlungen der deutscher Volkswirtschaft*, vol. I, pp. 51–2.

[2] The League of Agriculturalists (see above, p. 46) as reorganized in 1919.

policy gave him a position strong enough to preserve, together with his old ally Hindenburg, the appearances of a 'new Germany' peaceful as well as conservative so long as the influx of foreign credits kept up the façade of prosperity. Only the return to Conservative hands of the formal control of the Army (which was actually far to the right of parliamentary Conservatism) was needed to complete the reinstatement of the groups which had controlled pre-1918 Germany, purged from such irresponsible individuals as Wilhelm II and Ludendorff and adapted to the fact that the Junkers now had to play second fiddle to Big Business.

This change was completed in April 1925 by Hindenburg's election as Reichs-president; in the first ballot the several parties ran candidates of their own, with the result that none of them, not even Jarres, the joint candidate of the German National and German People's parties, could hope for the absolute majority needed for the second ballot; this would have to be fought out between the two large blocs into which public opinion was divided. The right-wingers replaced Jarres by Hindenburg following Stresemann's old suggestion;[1] the Social Democrats, in exchange for getting for their candidate, Otto Braun, the post of Prussian Prime Minister, withdrew him in favour of the Catholic candidate, Marx, who got only half of the Socialist's votes in the first ballot. As for the Communists, Maslow, with the support of the Comintern, suggested the withdrawal of their candidate, Thälmann, in favour of the Social Democrat. The issue arose before Braun's candidature was withdrawn by his own party; in the then conditions Communist support for Marx seemed out of the question.[2] In the second ballot, Thälmann got just that number of votes which, if *all* of them could have been transferred to the left-centre candidate, would have secured him a victory over Hindenburg. The actual importance of the Communist candidature is open to question; even if Maslow and the Comintern had got their way in the German Central Committee in time to make a definite offer, the Social Democrats would hardly have maintained their candidate (they could argue that right-wing Catholics and Democrats would prefer Jarres and even Hindenburg to a Socialist); and even if the Communist Central Committee had been ready to support the Catholic, their voters would hardly have done so. As things turned out, the Communist vote increased in the hopeless and dangerous second ballot in regions such as Saxony, where the rationalist Socialist workers' dislike of a Catholic was

[1] See above note [5] on p. 171.

[2] The presentation by Ruth Fischer (op. cit., pp. 421–2) is important as a refutation of the current myths about the part played in the events by the Comintern, but unhappily it omits the date of the German Central Committee's refusal to accept Zinoviev's and Maslow's proposal. My presentation is based on the assumption that this happened immediately after the Moscow discussion of April 2nd. At a later date—too late from the standpoint of the Social Democrats' negotiation with the Centre—withdrawal of Thälmann in favour of Braun was indeed suggested. Merker (op. cit., p. 119) makes the most of this suggestion.

predominant, while especially in Bavaria the Protestant Hindenburg collected right-wing Catholic votes at the expense of the official (and not left-wing) Catholic candidate; this tendency would have been stronger if Marx could have been denounced as sponsored by the Reds. The real chance of turning the scales in favour of a left-centre candidate by Communist intervention would have lain in a large-scale campaign to make him the symbol of left-wing resistance to the right, as eventually was done in the campaign for the expropriation of the Princes.[1] This was hardly possible in favour of a Catholic other than a definite left-winger such as Wirth, and the decision whether he would be nominated did not lie with the Communists. But certainly, whatever might have been the outcome of any alternative course, the course actually taken burdened them, in the eyes of many of their potential allies, with co-responsibility for all the fruits of Hindenburg's election.

(*d*) *The Trade Unions after 1918*

When the labour movement's future was transferred to the political field, its economic organization ceased to be of prime importance. Its growth was completed, however, during the period we are discussing; to the series of political defeats there corresponded a record of at least initial progress in the field upon which the advocates of gradualist advance to socialism had relied.

The climax of Central European trade unionism was reached in 1921, when trade union membership in Germany reached nearly ten millions —still only half of the workers and salaried employees—and in Austria 1·08 million, the bulk of the black-coated as well as of the manual workers. In Czechoslovakia the post-revolutionary maximum was not reached until 1924, when membership had risen from the 247,000 at the end of the war to 1·7 million, embracing 80 per cent of all employed personnel. Czechoslovakia was marked by the political diversity of its unions, thus contrasting with the predominance in Germany, and the near-monopoly in Austria,[2] of Socialist Trade Unions. These splits were perpetuated by the system of unemployment insurance,[3] but this prevented a later setback such as occurred in Germany and Austria; in Czechoslovakia, under penalty of having his unemployment benefit reduced to starvation level, no worker could remain outside all organizations, and under penalty of leaving its supporters exposed to the influence of competing parties, no party could afford not to have Unions of its own. These rulings preserved, though they did not cause, the political

[1] See below, pp. 280–1.

[2] Non-Socialist Trade Unions made some headway only after 1929, when the employers could apply pressure; at the end of the Republic the Christian Unions had about 100,000 members, the Nazi-controlled Unions some 60,000 (these latter mostly black-coated workers), while the Free Unions were reduced to half a million.

[3] See below, p. 299.

splits; at the climax in 1924, before the introduction of the Ghent system of unemployment insurance, 350,000 workers were organized by the Czechoslovak and 250,000 by the Sudeten-German Social Democrats, 300,000 by the Czechoslovak National Socialists, 200,000 by the Communists (the only party to have an inter-national organization), 120,000 in Czech and 20,000 in Sudeten German Christian Trade Unions, and 50,000 by the Sudeten German National Socialists. The rest were in 'non-political' Unions, mainly of civil servants. In 1930 1·22 million were organized in Czechoslovak, 0·48 million in Sudeten German, and 0·18 in Communist (inter-national) Unions; even in 1937, when the Henlein terror had reduced Sudeten German trade unionism of all kinds to just half its 1920 strength, 1·24 million workers and 0·98 million salaried employees were organized in Unions of one group or the other. These conditions were obviously special.

In Germany, apart from the 8 million Free Trade Unionists, there were 1·1 million in Christian Trade Unions, which now rallied the whole right-wing camp of trade unionism,[1] 225,000 (mostly black-coated workers) in the Hirsch-Duncker Unions, and a quarter of a million in Communist-influenced splits to the left of official trade unionism, mainly on the Ruhr. The growth in comparison with pre-war days was due to advance of already well-established Unions, which in most of the major enterprises had nearly reached a 'closed shop' position, as well as to the inclusion of strata previously excluded from trade union organization by conditions in imperial Germany; among the 8·1 million Free Trade Unionists counted in 1920 there were 1·65 million members of the Metal and Engineering Workers' Union (in 1913: 560,000);[2] 640,000 (210,000) Factory Workers in (the Chemical and similar industries), 570,000 (300,000) Transport Workers, 450,000 (100,000) Miners, 700,000 (20,000) Agricultural Workers, 430,000 Railwaymen (who until the revolution were prohibited from joining trade unions), 380,000 (30,000) Salaried Employees, 290,000 (50,000) Workers in State and Municipal Employment. The growth was comparatively smallest among the Building workers (470,000 as against 390,000), who were already well organized before the war. Evidently, agricultural labourers and railwaymen had been emancipated from a completely dependent status, and did not view the post-1918 development of German trade unionism with the same eyes as, say, Berlin engineering workers or builders who might look on it as a betrayal of the labour movement. When labourers and railwaymen got their share in the defeats of the labour movement they could no longer voice their disappointment within it, as, under heavy pressure from the employers, their organizations dissolved as quickly as they had grown.

Nor would it be correct to say that the German trade unions ceased

[1] See f.n. [3] below, p. 238.

[2] The numbers in brackets give the 1913 figure in each case.

to conduct industrial struggles. In his Memoirs,[1] Noske describes how he defeated not only political insurrection but also such economic strikes as he considered harmful to the national interest, by prohibiting strikes of railwaymen and miners, and even of the Berlin engineering workers, and encouraging the creation of a special body of strike-breakers, the famous TENO (Technical Emergency Help), many members of which later played their part in the Nazi movement, and were protected by heavy penalties, introduced by emergency decree, against interference or boycott. Trade Unionists, even very moderate ones, had to perform certain rituals of disapproval of such procedure even when they supplemented it by outlawing such strikes as did not fit into the framework of coalition policies. Very soon all strikes of railwaymen or of the workers in public utilities were unofficial; even the strikes of the agricultural labourers, whose newly awakened class-consciousness collided with the Junkers' old-standing claim to be the masters of the village, were unofficial more often than not. There were no clear borderlines between the two types of movements; a 'wild' strike, if strong enough to avoid being brought to an end by means other than the use of the official negotiation machinery, might be 'sanctioned' *post eventum* by the trade union leaders to enable them to take control, while the most lawful strike which went further than suited Social Democratic policies might, at a later stage, be declared 'wild' so as to let Noske intervene.

On the whole, there was a continuous increase of strikes, from 3,682 in 1919 to 4,348 in 1922 (the number of lockouts increased from 37 to 437); in 1919 and 1922 respectively, 2·75 and 2·5 million workers took part in labour conflicts, in the intermediate years only 2 million. There were thus nearly twice as many strikes and five times as many strikers as in the pre-war period. The number of industrial disputes in general increased even more than these figures show, because the progress of collective bargaining resulted in more disputes being settled without strike action. In 1920 every Free Trade Unionist took part on an average in about 1·66 disputes as against exactly 0·5 disputes in 1913;[2] but 86 as against 74 per cent of the disputes were settled without actual conflict; the percentage of strikes with no success had decreased from 19·5 in 1913 to 6·3 in 1920 (in 1919 it was a mere 4 per cent). True, in times of upheaval and monetary inflation, success is not necessarily interpreted by the workers concerned in the same terms as by the trade union officials; but however frequent the officials' complaints about the members' dissatisfaction and lack of discipline, there was no great movement away from the trade unions until their policies had resulted in a loss of influence over working conditions. At the end of 1922 collective agreements were in force for 890,000 enterprises with 14·26 million employees, and one year later only for 813,000 enterprises with 13·14

[1] Op. cit., p. 188.
[2] Umbreit, op. cit., p. 194.

million employees;[1] this fall also brought with it the first serious setback in membership figures, by nearly a fifth.[2] From these figures it is quite clear that the friendly society benefits offered by the unions played a much smaller part among the causes of their post-revoutionary growth than the workers' desire for an efficient representation of their interests; by 1922 there was no reason to bother about benefits which when they were paid would hardly purchase a loaf of bread.

The decline in membership set in when the unions proved obviously incapable of scoring any successes and when, because of the changed balance of power, in some enterprises, the smaller ones especially, it was useful to be a non-unionist; by the end of 1925 Free as well as Christian Trade Unions had lost about half their 1921–3 membership.[3] The recovery during the following years was slight and did not affect the larger undertakings in the main industries. At the 1924 Congress of the Metal Workers' Union Dissmann stated that in the Berlin engineering factories—the prime strongholds of the German labour movement—less than 40 per cent of the workers were organized, and in the Hamburg shipbuilding yards as well as in the Hamborn Thyssen works a mere 25 per cent. It should be added, however, that in the same speech Dissmann criticized the Düsseldorf engineers for striking against the advice of their officials. In the minds of some leading officials, unofficial strikes ranked with loss of members as symptoms of the decay of the movement; the new conditions of collective bargaining, it was asserted, called for close control of the members from above; 'sovereign personalities' were needed for 'sovereign action'. Elections of local officials were made to depend on the approval of the Union's central committee, and this could be refused if necessary to safeguard the principles of unified control and centralization. The literary advocates of the bureaucracy found this quite compatible with trade union democracy, the essence of which was that access even to the highest post of leadership should be open to everyone who showed his capacity therefor. The Advisory Councils[4] were the main stronghold of this type of trade union democracy.[5] It is difficult to avoid an interpretation in terms of Michels's comparison with bishops,[6] or, even more suggestively, in terms of the modern one-party State.

To such principles of organization corresponded a certain attitude to

[1] Seidel, op. cit., p. 39.

[2] Cf. the figures given by Ruth Fischer, op. cit., p. 299.

[3] According to the *Report* of the Central Committee of the C.P. to the Essen Congress, dated 15th March 1927, a mere 20 per cent of the workers of the heavy iron industries in the Ruhr, 35 per cent of the miners, 20 per cent of all the Berlin metal and engineering workers were unionists.

[4] We may remember the description of them, by a not very left-wing theoretician of trade unionism, as 'parliaments of paid officials'; see above, p. 74.

[5] Seidel, op. cit., pp. 37 and 141–3.

[6] See above, p. 78.

trade unionist action. In the winter of 1923–4 the Working Community[1] broke down because the employers, led by the heavy industrialists of the Ruhr, deemed an occasional resumption of trials of strength more profitable now that the threat of revolutionary action by the working class had been removed and the trade unions weakened. On the other side, occasional strike action was necessary in the area of bourgeois bloc Governments in order to assert the trade union bureaucracy's status as partner at the negotiating table. But so far as it was admitted at all, it was restricted to this purpose; any initiative from below for starting a strike, not to speak of continuing one against the union leaders' advice, was regarded as a subversive activity. The unorganized workers, whose ranks were swollen by these very tactics, were important only as an argument to prove the deplorable impossibility of strike action. The Communist attempts to rally the unorganized workers and to provide material support for them (and, of course, for organized workers whose strikes were disowned by the bureaucracy) were subversive because they undermined the idea that the Trade Union funds were the main source of working-class strength and the foundation of the claims of the controllers of those funds to control the movement. In some cases Communist Trade Union members were expelled because, in their capacity as municipal councillors, they had tabled motions for support from public funds for strikes which were sanctioned by the Union! During the strike of the Mansfeld copper miners in 1930[2] the Halle Consumers' Co-operative, which, under Communist control, sent food to the strikers (with the intention of strengthening the authority of the Communist-controlled committee which supported the unorganized workers) was not only expelled from the Consumers' Co-operative Association but actually made bankrupt by a boycott—the action being quite openly organized by the Social Democratic party. The relevant fact for us is not that the Social Democratic organizers of the German Consumers' Co-operatives wished to destroy Communist influence, but that they could use such an occasion as this without thereby destroying their own party's influence: the average Social Democrat was expected to regard any action which might break the Trade Union bureaucracy's monopoly in leading strike action as harmful in itself even if the strike, as in the case just quoted, was sanctioned by that very bureaucracy.

In such a scheme of things, participation by the unorganized workers in the formation of strike committees (which had been a common-place in the nineties, when the Trade Unions regarded themselves as the organizing and leading minority of a broader movement) was bound to be anathema to the Union leaders. Less natural, perhaps, was the fact that a considerable number of the Communist trade unionists resisted

[1] See above, p. 152.
[2] See below, p. 329.

the application of such methods, when demanded by their party,[1] not only for the possibly sound tactical consideration that their expulsion from the Union, which would inevitably follow such attempts, would do more harm than a broader strike committee could do good, but also because they shared in esteeming the non-union-member (i.e. 60 per cent of the German working class) as second-rate from the class point of view.

Such principles prevented a recovery of German trade unionism from its setback in 1923–4. The opportunity to strike an occasional bargain in favour of some individual group of workers returned, but there was no longer any question of the wholesale organization of the decisive groups of the working class. On the eve of the Great Depression little more than a third of the workers and salaried employees[2] were organized in bona fide trade unions, roughly the same proportion as immediately after the revolution; the degree of organization amongst workers and salaried employees was very similar, though the type of organization differed —amongst the salaried employees to such an extent that it might seem questionable whether the organization were really trade unionist in character.[3] Amongst the workers, there were 4·7 million Free Trade Unionists, 700,000 members of Christian, and 200,000 of Hirsch-Duncker Unions; with possibly another 200,000 organized in Communist and anarcho-syndicalist groups. Amongst the salaried employees the Christian group, with its German National appendix[3] predominant, had 590,000 members, the Free Trade Unions 460,000, and the Hirsch-Duncker Unions 335,000.

Perhaps more important than the proportionate strength of the various kinds of bona fide trade unions, which in most cases simply reflected the organized members' traditional background, was the comparative strength of the two trends within the 'class-conscious' labour movement. The strength of the left wing, represented at first by the left-wing Independents, and later by the Communists, was not reflected in

[1] See below, pp. 373–4.

[2] Conditions among civil servants, including salaried employees of the nationalized railways, were very different; nearly all of them were organized, but most of them in 'non-political' Unions. Cf. the figures given by F. David, *Der Bankrott des Reformismus*, Berlin, 1932, p. 255.

[3] The large majority of the Unions affiliated to the Christian Trade Union Centre for salaried employees was formed by the German National Commercial Employees' Association, which, before 1918, had been nearer to yellow than even to right-wing Christian Trade Unionism, with 400,000 members. Correspondingly, it is difficult to difficult to describe the parliamentary representation of Christian Trade Unionism as belonging unequivocally to the democratic elements in German life; of their 27 M.P.s in the Reichstag of 1924–8 only 17 belonged to the Centre (some of them, such as their leader Stegerwald, to its right wing), 2 to the German People's Party, 7 to the German Nationals, 1 even to the Nazi party. But nearly all the workers belonging to the Christian Trade Unions supported the left wing of the Centre Party.

that of the Communist-led splinter Unions; the latter really indicated two secondary elements of the situation: (1) radical, partly syndicalist, trends among various groups of workers (especially on the Ruhr) who simply refused to join the Free Trade Unions; and (2) the readiness or otherwise of the C.P. to compromise with such trends, or even to accept radical splinter Unions as an outlet for the activities of Communists who were expelled from the Free Trade Unions. Nor do the figures of C.P. membership amongst Union officials indicate very much, as they were dependent, apart from the political preferences of Union members, on the varying tactics[1] of the C.P. and on how far Trade Union central committees were prepared to tolerate well-known Communists within the Unions, especially as elected officials. Expulsions of Communists from the Unions, even where the Union leaders' case was extremely weak from the standpoint of the rules, date as far back as the existence of a Communist mass party,[2] but it depended on the C.P.'s varying tactics to make the Union leaders' task more or less difficult.

From Berlin, interesting data[3] are available on the positions held by Communists in the Trade Union hierarchy in 1927–8, a period when the C.P. was making maximum efforts to strengthen its position within the Unions, though with less success than before 1923. Of the 906,000 Berlin workers, 336,000 were organized in the Free Trade Unions. The proportion of Communist to Social Democrat votes at the general election was 611,000 to 816,000; this suggests near-equilibrium between Communist and Social Democrat supporters among the factory workers. But only 7·5 per cent of the 'men of confidence' and 8·5 per cent of the Trade Unionists elected to the Works' Councils were Communists; as also were 6·6 per cent of the delegates elected to the Regional Con-

[1] See below, p. 373.

[2] In answer to Levi's and his friends' reproach that the difficulties met with by Communist trade union officials were due to the existence of the Red Trade Union International, the *Report* of the Central Committee to the Jena (1921) Congress of the C.P. mentions (p. 33) a case which had arisen before that International was founded. The Berlin branch of the Railwaymen's Union had unanimously elected a well-known Communist as Chairman, and re-elected him twice when the assent of the Union's National Committee was refused. As the branch declined to change its mind, the elected Chairman was expelled from the Union, but, on his appeal, the Investigation Commission of the Union Congress *unanimously* decided that there had been no grounds for his expulsion. Then the National Committee forced the issue by threatening resignation if the expulsion was not upheld; under this pressure it was, at last, confirmed by the Congress with a narrow majority. Similar events occurred in all the workers' mass organizations. In 1927—a time when Communist tactics were certainly directed towards the preservation of status in the traditional organizations of labour—the Workers' Sport Association was split in Berlin because the Social Democratic minority, which was supported by the National Committee, declined to submit to the Communist majority in the Regional Comittee, which had just been backed by 60 per cent of the members. Cf. *Report* of the Berlin Regional Committee of the C.P. to the Regional Party Congress, 1929, pp. 105 ff.

[3] Ibid., pp. 256–7.

ferences of the individual Unions, 3·5 per cent of the Trade Committees, 2 per cent of the members of the wider committees of the individual Unions, 0·7 per cent of the members of their 'narrower' committees, and 0·2 per cent of the paid officials. At the same time the vote for Communist candidates at the election of delegates to the National Congress of those Unions wherein such delegates were elected by a general ballot of the members (amongst them the key Union of the Metal Workers) was 29,700 against 28,300 Social Democrat supporters:[1] i.e. just what might be expected from the vote in parliamentary elections. The higher in the Union hierarchy, the more efficient were the safeguards laid down by the rules (which were frequently amended for this purpose) in order to guarantee the continuance of control by the right-wing bureaucracy. The very few instances in which the Communists controlled the 'narrower', i.e. leading local committees of some Unions, or at least trade committees within their framework, concerned cases where tradition worked in favour of individuals or groups of individuals who had become Communists in the political split of 1920.

The elections to the Factory Councils worked perhaps the most important stage of the contest between the trends. In the Ruhr mines during the period under discussion a very large part of the Communist vote went to candidates of separate left-wing Unions; these polled, in 1921, about 30 per cent of the total vote against more than 40 per cent of the Free, and 25 per cent of the Christian and Polish Trade Unions. In 1924 the Communists increased their hold to 42·7 per cent, against 33 per cent for the Free and 20 per cent for the Christian Trade Unions; in the next year the position of 1921 was almost restored. In other enterprises the influence of the Communists could only be calculated indirectly, as they usually ran on Free Trade Union lists; even in the few cases where statistics are available, it is not clear how far Communists were elected merely *qua* exemplary Shop Stewards, and to what extent their election implied also a vote of confidence in their politics. For Berlin 1928 (where, as we have just seen, the proportion of Communists in the total of Union members elected to Works' Councils was a mere 8·5 per cent) we have statistics of the elections to 183 large factories with a total of 180,000 workers where a real electoral campaign took place; amongst 1,522 Works' Councillors elected in these factories there were 368 Communists and 323 non-party members known to be in sympathy with them, while the Social Democrats had 693 members and sympathizers elected.[2] These elections took place at a time when the Communists were trying to gain influence on the Works' Councils by

[1] Ibid., pp. 150–1. The percentage of Union members taking part in the contested elections varied between 15 in the chemical and tailoring industries, and 75 among the auxiliary workers of the graphic industries (in the largest Union, the Metal Workers, it was 56 per cent).

[2] Ibid., pp. 158–9.

being nominated on the lists of the Free Trade Unions. In a few instances they were not allowed to fight for the composition of these lists in plenary meetings of the Unionists employed in the factory (as prescribed by the rules of the T.U.C.), and entered on an open struggle before the whole electorate, with results much more favourable than had been offered them by the Social Democrat officials;[1] but the Communist Trade Union members elected on these lists were expelled from the Unions. There were individual instances in which only the rights of the majority of the factory Union caucus (sympathizing with the Communists) against the Social Democratic Union bureaucracy were defended; but in 1929, after another swerve in their tactical line,[2] the Communists made a general appeal to the unorganized workers by running independent lists against the official lists of the Free Trade Unions, and won clear majorities in nearly all the big engineering factories of Berlin, in the Central German chemical industries and in many mines (though few works of the heavy iron industries in the Ruhr). During the following years they lost many of these positions in spite of their increasing vote in political elections; apart from dismissals of Communists, this might be due to the workers' doubt of the capacity of Factory Councillors who were certain to be dismissed from the Union to defend their interests effectively. If anything can be deduced from the elections to the Factory Councils, it is that the workers in the big factories and mines were fairly equally divided between the two wings of the German labour movement.

[1] Ibid. In one of these works the Communists and their sympathizers were offered three out of eighteen seats, but won seven (in the following year, after the swerve in their Party line, a large absolute majority); in the other the (Communist) majority of the factory Union caucus had nominated two Social Democrats instead of the four demanded, and not those in whom the Social Democrats were most interested. In consequence, the Social Democrats entered a list of their own, and the Trade Unionists elected on the list of the factory caucus were expelled by the (Social Democrat) National Committee of the Union. Such incidents show how erroneous it is to interpret the eventual splits as mere outcomes of Communist policy decisions; what the Communist Party had actually to decide upon was how to behave towards a Social Democratic policy which clearly excluded the gaining of a Trade Union majority within the framework of the rules.

[2] See below, p. 373.

PART THREE

CENTRAL EUROPEAN DEMOCRACY AND ITS FALL 1924–1938

CHAPTER SEVEN

THE INSTITUTIONAL FRAMEWORK

(*a*) *The Political Parties*

CENTRAL European democracy was marked by the coexistence of a number of parties based on individual membership. With the quite insignificant exceptions of the 'Economic Party' in Germany and the 'Small Traders' Party' in Czechoslovakia,[1] each of them was based on a more or less definite social and political outlook, but was closely connected with the economic group organizations which they had at least helped to bring into being. The idea of a political party as the permanent centre of the political activities of citizens was taken for granted; when on 7th July 1929 the Supreme Court of the German Republic had to decide on what conditions a small party without parliamentary representation might enjoy those facilities for nominating candidates which the law granted to established parties, it defined a party as 'a stable combination of a fairly large number of citizens brought into being in order to achieve common political aims'; and enumerated as the normal characteristics of such a stable combination a fixed political programme, a developed organization, and a party Press: parliamentary representation was not considered essential. Few non-working-class party organizations in Britain, not to speak of the U.S.A. or even France, would have satisfied such a definition.

The accepted standard of party life was not equally complied with everywhere in this respect; the main distinction was between the political parties appealing to the working class and those of other groups. It is not true that in the political life of Central Europe (apart from Austria with its two-party system) the cleavage between 'Socialist' and 'bourgeois' parties was fundamental: the Social Democrats' relations with their 'bourgeois' coalition partners were much more friendly than with the Communists. But the working class, having initiated the system of economic and political organization and played the leading part in the struggle with autocratic monarchy, also set the standard of organization to which other parties conformed with moderate success.

[1] See below, pp. 259 and 302.

A not left-wing observer divided the German parties into two groups, according to how their activities were financed: those which collected comparatively small contributions from a large number of members, and those which, lacking sufficient members, appealed for large contributions, as regular as possible, from some wealthy adherents especially in commercial and industrial circles, who naturally 'would try to exercise their influence on the party in the sense of their private interests and thus might endanger its programmatic position'.[1] In the working-class parties of Germany and Austria a contribution of about 1 per cent of the member's total income was looked upon as the norm; an organized worker active in the movement might easily spend up to 5 per cent if trade union fees, subscription to the Party organ, expenditure on meetings, etc., were included. At the other end of the scale stood the people who undertook most of the National Conservatives' propaganda and, during the Republic's last years, the Nazi, who expected not only a good job in the event of his party's acceding to political power (as did many people in all parties), but even payment and regular support in return for his everyday activities.

Even further went the Austrian Heimwehren, whose members were known as 'five shilling men' because of the amount they were paid for each day's activities.[2] These were extreme cases, but undoubtedly the agricultural labourer who was a member of the German National Party or, as was more likely, of some para-military organization connected with it, quite apart from remaining on good terms with his employer, got more in immediate material benefits from his membership than it cost him. Various attitudes were represented in every party: there were Nazis who made serious sacrifices for their party without any other return than prospects for the day when it should eventually triumph, and there were Socialists and even Communists whose contributions to the Party funds were made out of a good salary earned in a job which would have been beyond their reach without the Party ticket—though a time might come when the temporary benefits would turn into the heaviest of sacrifices. In speaking of the typical case, however, we may safely say that membership in a right-wing party implied material benefits, in a centre party it was not costly, and was possibly a profitable profession of a political faith which was in any case inoffensive, while on the left it involved considerable sacrifices, at least in money and leisure.

The percentage of party members among voters for the Party varied according to the different degrees of political interest and activity and to the interpretation of the meaning and obligations of party membership, which might differ from country to country even within the same social stratum, and between parties with similar general concepts. One

[1] Roeder, op. cit., p. 59.

[2] For an honest explanation of the need for such a policy, from the industrialists' point of view, cf. Steeruwitz, op. cit., p. 230.

extreme was represented by the Austrian Socialist Party: its membership increased steadily from 90,000 before the war and a quarter of a million at the end of 1919 to a maximum of 718,000 in 1930; this represented 55 per cent of the Socialist vote and was far in excess of the membership of the Trade Unions. The increase was by far the greatest in Vienna, where the activities of the Socialist municipality made a strong impression even upon the lower middle classes and gave opportunities to bring pressure upon municipal employees; at the same time party life offered the increasing number of unemployed workers some substitute for that care which the Unions could not give them. The Vienna situation was exceptional, and the percentage achieved there was obviously incompatible with the making of any serious active demands on the party member; but even in 1914 20 per cent of the Socialist voters had been party members[1] and this percentage increased to 30 before the start of the drive 'to organize the electorate as fully as possible'. In Germany, political organization of as many as 20 per cent of the voters came about only before and immediately after the war; at their Kassel Congress in 1920 the Majority Socialists, who had just emerged from the election with 5·6 million votes, claimed 1·18 million members. While the party's vote had halved in comparison with the preceding year, its membership had increased by 15 per cent; it evidently replaced the workers lost to the Independents by new strata which could only be organized gradually.

The Independent Socialist Party, before the Halle split, claimed 750,000 members. This figure must have been inflated;[2] only 233,000 members (144,000 voting to join the Communists, 91,000 against) had taken part in the vital decision to elect delegates to the Halle Congress; neither the Communists nor the Socialists ever saw any considerable part of the remaining half a million. Part of the loss may have been due to the very fact of the split; most Socialists in both wings were convinced that the enormous strength of the Austrian Socialist Party, as distinct from the two German working class parties, was a result of its unity, quite apart from any implied opportunity for pressure; but most of the 'lost' members had only existed in the daydreams of the branch officers,[3] if not in deliberate falsifications on the part of the contending

[1] As women had no vote but could join the party (though very few did), the actual percentage may have been slightly lower.

[2] See above, p. 198.

[3] Incorrect figures were likely to be arrived at from the simple unwillingness of the local and district committees to recognize the obvious fact that, as in any German left-wing party (the Communists, later, provided further examples), a large proportion of the entrants left within a few months. The average worker would leave a party with which he disagreed, or with whose demands for active work and discipline he was no longer willing to comply, by ceasing on some pretext to pay his contributions. To exaggerate party membership, it was only necessary to take these pretexts at their face value.

factions. At a relatively stable time, the German Social Democratic Party on 1st January 1927 had 827,000 members; two years later 937,000, which in each case meant about 10 per cent of its vote. The membership of the C.P. from 1923 to 1932 remained at about 6 per cent of its actual (or probable) vote; at the two ends of the cycle, the culminating points of its influence, it had 295,000 and 360,000 members respectively, but dropped to 160,000 in the first years after the stabilization of the mark. The difference between the percentages of voters in the German Social Democratic and Communist Parties is sufficiently explained by the very different interpretations of the obligations implied in Party membership, seen even in their respective programmes.

Each of the working class parties had under its more or less stable influence a circle wider than its membership. In Germany of 1929 the Free Trade Unions had 4·4 million members—part of them under Communist influence—the Consumers' Co-operatives 2·8 million, the Social Democratic wing of the Workers' Sports Association 1·2 million, the Freethinkers' Association for Cremation 0·7 million. There was quite a lot of overlapping between these various organizations, and it was perfectly natural that the Social Democratic husband should be a Trade Unionist while his wife was a co-op member. But there can be little doubt that some five million people, half the Social Democratic voters, were bound to the Party's influence by the various mass organiaations. The overlapping of the diverse 'front' organizations set up by the Communists was even more obvious;[1] at no time do more than half a million workers appear to have been members of Communist-led organizations. These represented to a large extent the hard core, parts of which periodically joined the party or dropped their membership without ceasing to be in sympathy with it.[2] Such fluctuations were natural in view of the

[1] According to the *Report* of the Central Committee to the twelfth (1929) Party Congress the largest of the mass organizations, the *Rote Hilfe* (Red Help), providing support for persecuted workers in Germany and elsewhere, had 185,000 members, nearly half of them Party members, the International Workers' Help (welfare work and support for strikers) had 42,000 members. The Young Communist League reported with satisfaction that its membership had passed the 20,000 mark. Apart from the *Rote Hilfe*, whose members of course regarded their obligations as fulfilled by paying regular contributions for the benefit of imprisoned comrades, the largest Communist mass organization, with a membership of certainly over a hundred thousand, was the Red Front Soldiers' League, the fighting organization. Left-wing Trade Unions, among which there was an anarcho-syndicalist element, exceeded a quarter of a million members (see above, p. 238). In every one of these cases there was considerable overlap, especially with the Party itself, which, at that time, had 160,000 members.

[2] The *Report* of the Regional Committee submitted to the 1929 Congress of the Berlin-Brandenburg organization of the C.P. shows (p. 291) an increase in membership from 17,400 in 1927 to 18,500 in 1928; but over 6,000 members joined the Party during the year, of whom only 200 were recorded to have been lost by death, expulsion, or change of residence. According to these data, from a comparatively quiet period and from one of the most stable organizations of the German C.P., the

enormous demands made on the Communist party members' activities and on their readiness to face the disfavour of employers. Social Democracy, on the other side, was characterized by a stability in its membership which indicated tradition rather than active interest. According to the statistics of the Hanover and Bremen organizations submitted to the Kiel Party Congress in 1927, the main age-groups represented (each with about 15 per cent of the total membership) were 34–40, 41–45 (the largest), and 46–50. Twenty per cent of the members were in their twenties, and a similar percentage in their fifties; the percentage of those over sixty (6·8) was nearly as high as that of those under twenty-five (7.7).[1] On the assumption that in pre-war Social Democracy, just as in the post-war C.P., the typical member was in his later twenties or early thirties, 40 per cent of the Social Democratic Party members in these towns in 1927 would seem to have joined the Party before the war. Hanover especially was a centre where the split to the Left had been insignificant.

The non-working-class population was clearly less active in politics; the only precise figure available[2] concerns the German Democrats, who, even at a time when they hardly retained more than their hard core of voters, still remained substantially below the Social Democrats in the percentage of voters organized. Further to the right, in the political Catholic camp, the boundaries between membership in the party and in some organization controlled by and supporting it were already obliterated; while the Socialist worker was very conscious of the distinction between himself, as a Party member, and his fellow-worker who was a mere trade unionist and/or member of a Socialist Sports Association, the member of a Catholic Workers' Association,[3] if not of a Christian Trade Union, was likely to feel that by joining it he had given the Catholic party all the support that was expected from him. In the right-wing bourgeois parties the individual 'party members' represented little more than local committees.

Among the internal problems of Party life, that of bureaucracy, already familiar to us before the war, became of increasing importance because of the large number of State and municipal jobs open to members of the parties which took part in coalitions, while proportional representation ensured for any major opposition party a considerable

membership of the Berlin party organization would have been completely renewed every three years. There was, of course, a stable core of members; so the fluctuation amongst the rest must have been larger.

[1] Quoted from the *Report* of the C.C. of the C.P. to the 1929 Party Congress, p. 200.

[2] 132,000, that is 7–8 per cent of the poll then probable, in January 1926 (Roeder, op. cit., pp. 68–9). The possibility of exaggerated reports by branches in bourgeois parties is even higher than in Socialist parties, where accounts and the number of delegates to Party Congresses (which depended on the number of paid-up members) were thoroughly checked.

[3] See above, pp. 33 ff.

number of parliamentary seats, and, as a rule, a number of important positions in local government. True, the social structure of the Social Democratic organizations in these regions where the C.P. did not represent very serious competition within the working class remained fairly near to the pre-war standard;[1] for the party as a whole, however, there must have been some 15 per cent of members whose material status depended entirely on their keeping some share in the public jobs, or at least in an expanded organizational machine.[2] These conditions, together with the fact that the left wing of the labour movement was now organized as a separate party, as it had not been before the war, may explain the fact, surprising at first sight, that, unlike pre-war days, the Social Democratic party organization frequently stood to the right of the Trade Union leaders.[3] As long as there was some prospect of saving democracy (when it appeared to have gone, the right-wing Trade Unionists made desperate attempts to preserve some place in the new order for the 'estate of labour',[4] a trade union was a body concerned with having actual opportunity to bargain with the employers on terms of equality, while a Social Democratic party was a body of people concerned with having such a share in administration as was granted to every major party so long as it behaved loyally to the federal Government. There were many conceivable circumstances in which the Party's

[1] The statistics of the social position of party members submitted to the Kiel Party Congress of 1927, and based on investigations made in Hamburg, Bremen and Hanover, all centres where Social Democracy had retained the bulk of the working class, indicated in 1925–6 a percentage of 73·14 manual workers, 11·03 salaried employees, 6·66 independent craftsmen and professional workers and civil servants; for 9·17 per cent there were no data. This last percentage seems far too low to include non-working wives from the groups above mentioned, so we may suppose them to have been counted with their husbands.

[2] Statistics given by Weissmann (quoted in Merker's speech at the first Congress of the Revolutionary Trade Union Opposition, 1929, p. 9) enumerate 19,700 employees of the Social Democratic Party, Trade Unions, etc., 83,400 employees of co-ops and other economic enterprises of the labour movement, about 50,000 workers in social insurance, etc., 20,000 Social Democratic civil servants in the States. These statistics, which seem to have a Communist bias, include a further 113,000 persons who do not necessarily come under the heading of bureaucrats (elected representatives to various public and social insurance bodies, members of the Social Democratic Teachers' Association); and among the Co-op and even the Trade Union employees there may have been some non-party persons or even Communists. But it is quite likely that some 150,000 Social Democrats depended for their jobs on the Party; with their wives (who were under social pressure to join the party) they may easily have accounted for nearly a quarter of its membership (see above, p. 248). Even the figures given in the preceding note from centres where Social Democracy included a larger than average percentage of ordinary workers would lead to a fifth of the total membership consisting of persons dependent on 'bureaucracy' if it be assumed that a mere fifth of the workers worked in co-operative enterprises, etc. and half of the 'non-manual workers' were civil servants, or Party and Union officials.

[3] See above, p. 194 and below, pp. 317 and 327.

[4] See below, pp. 334–5 and 344.

ambitions could be satisfied, but not those of the Trade Unions.

Before things developed so far, there was always the alternative of being in the Government or forming the opposition; with the exception of Austria, where the Social Democratic Party preserved its unity by avoiding coalitions in unfavourable conditions, and made the necessary concessions in the relations of 'Red Vienna' to the Federal Government, this amounted to the alternative of accepting or rejecting conditions made by potential coalition partners for Social Democratic participation in the Government. At least in Germany and Czechoslovakia, where there were Communist mass parties, a Social Democratic worker was, by definition, a person who believed that the conditions of his class could be improved by its taking part in coalition Governments; no 'degeneration' must be seen in his leaders' acting on this assumption. But democracy itself might be undermined if the parties on which it rested were associated with a continuous loss of social achievements without any possibility of the worker identifying himself with the social system for whose development these sacrifices were made.[1] The scales within the party caucus might be heavily weighted because the association of Social Democratic party organizations with opportunities of getting public office increased the influence of actual or potential office-holders; and the filling of vacancies in the salaried service of the Party, and also of the Trade Unions, Co-operatives, and other associated organizations, might drain away opposition within the Party caucus of potential representatives.

The existence of a problem of bureaucratization was recognized within the labour movement, at any rate in theory.[2] The traditional answer to it, which had its rise in pre-war Social Democracy and continued to dominate the Communist approach, was not to allow the Party secretary or editor, who in most cases was of working-class origin,[3] to become a mere official. The average member of the editorial staff of a German Socialist paper, unlike that of a bourgeois one,[4] was not in the position of an employee who had to write as his master ordered, but really shared with the elected organs of the party caucus in working out his

[1] This point was missed in the familiar comparisons of the moderately conservative development in pre-1932 Central Europe with the enforcement of stricter labour discipline in Soviet Russia.

[2] Clearly it was not restricted to this movement; a trade union leader who changes sides in an industrial conflict is easily checked, but it is a matter of judgment to decide whether the relations of the secretary of an agricultural co-operative to a bank serve the former's or the latter's interests.

[3] According to Kantarovicz, op. cit., not more than 28 of the 241 editors of German socialist newspapers before 1914 had a university education; 80·2 per cent were of working-class origin, 8·4 per cent came from the lower and 11·3 per cent from the upper middle classes. I think that post-war conditions in the German working-class parties were similar, though there was a higher percentage of middle-class intellectuals among the more prominent leaders.

[4] Cf. ibid., pp. 101–2.

paper's policies; this difference was quite enough to make the service of the party, in spite of much lower pay at any rate for the higher ranks, attractive to the more ambitious and honest of the left-wing members of the journalistic profession.[1] In order not only to secure the best service possible but also to keep the Socialist journalist in permanent contact with the life of the organization, his tenure of office was largely dependent on his doing a large amount of party work in various honorary functions, some of them likely in themselves to satisfy his ambitions,[2] some of them shouldered because of the necessity of keeping in touch with the rank and file. This sytem has obvious advantages as long so the difference in outlook between party bureaucracy and rank and file can be considered as mere difference in experience; but once it is assumed that a Minister in a coalition Cabinet may represent interests different from those of his fellow party members, such a difference is made no less dangerous by the fact that, in his former capacity as an editor of the regional party paper, he has acquired strong influence in the regional caucus.

Another approach to the problem of bureaucracy presupposes the existence of distrust, but seeks to bring it into organized channels by giving workers at the bench a decisive vote against the party officials. The editors of pre-war Social Democratic papers were supervised by Press Commissions elected by the caucus; in the Central and District committees of the Communist parties a majority of workers still at the bench and a due share of women and young workers were secured by conventions of almost statutory force. True, the party official's superiority in persuasive power, which had brought him from the bench to his position in the party, was not likely to be less effective because of a predominance of the rank and file in the setting where the decisive argument had to be made. Even an active member of such a controlling body might contribute to its discussions mainly complaints on details or reports on experiences in the individual factory in the application of the party line, the correctness of which would hardly be directly questioned by the average factory activist in the face of his party's best-known leaders. It was different when he found these latter confronting a higher authority which commanded most of his allegiance; in such cases a majority of workers from the bench on the Central Committee might provide a guarantee against any mutiny by groups of Party leaders against the line of the Comintern.

It may be said that much of the educational value of Party life lies

[1] For Bebel's attitude to the problem, see above, p. 18.

[2] In 1914, of the 241 editors of German Social Democratic papers, 20 were M.Ps, 22 members of Diets, 58 municipal councillors, 47 members of the regional Party Committees. In post-war Social Democracy the proportion was certainly still higher, though the position of people with purely professional ambitions may have become more tolerable.

precisely in the fact that it gives the intelligent worker an opportunity to make contributions of the kind referred to; but this argument is substantially affected if it happens—and it is a very frequent experience of members of a radical labour movement—that the activist who has earned his place in the chief organs of his party by defending its views energetically in the factory is dismissed from his job, black-listed, and employed in the party machine, losing thereby the privileged position of a 'man at the bench'. If preference for the purest type of working-class leader 'from the bench' is combined with special regard for theoretical orthodoxy, the demands of which can hardly be satisfied even by working-class leaders with well-developed political gifts, all the conditions are thereby created for the growth of the most undesirable type of 'party intellectual', whatever his social origin, namely the man who cannot satisfy his ambitions in the regular way by combining high office with responsibilities, and who therefore works behind the scenes. For a party which accepted the Leninist concept of the 'professional revolutionary', that is, the man or woman so completely devoted to its cause that reminiscences of his parental home as well as the narrow trade unionist outlook become meaningless, such an attitude was certainly inconsistent, and harmful to the training of its working-class activists in actual leadership. For a reformist party which yet accepted the possibility of an actual divergence of views between the leaders and the rank and file, a broad party council might serve as a device to shift the responsibility for grave decisions from the leaders' shoulders; the Austrian Socialist party, the most cunning of all those with which we are concerned in this book, at all the crises of Austrian history established a special supreme organ, elected from its members still working in the factories, and expected to supervise and supplement the Central Committee in decisive issues of policy.[1] None of the devices successively applied to check the party bureaucracy could provide a substitute for adequate leadership, while each could easily degenerate into being a scapegoat for the average politician's shortcomings.

The reader, influenced by the tendency of most publications to overemphasize the shortcomings and difficulties of the Central European party system, may be surprised to learn that the fundamental trends discussed in the first two chapters of this book are entirely sufficient for a description of the basic facts of the system (as distinct from details, which had no more relevance than are, say, the existence of 'Bomb Berlin' candidates, or the habit of Conservatives to stand for election occasionally under the name 'National Liberal', 'National Labour', etc., for a description of British democracy).

The first and chief division to be made is that between the working-class parties and the others. In Austria, this exhausted the description of the party system; all the workers were Socialists, and the Christian

[1] See above, pp. 202 and 203, and below, p. 341.

Social party achieved the status of *the* non-Socialist party (the German Nationals being for all practical purposes absorbed, their eventual regeneration formed a mere transitional stage in the formation of the Nazi party after the actual destruction of Austrian democracy). In Germany and in Czechoslovakia (except in the Carpatho-Ukraine, where the C.P. came nearest to being the party of all the exploited and oppressed) the labour camp was split by the existence of strong Communist parties side by side with the Social Democratic ones, and in Czechoslovakia by the additional fact that, among the Czechs as well as amongst the Sudeten Germans, the National Socialist parties which in essence represented a breakaway of the black-coated workers from the traditional bourgeois parties, had also some influence amongst some groups of workers such as the railwaymen.

In Austria and in the Catholic parts of Germany the Catholic (Centre) party included nearly all the non-Socialist forces, from near-fascists and open representatives of the vested interests such as Papen and even Kaas or Brüning to advanced social reformers and to the working-class elements in the Christian Trade Unions. In Czechoslovakia, with her huge majority of nominal and moderate minority of practising Catholics, the Catholic party was one bourgeois party among others, restricted in its appeal by its specific relation to the national struggle. In Bohemia-Moravia, where its social composition was nearly as broad as that of the German Centre, it was affected by its past association with the Hapsburg monarchy, and in Slovakia its identification was near-fascist separatism.

Apart from the Catholic factor and outside Austria,[1] the position in the bourgeois camp was marked by the existence of one strong Conservative force based upon the organized agricultural interest. The political trends among the non-Catholic bourgeoisie can be described as a move of Big Business support and lower middle class sympathies away from the other traditional parties (which in Germany had been Liberal and temporarily inflated by the revolution, while in Czechoslovakia they represented the leadership of the urban middle-class in the past movement for national emancipation) to the party of the agrarian interest; this implied a further change in that party's structure. As in Czechoslovakia the National Democrats declined into insignificance, Big Business became a predominant factor in the councils of the Agrarian Party which, earlier, had been dominated by the leaders of the Agricultural Co-operatives and the civil servants connected with them and by such financial and industrial interests as were directly involved in agriculture.

[1] But even in Austria the bulk of the German Nationals in Styria and Carinthia (the only provinces where they were more than a sect) was formed by the supporters of the Agrarian League, which in these provinces, as compared with the Catholic Agricultural Co-operatives, had a greater propensity to represent the interest of the well-to-do farmer.

Within the German National People's Party, after 1925, the leadership of the old-Prussian Agrarian Conservatives (plus civil servants and army officers connected with the *ancien régime* and such support from the black-coated workers as the Protestant wing of Christian Trade Unionism could supply, which had accepted the Locarno settlement), was challenged by a Pan-German opposition on the lines of Ludendorff's policies during the war; the leader of this opposition was Hugenberg, a representative of Heavy Industry who after Stinnes's breakdown[1] had built up a powerful combination of newspapers and other means of propaganda, including Ufa, the leading film and cinema trust.

In October 1928, shortly after the formation of the last left-centre coalition Government, Hugenberg defeated the old Conservative leader Westarp in the Party caucus by a narrow majority; the party now joined the Nazi opposition against the Young Plan,[2] and later against the Brüning Government. The outcome was that the old-Conservative and agrarian interests were forced to leave the party, while the Nazis were much more successful in winning lower-middle-class support from their ally Hugenberg than in breaking the 'Marxist' influence over the workers; in September 1930 the official German National Party polled only 2·5 million votes, and another million voted for Agrarian lists. The moderate Conservatives were able to rally a mere 457,000 of the 1·9 million votes lost by the official German Nationals, and, like all the 'splinter parties' in Germany, were doomed to quick decline; but even the official German National vote dropped in July 1932 to a merely 2·2 million, a third of its strength eight years before. Yet it remained the most stable among the middle-class parties of Germany, apart from the Centre; the Democrats (originally the strongest of them) and the People's Party (the typical representatives of the bourgeois interest during the Republic) were practically annihilated.

Little change in the actual distribution of political power was implied in these dramatic changes of political representation and phraseology; especially as in Germany each of the larger trusts had its parliamentary representatives in every bourgeois party, and contributed to the funds of these 'competitors' in proportion as each had conformed with the requirements of the Trusts' parliamentary representatives; none of these party swamps saw anything blameworthy in accepting money which they had to share with representatives of the 'opposite' ideology. Their real relation was that of a division of labour between people who had to support certain interests by varying ideological arguments adapted to the specific demands of those among whom they had to agitate; as the political climate changed some of these agencies would become superfluous. The Nazis, who later did much the same, at least did not claim that there was any opposition between those of their agitators who

[1] See above, p. 231.
[2] See below, p. 282.

promised house-owners higher rents, and those who promised tenants cheaper lodgings.

The German party system during the democratic Republic can thus be described as a combination of a three-party system (a divided working class against a united agrarian-middle class bloc with some influence among the working classes) in the Catholic regions, and a four-party system (splits not only among the working-class parties but also between a more liberal party with its main strongholds in the towns and a conservative party based mainly upon the agrarian interest) in the Protestant parts. Including the Centre, which, from Wirth to Klöckner, contained the same political trends as were represented in the Protestant parts of the country by all the shades of opinion ranging from left-wing liberalism to Hugenberg's semi-fascism, every national election was contested by five major parties. In appearance, especially to foreign observers unfamiliar with the real state of things, the ballot-paper was further lengthened by including the names of those of the middle-class parties which had failed to preserve any real importance. In the last crisis of the Republic there was once again a five-party system, the Nazis being added to the two working-class parties, the Centre, and the surviving middle-class party (Hugenberg's German Nationals).

The Czechoslovak party system, as compared with the German, was complicated by a formal multiplication by three, because the corresponding parties of the diverse nationalities, at least after 1925, co-operated in fact but, with the exception of the Communists, did not dare appear on a common ballot; it was further complicated by the existence of a National Socialist Party with origins very similar to those of its Sudeten-German counterpart, but which, with the general democratic development of Czech nationalism, developed into a third party of labour, appealing mainly to the black-coated worker. The elimination of the traditional middle-class party, the National Democrats, was never as complete as that of the Liberals in Germany, and amongst the Czechs, as distinct from the Sudeten Germans and the Slovaks, there was no counterpart to German Hitlerism. There were differences between the nationalities of the Republic even as regards the labour movement: among the Slav peoples the left-wing Socialists, later Communists, were much stronger than in Germany, leading in the 1925 elections among the Czechs and Slovaks with three-fifths of the former united Socialist vote and, after a moderate setback in 1929, regaining a similar position, especially amongst the Slovaks, during the last years of the Republic (in the Carpatho-Ukraine the Communists always held an overwhelming majority of the working-class, and even occupied the first place among all the parties), while never more than a third of the Sudeten German workers followed the Communists; even this share was seriously reduced after 1929.

In the 1925 elections, when the anti-Hapsburg issue had lost its importance, the Catholic Party passed the National Democrats. The Agrarian Party, which formerly stood between Catholics and Socialists, had meanwhile become the main conservative force; only in Slovakia did it remain a Centre party, as did Czech political Catholicism in Bohemia and Moravia. Slovak Catholicism, which had split off from its Czech brother party for reasons similar to those for which in Germany the Bavarian Catholic party had split from the Centre, became under Hlinka's leadership a main force of fascism. Eventually it rallied more than a third of the Slovak electorate. Amongst the Sudeten Germans Henleinism absorbed all the bourgeois parties and reduced the workers' parties to mere fractions of their former strength.

(*b*) *Proportional Representation and the Party System*

Most foreign critics of Central European democracy have described proportional representation as its undoing. The main answer to their argument has already been given in the analysis of the party system and the conditions of its growth. There were no more parties of importance than were bound to arise in view of the whole social development of the countries under investigation; those which failed to satisfy a social need were eliminated in spite of proportional representation. Proportional representation arose not from any dogmatic considerations but from the very essence of Central European democracy. The parties were the only possible heirs to military-bureaucratic autocracy; unless one section of the population could establish its dictatorship,[1] their comparative strength had to be reflected in Parliament in such a way as to enforce the formation of coalitions, as in Germany and Czechoslovakia, or agreements with the opposition, as in Austria, where the second party was always strong enough to prevent constitutional amendments, without which Government was difficult in times of crisis. The ballot, so arranged that the voice of every important section was heard in the strength to which it was entitled by its ability to shape mass opinion, was the substitute for the bullet, in the most literal sense of the word; this was so generally felt that little argument on the issue was necessary.

Proportional representation, as distinct from general and equal suffrage for both sexes, had never formed part of a Socialist programme; in the atmosphere of 1918 its introduction was asked for by the bourgeois parties, who regarded themselves as likely to be the minorities in the coming times.[2] There was no serious objection from the Socialist side;

[1] But even the Communists, who had such a perspective, regarded parliamentary elections as an occasion for mass education and as a means to get positions from which Communist M.P.s could demonstrate their concepts of possible reforms in the working-class interest; from either point of view proportional representation was beyond reproach. Engels had said that within capitalist society general suffrage could be only a barometer indicating to both the fighting camps when the time was ripe for decision; the more precise this barometer the better.

[3] Cf. H. Preuss, op. cit., p. 391.

the measure was irreproachable from the standpoint of legitimizing the new régime, and the Social Democrats, pushed forward by their left wing, had no desire to obtain the appearance of a clear majority, which they would have had to use in accordance with the Party programme. The ostrich-like idea that one can dispose of a Communist mass party by demonstrating to the radical workers that they must not have an equal say in a parliamentary Republic did not occur to anyone until after World War II—since when it has become popular in France, and has also been imported by the Western Occupying Powers into Germany, with results which may be visible before this book is published. As Communism in Germany, and Social Democracy in Czechoslovakia, were strongly enough entrenched to ensure the polling of a strong protest vote, disfranchisement of labour's minority party would in most cases have secured victory for a bourgeois candidate, if the bourgeois camp was united—which in Germany was possible only under definitely right-wing leadership. I must leave it to the professional exporters of Anglo-Saxon institutions to say how they suppose Central European democracy could be stabilized by combining parliamentary majorities after the pattern of the Hindenburg election with a periodical demonstration to the most active sections of the working class that the ballot was a mere sham. No serious bourgeois politician of the Weimar Republic was so silly; at a time of crisis, he knew, he might have to fight the Communists, and he would fight them with the greater success the stronger within the working class (including the Communists themselves)[1] was the feeling that some achievements were possible within the constitutional framework; in ordinary times the Communist vote would function as a pressure group.

Moderate bourgeois thinkers agreed in disapproving of the two-party system; Thoma described it as 'a disaster in a modern industrialized State' which as a result of it would be exposed to 'some kind of legal revolution with every change of majority and government'.[2] Preuss expected a merger of the two class camps into two big parties 'to seal the fate of democracy and thereby of our national State'.[3] Stresemann, more realistic, warned his class-comrades that the balance between the two hypothetical big parties would move in the long run 'not to the right but to the left, all the more surely as the number of employees increases and as the Right is dominated by the employers' influence.'[4] All speculation, however, about the hypothetical merits and demerits of the two-party system supposed to be promoted by majority representation may be dismissed by the simple observation that the German and Czechoslovak many-party systems were an inheritance from pre-war majority

[1] See above, pp. 224–5.
[2] *Sinn und Gestaltung des deutschen Parliamentarismus*, vol. II, p. 104.
[3] *Staat, Recht und Freiheit*, p. 433.
[4] *Vermächtnis*, vol. III, p. 439.

representation, and that in Austria, where conditions were ripe for a two-party system, it came into being under proportional representation.

This fact, however surprising it may be to the advocates of the institutional approach, is easily explained by the character of the Central European mass parties. As a rule, any major trend would have at least a few strongholds in which it would obtain parliamentary representation even under majority suffrage, and even if all its opponents united against it; the party's close connexion with economic organizations would provide a purpose and a content for the activities of even those local organizations which under majority representation had no prospects of electing M.P.s. Some parties, such as the German Centre and the two main Austrian parties, would have fared just as well under majority representation as under P.R.; the latter's effect seen only in the composition of the parliamentary parties which included representatives from the regions where the party in question was in a definite minority, such as Austrian Social Democrats in the Alpine provinces, Christian Socials in Vienna, or Catholic workers in the definitely 'Red' centres of the Ruhr. Some other parties would, without proportional representation, have had to be satisfied with a few seats; in that event there would have been an obvious difference between the reactions of the Communists, in whose caucus the parliamentary party would have played an even smaller part than it actually did, and those of the liberal parties, whose electorate would have dissipated even more quickly if their loss of influence had been dramatized by the abrupt reductions probable under majority representation. The only parties which would not even have made a start under majority representation but obtained some influence under the proprotional system were the 'non-political' lower middle class parties such as the German *Wirtschaftspartei*, mainly representative of house-owners and small traders and the Czechoslovak Trades and Crafts Party; both were minor nuisances in the negotiations that preceded the formation of bourgeois coalitions, as they would otherwise have been within the conservative or liberal party caucuses. They might even be regarded as transitional stages in the progress of the lower middle classes from the traditional parties to fascism; certainly they played no large part in the fall of Central European Democracy. Seven parties in all contested the German elections of 1928; the rest of the thirty-three lists entered on that occasion, and frequently cited by foreign critics of proportional representation, consisted of five local descriptions of the National Conservative party,[1] five groups corresponding, in British conditions, to expelled members of major parties

[1] The Hanoverian Guelfs, and four regional lists of the League of Agriculturists, whose representatives, when elected, joined the Conservative (German National) Party.

standing as Independents,[1] one collective list of the national minorities, Poles and Danes, who thus helped each other to obtain a parliamentary mouthpiece for their grievances, and eleven lists corresponding to Independents representing some special 'protest' interest, from the 873 Unmarried Citizens who objected to extra taxation threatening them from the propaganda of the Fathers of Large Families, to the League of Small Savers who protested against their expropriation by the monetary inflation and gained the only success scored by these protest groups. In all this there was nothing that is unfamiliar—under other names—to the British system of representation; many people in this country would be glad to allow the Lord's Day Observance Society to have one or two outspoken representatives at Westminster and to let the rest of Parliament vote on what the majority of citizens regard as the basic issues of politics.

We here touch on one of the current reproaches against Proportional Representation; it is said to promote 'party spirit', i.e. to increase the weight of that large majority of a modern electorate which chooses its allegiance according to its attitude to basic social questions, and is therefore unlikely to change it on the basic issue of employer v. employee, as compared with those minorities which, under majority representation, might change their allegiance for the very reason that they regard such issues as Sunday observance, denominational education, capital punishment, etc., as more important than whatever decision on social insurance, steel nationalization, and so on may be taken as a by-product of their shifting their votes according to their favourite issues. Even under proportional representation a strong minority feeling on denominational education may have a bargaining power quite disproportionate to its strength, if it controls a party essential in the formation of coalition Governments as the Centre was in Germany; but this is not said to be a condition essential for the functioning of the system. Judgment on the merits or demerits of this argument depends essentially upon the critic's attitude to the fundamental issues of social organization; here it is enough to note that Central European democracy was based upon an appeal to civic activities which could develop only in service to one's section. In the absence of conventions which forced the majority of the day to show some consideration for the standpoint of the opposition, the equilibrium between the diverse sectional groups was believed to be insecure unless every important social group was granted an open say in Parliament and local government, and not merely a hypothetical chance of becoming an alternative Government unless before then it was disfranchised by the Government of the day or the powers of future Parliaments were restricted by amendments to the Constitution. For the benefit of admirers of parliamentary conventions

[1] Three groups were dissenters from the Socialist and Communist, two from the Nazi party.

we may add that proportional representation reduced not only the specific pressure-weight of the German counterparts of the Lord's Day Observance Society, but also the temptation to risk the reputation of one's party by the use of election manœuvres of the Red Letter type; to purchase three or four additional seats in Parliament by last-minute falsifications which would turn against their authors when discovered, was hardly worth while. Germany eventually had her Reichstag fire, with consequences more important and durable than those of the 1924 Red Letter in Britain; but as a result of the working of proportional representation, even after the fire Hitler had to arrest or hunt down the Communist and some other M.P.s in order to secure an artificial majority. No more can be asked of constitutional arrangements than that they bring violence into the open; no constitution can be a substitute for those social powers that can punish a breach of it.

Proportional representation had important implications for the internal life of the parties, but they did not all work in one direction. The importance of the regional organization, as the unit responsible for the large constituencies, as against the local one, was greatly increased; but in cases of disagreement on fundamentals, the regional was in a much better position than the local organization to withstand the National Committee, and proportional representation gave it a fair start in the event of a split. In any case it seems inconsistent for critics to reproach proportional representation for 'promoting party spirit' on the one hand and on the other for making easier the formation of 'splinter parties', which is itself the punishment for misuse of its powers by a national caucus. Certainly, P.R. fostered a tendency in the electorate to vote for party programmes rather than for individuals—which is quite general, even under the British majority system. It thereby reduced the power of the popular personage to split his party as long as he remained alone; but it also strengthened his power against the national caucus if he and his friends succeeded in rallying a group of organizations round their platform; the threat of a split might increase the power of an opposition group even though it was not carried out.

In general, complaints about the opportunities which P.R. gave to 'splinter parties' originated from the liberal groups, whose decomposition was hastened by opportunities for organized splits, rather than from the workers' parties, which were not afraid of letting their oppositions get some baiting at the hands of a well-disciplined electorate. These opportunities were not great; under the Austrian and Czechoslovak systems, the support of some 10 per cent of the electorate in one of the large constituencies was needed to win a seat, and that condition could hardly be fulfilled unless the opposition group carried with it the regional caucus of a major party. In Germany the support of about 3 per cent of the electorate in a very large constituency of about a million voters, combined with another 30,000 supporters in the neighbouring constituencies (or, alternatively, 60,000 votes in the main stronghold of the new party) was needed in order to get the first seat, as the condition for getting another from the residual vote in the rest of the country (which might be expected in the event of a split in a major party on all-national issues). There was only one instance of successful candidature because of a split in one of the existing political camps, and one of success because of an all-national issue with general appeal, respectively; the first success of the Communists (before their fusion with the left-wing Independents) in June 1920, and the above-mentioned victory of the League of Small Savers in May 1928; in each case half a million votes (which would have brought eight seats to a well-established party) were rewarded with two seats, one in the basic constituency (in the Communist case, Chemnitz) and one from the residual vote (no party could get more seats in the National List than it had got in the constituencies and their combinations). Both instances concerned issues of first-rate importance, non-registration of which would have been a real shortcoming in any electoral system, and nothing short of this produced successful 'splinter parties'. More than once, popular leaders of the Communists and, at least in the regional framework, of the Social Democrats were expelled from their party, secured the support of some local organization and even of one of the Party papers, and still failed to obtain the votes necessary for them to retain at least some of the seats which they had carried from their original party at the time of the split. (The practice in Germany allowed them to hold their seats till the next general election; in Czechoslovakia, the country which generally went furthest in identifying democracy with rule of the party bureaucracies, highly artificial arrangements were used to unseat dissenters even if they represented a major split within their party and could claim that they, as opposed to its Central Committee, adhered to the platform on which they had won their seats.)[1] The enormous power of resistance of established parties even against popular dissenters is well known, and was

[1] By a judgment of 22nd June 1923 against four left-wing dissenters of the Czech National Socialist Party the Electoral Court (composed of representatives of the major parliamentary parties, with a few judges added in a merely consultative capacity, declared that the votes of the electors were polled 'in favour of parties at elections, not of persons'. Unhappily, from the standpoint of the party bureaucrats who dominated the Court, the Czechoslovak constitution explicitly provided for unseating an M.P. only if his expulsion from his party had been caused by 'mean and disgraceful actions'; the Court explained away this restriction as made not in the public interest (which was evidently supposed to lie in an M.P.s unconditional obedience to his caucus) but in the private interest of M.P.s; therefore the M.P.s were allowed to contract out of that right, as they had done in the declarations signed by them at the time of their nomination (the expelled M.P.s, like other opposition M.P.s on similar occasions in Germany, had made the case that those declarations were invalid as contradicting the public interest that M.P.s should vote according to their understanding of the will of the electorate. F. Sander, *Verfassungsurkunde und Verfassungsbestirk der Tschechoslakwischen Republik*, Prague, 1934, pp. 119 ff.

once more exemplified in the British general election of 1950; it evidently holds good whatever electoral system is in vogue.

The relative power of the national in relation to the regional caucus increased for a number of reasons quite independent of the electoral system: the greater importance of national as compared with State and Provincial policies (in Austria, where Provincial and especially Viennese policies had greater importance because of the Federal constitution, the weight of the Provincial caucuses increased), centralization of the economic organizations with which the Party was connected (obviously only the national, and not the regional organizations of the Social Democrats could have direct relations with the T.U.C.), ideological appeals essential for the Party's cohesion (this was important especially for the Communists and the Catholics), the expenditure needed for modern means of propaganda, the use of broadcasting, etc., as a main means to win support for a party not strongly based upon mass-organization (this weighed heavily in the bourgeois parties, and decided Hugenberg's triumph within the German National caucus.[1] However it was conditioned, control of the party machine had to be secured by the nomination of a considerable number of M.P.s by the Party's Central Committee. As the German election law left it to the constituency (regional) organizations to decide whether their 'residual vote' was to be used in favour of their brother organizations in neighbouring constituencies or directly in favour of the party's National List, a national party caucus could either insist on the second alternative or on the nomination of candidates agreeable to it on the regional list. Only in a party ruled as dictatorially as Hugenberg ruled the German National Party (and needing the support of placemen of the 'big boss' as much as that did), could there arise the idea of permitting the compounding of the votes between the regional Party organizations on the condition that every second candidate was nominated by the national caucus;[2] the Central Committees of the left-wing parties would not have known what to do with the thirty to forty mandates secured to Hugenberg in this way. For the central organization of a left-wing party one or two dozen places on the national list, or set aside by agreement with the regional caucuses, were needed in order to provide seats for some leaders not sufficiently connected with some regional organization to prove attractive candidates, the representative of the Socialist (or Communist) medical men's organization, or that *rara avis*, the Socialist clergyman. In those parties, the Central Committee's influence on the regional caucuses was exercised to secure the nomination of such local repre-

[1] See above, p. 255.

[2] Lambach, op. cit., p. 139. As there was also the National List, this procedure implied an absolute majority of nominees of the national caucus in the parliamentary party.

sentatives as were regarded as reliable supporters of the party line rather than in favour of 'central candidates'.

(c) *The Formation of the Government*

In every country where no single party is in safe control of power, governments must be formed by compromise. On the British system this can be done by including planks in the party programme to attract the floating vote, and excluding proposals unpopular with the less decided parts of the electorate. Under a two-party system such as that of Austria (the stronger party's lead being secured for a considerable time by proportional representation) it was done by negotiating with the opposition. The need for this was increased by a constitution which called for frequent recourse to decisions for which a two-thirds majority was required, and even more by the impossibility of governing without the collaboration of the Vienna municipality (a Socialist majority would have faced the same problems with the Alpine provinces, whose Catholic majorities were safe for all practical purposes). Under a many-party system, with or without proportional representation, the compromises are made in negotiating the formation of a coalition Government.

Some parties in a manifest key position—the Centre in Germany, and the even stronger Agrarians in Czechoslovakia—could be regarded as certain participants in any conceivable Government; a circumstance which increased their attractiveness especially in the eyes of ambitious civil servants; their fates at the polls showed little more than what concessions they would have to make lest they should fare worse next time. Others—the Social Democrats, and on the bourgeois side the German People's Party until 1923, and the German National Party in Germany and Austria throughout the days of the Republic—were able to take part in the Government only as part of one of the possible combinations. In those cases where the negotiations which preceded the formation of a Government merely served to bring into being a bourgeois bloc honestly declared as such to the electorate, Thoma's remark held good that all such unaesthetic bargaining implied no more than 'making in public those compromises of interests and those tactical manœuvres which are in the councils of one of the large parties in Britain or the U.S.A,' carried out behind the scenes.[1] If the political alignment of the various parties was not made clear during the preceding electoral contest, unprincipled bartering by the intermediate groups (who would probably defend their attitude by 'changing tactical needs') took the place of what, under a two-party system with majority representation, would have been the abandonment by the majority party of some planks of the platform on which it had won the floating vote. In either case punishment could come only at the next appeal to the polls, and under a multi-

[1] See f.n. [2], p. 258.

party system it would be quite incapable of removing one of the centre parties from its key position, though it might strengthen within those parties the trends supported by the swing of public opinion. It is often said that an increase in the extremist vote for a party which had no chance of a share in the ministry, since in most cases it was gained at the expense of the neighbouring moderate party, reduced the latter's chances in a coalition and swung the pendulum in the opposite direction, but this assertion should be taken *cum grano salis*. The left-centre coalition under the progressive Catholic, Wirth, did not break down because, being a minority Government, it was merely tolerated by the Left, but rather because the bourgeois parties demanded 'compensation' by the broadening of the Government coalition to the right when it had achieved a safe majority through the Right-wing Independents joining the Majority Socialists, and obtained the backing of Ebert. Even the Communists would not have overthrown Wirth if he had carried out the policy he announced after Rathenau's murder; their objections 'on principle' to any collaboration with other parties developed in close parallel with the left-centre parties' links with the Right wing and with the Army.

But swings in public opinion were not the only, nor even necessarily the chief factor in influencing the formation of a Government. Under the established party order, the position of the Christian Socials in the Austrian two-party system, and of the Agrarians in the Czechoslovak multi-party system, was safely entrenched in the Army and the Civil Service; to govern in despite of them would have been difficult even if by some unexpected development they could have been outvoted in Parliament. In Germany, where no right-wing party was in a key position in Parliament (the Centre had a considerable left wing which might come to the fore in times of social crisis), the importance of the extra-parliamentary forces was brought into action by the position of the Army and its head, the President, who was elected by plebiscite.[1] Against the current opinion of competent jurists[2] his position had already been explained, during the period of bourgeois blocs in 1924–8, as giving him the power to decide not only what possible combination would be likely to obtain a vote of confidence in Parliament but also which would be viable (*tragfähig*), i.e. would enjoy the confidence of the Big Business combines, and, of course, of the Army. Governments formed merely by negotiations between parliamentary parties returned under general suffrage were bound to be either 'unviable' or 'untenable' in that they would fall to pieces as soon as they broke their promises to the electorate. The academic mouthpiece of the Employers' Association to whom we owe this honest presentation of the situation[3] concluded

[1] See below, p. 280. [2] See above, pp. 170–1.

[3] H. Heerfahrdt, *Die Kabinettsbildung nach der Weimarer Verfassung unter dem Einfluss der politischen Praxis*, *passim*, esp. p. 39.

that the President was under an obligation to prevent those interests that happened to form the majority of the electorate from overruling that other less numerous but more important part of the people without whose support no capable Government was possible. If a capable Government failed to command the support of a parliamentary majority, the President should represent against that majority 'the State and the commonweal', and apply emergency measures under Article 48 of the Constitution; he might even avoid the unnecessary bother of a dissolution, which could prove nothing more than the irrelevant fact that one part of the people was more numerous than the other and more important part. Presidential government presupposed a body of ministers fairly independent of party links; Heerfahrdt enumerated as an approach to it those 'permanent ministers' who survived the frequent Cabinet reconstructions under the bourgeois bloc;[1] to some of them he may have done an injustice by claiming them, at that time, for his interpretation of the Constitution (which corresponds rather to the post-1930 period). For the moment, parliamentary conventions were still respected; when the May 1928 elections much increased the strength of the Social Democrats and Communists, and brought a clear defeat of all the bourgeois parties, including the Centre, a Government of the Great Coalition was formed—the last parliamentary Government of the Weimar Republic. But even within the accepted conventions the President's powers were wide; Hindenburg, who in 1926 had prolonged the life of the bourgeois bloc by refusing Marx a dissolution on the question of compensation for the property rights of the former princes[2] crippled the new left-centre Government by insisting on the exclusion of Wirth, the most competent representative of the progressive Catholics.[3]

In these conditions there was quite a lot of squabbling between the coalition partners, but proper perspective would be lost if we forgot that most 'Cabinet crises' merely meant what in Britain would be called a 'reconstruction of the Government', the difference in terminology being due to the difference in party systems, because what within the Conservative Party would be a domestic dispute showed itself as a public conflict between the bourgeois parties in the coalition. During the thirteen years from the establishment of the Republic to the openly dictatorial Papen government (May 1932) Germany had 19 Cabinets, each of some 10 to 14 members; but during the period only 79 persons took part in the Government; each, on the average, was seven times in

[1] Gessler, Stresemann, Marx and Brauns; only the first-mentioned might at that time be regarded as a safe supporter of dictatorship (Jarres and Luther, who also might be regarded as permanent ministers, at that time were not sufficiently divorced from their party caucus to meet Heerfahrdt's requirements).

[2] See below, p. 281. It is clear, however, that the Centre, if it really insisted, could have forced a dissolution.

[3] Stampfer, op. cit., p. 472.

office, one even fourteen times. During the same period, Austria had 13 Governments with an even smaller total number of ministers; actually there were only two types of Government; Socialist and Catholic (in four variations), and Catholic-led bourgeois Governments with two subspecies, one of them based on agreement with the opposition, the other on preparation for open conflict.[1] Behind all the quarrelsome mechanism lay some comparatively simple trends; their parallelism in the three Republics shows how merely incidental were the mechanisms by which they were realized.

Apart from the short revolutionary transition in 1918–19, during which, in accordance with the different character of the forces supporting the revolution, Germany had a Socialist, and the two other Republics all-national coalition Governments, we can distinguish five definite periods. The elections held in the first months of 1919 were followed by coalitions between the Socialists and the bourgeois Centre; in Austria and Germany the Catholics (in Germany the Liberals also), in Czechoslovakia the Agrarians. These Governments enacted the social and agrarian achievements of the revolution (in Germany, from the very start, in definite reaction against what had been achieved in November 1918); they came to an end with the elections of 1920.

In the following period we have predominantly bourgeois Governments supported, in one form or another, by their former Socialist partners, on condition that they followed a fairly moderate policy. In Austria the Socialists never again entered the Government after 1920, but remained in friendly 'opposition' to a Conservative Government led by the more democratic element in the bourgeois camp (especially the peasant section of the Christian Social Party) until 1922, and afterwards during the two short respites in 1924 and 1931. In Germany, during that time, the Social Democrats twice entered the Government during reparations crises brought about by bourgeois bloc Governments,[2] and in Czechoslovakia the Social Democrat participation was gradually brought to an end.[3] 1922 in Austria, 1923 in Germany, and 1925 in Czechoslovakia opens the period of definitely bourgeois bloc Governments, which passed the deflationary and reactionary measures that followed on the post-war upheaval. It resulted in electoral defeats of the bourgeois blocs; in Austria in 1927, in Germany in 1928, and in Czechoslovakia in 1929. Developments in the three Republics then diverged; in Austria, the electoral success of the Social Democrats was followed by the opening of the Fascist offensive,[4] in Germany came the last two years of left-centre coalition, and in Czechoslovakia a similar coalition remained in office until the Republic was brought to an end by

[1] See above, p. 203, and below, pp. 322 and 336–7.
[2] See above, pp. 199 and 222.
[3] See above, p. 20.
[4] See below, pp. 314 ff.

outside intervention. On 22nd September 1938 the coalition Government was overthrown by a popular movement directed against the compromising policy of the Agrarian leaders, but after a few days of transition Czechoslovakia came under 'authoritarian', and soon after Fascist, government as the two other Republics had done already.

Within the period opened by the fall of the parliamentary bourgeois bloc Governments distinctions can be made according to the different conditions of each country. Germany, after the fall of the left-centre coalition in spring 1930, experienced three years of 'authoritarian' government before she became Fascist; Austria had in 1931-2 a last period of revival of parliamentary relations with the opposition as distinct from preparation for open civil war; Czechoslovakia, with no outward change in Government, experienced after 1935 a period marked more or less by *Front Populaire* policies, which comes outside our scope, as they clearly formed a sequel to Hitler's triumph in Germany.

(d) Government and Opposition

In general, the parties which formed a Government coalition ruled the country in the most open manner. If their leaders belonged to the Government, they regularly discussed all controversial issues; if they were 'outsiders', as were Otto Bauer and Seipel throughout most of the post-revolutionary coalition period in Austria, they constituted some formal or informal coalition committee to which the Ministers were really responsible. The most radical solution was the Czechoslovak *Pjetka*,[1] a kind of collective Prime Minister, or at least collective Chief Whip, to use terms familiar in Britain. Originating partly in the tradition of the national struggle for independence and partly in the need to control a 'non-partisan' Government, it later served to keep the 'all-national coalition' together by previous agreement on all parliamentary matters. This was necessary because a Government party might be put in an awkward position by motions appealing to the interests of those who had elected it, which might originate not only from the Communists but also from its brother-party in some other national camp, Sudeten-German or Magyar, kept outside the coalition. In these conditions quite an elaborate *Pjetka* machinery developed; apart from the committee of the Five party leaders there was a larger Committee of Ten, with special *Pjetkas* of specialists for all matters discussed. Such machinery might reduce Parliament to the role of a mere machine for registering decisions arrived at by the coalition, the collective Prime Minister (to use a British term) deciding authoritatively on the disposal of parliamentary time and on the acceptance or refusal of amendments, with the difference that the electorate had little opportunity to get rid of the five-headed chief of State. The abnormality of the situation was due, not to the mere fact of coalition between parties, formally indepen-

[1] See above, p. 201.

dent, but to its artificial construction according to racial and not to economic cleavages; when the Svehla Government returned to these normal lines of division[1] and the Sudeten German Social Democrats shared with their Czech comrades in opposition to the Government, the *Pjetka* was reduced to the status of an intra-coalition whip, and perhaps also of a kind of surrogate for the British convention (unknown on the Continent) which makes proposals for spending public money a prerogative of the Government. The Svehla Government also dared to do what the left-wing parties had been shy of doing, namely, to invite the members of the *Pjetka* to join the Government openly and to form an inner cabinet. Thus Parliament, including the opposition, was restored to its normal functions; when there was dissent in the ranks of the majority, as there was in 1929 on the question of social insurance, the *Pjetka* system did not prevent concessions to opposition amendments which went at least as far as would be conceivable under British conditions.

In all Central European parliaments most of the real work was done in Standing Committees, and not in the plenary meetings which often degenerated into a mere registration of speeches made before the Speaker, the official shorthand writers, a few unfortunate fellow-partisans of the speech-maker who had to form a chorus, the reporters of the Party Press (the only ones to report the speech) in the gallery, and, if the member speaking was lucky, a few opponents to supply interruptions. But in the committees, which played a much larger part than in Britain, the actual legislation was shaped, and the ordinary member of such a committee, even if he belonged to a radical opposition party, was expected to make his contribution. In the normal case, when he was nominated by his party on the proposal of some sectional organization, he had ample opportunity to make some definite contribution to the conditions of the group represented by him, and would thus find some satisfaction which the average back-bencher, with moderate hopes for a junior ministerial post, is denied in Britain. Some compensation for the lessened (in Austria almost non-existent) chances of the opposition's becoming the alternative Government under proportional representation was implied in the importance of Committee work; for example the Centre, even if it formed part of a bourgeois bloc, could hardly avoid nominating Christian Trade Unionists to represent it on the Committee for Social Policies, where they would not remain uninfluenced by the arguments put forward by Socialist and even Communist trade unionists. They would be afraid of being reminded, before a working-class electorate, of any amendment they had voted against; so they would support some opposition amendments, or at any rate, if party discipline prevented this, would cause such trouble within their own party caucus that they would be allowed to move at the Committee's

[1] See above, p. 201.

next meeting some more moderate amendments of their own, which, of course, would be presented to the electorate as the true solution of the problem on the initiative of the Christian Trade Unionists. This system of legislation, as well as the wide scope granted to local and Provincial government, reduced the amount of actual change in policy (as distinct from personnel) involved in changes in the Government coalition.

In Germany and Austria the importance of the work of the standing committees and of opposition participation in them was recognized by distributing their chairmanships among all the parties by proportional representation.[1] Even a Communist chairman of the German Standing Committee for Foreign Affairs would exercise his office in such a way as to prove his and his party's ability to carry out such tasks in a way likely to win the confidence of the electorate, though he would not attempt to prove his 'non-partisanship', which by a Central European electorate, and least of all by its working-class section, was not regarded as a virtue. The whole procedure clearly expressed a conception of democracy as joint rule by the democratic organizations, the electorate settling the proportions of their influence, but excluding none of them unless the organization ended in political bankruptcy. Naturally this concept collided with that of the actual holders of material power, who deemed that some organizations should be rewarded for faithful service by appropriate patronage, and others suppressed.

Equality of status among all the parliamentary parties was looked upon as a basic principle of democratic procedure; there was no restriction of legislative initiative, and no Government control of parliamentary time (except for the passing of the Budget, which was never obstructed). In Germany and Czechoslovakia Standing Orders made parliamentary obstruction difficult; the activities of the opposition had to be concentrated on preventing or weakening the legislation that was necessary to keep the Government coalition together. In Austria, the Standing Orders allowed of so much obstruction that hardly any legis-

[1] The D'hond system was applied; each party selected according to its strength the proper number of chairmanships from the established list. The strongest party had first choice; when its turn came again it took what it regarded as the 'best' chairmanship of those which the other parties had left. There was less controversy than might be expected at first sight; an opposition party would hardly be interested in the Finance Committee, whose chairman had to collaborate closely with the Government, nor would there be much disappointment in an agrarian party if a workers' party whose turn came before its own had preferred the chairmanship of the Committee for Social Policies to that for Agriculture. Thus each of the three or four strongest parties was likely to get one or two chairmanships which its electorate regarded as of first importance; this was what was intended by the shapers of the system, as distinct from the Czechoslovak distinction between privileged and underprivileged parties. It should be kept in mind that, unlike the practice in the U.S.A., the chairmen of committees were not the masters of their time-table; an opposition chairman of a committee could raise questions in which his party was interested, but could not prevent the Government from proceeding with its legislation.

lation could be passed without some at least tacit toleration by the opposition; unconstitutional interference with the latter's rights was prevented by the influential extra-parliamentary position of the Socialist Party, which could easily call a general strike and could rely on a large part of the Army and the Police. Obviously these powers could not be used except in cases where the opposition seemed clearly to be defending popular interests such as the right of railwaymen, etc. to strike, the right of combination for soldiers and policemen, the federal rights of Vienna (the infringement of which might also be prejudicial to those of the Catholic Provinces, and thus meet with resistance not only from the Viennese Socialists but even from the Alpine members of the Christian Social party) and, particularly, the Rent Restriction Act which allowed the Vienna municipality to proceed with its housing policy. Thus some taboos—none of them important for the peasant bulk of the Catholic party—were set up, the infringement of which by the Big-Business-controlled group within the majority party would be answered by parliamentary obstruction, with behind it the threat of a general strike and perhaps even of civil war. In other cases, including the most important issues of national policy such as the conditions for the League of Nations loan,[1] the weapon of obstruction would be applied only as a means of pressure to prevent the majority from abolishing parliamentary control of Government measures.

This case was typical not only of the kind of occasion when the weapon of obstruction could be applied in the national interest, but also of the limits to its use; after achieving the maximum concessions which the League of Nations was prepared to grant (to secure which, indeed, ought to have been Seipel's business, not the opposition's), the Social Democrats not only ceased to obstruct the passage of the reconstruction laws but even voted for them whenever that was necessary because they amended the constitution. This was an instance in which an obviously necessary measure (the stabilization of the currency) had to be carried out somehow, and where the task of the opposition was obviously to prevent the majority from using the occasion to make basic changes in the actual constitution of the country. But in spring 1929, after long obstruction and hard bargaining, the Socialists permitted the passage of bourgeois amendments to the Rent Restriction Act; in the autumn of that year they even voted for such amendments of the constitution in an 'authoritarian' direction as they were obliged to yield in negotiations which proceeded under the threat of civil war,[2] notwithstanding the fact that they regarded both amendments as harmful, and acceptable only in the sense that what remained of the bourgeois demands after the bargaining no longer seemed worth a trial of strength and the destruction of the position of the moderate elements in the

[1] See above, p. 209.
[2] See below, pp. 319–20.

bourgeois camp. Evidently the power of the Austrian opposition created conditions in which latent civil war between Social Democracy and the right wing of the bourgeois camp coexisted with hardly veiled coalition with the more moderate elements within the same camp; any shift in the relations of strength within the two main camps, or even between moderates and fascists in the Catholic party, might bring about the breakdown of the artificial equilibrium.

The Austrian case was an extreme one because of the existence of conditions for actual civil war as an alternative to compromise; but quite generally the need of a two-thirds majority[1] for amendments to the constitution, in which many of the revolutionary achievements had been included in order to secure them against occasional shifts in the electoral balance, resulted in a need for the Social Democrats to accept open responsibility for unpopular measures lest they were proclaimed by breach of the Constitution, and Social Democracy might have to face the alternative of either fighting such a breach or openly accepting it. Many of those who capitulated before this threat quite honestly believed that by saving the appearance of observing the Constitution they would preserve it for better times when it would once again serve for the enactment of social reforms; but they forgot that with every reactionary step which they concurred in so as to preserve constitutional appearances they also undermined the workers' feeling that the Constitution was worth defending.

(*e*) *Federal Institutions and Local Government*

The present writer has devoted a special study to the development of Federalism in Central and Eastern Europe;[2] we are interested in the subject here only as one of the institutional forms in which the principle of collaboration between political parties based on diverse sectional groups could be realized. Administrative devolution, and especially the transfer of some legislative powers to the lesser units, may give more scope for the development of the particular social attitude of the various communities that predominate in the different parts of a country; even the protection of minorities can be increased by giving them an opportunity to share as junior partners in regional self-government if there is some degree of equilibrium between the parts dominated by different sections.

[1] In Czechoslovakia a three-fifths majority, which was even more difficult to secure because of the racial divisions which involved the existence of large permanent opposition parties quite apart from the extreme left and right.

[2] *Federalism in Central and Eastern Europe* (London, 1945). It may be remarked that so important an application of federal institutions as that to the solution of the nationalities problem is excluded from the scope of the present study, as Czechoslovakia, the only one of the Central European democracies which had considerable national minorities, refrained from using devolution for such purposes.

Federalism offers no solution for such contradictions in terms as the search for a combination of complete internal self-determination of the unit with the preservation of all desirable links with its neighbours. It is impossible to have, within the borders of a single State, a planned nationalized economy and freedom of capitalist enterprise, a State religion protected by discrimination against dissenters and complete disestablishment, and so on. Still, some types of solution of the basic problems allow for minor variations, including such details as may appear to be a satisfaction of widespread desires. If the national solution involves some combination of private and public enterprise, the position of banks, railways, and basic heavy industries, the issue of land-nationalization, etc. must be decided on the national scale, or there is no unity in the national economy. But if these issues are decided in such a way that unofficial restrictions on regional autonomy (say discriminations in granting credits against municipalities which pursue building policies unpopular with High Finance) are made impossible, there is no strict need for homogeneous principles in housing, or even in the management of public utilities, to be applied all over the country. Nor need all parts of a country as large as Germany necessarily have the same law of inheritance of peasants' homesteads, etc. If there is national agreement on the desirability of an educational policy which denies a priviledged position to any religion (or even to religion in general as opposed to rationalism), but also avoids a hostile attitude to all religion and does not wish to put difficulties in the way of parents who wish their children to have religious instruction, a number of different solutions can coexist and may even be desirable if the normal attitudes of the majority of the people vary considerably in the diverse parts of the national territory. There are obvious limits to the reasonable extent of devolution of the various State functions:[1] one cannot have different housing policies in the various parts of a city, or different laws of inheritance in the diverse villages of a single agricultural region. Actual autonomy in matters of education presupposes units large enough to have their own secondary schools and teachers' training colleges, perhaps even their own universities. Obviously, the larger the unit within certain limits the more numerous the matters that can safely be left to its autonomy, and the stronger the case for it; the diverse German tribes, though not the individual villages or even dwarf States, each had their own specific traditions as to the indivisibility of peasants' homesteads.

Such an application of regional autonomy, however, was rendered

[1] The reader may notice that I take the interpretation of federalism as administrative devolution for granted. So it was with serious students at least for the territories under discussion (Kelsen, the framer of the Austrian federal constitution, called it a 'polite expression for far-reaching regional self-government'). In the book quoted in the preceding note, arguing against the advocates of a fashionable ideology, I tried to make the case that federalism makes no sense whatever in any other interpretation, whatever ideologies have grown up with it.

impossible in Central Europe by the unsuitability of the existing units; with the exception of Vienna's position as a separate province of the Austrian federation and of the fusion into one *Land* of the Thüringian dwarf States, the only instance in which the very cautious provisions of the Weimar position on the changes of *Land* borders were applied,[1] all the existing boundaries had been inherited from the pre-democratic, if not the pre-capitalist stage. They were preserved at the Revolution by an opposition to the centre which was based partly on the antagonism of the peasantry to food collections for the benefit of the towns,[2] partly on general opposition of the conservative element to the working-class influence on the post-revolutionary Governments, and in some Central German States also by working-class opposition to the left-centre coalition ruling in Berlin and especially to its compromises with the Prussian army. Most of the units thus preserved were quite unsuitable as expressions of distinct aspects of the national life. Catholic Upper Bavarian peasants and Protestant Franconian townspeople had little in common except that both had lived under the rule of the Bavarian kings and the Bavarian bureaucracy, and were accustomed to the latter's habits. On the other hand, the dismemberment of Prussia, which within borders explainable only by the acquisitions of the Hohenzollerns displayed most of those varieties of national life upon whose co-ordination normal federalism would have had to be based, was rejected as 'harmful to national unity'—this, evidently, being a synonym for the further progress of Prussian centralization.[3] In these circumstances, federalism meant mainly allowing every group of Germans to continue living under their traditional bureaucracy, and enforcing their submission to that bureaucracy, which could be trusted to conform with the actual centralist forces working within the Reich. Should the majority in some minor German State such as Saxony attempt to realize its principles in some field harmless to national unity, such as non-denominational education or the participation of working-class representatives in preparing bills on social policies, it would have to face a combination of the national with the local right wing, including the local bureaucracy.

The autonomy of the constituent parts of the federation, especially in Germany, was restricted not only by the forces supporting centralism (glorified by the traditions of the struggle for national unity and, on the Left, by a gross misunderstanding of the traditions of the French Revolution, which were interpreted in the Napoleonic rather than the Jacobin or Girondist sense without anyone, except a few specialists, noticing the difference) but even by the demands of the chief advocates of federalism, the Catholic parties; these strongly favoured federalism as a protection against the possible advent of a national left-wing

[1] See above, p. 168.
[2] See above, pp. 175–6, and my *Federalism etc.*, p. 86.
[3] See above, p. 168.

majority, but were little prepared to let the Left have its way in the regions where it was in the majority. They used their political key-position in Germany to impose in the Weimar Constitution rather narrow limits on the exercise of State autonomy in the educational field, and in Austria to prevent any federal legislation on matters of education and divorce with which any other party could agree. In consequence, apart from agricultural administration, the suitability of which for decentralization was not questionable, no clear delimitation of powers between Federation and States could be arrived at; really important Provincial competences, such as Vienna's housing policies, grew up behind the back of the framers of the Constitution. The resulting controversies on constitutional issues in Austria invited the frequent use of extreme devices such as parliamentary obstruction and threat of civil war;[1] in Germany they helped to promote an atmosphere in which Federal executive action was regarded as a legitimate means to bring into power the 'desirable' group in State politics.[2]

Because of the constitutional bargains through which Bismarck's empire had come into existence, the German States appeared to enjoy more legislative autonomy than the Austrian provinces, but in view of the realities of German constitutional life, their actual autonomy was much smaller. A Saxon Social Democrat, whose political outlook was very similar to that of his Viennese comrades,[3] mentioned as the main achievements of five years of left-wing Governments the laws on the elementary schools,[4] on ensuring the allegiance of civil servants to the Republic,[5] a law on local government, which after the Federal executive action was greatly modified, and the attempted establishment of a consultative Workers' Chamber,[6] the enactment of which was prevented by the Federal execution. In Vienna, it would have been unnecessary to enact the two laws last mentioned, since they formed part of the Austrian federal legislation, while in the two fields first mentioned the Viennese Socialists had to have recourse to administrative practice (for which the Austrian federal constitution allowed at least as much freedom as did the German for State legislation). As the right wing's federal strength was used mainly to preserve the *status quo*, administrative practice as a substitute for legislative reform had to be applied mainly by the left wing; Vienna's measures in these fields ranged from making

[1] See above, p. 271, and below, pp. 318 ff.

[2] See above, p. 227.

[3] Fabian, op. cit.,

[4] See above, note [1] on p. 169.

[5] Civil servants were prohibited from voicing anti-Republican views in office; in their private capacity as citizens they were allowed to propagate such views on condition that it was done without expressions of contempt or hatred. Such modest provisions were regarded by the Right Wing as 'Bolshevist'.

[6] See above, p. 173.

the attendance of school-children at church on Sundays voluntary[1] to introducing the institution of divorce where one of the spouses had been a Roman Catholic at the time of marriage[2] by the administrative practice of 'granting dispensation from the obstacle to a new marriage implied in the existence of a former marriage', provided the partners to the latter had been separated by Court decision. Such activities, though strongly attacked by the Catholic party, could not be interfered with before the fall of Austrian democracy because everyone, including most of the Viennese Catholics, regarded them as obvious necessities whose satisfaction by legislation had been sabotaged for doctrinaire reasons. But when the Prussian left-centre government promised to do away with capital punishment, which could not be abolished by federal legislation against the President and Federal Council, by the practice of reprieve, the attempt broke down on the occurrence of one of those specially abhorrent murders which are usually cited as arguments against its abolition. It is clear that administrative practice, as soon as it has to go into the merits of the individual case, is no substitute for legislation which draws a balance between the diverse types of case which arise in practice.

In the circumstances, the importance of State policies in Germany from the very start, and in Austria at least after 1927, lay not so much in the realization of the social and cultural ideas of the local majority as in the building up of positions for trials of strength in federal policies. So far as the constitutional aspects of such policies were concerned, State elections in Germany were important because they influenced the composition of the Federal Council. That Council's suspensive veto was an important factor in politics because, if it were supported by the President, it could be overruled only by a plebiscite, which never occurred. Such a combination between the centralist President and the Federal Chamber was conceivable only if the social interests of the right wing, and not mere interests of State autonomy, were involved. Since the members of the Federal Council were nominated by the State Governments, participation in which, after the trial of strength of 1923, was open to the extreme Right but not to the extreme Left, it was likely to differ from the Reichstag in favour of the moderate right wing. In Austria, the members of the Federal Council were elected by the Provincial Diets by proportional representation, which secured the position of the minorities (i.e. in the Alpine Provinces, the Socialists); as amongst the Provincial Catholics the moderate element was likely to prevail, the Federal Council, in the decisive crisis of 1933, proved to be to the Left

[1] As distinct from religious instruction, which was made obligatory by federal law.

[2] Austrian legislation, as inherited from the Empire, allowed divorce only in cases of non-Catholic marriages; marriages the parties to which had been Catholics at the time of marriage, unless the marriage were annulled by Canon Law, could only be separated by Court decision without the right to remarry.

of the Federal Government. Apart from all constitutional niceties, the State Governments, which in Germany controlled the Police, were looked upon as important strongholds in the event of civil war. We have seen how they were used in Bavaria and in Central Germany during the crisis of 1923; the complexion of German policies ensured that the Bavarian right wing, which had gone to the length of open mutiny, was integrated in the conservative government to come, while even the Social Democratic members of the Central German governments, whose attitude during the crisis had been a defensive one, were eliminated. Later, the idea that control of the State Governments was important in order to be sure of a police that could be relied upon in the event of a right-wing *coup* was to the front in the arguments used by the Prussian left-centre combination in defence of its continued collaboration with the dictatorial Reich Government; we shall see how it was exploded by the Prussian Government itself.[1]

There was no inherent reason why the granting of autonomy to local majorities which happened to be minorities in a larger unit should stop at the member-State of the Federation; the main sectional differences within the Central European democracies concerned the issue of town versus countryside. The example of the few cities that combined State with municipal rights[2] showed that far-reaching municipal autonomy was quite compatible with national economic unity. But municipal autonomy contradicted the policies of the alliance of political right-wing and traditionalist bureaucracy which dominated German and Austrian federalism: it was at this point that democratic and traditionalist concepts of administrative devolution parted.

The need to combine regional and municipal local government was recognized in Article 11 of Preuss's first draft of the Weimar Constitution of 3rd January 1919,[3] which, however, was defeated by the combination of the State bureaucracies with the Greater Prussian trend.[4] On

[1] See below, p. 331.

[2] Vienna in Austria, the three Hansa towns (Hamburg, Bremen and Lübeck) in Germany. Against the significance of these examples it might be argued that the exceptional position of these cities as economic centres of national importance was the very condition of their successful use of such far-reaching autonomy. But Vienna's most interesting policies in the fields of housing and culture had nothing to do with her monopolist position in commerce, banking, and tourist traffic, and could just as well be applied in any other industrial centre which enjoyed a similar degree of autonomy; capital does not move in search of higher rents, or for the religious education of children. Lübeck, nowadays a second-rate port, figured in the list merely for historical reasons; there was no reason why its autonomy should not be enjoyed just as well by Halle or Magdeburg, not to speak of Cologne or Munich. The functions of Hamburg and Bremen as national ports were even impaired by the historical boundaries of their State territory, which excluded important parts of the modern dock areas and industrial centres.

[3] Preuss, op. cit., 1928, pp. 160 ff.

[4] See above, p. 168.

the insistence of the Socialists, who were interested in the position of the industrial towns in the peasant-dominated Alpine Provinces, Article 42 of the Introductory Law to the Austrian Constitution ruled that those articles of the Constitution which granted the Provinces full autonomy, including the 'residuary powers' not explicitly reserved to the Federation, were suspended until the Provinces had enacted appropriate laws on municipal local government. The Catholic majorities in the Provincial Diets, however, trusting in their control of the Federal Government, preferred not to enjoy the enlarged autonomy offered to them on condition of their granting local autonomy in turn to their Socialist minorities. In 1925 the Socialists recognized that the provincial Catholics were somewhat less reactionary than the Viennese Big Business group which dominated the Federal Government: so they agreed to the Constitutional amendment by which the Provinces were granted the reserved powers without having fulfilled that condition. In Czechoslovakia, the centralist traditions of the old-Austrian civil service, combined with some verbiage about national unity, served the purposes of the Agrarian party which, as the mouthpiece of all the capitalist interests and by the use of its parliamentary key position, secured a permanent hold on the Ministry of the Interior and thereby on the Civil Service and on the 'supervision' of local government. Yet in spite of the unsatisfactory definition of its powers the average Central European town, because of the almost complete municipalization of public utilities, enjoyed some freedom of action in financial matters unless it was restricted by open interference by the national or State Government, perhaps by its share in the proceeds of general taxation normally due to the municipalities not being paid out unless its public utilities were operated in accordance with prescribed standards of financial self-support (which other people might describe as indirect taxation). As the municipal suffrage in Central Europe was not restricted to ratepayers nor based on any other kind of property qualification, quite a lot of interference with democracy which in traditional Britain was secured by the ratepayers' predominant position had to be carried out by direct orders from State and local bureaucracy.

While democratic principles of local government were consistently realized in Austria, in Germany and Czechoslovakia municipalities were subjected to direct supervision by the State (which in Czechoslovakia meant the central Government). In those parts of Germany which had been most influenced by French administrative tradition, bureaucratic control was almost unrestricted; the Prussian District Diets, at least in rural districts, were mere shadows of the Landrat whom they had to 'supervise'. In the Western parts of Czechoslovakia, the bureaucrats representing the central Government could disallow municipal decisions only if they were *ultra vires*; but the elected organs of district and provincial autonomy could nullify or alter any municipal decision they happened to disagree with, and the semi-official provincial Government could dissolve any municipal council for 'continuous failure to fulfil its duties' as the Government conceived them, and could even avoid awkward results at new elections by nominating a commissioner. The concepts of the moderate left-wing were reflected by the Saxon Law on Municipalities of July 1923, which preserved some supervision of the municipalities but offered guarantees against its bureaucratic misuse; municipalities could appeal against State organs which had vetoed their decisions to a municipal chamber elected by the Diet and composed of people with experience in local government. In 1925, this enactment of the Left Government was replaced by a new one providing for a two-chamber system in the municipality, with a mayor elected for life, and unrestricted State supervision of the municipalities.

In Austria, in western Czechoslovakia, and in Saxony under the law of 1923, municipalities were administered by an Assembly elected under general suffrage and proportional representation; Mayor and Town Council were its executive organs. Bavaria and Baden, typical peasant countries, came very near to this type of democratic government, the rights of the mayor, who in villages of under 3,000 inhabitants was directly elected by the people, being very restricted. In Prussia, the Council (called the 'Magistrate'), though in the long run dependent on the electorate, not only operated as a Second Chamber but also enjoyed a high degree of independence of the Assembly because of its lengthy tenure of office. The French influences, in their Napoleonic form, had produced the least democratic conditions in the Rhineland; there the Mayor (in this case more closely resembling an American City Manager) issued orders which the other members of the Magistrate (who were elected for shorter terms) had to carry out, and he had a veto on decisions of the Assembly, over whose deliberations he presided. In the Eastern parts of Prussia there was at least an elected President of the Assembly, independent of the Mayor; on the other hand, up to the end of 1927 one and a half million Prussians lived in 12,000 Estate Districts under the direct rule of the Lord of the Manor, as a substitute for local government; the abolition of this feudal institution was so long delayed because the left-centre coalition which governed Prussia waited—in vain—for a federal enactment on rural local government.

The relations between municipal self-government and the constituent units of the German and Austrian federations (apart from such a giant as Prussia) should not be described in terms of mere antagonism. Both had to deal mainly with social welfare and education, both stood comparatively close to the electorate, and both were frequent objects of attack by Big-Business-dominated national Governments and international organs of High Finance. The reparations agent, Parker Gilbert, opposed foreign loans to States as well as municipalities on the ground that they served 'non-productive purposes', while even the Communists demanded larger opportunities for States as well as municipalities in the interests of social welfare. Public opinion would draw the main dividing line between them and the Reich, and take sides according to the fundamental political issues. After 1927 the demand for 'unification of the Reich' became a rallying-cry of the right wing, and the specifically Prussian variety of Social Democracy would not fail to support it.

(*f*) *The Plebiscitarian Elements in the Constitution*

In origin[1] as well as in actual working, the German Presidency was an anti-democratic element in the constitutional framework. The course of the one election to the office which took place under democratic conditions illustrated the great advantage offered to the right wing by the very mechanism of election, at least in a country like Germany, where a chauvinist appeal, even under a defeated general, was the safest means of mobilizing the lower middle class vote.[2] Of the other plebiscitarian institutions of the German constitution,[3] the only one attempted on some occasions was the popular initiative; the results were immaterial from the practical point of view, but illustrate the inherent potentialities of a two-party system in Germany.

In autumn 1925, the former Princes' demands for the restitution of their property had excited large sections of the German population: not only the republican workers, but also the small savers who had just been expropriated by the monetary inflation. The Communists, who had just gone through an internal party crisis,[4] and wished to improve the relations between the two wings of the labour movement as shaped by the Socialist workers' reaction to the outcome of Hindenburg's election, proposed to the Social Democrats a joint initiative for the introduction of a law to expropriate the former Princes without compensation. There was a real popular movement in that direction, and the Social Democratic leaders had to agree; in the official initiative 12·5 million voters publicly entered their names on the lists, 1·8 million more than had voted in secret ballot, eighteen months before, for the two parties which supported the initiative. There could be no question of the Reichstag accepting the law, but the Centre parties felt uneasy in view of the

[1] See above, p. 170.

[2] See above, pp. 100 and 232–3.

[3] Referendum on presidential initiative, or to solve a deadlock between the constitutional elements, though envisaged, was never applied; nor were the corresponding institutions in Czechoslovakia. In Austria, plebiscitarian provisions of the German type were prevented by the Socialist influence in framing the Constitution of 1920, but direct election of the President was introduced, under right-wing pressure, by the amendments of 1929 (see below, p. 320). The Catholics, who had enforced the enactment, knew quite well that only the Nazis could profit by it; so they asked the Socialists to help in the enactment of a special law to have the next President elected in the old way; the demand was naturally complied with.

[4] See above, p. 230.

electors' probable reactions to the alternative, i.e. letting the Princes get from public funds everything that a sympathetic judiciary found it on some pretext possible to grant them.[1] Marx, who was Chancellor at the time, even proposed a dissolution in order to obtain authority for a settlement which would allow the Princes a certain proportion of their claims. Hindenburg refused the dissolution, and all the bourgeois parties, with the exception of a minority of the Democrats, who abstained, voted against the initiative, which was thus submitted to a plebiscite.

All the established powers, foremost among them the Catholic bishops in a collective pastoral letter of 1st June 1926, opposed the initiative as contrary to Christian morals and to the basic rights of private porperty; Hindenburg, by a letter to the Joint Committee of the bourgeois parties, gave the vote in the referendum for the initiative the character of a vote of no confidence against him.[2] The right wing deemed that in a secret ballot its cause might easily be lost; therefore it issued the slogan of abstention, thus making the vote open and exposing especially the labourers in the countryside and considerable parts of the Catholic population to the play of what Bismarck had once described as the 'God-willed dependences';[3] the Democrats alone countered this move by suggesting the casting of noes or blank ballots. One million voters followed this suggestion—amongst them, probably, some right-wing shopkeepers in the industrial centres, where open ballot might work the opposite way; 14·5 million, that is, nearly as many as had voted for Hindenburg in the secret ballot of the presidential election, supported the initiative; it was declared defeated, as less than half the total electorate had taken part in the vote. Those who took part, following the slogans of the Democrats, Socialists, and Communists, might be looked upon as definite opponents of Hindenburg's policies; the existence of a left-wing majority of the electorate, if rallied under a sufficiently attractive slogan, was thus proved. But the moral victory had no further practical implications, and it is hardly necessary to say that the Princes got all that they asked for.

As the plebiscite had proved an efficient means of mobilizing large

[1] Some of the demands made by the Princes and their relatives (in one case the mistress of a deceased Prince who had been promised an annuity from public funds) illustrated the shamelessness of the former rulers as well as the kind of judiciary on which they were able to rely.

[2] Stampfer (op. cit., p. 447) is mistaken, however, when he states that Hindenburg thereby contributed to the success of the initiative (which, as proposed by the Communists, does not enjoy his sympathies): as the right wing chose the method of open ballot, the authority of the national hero was quite helpful in strengthening the terror on which they relied. Most of those who wished to oppose Hindenburg while not supporting expropriation without compensation undoubtedly followed the Democratic slogan of casting invalid ballots.

[3] See above, p. 14.

masses, resort to it became a favourite device of opposition parties. The 'Small Savers'' group shortly afterwards failed ignominiously in an initiative demanding compensation, and the Communists did the same two years later in one against the building of the battle-cruisers; though this issue[1] had stirred up a large proportion of the Social Democratic workers, the initiative was supported by only 35 per cent of the voters which the Communists alone had mustered at the general election five months before. In 1929 Hugenberg and Hitler proclaimed the tactics of their Harzburg front by a popular initiative against the acceptance of the Young Plan; by a very narrow margin they mobilized, with 4·1 million sginatures for the initiative, the 10 per cent of the electorate necessary to compel a referendum. In the referendum itself they got merely 5·8 million votes: much less than, in the following year, Hitler himself was to poll. Evidently the bulk of the Conservatives had stayed at home. It had by now become the established tactic of the opponents of a referendum to suggest abstention; the right-wingers, who in the vote on the expropriation of the Princes had enforced an interpretation of the law which made the participation of half the electorate in a referendum a condition of its success,[2] turned round on this legal issue in order to interpret the vote of 15 per cent of the electorate against the Young Plan as its valid rejection; naturally Hugenberg found some High Court judges with a similar ability to adapt their legal views to political opportunism, to subscribe his memoranda. But this was too much even for German bourgeois stomachs, and the view that a plebiscite, to be valid, needed the participation of half the electorate became definitely established.

There was one other occasion on which this device was used and that in circumstances where, by all the rules of political arithmetic, the referendum should have been successful. In 1931 Hitler and Hugenberg started a popular initiative for the dissolution of the Prussian Diet, in order to get rid of the left-centre coalition Government in Prussia. It was subscribed by six million voters, 22·5 per cent of the Prussian electorate, at a time when a vote of 30–35 per cent for Nazis and German Nationals taken together could have been expected in a Parliamentary

[1] See below, p. 324.

[2] This was a condition made by Article 75 of the Constitution on the validity of referenda 'overruling enactments of Parliament', i.e. appeals from Parliament to the electorate. The framers of the constitution hardly envisaged the formal fact that between *every* popular initiative, even if intended to close gaps in existing legislation as in the case of the Princes, and the following referendum, Parliament was given an opportunity to accept, or to amend, the text of the law submitted by the popular initiative; if they had envisaged this, it would have been much simpler to say that *no* referendum originating in a popular initiative was valid unless half the electorate took part in the vote (which implied the possibility of its opponents making the ballot open and also counting in its favour all those who might abstain for non-political reasons, by simply issuing the slogan of abstention). But it is quite possible that the vagueness of the formulation was promoted by distrust of the popular initiative.

election. By a quirk of their inter-factional struggle the Communists, who had abstained from the initiative, found that the indirect support for the Prussian Government implied in abstaining from the plebiscite was incompatible with their principles (to speak more precisely, that on this issue the Neumann faction could defeat Thälmann in the internal caucus); so they decided to support the initiative, which, however, was now described as a 'Red' one. So also did the People's Party, the last of the opposition parties (without, of course, ceasing to describe the initiative as 'black-white-red'). On any sound estimate the total electoral strength of the parties which supported the plebiscite amounted to some 55 per cent, and it should easily have succeeded even against a slogan of abstention; but actually it got 9·8 million votes, just 37 per cent of the electorate; and Communists and 'black-white-red' right-wingers reproached each other for having brought about the failure. Probably both were right, and each side's normal followers were repulsed by their strange companions. In the elections which in due course, i.e. after eight months, followed the defeat of the plebiscite, the opposition got fourteen million votes, the Government only eight million. These figures represented the party allegiances of the electorate; the results of the preceding plebiscite, especially if compared with the very different results of the plebiscite against the Princes, showed the limits within which the electorate was at the disposal of the party leaders. There was a potential two-party system in Germany, with the electorate fairly equally divided, and with the party which took the initiative with a popular slogan or leader presumably in the advantage. It was based on such great issues as rich v. poor, monarchy v. republic, militarism v. peace. It contained the seeds of civil war, which was, indeed, the only alternative to a capitulation like that of 1933. The measure of any party was its capacity to rally superior forces for the inevitable trial of strength.

CHAPTER EIGHT

THE ACHIEVEMENTS

(*a*) *Land Reform*

It is no purpose of this book to describe even the most important achievements of the Central European countries in the cultural or educational fields; only occasionally have we glanced at issues such as religious education, which might illustrate the political balance in countries with powerful Catholic parties.[1] We are interested in achievements only in so far as they represented realization of sectional aims and may have affected the later balance of economic and political power. We began our description of the Central European setting with a short survey of the feudal elements which survived the revolution of 1848; we have to start our survey of the main economic results of the 1918 revolution by the statement that in that decisive field, at least at the decisive point, what was done amounted to nothing at all.

The decisive point was Germany: and the only reform worth mentioning there was the belated rescue of village government in the Eastern parts of Prussia from the grip of the landlords.[2] To some extent the failure to carry out a land reform was identical with the failure to settle accounts with the Junker-Big-Business combination which supported the Prussian army; but the negative attitude of German Social Democracy to the peasants' problem, developed long before the war,[3] produced suitable pretexts for such compromises with the powers that be. The awakening of the agricultural labourers (by which mainly the Majority Socialists profited in the absence of radical organizations in the countryside) interfered with the lower-middle-class utopia of turning Germany into a smallholders' country; resolutions of the Party Congresses of 1920 and 1921 showed a definite tendency to preserve the large estates (with or without verbiage about their eventual 'socialization'; this was the most elementary condition for the survival of the

[1] See above, pp. 169–70 and 276.
[2] See above, p. 279.
[3] See above, p. 86.

Agricultural Workers' Union. When that Union's influence was broken by the defeats of the labour movement in 1920–3, and when the prosperity which followed the acceptance of the Dawes Plan revived all kinds of lower-middle-class utopias, there was also a revival of the demands for 'settlement', which were quite harmless as, for the time being, Social Democracy was bound to remain an opposition party. Finally, at the Kiel Party Congress in 1927, a platform on the agrarian question was adopted, which borrowed from the former Revisionists the emphasis on medium-scale private enterprise, while the former Marxists (who, so far as they had remained in the Social Democratic Party, had now become defenders of the merits of large-scale enterprise pure and simple) secured the recognition of the economic importance of large estates; this platform implied a theoretical acceptance of the *status quo* in German agriculture.

In Austria, where large estates played a much smaller part, the political aspects of the problem should have appeared simpler. Those parts of the Catholic party with which the Social Democrats had any prospect of collaborating represented those very peasant small-holders to whose detriment latifundia had developed, and before the war had openly voiced their opposition to the landlords;[1] and Austrian Social Democracy had always been far less dogmatic on such matters than its German brother. But Big Business control of the Catholic party paralyzed even the representation of the peasant interest. Socialist pressure was needed to enforce the passing of the law of 31st May 1919 on the resettlement of lands taken from the peasants during the last ten years before the war. As abbeys and bishoprics were among the main beneficiaries by the expropriation of the peasants, their spiritual power was used to prevent believers from having recourse to the law as 'contradicting Christian morals'; and this protection was extended even to non-ecclesiastical landlords such as the Starhembergs. Of the 122,000 acres of peasant land which had been alienated during the period 1905–12 in Styria alone, a mere sixth was reclaimed by the peasants, and not even all of that was restored to them by the Courts. A little more successful was the land reform in the Burgenland (the former West Hungarian territories) where, as all over Hungary, a strong antagonism, in this case also national, divided the twenty Magyar aristocrats who owned the latifundia from the peasants; after 1929 the latter were allowed to buy from the landlords, for full compensation, the land they worked on. So only the well-to-do peasants could make use of the provisions of the law, and the landlords remained strong enough to press their tenants into the Fascist Heimwehren (as Prince Starhemberg could do even in peasant-dominated Upper Austria, thus forming his battalions of chasseurs, mainly from his foresters).

Only in Czechoslovokia was a land reform of any importance carried

[1] See above, p. 47.

out; and this reform, as well as most of the criticism levelled against it, was conditioned by the fact that in all the former Hungarian, and often in the former Austrian, territories the social antagonism between peasant and large landowner marched with the national enmity between Slav and Magyar or German. Under the impact of the Russian revolution, the inevitability of reform was obvious to all the Czech and Slovak parties, but during the winter of 1918–19 there was considerable argument about the amount of compensation to be paid (which as a result of the monetary inflation was eventually settled against the landlords, though the law gave them the pre-war value of the estates), and about the maximum size of the residual estate to be left to the landlords; the Socialists at first suggested 125 acres (rather more than was owned by the most prosperous peasants),[1] the Agrarians 2,500 acres (the upper limit of what could still be managed as a capitalist farm, as distinct from latifundia). The compromise enacted by the law of 16th April 1919 provided for a maximum of 1,250 acres. The peasants had to pay to the Land Office 50 per cent more than that office paid to the former owners, a provision which proved endurable only because the monetary inflation reduced the peasants' actual payments to about a quarter of the market value at the time of purchase, of which they had to pay in cash only 10 per cent of the price of the land and 50 per cent of the costs of the buildings, etc.; the rest was credited to them. Out of a total of £74 millions of credits thus granted, £46·7 millions had been repaid by the end of 1934; this seems to show that most of the new settlers were successful. The employees on the expropriated estates, including the farmhands, so far as they could get no land, received monetary compensation, which also, of course, lost much of its value by the inflation. As the Agrarian Party had practically complete control of the administration of the law, the provisions of the law on industrial enterprises connected with agricultural estates were executed in such a way that only those industries, mainly the distilleries, immediately connected with estate management were acquired, usually in favour of co-operatives formed by the peasants who shared the former estate, while so important an asset as the sugar refineries was left to the former owners. In administering the law, the provisions regarding estates in the preservation of which a 'national interest' was claimed to exist were interpreted in such a way that about 40 per cent of the areas originally sequestrated were returned to the former owners; the various branches of the Schwarzenberg family,[2] for example, under diverse pretexts retained 125,000 acres; and the estates owned by the Church were hardly touched at all. Racial discrimination in carrying out the reform was explicitly prohibited by

[1] The Socialists had also suggested that expropriated estates should be managed by co-operatives of the former employees; this demand, not very seriously put forward, was soon dropped.

[2] See above, f.n.[2] on p. 6.

the law; at least the provisions for turning small tenants into independent freeholders were sufficiently clear for even German tenants of expropriated Czech landlords to obtain their shares without undue difficulties.[1] A combination of national and social biases in the application of the law by the Agrarian Party resulted in lenient dealing with Czech latifundia-owners, some of whom had discovered their Czech nationality only after the fall of the Hapsburgs and forgot it again after Munich; some belated corrections had to be applied when the land reform of 1945 on avowedly nationalist lines expropriated all the Germans, including the Czech Quislings.

On the whole the land reform put private ownership on sounder and clearly capitalist foundations. The latifundia were reduced to more reasonable dimensions, and some of the semi-feudal features of society were abolished; the position of the small peasant proprietor was strengthened, and the status of the tenant-labourer, previously a semi-serf, was raised to that of a smallholding cottager. Along with the remnants of the original feudal landlord class a new stratum of purely capitalist acquirers of 'residual estates' came into being. In the end, out of 5,891 sequestered estates 2,994 were totally divided up and 1·79 million hectares (4,465,000 acres), i.e. 10 per cent of the agricultural and 18·2 per cent of the forest area of the Republic, changed hands. 783,000 hectares, of which 680,000 were agricultural land, were distributed among smallholders and peasants; a little more than half of the 1·25 million applications for new land were to some extent satisfied. Thus 235,000 applicants who had been landless (or mere tenants) and 404,000 holders of tiny holdings got an average of a little more than one hectare (2½ acres), each, while 40,000 hectares (100,000 acres) were distributed among a total of 3,068 cultivators (the average of 33 acres marked the position of an independent peasant). The privately owned (capitalist) 'residual estates' obtained 180,000 hectares of agricultural and 46,000 hectares of forest land, an average of 250 acres each. An insignificant part of the agricultural land but the bulk of the expropriated forests (more than 1·1 million acres) was retained by the State, which handed over about a fifth of this to the village communities.

(*b*) *Industrial Democracy*

From the Trade Unions' point of view, the main achievement of the revolution was the formal legalization of their status[2] which had already been foreshadowed during the war by the law on industrial service.[3]

[1] E. Wizkemann (op. cit., p. 152) notes that the Sudeten-German foresters of Southern Bohemia and the Böhmerwald, however grudgingly, always admitted that, by becoming masters of their huts and of the plots of land around them, they had been changed from serfs into men by the land reform of the Republic, which achieved what the reforms of Joseph II as well as the 1848 revolution had failed to do.

[2] See above, p. 152.

[3] See above, p. 127.

This enactment, however, might also imply restictions on the right to strike, which, as distinct from 'freedom of association', was *not* granted by Article 159 of the Weimar Constitution. By the German *Arbeitsgemeinschaft* agreement of 15th November 1918 the Trade Unions merely undertook to submit any dispute to the *Arbeitsgemeinschaft* of the industry concerned for discussion before going on strike; in the enactment of that agreement by the decree of 23rd December 1918 all that was provided for was the freedom of the parties to an industrial dispute to nominate an umpire Chairman of the Board of Arbitration, if they found this necessary. But by the Conciliation Order of 30th October 1923 the Chairman became obligatory and a Government nominee, with power to enforce his award against the will of the parties. An award by any of the twenty official mediators, who now formed a regular hierarchy, once it was declared 'binding' by the Government, had the legal force of a collective agreement; the trade union concerned, even if it had disagreed, was not allowed to support its members if they went on strike. Trade union leaders were thus allowed to avoid undesired strikes without shouldering formal responsibility for failure to satisfy the workers' demands.[2] Unofficial strikes thus became a trial of strength between official and unofficial trade unionism, the former being greatly interested in making the strike a failure and in applying suitable measures for this purpose, including appeal to the resources of a sympathetic police, while the Communists had a strong political interest in producing such lucid proofs of the Marxist-Leninist theories on the State and of the reformist bureaucracy. The dispute as to whether the opposition had been right in asserting that some additional pence of wage increase could have been secured if the official trade union representatives had taken a firmer stand in the negotiations, assumed the character of a trial of strength over the question whether the State and the employers' organizations could protect such an accommodating partner against opposition within the camp of labour. The split within the latter became incurable during the economic depression, when enforced 'arbitration' meant enforced lowering of wages and working conditions.[3] This fundamental pitfall was avoided in Austria, where no award could be enforced unless both parties agreed to it; the number of strikes was hardly greater and the position of the unions was preserved much better there than in Germany.

The differences between the attitude of German and Austrian trade unionism were most obvious in the enactments passed in all three Republics to establish what has frequently been called the 'constitutional enterprise', i.e. a legally guaranteed share by workers' representatives in

[1] See above, p. 152.
[2] On the changed position in the last period of the Republic see below, p. 325.
[3] See below, pp. 329–30.

the day-to-day affairs of the shop.[1] With all the authority of a united party and its record of advanced and fairly successful policies, the Austrian Socialists avoided the issue (familiar in Britain also) of shop steward v. Trade Union official; the Law on Works' Councils[2] simply recognized the long-standing trade unionist 'men of confidence'[3] as a legal institution and defined their duties in such a way as to spare them situations in which they would have to enforce on their fellows decisions of which they disapproved. They had to defend 'the economic, social, and educational interests of the employees', who had elected them; thus they could not, like the German Factory Councillors, be prosecuted for what the judiciary might interpret as failure to represent 'the interests of the enterprise'. The elections to the Austrian Works' Councils, unlike those in the two other Republics with their divided labour movements, remained an almost formal affair in that unopposed trade union lists were returned, at least until the last stage when the employers opposed the Free Trade Unions by suitable Heimwehr or Nazi surrogates. To avoid being identified with the employer's standpoint did not involve an attitude opposed to the interests of production. 'The more the employers recognized', wrote Otto Bauer[4] (speaking, it is true, of the revolutionary period), 'that only the influence of the Works' Committees made the restoration of discipline possible, the stronger was the influence which they were obliged to yield to them.'

In Germany the Law of 4th February 1920 regulated the legal status of the Shop Stewards, whose origins went back to the Factory Committees set up under the Law on Auxiliary War Service,[5] and who assumed wide responsibilities during the revolution, when they were recognized by the *Arbeitsgemeinschaft* agreement of 14th November 1918 in all factories with more than fifty employees. The law of 1920, the only enactment by which at least one of the promises made in Article 165 of the Constitution[6] was in part fulfilled, restricted the functions of the Factory Councils in relation not only to the demands of even the more moderate advocates of a 'system of Councils'[7] but also to their actual status. The Social Democratic *Vorwärts*, on 11th January 1920, noticed with satisfaction that in the deliberations of the Parliamentary Committee the functions of the Factory Councils had been greatly restricted in favour of the Trade Unions even in comparison with the original Government draft, which gave them some powers on

[1] In Czechoslovakia the term 'Works' Councils', current in the other republics, was avoided because of its 'Bolshevist' implications, in favour of 'Works' Committees'; but the results in practice were not very different from the German ones.

[2] See above, p. 179.

[3] See above, p. 69.

[4] The Austrian Revolution p. 141.

[5] See above, p. 127.

[6] See above, p. 172.

[7] See above, pp. 189–90.

such issues as strike ballots. The decisive vote, on 20th January, was accompanied by a general strike called by the Berlin Workers' Council and the Independent Socialist and Communist Parties, by a mass-demonstration, and a massacre before the Parliament building. In the law as enacted, the far-reaching ambitions for participation by the workers in the administration of the whole national economy, incapable of realization as they were in the existing relations of strength, were turned into a pretext for restricting the Shop Stewards' actual efforts to represent the employees' interests within the factory as against those of the employer; according to Article 1 of the law, their task of 'safeguarding the common economic[1] interest of employees' was to be combined with that of 'supporting the employer in the efficient conduct of his business'. The fulfilment of the second task might involve not only obvious contradictions to the first (which was the reason why it was enacted) but also support of monopolist combines against their competitors; this caused widespread, though unfulfilled, expectations that the Factory Councils, if not organs of a Works' Community or Corporative State in the Fascist sense, or tools of the employers against the Trade Unions, would at least promote an 'organic conception of society' in the sense of close collaboration of employers and employees within every industry as opposed to others. The right-wing Social Democrats, with their Trade Union backing, would clearly have preferred to have no Factory Councils at all, that is, to maintain a monopoly of the Trade Union bureaucracy as working-class representatives. As they had to compromise with the workers' demands,[2] they countered the left-wing threat to their monopoly by agreeing to a formulation of the law which might find support on the Right, i.e. from people who voted for Factory Councils only because they were expected to divert the workers from any kind of trade unionism and solidarity. After having given the law such a shape, the Trade Union leaders reproached the Councils for a supposed inclination to collaborate with the employers against the Trade Unions and the consumers.

In fact, the antagonism between Trade Unions and Factory Councils proved, in essence, to be an antagonism between right-wing and left-wing trade unionism. In a few cases, especially when the Berlin Committee of Fifteen, which claimed to have the support of 26,000 Works' Councils of the Region, took the initiative in overthrowing the Cuno Government,[3] the Factory Councils developed definite political activities; it is just possible that, with another turn of the German revolution, they might have become starting-points for German Soviets.[4] In any

[1] As distinct from Austria, 'social and educational' activities were not mentioned, evidently in order to avoid a loophole by which political activities might be legalized.

[2] See above, p. 172.

[3] See above, p. 222.

[4] See above, note 2 on p. 222.

case, the Factory Councils were closer to the workers at the bench, and, reflecting the left-wing trends in the German labour movement more accurately than the official Trade Union machinery did,[1] they might favour the replacement within the Trade Unions of professional by industrial organization, which was already much more developed in Germany than in Britain. To prevent the Councils from interfering on these lines with Trade Union organization was one of the main and avowed aims of the official organization of the Councils by the Unions;[2] in 1924, when the Union leaders deemed that events such as the anti-Cuno strike were no longer on the cards, the national office for Works' Councils established by the T.U.C. was abolished.

Of the original drive for workers' control and the later hopes for economic democracy, no more remained in the Law on Works' Councils than some provisions which, if honestly carried out, might have helped a Council to check the correctness of the employer's assertion that some legitimate demand could not be fulfilled because of the position of the business. Instead of direct access to the books, which had been called for by the left wing, the Works' Councils were granted only periodical information about the state of the business, which in practice was given in such a way as to produce whatever impression was desired. The author of the principal monograph on the Councils observes that the Works' Councillor who ventured to ask awkward questions (especially the salaried employee who, because of his special position, was most able to do so), even when he was within his legal rights, was likely to find himself marked down as a dangerous man, to be got rid of at the earliest opportunity.[3] The right of the Councils in works operated by joint-stock companies to nominate two representatives to the Company's Supervisory Council was usually circumvented by the transfer of all important decisions to a Special Committee of the Supervisory Council, from which employees' representatives were excluded. Guillebaud is probably right when he states that the workers obtained just enough of the information due to them according to the Law to realize that anything they were told, or allowed to see, concerning the financial results of the business, was not the whole truth.[3] During the first years, even such restricted rights to information about the business as the Law granted evoked the employers' protests. Later, when this question was settled, all the problems of the Works' Councils turned not on influencing the course of business but on securing, within a framework of complete control of the business by the employers, the best possible working conditions.

Once the general course of German industry was directed towards

[1] See above, pp. 239 ff.

[2] Guillebaud, op. cit., pp. 44 ff.

[3] Ibid., pp. 135, 240.

saving labour by 'rationalization', the statutory right and duty of the Works' Councillors 'by supporting management with advice to co-operate in securing the highest possible degree of working efficiency' (Article 66, 1 of the Law) was only one degree less dangerous from the workers' point of view than that notorious man-trap, the obligation of the Councillors (the representatives of a group whose strongest weapon was the strike) 'to guard the establishment against disturbances' (Article 66, 3). As failure to comply with this duty was the normal reason for obtaining the Court's permission to dismiss a Works' Councillor, a shrewd Councillor who was sure of getting the proper reaction from his fellows might combine fidelity to them with his legal obligations by asking a sufficiently prepared meeting 'to return to work, according to Article 66, paragraph 3 of the Law'.[1] In some cases, the Courts went to the length of constructing a duty of Works' Councillors to support the open shop because Article 66, 6, of the Law obliged them to protect the workers' freedom of combination.[2] The need for clever manœuvring by the Works' Councils in order to combine fulfilment of their main duties with avoidance of dismissal by the Labour Courts (which might be supposed to be hostile at any rate to the left-wing Works' Councillor) produced a field for the development of Communist tactics more elastic and practical than were required from a permanent opposition in Parliament. True, because of the smaller scale, only a long series of blunders in many factories could produce an external impression like that, say, of the participation in the plebiscite against the Prussian coalition Government,[3] but this does not exclude the possibility that in the actual course of events the positions for struggle available in the factories would weigh more heavily than the pretexts for avoiding the struggle which had been gratuitously supplied to the Social Democrats.

At first, a considerable part of the practical activities of the Works' Councils was concerned with wage issues, though their occupation with these problems always aroused suspicion on the part of the Trade Union bureaucracy. In fact, the very large-scale character of collective agreements implied some division of labour between Trade Unions and Works' Councils; the minimum wages fixed for whole industries over enormous areas remained, inevitably, far below the standards of the more advanced undertakings with the best labour organization. In industries as important as Ruhr metallurgy or Berlin engineering general

[1] Information by Mila Schlesinger. Less promising, in a suit before the Labour Court, would have been the argument suggested in the C.P.'s *Handbuch für Betriebsräte* (ed. 1926, pp. 87–8) that the enforcement of an agreement satisfying the workers' legitimate demands was the best means of 'guarding the establishment against disturbances'.

[2] Ibid., p. 113.

[3] See above, p. 283.

reductions of the wage standard by 10 to 20 per cent were quite feasible without direct interference with the regional wage scale; some of the largest industrial conflicts, indeed, developed because of attempts by employers to reduce 'over-scale wages'.[1] The Works' Council, apart from its general task of supervising the execution of the collective agreement within the enterprise, had also to defend, and if possible to increase, the factory's special achievements. After 1924, the Councils' relative strength receded at a quicker pace than that of the Trade Unions; as, eventually, even the latter became unable to defend the safeguards for 'over-scale' earnings, the Councils' practical opportunities were restricted to intervening in everyday disputes (especially over piecework) and other incidentals of factory life. During the Great Depression, their right to protest, in the Labour Courts, against dismissals 'which involved undue hardship (Article 84 of the Law) acquired great importance,[2] mainly as a controversial issue in conditions where the employer would ask the workers' representatives to suggest which dismissals involved the smallest hardships. Not only would right-wing Trade Unionists, against Communist resistance, suggest that women should be dismissed rather than men; if the issue was one of spinsters v. fathers of families, pressure would be brought by the bulk of the workers on Communist Works' Councillors who insisted on regarding themselves as representatives of *all* the workers (a split among whom was clearly to the interest of the employers and of the Nazis) and rejected the theory of the 'lesser evil' in this as well as in the political field. Certainly that theory corresponded to the ambiguous task forced on the workers' representative by a law which demanded that he support the employer 'in the efficient conduct of his business'.

The practical achievements were meagre even in almost uncontroversial concerns; the Nazis (who, it is true, enjoyed the support of the

[1] See below, p. 329.

[2] Earlier, the main disputes over dismissals arose in defence of the Works' Councillors' own immunity (which could be removed only by the Labour Court) and in their right to protest against any dismissal for political reasons. By the Conciliation Order of 30th October 1923, appeals arising from disputes with the Factory Councils were transferred from the Conciliation Boards to the highly legalist Labour Courts, where the burden of proof that the dismissal was not caused by urgent economic reasons (as the employer would assert) lay on the Works' Council. If the latter won the suit, the employer would have to pay a considerable compensation to the dismissed; this might be a deterrent against dismissals involving 'undue personal hardships', but certainly not against dismissals of persons whose removal was regarded as essential for the employers' control of the staff. The Works' Councillors themselves could not be dismissed without the approval of the Labour Court; if the employer had no sufficient case, he had to continue paying their wages as long as they were re-elected (which meant turning them into unofficial Union officers for the factory, whom, however, he could prevent from entering the premises, so that the meetings of the Council had to be held somewhere outside). A high degree of solidarity on the part of the workers was necessary for them to re-elect a Works' Councillor who could no longer assist them over their every day grievances.

employers) were left some scope for practical achievements even in such matters as cleanliness in the factory. But the experiment with the 'constitutional enterprise' contributed greatly to the self-education of men and women of the common people and to the growth of their capacity for leadership. To the present writer (and probably to everyone else who has had experience of the enormous difficulties inevitably met with in overcoming traditional prejudices) the data given by Guillebaud[1] to illustrate the restricted part taken by women in the activities of the Works' Councils would seem not unsatisfactory; there were 22 per cent women amongst the 3,417 Factory Councillors and 'men of confidence' (in smaller undertakings) elected in 374 Berlin works in various industries with a total of 280,000 workers, of whom 40 per cent were women; 12 per cent were women among the 640 councillors elected in 74 works in the Merseburg region with 58,000 workers, nearly 20 per cent of them women.[2] In the Chemnitz textile industry there were 70 per cent women amongst the workers, 63 per cent among the Councillors, and less than 50 per cent among the Chairmen of the Councils; evidently, in the average factory with a female majority a man (which usually meant a skilled worker) was preferred for the chairmanship. It was easier for the working-class organizations to secure the nomination of a certain number of women than to overcome, once the Council was elected, the traditional prejudice of men, and the reluctance of most of the women to assume a position of higher responsibility. A comparison of these figures with the percentage of women among Labour M.P.s in Britain and even on the Continent (including the Weimar Republic) may, however, be helpful as an indication of the place from which any serious training for democracy, as distinct from talk about democracy, has to start.

(*c*) *The Material Conditions of the Working Class*

In all three Republics the most important enactments of social legislation were passed in the first year after the revolution, when the working class had to be granted certain concessions as an alternative to far-reaching social changes. In Austria and Czechoslovakia these concessions were maintained till the end of the democratic régime, but in Germany they were greatly reduced during the winter of 1923–4; in most of the important industries the eight-hour was replaced by a nine-hour day, control of working conditions and of the guarantees given to the workers was largely removed from industrial self-government to the bureaucracy and the judiciary,[3] and the social services were much restricted on the pretext of economy.

During the first post-revolutionary period, monetary inflation in-

[1] Op. cit., p. 130.
[2] Mainly in the chemical industries.
[3] See above, pp. 292–3.

volved the virtual absence of unemployment and strengthened the workers' ability to enforce concessions; but so far as concerned wage standards these concessions were rendered meaningless by even greater increases in prices. Currency stabilization weakened the position of the working classes by increasing unemployment, but in spite of lost strikes and reduced wages those workers who remained in their jobs found their real income enhanced because the purchasing power of money had increased in comparison with the immediate post-war, though not with the pre-war level. In 1924 the average total wage (including over-scale payments) of a fully employed German worker amounted to 32·10 Mk. per week as against 31·05 Mk. in 1913, while the official cost-of-living index was 26 per cent higher. Even at that time, the productivity of labour had increased more than had wages; in the textile industry, where, it might be supposed, revolutionary upheaval was bound to result in an increase of many sub-standard wage-rates, there was a general and continuous reduction of the share of wages in production costs.[1]

During the following period of relative stability there was a continuous increase in wages, up to a peak of 52·91 Mk. in 1929, while the cost of living rose to about 50 per cent above pre-war. Not only was the loss in real wages between 1914 and 1924, which perhaps amounted to about 20 per cent, made good, but even the pre-war level was exceeded by some 10 per cent; during the year 1930, when general wage-scales still remained unaltered, the reduction in over-scale earnings [2]may have been compensated, for those workers who remained in full employment, by decreased cost of living. At that time, the average working hours, for those fully employed, were 10 per cent shorter than before the war, while the average output per working hour had increased by 20 per cent, undoubtedly to some extent at the expense of higher claims on the workers' health and strength. In Austria, where social reaction was kept more in check and the Trade Unions' position in the factories was unimpaired, the productivity of labour in 1925 just exceeded the pre-war figure, while money wages averaged 120 per cent of the pre-war level and the cost of living had arisen by the same amount. Thus in Austria[3] as well as in Germany (where, however, much greater demands were made on the workers' efforts) the pre-war level of real wages was reached in the third year after the stabilization of the currency. In Czechoslovakia workers continued to earn wages which were much below the German and even the Austrian level, but compared favourably with the pre-war level.

A different picture would result if, following J. and M. Kuczynski,[4]

[1] Cf. Seidel, op. cit., p. 62.

[2] See below, p. 329.

[3] B. Kautsky, in *Schriften des Vereins für Socialpolitik* (vols. 176–8), p. 95, and Layton-Rist, as cited p. 210 above, p. 40.

[4] *Die Lage des deutschen Industriearbeiters*, Berlin, 1930, pp. 14 ff.

unemployment and short time, minus public unemployment benefit, are taken into account, as a burden on the whole working class; but such an analysis (in which German pre-war real wages would have been achieved only for a short time) is unrealistic. The average worker who has to support his average unemployed fellow is a mere abstraction: in Germany, the building workers, the woodworkers, some of the miners, and especially the printers were much better off than the average, and textile workers and even some workers in the engineering industries much worse. Regional unemployment of textile workers in the Saxon Vogtland or, across the border, in the Sudeten German territories put no additional burden on the Berlin or Prague building worker (the latter would even be burdened, by Sudeten German nationalist propaganda, with responsibility for the unemployment in the Sudeten lands). Analyses of the position of 'the working class as a whole' miss a point important for the understanding of the events considered in the next chapter, namely the differentiation proceeding in its midst.

The gains made by women during the revolutionary period were largely lost during the political stabilization of the traditional order and of the prejudices involved in it: the wages of German unskilled women textile workers, which in 1924 amounted to 74 per cent of those of unskilled men[1] against 71 per cent in 1913–14, fell again to 70 per cent in 1930. But the wages of unskilled workers, e.g. in engineering (where many jobs formerly reserved for skilled were taken over by unskilled workers) continued to rise; the ratio of their wages to those of their skilled comrades amounted in 1913–14 to 64, in 1924 to 67, in 1925 and 1929 to 75 per cent. The salaries of the black-coated workers were not above the wages earned by the skilled worker; the increase in the salaries of German civil servants, against which the reparations agent, Parker Gilbert, protested on 20th October 1927, brought the *monthly* minimum up to 125 Mk. (£6 5s.) for the beginner, and 175 Mk. (£8 15s.) for the man with sixteen years' service. The security of employment and pension rights might make such jobs still attractive, but black-coated workers in private employment, who lacked that security, were hardly any better off; in 1929 the bulk (46·5 per cent) of the *male* salaried employees earned between 200 and 350 Mk. monthly, 16·8 per cent between 250 and 500 Mk., 3·1 per cent even more, i.e. had an income bringing them close to the middle class; but 18·2 per cent remained under 150 Mk. (the average standard of the *unskilled* worker) and another 15·4 per cent between 150 and 200 Mk. Amongst the women, 54·2 per cent remained

[1] We are here concerned only with the differentiation of incomes within the working class as existing, not with the general issue of women's emancipation, for which the different opportunities of access to the skilled jobs were essential. These differentiations were taken for granted until a recent enactment in the East German Republic, which was followed by large-scale efforts to train women for skilled and managerial jobs.

below 150 Mk., 26·7 per cent earned 150 to 200 Mk., 18 per cent from 200 to 350 Mk., i.e. incomes characteristic of the male skilled factory worker, and a mere 1 per cent earned over 350 Mk.[1]

Mass unemployment was the main threat to the economic position of the Central European worker. Amongst the members of the German Free Trade Unions—which comprised the more skilled portion of the working class, less exposed to unemployment for professional reasons[2] —2·3 per cent had been unemployed before the outbreak of World War I, but the percentage rose to 13·5 in 1924, 18 in 1926, 13·2 in 1929 and 23 in the first depression year, 1930. Apart from this, 15·3 per cent of the Union members worked part-time in 1924, 16 per cent in 1926, and 13·8 per cent in 1930: the total loss in wage-incomes of Trade Union members in 1924, 1926, and 1930 was estimated at 17·1, 22·4, and 26·4 per cent respectively. During the inflation, and also in 1925 and 1927–8, unemployment in Germany was low; but at least during the winters not less than 1½ million workers, 10 per cent of the German working class, were unemployed even in times of comparative prosperity. The Austrian standard was similar: 10 per cent in the best post-inflation year (1924), but 16–20 per cent during the following year, unemployment further increasing until the full impact of the economic depression was felt. Czechoslovakia fared a little better, but as Czechoslovak democracy survived the post-1930 depression it had to face the full weight of unemployment; there were 920,000 (or at least 30 per cent of the working class) unemployed in 1933.

The Central European democracies, restricted to orthodox capitalist ideas of what State interference was permissible in the economic sphere, disposed of small means to deal with unemployment at its source. During the revolutionary period, an Austrian enactment,[3] as a provisional emergency measure, enforced an increase of staffs by 20 per cent; the unemployment benefit formerly paid to the now reinstated workers was paid as a subsidy to the employer.[4] In 1935, at a time when democracy in the neighbour countries and liberal prejudices in the rest of the world had already disappeared, Czechoslovakia restricted the employer's freedom to close down his factory, or to dismiss at once more than 10 per cent of his employees at one time, or more than 40 per cent by instalments; in such cases he had to apply for the permission of the Factory Inspector, or if he intended to close down for more than three months, of the Minister of Labour, who were entitled to refuse

[1] According to the investigation of the GDA (the Centre of the Hirsch-Duncker Unions of Salaried Employees).

[2] Blacklisting because of orthodox Trade Union activities became negligible in the post-war period.

[3] See above, p. 180.

[4] In a different political setting, this device reappeared in Germany in 1932–3. See below, p. 331.

permission if such a course was not justified by the circumstances. In the absence of State supervision of the economy little use could be made of such measures except in cases where the employer depended on the good-will of the authorities, e.g. for public orders. The main advantage the employee obtained was two weeks' notice and a claim for compensation amounting to two, or in the case of salaried employees three weeks' wages (workers who had been employed for more than five years got an additional week's wage for every additional five years of service). Measures of this kind could not substantially influence the decisions of employers on whether to close down. It is interesting to note, however, that while the German and Austrian laws on Factory Councils protected the individual worker against dismissal for political reasons or when it caused social hardship, unless it were rendered necessary by economic depression,[1] the Czechoslovak law dealt only with mass dismissals caused by the depression without interfering with the employer's freedom to dismiss individual workers.

In the absence of effective protection against unemployment, the benefit paid to the unemployed from public funds became a political issue of central importance.[2] With the shift of political power to the bourgeois parties there was an increasing readiness in the labour camp to preserve the controlling influence of its representatives, to prevent the introduction of means tests, etc. even at the price of the workers' having to shoulder part of the burden, as was inevitable if State benefits were to be replaced by some form of obligatory insurance. The German Law of 7th December 1927 secured for 16·5 million employees (agricultural workers only being excepted) obligatory insurance against unemployment for twenty-six weeks, in case of necessity to be prolonged (as was accepted at the beginning of the Great Depression) up to a maximum of thirty-nine weeks. After that period, those who were still unemployed were supported by 'depression benefit' out of public funds, under a means test. Before its reduction by Brüning's reforms, the benefit varied from 6 Mk. weekly for the lowest income group with a weekly income of less than 10 Mk. to 22·05 Mk. for those whose former earnings were more than 60 Mk.; the average unskilled worker with a wage of some 60 Pfenning per hour might expect 10·80 Mk., the average skilled worker with 48 Mk. weekly about 17·85 Mk. unemployment benefit. Such amounts were above the destitution level, but far below what the employers feared as 'an incentive not to work'. The administration of the insurance was in the hands of equal numbers of employers' and employees' representatives. Employer and employee made equal contributions to the costs; 3 (after 1929[3] 3½) per cent of the worker's wage for each side.

[1] See above, p. 293 and note [2].
[2] See below, pp. 326–7.
[3] See below, p. 327.

In Czechoslovakia, disputes of the German type were avoided by the 'Ghent system' of unemployment benefit, which, in 1925, replaced benefit out of public funds; without interfering with the administration of trade union benefits except by a general system of supervision, the State granted every trade union which insured its members against unemployment under a prescribed scheme, a subsidy of twice or thrice as much as the members themselves contributed. Trade unions were thus stabilized in their hold on their membership; employers, as distinct from Germany, were excused any share in the costs of unemployment benefit; the State, finally, escaped responsibility for an unpopular branch of administration while it increased its influence on trade unionism and its power to bring strong pressure to bear even on radical opposition parties by the threat of dissolving Trade Unions in sympathy with them.

Under the Ghent system as it actually operated, the unemployed trade unionist received about two-thirds of his former wage, but the unorganized, the bulk of the agricultural workers (whose organization was prevented by every means by the Agrarian party which controlled administration) amongst them, were reduced to a rate of benefit near the destitution level and paid under a very stiff means test; Communist-controlled municipalities which treated their unemployed better than the Agrarian-controlled Ministry of the Interior thought proper, risked interference with their autonomy.[1]

To some extent, the differences in the conditions of the working classes were bridged, and some common interest in the working of democracy created, by what have frequently been called 'social wages', i.e. services provided by the community for the citizen (with a special view to working-class needs) irrespective of his capacity to pay for them out of his income, but without any 'charity' approach. The price charged for, say, the use of public baths can be fixed so low as just to prevent misuse but not to exclude anyone, even the long-term unemployed; and the costs can be raised by municipal taxation which will be exposed to little serious criticism[2] so long as the field in which public services are provided is of a generally recognized social importance.

New difficulties arise if, in a capitalist country,[3] the method is applied

[1] See above, p. 279.

[2] As distinct from expressions of blind partisan hatred (cf. the statements on Vienna's municipal services quoted in my *Federalism in Central and Eastern Europe*, London, 1945), p. 279, which, however, are hardly important for the actual working of a democracy; they are relevant only as agencies in its destruction.

[3] In a socialist economy where, in the absence of unemployment, differentiation in the satisfaction of personal needs is regarded as a main incentive to efficient work, other problems arise. The argument that, if services were offered at very low prices, the customer had little reason to make his patronage dependent on quality, was used when the Soviet theatres were made almost self-supporting by an increase in prices (cf. my *Spirit of Post-War Russia*, London, 1947, p. 50). In matters such as houses and places in rest-homes such a policy would not do without discriminating even against the considerably above-average worker in a lower grade and in favour of the

in order to supply one of the essential needs of the population which has traditionally been provided by private enterprise, perhaps with a long tail of vested interests (as is the case with large-scale building of houses for letting, financed by mortgages, as is usual on the Continent). If the publicly-built houses are let at lower rents than a private entrepreneur would charge, there must be careful selection among the applicants, the opposition of the entrepreneurs who miss their profits may be strengthened by that of taxpayers who have to pay part of the costs which the beneficiaries of the service could not meet without being among the selected ones. The obtaining of a stable majority in favour of municipal housing (and without a *stable* majority it would obviously be impossible) depends on isolating the first and obviously unappeasable group of opponents from the second. Existing tenants must be convinced that, even if they have no chance of getting one of the new flats, Tenant Protection, i.e. their own continuing to pay very moderate rents, depends on the possibility of avoiding recurrence to the private entrepreneurs' concepts of 'reasonable rents' by the use of alternative methods of satisfying the need for new dwellings. In this respect a comparison of the experiences in the three Republics (and in Austria also of the parts under Socialist and those under non-Socialist administration) is highly interesting.

In all three Republics, the monetary inflation had reduced rents to a nominal level; this increased the capacity of the national industry to compete in world markets, but destroyed the incentive for private capitalists to build new houses, or even to keep the existing ones in repair, and this was aggravated by building costs having strongly increased even in gold. In Germany the issue was further complicated by the desire to restore at least part of their savings to investors which had been lost in the monetary inflation;[1] that part of the pre-war rents which covered the service of the mortgages had to be restored, at least in part, apart from that portion which everywhere had to be restored to the house-owner in order to make it worth-while for him to administer and repair existing houses. But without a rent-level of 180 to 200 per cent of the pre-war standard there could be no private house-building for profit; and only middle-class people and, in Germany at least, an aristocracy of the skilled workers could afford to pay such rents in order to get a flat with modern amenities. The bulk of the working class was confined to the out-of-date, and increasingly overcrowded, pre-war

average, or even under-average worker or salaried employee in a higher grade; therefore the policy has been to keep prices comparatively low, but to transfer most of the housing to the enterprises which can discriminate according not only to the applicant's personal needs, but also to his merits as a worker, and can penalize him if he leaves his job.

[1] In Austria, this question was decided in the negative; in Czechoslovakia the inflation had been more moderate.

buildings which were bound to decay and could not be replaced on capitalist lines at any rent which the masses could afford without fundamental changes in the level of wages.

In theory, there were five possible solutions to this problem. Firstly, the rent-level might be left to the play of the free market, houses being built for a well-to-do minority, and the majority of the town-dwellers being reduced to slum conditions. Secondly, new house-building by private entrepreneurs might be subsidized by the community on condition that rents were kept at a tolerable level, rents for existing houses being restored only so far as would cover current repairs plus whatever income was regarded as desirable for mortgagors and house-owners, whether it was a sufficient incentive to private house-building or not. Thirdly, the municipalities might themselves build with borrowed capital, the subsidy being granted by letting the dwellings below production cost. Fourthly, the municipality could build the new houses *à fonds perdu*, raising the costs by taxation. Lastly, a combination of this method with the municipalization of existing houses would have made possible a reduction of the rents payable for these houses to the cost of repair plus a contribution by the tenants to the cost of house-building (provided that the compensation paid to former house-owners was nominal, as it might easily have been under conditions of monetary inflation).

Of these five methods, the first (which was fairly sure to open up the alternative between revolutionary upheavals and large all-round wage-increases with detrimental effects on the capacity of the national industries to compete on world markets), and the last, which involved an open and avowed interference with existing property rights, were ruled out by the balance of power that existed in all three Republics; the others were tried in different variations. Czechoslovakia and the Austrian Provinces other than Vienna restricted their interference with the capitalist method of catering for housing needs to protecting existing tenants by Rent Restriction Acts and subsidizing private capitalist building on certain conditions, or supplementing it by public building, the costs of which were raised by borrowing. The Austrian Rent Restriction Act, as distinct from its supplementation by public house-building, was a federal matter; its repeal, continually demanded by the bourgeois parties, was prevented by Socialist obstruction, and its amendment in 1929 allowed the house-owner, but not the mortgagor, a small profit over and above the cost of current repairs. Thus an Austrian province which, for political reasons, did not follow Vienna's example of municipal house-building was forced upon the second of the methods above mentioned. The same result was achieved in Czechoslovakia quite deliberately; in 1926 the bourgeois bloc began the gradual abolition of the Rent Restriction Act (which by the end of the Republic, protected only the poorest people with no more than one room for a family); on the other hand, individual or co-operative enterprise in building small flats was subsidized up to 85 per cent of the cost, on condition that the rents were kept within certain limits. In this way 41,650 houses with a total of 124,035 dwellings were built, i.e. the housing needs of about one-tenth of the urban population were satisfied; the State itself built only a very restricted number of houses for civil servants and the like.

In Germany, the idea of new house-building without public outlay was allowed to prevail over that of low rents, State interference mainly taking the form of redistributing rents. The federal Rent Law of 1922 created a position similar to that which was to be brought about in Austria by the compromise of 1929; rents for pre-war buildings were restricted to the 35 to 40 per cent of the pre-war level (in gold) necessary to cover the cost of repairs, etc. But, during that winter of reaction, 1923–4, the Third Emergency Decree on Finance contemplated the restoration of the pre-war rents not later than 1st April 1926; the subsequent legislation of the bourgeois bloc Governments, in opposition to the demands of the States and the municipalities, increased minimum rents to 110 per cent of the pre-war level by April, and 120 per cent by October 1927. Even this would not have made private house-building an economic proposition; a large part of the rents of old houses[1] was taxed away in order to subsidize the rents to be paid for new flats (mainly by cheap mortgages for private builders). Policies varied as to the distribution of the subsidies. The Berlin municipality, at the cost of a long waiting list, granted comparably high mortgages on a restricted number of buildings so as to achieve moderate rents (20 to 30 per cent over the post-war, i.e. 50 per cent over the pre-war rent of a comparable flat built before the war). Prussia granted many but low mortgages, with the result that the cost of a subsidized house was not very much below that of a flat offered on the free market independently of the waiting list, the cost being about three to four times that of a comparable pre-war flat. Many private builders, indeed, preferred building without cheap mortgages but with freedom to charge an 'economic rent' and without being bound to the priority list; during the Great Depression, when the black-

[1] In Prussia (cf. *Schriften des Vereins für Sozialpolitik*, vol. 177/I, p. 238) of the 120 per cent of the pre-war rent which the tenant had to pay, 20·5 per cent was destined for interest on old capital and mortgages; 48 per cent constituted the House Rent Tax, out of the proceeds of which the State subsidized new building; the rest went to the landlord, who had to account only for a third of that amount, devoted to current repairs. The key position of the Economic Party, which represented the urban lower middle classes (see above, p. 259), in German coalition policies had made the compromise very favourable to the landlords; *qua* administrators of their property (i.e. if the devaluation of existing capital concerned their mortgagors more than themselves, as was the rule) the landlords were better off than before the war, when, according to the explanations of the Berlin House Owners' Association, a mere 5 per cent of the rent had been regarded as compensation for the houseowner's activities, and 8 per cent had been needed for depreciation, and to cover the no longer existent risk of having vacant flats on his hands (*op. cit.*, vol. 177/III, p. 221).

coated and the upper stratum of the skilled workers could no longer afford to pay excessive rents, most of these landlords went bankrupt. As early as 1932 a practically uncontrolled housing market was achieved, but even in this, the richest of the three Central European countries, it was mainly by the destruction of 'illusionary' aspirations for a comfortable home.

Vienna's municipal housing policy, the classical example of the fourth of the five methods mentioned, was marked precisely by the desire to present the satisfaction of housing needs in the order of priority established by the 'normal' mechanism of a capitalist society, and by the consideration that low rents were necessary from the social as well as from the general economic point of view: there was neither any obstacle to nor bias against the private building of more luxurious homes, and indeed the Vienna municipality was rather glad not to have to cater for a demand of that kind. The Rent Restriction Law and the low level of wages forbade private building for mass consumption, and thus forced municipal building even upon those provinces of Austria which paid their tribute to capitalist orthodoxy by raising the costs in the money market (in the outcome, rents in these Provinces were three to ten times as high as those paid for comparable flats in Vienna). The specific conditions in Vienna favoured the approach of its Socialist municipality; even before the war it was usual to tax the housing expenditure of the masses (to a much higher extent than in the post-war period, and then not for housing but for general budgetary purposes); many types of business were concentrated in Vienna, including the banks and insurance companies which were still reaping enormous profits from their assets in the non-Austrian parts of the former Hapsburg monarchy. The decision to keep rents, and thereby the wages costs of Vienna's export industries, low and to let part of the bill for replacing the existing houses be born by general taxation of all businesses, might be looked upon as an essential step in adapting Austria's economy to the new conditions. This fact explains why Vienna's municipal housing policy, though opposed by all the current arguments of capitalist orthodoxy, could be carried as far as it was; but it also explains its eventual failure, and the failure of Austrian democracy in general; those very financial interests which represented the main obstacle to the adaptation of Austria's economy to the new conditions were the most powerful of the conservative forces in the country which enjoyed the strongest support from outside and actually controlled the Catholic party. There was nothing specifically socialistic in Vienna's policies; from the Marxist point of view, which was at least the official line of Austrian Social Democracy, house-building would seem a rather strange starting-point for the nationalization of production. 'Municipal socialism' was in issue only in the desire to make the municipally-built flats as impressive an argument as possible for the superiority of communal over private enterprise. The choice of housing as the field in which that superiority was to be proved was dictated by the tendency of Austrian Social Democracy to improve workers' conditions just where it could be done without interfering with the foundations of capitalist economics, and, indeed, in the well-understood interest of the more productive sections of Austrian capitalist enterprise. For this very reason Vienna's municipal flats have become a symbol; those who defended as well as those who attacked them—first by ordinary political means, later with heavy guns—realized that what was at stake was not some specialist experiment, but the worker's claim that his welfare should be regarded as more important than any obsolete vested interest.

The tenants' contribution to the cost of Vienna's municipal housing was represented by the special Building Tax, which in 1929 raised 33·4 million schillings, just a third of what the Catholic municipality had raised in 1913 by taxes on rent and surtaxes on State taxation of rent. The impost was a progressive one: 41·64 per cent of its proceeds were raised from the most expensive one-half per cent of the flats. Small dwellings, which in pre-war days had cost about 360 crowns (600 schillings) per annum, 40 per cent of this representing indirect taxation, after the war, apart from the 15 per cent of the pre-war value due to the house-owner for repairs and so on (until 1929) paid a mere 14·4 schillings as municipal housing tax; their total cost was thus about half that of the new flats, which were rather smaller, but more comfortable; one of 48 to 70 square yards in area would cost 16 to 20 schillings per month. In 1928, the share of housing in the average working-class family's expenditure (i.e. the combined average of the costs of old and new dwellings) amounted to 3·4 per cent, a fourth of the pre-war level;[1] the most expensive of the newly-built municipal flats cost three times as much. In 1929 the total expenditure on building amounted to 91·35 million schillings, only a third of which was covered by the municipal housing tax; the rest of the cost was raised, apart from minor taxes on luxuries, by the welfare duty on the wages and salaries of all Viennese enterprises. A total of 60,000 flats were built, i.e. accommodation for nearly an eighth of Vienna's population; this does not compare unfavourably with the proportions achieved by different methods in Czechoslovakia and Prussia.

The economic problems of Vienna's housing policies were political in origin; instead of being replaced by new agencies, the existing interest of High Finance in rent from houses had to be appeased. In order to keep the waiting list within reasonable limits and to reduce the difference in rent between old and new houses to what was justified by the different quality of the accommodation, the municipal Housing Tax would have had to be increased; if it had been possible, say, to double the small amount which the Viennese in 1929 had to pay to cover both rent and

[1] B. Kautsky (as cited above, note [3] on p. 295), p. 80.

municipal Housing Tax, this would have been sufficient to increase the annual rate of building by 50 per cent, and also to restore some balance to the market for flats, at prices not quite half the pre-war level. But the essential condition for this, of course, would have been that all the additional payments of the population remained at the disposal of the municipal housing agency. In 1929, under political pressure which went even to the length of threatening civil war,[1] Social Democracy had to agree to amendments of the Rent Restriction Law which provided for gradual increases in the amount due to the landlord up to 30 per cent of the pre-war rent in Vienna and 35 per cent in the Provinces; hence an increase of the municipal Housing Tax to provide for an increase in the rate of building was impossible without overburdening the tenants. As a counter-concession the Federal Government offered subsidies for house building in Vienna; this was no remedy for the growing waiting-list for municipal flats, as the right-wing Government expended its resources in supporting private builders, mainly of luxury houses, with an average subsidy of 75,000 schillings per building.[2] Within the given political framework, Vienna's municipal building policies had outrun their course; it is quite possible that the defeat of 1934 itself spared Austrian democracy this last disappointment.

(*d*) *The Aims: Functional Democracy*

The practical achievements of the Central European revolutions were modest; some of them, such as the Czechoslovak land reform, and Vienna's municipal housing policies, were obviously the result of local circumstances. Over the whole area, the achievements consisted essentially in recognition of the position of the trade unions—with important exceptions, particularly for the agricultural labourers—a certain status for the Shop Stewards in the decision of the everyday issues of factory life, and the creation of some opportunities for municipal reform policies (restricted by State supervision). From the standpoint of the everyday activities of the labour movement—those very activities which, according to the Revisionists' tenet, should have been 'everything'—this was quite a lot as long as the actual conditions of life were tolerable. When, in the Great Depression, conditions ceased to be tolerable, the test was to be made of the assertion that a movement could survive for which 'the final aim was nothing'[3], i.e. which had no prospect to offer except a glorification of existing conditions.

This statement may seem hard: after all, the Socialist parties at least had some general idea of the new society which would eventually grow out of the multitude of partial reforms. Aside from the classical Marxist

[1] See below, pp. 317. ff

[2] Cf. Bunzel, in *Schriften*, etc., pp. 134 ff.

[3] See above, p. 91.

programme, the defence of which, except perhaps in Austria, became a privilege of the Communists, the question is only whether such formulation of these ideas as was possible in the circumstances differed in any way from a glorification of the social and political *status quo*.

During the last years of the war, when the breakdown of the *ancien régime* was already manifest, and in the first revolutionary period, Rathenau, the founder of the AEG combine, and the most far-sighted politician that the German bourgeoisie has ever produced, worked out in a number of writings[1] the concept which later became popular under the name of a 'managerial society'. Being himself a manager with a big-business background and not a disappointed Trotskyist, he took the measure of the society to come, not by an egalitarian utopia, but by its prospects of offering equality of opportunity, of improving the standard of living of the masses and developing the resources of production. He was quite prepared to face the transfer of the property titles of large-scale enterprise to the State, but preferably by the radical taxation of inheritance, and the disappearance of the rentier class. In his writings of the revolutionary period, however, when disappointment outweighed hope, he deplored the inevitable doom of all the variety and individual choice implied in the cultural life of a bourgeois society. His organizational concepts of self-government by those engaged in diverse economic and cultural activities, under the supervision of a centralized State, came closer to the later ideas of the corporative State than to those of socialism; we should remember, however, that in the contemporary writings of the advocates of 'socialization'[2] the border-line between Socialism and all the conceivable concepts of a corporative order were left to say the least, very vague.

Stampfer later described the 1919 tendencies towards 'socialization' as having been, in fact, 'a struggle by the State to enlarge its sphere of influence within a privately-owned economy'.[3] This description is definitely incorrect, however 'socialization' is interpreted. The workers defined it as 'democracy in the factories with unified control of the whole industry, the replacement of capital as the dominant factor by the personalities who do the work';[4] the Majority Socialists, as Stampfer explains[5], objected to nationalization because it might result in sequestration of the nationalized enterprises by the Allies on account of repara-

[1] His *Nachgelassene Schriften* have been published (Berlin, 1928). Kessler's biography (English ed., London, 1929) has an evident bias in favour of the more conservative element in Rathenau's thought.

[2] The term 'nationalization' was avoided for fear of association with bureaucratic State management. See below, p. 307.

[3] Op. cit., p. 133.

[4] Minority Vote of the Independent Socialist members (Kautsky, Hilferding, and Lederer) of the Socialization Commission of 1919, *Report on the Socialization of Coal Mines*, p. 35).

[5] Op. cit., p. 130.

tions. Such tactical arguments were hardly more than a pretext for dropping a slogan which might be an obstacle to coalition policies; the Görlitz Programme of the (Majority) Social Democratic Party, 1921, looked to eventual nationalization of the land[1] with all its minerals, etc. as well as of water power, but called for more public supervision of capitalist enterprises, especially those controlled by monopolies. The only practical outcome of the 'socialization' campaign was the formation of mixed boards of employers and employees, the former together with the representatives of the consumer industries being in the majority, to administer the compulsory syndicates for coal and potash. In the practical working of these boards, the social divisions were not so important as those between producers and consumers; owners' and miners' representatives showed some propensity to vote together for high coal prices as against the coal merchants; in the Potash Board, where bread prices might be involved, there were instances of the miners' representatives supporting the representatives of agriculture against the mine-owners' demand for high prices.[2]

For the theoretical concepts of 'socialization' as distinct from the (negligible) practical outcome, Otto Bauer's *Way to Socialism*, published in 1919, may be regarded as fairly typical. All the emphasis is laid on the rejection of State management, which is denounced as inefficient and bureaucratic;[3] in his contemporary work, *Bolshevism and Social Democracy*,[4] Bauer stated that proletarian ideals had changed because of the very evolution of capitalism; while Marx confronted the anarchy of Manchester liberalism with the concept of socialism as economic planning by a democratic State, the bureaucratic autocracy of State capitalism, as developed under a war economy, should be answered by the Socialist principle of industrial self-government, i.e. by a systematic extension of democracy from the political to the economic sphere. Bauer was quite conscious that he was transferring the ideas of British Guild Socialism to Central Europe;[5] to the critic it is obvious that the

[1] The obvious non-topicality of this suggestion rules out any interpretation of the programmatic statement as a tactical restriction to such demands as were advisable under the reparations régime; the whole tendency of the Görlitz programme is to explain the outlook of Social Democracy in a way acceptable to partners in a coalition.

[2] Naphtali, op. cit., p. 46. The incident mentioned in the Potash Board of 1925 was followed the next year by the acceptance of a Government-sponsored compromise against the votes of the agriculturists, both mine-owners and miners supporting the proposal.

[3] P. 11 in the edition of 1921.

[4] Pp. 98–9.

[5] In *The Way to Socialism*, pp. 30 ff., the identity of Bauer's suggestions with those made in the Webbs' Constitution for a Socialist Commonwealth is emphasized. The Boards administering the socialized enterprises are seen as composed of one-third each of representatives of the employees, of consumers, and of the State, the last functioning as mediator between the opposed interests of the employees and the

democratic power to be extended according to his proposals was that of the organizations established by the workers and peasants in order to represent their sectional interests within a capitalist society for whose direction they were not responsible. The selection of the enterprises for immediate 'socialization' (Coal, Iron, Steel, Hydro-electric Power) was not self-effacing as with the German Majority Socialists,[1] but was not intended to cover even the key-positions of Austrian industry.[2] Besides, in a practical framework dominated by political compromise there would be only moderate differences between the 'socialized enterprises', whose boards would be formed by representatives of employees, State, and consumers, and other combines subject to mere supervision by mixed Boards, on which entrepreneurs too would be represented, and share in the distribution of profits; in a society with a still powerful private capitalist sector, public opinion would presumably see that many former entrepreneurs would be appointed as managers of 'socialized' enterprises, and that the compensation paid would be on an appropriate level. While vague on the issue of ownership, on which he laid all his emphasis, Bauer failed to foresee that, within ten years from the day when his book was written, 'organized capitalism' would produce such a degree of economic anarchy that the sympathies enjoyed by the Bolsheviks (even among the Austrian Socialist workers) would be based on the very rigidity of their planning, whatever bureaucratic traits it might include, and that the real alternative would lie not between State planning and liberal 'industrial self-government' but between planning by the State and planning by private monopolies.

When things had reached this point, Social Democracy had to make its choice. With a view to the approaching new coalition Government, which was to be the last in the history of the Weimar Republic, the Hamburg Congress of German Trade Unions in 1928 issued the slogan of Economic Democracy as a supposedly attractive battle-cry to replace 'socialization', which was compromised by the promises of 1918–19. The Trade Unions needed new ideological foundations for their activities;[3] such formulations should be neither unpopular with entrepreneurs, whose elimination had been the original purpose of 'socialization', nor too utopian in comparison with German reality. Economic Democracy was found both in the progress 'from individualistic capitalism of free competition to organized capitalism',[4] and in the increasing influ-

consumers as regards the price level. Bauer conspicuously overlooked the possibility that the State, as distinct from the engineering workers, the 'consumers of steel', might have interests in the output and price of steel over and above that of finding a proper compromise between their interests and those of the steel workers.

[1] See f.n. [1], p. 307.
[2] See above, p. 180.
[3] Cf. Herzig, op. cit., pp. 15 ff.
[4] Naphtali, op. cit., pp. 10–12.

ence of the State, both as direct owner of industrial property and as exercising influence on the private monopolies which 'organized' capitalism. In Naphtali's pamphlet, which represented the official explanation of the slogan on behalf of the T.U.C., the progress of rationalization, for example in the coalfields under the control of the mixed Coal Syndicate, and the growing interconnexions between the monopolies and the State, whose democratic character was evidently taken for granted, were described as characteristic of Economic Democracy. To-day, it is hardly necessary to put forward elaborate arguments in favour of what in those days was described by Naphtali and his friends as a Communist calumny, namely that many developments which they regarded as growing Economic Democracy were, in fact, elements of growing Fascism, of the transformation of the State into an instrument to organize production on behalf of monopoly capitalism.

In 1931–2, under Governments which were at least tolerated by Social Democracy and the Trade Unions, first in Austria, and later in Germany, all the economic key positions—the big Banks, and the Steel Trust—in consequence of the Great Depression actually came under State ownership. Nothing like Economic Democracy emerged; all that the State cared for was to restore these key positions to private ownership as soon as possible and at the cost of enormous sacrifice by the public. In his speech in the parliamentary debate on State aid for the Kreditanstalt, on 14th May 1931,[1] Otto Bauer, by far the best mind in the ranks of Central European Social Democracy, found it tragic that the State had to make a gift of hundreds of millions to private monopolists who happened to be in a key position for the employment of the Austrian workers; but he had nothing to offer except criticism of the details of the business from the Exchequer's and the taxpayers' point of view. Within the framework of such an argument, Juch, the Catholic who replied to Bauer, was quite right in claiming that the present made to the foreign shareholders was necessary in order to avoid the impression that investment in Austria was risky, and that international confidence in the Kreditanstalt could not be expected if it were known that a majority of its shares were State-owned (as Bauer had suggested they should be in order to get at least some value for the subsidies paid). There was, indeed, no way out of the dilemma short of freeing the capitalists—domestic and foreign—from the responsibility for investment. Otto Bauer had not dared to do it in 1919, when there was a possible political alternative to capitalist reconstruction;[2] he could not be expected to do it in 1931, when conditions were hopeless.

It was not the absence of clear economic prospects which destroyed Central European democracy; there have been many revolutions in history which found their path by trial and error. What was lacking was

[1] See below, p. 322.
[2] See above, p. 180.

any definite approach to the problem of political power. When in 1926, on the eve of the Fascist offensive, Austrian Social Democracy adopted the Linz Programme, it solemnly proclaimed that even if a temporary proletarian dictatorship should become necessary in the course of resistance to a bourgeois insurrection against parliamentary democracy, it would immediately give way to the latter as the normal condition of social progress (this might not have been the best method of discouraging the prospective sponsors of Fascist *coups d'état*). During the crisis of 1918–19 a certain set of conceptions as to the structure of the armed forces of the new democracies was fairly widespread within the moderate left-wing; they were accepted as a platform by the First Congress of the German Workers' and Soldiers' Councils[1] and in Austria they were actually realized.[2] The Austrian experience to which we turn in the next chapter shows that such a distribution of real power was incompatible with the restoration of a régime controlled by a High Finance; but the Austrian record studied in the first section of Chapter Six shows that it was perfectly compatible with bourgeois democracy carrying out a programme of moderate social reform. For the outcome, it did not so much matter whether the Central European democrats had a radical programme or by what name they would describe the régime they would have been forced to establish in the course of a consistent struggle for the defence of democracy as they understood it; what mattered was whether they were prepared to fight and, at every stage of the struggle, to take such measures as the emergency commanded. The experience of action was the only test of their capacity to produce something more democratic than the Russian régime of which even Rosa Luxemburg disapproved; but failure to act was surely the safest way to produce the very opposite of democracy.

Otto Bauer described Austria during the 1919–22 period as a People's Republic in the sense that neither class was strong enough to dominate the other, and therefore all classes had to share in political power; functional democracy, the pressure of the mass organizations of the workers and peasants, limited and corrected parliamentary democracy with its implication of majority rule.[3] Bauer's 'functional democracy' was the sectional interests as developed within capitalist society writ large, plus some delusions as to who it was he had to meet at the negotiating table;[4] he further confused the issue by adding that such equilibrium as was implied in functional democracy could not long continue, because each class aimed at replacing it by its own rule, as the bourgeoisie eventually did in Austria.[5] In fact, there never was such a

[1] See above, p. 157.

[2] See above, p. 175.

[3] *The Austrian Revolution*, German ed. (1923), p. 245. The decisive passages are not translated in the English edition.

[4] See above, p. 179.

[5] See f.n. [3], above.

thing as 'functional democracy' in the relations *between bourgeoisie and workers*, as control of Austrian economic life was never divided between the two classes; what actually happened was the replacement of a more civilized and organized way of settling differences between employers and employees within the capitalist frame-work, which had been forced upon the Austrian employers during the revolution, by a revival of the old aspirations of the masters as soon as they felt strong enough.[1] In the relations *between the workers and the peasants* there was only a moderate amount of functional democracy: these two groups used their powerful sectional organizations to wage with each other a struggle for food surpluses, and the peasants never managed to relieve themselves of bourgeois control as embodied in the Christian Social Party with its Vienna-dominated hierarchy. No inherent reason ruled out a more than ephemeral equilibrium between workers and peasants once the basic issues of social organization were solved. But they had to be solved by a showdown; the basic shortcoming of all those ideas about 'socialization', 'functional democracy', etc. was precisely that they gave birth to delusions about the possibility of avoiding a political decision.

[1] In his speech in Parliament after the events of 15th July 1927 (see below, pp. 314-5) Bauer put the question clearly enough; the great cleavage, he said, between his party and that of Seipel was on how to deal with spontaneous outbreaks of mass indignation. Bauer deemed that they had to be canalized into peaceful demonstrations; Seipel regarded them as an opportunity to make an example which would crush the workers' aspirations.

CHAPTER NINE

THE CATASTROPHE

(a) The First Fascist Offensive in Austria

At this point of our investigation, we must leave Czechoslovakia except for an occasional side glance. Perhaps because of the association of Fascist reaction in Germany and Austria with the traditional enemies of the Czech people, Czechoslovak democracy survived till it was destroyed by foreign intervention. This intervention found support among the Agrarians and in the bureaucracy they dominated, but it would be out of all proportion to analyze the germs of the authoritarian régime developed after Munich at the command of the Fascist and the Western Powers on the same level as those developments out of which Central European Fascism was born.

In Austria, with her well-developed two-party system, the transition from a parliamentary democracy to a bourgeois régime operating under extra-parliamentary pressure began very early, and so the dividing line drawn in the second section of Chapter Six may appear artificial. The interlude between the establishment of some degree of political equilibrium after the stabilization crisis and its shattering by a new right-wing offensive did not last longer than the two years—from autumn 1924 to autumn 1926—during which period the Government of the Provincial Christian Socials, under Ramek[1] was in office. The foundations of the new crisis were laid as early as the crisis of franc speculation[2] when the financial combines of the inflation period—in Austria the Castiglioni and Bosel, as in Germany the Stinnes—broke down, and leadership was restored to the solid banks of the old Empire that had weathered the storm.

In spring 1926 the Zentralbank der Sparkassen, the financial centre of the co-operative organizations linked with the Christian Social Party, especially of those in the Provinces, collapsed under the belated effects of the franc speculation crisis. Sieghard, the chief manager of the

[1] See above, p. 212.
[2] See above, p. 210.

Bodenkreditanstalt, was prepared to intervene on condition that Seipel, his closest political friend,[1] reassumed the direction of the party and the Government. This came about on 20th October 1926. Perhaps because he was afraid of an election struggle in which the bourgeois parties would reproach each other with the various financial scandals, but certainly at the special demand of the employers' organizations,[2] Seipel decided not to use the coming general election as an opportunity to absorb the German National Party,[3] but to accept it as a joint partner in an 'anti-Marxist bloc'.

The election struggle was fought with the appropriate 'anti-Marxist' means. Semi-military formations of former army officers, with ample subsidies from industry,[4] still survived in the eastern parts of the Republic from the days of the planned intervention against Soviet Hungary.[5] Though negligible in a general conflict with the working-class forces, an organization such as the Frontkämpferbund[6] was strong enough to provoke incidents with far-reaching implications; which was precisely why it was financed. On 30th January 1927, at an election meeting, groups of Frontkämpfer attacked Social Democratic workers in Schattendorf, Burgenland, and killed three of them. Strikes and protest demonstrations in Vienna followed; with some effort the Social Democratic leaders succeeded in keeping the movements to a demand for the punishment of the murderers by the courts. The unofficial provocation was soon followed by an official one; on March 2nd Seipel suddenly occupied the Vienna Arsenal to confiscate the arms which—with the knowledge and agreement of all the post-revolutionary Governments—had been kept there, under control of the Social Democratic Defence Corps, in case of a Hungarian-Hapsburg *coup* on the 1921 pattern.[7] There followed a few hours of crisis during which an armed conflict seemed imminent; as the Social Democrats were more interested in avoiding electoral demagogy than in keeping the arms, the con-

[1] And, by the way, the one among the Christian Social leaders whose personal integrity was beyond doubt. But this argument was overplayed at the time.

[2] In a speech made in spring 1927 at an employers' meeting Seipel enumerated the Industrialists' Association, the Chamber of Commerce, and the Tradesmen's League as the sources in contact with which 'the idea of a united front in the coming elections was born'.

[3] See above, p. 211.

[4] Julius Deutsch, op. cit., vol. II, p. 261, reports that in 1923 some Jewish members of the Industrialists' Association became afraid lest their contributions should be used to subsidize Nazis; they were satisfied by the President's statement that not the Nazi party *as such* but only 'para-party' right-wing associations such as Frontkämpfer and Heimwehren had a claim to subsidies.

[5] See above, p. 185.

[6] Its strength was estimated at 2,500 men in Vienna, 1,500 in Lower Austria, 1,000 in the Burgenland (where it continued the tradition of the Hungarian lands, see above, p. 205); but it was a very mobile organization, unlike the Heimwehren, who were hardly usable outside their own village.

[7] See above, p. 205.

flict was settled by a joint declaration which stated the facts, after which the arms were transferred to Government custody.

After all these incidents, the elections of April 1927 brought Social Democracy an enormous success; with 42·3 per cent of the total vote, it exceeded even the maximum of 1919, 40·8 per cent. In Vienna it polled 693,000 votes against 423,000 for the united bourgeois parties, and in the Provincial towns and villages with over 2,000 inhabitants 425,000 against 391,000, though in the smaller villages it received only 420,000 votes to 1,168,000. Even in the bourgeois camp the League of Agriculturists, which, unlike the official German Nationals, had contested the election with independent lists, fared so well that it was needed for the formation of the new Government; the permanent opposition status of the Social Democrats was already guaranteed by the programme on which the contest had been fought. It was, however, a powerful opposition, and Seipel's effort would have failed had he not found the means to break it. Riehl, the leader of the Austrian Nazis, in a speech of July 4th described the results of the general election as a Jewish challenge, for which the Jews should be punished. On the same day the Heimwehr leader, Steidle, speaking at Wels, talked of the 'veiled Red dictatorship' existing in Austria; if the Viennese Parliament could not take proper measures, the Provincial Governments should act in its stead; if necessary, arms would have to be used.

On July 5th the trial of the murderers of Schattendorf began, evoking the widest public interest. They were defended by Dr. Riehl, whose acquaintance we have just made, and the auditory was properly prepared; the trial was accompanied by provocative demonstrations of Frontkämpfer in Vienna working-class quarters. On the evening of the 14th, the jury returned a verdict of acquittal; Seipel, explaining this verdict later in Parliament, said that honest members of the public did not get the impression that men like the Schattendorf Frontkämpfer, even though they had resisted their opponents, were murderers. On the same evening the Vienna electricity workers demanded that the Socialist Party headquarters should give orders as to what should be done; Otto Bauer later described it as his biggest mistake that he had not directed the natural indignation of the masses into the outlet of an organized demonstration. The absence of any radical concepts on his side is sufficiently indicated by his reasons for this omission; the demonstration would have assumed the character of a manifestation against the institution of juries, and thus would have fitted in with Seipel's plans.

Thus spontaneity took its course. The electricity workers insisted on a short protest strike, combined with a street demonstration, and other workers followed their example. The police attacked, and the first four demonstrators were killed,[1] while the Social Democrat leaders attempted

[1] The Social Democrats' complete surprise at the behaviour of the police is indicated by the fact that shortly before Julius Deutsch had asked for increased, but

to calm the workers, and thus indeed enabled the police who were involved in the fighting to retreat to safety. The Government decided on a trial of strength; Schober moved masses of police, carrying heavy firearms and inspired by all kinds of atrocity stories, into action, while new masses of workers moved into the city centre. In a few hours 100 persons were killed, and the Ministry of Justice, which the masses treated as the symbol of a hated system, was in flames. The Social Democratic leaders now proclaimed a one-day general strike, which actually meant only the proper organization of the action already in full swing, and a strike of the railwaymen which was to continue until an investigation of the causes of the massacre was granted. The evident intention was to force Seipel to enter a new coalition Government; as late as July 23rd the Central Committee demanded and obtained from a national Party Conference full powers to take the necessary decisions. The Government replied to the railway strike by letting the stations in the Alpine Provinces be occupied by *Heimwehren*; in the given conditions of strength only in the Tyrol did the measure assume a threatening character, and even there only a small minority of the railwaymen offered their services as strike-breakers. But a real trial of strength was the last thing the Social Democrats desired; even if it were successful, it might destroy their last hopes of agreement with at least some sections of the Catholic party. On July 18th it was decided to call off the railway strike unconditionally.

In a sober analysis, the events of July 1927 were one incident like many others in the history of the Austrian labour movement which could not fundamentally affect the relations of strength. An extreme provocation had produced one of the familiar outbreaks of spontaneity by the Austrian workers;[1] the right-wing Government had used the opportunity to show what fighting forces it had available in case of civil war, and Social Democracy could not call the bluff because the last thing it wanted was a civil war, even if it were to be victorious. But the position of Social Democracy rested to a large extent on its extra-parliamentary means of pressure; once it was shown that these would not be

inoffensive, police patrols, as the Social Democrat Defence Corps could not be mobilized quickly enough to keep order at the demonstration (cf. Geyde, *Fallen Bastions*, p. 30). The police chief Skubl, who ordered the attack, eventually reached high office under Schuschnigg, and even higher under the Nazi régime.

[1] Both aspects of the situation were evident even to the bourgeois Press until the myth of the victorious side (which also dominated most English publications on the subject) had had time to establish itself. The *Neue Freie Presse* on the morning of July 15th described the jury's verdict as 'most controversial'; the Conservative Berlin *Kreuzzeitung*, as late as July 23rd, regarded the events—which it evidently did not regard as a defeat of the workers—as an argument *against Anschluss*: Austria and Prussia, the paper said, could not be included within one political unit without destroying the essence of the latter and even risking turning the *Reichswehr* into a Red army.

used to the limit to enforce punishment for those responsible for a massacre in the streets of Vienna, it was not likely that they would be used to defend the right of combination of the soldiers, or even that of the workers of the heavy iron industries in Styria; this demonstration was precisely what Seipel and the men who had ordered him to form his 'anti-Marxist bloc' needed. On some pretext the bodies of the Soldiers' 'men of confidence' which had been re-elected in the preceding October were dissolved; in the new elections the percentage of votes cast for the Social Democratic Soldiers' Union fell from 75 to 60. Not even this figure was very satisfactory for a Government waging a civil war against Social Democracy. Much less favourable for the latter was the result of the elections to the representative bodies of the police in Vienna and Graz, which were dissolved immediately after July 15th; a combination of mass-dismissals of Social Democratic policemen with public expressions of gratitude to the 'heroes of July 15th' produced secure right-wing majorities (in the elections of 1st March 1927, 4,000 of the 5,500 Vienna policemen had voted for the Socialist Union). In the Provinces, industrial employers, especially the managers of the Alpine Montan Company, the heavy iron industry of Styria, now controlled by the German Steel Trust, put direct pressure on the workers to make them join the Heimwehren,[1] into which bodies such as the Frontkämpfer were integrated (the description was chosen in deference to the right-wing peasant tradition;[2] actually, the peasant element in the Heimwehren was numerous but was not remarkable for its initiative and fighting strength). The reliability of the industrial element mobilized by the employers was open to question;[3] as late as 1929 the elections to the Work's Councils of the Alpine Montan Company brought the Heimwehr 'trade unions' a 55 per cent majority in the Donawitz, but minorities, sometimes insignificant, in the other works. The employers, of course, used the position of the yellow Trade Union as an occasion to conclude the appropriate 'collective agreement' and thus to get back the money they had invested in the Heimwehren.[4] The total strength of the Austrian Free Trade Unions, which was 756,000 at the end of 1926, 772,000 at the end of 1927, and 766,000 in 1928, had dropped only

[1] Cf. Steeruwitz, op. cit., p. 230. Steeruwitz, who was the industrialists' representative on the Christian Social caucus, and later (see below, p. 318) became Prime Minister, is a most competent source on these matters, as his right-wing bias is incontestable; he wrote under the Dollfuss régime, and therefore had no need to be afraid of saying honestly who had organized the Heimwehren.

[2] See above, p. 202.

[3] Deutsch, op. cit., vol. II, p. 238 ff. calculates that nearly half the members of the Free Trade Unions still existing in the works of the Alpine Montan Company must have been doubly organized, paying their contributions to the Free Union in secret, and allowing their contributions to the yellow Trade Union to be withheld from their wages.

[4] See f.n. [1], above.

slightly at the end of 1929; the following years (in which the Great Depression had already begun) saw an annual loss of 60,000–75,000 members until by the end of 1932 the strength was only 520,000.

Austrian Social Democracy's answer to the reactionary offensive was a cautious one. At its October congress in 1927 it rejected the suggestions of a 'right wing' under Renner who, even at the risk of an internal split, demanded a coalition policy on the German pattern even in situations when nothing more could be achieved than to prevent the majority from using its power in excessive, fascist ways;[1] this implied acquiescence in, and even support of, the use of this power for ordinary bourgeois reaction. On the other hand, its answer to the Heimwehr threat and to Seipel's provocations was restricted to the propagandist field,[2] and so further trials of strength were avoided. On 7th October 1928 Seipel and Vaugoin deemed conditions ripe for a showdown;[3] Heimwehren from all over Austria were ordered to demonstrate at Wiener Neustadt, a notoriously working-class centre. The Social Democrats called a counter-demonstration in the expectation that the Government would prohibit both; but Seipel mobilized the Army, which now took up a position between the demonstrations, of which that of the workers was naturally the stronger, so as to demonstrate its 'authoritarian' attitude. It was not further tested, as both sides were afraid to launch a civil war. On 14th February 1929 Schober, acting on Seipel's orders, began a provocative search for weapons in Social Democratic headquarters; this time the Trade Union leaders suggested assembling the workers before the Party building and risking a test of strength before it was too late from the standpoint of the workers' fighting strength in the factories. The majority of the Central Committee rejected the suggestion, and restricted itself to an indirect answer, namely parliamentary obstruction to the amendments to the Rent Restrictions Law in which the bourgeois parties were interested. On April 3rd, indeed, Seipel resigned 'in order to relieve the internal tensions'; by this he meant the parliamentary obstruction as well as the propaganda for leaving the Church,[4] which had raised doubts in his ecclesiastical

[1] Proceedings of the Congress, p. 147.

[2] Some part amongst them was played by the suggestion that those Party members who had no religious convictions but were still formally Catholics (as many Austrian workers were) should leave the Church in protest against Seipel's 'no mercy' statement in the parliamentary debate on the events of July 15th. The numerical results of the campaign were not very considerable; the number of resignations from the Church, which before had averaged between 8,000 and 9,000 per annum, rose in 1927 to 28,000 and in 1928 to 31,000, to fall gradually thereafter. But as a warning to the Church authorities it was certainly effective (see below in text) so long as the Church had not means of repression at its disposal. After 1931 Fascist policies far more outspoken than those of Seipel were solemnly supported by Church authorities much higher than an individual prelate (see my *Federalism*, etc. pp. 288 and 290).

[3] See f.n. [1], p. 316.

[4] See f.n. [2], above.

superiors as to the advisability of directly linking the authority of a leading Churchman with the launching of the civil war. For this was the next item on the order of the day for Seipel and, we may suppose, his industrial and ecclesiastical advisers; he informed his successor, Steeruwitz,[1] that he 'expected from me (Steeruwitz), as an old army officer and industrial leader, the application of the energy which he possessed in sufficient degree but, being a priest, for obvious reasons could not easily put in motion'.

After a short interlude, during which the Christian Socials, in exchange for Seipel's replacement by Steeruwitz, got their compromise on the Rent Restriction Law, the Heimwehren offensive was reopened, in the Upper Styrian strongholds of the Alpine Montan Company. But meanwhile the Social Democrat workers' will to resistance had been strengthened. An attack by heavily armed Heimwehren on a meeting of workers at Sankt Lorenzen resulted in roughly equal losses on both sides; this time even the justice of the Austrian Republic realized that complete silence was the only means to save those who had begun it. By an extreme effort the Social Democratic leaders prevented a general strike being proclaimed and diverted the general indignation into the channel of reinforcement of the League for the Defence of the Republic, one of whose main functions, at that time, was the prevention of 'undisciplined', i.e. spontaneous, action by the workers. The leaders of the Heimwehren—which in practice meant Seipel—now announced for September 29th four big demonstrations at places round Vienna, which might start off a 'march on Vienna' to enforce a revision of the Constitution in the Fascist direction. The Social Democrats answered with external caution[2] but proclaimed that armed resistance would be offered to a *coup d'état*. When Steeruwitz, to Seipel's great disappointment,[3] declared that he would defend the public authority against all comers, he came under the wildest personal attacks from Major Pabst,[4] who since 1927 had found a congenial field of activity as military adviser to the Heimwehren, as well as from the League of Industrialists.[5]

[1] Cf. his op. cit., p. 413. From the standpoint of 1934 he (ibid., p. 227) draws up the balance sheet of his disagreements with Seipel; Seipel had been right in expecting an international development towards fascism in which Austria should play her part, but he had been mistaken when demanding from Steeruwitz, in 1929, military pressure against Social Democracy; this would have resulted in a civil war in which the right wing, as distinct from what eventually happened in 1934, would have had no chance.

[2] They went to the length of calling their counter-demonstrations against the Fascist threat for the preceding day.

[3] See f.n. [1], above.

[4] See above, p. 163.

[5] Steeruwitz (op. cit., p. 412) declares that he expected that a movement so completely dependent on the Industrialists as the Heimwehren would be kept under control by them. Accordingly he informed Urban, the Chairman of the Industrialists, of the preparations for a *coup d'état*, which, in Steeruwitz's opinion, had almost no

Though he was still supported by a majority of the Christian Social Parliamentary Party,[1] Steeruwitz was threatened by the Heimwehren that unless he resigned the demonstrations of 29th September (the mere announcement of which had caused large-scale withdrawals from the banks) would not pass without incident. On the 25th Pabst got Seipel's promise that, before the day had passed, Steeruwitz would be removed; by the resignation of his German National friends Seipel, as so often before,[2] could easily overthrow a Government. The new Cabinet was ready; Schober became its non-political head and Vaugoin, Seipel's special man of confidence, his deputy.

It was a Pyrrhic victory; on 6th October, a week before the first crisis on the New York Stock Exchange, Sieghard's Bodenkreditanstalt broke down, to a large extent as the effect of the withdrawals of deposits which had been provoked by Sieghard's and Seipel's dalliance with civil war. It was absorbed by Rothschild's Kreditanstalt, to whose eventual breakdown the operation contributed, and which of all the Austrian banks was the one which had the strongest Western connexions and the least interest in political adventures.[3] Schober, who may have been playing a double game from the very moment when he assumed office,[4] introduced far-reaching constitutional amendments in the 'authoritarian' if not in the Fascist sense, but sat down at the negotiating table after the Social Democrats (without whose agreement no constitutional amendment was possible) in a series of special national conferences of the Trade Unions and of the League for the Defence of the Republic had

military chances of success, but the very attempt at which was bound to result in a financial breakdown of Austrian business; he added that he would resist a *coup*, however reluctantly. This letter of the Prime Minister was sufficient to range the League of Industrialists among the forces aiming at his fall.

[1] Apart from the long-standing differences between the Provincial Catholics and Vienna High Finance, some tension even within the Vienna Christian Social organizations had arisen from the attempt of the Heimwehren, or to speak more precisely, their industrial backers, to repress even the Christian Trade Unions, and also because of the part played in at least the Viennese Heimwehr organization by ordinary criminals. Cf. Kunschak's speech on 14th October 1929, made in opposition to a speech by Seipel's supporter Vaugoin, delivered at the same Party meeting, which was evidently carried by Kunschak.

[2] See above, pp. 204 and 208.

[3] In his Memoirs (p. 410) Steeruwitz, together with the catastrophe of the Bodenkreditanstalt, mentions foreign warnings, as expressed in *The Times*, October 6th, and the *Daily Telegraph*, October 11th, as reasons for the peaceful settlement of the constitutional crisis.

[4] This was suggested in an article signed 'Spectator Noricus' published in the *Volkswohl*, the Christian Social periodical, January 1931, under the heading 'Fro Seipel to Schober' (see below, p. 321), which originated if not from Seipel himse from his immediate circle. Schober's unfaithfulness was described as the more worthy of reproach as in July 1927 he had been saved only by Seipel from the consequences of his action (see above, p. 315) which thus appears to have been not quite so much within the scope of the law as Seipel publicly asserted.

declared that they would reply to a *coup d'état* by a general strike and civil war. After having demonstrated their will to resistance against the original draft, the Social Democrats were evidently interested in letting their partners have *some* constitutional amendment which would strengthen the advocates of negotiation in the bourgeois camp; they remained firm on all points where Vienna's authority was involved, but made concessions as regards the widening of the powers of the Government, including 'emergency' legislation, which, however, was not quite up to the German standard, as the agreement of a special parliamentary committee was required for such measures.

The 1929 amendments to the Constitution were of little importance to the coming crisis of Austrian democracy; the important point was that, in an issue where Social Democracy was under no constitutional obligation to give way, it supported amendments which it looked upon and openly described as harmful, in order to avoid a trial of strength. This was done under conditions where victory would probably have resulted in a split in the adversary's ranks and in opportunities for coalition with the more moderate elements in the bourgeois camp. The onset of the World economic depression, which was fully commented on in the Austrian political statements of those days, at first weakened the position of the only serious supporters of the reactionary forces in that it made a *coup d'état* a synonym of their suicide;[1] it was not used by Social Democracy to assume responsibility. It was not even used to force on the bourgeois parties a formal renunciation of their more long-term projects; they described the concessions made by the Social Democrats as a mere first instalment, and voted for their far-reaching, near-Fascist amendments, which thus received a simple majority, but not the two-thirds majority demanded by the Constitution. Their contribution to the compromise consisted merely in the declaration that they would not react to this partial parliamentary defeat by civil war.

They had, however, promised their supporters a civil war lest the Social Democrats should capitulate completely; 'these beasts must be shown the scourge', to quote the phrase used by the Heimwehr leader Steidle during the demonstration of September 29th. The mere fact of compromise was sufficient to produce a crisis within the Heimwehren. At the Korneuburg meeting of their Lower Austrian organization, on 10th May 1930, they openly mutinied against the Christian Social Party caucus, denouncing 'Western democratic parliamentarism' and the 'parties' State'; all present were invited to take an oath of obedience to the Heimwehren command against any other authority, including that of their parties; the Christian Social M.P.s present, Rintelen,[2] foremost among them, did not hesitate to take this oath. Schober now expelled Pabst as an undesirable alien. The Heimwehren replied with a rebellion

[1] See f.n. [5], p. 318.
[2] See above, p. 185, and below, p. 345.

of the more or less declared Nazis, under Starhemberg and Fey, against the 'compromisers' such as Steidle who had based themselves too much upon Fascist Italy, and accepted the Korneuburg resolution as their national platform. Seipel used the opportunity to replace Schober's Cabinet by another of the 'strong hand' under his friend Vaugoin;[1] the Heimwehr leaders of all factions took part, Starhemberg, who took the Ministry of the Interior, joined the Government against Hitler's advice; but in any case he appreciated the Führer's suggestions sufficiently to reject Seipel's proposal to enter the elections as part of a renewed anti-Marxist bloc. Schober took his revenge by using the Strafella scandal[1] as an opportunity to rally the more sober elements of the bourgeoisie in a special bloc, with emphasis on the pan-German appeal; in the general elections of 9th November 1930 he obtained a vote slightly higher than that of the German Nationals in the 1923 elections, the last in which they had taken an independent stand.

Austria had a three-party system once more; if the Heimwehren, who got 227,000 votes, were included, there were even four parties.[2] In an

[1] The way in which the change was made was characteristic of Austrian conditions. Seipel foresaw the next attack to be made against the Railwaymen's Trade Union and wished for the nomination, as General Manager, of a certain Strafella, who as Deputy-Mayor of Graz had become popular among local right-wingers for his energetic treatment of the tramway workers. Unhappily, he also had a non-political record, the description of which in the Social Democratic Press as corrupt had been accepted as justified by the judge in a libel suit. In these circumstances the President of the Austrian Federal Railways, Banhans, a conservative bureaucrat with old-fashioned ideas of political honesty, refused Strafella's nomination, at least until he had been cleared by the Court of Appeal, and was supported by Schober. Now Vaugoin declared that Banhans' views on political morals were clearly connected with his propensity to negotiate with trade unionists on friendly terms, and the Christian Social ministers resigned.

[2] The November general election of 1930 was the last in pre-Nazi Austria. Additional information on the trend of opinion in Austria under conditions of free election can be gained from the local elections which took place on 24th April 1932 in Vienna and some of the Provinces. In Vienna and Lower Austria the Social Democrats practically preserved their 1930 position, with slight losses to the Communists, who, however, did not surpass the status of an almost uninfluential sect; the Christian Socials suffered heavy losses to the Nazis in Vienna, but none in Lower Austria, where they had suffered their Heimwehren split in 1930. In Carinthia Social Democrats as well as Christian Socials made some slight progress; the Nazi successes were entirely due to the absorption of the German Nationals and the Heimwehren. In Salzburg both the major parties suffered minor losses to the Nazis' benefit; the same happened one year later (at the time of the complete Nazi triumph in Germany) in the municipal elections at Innsbruck. Heimwehren and German Nationals were virtually absorbed by the Nazis all over Austria as early as 1932.

A tentative estimate of the strength of the Austrian parties in 1932—practically at the end of the democratic republic—would give some 1·4 million voters for the Social Democrats, 1·2 million for the Christian Socials, 0·8 million for the Nazis, of which a mere 150,000 can have come from the two major parties, apart from the supply of 200,000 Heimwehr votes by the Christian Socials in the preceding year. The extreme political stability both of the labour movement and of political Catholicism is thus election campaign which had been carried on under open threat of civil war made by members of the Government, Social Democracy had held its own; losses, especially in Upper Styria, though that involved its working-class support, were almost compensated by gains elsewhere, especially in Vienna and Carinthia (as the Viennese workers had long since voted Socialist, these successes seemed to indicate progress among the lower middle class). Seipel's party, at whose expense the Schober bloc as well as the Heimwehren had scored their gains, was the actual loser, forming with 1·3 million votes the second party after the Social Democrats, whose 1·5 million nearly equalled their strength in 1927. The bankruptcy of Seipel's policy was now evident; his initiative, taken jointly with the Heimwehr leaders, to restore the anti-Marxist bloc failed, and the new Government was formed by Ender, a moderate Catholic, with Schober as Foreign Minister. A renewed internal crisis of the Heimwehren followed their political defeat.[1]

Like other Governments representing the moderate wing of the Austrian bourgeoisie, that of Ender-Schober depended on Social Democratic support. This was willingly given, not only for fear of the Seipel-Starhemberg alternative; in March 1931 Schober concluded his agreement with Curtius on an Austro-German Customs Union; and this approach to *Anschluss* was greatly applauded by the Social Democrats. Early in 1927 Otto Bauer had explained that the Social Democrat demand for *Anschluss* would not be realized by Hindenburg's Germany; now Hindenburg and Brüning had evidently been promoted to the status of potential coalition partners. The attempt broke down when French financiers reacted to the Customs Union agreement by withdrawing their credits from Austria; May 11th saw the bankruptcy of the Kreditanstalt, which, since 1929, had been the monopolist financing organization of Austrian industry; Social Democracy had to support enormous gifts made from the public purse to the shareholders to preserve the confidence of the foreign investors.[2] The Customs Union was buried when Austria had to apply for renewed League of Nations sup-

illustrated once more; the latter's losses concern the specifically 'anti-Marxist' element of Seipel's policy. The post-war elections in Austria show a similar structure, with the Communist vote increased to 200,000.

[1] Some information as to its background was eventually gained from these internal disputes. At a Press conference on 28th January 1931 Steidle explained that the name of Starhemberg 'had attracted a number of juvenile forces' but sympathy, 'especially in economic circles', was lost by his policy, particularly by the Heimwehren's operating as a separate group distinct from the old-standing bourgeois parties. Starhemberg answered the following day with the statement that Steidle, Fey, and their Lower Austrian friends had pressed him to enter the Government, but that he had made a very difficult stand against their urge to reply to the election defeat with a hopeless *coup de état*.

[2] See above, p. 309.

port and so to accept renewed League of Nations control; and the Social Democrats accepted even the appropriate deflationary measures.

An opportunity to end at least the open and avowed Fascist threat came when, on September 13th, the Starhemberg-Pfriemer wing of the Heimwehren, driven more by internal competition than by any appreciation of political realities, started an insurrection. In order to avoid a conflict with the Government, Social Democracy left to it all the initiative in liquidating the *coup*, and restricted itself to a dissolution of those, but only those, Heimwehr formations which had shared in it, a demand which Schober accepted. Under purely demonstrative pressure by the Army the Putschists withdrew with their arms, and their leaders were arrested for a few days; then Seipel intervened to settle the intra-Heimwehr dispute. Starhemberg, who was immediately discharged, in agreement with Steidle resumed the leadership and broke with the official Nazis. Word came from the Austrian representative at Geneva that energetic measures against the Heimwehren would weaken Italian and French support for Austria's demands, and the whole matter was silently dropped.

(*b*) *The Fall of Democracy in Germany and Austria*

In this chapter we have devoted our attention first to Austria because the anti-democratic reaction in that country grew up long before the Great Depression, and because it is clearly impossible to explain its early stages, including the growth of the local variety of Fascism, by a split in the labour movement or by any specifically Prussian phenomena. As the *ancien régime* in Austria was completely disorganized by the fall of the monarchy, the counter-revolutionary forces had to be reconstructed; but as soon as this had been done, they resumed an offensive which, with short interruptions, came to an end only in February 1934. In Germany, where much more of the *ancien régime* had been incorporated into the firm positions of the right wing, there had been a definite recoil from the extreme tensions of 1923 as soon as parliamentary rule by the bourgeois bloc was secured.[1] It was put in question once more when the elections of 1928 returned a left-centre majority; what had been little more than hypothetical speculations by more or less responsible outsiders[2] and systematic attempts within the

[1] There was an almost uninterrupted chain of conspiracies, especially in connexion with the political crisis caused by the initiative on the expropriation of the Princes: some developed fairly close to Hindenburg's personal circle (cf. the material reproduced in Merker, op. cit., pp. 123–5, and O. Braun, op. cit., pp. 195 ff.). But the importance of these incidents in the whole development of German reaction (and in comparison with what preceded as well as what followed) was certainly no more than, if subsequent events had had a different outcome, would have made them incidents in the consolidation of a bourgeois Republic. They had much less importance than comparable incidents in France after 1871.

[2] See above, pp. 265–6.

framework of the constitution to increase the powers of the President as the mouthpiece of the Army and Big Business, now became a definite attempt to break up that framework.

The outcome of the elections of 1928 marked the opening of the crisis of the Weimar Republic in a twofold sense. In the two principal bourgeois parties, the reply to the election defeat was a triumph of the extreme right wing within the Party caucus: Hugenberg conquered the German National Party and Kaas became leader of the Centre. The second event supplied Hindenburg's Army clique with a tool for establishing its dictatorship without driving the Catholic part of the population into opposition, as other Prussian dictators had done; the first gave rise to the formation of moderate Conservative blocs of Agrarian and Christian Trade Unionist representatives.[1] This aroused in Hindenburg and his circle (to which Treviranus, a leader of these groups, belonged) the delusion that a conservative rally was possible without adventures into the field of foreign policies, such as Hugenberg demanded. Within Social Democracy, the realization that the appearances of power were due to the favour of Hindenburg produced a determination to exercise that 'power' in such a way as to win the confidence of Germany's real masters and to establish a precedent such that the left-wing Governments would no longer thereafter be regarded as a disturbance of the 'normal' German state of affairs. Such a resolve, which could easily have been foreseen in view of the antecedents of German Social Democracy and was proclaimed frankly enough on the eve of its electoral triumph,[2] invited its opponents to allow it to destroy itself by purchasing a short term of office with a refutation of all the arguments on which it had based its propagandist appeal.

A beginning was made with the pacifist slogan. Immediately before its mandate ended, the bourgeois bloc government had decided to begin building of the later famous 'pocket battleships'; this decision, in itself of secondary importance in comparison with what happened in other fields of German rearmament, had formed a main point in the left wing's election propaganda. As soon as the left-centre Government under the Social Democrat Müller had taken office, it was ordered by Hindenburg and the Generals to carry out the decision envisaged by its predecessor. The Social Democrat Ministers had no objection, but the Party caucus got into great internal difficulties and the Communists made the most of the Social Democrats' betrayal of their election promises. So it was decided to make a virtue of necessity, and to enlighten their Party members on the merits of German rearmament from the standpoint of a democratic foreign policy. The Magdeburg Congress of May 1929 accepted a platform on these lines without meeting with resistance on the point of principle except from minor groups. A stronger opposition

[1] See above, p. 255.

[2] See above, pp. 285 and 308.

was formed on the motion that, in future, Ministers should consult the caucus before taking decisions important in view of the Party's general appeal; this was defeated by 199 votes to 167. The margin was narrow, but noteworthy in that the statement of principles once commonplace in the Party[1] was now reserved to a minority which never again obtained anything approaching a similar strength. Its most consistent representatives were eventually driven out of the Social Democratic party, and formed an opposition group which at a later date played some part in underground work against Hitler, and later still in the formation of the Socialist Unity Party in Eastern Germany. But its electoral appeal proved no greater than that of other splinter groups in the German labour movement.

The next pitfall involved the very substance of Social Democratic policy, namely the theory of 'political wages', according to which participation in the Government meant the use of the Government's power in the interest of the legitimate claims of the Trade Unions. When the collective agreement of the Ruhr metal workers was to be renewed in September 1928, the Union demanded a wage increase of 15 Pfennig an hour, while the employers refused any increase. The Public Mediator decreed a compromise, an increase of two Pfennig an hour for the piece-workers, who formed 90 per cent of the total labour force, and 6 Pfennig for the others. Both parties to the dispute voted against the award, but in accordance with the established procedure[2] the Minister of Labour, a Social Democrat, declared it legally binding. The Trade Union gave way, but the employers proclaimed a lock-out, and the Government refused to interfere; eventually it withdrew the Arbitration award which it had itself declared binding and ordered a new mediation which was more favourable to the employers. 'In full consciousness of the political implications of its decision', i.e. in order to save the Government coalition, the Delegates' Conference of the Metal Workers' Union, by a two-thirds majority, accepted the decision on 2nd December and work was resumed. On December 21st, when the Christmas holidays made a strike movement unlikely, the new mediator, Severing, issued his award; the pieceworkers received no increase at all, a small minority of the time workers a very small one. The legal issues raised by the employers' successful resistance were left to the Supreme Labour Court, which, by its decision of 22nd January 1929, reversed the former practice; henceforth no arbitration award could be declared binding unless it had been supported by a majority of the Arbitration Commission, that is, apart from the Mediator, either by the employers or by the union concerned. This meant that, in the coming days of wage reductions, the unions, unless they were prepared to fight, had to vote for the wage reduction suggested by the Mediator lest he should support the

[1] See above, p. 115.
[2] See above, p. 288.

full demands of the employers because of 'the public interest in industrial peace'.

The lock-out of the 200,000 Ruhr metal workers had contributed to a renewed increase of tension within the labour movement; the Social Democratic Trade Union leaders had resisted by every means the suggestions of the Communists to support the unorganized workers involved in the lock-out to meet the employers' refusal to accept the award by solidarity strikes in other industries. The next contribution to bringing these tensions to the breaking-point was made by the initiative of the Prussian Social Democratic ministers. In Berlin a Police order prohibiting public demonstrations had been in force for some time because of some minor incidents with the Fascists; Zörgiebel, the Social Democrat chief of the Berlin Police, refused to lift it for the traditional demonstration on May Day 1929, and in spite of some protests from the Berlin Social Democratic organization, he was supported by the Prussian Minister of the Interior, Severing.[1] It was obvious that the Communists would use the opportunity to demonstrate that they were the only upholders of the traditions of the labour movement; evidently the Social Democrat Ministers considered that this price must be paid in order to indicate to their bourgeois coalition partners their own readiness not to be bound by those traditions.[2] But even this was not enough. Zörgiebel felt that he would not have sufficiently fulfilled his task if he, like his predecessors under the Hohenzollern régime, kept the holders of the illegal demonstration on the move and let them satisfy themselves by having the banned outdoor meeting replaced by some cheers and songs in opposition to the police prohibition; his police attacked the points of assembly in the working-class suburbs. In two areas barricades were raised, at first only in order to impede the attacking police, but later they were defended; street-fighting continued for three days and claimed thirty-three victims, most of them innocent passers-by. A Communist attempt to call a protest strike failed, but the incident definitely gave the Communists ascendancy amongst the workers of the capital, and strengthened the position in the Communist caucus of those who thought that any attack against the bourgeoisie would have first to meet the 'social fascists' as its main defenders.[3]

The last attacks, which eventually broke the position of Hermann Müller's cabinet, began on the issue of unemployment benefit. As early as the summer of 1929 the bourgeois partners in the coalition called for its reduction, and especially the exclusion of many seasonal workers, in order to restore both the financial equilibrium of the public Unemploy-

[1] It may be remarked that Zörgiebel and Severing (see also above, pp. 194–5) shared with Noske the questionable honour of having their pensions continued under the Hitler régime.

[2] See above, p. 324.

[3] See below, pp. 377–8.

ment Insurance scheme and a proper degree of pressure on the labour market. The compromise left the benefits unaltered, but increased both workers' and employers' contributions from 3 to 3½ per cent of wages; on the bourgeois side it had a narrow passage. On October 3rd, during his last illness, Stresemann intervened with his party to preserve the coalition; a Government crisis at that moment would interfere with the progress of the Hague Conference on the Young Plan. On Hindenburg's orders and jointly with Big Business representatives, Schleicher, Treviranus, and Brüning were already preparing a new Government; they agreed, however, that the Social Democrats should not be dropped until after they had shouldered the responsibility for signing the Young Plan, which had just provided a main object for Nationalist demagogy.[1] On December 25th Brüning was ordered by Schleicher to make preparations for the new Government which was to take office immediately after the Young Plan was signed.[2]

On December 5th Schacht, the chief representative of Germany at the Hague Conference, had already protested against the Young Plan as well as against the Government's financial policies which were alleged to contradict the preliminary conditions of its fulfilment; as President of the National Bank he called for so deflationist a step as the immediate repayment of 450 million of public debt. The Finance Minister, Hilferding, resigned as a protest against Schacht's assuming control of the budget, but the rest of the Cabinet gave way; on 20th January 1930 the Young Plan was signed. At once the Government had to face another demand by its partners in the coalition for a reduction of Unemployment Benefit to balance the budget. The Social Democratic leaders tried to save the coalition, but the T.U.C. and a large majority of the parliamentary party refused to submit; on March 26th the last Cabinet of the German Republic to derive its authority from the votes of the electorate resigned, and Brüning's Cabinet took office. It was intended as another bourgeois bloc, including the German Nationals; but the majority of these proved to be controlled by Hugenberg; he refused to support Brüning, who had included in his Cabinet representatives of the German National opposition such as Schiele and Treviranus. Brüning now had his financial programme proclaimed by Hindenburg, under the emergency Article 48 of the Constitution, which from now on was used as a substitute for ordinary legislation.

The Social Democrats and Communists demanded the withdrawal of the emergency decrees, and Hugenberg declared that he would not support Brüning unless the latter included his own party and the Nazis in the Reich Government and enforced the formation of a similar Government in Prussia. Brüning, as he remained in a small minority, got from Hindenberg a dissolution and full powers to govern with the aid of the

[1] See above, p. 282.

[2] Merker, op. cit., p. 177.

emergency article. He may have regarded these merely as transitional measures pending the formation of a parliamentary Government of the moderate right; but the elections of 14th September 1930 brought a breakdown, not only for Hugenberg, but also for the Conservative opposition[1] and for the German People's Party, which lost 900,000 votes. On the left, the Communists won 1·3 million votes, 571,000 of them from the Social Democrats; but the Nazis, who increased from 0·8 to 6·6 million, had absorbed the bulk of the losses of the old bourgeois parties, including that of their ally Hugenberg, as well as a majority of the new voters.

With this election, any possibility of a parliamentary majority, short of a coalition between the moderate right as represented by Brüning and Social Democracy, had definitely come to an end; and the later shifts in the electorate in favour of the Nazis and the Communists ruled out even this possibility. But Brüning had been installed by the Hindenburg clique precisely in order to exclude the Social Democrats, still the strongest party, from the Government; afraid of an alliance between Brüning and the extreme right, the Social Democrats now allowed him to govern by emergency decrees, voting against the demands for the repeal of those decrees moved by the opposition parties. They thus shared in the responsibilities of government without having any share in its decisions; Brüning openly declared that he was responsible to Hindenburg, and to no one else. He was duly removed when Hindenburg, re-elected to the Presidency with the help of Brüning and the Social Democrats, thought that a Government clearly working by favour of the Junkers and of Heavy Industry and without any parliamentary support would pay larger subsidies to bankrupt Junkers. All this belongs to the struggle of corrupt cliques that came to an end only when the most corrupt of them all finally put the Nazis in control; the history of German democracy practically came to an end with the establishment by emergency decree of Brüning's Cabinet and Government.

The decisive steps in the development towards 'authoritarian' government had been taken before the onset of the Great Depression, the effect of which was not felt in Germany until the spring of 1930, though unemployment gradually increased from 940,000 in 1927 to 1,260,000 in 1929; the employers' first major attack against the positions of the trade unions and the Government[2] was still directed against wage increases awarded in a period of apparent prosperity. But immediately after the nomination of Brüning's Government the first reflections of the World economic depression were accompanied by outright demands for wage reductions. The ultimate acceptance of these demands by the trade unions led to a breakdown of their authority corresponding to that experienced at the same time by Social Democracy as a political party.

[1] See above, p. 255.
[2] See above, p. 325.

In March 1930, on the initiative of the Christian Trade Unions, the employees of the Becker Steel Works in the Ruhr had accepted a 10 per cent wage reduction imposed as an alternative to the closing down of the works. Demands for wage reductions were presented successively to the workers in the copper mines and refineries in the Mansfeld region (in May), in the Ruhr heavy industries (in June) and in the Berlin engineering industry (in October 1930). In the first case at Mansfeld the reduction was demanded for a particular industry of local importance in connexion with the general fall in prices of raw materials; in the Ruhr the employers' attack was directed against the piece-workers' 'over-scale' earnings, which, however, represented an essential element in their standard of living; in the Berlin issue, which followed on the Nazi success in the elections of September 1930, reduction of the agreed wages scales was demanded from the workers in a basic industry. Accordingly there were differences in the reactions of the trade unions. In the Mansfeld and Ruhr cases they offered a token resistance;[1] only in the first case, because of the initiative of a Communist-led opposition,[2] did it turn into a serious strike, which lasted for eight weeks. On the Ruhr, the Christian Trade Unions' refusal to back resistance and the acceptance of the new terms in some works which followed on this served the leaders of the Free Trade Unions as a main argument against the Communist attempts to continue strikes in those works where the workers had stood firm. The challenge to the workers of the Berlin engineering industries was taken up more seriously by the local Trade Union leaders, some of whom were definite supporters of opposition to

[1] i.e. they rejected the award (on the new interpretation of the Arbitration Law, see above, p. 325, this deprived it of binding force), and advised the workers to strike, but avoided the action that was necessary to overcome hesitation on the part of workers faced with complicated issues. In the Ruhr heavy industries, workers who continued to work on July 1st were supposed by the law to have agreed to the reduction in the piece rates, which were carried out in the individual works and shops; the Union leaders emphasized that every group of workers which did not strike on that date was under a legal obligation to work even if others were on strike. At Mansfeld, the wages reduction came into force on a Sunday, when the mines, but not the metal works, were closed: in the circumstances the Union leaders' failure to call a strike, had it not been countered by the Communist initiative, would certainly have caused the former to regard their cause as lost and, by working under the new conditions, to accept the wage reduction.

[2] By mobilizing the unemployed workers for mass-picketing it gave the metal workers (see preceding note) a lead to strike, which was followed by official sanction of the strike by the Union. During the whole period of the strike two sets of strike committees existed in the large area involved, Communist initiative being conspicuous in support of the unorganized workers as well as in the sometimes drastic measures taken to counter the employers' attempts to introduce strike-breakers. The workers' sympathies were clearly with the more energetic methods of carrying on the strike, but disappeared as soon as the Social Democrat Trade Unionists, submitting to a second award, recommended acceptance of a wage reduction only slightly smaller than that originally demanded by the employers. Subsequently, the Nazis gained a strong influence in the region.

the Brüning Government; from the first, the Communists' function in this movement was restricted to propaganda on behalf of the strike and for maximum collaboration with the unorganized workers.

Brüning had entered on a trial of strength with this best-organized group in the German key-industries by nominating as arbitrator, instead of the Social Democrat who normally acted as Mediator for Berlin, a leading representative of the People's Party; his award provided for a reduction of wages by 8 per cent. As Brüning had not a parliamentary majority at his disposal, a resolution of the Reichstag invited him not to declare the award legally binding, as the employers had demanded. But meanwhile the Social Democratic parliamentary party had decided to 'tolerate' the Brüning Government.[1] In these circumstances, the national leaders of the Metal Workers' Union agreed with the employers on a new mediation procedure which eventually gave the employers everything they had demanded; on the Union leaders' advice, work was immediately resumed in a key work even before the ballot arranged by the Berlin local Union group had been taken. As a result, a majority even of those who still took part in the ballot voted against continuing the strike. In this, as well as in the preceding Mansfeld case, the Communists failed in their attempts to continue the strike after the Union leaders had ordered its end.

The outcome of the Berlin metal workers' vote does not suggest that a determined readiness to fight existed in more than a minority of the workers; in all the movements mentioned, the Communists had the support of about a fourth of the strikers. Trade Union leaders with a clear conception of the prospects might have given the wavering majority a lead; those who had been produced by the whole development of the German labour movement increased its vacillations by every kind of procedural device, and afterwards quoted the Communists' failure to overcome the long-established discipline of German trade unionism as a proof of the necessity of accepting wage reductions. Although the Communists succeeded here and there in countering some wage reduction by a local strike, which usually broke down after a few days but was used as propaganda for their renewed attempts to create independent left Unions,[2] the outcome of the three major movements of summer 1930 marked the end of large-scale resistance to the employers' demands. The lowest point was reached when on 1st January 1932 Brüning decreed a further general reduction of all wages by 10 per cent, with the Social Democrats supporting this emergency decree as they had the others, and the Communists failing to call out more than a few thousand workers, and those only for a few days. The 'political path' so much cried up by Social Democracy had resulted only in the Party's giving its support to large-scale wage reductions if carried out by that bourgeois

[1] See above, p. 328.
[2] See below, p. 380.

Government which was described as the lesser evil because it was only the preparatory stage for worse things to come.

A short-term revival of the labour movement started again from a political event, but because of Hitler's access to power it had no opportunity to develop fully. On 20th July 1932 Papen deposed the Prussian Government by an obviously unconstitutional procedure. The Social Democrat Ministers, who had for so long described their position and their control of the Prussian police as the main stronghold of German constitutionalism, capitulated without more than juridical protests, and denounced the Communist appeals to strike as 'provocation'; a few Berlin Trade Union leaders, some of the higher police officers, and, characteristically enough, some of the liberal members of the coalition Government, were the only persons outside the Communist camp in favour of resisting the *coup d'état*. But the description of Hindenburg's nominees as the 'lesser evil' had been carried *ad absurdum*; and the elections which followed ten days later showed a clear turnover of some 600,000 Social Democratic votes to the Communists, who until then had registered their principal gains among the unemployed. As Papen failed to satisfy all the aspirations of the Nazis, the Government of the Herrenklub (Club of the Masters) got an almost unanimous vote of no confidence; only the thirty M.P.s that were left of the Hugenberg party were prepared to support it. Schleicher, the army leader, described the situation as 'the uncomfortable state of having no cushion to sit on but one of bayonets'. So long as Schleicher provided the bayonets, Papen had his cushion, and Hindenburg's signature to whatever emergency decrees the Club of the Masters desired. But by over-estimating the extent to which the German workers were silenced, he broke the neck of his régime.

As the worst period of the Great Depression was now passing, Papen offered employers an incentive to reinstate their unemployed workers; they were allowed to reduce the wages of employed workers by a percentage corresponding to the increase in the numbers they employed; the remainder of the increased wage-bill being made good by a State subsidy corresponding to the saving in unemployment benefit.[1] This procedure concentrated the trial of strength in individual enterprises which, by their very attempt to apply the decree, proved that they had orders to fulfil; the workers did not fail to notice this. Resistance was fairly general and in most cases successful even before a strike was called, the employers dropping the demand for wage reduction and contenting

[1] One year later Hitler enforced a similar device by regulation, instead of leaving the initiative to employers; they had to reinstate a certain percentage of unemployed, paying them a wage slightly above the unemployment benefit paid to them before, the additional cost being borne by a 3 per cent deduction from the wages of those employed (apart from the fact that the creation of two types of workers naturally promoted a tendency to level down wages). At that time, no more serious resistance was possible.

themselves with the State subsidy. In those cases where the employers insisted on the wage reduction the ensuing strikes were supported by all the employees, whatever their political standpoint; in many cases Nazis joined in mass picketing with their Social Democrat, Communist, and Christian comrades. By a special emergency decree of October 4th Papen prohibited trade unions from supporting these strikes; it was of no consequence, as the workers could easily manage without official support the short strikes necessary to enforce the employers' withdrawal. Papen's wage-reduction decree remained a dead letter; few noticed when it was withdrawn by Schleicher, who thus dissociated himself from his predecessor.

The wave of Papen strikes culminated, after a short strike by the Hamburg transport workers early in October, in the famous strike of the Berlin transport workers, 2nd to 6th November 1932. The national trade union leaders had concluded an agreement with the management (i.e. the Berlin municipality) providing for a reduction, by two Pfennig, of the hourly rate in fulfilment of a Papen decree by which the wages of municipal workers had to be adjusted to those reduced by the Federal Government; they were very proud of this achievement, and did not even think of the possibility of a conflict with their Social Democrat fellow party members in the municipal government. They were also, though wrongly, fairly sure of their Social Democrat fellow-workers who formed the decisive section of the staff (of 22,000 workers 6,000 were organized in the Free Trade Union, 1,200 in Christian and similar Unions, 1,500 in the Communist-controlled RGO-Trade Union Opposition; in the elections to the Works' Council, 45 per cent of the workers had supported the Free Trade Union, 33 per cent the Communists, 10 per cent the Nazis, and the rest, mainly black-coated workers, the Christian, National, and similar Unions).[1] When the Communists

[1] It may be worth while to give the results of the elections to the Works' Council (from the *Report* to the 19th Regional Party Congress of the C.P., Berlin, 1932, pp. 31–2):

	1929	1930	October 1931
Free Trade Unions	5,934	10,155	8,150
R.G.O. (Communists)	10,747	6,321	6,306
Christian Nationals	373	801	628
German Nationals	1,811	1,643	930
Nazis	—	1,346	1,544
Gewerkschaft der Eisenbahner (Hirsch-Duncker)	1,593	1,947	1,390

The figures are also interesting in that they show the extent to which, in an enterprise certainly near to the black-coated workers' outlook the Nazis may have made gains from the Communists or Social Democrats, as distinct from competition between diverse right-wing groups; the number cannot have amounted to more than a few hundred in either case (nearly all the Communist losses between 1929 and 1930 represented Social Democratic gains).

Among the over 8,000 non-Communist workers who voted for a strike on 1st started propaganda and preparations for a strike, the Trade Union leaders agreed to a secret ballot 'to stop the Communists' mouths'; they were greatly disappointed when it resulted in a majority of 14,471 against 3,993 in favour of a strike. They attempted to deny the existence of the three-quarters majority demanded by the rules by claiming the 3,335 employees who had not taken part in the ballot (2,900 of them were on sick or other leave) as 'Nos';[1] but immediately after receiving the result of the ballot the delegate meeting which had been called by the Communists called the strike, elected a strike committee (amongst whose members were sixteen members of the Free Union, and four Nazi workers) and, with the help of the Berlin party organization of the C.P., organized mass picketing. Within a few minutes of the appointed hour the strike was complete; only after the event did Goebbels come to the conclusion that he was incapable of preventing the Nazi workers from joining in the strike, and made a virtue of necessity.[2] On the second day the award was declared by Papen to be legally binding, and the Trade Union leaders made energetic attempts to break the strike; when street battles developed with the strike-breaking minority (only for a few hours did the management succeed in resuming some 5 per cent of their services), Nazi storm-troopers joined with the Communist workers. The strike committee had to go underground to avoid arrest and a delegate meeting of the other public utilities which discussed extending the strike was actually arrested: for the first—and last—time the Communist opposition succeeded in upholding for a few days a major strike in open conflict with the Trade Union leaders and the government.

The workers themselves seem to have regarded the strike, the material issue in which was indeed of minor importance, as a political demonstration connected with the general elections; as soon as the ballot-boxes had closed on the evening of November 6th and the Nazis, as was to be expected, had ordered their supporters to resume work, many of the Social Democratic workers, who up to that moment had defied their leaders, also resumed work; the Communists had to follow their example the next day. The election resulted in large Communist gains

November 1932 must have been three-quarters of the Social Democrats even on the assumption that two-thirds of the Nazis and Hirsch-Duncker Unionists voted for a strike (the members of the conservative groups certainly did not). As the 'No' votes were concentrated in the offices, it is obvious that the number of Social Democratic transport workers who voted against the strike was negligible; but it is just possible that in some offices the typical voter for a strike was a Nazi, and those who voted for continuing work right-wing Social Democrats, strongly connected with his municipality. Amongst the workers, the strike was a Social Democrat as well as Communist affair, and hardly at all a Nazi one.

[1] *Vorwärts*, 3rd November 1932.

[2] J. Goebbels, *My Part in Germany's Fight*, English ed., of 1935, p. 181

at the expense of both Social Democrats and Nazis.[1] Goebbels's manœuvre had no result beyond restricting the Nazi losses to somewhat below their level in other parts of the country. Social Democratic *émigré* publications have since built up the culmination point, modest as it was, of the German workers' struggle against the Fascist reaction into an alleged cause of the Nazis' triumph, thereby influencing most Western publications on the subject. At the time of the event, no serious observer shared this view. *Der Deutsche Volkswirt*, one of the most intelligent of the organs of High Finance, said in its issue of November 11th:

> 'There can be no doubt: notwithstanding the implied inconveniences, and in spite of the numerous sabotage actions which even a numerous police force was incapable of preventing, the strike movement was supported by the sympathies of the masses of the people. Here came into the open the effects of events not logically connected with the strike: the reduction of social benefits, the Government's statements on the obsoleteness of the welfare State, July 20th [i.e. the removal of the Prussian Government by von Papen—R.S.] Numerous workers and employees with no direct stake in the issue felt a deep satisfaction in noticing that such a sharp weapon was still left to the working class.'

With enthusiasm the leading liberal organ, the *Berliner Tageblatt*, wrote on the strike and the outcome of the elections:[2] 'The wind is in the country again.' Papen had to go; his successor, General Schleicher, came to the conclusion that continued government against an almost compact working-class opposition was impossible. He attempted to form a Government which would be based upon the para-military formations, from the Nazis (whose storm-troopers, at that time, were in partial revolt against Hitler's leadership) to the Social Democrat *Reichsbanner*, to be attached to the army; a combination of Social Democrat and Christian Trade Unionists with the left wing opposition in the Nazi camp (under Gregor Strasser) would supply the workers' element in this new, 'social', version of army dictatorship. The leaders of the Free Trade Unions were prepared to join, but were disowned, on 4th December 1932, by the Central Committee of the Social Democrats, and Gregor Strasser failed to split the Nazi party. Thus Schleicher was left alone with the Trust magnates, who soon came to the conclusion that a less 'social' and more demagogic dictatorship was to be prepared. The further course of events has often been described; it has no place in a study dedicated to the history of democratic organization.

We need only devote a few pages to the formal procedure by which the German workers' organization was introduced into the framework of the totalitarian State. If there was logical consistency on the road from Ebert's and Noske's rearming of the monarchist officers against

[1] In comparison with the elections of July 31st of the same year the Communists gained in Berlin 140,000 votes, the Social Democrats lost 76,000, the Nazis 38,000.

[2] The liberal (Democratic) party had already disappeared in earlier elections.

the radical wing of the labour movement to Severing's capitulation before Papen's *coup d'état* and the Trade Union leaders' attempt to find some place for their organizations within Schleicher's schemes, then there was also some consistency on the road from this last step to integration in the German Labour Front. The former Head of the Bernau Trade Union School, who acted as adviser to Leipart and Grassmann in their negotiations with Schleicher, but with less moral control and greater political consistency joined Hitler's camp as early as January 31st, wrote in his diaries during the period of the Schleicher's negotiations (17th to 18th January 1933):

'Socialism will not come from below. It will not be given its shape by those who emerge from the ranks of the workers, least of all by trade union or party officials. The transformation must come from above, from those who stand *above* the working class, a staff of leaders and an army of retainers (*Gefolgsleuten*) who from the experience of work are led towards that of national community. . . . The end of parliamentarism implies the need for a new attitude on the part of trade unionism.'[1]

A memorandum submitted to Hitler by Leipart and Grassmann on 30th March represented the last platform on which reformist Trade Unionism, as distinct from the open renegades, tried to find its place in the new order: trade unions had taken their rise as the workers' organized system of self-help, and their social tasks had to be fulfilled under any régime: by their recognition of the public arbitration procedure they had accepted the State's right to settle industrial disputes in the public interest. They would claim no right to interfere in politics, i.e. they would dissolve their traditional association with Social Democracy; nor would they claim a monopoly for themselves, i.e. they would not object to the Nazi competition in the field of labour organization. Three weeks later the T.U.C. called the workers to participate, 'conscious of belonging to their estate',[2] in the celebration of the National Day of Labour arranged for May 1st. But on the day after the Trade Unionists had thus been introduced into the 'national community', the Trade Union offices were occupied by the Nazi organization. On 13th May the Trade Unions' property was confiscated, with characteristic demagogy by the department of the Prussian C.I.D. concerned with the prosecution of cases of corruption.[3] The leaders of the Christian, National and Hirsch-Duncker

[1] H. Salbach, *Das Ende der Gewerkschaften*, Berlin, 1934, pp. 7–8.

[2] *Stand* as distinct from class, the term formerly used on such occasions. Yet the slogan still denotes a claim to some special position for labour within the new order.

[3] A combination of demagogy of this type with additional taxation of the workers was quite ordinary in those days, especially in the few organizations whose leaders had transferred funds abroad for purposes of future anti-Nazi propaganda. For this reason, for example, the members of the Freethinkers' Association for Cremation, whose leaders had removed part of the funds abroad on the eve of Hitler's accession to power, evidently with the intention of having a reserve for Social Democratic underground activities, were informed by the Nazi Commissioners that they would

Unions carried the attempt at collaboration so far as to join the leading organs of the German Labour Front; but as they still continued to speak of special interests of employees distinct from those of employers, and of the necessity for a special organization for labour, they were expelled on June 23rd, and their offices occupied by the Nazis. On 20th January 1934 the Law on the Regulation of National Labour conferred on the employers as the 'leaders of the enterprise' the right to regulate working conditions in the factory; the 'retinue' was subject to their full discipline.

The Works' Councils proved the only organ of the German labour movement to resist 'unification'. On 21st March 1933, at the culmination of the wave of terror which succeeded the Reichstag fire, they were re-elected all over Germany, with the result that the Nazis themselves did not claim to have received more than an average of 25 per cent of the votes. Most of the new Works' Councillors had to be removed by physical force, and their offices occupied by Nazi representatives. The Law on the Regulation of National Labour replaced the Works' Councils by 'Councils of Confidence' whose members were to be nominated by agreement between employer and Nazi organization and confirmed by a vote in the factory; the first vote of this kind, in March 1934, was also the last, as the majority of the workers made their votes invalid. Hence the reserve provision of the law, according to which the Councillors of Confidence could be confirmed by the State Representative for Labour Issues (*Treuhänder der Arbeit*) became the general rule.

The end of Austrian democracy followed, at some distance, the course of events in Germany. After the local elections of April 1932, the Social Democrats moved for a dissolution, which, if the framework of parliamentary democracy was to be preserved, would have left the Christian Socials with the alternative of coalition either with the Nazis, which was impossible, or with the Social Democrats, who in such a case would have been the stronger partner.[1] The Christian Socials purchased the

have to pay over again for their funerals because the first contribution had been 'stolen' by the former leaders.

[1] See note [2] above, p. 321. Later (op. cit., 1934, p. 40) Otto Bauer described the Social Democrats' insistence on the motion for dissolution as a tactical mistake which may have forced coalition with the Heimwehren on the Christian Socials (Buresch, the moderate Catholic who was then Prime Minister, had warned the Social Democrats that his resignation would be unavoidable if they insisted on their motion); Bauer explains his behaviour in 1932 by the catastrophic experiences brought about by the German Social Democrats' toleration of the Brüning Government. Indeed, a complete repetition of that policy would have been the alternative to the course the Austrian Social Democrats actually took: as the Geneva protocols were bound to come up in Parliament and the Heimwehren, unless paid their price, would not have voted for them, the Social Democrats would have had to vote for extreme deflationist measures carried out by a Government in which they were denied any share; the move for dissolution itself implied an offer of coalition after the elections, as the

support of the Heimwehren for avoiding a dissolution by a Cabinet reconstruction under Dollfuss,[1] Rintelen and Starhemberg being included; by a one-man margin they managed to get the new League of Nations control accepted in Parliament. The Social Democrats naturally voted against this, and thus deprived the Nazis of an obvious line of nationalist demagogy, but they showed no tendency to compromise with the 'revisionist' camp in international policies. On January 8th they published materials about ammunition supplies sent on Italian account to Hungary, with the obvious intention of increasing that country's pressure on Czechoslovakia. The formal merits of the issue were clear, and Dollfuss could no more defend Mussolini's arms than the Social Democrats had been able to defend their own in 1927.[2] A motion in favour of Austria's strict neutrality was carried unanimously in the Political Committee of Parliament. But Dollfuss, and his Italian backer, strongly resented this defeat, which grew worse when the Social Democrats further announced that Seefehlner, the General Manager of the Federal Railways, who had been nominated by Vaugoin when Strafella[3] had proved untenable, had tried to bribe the leaders of the Railwaymen's Union in order to enable the confiscated arms to be passed on to Hungary. Seefehlner had to be dropped, but at Mussolini's explicit demand the arms were put at the disposal of the Austrian Heimwehren, who were allowed to 'steal' them on the return journey to Italy, and the attack on the Railwaymen's Trade Union, long since a first priority in the Austrian right wing programme, was opened.

A pretext was easily found; on March 1st the railway management announced that it was incapable of paying the salaries due on that day otherwise than by delayed instalments, and, to make the provocation complete, added a reduction of the railwaymen's pension rights. All the Railwaymen's Unions, including the Catholics and the Nazis, answered with a protest which, in order to avoid a conflict with the Government, was limited to the modest measure of a two-hour stoppage. But Hitler

Social Democrats could not be supposed to leave the Catholics no alternative other than coalition with the Nazis. Even a vote on dissolution was unavoidable, as the Nazi members of the Heimwehren would have moved it in any case; to vote against it would have meant involving Social Democracy in the Nazi reproach that Parliament was afraid to face the electorate.

[1] Dollfuss himself, up to then prominent only as the parliamentary representative of the Peasants' Co-operatives, was not regarded as a right-wing Christian Socialist; in the frequent negotiations in which he was engaged with Otto Bauer on agricultural matters he assured the latter that he too regarded co-operation between peasants and workers as the only political system feasible in Austria (cf. Pertinax, op. cit., p. 150). The Heimwehr leaders, indeed, at the beginning distrusted Dollfuss, and wished to replace him by Rintelen; the details were fully discussed on the occasion of the latter's trial for the *coup* of July 1934.

[2] See above, p. 313.

[3] See f.n. [1], p. 321.

had just managed his Reichstag fire, and Dollfuss deemed that the time to show 'the strong hand' had come in Austria also; the Army occupied the railway stations, and arrested the strike committees, their members, after a few hours, being discharged, but dismissed from their jobs.

The simplest answer might have been the calling of a general strike for which, in view of its origins, the railwaymen's support would have been certain. The Social Democrats preferred a parliamentary protest, for which a majority seemed assured, as the German Nationals could not leave their dismissed supporters among the railwaymen in the lurch;[1] evidently they did not realize that they would thereby remove the trial of strength from the issue of the railwaymen's right of combination to that of the Constitution. It may be added, however, that in those very days—between the Reichstag fire and the German elections of 5th March 1933 which broke the power of Bavarian political Catholicism—hopes that South Germany would resist the Berlin Government were widespread even among German left-wingers; the Austrian Social Democrats may have expected that, in such a situation, the Austrian Christian Socials would follow the example of their Bavarian brethren and enter a coalition to defend Austria's independence. The vote of March 4th gave the Government a narrow majority but resulted in a dispute on procedure, during which the three Presidents of the House resigned. On March 5th Hitler's triumph in Southern Germany was decided. It is possible that in those very days the Vatican took its decision on collaboration with Hitler. Be this as it may, on March 7th Dollfuss suspended by emergency decree[2] the constitutional guarantees, alleging that Parliament was unable to function. When Renner, the first of the three Presidents who had resigned, called a new meeting of Parliament for its Praesidium to be re-elected, Dollfuss announced that he would prevent the meeting by physical force. Clearly this would have been the most suitable occasion for a trial of strength from the point of view of democracy. The Social Democrats were well informed about the issue: on March 8th Dollfuss negotiated with Danneberg, offering no concessions, but inviting the Social Democrats to make a peaceful retreat; he claimed that no more was intended than the amendment of

[1] Even the Christian Socials could not avoid moving, as distinct from the vote of no confidence, a demand for clemency for the dismissed railwaymen; indeed, Dollfuss found it politic to reinstate most of them when his *coup d'état* was carried out a few days later.

[2] As the constitutional compromise of 1929 had not given him the necessary powers, Dollfuss used as a constitutional pretext—for actually abolishing the constitution—a law on war-economic emergency legislation enacted by the Imperial Government during World War I, the formal repeal of which (of course without foreseeing such potentialities as those of March 1933) had frequently been demanded by the Social Democrats, but refused by the Christian Socials. Waste of time over arguments about Dollfuss's legality can easily be avoided by reading the last of his emergency decrees of 7th March 1933, which prohibited the Constitutional Court from dealing with complaints about the legality of the Government's measures.

the Constitution in the direction of the principle of 'estates'[1] which had failed in 1929; by the end of March Dollfuss would submit his proposals and, as soon as an agreement was reached, Parliament could be recalled, evidently in order to abolish parliamentarism. But the Social Democrats must understand that an anti-Nazi policy, as aimed at also by Dollfuss, must be carried out within an anti-Marxist framework (i.e. by the elimination of Social Democracy as an independent factor); otherwise the Nazis would annihilate the Christian Socials just as they had done in Germany.

This was clear enough; Bauer's later complaints[2] that he was betrayed by Dollfuss can affect nothing but details, such as the part to be allowed to parliamentary institutions within an 'anti-Marxist' order based on 'estates', i.e. the more or less civilized forms of Fascism[3]. For days discussions continued amongst the Social Democrats on whether they should offer resistance, and on the technical issues involved; a date for decision was fixed by the fact that the last of the three Presidents who had resigned, a German National, called a meeting of Parliament for March 15th to elect a Praesidium and Dollfuss proclaimed he would use the police to dissolve the meeting by force. On the 13th Otto Bauer spoke in the Social Democratic Central Committee against 'preventive war', that is, against acceptance of a trial of strength on the mere consideration that conditions would get worse if it were delayed; this argument shows that he regarded the defence of the democratic Constitution, which clearly could not be delayed, as of secondary importance. On the 15th, in the last hours before the announced meeting of Parliament, the Trade Unionists insisted on accepting the struggle before the workers' self-confidence was broken. General Körner, the leader of the Republican Defence League, remarked on the absence of spontaneous action on the workers' part; he did not take it into account that his organization's activities, at least since 1927, had been directed precisely towards quelling any such initiative, in expectation of the day when they would be called to disciplined action. The parliamentarians suggested caution. While Dollfuss's police were occupying the Parliament building, a comedy was carried out: those M.P.s who had managed to enter the House assembled for a few minutes in order to demonstrate the continuing existence of Parliament, and then dispersed without

[1] *Ständische Verfassung*—the term used at that time by Fascists of all kinds to describe a system of representation according to professional and economic groups, the scales being properly weighted in favour of agriculture and of the employers' interests. See above, note [2] on p. 335.

[2] Op. cit. (1934), pp. 42 ff. Much of the following presentation is based upon Pertinax's well-informed book.

[3] The Christian Social speakers in the Lower Austrian Diet on March 14th (in which the Social Democratic motion for disapproval of the policies of the Federal Government was accepted) argued mainly by comparisons with the pogroms and terror proceeding at that time in Germany.

passing to the order of the day. Dollfuss quickly removed one democratic institution after another by emergency decree. When, at the end of the month, the Social Democrats inquired about the promised negotiations on constitutional reforms, they were informed that Dollfuss would not negotiate with the existing leaders of the Party. Other and more acceptable negotiators were proposed to him, but Dollfuss refused to accept even them.[1]

One year later, when all was lost, Otto Bauer wrote of the events of 15th March 1933:

'We could have responded by calling a general strike. Never were the conditions for a successful strike so favourable as on that day. The counter-revolution which was just then reaching its full development in Germany had aroused the Austrian masses. The masses of the workers were awaiting the signal for battle. The railwaymen were not so crushed as they were eleven months later. The Government's military organization was far weaker than in February 1934. At that time we might have won. But we shrank back dismayed from the battle. We still believed that we should be able to reach a peaceful settlement by negotiation. Dollfuss had promised to negotiate with us at an early date . . . concerning a reform of the Constitution and of the Parliamentary agenda, and we were still fools enough to trust a promise of Dollfuss. We postponed the fight because we wanted to spare the country the disaster of a bloody civil war. The civil war, nevertheless, broke out eleven months later, but under conditions that were considerably less favourable to ourselves.'[2]

With this post-portem verdict by one of those who bore the main responsibility for the decision, we might conclude our record of the fall of Austrian democracy had not 'spontaneity' at last had its say after the huge and elaborate machinery of the labour movement had capitulated.

While friction with the Nazis—who as early as April 18th were joined by the majority of the Styrian Heimwehren—alternated with negotiations, which continued all through the autumn of 1933,[3] Dollfuss quickly proceeded from abolition of the right to strike in public enter-

[1] Bauer, Op. cit. (1934), p. 20.

[2] Op. cit. (1934), pp. 72 ff.

[3] According to the official Austrian publications (*The Death of Dollfuss*, pp. 92–4, and Schuschnigg's *Farewell Austria*, pp. 198–200), in these negotiations the difference was eventually reduced to the issue whether the Austrian Nazis should be integrated within the united Austrian Patriotic Front, or be accepted into the Austro-Fascist framework as a separate party. On December 27th Dollfuss gave way even on this point and expressed his readiness to negotiate with the Nazi party representative, Habicht, on the single condition that, for reasons of prestige, Habicht should make the formal approach, but be formally authorized by Hitler so as to have some guarantee for the fulfilment of agreements reached. According to Pertinax, who wrote before the Austrian documents were available and on the basis of independent information, Schuschnigg served as an intermediary in this last step. The negotiations were broken off because Fey, the leader of the pro-Italian minority of the Heimwehren, was informed, and threatened to arrest the Government, in which he was deputy Prime Minister, if they were continued behind Mussolini's back.

prises and the establishment of a preliminary censorship for the Social Democratic press to the proclamation, on May 1st, that the new State would be based upon the teachings of the encyclical *Quadragesimo Anno*; there could be no place in the new Austria for Socialism in its traditional, international form. The meeting of the Austrian Catholics, September 9th–11th, served as the occasion for the official proclamation of Catholic Fascism; it was duly authorized by Mussolini, at his preceding meeting in Riccione, and duly blessed by Pius XI in a speech of October 7th. The Bishops elaborated the subject in their Christmas encyclical of 21st December 1933:

'However small a State may be, it needs a Führer . . . a master whom the others obey. . . . The people, too, have to obey and to serve, not to decide according to their whims. . . . The frequently misinterpreted phraseology about popular sovereignty is not only unreasonable but also unchristian, and in the long run even atheist.'

The Social Democrats reacted to Dollfuss's proclamation of September 9th–11th by the statement, at a special Party conference, of the 'four issues' on which they would face a decisive struggle: the introduction of a Fascist constitution by unconstitutional means; the unconstitutional abolition of Vienna's autonomy; the outlawing of the Party; the dissolution or *Gleichschaltung* of the Trade Unions. The intention was to avoid a battle except on issues which would be regarded as essential by the whole working class; the result, which might easily have been foreseen, was a hint to the opponent that, for the time being, he had to proceed by roundabout measures until Social Democracy was sufficiently weakened to have its whole moral position destroyed. In turn, railwaymen and workers employed on public emergency works were faced with the alternative of joining the Patriotic Front or becoming unemployed; the Trade Unions advised the workers not to submit to the Government, yet would not accept a struggle in defence of those dismissed.

At the Party Congress on October 14th the policy of the Central Committee was questioned by two oppositions; the right wing under Renner suggested the acceptance of Dollfuss's corporative State in order that as many Social Democrats as possible, if not Social Democracy as an organization, might be integrated into its framework, and the left wing, in view of the experience with the policy of the 'lesser evil' in Germany, demanded that the Party should accept the decisive struggle even in a hopeless situation in order to preserve the traditions of the Austrian labour movement. Otto Bauer attempted to preserve party unity by the institution of a Party Council, composed of factory representatives which should decide, within the framework of the Four Points, whether a decisive struggle was necessary (this Council played no part in the events of February 1934). Bauer went to the length of offering the Government full powers to govern for two years by emergency decree, on the sole condition that these powers should be enacted in the constitutional way and that Social Democracy should be allowed a certain degree of freedom of propaganda; he was even ready to accept 'corporative concepts' of social and political organization as the basis of the new Constitution.[1] It was all in vain; Dollfuss refused to enter into any negotiations, and proceeded with his piecemeal offensive. By January 1st Vienna's legislation on taxation was amended, by (unconstitutional) Government decree, in accordance with the employers' demand; the Workers' Chambers and the Factory Councils of public enterprises were transformed from elected organs into bodies made up of Government nominees. There were protests and quite impressive demonstrations, but no official Party action. When Dollfuss came under heavier pressure from the Nazi wing of the Heimwehren as well as from the Italian Government, he reacted by a sharper attack on the Trade Unions; their members were excluded from public works and employers who had Government orders had to replace their Union workers by members of the Patriotic Front until the latter made up at least 80 per cent of the staff. In a declaration of January 28th the Social Democratic Party Council repeated the offer of collaboration with Dollfuss; Schmitz answered in a leading article in the Christian Social Party's central organ that, in the new Austria, there would be no independent trade unions, but only corporations under State supervision and without the right to strike.

Dollfuss's clever manœuvring was disturbed by the latent disputes in the Fascist camp. In the last days of January there were local conflicts with the Nazis; the pro-Italian wing of the Heimwehren, who had been given powers by Dollfuss, immediately went into action not so so much against the Nazis as against the provincial Governments which were composed mainly of Christian Socials who might be suspect of preserving some kind of legality and also of collaborating with the local Social Democrats against the Nazis. On February 5th the Heimwehren began a *coup d'état* in Innsbruck, against the protests of the local Catholics; things had gone so far that, on the same day, the leaders of the Christian Socials of Lower Austria, at a Party conference, had to make speeches in favour of their party's right to continued existence 'so that the people may have some say even in the new State'. During the following days Heimwehr *coups* were carried out in other Provincial capitals; most of the Christian Social heads of Provincial Governments protested. On February 8th Fey arrested most of the Viennese leaders of the League for the Defence of the Republic; the finding of a depot of arms at Schwechat near Vienna was worked up, in good Nazi style, as the happy prevention, at the very last minute, of a Bolshevik con-

[1] Op. cit. (1934), pp. 21–2. In Bauer's interview with the *Sunday Times* it was stated that the Government's 'emergency' powers should be exercised with the assent of a small parliamentary committee, on which it was assured of a majority.

spiracy against State security. On February 9th Dollfuss returned from a conference at Budapest where, evidently, the decisions had been taken; on the following evening he declared: 'We shall realize our plans very soon.' On the 11th Fey promised the Heimwehren: 'To-morrow we shall start, and we shall make a good job of it.' The Social Democrats, answering Fey's allegations, protested their readiness to defend the Republic; at the same time they arranged, for the next morning, negotiations with the Lower Austrian Christian Socials on how the threatening catastrophe could be avoided. These negotiations were eventually to end with the arrest of the negotiators.

On February 11th the Linz organization of the Social Democrats was informed that Fey had prepared the occupation of their Party building and the confiscation of their arms for the following morning. They informed the Central Committee that they would join battle on their own responsibility, and expected not to be left in the lurch.[1] Otto Bauer advised against accepting battle, as the situation was bound to be cleared in the next few days. The telegram fell into the Government's hands, and may have contributed—if it were necessary—to bring about Fey's decision; on the morning of February 12th his troops moved against the Linz party building. The workers accepted battle; the Factory Councillors of the Viennese district of Floridsdorf, who were just discussing whether they should reply to the arrest of one of their leaders by a protest strike, immediately on receiving the message decided to go into action. While in Linz the guns were already at work, the Social Democrat Committee, by a narrow majority, decided to fight, and called a general strike. The carrying out of the decision was sabotaged by the right wing: in practially the whole of Lower Austria and some of the Viennese districts no arms were distributed, nor were the fighting squads assembled. There was virtually no leadership, and the local fighting soon assumed a defensive character.

While the general strike was starting in Vienna, there was near-agreement between the moderates on both sides, the official Christian Socials and the Lower Austrian Social Democrats: one of the former had already been suggested as the new Prime Minister when Dollfuss's police arrived to arrest his partners in the negotiations. In the afternoon Dollfuss proclaimed martial law in Vienna, where, up to that time, not a single shot had been fired, and abolished Vienna's autonomy.

Apart from the chance, ruled out by the Party's passive attitude, of encouraging by a surprise offensive a split in the Government camp,

[1] The text of the letter is given in Schönau's booklet *The February Insurrection in Austria*, Modern Books, London, 1934. The presentations given by Bauer (op. cit., 1934) and Gedye (*Fallen Bastions*, London, 1938, a secondary account based upon Social Democratic sources), differ in details, especially as regards the contents and meaning of the telegram sent from Vienna to Linz, but do not affect the main facts as mentioned above in the text.

the conditions in which battle was accepted by the workers were practically hopeless; the railwaymen, who in March 1933 would have been in the foreground of the struggle, were now demoralized by the destruction of their Trade Union; groups such as the printers were affected by the earlier discussions about the possibility of their finding some place in the corporative order. The brunt of the battle—in those parts of the country where it was fought at all—was borne by the municipal workers and by the unemployed, who formed the core of the fighting formation, a total of perhaps 15,000 to 20,000 fighters[1] against 50,000 men available to the Government (amongst them 10,000 Heimwehr men, who proved of little use for purposes other than torturing prisoners). The 'civilian' population of the quarters where the battle raged behaved as sympathizers to the League for the Defence of the Republic, but did not take an active part. Nor were they invited to do so; for years past disciplined action by the fighting organization, the unofficial army of Social Democracy, had been lauded as the highest of virtues. Now it had to fight under conditions in which the main advantage of a disciplined army, centralized leadership which made offensive action possible, was conspicuously absent, and where the betrayal of some local leader might keep out of action hundreds of fighters who had been taught to wait until they were given arms by the proper official, instead of taking them from the partly disorganized Government forces. The remarkable thing is not that the Socialist workers were defeated, but that they fought as well as they did; in the working-class quarters of Vienna, in parts of Upper Austria and Upper Styria large areas were held against much superior forces for from forty-eight to seventy-two hours. Then the hangman went into action—with moderation in comparison with neighbouring Germany, as the Government still felt its weakness. Party and Trade Unions were outlawed. On May 1st the Constitution for the 'Christian German Federal State on a corporative basis'[2] was 'given to the Austrian people . . . in the name of Almighty God, from whom

[1] In the first publications after the events the number of the fighting workers was greatly exaggerated by the Government (which had an interest in overestimating the number of the opponents which caused its army such difficulties; the number of the defenders of the Ottakring Workers' Home, for instance, was overestimated tenfold) as well as by the Communists, who had an interest in proving that bad leadership had spoiled a situation which should still have been full of promise. Schönaü, whose booklet is a collection of his articles in the German edition of *The Communist International*, gives, for example, the number of the Floridsdorf fighters as 6,000. Roscher, their leader, in a very instructive article published in the same periodical in 1935, gave their number as 2,000. In its best days the League for the Defence of the Republic had 80,000 members; in February 1934 hardly more than half as many, and many regions, because of disorganization, or direct intervention by their leaders, were prevented from acting. According to Pertinax, only half the members in Vienna took part in the fighting, which in the given conditions was not unnnatural.

[2] The formula, of course, represented a compromise between the various Fascist trends, and also a concession to the Provincial Catholics ('Federal').

emanates all law'. Three months later Dollfuss was killed by the Nazi wing of the Heimwehren, supported by right-wing Christian Socials such as Rintelen, in conditions where some of his own supporters such as Fey behaved in a suspect manner, to say the least. The weak resistance put up in the following days by the Nazis who were much better armed, controlled three times as large a territory, and enjoyed the sympathies of a neighbouring Great Power, puts the resistance of February 1934 in the proper perspective.

Since the labour movement had not suffered a moral breakdown such as it had in Germany, and continued with quite successful underground activities,[1] the trade union problem proved much more difficult for the conquerors of Austrian democracy than for the Nazis in Germany.[2] The Christian Trade Unionists, long since in clear conflict with such obvious tools of the employers as the Heimwehren,[3] wanted to preserve their position as the only independent Trade Unions surviving after the suppression of the Free Unions and, by offering the old Free Trade Unionists some scope for activity within their framework, hoped to attract the support of at least the right-wing Social Democrats. For this very reason such a solution was inacceptable to Dollfuss; after he had failed to win support from some former Trade Union leaders he established by decree a State-controlled Unified Trade Union which claimed, at the end of June 1934, to have 148,000 members. At the end of 1932 the Christian Trade Unions, amongst whose members some readiness to collaborate with the Government might be supposed to exist, had had 101,000 members; 96,000 members of the Free, and presumably the overwhelming majority of the 53,000 members of the Nazi Trade Unions had been railwaymen and public employees, i.e. people who could not easily withstand official pressure; apart from these, the Heimwehr 'Trade Unions' established by the employers had had at least some members.[4] In these circumstances, it is remarkable that the Government did not succeed at the start in rallying in its Unified Trade Unions more than half of those who for professional or political reasons were obvious candidates for recruitment.

At first, the underground labour movement advocated a boycott of the Unified Trade Unions. This slogan was strictly followed, with the sole exception of the printers,[5] who had stood aside during the February strike and whose attitude had always been largely dominated by their claims to friendly society benefits, which would have been lost if they had not joined. Later the pressure on the unemployed, who could not

[1] During the first years, the Social Democrat *Arbeiterzeitung*, published abroad and imported illegally, had 60,000 subscribers; the organizational activities of the Communists had greatly increased as compared with the time of their legal existence.

[2] See above, p. 336.

[3] See above, note [1] on p. 319.

[4] See above, p. 316.

[5] Otto Bauer, *Die illegale Partei*, p. 86.

get work unless they became members of the Government-sponsored 'Trade Union' became effective, and employers who could not get Government orders unless their workers were organized in that Union began to exercise pressure on their workers; if things could not be managed otherwise, they paid the contributions to the Unified Trade Union on their workers' behalf out of their own pockets. Within the underground labour movement the Communists, whose ranks had been strengthened by disappointed fighters, realized the impossibility of continuing the boycott *in infinitum*, and insisted on use being made of the few legal opportunities for working-class activity that were available; they did this in opposition to the Revolutionary Socialists (the name assumed by those Social Democrats who continued to work underground), who, in general, showed some tendency to take up a radical position of a Trotskyist colour. Apart from all theoretical considerations, there was some practical pressure from the workers who wished to keep their old-standing 'men of confidence' in an officially recognized status. This could only be done by allowing them to enter the Unified Trade Union; in many cases the 'Trojan Horses' thus sent into the Government-sponsored Union asked some of their fellows to follow them in order to give them some backing. By the end of 1934 the Unified Trade Union had 261,000 members, a year later 338,000—half as many as Free and Christian Trade Unions together had numbered under free conditions. The actual relations of strength are well enough indicated by the fact that, when in the last days before the Nazi invasion in 1938 Schuschnigg had to make an appeal to organized labour, this was regarded by everyone as synonymous with a restoration of the Socialist-dominated labour movement.

On 3rd March 1938, while Hitler's armies were massing on the frontier, Schuschnigg had to negotiate with a delegation of workers of the principal factories of Vienna on the restoration of some legal scope for the activities of the real labour movement. On March 7th, again, for the first time for four, and for the last time in seven years, a conference of 350 workers' delegates met free from police control; they sang the old songs, and representatives of the underground parties spoke. Collaboration was promised to Schuschnigg if he fulfilled certain conditions, among them free election of workers' delegates to all economic organizations, restitution of the property of the workers' organizations confiscated in favour of those sponsored by the Government, and permission to publish an independent workers' newspaper. Over the second point there were prolonged negotiations, as those who had benefited by the confiscation, including the Catholic organization, tried to defend their prey to the last; the fourth point was granted only at the very last moment when all was already lost.

Mr. Eden had been dismissed by Chamberlain a few days before; even if Schuschnigg had found the strength to accept the fact that

Austria's independence could be defended only on the basis of restoring democracy, he could not have achieved more than an honourable defeat such as the Austrian workers had suffered in February 1934. In the light of what now followed everything, February 1934 included, was buried: on lorries, under Swastika flags, the Nazis brought Social Democratic workers, liberated from Schuschnigg's concentration camps, back to their homes. Since March 1933, Dollfus and Schuschnigg had won a Pyrrhic victory; the Nazis, however, had the slogans with which to appeal to the masses. They might have been resisted if the idea of Austrian independence had real roots; but while Otto Bauer opposed it and linked the fate of the Austrian workers with that of the German working class, Seipel, Dollfuss, and Schuschnigg had conceived Austria's independence as a Big Business paradise, enlightened by the hymns of the Catholic Church and supported by armed right-wingers with no inspiration other than rabid anti-Semitism and German nationalism.

(*c*) *Authoritarian Government*

The events discussed in the preceding section are the answer to all statements about a supposed Fascist revolution. There was nothing of the kind, not even in Italy. The reformist movement withdrew under the pressure of Big Business and the traditional right-wing politicians; in the latter's armoury the threat to let loose the Nazis played some part in Austria in 1933 as well as in Germany in 1930–2, and there was some mutual borrowing of phrases between Nazis and traditional right-wingers. But the Nazis had no serious offensive power. In Germany they endured electoral setbacks shortly after Social Democratic policies had suffered the bankruptcy of 20th July 1932, but were eventually rescued by the operation of combinations within the Junker-Big-Business camp. In Austria, after most of the Government-sponsored Fascist organizations had entered their camp, they attacked on 25th July 1934 a Government which had no serious support in the country; yet they suffered an ignominious defeat which was made good, in due course, only through the effects of the Chamberlain-Daladier combination. The Nazis got possession of Central Europe not because they defeated anyone, but because the labour movement was incapable of conquering, and Big Business incapable of governing it.[1]

[1] K. Polanyi (*Origins of Our Time*, London, 1945, p. 236) defines a revolutionary situation as marked by the absence of resistance; therefore the 'Fascist situation' of 1933 was genuine. To this I would simply remark (*a*) that, although a revolutionary situation presupposes some disintegration of the forces of potential resistance, it certainly, first of all, implies the existence of the revolutionary mass movements; (*b*) that the interest against which a revolutionary movement is defined should, in any case, be interpreted as being opposed to it, which can hardly be said of the Big-Business-Junker combination which transferred power to Hitler in January 1933. Everything which followed was merely a struggle between cliques all of which belonged, and continued to belong, to the new framework.

In a letter to Marx of 13th April 1866, Engels expressed his growing conviction that the bourgeoisie was unable to exercise direct rule; unless, as in England, an oligarchy was ready to lead State and society in return for good remuneration, Bonapartist semi-dictatorship was the normal instrument of Government on behalf of the bourgeoisie. This statement was made at the time of the developments with which our investigation started; Napoleon III in France and Bismarck in Germany appealed to the general suffrage because great tasks were in the air whose accomplishment might earn popular support for a dictator, after the professional bourgeois politicians had failed. At the time of which we are speaking there were no longer any tasks of bourgeois reconstruction to be fulfilled, and there was so much disillusionment about the working of bourgeois society that any government which honestly aimed at preserving it was bound to remain in a minority at the polls. What was in the air was the socialist transformation of society, which served as the bogey to keep the lower middle classes within the bourgeois framework; this attempt, however, was breaking down under the effects of the experiment made with bourgeois bloc Governments even before the onset of the Great Depression.[1] Before the bourgeoisie resorted to the Fascist tool, whose propensity to become the master of those who employed it was realized at least by the more intelligent bourgeois policitians,[2] full authority was transferred to a more familiar instrument whose reliability could be taken for granted; the State machine of the *ancien régime*. The preservation or restoration of this machine after the revolutionary upheaval provided the main extra-parliamentary backing for government by the bourgeois parties. Now, when the legitimation of bourgeois government by general suffrage had disappeared, that machinery should rule itself, although, in the upheaval of world war and revolution, it had lost that irrational legitimacy which had been provided earlier by Monarchy by the Grace of God.

Under these conditions the 'realistic' interpretation of government by Power pure and simple became predominant in German political thought. As the bureaucracy and Army gradually moved from the status of a guarantee against the 'unreasonable' working of parliamentary government under adult suffrage to that of the last resort of law and order, the German jurists gradually realized that what they understood by the Rule of Law had to be divorced from the question whether the law was properly enacted. We have noticed[3] statements to the effect

[1] Stresemann was among those who fully realized this trend, though he still searched for an answer within the field of the traditional multiparty system. See above, p. 258.

[2] See note [1] below, p. 363. Further hesitations may have been produced by the fear that the tool might break down, with the result that the disappointed Nazis would swell the Communist ranks. Knickerbocker's book *Germany: Fascist or Soviet* ?, London, 1932, is a good presentation of the atmosphere by an intelligent foreign observer.

[3] See above, pp. 265–6.

that it was the task of the Reichspresident to correct the working of parliamentary democracy if the bourgeois bloc should find itself in a minority. Even at the time when the overthrow of the last parliamentary Government, that of Hermann Müller, was being prepared, an academic supporter of the right wing, Pötsch-Heffter, interpreted German constitutional law in terms befitting the traditions of Prussian militarism: 'The dependence of the Chancellor on the confidence of Parliament is dependence of the leader on the confidence of the led; but the relation of confidence between President and Chancellor should correspond to the relations of confidence between the High Command and the commanding officer of an army group who needs to enjoy some initiative in action.'[1] This theory fairly describes the eventual relations of Brüning to his commander-in-chief, though the way in which he was dismissed by the latter because of his lack of readiness to subsidize bankrupt Junkers may seem more suitable to old feudal concepts of the behaviour due to disobedient servants than normal relationships between commanders-in-chief and commanders of independent army groups.

In these theories the existence of all the constitutional factors provided by the Weimar Constitution was still supposed; only the interpretation of their respective rights and powers was weighted in favour of the one of them who, himself of plebiscitarian origin, might be regarded as the most reliable from the standpoint of Big Business as well as of the army. We already find, in such statements, however, the first elaboration of the authoritarian ideology: the executive power claims obedience, even if, and especially if, it is exercised in opposition to legal or democratic principles; if, for example, a President of the German Reich, or a Chancellor of the Austrian Republic, breaks his oath to the Constitution,[2] dissolves Parliament against its explicit provisions, removes a constitutional State government, etc. Though most authoritarian governments try to give reasons for their actions, authoritarianism is something different from 'revolution from above' which makes the legitimacy of its action depend on the alleged need to violate the laws in the interest of the nation; the concept of Enlightened Absolutism implies the existence of unenlightened absolutism, of tyranny, which may legitimatize even revolution from below —as most of the princely representatives of eighteenth-century

[1] *Handbuch des deutschen Staatsrechts*, ed. 1930, p. 514. At that time, such conceptions of the powers of the President were shared only by a minority of the teachers of German Constitutional Law. Cf. ibid, p. 508 quoted above, p. 170

[2] As no modern State can be governed without lawyers, and as lawyers differ in their moral standards, lawyers will everywhere be found who interpret the Constitution in such a way that it appears not to have been broken; the importance of the theories to be discussed in the next paragraph lies precisely in that they allow the more intelligent type of right-wing lawyer to dispense with dishonest statements (or at least to reduce them to the status of propagandist by-products in the defence of a régime whose claims are proved in a more serious way).

enlightened absolutism would, if only in theory, have recognized.

Authoritarian ideology proceeds from the State, not from the nation. In the debate on the constitutional amendments demanded by the Heimwehren, Schmitz, a leading right-wing Catholic, stated on 22nd October 1929 that the State, while still preserving its identity, could change its Constitution in two ways; either by the normal constitutional procedure, or, if that procedure should fail (i.e., if Social Democracy, disposing of more than a third of the parliamentary seats, should vote against the amendments demanded by the Heimwehren), by a higher Right of Emergency. 'If the State's institutions fail, it produces new ones.' Four years later the Austrian bishops solemnly declared that 'every State needs a Führer, a master whom the others must obey'.[1] The typical addressee of the authoritarian ideology is the lower-middle-class person afraid of having to think for himself and easily convinced by those who have good reasons to finance authoritarian propaganda that all the evil in the world results from argument, disorder, party strife, dissolution of coalitions, etc. Peoples like the German and Japanese, in whose record of national unification militarism played a large part, are most exposed to authoritarian propaganda, but it would be an error to suppose that it was confined to such countries;[2] even in Germany it soon had to give way to the type of the 'political soldier' following charismatic leadership. Authoritarianism has a certain place in history, namely as the most obvious symptom of the approaching death of a society which can find no other justification for its continued existence than its possession of administrative and military power.

One of the most gifted and also the most versatile of German legal theorists, Karl Schmitt, developed the theory of the authoritarian State; the sovereign power in a State, in the Austinian sense, is that which can make us of the 'State of Emergency'. With Schmitt,[3] how-

[1] See above, p. 341.

[2] While, in such countries, the authoritarian argument can make some appeal to national tradition, in others it amounts to more or less obvious betrayal of that tradition. An editor of the *Prager Presse* (an organ that had been established to propagate the democratic views of the Masaryk-Beneš group) found it decent, or at least convenient, to celebrate the anniversary of the Czechoslovak Independence Day which followed the Munich catastrophe with an editorial headed 'World Authority, not World Revolution' (an allusion to the title of Masaryk's chief work, which was published in Czech and German under the title *World Revolution*, and not the English title *The Making of a State*). The implication was that the democratic wave supposed by Masaryk had been superseded by a world-wide authority emanating from Munich and, for Czechoslovakia, from that party to the Munich Agreement to which the country was delivered over.

[3] *Political Theology* (reprint of 1934), pp. 18–19. The book was originally (1922) written as a polemic against Kelsen, who denied the existence of the State (in the legal sense) except as a synonym of the legal order. Schmitt's theories were pushed to extremes by the Sudeten-German F. Sander (*Allgemeine Staatslehre*, Prague, 1936) who defined the sovereign organ in a State as that which is capable of carrying out a

ever, the State of Emergency is no mere measure[1] intended to overcome the temporary impossibility of preserving in an emergency some elements of the legal order: it is the power to suspend the whole existing constitution. Once it is realized, he says, that the supreme power in the State consists in the right to overthrow the legal order,[2] then it is obvious that, in such a case, the State continues to exist though the concept of Law disappears. In the legal sense[3] such a State has still a (dictatorial) constitution but no legal order. In another work,[4] in recognizing the fact of social and political struggle and the element of violence essential to the State, Schmitt went so far as to describe as 'the essence of politics' the power 'to nominate the enemy', external or internal, who ought to be annihilated. The disillusionment with the Weimar idyll of peaceful collaboration between classes and nations was thus carried to its extreme. To the lower middle class man, who, horrified by the phenomenon of class struggle, had called for 'authoritarian government' to protect 'law and order', Schmitt explained that the truly authoritarian power in government was that of overthrowing the law, and that the only order essential to the State was that which is preserved by military police or Gestapo in the rear of—it might be hoped—advancing armies. It was a truly Prussian theory: but even the Prussian soldier did not like dying without being told what he was dying for.

Authority as the ultimate legitimation of government is the true police State. Authoritarian government professes its civilized character, and its preparedness to preserve the Rule of Law (of course, of a law serving the vested interests); in every case an attempt is made to interpret away the violations of the legal order. Lawyers honest enough to recognize what they are doing in such a State use the excuse that they are thus preserving at least the foundations of the legal order. In fact, the social forces which back 'authoritarian' government are not interested in Party tickets being produced by insolvent debtors, or in thefts being committed by gangs which can successfully

coup d'état by 'emergency legislation' and of overthrowing the Constitution. In Austrian terms, the progress from Schmitt to Sander represents the political progress from Schmitz in 1929 (see above, p. 350) to Dollfuss in 1933 (see above, p. 341).

[1] It is no fault of mine, but that of German academic writings, that an ample German terminology if translated into sober English produces contradictions in terms. By a very elaborate terminology (the contribution to which of some terms of their own is regarded by most German writers as more important than making any original contribution to sociological thought) the German reader has become accustomed not to laugh at someone who assures him, in a scientific work, that the *Ausnahmezustand* is no mere *Notstandsmassnahme*, or that a State *im juristischen Sinne* can exist *ohne Rechtsordnung*.

[2] *Der Begriff des Politischen*, reprint 1933, pp. 28–9.

[3] See f.n. [1], above.

[4] See f.n. [2], above.

claim that they have deserved well of national regeneration, or that the victim was of non-Aryan origin. Big-Business men, when travelling abroad, do not like even to hear too much of atrocities committed in their concentration camps against actually subversive elements.

Such a régime may, indeed, use less violence than an honestly Fascist one; unhappily, however, it can produce no justification for such violence and brutality as it has to apply—and in cases such as the events of February 1934 there is quite a lot of it. It honestly protects the vested interests, and no insurmountable difficulties prevent this fact from being known. There is quite enough political and social oppression to arouse protest, though not enough to suppress it. 'Underground' publications with a circulation similar to that of their legal predecessors,[1] and full use by the opposition of the organizations created by the régime for its own purposes, turn 'authority' into its opposite: a régime whose validity depends on general reverence for the police undergoes a political defeat every time a group of youths succeeds in painting some forbidden slogan on a wall at night behind the back of some sleepy policeman. Within the 'authoritarian' world a President prepared to break his oath to the Constitution can easily procure the arrest, by a few soldiers who need only to apply a little symbolic force, of a Prussian Government composed of good subjects accessible to authoritarian ideology and fearful of 'greater evils', even if they can dispose of 100,000 well-armed and politically reliable police. But the same President has to dismiss his favourite when 20,000 Berlin Transport workers strike for a few days. In the state of latent civil war symbolized by 'authoritarian government' there is either complete obedience, or something hardly definable which may be to-day a group of youths defying the police, and to-morrow a successful insurrection. Therefore it has to be replaced by open violence with the enemy clearly identified (to speak with Schmitt) and subject to a continuing process of annihilation by the 'political soldiers' of a Fascist régime. Unhappily, political soldiers are not much given to the virtue of gratitude, even towards those who have put them in power. Nor can a thousand victories won in the torture-chamber atone for a defeat on the battlefield against a well-armed enemy who know what to fight for.

(*d*) *The External Conditions*

Most Western writings on the fate of the Central European democracies are dominated by the complaints of those who failed to make them a success, and protested against the lack of support from those who ought to have been interested in their success. This is not the place to discuss whether there is or is not an address to which such complaints should be directed. Classes and nations, not to speak

[1] See above, note [1] on p. 345.

of such hypothetical entities as 'Western Democracy', are made up of groups which pursue each their different interests; they should not be regarded as responsible if such a pursuit has results which are disagreeable from the standpoint even of all the groups concerned. Any complaint by unsuccessful politicians that they have been faced with difficult conditions is simply another way of admitting that they have failed to overcome those difficulties. And there was nothing out of the way in the difficulties that faced the Central European democracies.

For a long time, lost wars have provided favourable conditions for revolutions; but lost wars have a deplorable tendency to result in unfavourable peace treaties. Versailles was no worse than many other examples of the kind, not to speak of Brest-Litovsk, or of the difficulties which Eastern as well as Western Germans now have to face after the Hitlerite catastrophe. To complain of the hardships of the Versailles Treaty, which it is said, prevented German democracy from turning out a success, is either another way of saying that German Social Democracy did not want to obtain power under the only conditions in which it could be obtained (a victorious Hohenzollern would certainly not have resigned) or to shift on to others the responsibility for its own obvious mistakes. From the Independent Socialists' initiative in favour of signing the Treaty of Versailles[1] up to the last Left-Centre government's eagerness to remain in office as long as was necessary to sign the Young Plan[2] runs a chain of offences by the German moderate Left against the most elementary rule of politics that he who holds actual power must also take the responsibility for unpopular decisions, and that no one is under any obligation to share in such responsibility unless he is granted such actual power as he deems necessary in order to distribute the consequences of those decisions in what he considers the appropriate way—in this case, to let those who would have gained most from Wilhelm's war, had it been successful, also bear its burdens when it was lost. The moderate left wing's failure to observe these elementary rules was continued, in the emigration, by attacks on the Communists who did attempt to follow them; indeed, every attempt the Communists made not to let the disappointed lower middle classes become an easy prey to demagogy financed by Big Business nor to allow the whole of the Left to be regarded as an agency of Western Imperialism[3] survives in the mem-

[1] See above, p. 174.

[2] See above, p. 327.

[3] See above, p. 220 and f.n. [1]. It should be noted that none of the Communist criticisms of Versailles dealt with issues other than Reparations, the Saar, and (in some phases of Communist and international policies) the *Anschluss* question; Poland's right to her new territories was always recognized, and the Alsace-Lorraine issue was raised only by a right-wing opposition group which was expelled from the German as well as from the French party, and whose members later acted as German quislings.

ory of Western readers as an alleged contribution to the Nazis' accession to power.

Nor was there anything abnormal in the Central European democracies' need to face the Great Depression. The propensity of capitalism to produce periodical depressions was taken for granted by all Central European economists, especially by the Socialists; no one could enter politics, least of all Socialist politics, without being prepared to face problems of that kind. To say that a political system can function only in times of economic prosperity is simply another way of saying that it is bankrupt from the very start. Certainly, if democracy be defined as a political system under which the masses always get small benefits but are discouraged from making the efforts, and the sacrifices, necessary in order to bring about a fundamental change in the social structure, it follows that a lost war and an economic depression provide the least suitable opportunities for practising democracy of that type, however favourable the former may be to the conquest of political power and however many opportunities the latter may offer to nationalize the key industries even without offending the theoretical sanctity of private property.[1] Because of the close association of Socialism with the reforms achieved by the everyday work of their organization, the masses were inevitably exposed to such errors; but serious democratic politicians had to use the time available to replace the erroneous concept by another and a more realistic one, instead of leaving control of the country to the deadly enemies of democracy.

The alleged connexion between the Great Depression and the fall of Central European democracy is highly artificial. The anti-democratic reaction began in Austria long before,[2] and even in Germany preceded it; reaction was provoked not by the Depression but by the growth of the moderate left, during the preceding period of prosperity, to a strength incompatible with what Big Business regarded as its proper claim to profits. Fascism was pushed into power when the nadir of the Depression had been passed; in Germany because the local, in Austria and Czechoslovakia because the international representatives of the vested interests deemed that even such disagreeable experiences as they expected would be a lesser evil than the consequences of a disintegration of German National Socialism. This is not the place to discuss whether they were right from their point of view in spite of the evident underestimation of the autonomy of the 'tool' by the Schachts, Krupps, and Thyssens, and the eventual inability of the appeasers of 1938 to avoid World War II; they could still have made the case that the alternative evil would indeed have been greater;[3] as we have not seen it, there is little sense in arguing about it.

[1] See above, p. 309 and below, p. 360.

[2] See above, pp. 313 ff.

[3] I would still doubt it (of course in an analysis from the point of view of the Big.

All this is not intended as a denial that the actual course of events, with their catastrophic outcome, was to some extent shaped by the international setting; the only point which I wish to make is that that setting involved no necessity for defeat except for concepts ridden by inherent contradictions, and that there is no reason to suppose that any variation in the setting would have produced a very different external result. Moreover, that setting was itself so closely connected with the internal developments in the Central European countries that the legitimacy of looking for even a purely theoretical contrast between the sets of facts is open to doubt.

From the very start, before the growth of its Communist sector, Central European democracy, though it had developed under the influence of the Russian Revolution, was dominated by forces which clearly supported the anti-Bolshevist intervention. The German 'People's Commissaries' refused to establish economic and diplomatic relations with Soviet Russia in a provocative way[1] while the Baltikum divisions, taking an active part in the war of intervention against Soviet Russia, became a main force of counter-revolution within Germany. While in Czechoslovakia itself the emancipation struggle proceeded under evident inspiration from the Bolshevist revolution,[2] the Czechoslovak legions acted as a main force of anti-Bolshevist intervention within Russia; this function, indeed, was the basis on which the *émigré* group of Masaryk and Beneš overcame the pro-Hapsburg sympathies in the Allied camp

Business interests): as the Nazis had attracted mainly the lower middle class and blackcoat vote, their breakdown (which would have been unavoidable if they had not been allowed to assume power) would have strengthened the Social Democrats much more than the Communists. A strong shift in the working-class camp in favour of Communism would have remained as an element in the future situation (if the election results of 1932 are taken as a standard, and even if it is assumed that all the working-class elements, as distinct from the black-coated workers, disappointed by the Nazis would have found their place in the Communist camp, the comparative strength of Communism among the German workers would still have remained inferior to, say, its position in present-day France or Italy). To speak in parliamentary terms, in the party system as it was likely to be consolidated after the end of the depression the Social Democrats would have been left with the alternative of combining with the Communists or with the Centre (whose left wing would also have been strengthened under such conditions): they were not likely to be inclined towards the former combination, but might still use it as a threat to enforce favourable terms for a left-centre coalition. As Stresemann had rightly foreseen (see above, p. 258) parliamentary government of the right would have been for ever excluded; it was this prospect which caused Big Business to destroy the parliamentary framework. Of course, if it had revolted against the disagreeable working of a re-established parliamentary democracy, the chances of the Communists becoming the victors in the resulting civil war would have been increased by their stronger position within the working class; but it is not true that the alternative, in 1932–3, lay between a Communist and a Fascist dictatorship. Big Business simply did not accept the prospect of having to work under a Government not formed by its own representatives.

[1] See above, p. 155.

[2] See above, pp. 137 and 141.

and secured recognition for Czechoslovakia's independence before the War had been won. Only the Austrian Social Democratic party succeeded in preserving neutrality in the struggle between Soviet Hungary and her neighbours, who belonged to the French system of alliances; this attitude (which corresponded to that of the bulk of the Russian Mensheviks as distinct from people like Kerensky and the right-wing Social Revolutionaries) may have been promoted by the Austrian Social Democrats' emphasis on continuity with the record of 1848, when the revolutionaries of Vienna fought in alliance with the Hungarians and Italians against the Hapsburg monarchy which was supported by a majority of the Austrian Slavs.[1]

When the possibilities of Socialist revolutions in Central Europe receded, and much of the international relations of the region took the form of a continuation of the struggle of the Austro-Hungarian Slavs against the Hapsburg monarchy, now represented by Hungarian revisionism, which soon secured Italian and German backing, the Austrian Social Democrats found themselves involved in a hopeless contradiction between their anti-Slav and pro-*Anschluss* tradition and the necessities of a situation in which, as they well realized, all practical chances of preserving democracy lay in alliance with Czechoslovakia; it is quite possible that reluctance to accept the implications of a victory over Austrian Fascism contributed to the withdrawals of 1931 and even 1933. On the other hand the Czechs, although under the impact of the experience of their legions in Siberia they became a comparatively moderate force within the French camp as early as the Polish-Soviet war of 1920, remained the prisoners of their protecting power, whose status as a 'Great Power' did not become obviously problematic until 1938-40. With due respect to their protector's vacillations, they avoided even such initiative as would have strengthened their position in relation to Austrian democracy[2] and thence their ability to play a leading part in Central Europe. The Masaryk-Beneš group simply did not dare to readjust relations with the U.S.S.R. after Hitler's accession to power before the French seemed to be ripe for a similar step; when confronted with the Henleinite pressure they made, however reluctantly, such concessions as were demanded by their Western allies and by the Agrarian party which in the course of such policies had become the key party of the country. The end has been described by a leading member of the group, whose bias is certainly not anti-Western, in the following words:

'It would [in September 1938] have been more than dangerous to ask Russia to help us independently of France and the League of Nations, for Britain and France, who were supporting German claims in the dispute, and who were therefore opposing us, would have considered such Russian intervention on our behalf as a dangerous expansion of "Bolshevism" in Europe. In the

[1] Even this tradition had some continuation in 1919; see above, pp. 186–7.
[2] See above, p. 209.

"ideological war" which might have ensued . . . the Great Powers of the West would undoubtedly have sympathized with the Berlin-Rome Axis, as the defenders of "order and European civilization" against "Bolshevist disruption and decay". To ask for help from Soviet Russia alone would have been dangerous for internal Czechoslovak reasons also, for, although all our political parties were united in favour of seeking help from France and Russia combined, the parties of the Right would certainly have protested against accepting help from Russia alone. The resulting internal dissension would have dangerously weakened our national resistance.'[1]

Thus ended that one of the Central European democracies which could associate the defence of liberal democracy, as established in the aftermath of World War I, with the national tradition. Conditions in Czechoslovakia were incomparably more favourable than in Germany, where democracy was associated with national defeat, and even in Austria, where, as we have just seen, the one existing democratic party would have needed to break with the traditions which inspired it if it wished to identify resistance to the Fascist threat with the growth of a new national tradition. Unless identified with national tradition, democracy, in whatever interpretation, was a synonym of subservience to some protecting power, dependent for its authority on that power's material strength; it was deprived of any deeper meaning when the internal development of these protecting countries was reflected in their treatment of the pawns on the chessboard. The kind of democracy realized in post 1918 Central Europe had been born on the battlefields of World War I: it was destroyed at Munich, and the apparitions of its ghost are now limited by American considerations about the conditions under which the maximum support can be obtained from ex-Nazi soldiers for the Atlantic Pact effort.

Against these fundamental difficulties of the situation, any details of the diplomatic game are of secondary importance. Before Russia's recovery from the crisis of the civil war, the European scene had become dominated by the Anglo-French antagonism. France, as the organizer and protector of the *cordon sanitaire*, and also the main claimant for reparations, shouldered most of the antagonism the Peace Treaties aroused. Britain, following the inertia of her political tradition, saw merely the obvious fact, French claims to hegemony on the Continent, and not its real reasons, France's extreme weakness and Germany's

[1] H. Ripka, *Munich, Before and After*, London, 1939, p. 83. The author's statement that all parties were in favour of seeking help from Russia and France combined, is correct so far as the parliamentary parties, or at least their majorities, are concerned; it is incorrect as regards the highly influential Big Business and financial groups within the Agrarian Party, who behaved like ordinary traitors. Ripka, like most people who were on the spot, takes the availability of the alternative, i.e. Soviet readiness to offer Czechoslovakia even single-handed support, for granted; it may be worth mentioning that this has now been confirmed by an official Soviet publication (*Diplomatichesky Slovar*, vol. II, 1950, p. 198).

potential strength. This gave the German right wing, in face of the left-centre advocates of 'fulfilment', a clear line in foreign policy from the days when Wirth's left-centre government was replaced by the right-centre combination of Cuno (who, in fencing with Poincaré, provoked the occupation of the Ruhr, and earned his meagre reward in the shape of friendly speeches from British politicians) up to the Anglo-German Naval Agreement of 1935. Hitler developed his platform on foreign policies in the aftermath of the Ruhr conflict; he would indeed have been a political suckling had he not learnt the obvious lessons.

From 1922 onwards, relations with Soviet Russia became a key problem in German politics. If anyone in Germany aimed at finding some half-way house between the Russian form of socialism and Western Big Business rule, Germany's geographical position between the two centres was a godsend, as of course it was also from the standpoint of any shrewd diplomatist pursuing imperialist aims. In fact, Wirth and Rathenau remained the first and last left-centre politicians who dared to do the obvious (characteristically, they represented bourgeois parties). In the following period, the establishment of friendly relations with the U.S.S.R. was left to Big Business and the Reichswehr; Social Democracy developed a peculiar kind of pacifism which consisted mainly in attacks on the Soviet Union.

The German Social Democrats and their various literary successors asserted and still assert that the Russians, for reasons of foreign policy, supported the German right wing against the left centre, and induced the German Communists to do the same: evidently the German Social Democrats could not imagine that anyone could honestly oppose their policy because of its own failings. The Russians knew quite well that the Reichswehr, when entering into agreements with them on technical collaboration, did so in order to prepare for war against them, and they used that technical collaboration to get ready for the eventual war against the Reichswehr; they also knew that the Ebert who allowed the Reichswehr to enter into technical agreements with them was the Ebert who had opposed Rapallo, prepared Locarno, and encouraged his party's anti-Soviet propaganda. Nor did the German Communists need any special encouragement in order to devote their main propagandist attention to their competitors within the labour movement and to reserve their bitterest attack for opponents whose advocacy of a possible war with the U.S.S.R. might influence the working class, as distinct from others who could be sufficiently characterized by quotations from *Mein Kampf*, Hugenberg's speeches, and even Stresemann's official proclamations. There was always a clear distinction between propaganda directed towards inducing a—preferably left-centre—government of the German bourgeois republic to develop friendly relations with the U.S.S.R., and propaganda to induce lower-middle-class people influenced by the Nazis to break with them and to support the C.P. in its struggle against domestic and foreign Big Business.[1]

The serious point in the position was not that anything was done which was not natural in view of the existence of a left-wing opposition to German Social Democracy (however unnatural this fact might seem to the latter), but that some things were *not* done which could have born fruits if the German left-centre parties, however unsatisfactory their domestic policies were bound to appear to the extreme Left, had differed in their foreign policies from the leading bourgeois parties by greater friendliness not only to France, but also, and at least as much, to the U.S.S.R. Nothing of that kind was to be seen. On the contrary, the typical Social Democratic speech which was mainly directed towards discrediting the Communists' principal propaganda asset differed, not unnnaturally, from the typical speech of Stresemann or any other bourgeois Minister by a more provocative anti-Soviet note. It followed that by the mere pursuit of their party propaganda and by using a politician's attitude to the U.S.S.R. as a main criterion in his evaluation, the Communists destroyed any idea that there might be a practical difference between the foreign policies of a left-centre and those of a right-wing government. There was never anything like a 'Nazi-Communist alliance', but there were trends within the German C.P.—for some time predominant—which considered that the choice between Marx and Hindenburg or the risk of a replacement of the Prussian Government by Hugenberg's nominees should not distract the Party's attention from its main purpose of developing the most radical opposition propaganda. The results were disastrous for the Russians; not because they entertained any illusions about the German right wing's foreign policies, but because they failed to bring home to the German Communists that even a very unsatisfactory result in domestic policy, if it resulted in keeping German imperialism weak, might preserve the lives of millions of people, Germans as well as Russians. The question remains whether even the best conceivable policy on the part of the German C.P. could have saved the situation;[2] it is true, however, that even a narrower margin of defeat would have affected the course, and especially the aftermath, of World War II.

We are applying immanent criticism to the forces that shaped the external environment of the Central European tragedy; more legitimate subjects of this criticism than the Russians, who regarded bourgeois democracy as a delusion to be speedily overcome, are the social forces dominating the Western countries whose concepts of democracy were applied in post-1918 Central Europe. In all their activities in the financial and economic field, these forces behaved as if it was their intention to destroy whatever delusions were abroad about the kind of democracy

[1] See above, pp. 214–15, and note [1] p. 220.

[2] See below, p. 384.

they favoured, in conditions where the destruction of these delusions was bound to strengthen Nazism.

On the surface and according to its own ideology, the 'practical pacifism' of business men and bankers operated as a conciliating factor, bridging the chasms allegedly opened by 'the politicians', i.e., the honest play of power politics. When the League of Nations credit was granted to Austria, or the Reparations problem was settled by the Dawes Plan, the conditions, in their political aspects, were more favourable to the debtor than would have been the results of the French-Italian antagonism for control of the Danube basin, or than had been the French occupation of the Ruhr. Nothing more was insisted on than the deflationist standards of orthodox finance; but these were insisted on with a consequence intentionally strengthened by the fact that the controller was located abroad and could not be brought under the direct pressure of an electorate which had to suffer beneath a deliberately and artificially intensified depression.[1] Even in Czechoslovakia, which as a 'victor country' was spared the worst humiliations and where inflation had never proceeded to a point threatening actual catastrophe, the return of 180,000–200,000 workers alleged to be superfluous in industry to the villages, from which they had migrated to the towns just because they had become superfluous in agriculture, was looked upon as a perfectly legitimate aspect of monetary deflation.[2]

International financial intervention during the first post-war period brought with it at least some material benefits, if only in the shape of the encouragement of private investments. Austria received a loan which was not needed for the stabilization of the currency and after hard struggles could be used for internal investment; Germany received a total of twenty milliards in credits (eleven of them, true, only on short-term) which did more than compensate for the reparation payments. During the Great Depression, 'help' from international finance took the form of naked pressure on the living standards of the masses without offering any more than the prospect that no more foreign credits would be withdrawn. In the Geneva negotiations of November 1931[3] the Austrian Chancellor undertook 'in the interest of the stability of the currency' to adapt the standard of life of the population 'to the changed situation', i.e. to the bankruptcy of the Kreditanstalt. To preserve the confidence of foreign investors, the Austrian Government had to make large presents to the bankrupt bank; when it had contributed more than the total value of that bank's assets and therefore could not avoid formal ownership, it undertook 'not to interfere with the commercial management of the Kreditanstalt (the controller of the larger part of Austrian industry) except for the purpose of safeguarding its interests

[1] See above, pp. 211 and 279.
[2] G. Georges-Picot, *La Politique de déflation en Tchéchoslovaquie*, Paris, 1925, p. 65.
[3] See above, p. 323.

as guarantor'. It was not allowed to interfere for the purpose of preventing unemployment. Even when deciding to shut down whole industries the General Manager of the Kreditanstalt, who was nominated with the approval of the League of Nations Finance Committee, needed the consent of the Executive Committee, on which the Austrians were in the majority, only in cases where 'the continuance of the industry does not necessitate the granting of further credits'. In exchange for such far-reaching restrictions on Austria's economic independence the foreign creditors, who to a large extent were actually identical with the bankrupt debtor, the Rothschild-owned Kreditanstalt, promised no more than not to withdraw 'a substantial majority' of their former credits to the bank; even the withdrawal of a considerable part of the credits still left the Austrian Government under the control of its 'benefactors'.

In later years, States much wealthier than Austria replied to similar threats by simply freezing the foreign investments by national enactment; the use of such a device, however, would have contradicted the interests of powerful groups inside Austria, and even the Social Democrats did not dare to contemplate breaking the golden chains by which the country was fettered.[1] The foreign financiers did not bother to produce any delusions about what was on the cards; an American advocate of the Tardieu Plan (which was offered as an alternative to the Schober-Curtius agreement abandoned under the pressure of the withdrawals of credits) advised the Danubian governments 'stoically to accept the fact' that the necessary reduction of tariffs would 'entail immediate loss and suffering to certain groups of their citizens', which, however, would be preferable to the alternative of 'uprisings which would transform the whole established social order'.[2] Central European democracy was bankrupt when no one outside the Communist camp dared to state, with similar honesty, that a transformation of the whole established social order was precisely what was wanted. With the foreign credits bourgeois democracy in Central Europe came to an end; not because it was incapable of working without a deficit, as its opponents alleged, but because its liberal framework, which had been to a large extent preserved out of respect for foreign investors, precluded it from making full use of the existing capacities for production. A solution in which the framework was exploded but democracy was preserved was conceivable; but foreign capitalist help had been efficient enough to stabilize the framework of social relations even when it ceased to include the free movement of goods and capital.

(*e*) *The Policies of the Labour Movement*

There is no sense in criticizing the policies of a political party from

[1] See above, pp. 180 and 309.

[2] H. F. Armstrong in *Foreign Affairs* (New York), vol. X, p. 614.

any standpoint other than that of its own principles. Central European Democracy had been established against the will of the bourgeois parties (with the exception of one wing of the national liberation movement in Czechoslovakia); it is pointless to reproach them for having failed to prevent its fall. Liberalism, as a trend represented in political parties, had been destroyed by the course of its own internal development (again with the exception of Czechoslovakia), and the left wing of political Catholicism had submitted completely to the nominees of Krupp and Klöckner. There were brave individuals who, even in the torture chamber, defended the ideas for which they stood, but there was no political party outside the labour movement which could reasonably be reproached for not having offered resistance; ought they to have fought against a different representation of the interests for which they themselves stood? I am not speaking here of the issues of foreign policy: resistance to the Nazi régime for the sole reason that it would land Germany in external defeat, however legitimate, would not have been a defence of democracy. The classical instance of the behaviour of the German bourgeois parties is that of the Centre, which practically disappeared from the political scene—its leader, Kaas, who had done so much to bring Hitler into power, retiring to Rome—as soon as Hitler had bought off Vatican opposition by a Concordat. The later disagreements between Hitlerism and the Churches belong to a history of German Fascism.

In speaking of political capitulation we must first of all speak of German Social Democracy: it stood for something definitely incompatible with a Fascist order, namely the separate representation of the interests of labour as distinct from those of employers. But it submitted without any resistance except for a vote of no confidence against Brüning, which was not repeated after Brüning was seen in the light of the 'lesser evil', and for a lawsuit before the Supreme Court after Papen had destroyed its main position of power by a *coup d'état*. On the eve of Hitler's accession to power on 30th January 1933 an editorial in *Vorwärts* enumerated a whole series of 'lesser evils', even a Hitler Government established by legal means being preferable to one established by illegal means amid bloodshed. On March 25th those Social Democratic M.P.s who had neither been arrested nor had emigrated declared their support for Hitler's foreign policy; on May 17th the declaration was solemnly repeated. On April 27th a national conference decided to carry on with the Party's work 'within the given legal framework', and Socialist Youth organizations which started underground work were expelled. When the 'legal framework' developed in such a way that most of the leaders had to emigrate, and use the publication facilities available abroad, another national conference was held on July 19th to elect a new Central Committee (with due allowance for the exclusion of Jews from political life) and to denounce the activities of the emigrated members of the Central

Committee. Four days later Hitler ended the comedy by suppressing the Social Democratic Party, unseating its M.P.s, and arresting all its leaders. The statement of some of the theoreticians of the Schleicher policy that the principle of the 'lesser evil' was the substance of Social Democratic policies in general[1] seems amply proved by its whole record; this record also provides the most impressive of the many refutations of this political principle available in historical experience.

It seems to follow that Social Democracy, at least under German conditions, was a self-contradiction, bound to destroy itself; if revolution was an evil 'to be feared like sin', and if, on the other hand, there was a ruling class which, on a suitable occasion, such as the Great Depression with its effects on the lower-middle-class vote, would exclude workers' representatives from taking any part in public administration and even from having a say in the factory, such exclusion had to be accepted without resistance. That acceptance might, indeed, be accompanied by pious hopes that the new system would not work and that its leaders would be forced to recall the experienced saviours of society, as Ludendorff had been in September 1918. The main difficulty in this concept was that the new system, unless it were actively opposed by the working class, could break down only as a result of external adventures, opposition to which would also provide those 'more reasonable bourgeois politicians' who were needed as prospective partners in a coalition; but Social Democracy did not, and could not, wish for Germany's external defeat. There is no case for defeatism except as an element in a revolutionary outlook; any group which desires the defeat of its own

[1] *Führerbriefe*, issues No. 72 and 73 of 13th and 20th September 1932 (quoted in part by Merker, op. cit., pp. 269–70). The whole argument of the document (whose terminology shows extensive borrowings from Marxism, which were quite common among the more intelligent of the Army officers) is interesting: as the bourgeoisie had narrowed down too much for it to be able to rule post-war Germany by its own forces, the consolidation of its rule (which was regarded by the authors as the desirable political aim) called for support from some mass-movement which would split the ruled. Social Democracy suited the purpose well because, as a sectional movement, it had no aspiration to control society as a whole; it sought only for a share in the State. On the other hand, National Socialism, having no social basis of its own, was bound to aim at substituting for it a monopoly of political power. This was unacceptable to the group for which the authors spoke, but, they considered, Social Democracy could no longer serve the purpose of splitting the working class because the economic depression had made it impossible to grant economic concessions to that part of the working class represented by the Social Democrats. The Trade Unions were more interested in their connexions with the State than in those with Social Democracy, which would come to an end with the expected end of parliamentarism, and they could then be integrated into any bourgeois State which was prepared to find a place for them; National Socialism might find a new (sectional) function in representing them within a corporative order and might thus be diverted from aiming at a political monopoly and at a solution of the unemployment problem by purely military methods of planning which might leave bourgeois rule no more than an empty shell.

country except as an occasion for destroying its domestic oppressors stamps itself thereby as an agency of the foreign country whose triumph it advocates. Stampfer is mistaken in describing the last acts of the Social Democratic parliamentarians who supported Hitler's foreign policy as a mere expression of human weakness, or of consideration for the fate of the party comrades in the concentration camps; in fact they, and not Stampfer, were the consistent Social Democrats. What sense would there have been, within the context of Social Democracy (not to speak of political Catholicism), in calling on the people to oppose Hitler's aggressive policy so as to bring about defeat in war at the price of millions of lives, and later to write, as Stampfer did in *Neuer Vorwärts* after the British General elections of 1934 which gave the Tories control: 'If you wish to know what we want to see established in place of Hitler, look at the British elections'?

In the Anglo-Saxon countries, explanations of the breakdown of German Social Democracy as a result of local conditions can be put forward; in Germany it is impossible to do this without at least locally making the case for Communism, and, moreover, dropping all the traditions of the Second International for which the German and Austrian parties were the model ones. Within the traditional framework of the Central European labour movement explanations of the breakdown had to be based on the existence of factional strife; the Communists accused the Social Democrats of having prevented them from establishing a proletarian dictatorship, the Social Democrats accused the Communists of having prevented them, by pursuing their own separate aims, from efficiently defending working-class interests within the Weimar Republic, and that Republic itself. Assuming that there were at least a few occasions when a united working class might have assumed power in Germany, the Communist case (on the assumption that proletarian dictatorship is in itself desirable, as according to the traditions of pre-1914 Social Democracy it was) is stronger than that of the Social Democrats (on the corresponding assumption that a State such as the Weimar Republic ought to be defended on its own merits); clearly, one half of the working class cannot make a proletarian revolution, but even half of it (and in fact it was the larger half) should be able to provide a quite efficient opposition in a bourgeois-democratic republic and to prevent attacks on it by the right wing, especially if the threats and pressure of the other half strengthen the most cautious trends within the bourgeois camp. Besides, an attitude of opposition, departed from only in those cases where participation in a Government provided an opportunity of securing obvious benefits for the workers, would have been the surest way to weaken the Communists.

This argument is so obvious that it was used from the very start. In the Berlin Independent Socialist *Freiheit*, on 3rd January 1922, Otto Bauer criticized the participation of German Social Democracy in a

Government which left all economic and military power in the hands of the bourgeoisie, and burdened Social Democracy with the responsibility for the use of that power against the working class, as compared with Austrian coalition policies which were supported by working-class control of the Army and of the transport system. Kautsky[1] replied that only because the Austrian Socialists had secured such positions of power outside Parliament could they dare to leave the Government without running the risk of actual counter-revolution: in a country where the Army was not in the hands of the working class, the consequences of leaving its control in the hands of purely bourgeois Governments might be harmful. He elaborated his standpoint by replacing Marx's statement, in the *Critique of the Gotha Programme*, that 'to the period of revolutionary transformation of capitalist into communist society there corresponds a political transition period in which the State can be nothing but the *revolutionary dictatorship of the proletariat*' by a new formula, according to which 'between the period of bourgeois and that of working-class rule in a democracy lies a transition period characterized by coalition government'.[2] Not a year had passed since these lines were written when their true meaning was illustrated by the Reichswehr which, on the orders of a Social Democratic President of the Republic and of a coalition Government, invaded Saxony and Thüringia to remove Social Democratic Ministers. Throughout its career German Social Democracy, out of all the evils available, consistently chose the greatest, namely, to leave real power in the hands of forces bound to destroy democracy while splitting the ranks of democracy by identifying the Republic with a régime controlled by the Reichswehr. Without the split in the ranks of the working class and with a real two-party system in Germany there might have been civil war; but the actual choice was not between peaceful and gradualist democracy and civil war, but between civil war won on the barricades and civil war lost in the torture chambers. It may be true that civil war won even more than civil war lost (after which there might have been a short-term revival because of foreign intervention) meant the end of what traditional Social Democracy stood for; in view of the historical record, however, this is merely another way of saying that Social Democracy stood for something that could not be achieved; if there was a choice, it was between the actual course of events and an attempt to bring the practical alternative as near as possible to the traditions of German Socialism, at a time when even partial success in this attempt would have shaped the outlook of the world to come.

The split which German Social Democrats quote as an excuse for their failure was one of their own making. If, during the War, they had accepted the fact of a divergence in their ranks over the attitude towards

[1] *Die proletarische Revolution und ihr Programm*, Stuttgart, 1922, pp. 104–5.
[2] Ibid., p. 106.

the war and had not been afraid of losing the High Command's favour because of the presence of a pacifist minority in their midst, there would have been no Independent Socialist Party. If in 1919 they had not sent the Army against the workers, and if in 1920 they had disarmed the Kappists, the split (apart from a small Communist propaganda group) would have remained a passing affair; if, in 1923, of Stresemann's three alternatives[1] they had rejected the one he preferred and had faced Ebert with the alternative of either *not* sending the army against Saxony and Thüringia or being expelled from their party, which had joined with the Communists and its own Saxon fellows in a general strike all over Germany, the right-wing majority of the C.P. would have remained in control of the caucus and the split in the labour movement would have been either healed or reduced to such mere competition in propaganda as flourished, for example, in Czechoslovakia without threatening the Republic or even the possibility of joint action by all the working-class parties in face of a common danger.

After all that had happened in Germany, the split and its accompaniment by demagogy and shrewd manœuvring on both sides was an accomplished fact. When, in 1928, the Social Democrats decided to link their fates once more with bourgeois partners in a coalition (who meanwhile had moved even further to the right) and continued to support even Brüning's dictatorship, they could not complain if their opponents on the left made the most of it. By the time Brüning fell, however, those trends within the C.P. which might have refused to collaborate with a Social Democracy prepared to oppose reaction were defeated,[2] and, as the Social Democratic leaders very well knew, it depended solely on them whether a joint struggle against Papen could be organized. In fact, they went just to the point of semi-official negotiations on Communist support for the Prussian Government in Parliament. These negotiations were betrayed to Papen by a Nazi spy,[3] and this hastened Papen's *coup d'état* against the Prussian Government. This experience was used in the Social Democratic caucus as an argument, not against collaboration with people who might reply by *coups d'état* to the possibility of State Governments they disliked obtaining a parliamentary majority, but against negotiation with a party unpopular with such people; in its appeal to the Supreme Court Braun's Government claimed, quite rightly, that the Prussian police had killed many more left-wingers than they had Nazis. The Communist proposal to reply to Papen's *coup* by a general strike was denounced as a provocation. In his *Memoirs*[4] Braun himself asserted the complete bankruptcy of Social Democratic policies

[1] See above, p. 222.
[2] See below, p. 382.
[3] Cf. Merker, op. cit., p. 253. Dr. Diels, at that time Severing's secretary, later became chief of the Gestapo in Prussia.
[4] Op. cit., 1940, p. 410.

by asking the rhetorical question for what cause he ought to have called the Republicans to fight against heavy odds; 'Was it in order to overthrow the Reichspresident [whose election, it is true, had been supported by the Social Democrats on Braun's own initiative—R.S.][1] and his Government, or to stabilize the Weimar Republic, which had been rejected by much more than 50 per cent of the electorate, or to establish a Soviet dictatorship?' Braun, who in my view was simply honest and consistent, might be described as a representative of his party's extreme right wing (though he was its most outstanding leader after Ebert's death), but the near-unanimity with which his course was supported by at any rate the upper strata of Social Democracy is illustrated by the very few instances of opposing opinions which Merker, strongly interested in potential Front Populaire partners as he was when writing his book, was able to enumerate.[2]

Braun may have been mistaken in his denial that there was any chance of restoring the bourgeois-democratic Republic; but it certainly could not be restored without fighting the powers that Social Democracy itself had put into office as the 'lesser evils'. Even if for some mysterious reason of solidarity with their Berlin Magistrate the Social Democrats could not start the Transport Workers' strike, they had no need to oppose it, and could easily have let it run its course until it resulted in a general movement against Papen, with which ordinary liberals would have been quite sympathetic,[3] and faced Goebbels with the alternative of having his demagogy completely unmasked before the workers or of losing Thyssen's subsidies. That the Social Democrats not only did not choose such a course but even to this day use the fact that the Communists did choose it as a main reproach against them, is the best illustration of their complete inability to appreciate the use of weapons other than the casting of votes in a House which would be dissolved immediately it passed a vote of no-confidence, and the entering complaints about such procedure before the Supreme Court. In the context of such a general attitude, the disowning by Social Democracy of the Trade Union leaders' attempt to give the army dictatorship a more 'social' aspect and to support the Strassers against the Hitlers and Hugenbergs and the A.E.G. against Krupp and Thyssen meant, at best, washing one's hands in innocency; on the lines of the scale of 'lesser evils', Schleicher deserved support; on those of a struggle for democracy the Social Democrats had to accept the Communist suggestions for joint action, whether they liked the Communists or not. It may be

[1] Ibid., p. 372.

[2] S. Aufhäuser, the representative of the black-coated workers on the General Council of the T.U.C., whose personal influence was considerable only in Berlin, and the Union of Engine Drivers and Firemen, which was not of great importance. As mentioned above (p. 331), opposition to the capitulation of the Prussian Government by liberals within and outside it was stronger.

[3] See above, p. 334.

argued that a joint struggle against Hitlerism, especially had it been successful, might have given Communism the upper hand over its allies, and that the prevention of Communist ascendancy is the supreme purpose of democratic policies; if such an attitude be adopted the Social Democratic leaders were right, just as it would be right once more to establish a Nazi dictatorship if this should prove to be the only means of keeping Western Germany on the side of the Atlantic powers. This is not the place to argue about such a policy: suffice it to say that 'democracy', thus defined, contradicts democracy as defined in the growth of the Central European labour movement much more than would the dictatorship of one of the parties that grew up within its framework; the argument just put forward is another way of saying that the preservation of democratic institutions should be subordinate to the preservation of the capitalist mode of production.

A practical criticism of the attitude of the German Social Democrats, on the general lines of Social Democratic concepts, seems to be supplied by the Austrian experience. The Austrian party, like the German, had a pacifist wing as well as a 'social-patriotic' one; partly[1] because Parliament was not assembled before the Russian March Revolution had had its effect upon the Socialist and national movements, the dispute could be kept within the framework of one caucus; the minorities who wished to push the strikes of January 1918 and the revolution of 1918–19 beyond the limits of a bourgeois-democratic outlook remained isolated. Without continuing to take part in the Government for longer than seemed acceptable to advanced working-class opinion,[2] the party built up strongholds which forced every bourgeois Government to compromise, under penalty of a civil war in which the dice would be heavily loaded against reaction. Seipel called the bluff by opening the Fascist offensive, which could easily have been countered had Social Democracy been ready to risk the consequences of a victory in civil war; as it was not, retreat was unavoidable, and proceeded as far as was compatible with the preservation of firm strongholds of the labour movement in a bourgeois régime.

At that time, the bourgeoisie itself was not prepared to advance further, so a new equilibrium of forces was established and continued until Dollfuss got orders from Mussolini to go ahead with full-blown dictatorship. The offensive could have been stopped once more[3] and

[1] The argument should not be overemphasized, as is done by many authors: such crises develop within every party caucus, and every member of the Austrian Social Democratic Party would realize clearly from the Party Press that the Central Committee was 'social-patriotic' at that time. To say that a split would have been unavoidable if there had been meetings of Parliament and opportunities for the opposition to defy party discipline in public is to beg the question how the Party majority (which in Austria was quite used to splits on national lines) would have reacted to such an event.

[2] See above, p. 202.

[3] See above, p. 340.

this time there was no risk of Social Democracy being driven further than it desired; a victory in March 1933 would have resulted in a renewed coalition with the left wing of the Catholics, who, after the German experiences, might have been ready to form a Government of national resistance. Subsequent events followed fairly closely the course of German Social Democracy three years earlier, which had accepted concepts of a gradually more 'authoritarian' régime as the 'lesser evil': the Austrian Trade Unions were already leading to imitate the policies of the German T.U.C., which had sought integration in Schleicher's 'social dictatorship'. Perhaps Austrian Social Democracy might even have accepted the counterpart of Papen's *coup* of 20th July 1932 (which under Austrian conditions would have been the abolition of Vienna's autonomy); the initiative of the Linz workers, who were fed up with a gradual retreat hardly to be distinguished from a rout, forced on the party the trial of strength of February 1934. Only a minority in the Central Committee actively supported the struggle; but it must be said in honour of the Austrian right-wing Social Democrats that, while they did everything in their power to restrict the fighting, which they regarded as hopeless, they did not fall into the abomination of their German comrades, who in July 1932 denounced those who wanted to fight as provocators; on the contrary, they went to prison in a situation analogous to that in which their German comrades had found it fit to support Hitler's foreign policies.

The result was that the Austrian labour movement remained substantially united,[1] and Austrian Fascism so weak that a restoration of democracy seemed imminent when Schuschnigg made his slight attempts at resisting the Hitlerite invasion. No more came out of these movements: all strata of Austrian society had been so deeply permeated by the pan-German ideology that Schuschnigg's own foundations disappeared under his feet. The Social Democratic workers, whose support for Schuschnigg would have taken the form of taking sides in a German civil war, after his capitulation accepted the Greater German empire with rather less resistance than the left wing of the German labour movement had offered in the underground.

What light can be gained for this record on our problem whether capitulation was inevitable from the standpoint of Social Democracy in general, as distinct from its specific Prussian variety? On two occasions —when it kept its unity in the war crisis, and again in February 1934— Austrian Social Democracy, against the wishes of most of its leaders, behaved properly because the results of the opposite kind of behaviour had just been seen in Germany. How modest were the limits of its

[1] The division from the Revolutionary Socialists, who started underground work, remained in essence a division of labour, and, while many underground workers turned towards Communism, the relations between the two parties allowed of United Front policies.

adaptability is shown by the fact that six weeks proved too short a time for it to learn the lessons of 30th January 1933; a year was needed, and by then no more than honour could be saved. Further, from January 1918, when Otto Bauer did not dare to undertake joint action with the Czechs, until the very end Austrian Social Democracy was paralysed by its pan-German ideology. Still, these are criticisms within the Social Democratic setting; to say that a party was slow to learn from the experience of a brother party and that it was successful in so far as it did so, is another way of saying that the brother party itself, had it had better leaders, might have avoided catastrophic mistakes. And there is no inherent reason why every Social Democratic party should be infected by the nationalism of a neighbouring Great Power; though there was some necessary connexion between the Austrian Social Democrats' reformism and their attachment to the nationalism of the most advanced and aggressive capitalist nation of the Continent, as against the Slavs who in the old Austro-Hungarian Empire had been reduced to the status of underdog.

Yet on two occasions of historical importance—in January 1918[1] and in the spring of 1919[2]—the leading group of Austrian Social Democrats under Otto Bauer shrank from action which might have changed the course of world history, and that in conditions where victory—immediate or (as might have been the case in the conditions of 1918) delayed—need not have resulted in the hegemony of the Russian Bolsheviks; Communism has become Russian-dominated precisely because the Bolsheviks were shunned by Western Socialists. Unlike its close counterpart, the Martov-Dan group in Russian Menshevism,[3] the Austro-Marxist school could not even plead an accepted theoretical convention that the country was not ripe for a Socialist revolution and that, for that reason, leadership in the transformation must be left to the bourgeoisie. Nor would action on either occasion have been confined to a dwarf-State surrounded by superior Powers, as was often argued in later statements about Austrian Social Democracy; it would have been

[1] See above, pp. 137–8.

[2] This, of course, is not to say that there would have been any chance of successful action by the small C.P. of Austria (see above, p. 183); we are discussing here the possible outcome of support of the Hungarian Soviet Government (itself a coalition between Social Democrats and Communists) by the party which commanded the support of practically the whole Austrian working class and still held great authority among the workers in the other Succession States.

[3] With which Bauer closely collaborated when released (he was a prisoner of war in Russia) after the February revolution. Complaints about the Russian Mensheviks' collaboration with such 'suspect foreigners' were part of the armoury of the Russian bourgeoisie and its foreign sympathizers (cf. Tyrnova-Williams, *From Liberty to Brest-Litovsk*, London, 1919, p. 104). In their lacking of understanding of the political position of Menshevism they are equalled by contemporary British right-wing statements about Otto Bauer and Austrian Social Democracy in general (see above, note [3] on p. 145).

action taken by the leading part of the working class of a Great Power, or of the group of States springing from its dissolution (and the working classes of some of the other Succession States of Austria-Hungary were definitely to the left of their Austro-German fellows). In his book on *The Austrian Revolution*, Otto Bauer described the victory of the Allies in World War I as the greatest bourgeois-democratic revolution in history (by his Menshevist outlook in Russian affairs he was prevented from seeing the other aspect of the event, the historical importance of the Bolshevist revolution). Yet there was no reason in the accepted teaching of the 'Marxist Centre' why such an event might not be followed by Socialist revolutions in other industrial countries, unless it be tacitly supposed that revolutions must always start with the working classes of those countries which appear to be at the zenith of their external power; we need scarcely dwell on the completely unhistorical character of such an assumption. Bauer refrained from action in January 1918 for fear of the Germans, whose revolution might have been unleashed precisely by action in Austria,[1] and in spring 1919 for fear of the Western Allies, out of respect for whom he dropped even his very modest nationalization programme.[2]

All this may still be explained by assuming that Austrian Social Democracy was in fact a bourgeois-democratic party, the heir of the traditions of 1848, its Socialist phraseology being mere ideological trimming to be explained away by interpretations to the effect that external conditions, unfortunately, prevented its realization. Yet in a whole series of crises between 1927 and 1933 the Austrian Social Democrats could have effectively defended bourgeois democracy without any risk of being driven further than they desired to go, for at that time international conditions would in fact have prevented the Austrian workers from using a victory for any other purpose than the re-establishment of liberal democracy, with some institutional guarantees that they should have their say in its shaping. It did not act, but withdrew as far as seemed necessary in view of the need to preserve powerful foreign sympathies, including those of financiers who made the preservation of their arms by the Austrian Heimwehren a condition of such help as they had to offer; sympathies which eventually resulted in putting the Dollfuss Government in power.[3] The attention devoted by Austrian Social Democracy to international problems was merely another aspect of its unwillingness to act on the national scale, just as its faithfulness to the national traditions of 1848 was another aspect of its incapacity to fight within that framework (not German-dominated) in which the democratic traditions of 1848 could have been vindicated. Austrian Social Democracy did not send armed gangs against the workers, did

[1] See above, pp. 138–9.
[2] See above, p. 180.
[3] See above, p. 323.

not encourage the murder of opposition leaders, did not hail a legal in comparison with an illegal Hitlerism as the 'lesser evil', and did not support Hitler's foreign policy; its bankruptcy shows that Central European democracy was not only betrayed by some corrupt representatives, but failed in its very substance. Its basic limitation was that no one except the labour movement was interested in it, and that the reformist labour movement defended the interests of labour within a setting supposed to be controlled by a class which had no real interest in democracy.

Comparison between the different courses followed by the German and the Russian revolutions respectively dominated the internal development of German Communism in the crises which followed the defeat of 1923.[1] There can be no doubt that a party of the Russian Bolshevik type, if one had existed in Germany between January 1918 and August if not October 1923,[2] would have found half a dozen opportunities to seize power in conditions quite favourable for subsequent Socialist reconstruction. Under the Communist analysis of the general conditions of decaying capitalism it followed that such a party, if created during the 'temporary stabilization of capitalism', would find its opportunity when this stabilization came to its inevitable end: the task consisted simply in breaking the links which connected German Communism with its Social Democratic past while, at the same time, learning from the Bolsheviks how to manœuvre during the difficult period that was bound to come before the large majority of the working class was prepared for a decisive struggle. The solution of this task was attempted in two crises, those of 1923–4 and 1925–6; in the first the Party, going far beyond the advice of the Comintern, removed from its leadership all those who were involved in alliance with Social Democracy; in the second the Comintern took the initiative in establishing a leadership which would collaborate with the Social Democrats for definite purposes without losing its identity, and would resume the Communists' work in the Trade Unions which had been discredited in their ranks as almost equivalent to the acceptance of the leadership of the Trade Union bureaucracy. The new policy brought to the Communists the moral success of the popular initiative on the expropriation of the Princes and some degree of restoration of their position in the Trade Unions, though it never recovered its pre-1923 level. These successes were conditioned by the rule of bourgeois bloc Governments which allowed the Communists to play the part of the more consistent of two working class parties both opposed to these governments; but in a situation in which the Social Democrats could again participate in a coalition Government (and pay the necessary price by adopting the corresponding attitude in such matters as rearmament)[3] and the

[1] See above, pp. 229–30. [2] See above, pp. 139, 162, 193–4 and 222.
[3] See above, p. 324.

Trade Unions would prevent collision with the employers, the Communists were left with no choice save either to resume open warfare on Social Democracy or to become an opposition group within its camp differing from the Social Democrat left wing mainly in that its separate existence as an organization freed it from the shackles of party discipline, and with its main prospects set on the hope that its example might inspire a successful opposition within Social Democracy itself.

Different answers to this dilemma were attempted by the two wings of the coalition of the moderate Left and the moderate Right[1] of the C.P. which controlled the Party after 1925. It nearly exploded in spring 1928 when the Fifth International Congress of Communist Trade Unionists suggested replying to the increasing restrictions on Communist activities in the Trade Unions by a more independent initiative; in the elections to the Works' Councils independent lists of candidates ought to appeal also to the unorganized workers in sympathy with the Communists, and in times of strikes, wide strike committees should be formed to include representatives of the organized workers (in all the trade unions) as well as of the unorganized workers taking part in the strike. Modest as the issue might appear, it had far-reaching practical and theoretical implications; the Trade Union bureaucracy would expel members who fought an electoral battle against the lists of candidates nominated with its support,[2] or who wanted to influence the course of a strike in other ways than by making their voice heard within the Trade Union machinery in accordance with the rules. The resultant weakening of the Communist position within the Trade Unions was tolerable only on the assumption that the organized workers were not the only, and not necessarily the most active, part of the working class; an eventual upheaval presupposed an appeal by the Communists to all the workers, including the unorganized ones, a very large part of whom were so only because they had lost their faith in the Unions' capacity to defend their interests after the reaction of the winter of 1923–4. The two possible answers to these practical and theoretical problems supposed two

[1] The description of the group—under Ernst Meyer, Evert and Gerhard Eisler—was Versöhnler ('appeasers', with the appropriate analogies to some episodes in Russian Party history) in view of their relationship to the open right-wing of the party, under Brandler, which bore responsibility for the events of 1923 and was excluded from leading positions (in the Russian analogies, the 'appeasers' had been defined in relationship to the Mensheviks). In fact, the Versöhnler were the actual right wing of the Party, i.e., those who gave one of the possible answers to the current questions as formulated above in the text; the official Right stood outside the framework of German Communism as it was shaped since the experience of 1923. When Brandler returned from Moscow in 1928 it was only to begin another of those factional disputes in which uninfluential groups split away from the two main parties of the German labour movement.

[2] See above, p. 241.

different interpretations of the situation. If capitalism were entering on a period of prolonged prosperity, whatever its limitations,[1] there was some point in advising the unorganized workers who sympathized with the Communists that they should enter the Trade Unions as the bodies wherein working-class policies were shaped, and in advising the Communist Trade Union members to avoid action which would supply the Trade Union bureaucracy with pretexts for their expulsion, even though at the price of limiting the expression of the party's strength. But if a new period of depressions and warlike catastrophies was imminent,[1] the problem of the unorganized workers—the major half of the German working class—could not be tackled by advising them to join the Trade Unions; this would have been another way of telling them that the C.P. was not interested in their fate,[2] and of leaving them an easy prey to Nazi demagogy. Opponents of a Communist policy which implied a contest with the Nazis for the sympathies of the unorganized workers would reproach it for destroying the prestige of the Weimar Republic without enabling the C.P. to supersede it; to which the Communist Left would answer that the prestige of the Weimar Republic was already destroyed, chiefly by the activities of its supporters, and that if the Communists failed to show that there was a left-wing alternative to

[1] In the factional dispute within the C.P.S.U., where in the summer of 1928 the differences between the right-wing led by Bukharin (at that time Chairman of the Comintern) and Stalin's group were just coming into the open, the issue took the shape of a struggle over the interpretation of an ambiguous formula adopted as a compromise. The theses of the Sixth Comintern Congress on the international situation stated the obvious fact that the revolutionary period immediately following the war, and the subsequent period of comparative prosperity (the 'relative stabilization of capitalism' in Communist jargon) were being followed by a new stage; it was left open whether this stage would itself be (as interpreted by Stalin and the left wing in the Western parties) or merely be followed by (as Bukharin and the right wing considered) a new wave of crises, wars, and revolutions. The former interpretation called for the political consequences drawn by the Left; in the second, the stage immediately impending (the 'third period') would be marked even by increased strength in capitalist society, whose ultimate limitations were denoted merely by a hint at the catastrophes to which it would eventually lead (as imperialism must do in any case, according to Communist theory).

[2] Analogies with Rosa Luxemburg's emphasis on the part played by the unorganized workers in revolutionary crises (see above, pp. 109–10) are inviting but misleading. First, Rosa Luxemburg's whole position belongs to the pre-history of the C.P. as such, not merely to that of one of its factions; her problem was not how the Trade Union bureaucracy could best be opposed, but the much more elementary one of showing that the machinery commanded by that bureaucracy was not identical with the labour movement. Secondly, when Rosa Luxemburg spoke of the unorganized workers, she meant mainly whole industries (key industries such as steel, railways, agriculture among them), the workers in which were prevented from organizing by the conditions existing; the Communist arguments since 1928 dealt with the relations existing within nearly all industries (with the partial exception of agriculture) between the workers who had remained in the Unions after the setback of 1923–24, and the others who in despair had left them.

Weimar they would leave Hugenberg and Hitler uncontested heirs to its estate.

In retrospect it is clear that a victory of the right wing within the Communist party caucus would in no way have prevented the German Social Democrats from following the course they eventually took (they submitted to Brüning's dictatorship because they were afraid of the Nazis, not of the Communist competition), and that this course was bound to lead to situations such as the vote for Hindenburg as the 'lesser evil', where it could not be followed by the Communists without their betraying their principles; there is a large difference between what an underground party can do in a dispute raging openly between two cliques in the camp of its oppressors and what a legal party can explain to an electorate which expects from it a defence of its principles. Disputes between close political neighbours tend to be the most bitter of all; supposing the C.P., led by its right wing, had succeeded in making itself the mouthpiece of a broader left wing within Social Democracy and the Trade Unions (and this was the only purpose that the right-wing Communists could reasonably pursue) that need not have made a united front with them more acceptable to the right wing Social Democrats than the excesses of demonstrative opposition to the moderate republicans eventually did. The case for the policy of the right-wing Communists in 1928–9 is not that it might have prevented the catastrophe, but that it might have made easier the re-emergence of a united labour movement after the Social Democrats had learned their lessons from defeat. Actually there was some *rapprochement* between Social Democrats and Communists in the underground; the long duration of the Fascist régime (which was foreseen by neither of the Communist factions before 1932) allowed for an interlude of internationally conditioned *Front Populaire* policies between the cleavages caused by the agony of the Weimar Republic and those others caused by the Soviet-American tension after World War II.

The chief reproach that must be levelled against the Communist left-wing is that it indulged in wishful thinking on the immediate outcome of the impending crises—doubts as to their ultimate outcome would have prevented anyone from remaining a Communist. The Communists would have betrayed the cause if they had left the unorganized part of the German working class (soon to number in its ranks six million unemployed) to the Nazis without any resistance other than praise of a bankrupt system of organization; but if there were hard times to come, it was good policy to enter on them with a record which might help the German working class to forge its unity in underground activity. Keen criticism of the Social Democrats—including practical criticism by actions which they disliked, but which were undoubtedly directed against the bourgeoisie, such as the Berlin Transport Workers' strike—was the essence of any Communist policy which was to make sense: but there was no sense in expressions of that criticism which seemed to an ordinary Social Democrat worker (not the bureaucrat, who was bound to resent competition as such) to be a mere product of competition between factions. The very mechanism by which the Communist party caucus worked promoted statements and actions which were directed towards the proof of controversial tenets of the Communist analysis and tactical principles, such as the comparative danger involved in the bourgeoisie itself and in workers' parties which compromised with it, the need to direct 'the main thrust' against such parties, etc. Worst of all, this mechanism was conditioned not only by the internal operation of factional strife within the German Communist caucus—the mechanism by which the objective needs of changing conditions are actualized in any party—but, additionally, by the interplay with analogous[1] conflicts in another caucus, the Russian. The latter's predominant position gave any decision it reached an abrupt and in many cases exaggerated character, even if we assume that it pointed in the same direction as it would have done if built on the forces within the German caucus,[1] and that in many cases the Russians proved a moderating force so far as the contents of the policy adopted (and distinct from the methods of its adoption) are concerned.[2]

Immediately after the differences had been somewhat patched up at the Sixth Comintern Congress, the latent party crisis in the U.S.S.R. —and, presumably, misleading information about its likely outcome[3]—

[1] This qualification should be kept in mind; when the C.P.S.U., through the Comintern, interfered in German Communist policy, it did so not merely from the standpoint of the interests of the Russian State (this criticism, very frequently made, is quite irrelevant since Communist policies clearly aim at the preservation and strengthening of the Soviet power in Russia); it reacted to a situation which had differing aspects for Russian and German Communism: for the former, whether it should be confronted with foreign intervention, for the latter, whether it should be driven underground. The first aspect of the matter was as disagreeable as the second, and there is no need to suppose any inherent contradiction between Russian and Western Communist interests. This contradiction arises only in the Trotskyist concept by which the development of class struggle in the West, even if it does not lead to the immediate conquest of State power by any Western Communist Party, is the main, and the preservation of the (allegedly non-socialist) State power in Russia, if cherished at all, is a secondary issue. The Communist parties in the period of which we are speaking had clearly rallied on an anti-Trotskyist platform; immanent criticism of their policies should not start from the Trotskyist scale of values.

[2] See above, pp. 329 and 232, and below, p. 378.

[3] Though I myself stood close to the events (though not to the persons concerned) I can offer no proof for this hypothesis except that nothing else can explain the course of affairs. The pretext for Thälmann's removal was the fact that—as everyone knew, under conditions of sharp but underground factional struggle—he had hushed up a case of embezzlement of Party funds in the Hamburg organization with the evident intention of having the sinner—a member of his own faction—silently removed to Russia rather than cause a scandal within the German party which would be promptly used by the opposite faction. No one who knew Thälmann could believe

enabled the right wing of the German C.P., i.e., the supporters of Bukharin, to rally an overwhelming majority of the Central Committee against the Party's official leader Thälmann. There was a sharp reaction on the part of the rank and file; the left wing was already in control of most of the Party organizations when the slow machinery of the Comintern (within which the German dispute had brought the Bukharin-Stalin conflict into the open) came out in support of Thälmann, and also sought to moderate the efforts of the left wing which immediately began to purge the leading Party organs of its antagonists. In the ideological dispute that followed, the left wing, now in control of the Party, tried to prove the impossibility of a policy of alliance with the Social Democrats because the latter, by the very logic of their evolution, were bound to become a stronghold of bourgeois counter-revolution; and the Social Democrats' behaviour before and after the formation of the Hermann Müller Government[1] certainly did not make the task of the Communist theorists difficult. When Zörgiebel let his police fire on the Berlin workers who were celebrating May Day, and when Wels explained at the Magdeburg Congress (in support of a programme of German re-armament) that, if dictatorship was needed in Germany, Social Democracy would establish it,[2] the ingredients for the description of Social Democrat policies as 'social fascist' were supplied; to anyone who was convinced that monopoly capitalism needed Fascist forms of social discipline, the statements made by Social Democrat theorists to show that monopoly capitalism, being interwoven with the democratic State,

that he acted from other than political considerations; and everyone who knew anything about politics knew that cases of this kind occur in all political parties. So everything amounted to the question whether Thälmann, in principle, had been right in opposing the party's right wing by a faction of his own. Some people who were not in sympathy with the former none the less disapproved of Thälmann's basing his political operations on a close circle of personal friends; yet they cannot have overlooked the fact that Thälmann's removal was a political victory for the Versöhnler (see note [1], p. 373) who were quite outspoken about it. A measure such as the removal of Thälmann (who was a member of the Executive Committee of the Comintern) and especially its publication (which, indeed, excluded correction by means other than an open Party crisis) without consultation with the Comintern was prohibited by the latter's statutes; if the majority of the German C.C., usually not very prone to offend the Comintern even in matters left to tact and goodwill, decided to take such a step, it evidently did so on the assumption that the Comintern, headed by Bukharin, would not object, and that Stalin, whose opposition to Bukharin must have been plain to all those who took part in the Comintern Congress, would be incapable of interference.

[1] See above, pp. 324 ff.

[2] Wels made this statement in opposition to the manœuvres of Hindenburg's clique which eventually (see above, p. 327) resulted in the establishment of Brüning's dictatorship. He wished to make the case that if government by emergency decree was needed the Social Democrats, as the strongest party, had a claim to exercise it. From the point of view of the Communist theories explained below in the text these subjective intentions, however honest, obviously proved *quod erat demonstrandum*.

became democratic, was another way of saying that bourgeois democracy, being interwoven with the power of private monopolies, had to turn fascist. At that time, Hitlerism was one of the minor groups competing for influence in the German right wing, and at least as prominent for German Communists as the Italian model was the example of Poland, where a right-wing Social Democrat with his immediate clique, ultimately acting against his own party, had established an at least semi-fascist dictatorship.[1] No one among the Communist theorists suggested that German Social Democracy would be more than one—and not necessarily the most prominent—of the tools by which Big Business would establish a fascist or semi-fascist dictatorship; if Schleicher's later attempts to establish his 'social dictatorship' with support from Strasser to Leipart had succeeded, the part played by the Trade Unionists in that Government would have been precisely what the framers of the concept of 'social fascism' had had in mind. In such a case, however, the C.P. would hardly have offered more than propagandist resistance to Schleicher so long as he was the alternative to the Hitlerite dictatorship; all the statements about 'social fascism' would have amounted to the true, but not very illuminating, thesis that all the varying factions, amongst which the C.P. would have supported the least dangerous one, belonged not to a democratic but to a fascist framework.

Yet the political outcome of the theoretical statements on 'social fascism' did not depend on the amount of truth they might contain, nor even on the fantastic exaggerations with which they were occasionally applied in the party's propaganda; most of this exaggeration has become known to wider circles precisely because of the sharp criticism and correction to which they were subjected by the Party leaders in spring 1930, after the publication in Russia of Stalin's *Dizzy with Success*.[2]

[1] O. Braun (op. cit., pp. 365–6) mentions the suggestions made by the right-wingers that he should be appointed head of a dictorial régime, and states that he always refrained from encouraging such projects, being convinced that, as in the Polish case, the persons involved would be driven by the logic of the situation to the application of Fascist methods.

[2] It is not the task of this book to go into the complicated inter-connexion between Soviet and German Communist policies. The very essence of the Communist analysis implies the feeling that some logical interconnexion exists—i.e. that the same analysis of the international situation which demanded the overthrow of Bukharin and the quick start with wholesale collectivization in Russia also demanded the elimination of the Versöhnler which would make the German C.P. an annex to the Social Democrats' inevitable capitulation before the Fascist threat (this interconnexion was felt by the right wing as well, see note [3], p. 376). The same mechanism of internal party life which produced excesses in collectivization in Russia might also have produced illegitimate generalizations even from correct descriptions of the essence of Social Democrat policies. The very existence of the Comintern implied a special mechanism by which necessary changes were carried out, and this mechanism might easily defeat their purpose. In the case under discussion, a group in the German Central Committee led by H. Neumann, who was closely linked with that group in the C.P.S.U. under Lominadze who had been associated with the excesses of the collectivization

It depended on the limitations which were set by the party's theoretical analysis to the adaptation of its policies to changing circumstances. When in spring 1930 the left-centre Government was thrown out by Hindenburg's clique and a strong wing of Social Democracy (including most of the Trade Unionists) for a while resisted toleration of the Brüning Government, it would have been good policy for the Communists not only to vote in Parliament for anti-Brüning motions made by the Social Democrats, as they did, but to make to Social Democrats and Trade Unionists an offer of collaboration against the dictatorship as an alternative to its toleration. Such an offer would have put the unavoidable cleavage between the right-wing Social Democrats and the Communists on the appropriate basis; in the actual setting, as described in the Communist theories on 'social fascism', the unavoidable reactions of the Communist caucus to the Social Democrats' capitulation took on the character of a dispute about the best means by which the enemy thus described might be fought.

That part of the C.P.'s left wing which had taken the initiative in defeating the right-wing used its moral—though never organizational—preponderance within the caucus for a large-scale application of those concepts of economic struggle in opposition to which the Versöhnler had revolted.[3] The elections to the Works' Councils were contested everywhere, and the impressive vote achieved in the largest factories strengthened the Communists' feeling that the time had passed when they could consider themselves as a mere minority pressure group within the Trade Unions. With all energy new methods of strike organization by broad committees comprising unorganized as well as organized workers, mass-picketing, and organization of the support of the strikers by all the working-class population were developed and applied in the series of strikes that marked the opening of the Great Depression;[3]

drive (he later turned round and joined forces with Bukharin's group) turned the reaction against leftist excesses in the treatment of the Social Democrats against P. Merker, who had been more or less accidentally associated with them, but was one of the chief representatives of the tendency to independent organization of the economic struggles by the C.P. In the outcome (see below in text) an impolitic approach to the Social Democrat workers was replaced by intentional attempts at splitting the Trade Unions, which did not make things any better.

[1] The Versöhnler—or party activists in sympathy with their principles who paid due lip-service to motions endorsed by the Comintern—never ceased to be a more important factor in party life than would appear from the overwhelming majorities with which their policies were disapproved; within the left wing the tendencies which soon crystallized in the 'Neumann group' long remained preponderant within the Central Committee, in spite of Thälmann's leadership, which, from the first, mainly sought for a compromise within the left wing.

[2] See above, p. 373.

[3] See above, p. 329. The Social Democratic Trade Unionists reproached the Communists with reviving primitive methods of class struggle (see above, pp. 53 and 63–4) which, they said, had since been outmoded by the development of working-class

the mass expulsions of Communists from the Trade Unions which followed such breaches of the rules were regarded as an unavoidable by-product of the extension of the class struggle which would matter little once that struggle had culminated in a wave of political mass strikes. Such tactics were linked with an analysis of the situation which proved mistaken when the Great Depression, which had been correctly forecast by the left wing of the C.P., failed to produce the revolutionary wave expected by it.

A reaction within the Party caucus was unavoidable. In the setting created by the preceding disputes it turned out in favour not of the Versöhnler but of a group led by H. Neumann, which, while maintaining the denunciation of Social Democracy, followed it up, not by independent attempts by the Communists to organize mass-movements, but by the usual devices of organizational competition. After the strike of the Berlin engineering workers[1] every occasion was used (and sometimes even provoked) to establish independent Communist Trade Unions. They proved a conspicuous failure,[2] but they helped to purge the Free Trade Unions of such active Communists as might still be left in them after the initiative with independent candidates for the Works' Councils. Even worse than these attempts, which were no novelty in the history of the German labour movement,[3] were the excesses to which the avoidance of even the slightest suspicion of identification of the C.P. with Social Democrat policies was driven in parliamentary moves; the support given to the right-wing initiative for the removal of the Prussian Government[4] made it certainly easier for the Social Democrat leaders, in the following year when the C.P.s policy had changed, to reject all its offers of collaboration against Papen and Hitler. At almost every three-cornered election, in more stable democracies, the extreme left is re-

organization. The Communists would accept the analogy, but explain it by the statement that they as well as the Social Democrats of the nineties regarded the economic struggle not as an end in itself but as a preparation for the decisive political struggles. In fact, some, such as mass-picketing, methods of strike organization developed by the German left wing in 1929–30, though they failed in their country of origin, have since become widely accepted by the labour movements of other countries.

[1] See above, pp. 329–30.

[2] The Report to the 19th Regional Congress of the Berlin Party organization gives, for 1st October 1932, a total figure of 50,354 members of the Red Trade Unions and the Revolutionary Trade Union Opposition (in those industries where there were no Red Unions, nearly half of the total) at a time when the party had 46,600 members and got 860,800 votes (on 1st July 1932, when the party had 140,000 voters less, there had been 600 more members in its Trade Union organization). The strongest of the Red Unions were the Engineers (in Berlin's main industry) with 13,600 and the Builders with 8,950 members; 7,800 workers of the municipal undertakings (including transport) were members of the Revolutionary Trade Union Opposition (no other group exceeded even the 3,000 mark).

[3] See above, p. 234.

[4] See above, p. 283.

proached by the moderate left with supporting the right-wing candidate; but these were no normal times, and the ballot had no longer much importance in Germany except as indicating in what direction the bullets would eventually be fired. To avoid possible misunderstandings in this regard, the Neumann group supplemented its anti-centre organizational and electional activities by anti-Nazi military activities of the most simplified type; the slogan 'Hit the Fascists wherever you meet them' gave every Communist youth who had his gun handy when he met a Nazi gang full powers to involve his party in a conflict with the (usually Social Democrat) police. A general atmosphere created by moves such as the 'red plebiscite'[1] certainly did not invite Social Democratic sympathies with the Communist party to the collision; not to speak of further excesses, which had to be corrected by a special Party decision 'against individual terrorism'.

Even the supporters of the Neumann group were not such political babes that they overlooked the harm done by all these things to the possibility of the C.P.'s initiating mass action against the Fascist threat; their conscience, however, was appeased by the consideration, quite widespread in those days,[2] that a temporary triumph of the Nazis, unavoidable as it might be, would form a mere prelude to the Communists' accession to power. It followed that attention should be directed not so much to preventing this prelude as to creating safeguards against its being followed by a restoration of the Weimar Republic; whatever helped to discredit the latter might bear revolutionary fruit in the future. At the end of 1931 Thälmann attacked the Neumann group on this very point: referring to the Italian experience, he showed that there was no guarantee whatever that a Fascist régime would remain a short interlude. It followed that it must be prevented; the obvious means for this was united action by the Social Democrat and Communist workers. Being entangled, however, in the framework of Communist orthodoxy (violation of whose rules would have given the Neumann group as easy victory) Thälmann had to explain that such united action was the surest means of breaking the Social Democrat leaders' hold on their supporters; such arguments, put forward in public, supplied the Social Democrat leaders with an easy answer to the Communist suggestions of united action. Neumann used an apparent setback in the Second Ballot in the Presidential elections of 1932[3] as an

[1] See above, p. 283.

[2] See above, note [2] on p. 348.

[3] The circumstances are characteristic: in the second ballot (at which a relative majority sufficed) Thälmann lost a fourth of the five million votes polled for him in the first ballot, in which a draw was generally foreseen and, in any case, an absolute majority was needed for the successful candidate (Hindenburg and Hitler were the other candidates); evidently the memories of Hindenburg's election in 1925 (see above, p. 232) were so strong that even a large part of the Communist voters preferred to play safe in the second ballot and to vote for Hindenburg lest Hitler might

opportunity for a counter-attack against Thälmann's leadership, but merely secured thereby his rapid fall by a combination of all the other trends within the party. Now the party could go ahead with suggestions for joint action committees in the local areas against the Nazi threat and with the demand for a general strike to reply to the removal of the Prussian Government; this demand was rejected by the Social Democratic leaders as a 'provocation'.[1] It did not make action dependent on the Social Democrat leaders' approval; the chain of the 'Papen strikes' and the election victory of 6th November 1932 won at the expense of both Nazis and Social Democrats marked the summit of the C.P.'s strength. In January it made some progress on the question of joint demonstrations with the Social Democrats, but could not get their leaders to agree to any joint action against Hitler's nomination; there was no question of resistance with the C.P.'s own forces.[2] With a last

be elected. In fact, such precautions were unnecessary; Hindenburg got an absolute majority, which he used in the way we have seen above. The Communist electorate had no tendency to decrease; on 31st July, 5·2 million votes were recorded. Vacillations in its attitude could in fact only prove Thälmann's case by showing how widespread were the concepts of the 'lesser evil' even among the left wing of the labour movement.

[1] See above, p. 331.

[2] This question should be clearly distinguished from that of what a united front of labour should have done, even if defeat had been certain (as it was not, in view of the tensions existing between the Schleicher and Papen-Thyssen groups). Honourable defeats, like that of February 1934 in Austria, have value only in that they create a tradition for the future revival (in this sense, they would certainly have justified even the heaviest sacrifices conceivable in January 1933): they give no sense if the fighters are burdened by a competing group in the camp of labour with the responsibility for the white terror which allegedly could have been avoided without their 'provocative' action; this would have been the certain outcome of a Communist action against Hitler's access to power which could only have had an armed character (strikes were attempted, but clearly failed because of the widespread consciousness that they were useless unless they were backed by both wings of the labour movement). The question who would have been the beneficiary of armed actions by isolated Communist groups was best answered by Hitler, who, in the absence of the real thing, attempted to fake it.

The general feeling that the events of January 1933 were a defeat of historical importance produced much heart-searching among the Communists. Though the factional disputes, on issues such as whether the Trade Unions, dissolved by Hitler, should be reorganized in the underground on a 'red' or on a revived 'Free' basis, continued for years in the underground, none of the major trends within the party has suggested that armed resistance was possible in 1933; criticism on these grounds was reserved to outside factions to which, at that time, belonged not only the Versöhnler but the Neumann group also. In documents originating from those sides there has been considerable speculation about the dates 'missed'. The only one for which a serious case could be made was 22nd January 1933, when, under pressure from the very people who removed him one week later, Schleicher had to allow a provocative Nazi demonstration before the Communist headquarters; the intention was, evidently, to face the Party with the alternative between a loss of face in a critical situation and an armed conflict with Schleicher's forces which would drive the latter into the arms of the Nazis. Schleicher saw the trap and warned the Communists, impressive demonstration on the eve of Hitler's nomination it went underground, only gradually to realize that Hitlerism was to stay for a long time and that the internal crises which accompanied its first year of power were only by-products of its consolidation.

German Communism succeeded neither in assuming power nor in preventing Social Democracy from dominating the last phase in the history of the German labour movement according to its own laws; this implied the triumph of Fascism once the predominant forces in the bourgeois camp had decided in its favour. It may be asked whether the second failure was not implied in the first, i.e. whether a Weimar Republic not overthrown, in time, by the Left was not bound to be transformed, in due course, according to the right-wing's needs. There is no need to follow up this argument, as the C.P.—with the possible exception of the Neumann interlude—pursued the aim of preventing a Fascist régime; it must be criticized in the light of the question whether it pursued this aim with all the energy possible. The best criticism of the line applied by the German Communists during the last crisis of the Weimar Republic is that it had to be corrected three times between summer 1928, when the essential data were available and could be appreciated with some critical foresight, and summer 1932, when it had to be applied on the occasion of Papen's *coup d'état*; a fourth correction, which involved the acceptance of *Front Populaire* policies, was carried out after prolonged discussions in the underground in 1933–5. A party's ability to correct its line is not a weakness; the internal crises of the Communist caucus compare favourably with the stubbornness with which the Social Democrats—save for a short vacillation during the first months of Brüning's Government—pursued their original line to the extent of self-destruction. But while a party's capacity to learn from mistakes is a first condition for its being a serious factor, its institutional

giving them the compensation of a counter-demonstration three days later, which proved very impressive. Supposing that the Communist C.C. had realized that there was no more to be won in the interplay between the diverse right-wing cliques and that the only thing to be achieved was an honourable ending to the Party's career (but still there would have remained the certainty after the defeat of being denounced by the Social Democrats as being responsible for the advent of German Fascism), an armed conflict might have been opened by firing on the Nazi columns passing the Party house, which in themselves presented an obvious provocation. But it is difficult to see how the Communists, in such a case, could have avoided casualties mainly among the police who (very reluctantly) shepherded the Nazi demonstration; such casualties were most likely to give the conflict an anti-Social-Democrat instead of an anti-Nazi character. In fact the C.P. organized an (illegal) demonstration against the Nazis (which passed without major incidents, as the police confined themselves to slowly driving the counter-demonstrators away, and the Nazis preserved discipline in what must for them have been a distasteful situation) but made no major efforts to use those incidents as an occasion for a political strike, which would have been most unlikely to become impressive. In the situation of January 30th, another of the dates mentioned in these factional disputes, there was not the slightest possibility of Communist counter-action.

structure and methods should also be measured according to the elasticity and speed with which such corrections can be carried out. The complicated interplay[1] of factional disputes in the German and Soviet party caucuses made corrections possible by eliminating leaders who clung to obsolete tenets; but it also restricted the scope of correction by offering usually only two sets of alternatives. When the Versöhnler were defeated (rightly, for they overlooked the approach of the Great Depression and would have bound up the Party's fate with the capitulation policy of Social Democracy) quite a number of incorrect statements, born partly of wishful thinking, partly from mechanical application of the Stalinist theory, had to be accepted too.

Similar things happen in many parties; but this was an extraordinary time; 1928 was, perhaps, the last moment at which the adoption of a correct line might have given the C.P. *some* chance of preventing the Social Democrats from controlling decisive parts of the working class at the time of their final capitulation, and even if Fascism could not have been prevented, might have rendered that capitulation the definite end of the Social Democrat traditions within the German labour movement. In the actual course of events, the Communists entered the decisive crisis with a line which was just sufficient to shift the responsibility for action or inaction to the Social Democrats (who had been supplied with many pretexts for inaction by the C.P.'s preceding vacillations) and would have secured for the party the position of major factor in the German labour movement if democracy had been restored by a failure of the Fascist cliques to agree on joint action; the progress made by the Communists in that direction was just sufficient to render such agreement most desirable from the Big Business point of view. In the circumstances, restoration of the German labour movement (with the balance shifted to its left), however likely it appeared in November 1932 to many observers, German Liberals as well as to Otto Bauer, would have been a godsend; it could not be expected according to the Marxist thesis that disorganization in the ranks of the ruling class occurs as a by-product of the revolt of the oppressed. The naked, however disagreeable, balance was that the type of democracy developed by the sectional labour movement was incapable of defending itself once the vested interests found it advisable to destroy it, and that the opposition that had grown up in its ranks under the impact of the Russian revolution was incapable of wresting the initiative from them.

[1] For the period under discussion, we must speak of interplay, not, as is frequently done, of one-way domination of the German by the Russian caucus. Perhaps the latter (i.e. transfer of Bolshevist experiences to Germany, however likely to be wrong when applied in a very different environment) would not have been quite so bad as was interference by the predominant Soviet faction born of the knowledge that the German sympathizers of its opponents used the German issues, as an opportunity to strike against it (see f.n. [3], p. 376 and f.n. [2], p. 378).

CONCLUSION

THE type of democracy discussed in this book was marked by the close interconnexion between political and economic group organizations; these organizations tended to embrace the broad masses of the population and, in their activities as well as in their final crisis, were subject to the test whether they could act on behalf of those masses. Failure to act in time resulted in lack of confidence. The result was destruction. In Austria, the leaders lost control at the end; the outcome, February 1934, was and is generally regarded as at least preferable to the shame of the German capitulation. The existence of real chances of success at a date as late as March 1933 has been asserted from the most competent quarter.[1]

The eventual degeneration was prepared for by the identification of the sectional organization with a large number of functions which could eventually be taken over by the State whatever the character of its government, if not by the sectional opponents of the labour movement. Yet it would be a mistake to ascribe the catastrophe to atrophy because of loss of functions of importance to the social groups which the organizations served. Of all the movements we have discussed, German Social Democracy suffered by far the worst moral bankruptcy; but in its present sphere of activity (which it owes to forces not of its own making) the business of collective agreements, strike ballots, mediators, etc. continues as if nothing had happened. Evidently these things *are* necessary in a certain kind of society. The Social Democrat slogan of 'political wages' was in itself correct: if anything has become evident from the record we have discussed, it is the impossibility of conceiving economic conflicts in isolation from their political framework. What was erroneous in the Social Democratic concept was the assertion that the economic interests of the working class would necessarily be served by collaboration with the existing government; as government was controlled by forces which demanded a monopoly of power, this amounted to political suicide on the part of Social Democracy.

Yet clearly the alternative to collaboration within the established system is readiness to overthrow it, at least as a last resort if it fails to

[1] See above, p. 340.

satisfy certain minimum demands. This has nothing to do with details of political organization, and least of all with the specifically Russian methods of revolution. The greatest of the decisions discussed in this book belong to the period before the Russian pattern of Communism was definitely established. That the world, to-day, is divided between two main patterns of political and social organization—with some prospect that a new diversity may develop from variations in either camp—this is largely due to the facts discussed, both in their direct outcome (in that the Central European labour movements failed to produce some variety of socialism different from that of Soviet Russia) and in their indirect effect, in that their breakdown and the temporary triumph of Hitlerism made war rather than the dynamic of internal development the great shaper of contemporary society, including the society of the U.S.S.R. War and the results of war have also given to what survives of the trends discussed in this book their respective spheres of influence and activity. The historian will remember that similar things have happened before, in the aftermath of all the great revolutionary periods; when the principle *cujus regio ejus religio* was established, it was not just a moral triumph, nor was it the end of the spiritual influence of the Reformation. The real indication of the decay of Central European Democracy was not its inability to play a leading part in a period when the historical importance of Europe as a whole is decreasing, but the completely passive character of the role assumed by the movements discussed in this book. The Germans' greatest author told them, a hundred and fifty years ago, that there was no choice except to be a hammer or an anvil; they have been fonder of applying this lesson abroad than at home. The results we see to-day.

Against the greatness of such a historical test (which, we remember, did not culminate at any single moment but offered ample opportunity for the correction of initial mistakes) the explanations current in the literature on the subject seem makeshifts. Central European democracy was not defeated because of its institutional framework; on the contrary, if democracy in the Western sense (in the widest sense of the word, for an identification with specifically Anglo-American institutions would beg the question) was possible at all in Central Europe, it had to be based upon mass-parties of the type discussed (which embodied the only democratic forces of those countries), proportional representation, etc. If it was not possible—and for that a reasonable case can be made—the lack of its preliminary conditions was bound to be expressed in its institutional framework, though 'mistakes' on the part of individual parties, failure to produce the necessary type of leader, and so on.

Similarly, the statement that Central European democracy was defeated by its international environment is correct only if we take it for granted that democracy has to offer short-term benefits to all the electorate; on this assumption, the aftermath of a lost war and the

Great Depression, however favourable to a thorough transformation of society, were certainly unfavourable to the democratic experiment. But in the historical record as distinct from the ideological applications of the term since it has become fashionable, democracy has always been relevant as an attempt to find solutions to problems of social crisis: if an idea of democracy fails to answer this elementary need, it has to be reinterpreted.

Finally, it is not true except in appearance that Central European democracy was defeated by splits in the labour movement; in Austria there was no such split, and in Germany and Czechoslovakia the most important decisions were taken before the irrevocable split occurred. At the decisive point, i.e. in Germany, the split occurred, and became definitive, just because a particular policy which contradicted its original tenets was pursued by the leaders of the Social Democratic Party.[1] Subsequently, there were plenty of blunders on the Communist side which supplied as many pretexts for Social Democrats who preferred co-operation with Hindenburg's army to resistance in alliance with Communism; their basic decision, however, was that of collaborating with the forces which controlled the Prusso-German State. From this decision the split followed, as well as the many opportunities offered by the dynamic of intra-factional strife to everyone who wished to continue that policy of collaboration even when it amounted to political suicide.

From the standpoint of those concerned, the stubbornness with which this fatal path was pursued might be explained by the increasingly repellent character of the alternative which became the more definitive the more their own politics developed. Scheidemann, Ebert, and Noske supplied the Comintern with its German section; they had Rosa Luxemburg killed at a time when her politics represented a potential alternative to the course which the left wing under Russian leadership was eventually to pursue. Yet once irrevocable things had been done, to enter on a decisive struggle with the bourgeoisie meant, in the event of success, having to compete with the Communists in the atmosphere of a revolutionary upheaval, which would strengthen their appeal to the masses. Speaking of the record of the Russian revolution, Prof. Carr noticed that 'once bourgeois democracy was recognized as a stepping-stone to socialism, it could be brought into being only by those who believed also in socialism'.[2] Ought we to add that, once joint resistance to Kornilov's attempt at counter-revolution had proved to be a stepping-stone to the triumph of the Bolshevik revolution in Russia, only people who were at least prepared to prefer Bolshevism to Fascism could offer serious resistance to a Fascist counter-revolution? But if this be so, it would only strengthen our refusal to ascribe the catastrophe to the mere blunders or betrayals of individuals.

[1] See above, pp. 116–7.

[2] *The Bolshevik Revolution*, 1917–23, vol. I, London, 1950, p. 42.

If Schleicher's attempt at basing a 'social army-dictatorship' upon support from Strasser to Leipart had succeeded, he would have realized, under different conditions, Lassalle's conception of the 'social monarchy' as well as proving the Communist attacks against 'social fascism'; however the two descriptions differed in evaluation, they referred to one thing which was within the realm of possibility in 1932, if not in 1862. But Lassalle had also said that the workers would form the Church of the future. Clearly he did not wish thereby to assert what Marx, in those same years, expressed in the statement that 'the emancipation of the working class can only be the work of the workers themselves'; in this concept, there was no place for Lassalle's appeal for State help where it was the State of Prussian Junkerdom to which they would be addressed. But certainly Lassalle did not merely wish to foretell that something like the Nazis (whether Hitler or Strasser) would have to disguise themselves as a 'workers' party'. What he meant was that the State would have to face, and would be capable of facing, the new tasks of the industrial age by a mere shift in its political appeal, without a thorough revolution; his true pupil was Ebert, who hated revolution 'like sin',[1] and yet believed that a saddler's rise to head the German empire was a symbol of the emancipation of the German workers. As opposed to some of Marx's more utopian statements Lassalle may have been right in guessing that Socialism would be national; but Marx was right in understanding that it presupposed a quite definite procedure of national regeneration. The German labour movement paid its tribute to Marxism mainly by accepting such of its tenets as seemed suitable objects for hymn-singing in the Church of the Future; reality was taken care of by comparisons between the Russian and the German food rations. But peoples and classes cannot be masters of their future without, if necessary, accepting low rations and even some casualties.

The plain lesson of the record seems to be that the sectional mass movement, unless it gives birth to something which outgrows its limitations, is incapable of creating the setting in which its inherent potentialities can develop. We have no historical experience of the application of Guild Socialism, and I suspect that for the reasons just mentioned we shall have none. There was no inherent economic contradiction in Hillmann's expectation[2] that, eventually, capitalism would develop a new social structure by integrating the trade unions into its framework; the practical application of such concepts, however, was bound to lead to Naphtali's statement[3] that the German trusts were becoming democratic because the German Trade Unions had been integrated in their State. Democracy is a concept open to diverse interpretation, and no extraneous criticism should be applied to the outcome. But surely, the

[1] See above, p. 148.
[2] See above, p. 22.
[3] See above, p. 309.

most immanent criticism of sectional mass organization is the concept of maximum development and autonomy of trade union functions. It is quite obvious that sectional organization in Central Europe developed, one by one, a set of functions which could easily be taken off its shoulders in favour of the State—which, thereby, did *not* become more democratic. The only function in which Fascism proved a conspicuous failure was the representation of the workers' interests in the individual shop; but the Workers' Councils themselves had never been popular with the German Trade Union bureaucrats. In the outcome the State, with a set of functions which in Lassalle's days would have been anathema to any Liberal or Conservative, became something which it had not been before; even the employer, called by Hitler the 'leader of the enterprise' was no longer the 'master in his own house' of Lassalle's and later days. There was less destitution, but hardly more freedom than before. And the price that had to be paid for full employment was war.

In the second chapter of this book we have seen how the democratic movement, passing in the aftermath of the abortive revolution of 1848 from one social group to another, inspired and created sectional mass-organization; in the last chapters we have seen how the working and the limitations of sectional organization, after the abortive revolution of 1918, brought bourgeois democracy to an end. It had not been in vain; the world was different from what it had been in the days when it began. But it was the close of a chapter of history, and there is no sense in reopening it. Its contribution to the future is to be found in the lessons that can be drawn from its defeat for the synthesis to come.

BIBLIOGRAPHY

This list does not include all the books which I have consulted in writing this study, but only those from which I have frequently quoted or which I would suggest as likely to be useful to future workers in the field. In a few cases a note is added drawing attention to the scope and standpoint of the book referred to; this has been done particularly with regard to some books which cannot be supposed to be well known in Britain. The absence of such a note (save for a few of the older publications now outdated) must not be taken as any indication that it is considered as of minor importance: indeed, I have made no comments on those books whose importance I have felt justified in assuming to be already recognized.

Reports and Proceedings of party or trade union congresses and similar publications which every specialist student will know how to find but which will not be ordinarily available to the general reader are not listed here.

Friedrich Adler vor dem Ausnahmegericht: Protokoll der Verhandlung. Berlin, 1919. One of the most important sources for the war-time history of Austrian Social Democracy.

Bachem, Karl. *Vorgeschichte, Geschichte und Politik der deutschen Zentrumspartei.* 7 vols. Cologne, 1922 ff. The standard work on the subject.

Bauer, Otto. *Die Oesterreichische Revolution.* Vienna, 1923. A much abridged English version was published in 1927, and has as far as possible been used in this book.

Der Kampf um Wald und Weide. Vienna, 1925.

Austrian Democracy under Fire. London, 1934.

Die illegale Partei. Paris, 1939 (posthumous).

Bebel, August. *Aus meinem Leben.* 3 vols. (reprint) Dietz-Verlag, Berlin, 1946.

Beneš, Eduard. *My War Memoirs.* English edition. 1928.

Bergsträsser, Ludwig (*ed.*). *Der politische Katholizismus, Dokumente seiner Entwicklung.* Munich, 1921.

Bernstein, Eduard. *Evolutionary Socialism*. English edition. London, 1909.
Die deutsche Revolution. Berlin, 1921. Interesting collection of documents.
Braun, Adolf. 'Allgemeines und Spezielles zur Buchdruckertariffrage.' In: *Neue Zeit*, vol. XVIII, i, 1900.
Die Gewerkschaften vor dem Kriege. Berlin, 1921.
Braun, Otto. *Von Weimar zu Hitler*. New York, 1940.
Bringmann, A. *Beiträge zur Geschichte der deutschen Zimmererbewegung*, 2 vols. Stuttgart, 1903. The most important general collection of materials on the early development of trade unionism in Germany.
Bruegel, Ludwig. *Geschichte der österreichischen Sozial-demokratie*. 5 vols. Vienna, 1922–5.
Chmelar, J., *The Political Parties in Czechoslovakia*. Prague, 1926.
Denis, Ernst. *La Bohème depuis la Montagne Blanche*. Vol. 2: 'La Renaissance tschèque; vers le féderalisme.' Paris, 1903.
Deutsch, Julius. *Geschichte der österreichischen Gewerkschaftsbewegung*. 2 vols. Vienna, 1927–30. (First edition of vol. 1, 1908; quotations refer to this edition.)
Aus Oesterreichs Revolution. Vienna, 1920. Early history of the Austrian Republican Army.
Der Bürgerkrieg in Oesterreich. Prague, 1934. Reports of eye-witnesses of the events of February 1934.
Deutscher Buchdruckerverband. Kurze Verbandsgeschichte. 2nd edition. 1925.
Deutscher Liberalismus im Zeitalter Bismarcks, eine politische Briefsammlung. Ed. J. Heydenhoff. Stuttgart, 1925.
Deutscher Textilarbeiterverband: Mein Arbeitstag, mein Wochenende. Contributions from 150 women textile workers. Berlin, 1930.
Digby, M. *Agricultural Co-operation in Czechoslovakia*. London, 1930.
Ebert, Friedrich. *Kämpfe und Ziele*. Berlin, 1926. A collection of political notes, published by his party.
von Elm, A. 'Zur Frage der Neutralisierung der Gewerkschaften.' In: *Neue Zeit*, vol. XVIII, 1, 1900.
Erdmann, A., *Die Christliche Arbeiterbewegung in Deutschland*. Stuttgart, 1907.
Fabian, W. *Klassenkampf im Sachsen*. Loebau, 1930.
Fischer, Ruth. *Stalin and German Communism*. Harvard Univ. Press, 1948.
Guillebaud, R. *The Works' Councils in Germany*. Cambridge, 1928.
Hänisch, Konrad. 'Zur Frage der gewerkschaftlichen Arbeitslosenunterstützung. In: *Neue Zeit*, XVI, ii, 1898.
Heiss, F. 'Die gelbe Arbeiterbewegung.' In: *Schmoller's Jahrbuch*, vol. XXXV.

Herkner, Heinrich, *Die Arbeiterfrage*. 6th edition, 1916. The classical German academic treatment. References are to vol. II.

Herzig, J., *Die Stiellung der deutschen Arbeitergewerkschaften zum Problem der Wirkschaftsdemokratie*. Jena, 1933.

Jäck, H., *The New Germany*. London, 1927.

Jostock, P., *Der deutsche Katholizismus und die Ueberwindung des Kapitalalismus*. Regensburg, 1932.

Kantarowicz, L. *Die sozialdemokratische Presse. Deutschlands*, Tübingen 1922.

Kautsky, Karl. 'Zur Frage der gewerkschaftlichen Neutralität.' In: *Neue Zeit*, vol. XVIII, ii, 1900. (Quotations refer to this article.)

Der politische Massenstreik. Stuttgart, 1914.

Die Internationalität und der Krieg. Berlin, 1915.

Kessler, H. Count. *Rathenau*. London, 1929.

Klüss, F. *Der Allgemeine Deutsche Zigarrenarbeiterverein*. Volkswirtschaftliche Abhandlungen der badischen Hochschulen, 1905. A study of Germany's first Trade Union.

Kuczynski, J. and M. *Die Lage des deutschen Industriearbeiter*. Berlin, 1930.

Kulemann, F. *Die Bernfsverbände*, 2 vols. 1908 ed. An academic presentation from a standpoint less friendly than that of the Academic Socialists, e.g. Herkner.

Lambach, W. *Die Herrschaft der Fünfhundert*. Berlin, 1925. An intelligent and comprehensive description of the working of the parliamentary machinery of the Weimar Republic by a moderate Conservative.

Layton, R. T., and Rist, C. *The Economic Situation in Austria*. League of Nations Publication, 1925.

Legien, Karl. *Die Gewerkschafssbewegung in Deutschland in Jahie 1896* In: *Neue Zeit*, vol. XVI, 1.

Luxemburg, Rosa. *Werke* (*ed.* Fröhlich). Incomplete: references in this book are to vol. IV, 'Gewerkschaftskampf und Massenstreik'.

Sozialreform oder Revolution? 1898. Second edition. Berlin, 1908. Her polemic against Bernstein.

Massenstreik, Partei und Gewerkschaft. Stuttgart, 1906.

Marx-Engels Correspondence. Complete German edition, Marx-Engels Institute, Moscow.

Masaryk, T. G. *Palacky's Idee des böhmischen Volkes*. Prague, 1898.

The Making of a State. English edition. London, 1926.

Mayer, Gustav. *J. B. von Schweitzer und die Sozialdemokratie*. Leipzig, 1909.

Mehring, Franz. *Geschichte der deutschen Sozialdemokratie*. 4 vols. 1904, reprinted 1922. Quotations not specially indicated refer to this enlarged edition of this standard work, first published in 1893. Before he became a Social Democrat Mehring, from a National

Liberal point of view, wrote a short book under the same title in 1878, to which occasional reference is made.

Merker, Paul. *Deutschland, Sein oder Nichtsein?* Vol. I, Mexico City, 1944. The only comprehensive presentation of the fall of the Weimar Republic from the (at the time of publication official) Communist standpoint.

Michels, R. *Political Parties; A Sociological Study of the Oligarchical Tendency of Modern Democracy*. English edition, London, 1915.

Michels, R. and G. 'Das Problem der Arbeitslosigkeit und ihrer Bekämpfung durch der deutschen Gewerkschaften. In: *Archiv für Sozialwissenschaft*, vol. XXXI. 1910.

Milhaud, E. *La Democratic socialiste allemand*. Paris 1903.

Müller, O. 'Die Christliche Gewerkschaftsbewegung Deutschlands.' mit besonderer Berück sichtigung der Bergarberter und Textilarbirter, In: *Volkswirschaftliche Abhandlungen der badischen Hochschulen*, Vol. 8, 1897.

Naphtali, Fritz. *Wirtschaftsdemokratie*. Berlin, 1928. An official publication of the German T.U.C.

Nestriepke, Siegfried. *Die Gewerkschaftsbewegung*. 2 vols. Stuttgart, 1920–4. The standard work from the viewpoint of a somewhat critical representative of German Trade unionism. Quotations refer to Vol. I, which deals with the pre-war period.

Noske, G. *Von Kiel bis Kapp*. Berlin, 1920.

Oncken, L. *Lassalle*. The standard biography: various editions.

Palacky, F. *Politisches Vermächtnis*. German ed. Prague, 1872.

Payer, Max. 'Gewerkschaften und Sozialdemokratie.' In: *Süddeutsche Monatshefte*, 1906.

Pertinax (pseudonym of a leading left-wing Social Democrat). *Oesterreich* 1934. Europa-Verlag. Zürich, 1935. (The standard work on the fall of Austrian Democracy from the standpoint of the Labour movement.)

Pörsch, B. 'Die Gewerkschaftskartelle.' In: *Neue Zeit*, vol. XVI, i.

Polin, R., and Claron, J. G. *Les co-operatives rurales en Tchécoslovakie et Roumanie*. Paris.

Prager, R. *Geschichte der U.S.P.D.* Berlin, 1921.

Preuss, H. *Staat, Recht, Freiheit*. Tübingen, 1921. Collected papers, partly posthumous.

Rathenau, Walter. *Nachgelassene Schriften*. Berlin, 1928.

Riehn, R. 'Das Konsumvereinswesen in Deutschland.' In: *Volkswirtschaftliche Abhandlungen*. Stuttgart, 1902.

Röder, F. *Parteien und Parteinstaat in Deutschland*. Munich, 1930.

Rohrbach, H. 'Die Entstehung des deutschen Metallarbeiterverbandes.' In: *Neue Zeit*, vol. XI, ii. 1897.

Rosenberg, Arthur. *A History of the German Republic*. London, 1936.

Sadbruch, H. *Das Ende der Gewerkschaften.* Berlin, 1934.
Schär, J. F. 'Konsumverein und Warenhaus.' In: *Archiv für Sozialwissenschaft*, vol. XXXI, 1910.
Scheidemann, Philipp. *Memoirs of a German Social Democrat.* 2 vols. Unless otherwise stated, the German edition is quoted: there is an English edition dated 1929. A main source for the events of 1918–20 from a right-wing Social Democrat standpoint, but by an author who later became slightly more critical.
Schlesinger, Rudolf. *Federalism in Central and Eastern Europe.* London, 1945.
Schröder, W. *Handbuch der Sozialdemokratischen Parteitage.* Useful for the student who has no complete set of the Reports available, but sometimes needs checking.
Seidel, R. *Die Gewerkschaften nach dem Kriege.* Berlin, 1925. Represents the official Trade Union view.
Seipel, Ignaz. *Der Kampf um die österreichische Verfassung.* Vienna, 1940. Collection of his speeches.
Sigl, E. *Die soziale Struktur des Sudetendeutschtums.* Leipzig, 1938. Far above the usual level of Nazi publications.
Sonter, P. *Der neue deutsche Imperialismus.* Berlin, 1934.
Stampfer, Friedrich. *Die* 14 *Jahre ersten deutschen Republik.* Karlsbad, 1936. The most comprehensive of the Social Democrat publications.
von Steeruwitz, E. *Wie es kam.* Vienna, 1934. The by far most serious account of the fall of Austrian democracy from the right-wing standpoint perhaps because of the author's later outside position.
Stresemann, Gustav. *Vermächtnis.* 3 vols. Leipzig, 1930 ff. Diaries, etc.
Strong, David F. *Austria: October* 1918–*March* 1919. New York (Columbia Univ. Press), 1939.
Stumm, T. 'Die Aufgaben der Gewerkschaftskartelle.' In: *Neue Zeit*, vol. XV. 2.
Tanzler, F. *Die deutschen Arbeitgeberverbände*, 1904–29. Berlin, 1929. Official publication of the Employers' Association.
Textor, L. E. *Land Reform in Czechoslovakia.* London, 1923.
Umbreit, Paul. 'Die deutschen Gewerkschaften im Kriege.' In: *Economic and Social History of the World War.* German series, vol. VI. Stuttgart, 1928.
Untersuchungsausschuss des deutschen Reichstages: Die Ursachen des deutschen Zusammenbruches im Jahre 1918. Vierte Reihe. Vols. 4–7. Berlin, 1928. Most documents are reprinted in *Documents of the German Revolution*, ed. Lutz, Stanford University Press and Oxford Univ. Press, 1932.
Webb, S. and B. *A History of Trade Unionism.* 1920 edition.
Weber, Adolf. 'Die Bürokratisierung der Gewerkschaften und die gelbe Arbeiterbewegung.' In: *Archiv für Sozialwissenschaft*, vol. XXXVII.

Winnig, A. *Von Proletariat zum Arbeitertum*. Hamburg, 1930.
Wizkemann, Elisabeth. *Czechs and Germans*. London, 1938.
Yerusalimsky, A. S. *The Foreign Policy and Diplomacy of German Imperialism at the end of the* 19*th Century* (in Russian). Academy of Sciences of the U.S.S.R., 1948. Attempts beyond its immediate subject, to give the political and social background.
Zeidler, H. 'Geschichte des deutschen Genossenschaftswesens der Neuzeit.' In: *Staatswissenschaftliche Beiträge*. Leipzig, 1893.
Ziegler, W. *Die deutsche Nationalversammlung* 1919–20 *und ihr Verfassungswerk*. Berlin, 1932.

INDEX

(No names quoted as mere references, nor institutions the treatment of which is fully indicated in the Contents, are included)

Made in the USA
Las Vegas, NV
29 October 2024

10619571R00233